Lecture Notes in Computer Science 11779

More information about this series at http://www.springer.com/series/7409

Chiara Ghidini · Olaf Hartig ·
Maria Maleshkova · Vojtěch Svátek ·
Isabel Cruz · Aidan Hogan ·
Jie Song · Maxime Lefrançois ·
Fabien Gandon (Eds.)

The Semantic Web – ISWC 2019

18th International Semantic Web Conference
Auckland, New Zealand, October 26–30, 2019
Proceedings, Part II

Editors
Chiara Ghidini
Fondazione Bruno Kessler
Trento, Italy

Maria Maleshkova
University of Bonn
Bonn, Germany

Isabel Cruz
University of Illinois at Chicago
Chicago, IL, USA

Jie Song
Memect Technology
Beijing, China

Fabien Gandon
Inria Sophia Antipolis - Méditerranée
Sophia Antipolis, France

Olaf Hartig
Linköping University
Linköping, Sweden

Vojtěch Svátek
University of Economics Prague
Prague, Czech Republic

Aidan Hogan
University of Chile
Santiago, Chile

Maxime Lefrançois
Mines Saint-Etienne
Saint-Etienne, France

ISSN 0302-9743 ISSN 1611-3349 (electronic)
Lecture Notes in Computer Science
ISBN 978-3-030-30795-0 ISBN 978-3-030-30796-7 (eBook)
https://doi.org/10.1007/978-3-030-30796-7

LNCS Sublibrary: SL3 – Information Systems and Applications, incl. Internet/Web, and HCI

This Springer imprint is published by the registered company Springer Nature Switzerland AG
The registered company address is: Gewerbestrasse 11, 6330 Cham, Switzerland

Preface

Knowledge graphs, linked data, linked schemas and AI ... on the Web.

Now in its 18th edition, the ISWC conference is the most important international venue to discuss and present latest advances and applications of the Semantic Web, Linked Data, Knowledge Graphs, Knowledge Representation, and Intelligent Processing on the Web. At the beginning of the 2000s this research community was formed, starting with the first international Semantic Web Working Symposium (SWWS), a workshop held in Stanford, Palo Alto, held during July 30 to August 1, 2001. The following year the symposium became the International Semantic Web Conference (ISWC) series in Sardinia, Italy, and at that time the website was predicting that it would be a major international forum at which research on all aspects of the Semantic Web would be presented. And indeed, as in previous editions, ISWC 2019 brought together researchers and practitioners from all over the world to present fundamental research, new technologies, visionary ideas, new applications, and discuss experiences. It featured a balanced mix of fundamental research, innovations, scientific artefacts such as datasets, software, ontologies, or benchmarks, and applications that showcase the power and latest advances of semantics, data, and artificial intelligence on the Web.

In 2019 we celebrated the 30th anniversary of the Web [2]. Happy birthday to you, Web! But our community also remembers that 25 years ago, Tim Berners-Lee et al. were already proposing in an article of the Communications of the ACM August 1994, to provide on the Web "more machine-oriented semantic information, allowing more sophisticated processing" [1]. And since the beginning, the Semantic Web community in general, and ISWC participants in particular, have always been interested in providing intelligent processing of the linked data and linked schemata of the Web, starting with querying, reasoning, and learning [3, 4]. This remains a core challenge of our community, tackling problems in using open data of very different sources and quality, as well as ensuring the best results possible and scaling the methods so they can face the real World Wide Web. For these reasons, and to explore the links between the Semantic Web and the latest advances in AI and knowledge graphs, the motto for ISWC 2019 was "knowledge graphs, linked data, linked schemas and AI on the Web."

Several facets of this topic were addressed in three distinguished keynote talks and a panel. Dougal Watt's keynote is entitled "Semantics: the business technology disruptor of the future" and defends the role of semantics in bringing meaning to business data. The keynote of Jerôme Euzenat is entitled "For Knowledge" and defends the grand goal of formally expressing knowledge on the Web and supporting its evolution, distribution, and diversity. After this keynote, a panel entitled "How Much Semantics Goes How Long a Way?" continued the discussion on linked knowledge, schemas, and ontologies on the Web. Finally, in her keynote entitled "Extracting Knowledge from the Data Deluge to Reveal the Mysteries of the Universe," Melanie Johnston-Hollitt introduced us to one of the most data-intensive research fields (radio astronomy) that requires many innovations to achieve scalability and the "big data" regime.

The proceedings of ISWC 2019 are presented in two volumes: the first one containing the research track papers and the second one the resource track and in-use track papers. All these papers were peer reviewed. Combined, these tracks received a total of 283 submissions of which 443 reviewers accepted 74 papers: 42 in the research track, 11 in the in-use track, and 21 in the resource track. Beyond these three tracks and at the moment of writing this preface, this edition of the international conference ISWC already involved more than 1,300 authors of submitted papers, demos, posters, etc. and more than 660 reviewers for all the tracks, amounting to them being of 44 different nationalities. This year again, the number of papers in the resources category attests the commitment of the community to sharing and collaboration.

The excellent reputation of ISWC as a prime scientific conference was confirmed again this year. The research track received 194 valid full paper submissions, out of which 42 papers were selected, leading to an acceptance rate of 21.6%. This year, a double-blind approach was applied to the reviewing process; that is, the identity of the submission authors was not revealed to the reviewers and vice versa. The Program Committee (PC) comprised 26 Senior PC members and 270 regular PC members. In addition, 70 sub-reviewers were recruited to help with the review process. The PC chairs thank all these committee members for the time and energy they have put into the process. ISWC has very rigorous reviewing criteria. The papers were assessed for originality, novelty, relevance and impact of the research contributions, soundness, rigor and reproducibility, clarity and quality of presentation, and grounding in the literature. This year, the vast majority of papers were reviewed by a team comprising four reviewers and a senior PC member, who engaged in a discussion phase after the initial reviews were prepared and the authors responses were made available. Each paper was then discussed among the research track PC chairs and the senior PC members, so as to reach a consensus on the final list of accepted papers.

For the first time in the history of ISWC, we organized a specific initiative to evaluate the reproducibility of research papers. This innovative track was led by Alejandra Gonzalez-Beltran and Michael Cochez. Authors of accepted papers were invited to share their experimental setup and code for evaluation. We received 11 submissions which were assessed in their varying degrees of reproducibility by a member of the Reproducibility Committee. The 'reproducer', rather than reviewer, interacted with the authors and aimed to execute the code and obtain results similar to what was reported in the paper. If the results were reproducible, the paper received the reproducibility label.

The resources track promoted the sharing of high-quality information artifacts that have contributed to the generation of novel scientific work. Resources could be datasets, ontologies, vocabularies, ontology design patterns, benchmarks, crowdsourcing designs, software frameworks, workflows, protocols, or metrics, among others. This track demonstrates how important it is for our community to share reusable resources in order to allow other researchers to compare new results, reproduce experimental research, and explore new lines of research, in accordance with the FAIR principles for scientific data management. All published resources address a set of requirements: persistent URI, indicator for impact, support for reuse, license specification, to mention a few. This year the track chairs Maria Maleshkova and Vojtěch Svátek received 64 submissions, of which 21 were accepted (a 33% acceptance rate), covering a wide range of resource types such as benchmarks, ontologies, datasets, and software frameworks, in a variety of domains such as music, health, scholar, drama, and audio, and addressing multiple problems such as RDF querying, ontology alignment, linked data analytics, or recommending systems. The reviewing process involved 87 PC members and 7 sub-reviewers, supported by 8 senior PC members. The average number of reviews per paper was 3.1 (at least three per paper), plus a meta-review provided by a senior PC member. Papers were evaluated based on the availability of the resource, its design and technical quality, impact, and reusability; owing to the mandatory dereferenceability and community-visibility of the resources (precluding the author anonymity), the papers were reviewed in a single-blind mode. The review process also included a rebuttal phase and further discussions among reviewers and senior PC members, who provided recommendations. Final decisions were taken following a detailed analysis and discussion of each paper conducted by the program chairs and the senior PC.

The in-use track aimed to showcase and learn from the growing adoption of Semantic Web and related technologies in real-world settings, in particular to address questions such as: where are such technologies being used, what are their benefits, and how can they be improved with further research? The track chairs Isabel Cruz and Aidan Hogan received 25 paper submissions and 11 papers were accepted, giving an acceptance rate of 44%; this reflects a significant increase in papers accepted over previous years, indicative of a growing maturation and adoption of Semantic Web and related technologies. In the in-use track, 39 PC members contributed three reviews per paper and took part in an extensive discussion on each paper, to ensure a high-quality program. The accepted papers describe successful applications of technologies including ontologies, knowledge graphs, linked data, and RDB2RDF. The results described by these papers were developed in whole, or with collaboration from, both large companies (e.g., Pinterest, Springer Nature, IBM, and JOT Internet Media), start-ups (Capsenta), as well as public organizations (e.g., Norwegian Institute for Water Research and European Commission).

The industry track provided an opportunity for industry adopters to highlight and share the key learnings and challenges faced by real world implementations. This year, the track chairs Anna Lisa Gentile and Christophe Guéret received 24 submissions from a wide range of companies of different sizes and 16 submissions were accepted. The submissions were assessed in terms of: quantitative and/or qualitative value proposition provided; amount of discussion of innovative aspects, experiences, impact, lessons learned, and business value in the application domain; and degree to which semantic technologies are critical to the offering. Each paper received 3 assigned reviewers from a panel of academic and industry Semantic Web experts.

The main conference program was complemented by presentations from the journal, industry, and posters and demos tracks, as well as the Semantic Web Challenge and a panel on future trends in knowledge graphs.

The journal track was intended as a forum for presenting significant Semantic Web-related research results that have been recently published in well-known and well-established journals but that have not been presented at a Semantic Web-related conference. The goal was to highlight these results at ISWC and promote discussions potentially leading to meaningful multi-disciplinary collaborations. Traditionally only articles published in the *Journal of Web Semantics* (JWS) and the *Semantic Web Journal* (SWJ) were considered for the ISWC journal track. However, with the goal of enabling cross-fertilization with other related communities, this year our two chairs Claudia d'Amato and Lalana Kagal included additional journals such as: the *Journal of Network and Computer Applications*, *IEEE Transactions on Neural Networks and Learning Systems*, the *Journal of Machine Learning Research*, the *Data Mining and Knowledge Discovery Journal*, *ACM Transactions on the Web*, *ACM Computing Surveys*, *IEEE Transactions on Knowledge and Data Engineering*, *ACM Transactions on Computer-Human Interaction*, *Artificial Intelligence Journal*, *Proceedings of the Very Large Database Endowment*, and the *Journal of Information Science*. Papers that fell within the ISWC topics which had been published within the listed journals starting from January 1, 2017, were considered eligible for submission to the journal track. We received 24 extended abstract submissions, out of which 13 were accepted and collected as CEUR proceedings. Each submission was reviewed by at least two members of the PC in order to assess how interesting it was as well as its novelty, relevance, and attractiveness for the ISWC audience. Also taken into consideration was the quality of the extended abstracts and the diversity of the topics, spanning from scalable reasoning and triple storage, machine translation, fact predictions on (probabilistic) knowledge graphs, modeling linked open data for different domains, and semantic sensor networks.

The conference included several events appreciated by the community, which created more opportunities to present and discuss emerging ideas, network, learn, and mentor. Thanks to H. Sofia Pinto and 武田 英明 (Hideaki Takeda), the workshops and tutorials program included a mix of established topics such as ontology matching, ontology design patterns, and semantics-powered data mining, as well as analytics alongside newer ones that reflect the commitment of the community to innovate and help create systems and technologies that people want and deserve, including semantic explainability or blockchain enabled Semantic Web. Application-centric workshops ranged from solutions for large-scale biomedical data analytics to health data management. The tutorials covered topics such as scalable sustainable construction of knowledge bases, linked data querying, reasoning and benchmarking, GraphQL, solid and comunica, blockchain and Semantic Web, provenance for scientific reproducibility, and an historical perspective and context on the roots of knowledge graphs.

The conference also included a Doctoral Consortium (DC) track, which was chaired by 乔淼 (Miao Qiao) and Mauro Dragoni. The DC afforded PhD students from the Semantic Web community the opportunity to share their research ideas in a critical but supportive environment, where they received feedback from both the senior members of the community and the other students. Indeed, students participated also in the review process in order to have a first tangible experience of it. This year the PC accepted 13 papers for oral presentation out of the 16 submissions received. All student participants were paired with mentors from the PC who provided guidance on improving their research, producing slides and giving presentations.

This program was complemented by activities put together by our student coordinating chairs ඔෂානි සෙනෙවිරත්න (Oshani Seneviratne) and 岑超榮 (Bruce Sham), who secured funding for travel grants, managed the grants application process, and organized the mentoring lunch alongside other informal opportunities for students and other newcomers to get to know the community.

Posters and demos are one of the most vibrant part of every ISWC. This year, the track was chaired by Mari Carmen Suárez-Figueroa and 程龚 (Gong Cheng). For the first time, poster submissions were subject to double-blind review, whereas demo submissions were single-blind as in previous years due to the possible inclusion of online demos. We received 59 poster and 43 demo submissions. We had to remove four poster and one demo submissions, as they exceeded the page limit. The PC, consisting of 41 members for posters and 44 members for demos, accepted 39 posters and 37 demos. Decisions were mainly based on relevance, originality, and clarity. Additionally, we conditionally accepted one poster that was transferred from the industry track.

The Semantic Web Challenge has now been a part of ISWC for 16 years. The 2019 edition of the challenge followed a new direction started in 2017: all challenges define fixed datasets, objective measures, and provide their participants with a benchmarking platform. In contrast to 2017 and 2018, this year the challenges were open. This means that a call for challenge was issued and potential challenge organizers submitted proposals for challenges, which were reviewed by the organizers. Two challenges made the cut. The aim of the first challenge was to evaluate the performance of matching systems for tables. The participants were to devise means to link entries in tables to classes, resource, or relations from a predefined knowledge graph. The second challenge evaluated the performance of fact validation systems. For each fact in the benchmark data, the participants were to return a score which expressed how likely said fact was to be true. The best solutions were then presented and discussed at the conference in a dedicated challenge session and during the poster session.

Newly reintroduced last year after an initial showing in 2011, the outrages ideas track solicits visionary ideas, long term challenges, and opportunities for the Semantic Web. This track was chaired by Maria Keet and Abraham Bernstein and it featured a special award funded by the Computer Community Consortium's Blue Sky Ideas initiative. We received nine submissions of which two were accepted.

Finally, the Minute Madness is a tradition at the International Semantic Web Conference that started back in 2011. It usually provides conference participants with a quick and fun overview of the presented works at the conference, since each speaker is allowed to pitch his/her work with a 60 second speech. This year, the two chairs Irene Celino and Armin Haller split the Minute Madness into two separate sessions, both in plenary: the traditional slot for poster and demo authors, to generate interest and traction for the following dedicated event, and a stand-alone session, open to all conference participants, allowed to submit their contribution proposal through the dedicated Minute Madness call.

Organizing a conference is so much more than assembling a program. An international event of the scale and complexity of ISWC requires the commitment, support, resources, and time of hundreds of people, organizers of satellite events, reviewers, volunteers, and sponsors. We are very grateful to our local team at the University of Auckland, and in particular to the local chairs, 孙敬 (Jing Sun) and Gill Dobbie as well as their Conference Coordinator Alex Harvey. They expertly managed the conference logistics down to every detail and make it a splendid event that we want to attend every year. This year again, they helped us grow this exciting scientific community and connect with the local scientific community of the venue.

Our thanks also go to Valentina Ivanova and فؤاد زبليط (Fouad Zablith), our proactive publicity chairs, and นชา ชลดำรงค์กุล (Nacha Chondamrongkul) our hyper-responsive Web chair - they played a critical role in ensuring that all conference activities and updates were communicated and promoted on the Web and across mailing lists and on social media. Maribel Acosta and Andrea Giovanni Nuzzolese were the metadata chairs this year and their ensured that all relevant information about the conference was available in a format that could be used across all applications, continuing a tradition established at ISWC many years ago. Also, we are especially thankful to our proceedings chairs, 宋劼 (Jie Song) and Maxime Lefrançois, who oversaw the publication of these volumes.

Sponsorship is crucial to realize the conference in its current form. We had a highly committed trio of sponsorship chairs, 彭麗姬 (Lai Kei Pang), Cédric Pruski, and Oktie Hassanzadeh, who went above and beyond to find new ways to engage with sponsors and promote the conference to them. Thanks to them, the conference now features a social program that is almost as exciting as the scientific one.

Finally, our special thanks go to the Semantic Web Science Association (SWSA) for their continuing support and guidance and to the organizers of the conference from 2017 and 2018 who were a constant inspiration, role models, and source of knowledge, advice, and experience.

August 2019

Chiara Ghidini
Olaf Hartig
Maria Maleshkova
Vojtěch Svátek
Isabel Cruz
Aidan Hogan
宋劼 Jie Song
Maxime Lefrançois
Fabien Gandon

References

1. T. Berners-Lee, R. Cailliau, A. Luotonen, H. F. Nielsen, and A. Secret. The World-Wide Web. *Commun. ACM*, 37(8):76–82, Aug. 1994.
2. F. Gandon. For everything: Tim Berners-Lee, winner of the 2016 Turing award for having invented… the Web. *1024: Bulletin de la Société Informatique de France*, (11):21, Sept. 2017.
3. F. Gandon. A Survey of the First 20 Years of Research on Semantic Web and Linked Data. *Revue des Sciences et Technologies de l'Information - Série ISI: Ingénierie des Systèmes d'Information*, Dec. 2018.
4. F. Gandon, M. Sabou, and H. Sack. Weaving a Web of Linked Resources. Semantic Web Journal Sepcial Issue, 2017.

Organization

Organizing Committee

General Chair

Fabien Gandon	Inria, Université Côte d'Azur, CNRS, I3S Sophia Antipolis, France

Local Chairs

孙敬 (Jing Sun)	The University of Auckland, New Zealand
Gill Dobbie	The University of Auckland, New Zealand

Research Track Chairs

Chiara Ghidini	Fondazione Bruno Kessler (FBK), Italy
Olaf Hartig	Linköping University, Sweden

Resources Track Chairs

Maria Maleshkova	SDA, University of Bonn, Germany
Vojtěch Svátek	University of Economics in Prague, Czech Republic

In-Use Track Chairs

Isabel Cruz	University of Illinois at Chicago, USA
Aidan Hogan	DCC, Universidad de Chile, Chile

Reproducibility Track Chairs

Alejandra Gonzalez-Beltran	Science and Technology Facilities Council, UK
Michael Cochez	Fraunhofer Institute for Applied Information Technology, RWTH Aachen University, Germany, and University of Jyvaskyla, Finland

Industry Track Chairs

Anna Lisa Gentile	IBM Research, USA
Christophe Guéret	Accenture Labs Dublin, Ireland

Journal Track Chairs

Claudia d'Amato	University of Bari, Italy
Lalana Kagal	MIT, USA

Workshop and Tutorial Chairs

H. Sofia Pinto	INESC-ID, Instituto Superior Técnico, Universidade de Lisboa, Portugal
武田 英明 (Hideaki Takeda)	National Institute of Informatics, Japan

Semantic Web Challenges Track Chairs

Gianluca Demartini	The University of Queensland, Australia
Valentina Presutti	STLab-ISTC, National Research Council, Italy
Axel Ngonga	Paderborn University, Germany

Poster and Demo Track Chairs

Mari Carmen Suárez-Figueroa	Universidad Politécnica de Madrid (UPM), Ontology Engineering Group (OEG), Spain
程龚 (Gong Cheng)	Nanjing University, China

Doctoral Consortium Chairs

乔淼 (Miao Qiao)	The University of Auckland, New Zealand
Mauro Dragoni	Fondazione Bruno Kessler, Italy

Student Coordination Chairs

ඔෂානි සෙනෙවිරත්න (Oshani Seneviratne)	Oshani Rensselaer Polytechnic Institute, USA
岑超榮 (Bruce, Chiu-Wing Sham)	The University of Auckland, New Zealand

Minute Madness Chairs

Irene Celino	Cefriel, Italy
Armin Haller	Australian National University, Australia

Outrageous Ideas Track Chairs

Maria Keet	University of Cape Town, South Africa
Abraham Bernstein	University of Zurich, Switzerland

Proceedings Chairs

宋劼 (Jie Song)	Memect Technology, China
Maxime Lefrançois	MINES Saint-Étienne, France

Metadata Chairs

Maribel Acosta	Karlsruhe Institute of Technology, Germany
Andrea Giovanni Nuzzolese	STLab, ISTC-CNR, Italy

Publicity Chairs

Valentina Ivanova	RISE Research Institutes of Sweden, Sweden
فؤاد زبليط (Fouad Zablith)	American University of Beirut, Lebanon

Sponsorship Chairs

彭麗姬 (Lai Kei Pang)	University of Auckland Libraries and Learning Services, New Zealand
Cédric Pruski	Luxembourg Institute of Science and Technology, Luxembourg
Oktie Hassanzadeh	IBM Research, USA

Web Site Chair

นชา ชลดำรงค์กุล (Nacha Chondamrongkul)	The University of Auckland, New Zealand

Program Committee

Senior Program Committee – Research Track

Lora Aroyo	Google
Paul Buitelaar	Insight Centre for Data Analytics, National University of Ireland Galway
Emanuele Della Valle	Politecnico di Milano
Gianluca Demartini	The University of Queensland
Armin Haller	Australian National University
Annika Hinze	University of Waikato
Katja Hose	Aalborg University
Andreas Hotho	University of Wuerzburg
Wei Hu	Nanjing University
Mustafa Jarrar	Birzeit University
Sabrina Kirrane	Vienna University of Economics and Business
Markus Luczak-Roesch	Victoria University of Wellington
David Martin	Samsung Research America
Tommie Meyer	University of Cape Town, CAIR
Matteo Palmonari	University of Milano-Bicocca
Jorge Pérez	Universidad de Chile
Achim Rettinger	Trier University
Marco Rospocher	Università degli Studi di Verona
Hideaki Takeda	National Institute of Informatics
Valentina Tamma	University of Liverpool
Kerry Taylor	Australian National University and University of Surrey
Tania Tudorache	Stanford University
Axel Polleres	WU Wien
Maria Esther Vidal	Universidad Simon Bolivar
Paul Groth	University of Amsterdam
Luciano Serafini	Fondazione Bruno Kessler

Program Committee – Research Track

Maribel Acosta	Karlsruhe Institute of Technology
Harith Alani	The Open University
Jose Julio Alferes	Universidade NOVA de Lisboa
Muhammad Intizar Ali	Insight Centre for Data Analytics, National University of Ireland Galway
Marjan Alirezaie	Orebro University
Tahani Alsubait	Umm Al-Qura University
José Luis Ambite	University of Southern California
Renzo Angles	Universidad de Talca
Mihael Arcan	Insight @ NUI Galway
Manuel Atencia	Université Grenoble Alpes
Maurizio Atzori	University of Cagliari
Payam Barnaghi	University of Surrey
Pierpaolo Basile	University of Bari
Valerio Basile	University of Turin
Srikanta Bedathur	IIT Delhi
Zohra Bellahsene	LIRMM
Ladjel Bellatreche	LIAS/ENSMA
Maria Bermudez-Edo	University of Granada
Leopoldo Bertossi	Relational AI Inc., Carleton University
Eva Blomqvist	Linköping University
Fernando Bobillo	University of Zaragoza
Alex Borgida	Rutgers University
Stefano Borgo	Laboratory for Applied Ontology, ISTC-CNR (Trento)
Loris Bozzato	Fondazione Bruno Kessler
Alessandro Bozzon	Delft University of Technology
John Breslin	NUI Galway
Carlos Buil Aranda	Universidad Técnica Federico Santa Maria
Marut Buranarach	NECTEC
Aljoscha Burchardt	DFKI
Elena Cabrio	Université Côte d'Azur, CNRS, Inria, I3S
Jean-Paul Calbimonte	HES-SO University of Applied Sciences and Arts Western Switzerland
David Carral	TU Dresden
Vinay Chaudhri	Independent Consultant, San Francisco Bay Area
Huajun Chen	Zhejiang University
Huiyuan Chen	Case Western Reserve University
Gong Cheng	Nanjing University
Philipp Cimiano	Bielefeld University
Michael Cochez	Fraunhofer Institute for Applied Information Technology
Jack G. Conrad	Thomson Reuters

Olivier Corby	Inria
Oscar Corcho	Universidad Politécnica de Madrid
Francesco Corcoglioniti	Fondazione Bruno Kessler
Luca Costabello	Accenture Labs
Fabio Cozman	University of São Paulo
Isabel Cruz	University of Illinois at Chicago
Philippe Cudre-Mauroux	University of Fribourg
Olivier Curé	Université Paris-Est, LIGM
Claudia d'Amato	University of Bari
Mathieu D'Aquin	Insight Centre for Data Analytics, National University of Ireland Galway
Jérôme David	Inria
Jeremy Debattista	Trinity College Dublin
Thierry Declerck	DFKI GmbH and University of Saarland
Daniele Dell'Aglio	University of Zurich
Elena Demidova	L3S Research Center
Chiara Di Francescomarino	FBK-irst
Stefan Dietze	GESIS – Leibniz Institute for the Social Sciences
Mauro Dragoni	FBK-irst
Jianfeng Du	Guangdong University of Foreign Studies
Michel Dumontier	Maastricht University
Shady Elbassuoni	American University of Beirut
Lorena Etcheverry	Instituto de Computación, Universidad de la República
Jérôme Euzenat	Inria, Université Grenoble Alpes
Stefano Faralli	University of Rome Unitelma Sapienza
Alessandro Faraotti	IBM
Catherine Faron Zucker	University Nice Sophia Antipolis
Anna Fensel	Semantic Technology Institute (STI) Innsbruck, University of Innsbruck
Alba Fernandez	Universidad Politécnica de Madrid
Miriam Fernandez	Knowledge Media Institute
Javier D. Fernández	Vienna University of Economics and Business
Besnik Fetahu	L3S Research Center
Valeria Fionda	Università della Calabria
Antske Fokkens	Vrije Universiteit Amsterdam
Flavius Frasincar	Erasmus University Rotterdam
Fred Freitas	Universidade Federal de Pernambuco (UFPE)
Francesca Frontini	Université Paul-Valéry Montpellier 3, Praxiling UMR 5267 CNRS
Naoki Fukuta	Shizuoka University
Michael Färber	University of Freiburg
Luis Galárraga	Aalborg University
Raúl García-Castro	Universidad Politécnica de Madrid
Daniel Garijo	Information Sciences Institute
Anna Lisa Gentile	IBM
Aurona Gerber	CAIR, University of Pretoria

Jose Manuel Gomez-Perez	ExpertSystem
Rafael S. Gonçalves	Stanford University
Guido Governatori	CSIRO
Jorge Gracia	University of Zaragoza
Dagmar Gromann	TU Dresden
Tudor Groza	The Garvan Institute of Medical Research
Claudio Gutierrez	Universidad de Chile
Peter Haase	metaphacts
Andreas Harth	University of Erlangen-Nuremberg, Fraunhofer IIS-SCS
Bernhard Haslhofer	AIT Austrian Institute of Technology
Oktie Hassanzadeh	IBM
Pascal Hitzler	Wright State University
Rinke Hoekstra	University of Amsterdam
Aidan Hogan	DCC, Universidad de Chile
Geert-Jan Houben	Delft University of Technology
Wen Hua	The University of Queensland
Eero Hyvönen	Aalto University and University of Helsinki (HELDIG)
Luis Ibanez-Gonzalez	University of Southampton
Ryutaro Ichise	National Institute of Informatics
Nancy Ide	Vassar College
Oana Inel	Delft University of Technology
Prateek Jain	Nuance Communications Inc.
Krzysztof Janowicz	University of California
Caroline Jay	The University of Manchester
Ernesto Jimenez-Ruiz	The Alan Turing Institute
Lucie-Aimée Kaffee	University of Southampton
Evangelos Kalampokis	University of Macedonia
Maulik R. Kamdar	Stanford Center for Biomedical Informatics Research, Stanford University
Megan Katsumi	University of Toronto
Tomi Kauppinen	Aalto University School of Science
Takahiro Kawamura	Japan Science and Technology Agency
Maria Keet	University of Cape Town
Mayank Kejriwal	Information Sciences Institute
Thomas Kipf	University of Amsterdam
Matthias Klusch	DFKI
Stasinos Konstantopoulos	NCSR Demokritos
Roman Kontchakov	Birkbeck, University of London
Dimitris Kontokostas	University of Leipzig
Manolis Koubarakis	National and Kapodistrian University of Athens
Kouji Kozaki	Osaka University
Adila A. Krisnadhi	University of Indonesia
Tobias Kuhn	Vrije Universiteit Amsterdam
Tobias Käfer	Karlsruhe Institute of Technology
Jose Emilio Labra Gayo	Universidad de Oviedo

Patrick Lambrix	Linköping University
Christoph Lange	University of Bonn, Fraunhofer IAIS
Danh Le Phuoc	TU Berlin
Roy Lee	Singapore Management University
Maxime Lefrançois	MINES Saint-Étienne
Maurizio Lenzerini	Università di Roma La Sapienza
Juanzi Li	Tsinghua University
Yuan-Fang Li	Monash University
Chunbin Lin	Amazon AWS
Alejandro Llaves	Fujitsu Laboratories of Europe
Thomas Lukasiewicz	University of Oxford
Carsten Lutz	Universität Bremen
Gengchen Mai	University of California
Ioana Manolescu	Inria Saclay, LRI, Université Paris Sud-11
Miguel A. Martinez-Prieto	University of Valladolid
John P. McCrae	National University of Ireland Galway
Fiona McNeill	Heriot Watt University
Christian Meilicke	University of Mannheim
Albert Meroño-Peñuela	Vrije Universiteit Amsterdam
Pasquale Minervini	University College London
Daniel Miranker	Institute for Cell and Molecular Biology, The University of Texas at Austin
Dunja Mladenic	Jožef Stefan Institute
Aditya Mogadala	Universität des Saarlandes
Pascal Molli	University of Nantes, LS2N
Elena Montiel-Ponsoda	Universidad Politécnica de Madrid
Gabriela Montoya	Aalborg University
Takeshi Morita	Keio University
Regina Motz	Universidad de la República
Hubert Naacke	Sorbonne Université, UPMC, LIP6
Sven Naumann	University of Trier
Axel-Cyrille Ngonga Ngomo	University of Paderborn
Andriy Nikolov	metaphacts GmbH
Leo Obrst	MITRE
Alessandro Oltramari	Bosch Research and Technology Center
Magdalena Ortiz	Vienna University of Technology
Francesco Osborne	The Open University
Ankur Padia	UMBC
Jeff Z. Pan	University of Aberdeen
Peter Patel-Schneider	Samsung Research America
Terry Payne	University of Liverpool
Tassilo Pellegrini	University of Applied Sciences St. Pölten
Catia Pesquita	LaSIGE, Faculdade de Ciências, Universidade de Lisboa

Giulio Petrucci	Google
Rafael Peñaloza	University of Milano-Bicocca
Patrick Philipp	Forschungszentrum Informatik (FZI)
Reinhard Pichler	TU Wien
Giuseppe Pirrò	Sapienza University of Rome
Alessandro Piscopo	BBC
Dimitris Plexousakis	FORTH
María Poveda-Villalón	Universidad Politécnica de Madrid
Guilin Qi	Southeast University
Yuzhong Qu	Nanjing University
Alexandre Rademaker	IBM Research Brazil, EMAp/FGV
Maya Ramanath	IIT Delhi
David Ratcliffe	Defence
Simon Razniewski	Max Planck Institute for Informatics
Blake Regalia	University of California
Georg Rehm	DFKI
Juan L. Reutter	Pontificia Universidad Católica
Martin Rezk	DMM.com
Giuseppe Rizzo	LINKS Foundation
Mariano Rodríguez Muro	Google
Dumitru Roman	SINTEF
Gaetano Rossiello	University of Bari
Ana Roxin	University of Burgundy, UMR CNRS 6306
Sebastian Rudolph	TU Dresden
Anisa Rula	University of Milano-Bicocca
Harald Sack	FIZ Karlsruhe – Leibniz Institute for Information Infrastructure, KIT Karlsruhe
Angelo Antonio Salatino	The Open University
Muhammad Saleem	AKSW, University of Leizpig
Kai-Uwe Sattler	TU Ilmenau
Simon Scerri	Fraunhofer
Ralph Schaefermeier	University of Leipzig
Bernhard Schandl	mySugr GmbH
Ralf Schenkel	University of Trier
Stefan Schlobach	Vrije Universiteit Amsterdam
Andreas Schmidt	University of Kassel
Giovanni Semeraro	University of Bari
Juan F. Sequeda	Capsenta Labs
Gilles Serasset	LIG, Université Grenoble Alpes
Yanfeng Shu	CSIRO
Gerardo Simari	Universidad Nacional del Sur, CONICET
Hala Skaf-Molli	University of Nantes, LS2N
Sebastian Skritek	TU Wien
Dezhao Song	Thomson Reuters

Steffen Staab	Institut WeST, University Koblenz-Landau and WAIS, University of Southampton
Armando Stellato	University of Rome
Simon Steyskal	Siemens AG Austria
Markus Stocker	German National Library of Science and Technology (TIB)
Audun Stolpe	Norwegian Defence Research Establishment (FFI)
Umberto Straccia	ISTI-CNR
Heiner Stuckenschmidt	University of Mannheim
York Sure-Vetter	Karlsruhe Institute of Technology
Pedro Szekely	USC – Information Sciences Institute
Mohsen Taheriyan	Google
Naoya Takeishi	RIKEN Center for Advanced Intelligence Project
Sergio Tessaris	Free University of Bozen-Bolzano
Andrea Tettamanzi	University Nice Sophia Antipolis
Kia Teymourian	Boston University
Harsh Thakkar	University of Bonn
Andreas Thalhammer	F. Hoffmann-La Roche AG
Ilaria Tiddi	Vrije University
David Toman	University of Waterloo
Yannick Toussaint	Loria
Sebastian Tramp	eccenca GmbH
Cassia Trojahn	UT2J, IRIT
Anni-Yasmin Turhan	TU Dresden
Takanori Ugai	Fujitsu Laboratories Ltd.
Jürgen Umbrich	Vienna University of Economy and Business
Joerg Unbehauen	University of Leipzig
Jacopo Urbani	Vrije Universiteit Amsterdam
Dmitry Ustalov	University of Mannheim
Alejandro A. Vaisman	Instituto Tecnológico de Buenos Aires
Marieke van Erp	KNAW Humanities Cluster
Jacco van Ossenbruggen	CWI, VU University Amsterdam
Miel Vander Sande	Ghent University
Ruben Verborgh	Ghent University – imec
Serena Villata	CNRS – Laboratoire d'Informatique, Signaux et Systèmes de Sophia-Antipolis
Boris Villazon-Terrazas	Majorel
Piek Vossen	Vrije Universiteit Amsterdam
Domagoj Vrgoc	Pontificia Universidad Católica de Chile
Simon Walk	Graz University of Technology
Kewen Wang	Griffith University
Xin Wang	Tianjin University
Zhichun Wang	Beijing Normal University
Grant Weddell	University of Waterloo
Gregory Todd Williams	Hulu

Frank Wolter	University of Liverpool
Josiane Xavier Parreira	Siemens AG Österreich
Guohui Xiao	KRDB Research Centre, Free University of Bozen-Bolzano
Fouad Zablith	American University of Beirut
Ondřej Zamazal	University of Economics in Prague
Veruska Zamborlini	University of Amsterdam
Amrapali Zaveri	Maastricht University
Sergej Zerr	L3S Research Center
Kalliopi Zervanou	Eindhoven University of Technology
Lei Zhang	FIZ Karlsruhe – Leibniz Institute for Information Infrastructure
Wei Emma Zhang	Macquarie University
Xiaowang Zhang	Tianjin University
Ziqi Zhang	Sheffield University
Jun Zhao	University of Oxford
Lihua Zhao	Accenture
Antoine Zimmermann	MINES Saint-Étienne
Amal Zouaq	University of Ottawa

Additional Reviewers – Research Track

Dimitris Alivanistos	Elsevier
Andrea Bellandi	Institute for Computational Linguistics
Mohamed Ben Ellefi	Aix-Marseille University, Lis-Lab
Nabila Berkani	ESI
Federico Bianchi	University of Milan-Bicocca
Zeyd Boukhers	University of Siegen
Marco Brambilla	Politecnico di Milano
Janez Brank	Jožef Stefan Institute
Angelos Charalambidis	University of Athens
Marco Cremaschi	Università di Milano-Bicocca
Ronald Denaux	ExpertSystem
Dimitar Dimitrov	GESIS
Monireh Ebrahimi	Wright State University
Cristina Feier	University of Bremen
Oliver Fernandez Gil	TU Dresden
Giorgos Flouris	FORTH-ICS
Jorge Galicia Auyon	ISAE-ENSMA
Andrés García-Silva	ExpertSystem
Genet Asefa Gesese	FIZ Karlsruhe
Pouya Ghiasnezhad Omran	Griffith University and Australian National University
Simon Gottschalk	L3S Research Center
Jonas Halvorsen	Norwegian Defence Research Establishment (FFI)
Dave Hendricksen	Thomson Reuters
Annika Hinze	University of Waikato

Yuncheng Hua	Southeast University
Gao Huan	Southeast University
John Hudzina	Thomson Reuters
Robert Isele	eccenca GmbH
Chen Jiaoyan	University of Oxford
Anas Fahad Khan	Istituto di Linguistica Computazionale Antonio Zampolli
Haris Kondylakis	FORTH
George Konstantinidis	University of Southampton
Cedric Kulbach	FZI - AIFB
Artem Lutov	University of Fribourg
Andrea Mauri	Delft University of Technology
Sepideh Mesbah	Delft University of Technology
Payal Mitra	.
Piero Molino	Università di Bari Aldo Moro
Anna Nguyen	Karlsruhe Institute of Technology
Kristian Noullet	University of Freiburg
Erik Novak	Jožef Stefan Institute
Inna Novalija	Jožef Stefan Institute
Wolfgang Otto	GESIS
Romana Pernischová	University of Zurich
Freddy Priyatna	Universidad Politécnica de Madrid
Joe Raad	Vrije Universiteit Amsterdam
Jan Rörden	AIT Austrian Institute of Technology
Leif Sabellek	University of Bremen
Filipe Santana Da Silva	Fundação Universidade Federal de Ciências da Saúde de Porto Alegre (UFCSPA)
Lukas Schmelzeisen	University of Koblenz-Landau
Miroslav Shaltev	L3S
Cogan Shimizu	Wright State University
Lucia Siciliani	University of Bari
Alisa Smirnova	University of Fribourg
Blerina Spahiu	Università degli Studi di Milano Bicocca
Nicolas Tempelmeier	L3S Research Center
Elodie Thieblin	IRIT
Riccardo Tommasini	Politecnico di Milano
Philip Turk	SINTEF
Rima Türker	FIZ Karlsruhe
Roman Vlasov	IDA GmbH, RSM Intelligence
Zhe Wang	Griffith University
Kemas Wiharja	University of Aberdeen
Bo Yan	University of California
Dingqi Yang	eXascale Infolab, University of Fribourg
Lingxi Yue	Shandong University
Rui Zhu	University of California
Thomas Zielund	Thomson Reuters

Sarah de Nigris	Institute WeST, Koblenz-Landau Universität
Remzi Çelebi	Ege University

Senior Program Committee – Research Track

Anna Lisa Gentile	IBM
Sebastian Rudolph	TU Dresden
Heiko Paulheim	University of Mannheim
Maria Esther Vidal	Universidad Simon Bolivar
Agnieszka Lawrynowicz	Poznan University of Technology
Stefan Dietze	GESIS – Leibniz Institute for the Social Sciences
Steffen Lohmann	Fraunhofer
Francesco Osborne	The Open University

Program Committee – Resources Track

Muhammad Intizar Ali	Insight Centre for Data Analytics, National University of Ireland
Ghislain Auguste Atemezing	Mondeca
Maurizio Atzori	University of Cagliari
Elena Cabrio	Université Côte d'Azur, CNRS, Inria, I3S
Irene Celino	CEFRIEL
Timothy Clark	University of Virginia
Francesco Corcoglioniti	Fondazione Bruno Kessler
Victor de Boer	Vrije Universiteit Amsterdam
Daniele Dell'Aglio	University of Zurich
Emanuele Della Valle	Politecnico di Milano
Anastasia Dimou	Ghent University
Ying Ding	Indiana University Bloomington
Mauro Dragoni	FBK-irst
Mohnish Dubey	University of Bonn
Marek Dudáš	University of Economics in Prague
Fajar J. Ekaputra	Vienna University of Technology
Ivan Ermilov	Universität Leipzig
Diego Esteves	Fraunhofer
Michael Färber	University of Freiburg
Michael Galkin	Fraunhofer IAIS University of Bonn and ITMO University
Aldo Gangemi	Università di Bologna, CNR-ISTC
Raúl Garcia-Castro	Universidad Politécnica de Madrid
Daniel Garijo	Information Sciences Institute
Jose Manuel Gomez-Perez	ExpertSystem
Alejandra Gonzalez-Beltran	University of Oxford
Rafael S. Gonçalves	Stanford University
Alasdair Gray	Heriot-Watt University
Tudor Groza	The Garvan Institute of Medical Research

Amelie Gyrard	Kno.e.sis – Ohio Center of Excellence in Knowledge-enabled Computing
Armin Haller	Australian National University
Karl Hammar	Jönköping University
Rinke Hoekstra	University of Amsterdam
Antoine Isaac	Europeana, VU University Amsterdam
Ernesto Jimenez-Ruiz	The Alan Turing Institute
Simon Jupp	European Bioinformatics Institute
Tomi Kauppinen	Aalto University School of Science
Elmar Kiesling	Vienna University of Technology
Tomáš Kliegr	University of Economics in Prague
Jakub Klímek	Charles University
Adila A. Krisnadhi	University of Indonesia
Markus Krötzsch	TU Dresden
Christoph Lange	University of Bonn, Fraunhofer IAIS
Maxime Lefrançois	MINES Saint-Étienne
Ioanna Lytra	Enterprise Information Systems, University of Bonn
Simon Mayer	University of St. Gallen and ETH Zurich
Jim McCusker	Rensselaer Polytechnic Institute
Fiona McNeill	Heriot Watt University
Nicole Merkle	FZI Forschungszentrum Informatik am KIT
Nandana Mihindukula-sooriya	Universidad Politécnica de Madrid
Raghava Mutharaju	IIIT Delhi
Lionel Médini	LIRIS, University of Lyon
Giulio Napolitano	Fraunhofer Institute, University of Bonn
Mojtaba Nayyeri	University of Bonn
Martin Nečaský	Charles University
Vinh Nguyen	National Library of Medicine, NIH
Andrea Giovanni Nuzzolese	University of Bologna
Alessandro Oltramari	Bosch Research and Technology Center
Bijan Parsia	The University of Manchester
Silvio Peroni	University of Bologna
Guilin Qi	Southeast University
Mariano Rico	Universidad Politécnica de Madrid
German Rigau	IXA Group, UPV/EHU
Giuseppe Rizzo	LINKS Foundation
Mariano Rodríguez Muro	Google
Edna Ruckhaus	Universidad Politécnica de Madrid
Anisa Rula	University of Milano-Bicocca
Michele Ruta	Politecnico di Bari
Satya Sahoo	Case Western Reserve University
Miel Vander Sande	Ghent University
Marco Luca Sbodio	IBM
Stefan Schlobach	Vrije Universiteit Amsterdam
Gezim Sejdiu	University of Bonn

Nicolas Seydoux	LAAS-CNRS, IRIT
Ruben Taelman	Ghent University – imec
Harsh Thakkar	University of Bonn
Allan Third	The Open University
Krishnaprasad Thirunarayan	Wright State University
Konstantin Todorov	LIRMM, University of Montpellier
Priyansh Trivedi	University of Bonn
Cassia Trojahn	UT2J, IRIT
Federico Ulliana	Université Montpellier
Natalia Villanueva-Rosales	University of Texas at El Paso
Tobias Weller	Karlsruhe Institute of Technology
Fouad Zablith	American University of Beirut
Ondřej Zamazal	University of Economics in Prague
Amrapali Zaveri	Maastricht University
Jun Zhao	University of Oxford

Additional Reviewers – Resources Track

Pierre-Antoine Champin	Universite Claude Bernard Lyon 1
Nathan Elazar	Australian National University
Kuldeep Singh	Fraunhofer IAIS
Blerina Spahiu	Bicocca University
Xander Wilcke	Vrije Universiteit Amsterdam
Tianxing Wu	Nanyang Technological University
Hong Yung Yip	Wright State University

Program Committee – In-Use Track

Renzo Angles	Universidad de Talca
Sonia Bergamaschi	University of Modena
Carlos Buil-Aranda	Universidad Técnica Federico Santa María
Irene Celino	Cefriel
Oscar Corcho	Universidad Politécnica de Madrid
Philippe Cudre-Mauroux	University of Fribourg
Brian Davis	National University of Ireland Maynooth
Mauro Dragoni	Fondazione Bruno Kessler
Achille Fokoue	IBM
Daniel Garijo	Information Sciences Institute, University of Southern California
Jose Manuel Gomez-Perez	ExpertSystem
Rafael Gonçalves	Stanford University
Paul Groth	University of Amsterdam
Tudor Groza	The Garvan Institute of Medical Research
Peter Haase	metaphacts
Armin Haller	Australian National University
Tomi Kauppinen	Aalto University
Sabrina Kirrane	Vienna University of Economics and Business

Craig Knoblock	USC Information Sciences Institute
Freddy Lecue	CortAIx, Canada, and Inria, Sophia Antipolis
Vanessa Lopez	IBM Research Ireland
Andriy Nikolov	metaphacts GmbH
Francesco Osborne	The Open University
Matteo Palmonari	University of Milan-Bicocca
Jeff Z. Pan	University of Aberdeen
Josiane Xavier Parreira	Siemens AG Österreich
Catia Pesquita	LASIGE, University of Lisbon
Artem Revenko	Semantic Web Company GmbH
Mariano Rico	Universidad Politécnica de Madrid
Dumitru Roman	SINTEF AS, University of Oslo
Anisa Rula	University of Milan-Bicocca
Juan F. Sequeda	Capsenta Labs
Dezhao Song	Thomson Reuters
Thomas Steiner	Google
Ilaria Tiddi	VU Amsterdam
Anna Tordai	Elsevier
Raphaël Troncy	EURECOM
Benjamin Zapilko	GESIS – Leibniz Institute for the Social Sciences
Matthäus Zloch	GESIS – Leibniz Institute for the Social Sciences

Additional Reviewers – In-Use Track

Akansha Bhardwaj	eXascale Infolab, University of Fribourg
Luca Gagliardelli	Università degli Studi di Modena e Reggio Emilia
Elena Montiel-Ponsoda	Universidad Politécnica de Madrid
Nikolay Nikolov	University of Oxford
Joe Raad	Vrije Universiteit Amsterdam
Giovanni Simonini	MIT
Ahmet Soylu	Norwegian University of Science and Technology

Sponsors

Gold Plus Sponsor

IBM **Research**

http://www.research.ibm.com

Gold Sponsor

https://metaphacts.com

Silver Sponsors

GE Global Research

https://www.ge.com/research

Google

https://www.google.com

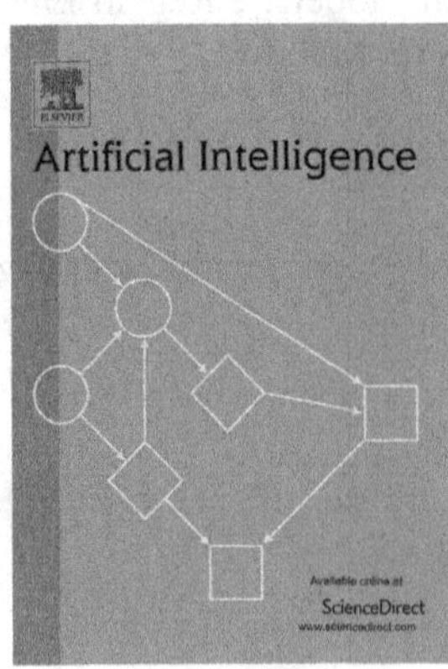

https://www.journals.elsevier.com/artificial-intelligence

100% PURE NEW ZEALAND

https://www.tourismnewzealand.com

Bronze Sponsors

https://www.springer.com

https://www.auckland.ac.nz/en/science.html

http://aucklandconventions.co.nz

http://cs.auckland.ac.nz

Other Sponsors

https://franz.com

https://www.inria.fr/en

Student Travel Award Sponsors

http://swsa.semanticweb.org

https://www.nsf.gov

Contents – Part II

Resources Track

In-Use Track

Contents – Part I

Research Track

Resources Track

The KEEN Universe

An Ecosystem for Knowledge Graph Embeddings with a Focus on Reproducibility and Transferability

Mehdi Ali[1,2(✉)], Hajira Jabeen[1], Charles Tapley Hoyt[3], and Jens Lehmann[1,2]

[1] Smart Data Analytics Group, University of Bonn, Bonn, Germany
{mehdi.ali,jabeen,jens.lehmann}@cs.uni-bonn.de
[2] Department of Enterprise Information Systems, Fraunhofer Institute for Intelligent Analysis and Information Systems (IAIS), Sankt Augustin and Dresden, Germany
{mehdi.ali,jens.lehmann}@iais.fraunhofer.de
[3] Department of Bioinformatics, Fraunhofer Institute for Algorithms and Scientific Computing (SCAI), Sankt Augustin, Germany
charles.hoyt@scai.fraunhofer.de

Abstract. There is an emerging trend of embedding knowledge graphs (KGs) in continuous vector spaces in order to use those for machine learning tasks. Recently, many knowledge graph embedding (KGE) models have been proposed that learn low dimensional representations while trying to maintain the structural properties of the KGs such as the similarity of nodes depending on their edges to other nodes. KGEs can be used to address tasks within KGs such as the prediction of novel links and the disambiguation of entities. They can also be used for downstream tasks like question answering and fact-checking. Overall, these tasks are relevant for the semantic web community. Despite their popularity, the reproducibility of KGE experiments and the transferability of proposed KGE models to research fields outside the machine learning community can be a major challenge. Therefore, we present the KEEN Universe, an ecosystem for knowledge graph embeddings that we have developed with a strong focus on reproducibility and transferability. The KEEN Universe currently consists of the Python packages PyKEEN (Python KnowlEdge EmbeddiNgs), BioKEEN (Biological KnowlEdge EmbeddiNgs), and the KEEN Model Zoo for sharing trained KGE models with the community.

Resource Type: Software Framework
License: MIT License
Permanent URL: https://figshare.com/articles/The_KEEN_Universe/7957445.

Keywords: Knowledge graph embeddings · Machine learning · Semantic web

C. Ghidini et al. (Eds.): ISWC 2019, LNCS 11779, pp. 3–18, 2019.
https://doi.org/10.1007/978-3-030-30796-7_1

1 Introduction

In the last two decades, representing factual information as knowledge graphs (KGs) has gained significant attention. KGs have been successfully applied to tasks such as link prediction, clustering, and question answering. In the context of this paper, a KG is a directed, multi-relational graph that represents entities as nodes, and their relations as edges, and can be used as an abstraction of the real world. Factual information contained in KGs is represented as triples of the form (h, r, t), where h and t denote the head and tail entities, and r denotes their respective relation. Prominent examples of KGs are DBpedia [18], Wikidata [25], Freebase [5], and Knowledge Vault [10]. Traditionally, KGs have been processed in their essential form as symbolic systems, but recently, knowledge graph embedding models (KGEs) have become popular that encode the nodes and edges of KGs into low-dimensional continuous vector spaces while best preserving the structural properties of the KGs. The learned embeddings can be used to perform algebraic operations on the corresponding KGs, and common tasks are link prediction and entity disambiguation [26]. Furthermore, we can observe that KGEs are applied in downstream tasks such as question answering (QA) [23].

Although KGEs are becoming popular, the reproducibility of KGE experiments and the transferability of the proposed models to research fields outside the machine learning community such as the semantic web or the biomedical domain remains a challenge. Depending on the used hyper-parameter values and the optimization approach, the model performance can vary significantly. For instance, in the experiments performed by Akrami *et al.* [2] an increase of 14.4% for the TransE model and 23.6% for the DistMult model in the *hits@k* metric has been reported. However, the reasons for the performance discrepancies are often not discussed in depth [29,30], impeding the reproducibility of experiments. Furthermore, applying proposed KGE models requires both expertise in KGEs and in implementing these models which can be obstacles for non-machine learning researchers. These are significant shortcomings considering that in research fields like the semantic web or the bioinformatics community, KGs are widely applied, and KGE models might have a strong potential to be used in many tasks. Initiatives like the SIGMOD[1] guidelines defined by the database community or the FAIR data principles [28] highlight that reproducibility and transferability is not only a fundamental challenge inside the research field of KGEs, but it is a cross-domain issue.

In this paper, we describe a software ecosystem that we have developed with a strong emphasis on reproducibility and transferability. Our contribution is the KEEN Universe that currently consists of: (i) PyKEEN (Python KnowlEdge Graph EmbeddiNgs), a Python package encapsulating the machine learning functionalities, (ii) BioKEEN (Biological KnowlEdge Graph EmbeddiNgs) [3], a Python package specifically developed to facilitate the use of KGEs within the bioinformatics community and (iii) the KEEN Model Zoo, a platform to share

[1] http://db-reproducibility.seas.harvard.edu/.

pre-trained KGE models. Furthermore, we evaluate the usability of the KEEN Universe on two case scenarios from the area of scholarly metadata research and bioinformatics.

2 Impact and Use Cases

2.1 Impact

Impact on the KGE Community. By providing an ecosystem that enables researchers to easily share code, experimental set-ups and research results without requiring additional overhead, the KEEN Universe is an essential step in the direction of reproducible KGE research. Specifically, researchers can integrate their new KGE models into our ecosystem to enhance comparability with existing approaches as well as to share their trained models through our model zoo to make it easily accessible for the community. The functionalities provided by the KEEN Universe will save researchers significant amount of time and facilitate the work on complex tasks.

Impact Beyond the KGE Community. KGs have become a standard in representing factual information across different domains. Considering that KGs are often incomplete and noisy, the KEEN Universe can be applied in numerous applications to derive new facts. For instance, the KEEN Universe has been used on scholarly KGs to provide research recommendations [14] and on biomedical KGs to predict associations between biomedical entities [3,17]. Moreover, it can be used in downstream tasks like QA and dialogue generation [6,19].

Impact on Industry. KGs are established in several major companies such as Google, Facebook, Bayer, Siemens, and KGEs are for instance used to build KGE based recommender systems [6,15]. Furthermore, the evolution of industry to *Industry 4.0* paves a new way for KGEs to be applied in the observation of manufacturing processes: (knowledge) graphs are a convenient approach to model the data produced by sensors which can be used to model the status of production pipelines. The encoded information can be fed to machine learning based systems for predictive maintenance. Instead of performing feature engineering which is time-consuming and complex, KGEs can be used to encode the information of KGs [11]. Enterprises could use the KEEN Universe to experiment with KGEs before performing major investments to build their own specialized systems.

Impact on Teaching. The KEEN Universe can be used by students to learn how KGE models and their training and evaluation procedures are implemented which helps them to implement new KGE models that in turn could be integrated into the KEEN Universe. It has been already successfully applied in two master theses and currently, it is being used in a further master thesis to compare link prediction approaches based on handcrafted KG features against KGEs based link prediction approaches. Furthermore, it is used in the Knowledge Graph Analysis Lab (University of Bonn) to introduce KGE models to master students.

2.2 Use Cases

Bioinformatics. Bio2Vec[2] is a project that aims to provide a platform to enable the development of machine learning and data analytic tools for biological KGs with the goal of discovering molecular mechanisms underlying complex diseases and drugs' modes of action. This project also aims to provide pre-trained embeddings for existing biological data, and additional data created and produced within this project. BioKEEN and PyKEEN have been applied already within Bio2Vec to predict hierarchies and cross-talks between biological pathways [3] and to predict protein-protein interactions [17]. Furthermore, the model to predict interactions between biological pathways has been shared through the KEEN Model Zoo (https://github.com/SmartDataAnalytics/KEEN-Model-Zoo/tree/master/bioinformatics/ComPath/compath_model_01).

Bayer Crop Science R&D. The department of Computational Life Science (CLS) at Bayer Crop Science R&D[3] developed a large knowledge graph to describe field trial experiments in which candidates for crop protection products are tested across many experimental settings. The knowledge graph is augmented with trial properties, wherein each node contains information beyond the graph structure. However, a subgraph of the property graph can be extracted in such a way that only important relationships are preserved between nodes. This subgraph is stored as a collection of subject-predicate-object triples to allow for a range of embedding techniques to be easily applied. Since different use cases may require a different approach to mining the graph structure for suggested links or node similarities, it is necessary to have a framework that can simply consume the same graph data and apply new models without a large time investment.

The modular design of PyKEEN makes it a perfect fit for the needs of Bayer CLS researchers. The knowledge graph contains nodes of various categories and relation types, as well as many-to-one and one-to-many relations, requiring the use of advanced embedding methods. In addition, new embedding algorithms can be simply added to or modified from the existing framework. As an initial use case, Bayer CLS researchers implemented the included TransR embedding method to their subgraph and, with very little effort, produced an embedding space that demonstrated clear clusters between node categories. Additionally, they were easily able to add node category support to PyKEEN in order to extend the functionality of the existing TransD algorithm. The team at Bayer CLS expects to provide insights into field trial design, future field trial planning, and data quality checks using link predictions from graph embeddings trained and optimized within PyKEEN.

3 System Description

To improve the reproducibility of KGE experiments, we have defined the following requirements for our ecosystem: (i) provide users the full control of the experimental setup, (ii) provide transparent training procedure for all KGE models,

[2] http://bio2vec.net/.

[3] https://agrar.bayer.de/.

and (iii) provide identical evaluation procedure for all KGE models. To enable the transferability of KGE research, we have defined two requirements: (i) enable experts and inexperienced users to use the ecosystem, (ii) easy to specialize for requirements in different domains. In the following, we explain how these requirements are addressed within the KEEN Universe. First, we describe PyKEEN (Sect. 3.1), then we introduce BioKEEN (Sect. 3.2), and finally, we present the KEEN Model Zoo (Sect. 3.3).

3.1 PyKEEN

Here, we present PyKEEN's software architecture, give an overview of the supported data formats, explain our approach for configuring KGE experiments, describe the training and evaluation procedures, describe which experimental artifacts are exported and finally, we present our inference workflow.

Software Architecture. PyKEEN consists of a *configuration* and a *learning layer* (Fig. 1). In the configuration layer, users can define their experiments, i.e. select the KGE model, its hyper-parameters, and define the evaluation procedure. The experimental setup is saved and passed to the learning layer that executes the experiment. In PyKEEN, a KGE model can be trained based on user defined hyper-parameter values or a hyper-parameter optimization can be performed to find suitable values. Finally, the experimental artifacts are exported.

PyKEEN has a modular architecture (Fig. 2) and depending on the task different modules are executed and interact with each other. The *command line interface (CLI)* module enables users to configure experiments through a terminal, the *Pipeline* module starts and controls the configured experiment, *KGEModel* modules represent KGE models, the *Training* module is responsible for training a *KGEModel* module and the *Evaluator* module for its evaluation. A *HPOOptimizer* module performs the hyper-parameter optimization (currently only *random search* is available). To perform inference the *Inference* module has been developed.

Supported Data Formats. PyKEEN supports KGs represented as RDF, from NDEx [22], and as tab-separated values. We provide support for RDF, because it is an established data format to represent KGs [19]. Examples of popular KGs available as RDF are DBpedia [18] and Bio2RDF [4]. NDEx is an online commons for exchanging biological networks, and of interest for life science researchers. Finally, a tab separated file containing the triples of a KG can also be provided directly to PyKEEN. Overall, by supporting these data formats, many KGs can directly be used, allowing users to focus on their experiments rather than on data pre-processing.

Configuration of Experiments. To provide users full control of the experimental setup we have developed the configuration layer (Fig. 1) that enables users to specify every detail of an experiment, i.e. the datasets, the execution mode (training or HPO mode), the KGE model along with its hyper-parameter values, the details of the evaluation procedure, the seed for the random generator,

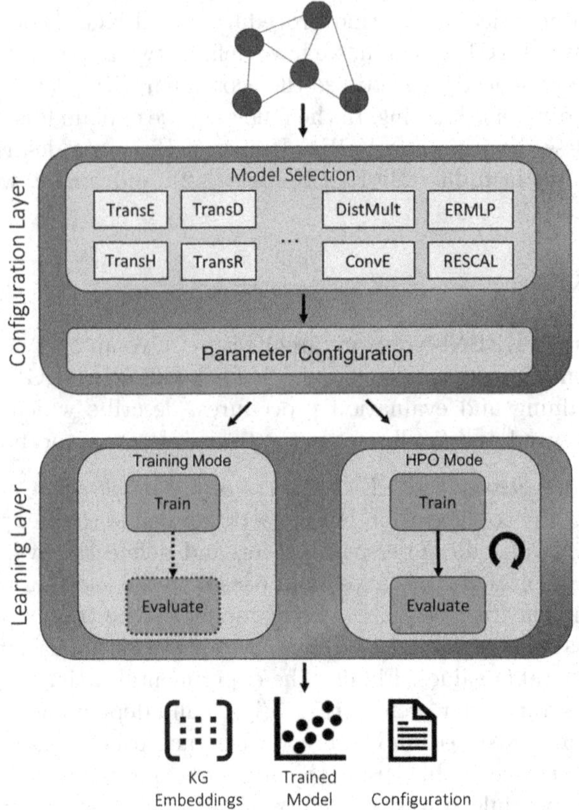

Fig. 1. Software architecture of PyKEEN: (1) the configuration layer assists users to specify experiments and (2) the learning layer trains a model with user-defined hyper-parameters or performs a hyper-parameter search.

and the preferred training device (graphics processing unit (GPU) or CPU). To address experts and inexperienced users, experiments can be either configured through the interactive command line interface (CLI) that assists inexperienced users, or programmatically. The CLI ensures that an experiment is configured correctly. In case that users provide an incorrect value for a hyper-parameter such as a negative number for the embedding dimension, the CLI notifies the users and provides an example of a correct input.

Training of KGE Models. In PyKEEN we have clearly defined training procedures: KGE models are trained based on the *open world assumption* i.e. triples that are not contained in a KG are not considered as non-existing, but as unknowns which might be true or false facts. The models are trained according the algorithm described by Bordes *et al.* [7], and the margin ranking loss and the binary cross entropy are used as loss functions [19]. Selecting suitable hyper-parameter values is fundamental for the model performance and strongly

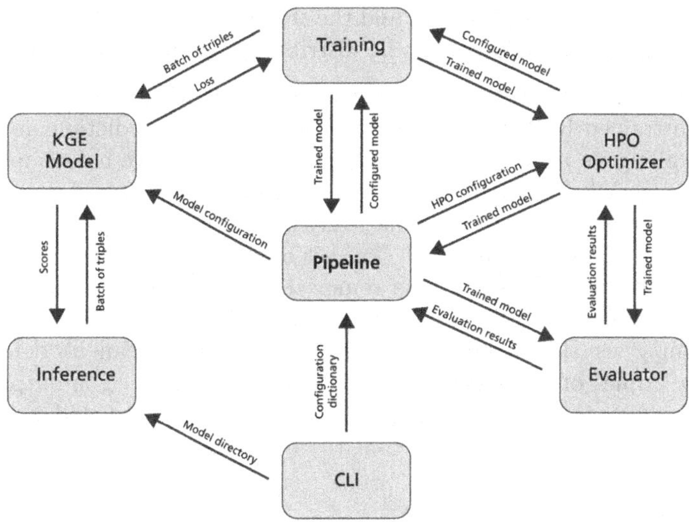

Fig. 2. PyKEEN's modules and their interactions [3].

depends on the expertise and experience of the users. To address both, experienced and inexperienced users, we have developed the *training* and *hyper-parameter optimization mode (HPO)*. In training mode users provide for each hyper-parameter the corresponding value. Optionally, a trained KGE model can be evaluated in training mode. In HPO mode, users have to define for each hyper-parameter a set of possible values (or single values) and PyKEEN assists users to find suitable hyper-parameter values by applying *random search* [12]. The hyper-parameters obtained by the hyper-parameter optimization can be used later to train the final model in training mode.

Evaluation of KGE Models. Within PyKEEN all the KGE models are evaluated based on the procedure described in Bordes *et al.* [7] and the widely applied metrics *mean rank* and *hits@k* are computed [7]. Users can provide a set of test triples, or they can use PyKEEN to automatically split the input KG into training and test triples based on a user defined splitting ratio. This is especially relevant if a separate test set is not available. Furthermore, users can specify whether they want to compute the mean rank and hits@k in the *raw* or *filtered setting*. In the filtered setting, artificially created negative samples that are contained as positive examples in the training set will be removed [7]. Usually, results for both settings are reported.

Exporting Experimental Artifacts. To ensure the reproducibility of a KGE experiment, we export all relevant experimental artifacts after an experiment is conducted. Specifically, we export a configuration file (JSON) describing the experimental setup, the evaluation results (as JSON file), mappings of entities and relations to unique IDs (JSONs), mappings of entities and relations to their learned embeddings (JSONs), and the trained model in a serialized format (pickle). The exported artifacts can be distributed by our model zoo.

Inference. Inference can be performed in two ways within PyKEEN. On the one hand, a trained KGE model can be used to provide predictions for a set of triples by calling its *predict* function. On the other hand, we have implemented an inference workflow that provides additional functionalities: for a set of user defined entities and relations, automatically all triple-permutations are created for which predictions are computed. The set of generated triples can be filtered by providing triples that should be removed. This is for instance relevant in a setting, in which predictions for all possible triples except those contained in the training set should be computed. Furthermore, it can be defined that all reflexive triples of the form (e, r, e) should be excluded. The output of the inference workflow is a file containing the triples and their predicted scores where the most plausible triples are located at the beginning of the file.

3.2 BioKEEN

With the development of BioKEEN we demonstrate how KGE research can be transferred to research domains outside the machine learning community. While developing BioKEEN we took into account that expertise in KGE models and in their implementation might be limited in the bioinformatics community. Within BioKEEN we provide direct access to numerous biomedical databases without requiring the user to process them.

Software Architecture. BioKEEN consists of a three-layered architecture (Fig. 3). Its *configuration layer* is an extension of PyKEEN's configuration layer and enables users to select one of the biomedical databases that are directly accessible through BioKEEN, the *Data Acquisition Layer* provides access to these databases and the learning layer (part of PyKEEN) performs the training of the KGE models.

Easy Access to Numerous Biomedical Databases. Within the biomedical domain, numerous databases containing structured knowledge are available [4]. However, data pre-processing is a time consuming process. For this reason, we have created the *Data Acquisition Layer* that automatically retrieves and converts the content of numerous biomedical databases and makes it available within BioKEEN (a full list is available at https://biokeen.readthedocs.io/en/latest/bio2bel_repositories.html). The data acquisition layer makes use of the Bio2BEL [16] software to access the databases. Bio2BEL is a framework that gathers biological data sources and represents them in the Biological Expression Language (BEL)[4]. By integrating the Bio2BEL software users have direct access to several biomedical databases, can automatically update the database version, and retrieve further databases as they are integrated to Bio2BEL. This functionality allows bioinformaticians to focus on their experiments instead of data pre-processing.

[4] http://openbel.org/.

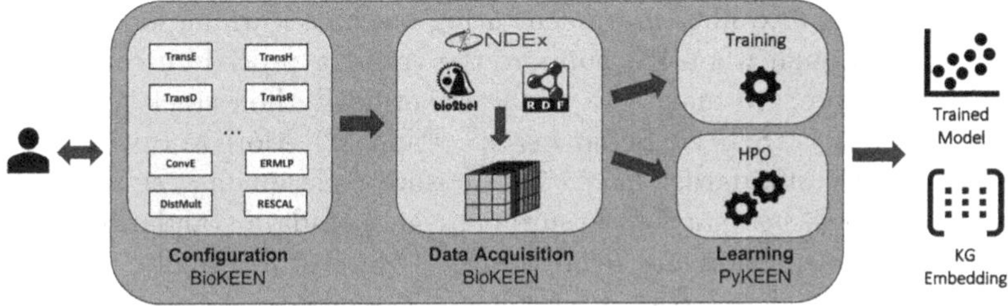

Fig. 3. BioKEEN's Software Architecture [3].

Overall, the data acquisition layer, the HPO mode and the interactive command line interface are essential features to make KGE research transferable to the domain of bioinformatics considering that the expertise in KGE models and their implementation might be limited.

3.3 KEEN Model Zoo

We have created the KEEN Model Zoo as a GitHub project to provide a platform on which researchers can share their experimental artifacts (i.e. trained KGE models, configuration files, evaluation summaries, etc.) that have been created using components of the KEEN Universe. Providing these artifacts publicly will improve the reproducibility of KGE research, and we aim the community to contribute to this project.

To ensure the quality of the model zoo, we have defined following requirements: (i) conducted experiments must be reported in a scientific paper, (ii) all experimental artifacts that have been created by Py/BioKEEN for an experiment needs to be provided, (iii) the used datasets have to be publicly accessible, (iv) a description of the experiment must be provided, (v) a unit test needs to be implemented checking that the provided model can be instantiated. Within the model zoo, we split experiments based on their research domains (e.g. bioinformatics, scholarly metadata research, etc.), and within each research domain, the experiments are categorized according to the datasets on which the experiments have been conducted.

Researchers that want to share their experimental artifacts are asked to create a *pull request* that will be reviewed and *merged* into the *master branch* if all requirements are fulfilled.

4 Implementation

We have implemented PyKEEN and BioKEEN in Python since it is an established programming language for implementing machine learning models[5]. PyTorch [21] has been used as the underlying machine learning framework,

[5] https://github.blog/2019-01-24-the-state-of-the-octoverse-machine-learning.

because it provides flexibility in implementing machine learning models, is easy to debug and through it's GPU support the training procedure can be accelerated. Furthermore, we make use of the scientific Python stack for scientific computing (NumPy[6], SciPy[7], Scikit-Learn[8], Pandas[9]). Moreover, we apply following community standards: *flake8*[10] to ensure code quality, *setuptools*[11] to create distributions, *pyroma*[12] to ensure package metadata standards, *sphinx*[13] to build our documentation and *Read the Docs*[14] to host it. Finally, *Travis-CI*[15] is used as continuous integration server.

Extensibility. The KEEN Universe can be extended in various ways. New machine learning related components can be added (extension of PyKEEN is required), further data reader can be implemented to load additional data formats (extension of PyKEEN), further components specifically relevant for the bioinformatics community can be integrated (extension of BioKEEN is required), finally extensions of PyKEEN specialized for further research domains can be created. Here, we describe how new machine learning components can be integrated into our ecosystem by extending PyKEEN. Figure 2 depicts the sub-modules of PyKEEN and the most relevant with regards to an extension are the *KGE-Model* and the *HPOOptimizer* modules. The modular architecture of PyKEEN facilitates its extension.

Integration of an Additional KGE Model. Within PyKEEN, a *KGEModel* module interacts with the *Pipeline*, the *Training*, and the *Inference* module (Fig. 2). To ensure that a new KGE model can interact with these modules, it needs to provide implementations of a *forward()* and a *predict()* function. The *forward* should expect two multi-dimensional arrays (tensors) containing the batch of positive and negative training triples (or a batch of training triples and corresponding labels; depends on the KGE model) and return the loss value computed for this batch. The *predict* function should expect a tensor of triples for which predictions should be computed and returned. There are no further constraints for the model implementation.

Integration of an Additional Hyper-Parameter Optimization Algorithm. Currently, random search is applied to perform hyper-parameter optimizations and *RandomSearchHPO* is the corresponding module. It extends our abstract class *AbstractHPOoptimizer* which contains the two abstract functions *optimise_hyperparams* and *sample_parameter_value*, where the former is used to

[6] http://www.numpy.org/.
[7] https://www.scipy.org/.
[8] https://scikit-learn.org/stable/.
[9] https://pandas.pydata.org/.
[10] http://ake8.pycqa.org/en/latest/.
[11] https://github.com/pypa/setuptools/tree/master/setuptools.
[12] https://github.com/regebro/pyroma.
[13] http://www.sphinx-doc.org/en/master/.
[14] https://readthedocs.org/.
[15] https://travis-ci.org/.

initiate the optimization procedure and the latter is called in each optimization iteration to sample new hyper-parameter values. To add a new hyper-parameter optimizer, the respective module has to extend the abstract class *AbstractHPOoptimizer* and provide implementations for its two abstract functions to ensure that the optimizer can interact with the *Pipeline*, the *Training*, and the *Evaluator* module.

Overall, the modular architecture of PyKEEN and the simple API of the KGE and hyper-parameter optimization modules facilitate the integration of new machine learning components to PyKEEN.

5 Availability and Maintenance

Availability. PyKEEN, BioKEEN and the KEEN Model Zoo are available at our GitHub repositories under the MIT License. Furthermore, PyKEEN and BioKEEN are also available through PyPI enabling users to install the software packages easily through **pip**.

Maintenance. We aim that researchers from different communities (e.g., semantic web, machine learning, bioinformatics, crop science) will support us in maintaining and extending the KEEN Universe. Before this state is reached, the maintenance of the KEEN Universe is ensured through the Bio2Vec[16] and the German national funded BmBF project MLwin[17] at least till 2022.

6 Evaluation of the Usability of the KEEN Universe

Usability is defined as the extent a software system can be used to achieve a goal with *effectiveness* (extent to which the tasks can be completed), *efficiency* (resources required to achieve the goals) and *satisfaction* (feeling of the users towards the software) in a specified context [1]. We evaluate these aspects based on two case scenarios: co-author recommendations for a scholarly KG, and the predictions of crosstalks and hierarchies between biological pathways.

6.1 Co-author Recommendations Based on KGEs

In the work of Henk *et al.* [14], PyKEEN has been used to provide co-author recommendations based on KGEs for a scholarly KG. The KG contains the entity types *author*, *paper*, *department* and *event*. Furthermore, it contains the relationship types *isAuthorOf*, *isCoAuthorOf*, *isAffiliatedIn* and *isPublished*. The goal was to evaluate co-author recommendations i.e. triples of the form (*author*, *isCoAuthorOf*, *author*). For additional information including the experimental set-up and the evaluation, we refer to [14] and the final experimental artifacts are available at our model

[16] http://bio2vec.net/.
[17] https://mlwin.de/.

zoo (https://github.com/SmartDataAnalytics/KEEN-Model-Zoo/tree/master/scholarly_data_related_recommendations/SG4MR/sg4mr_model_01).

Effectiveness. The KEEN Universe provides all components to completely achieve the goal: PyKEEN has been used to train four KGE models (DistMult, TransE, TransH and TransR) on the KG, and through the hyper-parameter optimization mode, a suitable combination of KGE model and hyper-parameter values has been automatically determined. Based on the model that performed best, we have used the inference workflow to provide co-author recommendations which have been manually evaluated by a domain expert that classified the top predictions as valid recommendations.

Efficiency. Considering efficiency with regards to the computation time, we made use of the GPU support of PyKEEN (PyTorch) to reduce the training time. The models have been trained on a single GPU. Efficiency with respect to the time necessary to learn the software to be able to solve the task, the main author could quickly set-up and run her experiments through the command line interface which assisted and ensured that the experiments have been configured correctly. The whole process has been performed without any programming required by the author.

Satisfaction. The main author didn't have any prior knowledge about KGEs and the software ecosystem, but she could easily achieve her goals. This positive experience has helped her to get into the field of KGEs.

6.2 Prediction of Cross-Talks and Hierarchies Between Biological Pathways

In the work of Ali *et al.* [3], BioKEEN has been used to predict novel cross-talks and hierarchies between biological pathways. ComPath [9], a novel database for biological pathways has been used to train the KGE models. ComPath contains two types of relationships: *equivalentTo* expressing that two pathways correspond to the same biological process, and *isPartOf* expressing a hierarchy of pathways. Again, we refer to [3] for additional information and to https://github.com/SmartDataAnalytics/KEEN-Model-Zoo/tree/master/bioinformatics/ComPath/compath_model_01 to access the experimental artifacts of the final model.

Effectiveness. The KEEN Universe provides all components to completely achieve the goal: We have used BioKEEN to train five KGE models (UM, DistMult, TransE, TransH and TransR) on ComPath that is directly accessible through BioKEEN. We performed a hyper-parameter optimization to find the best combination of KGE model and hyper-parameters, showed the sensibility of choosing appropriate hyper-parameter values and the effectiveness of the HPO mode to find suitable hyper-parameter values (performance increase from 19.10% to 63.20% for the hits@k metric). The final model has been used to predict new interactions between pathways based on the inference workflow.

The top predictions have been evaluated by domain experts and we found following novel links that have been added to ComPath: the first link states that the *TGF-beta signaling pathway* is equivalent to the *TGF-beta Receptor Signaling* pathway, and the second link expresses that *Lipoic Acid* is part of *Lipid Metabolism*.

Efficiency. Because ComPath is not a large KG, we trained the KGE models on a single CPU (efficiency regarding computation time). Furthermore, no pre-processing of the dataset was required since it is directly accessible within BioKEEN. Although the primary author has no domain expertise regarding pathway interactions, he effortlessly provided new predictions to domain experts who validated them (efficiency with respect to use the software for solving the task).

Satisfaction. Through BioKEEN the main author was able to get to know a new application area in the field of bioinformatics. Furthermore, researchers from different research fields could work successfully in an interdisciplinary team.

7 Related Work

Supported KGE Models. KGE models can be divided into *translational distance models (TDM)* and *semantic matching models (SMM)* where the former compute the plausibility of a fact by a distance function (e.g. using the Euclidean norm) and the latter apply similarity-based scoring functions (considering the similarity of the latent features of the entities and relations) [26]. Table 1 lists all the KGE models that are currently available within the KEEN Universe.

Existing Ecosystems for KGE Models. The available software for KGE models is limited, and an ecosystem like the KEEN Universe is to the best of our knowledge unique. However, there exist software projects that provide implementations of different KGE models. One of them is scikit-kge[18] that provides implementations of three KGE models and different negative sampling approaches. The project doesn't seem to be maintained since the last commit dates back to the year 2016. A recently published framework which enables users to train and evaluate several KGE models is OpenKE [13] that can be compared to PyKEEN (Sect. 3.1). While allowing users to reproduce KGE experiments, we argue that it has not been developed with the goal of making KGE research transferable to domains outside the machine learning community and usable for both, experts and non-experts. For instance, it supports only one data format (a text-file consisting of three columns) whereas within PyKEEN a KG can be provided as tab separated values, RDF and from NDEx (Sect. 3.1). Users without expertise in programming might face difficulties to run the software since it doesn't provide an interactive command line interface, and users without expertise in KGE models might have issues in finding appropriate combinations of

[18] https://github.com/mnick/scikit-kge.

Table 1. KGE Models available within the KEEN Universe.

Type	Reference	Model
TDM	[26]	TransE
	[26]	TransH
	[26]	TransR
	[26]	TransD
	[26]	Unstructured Model (UM)
	[26]	Structured Embedding (SE)
SMM	[20]	RESCAL
	[26]	DistMult
	[26]	ERMLP
	[8]	ConvE

KGE models and corresponding hyper-parameter values since it doesn't provide a hyper-parameter optimization procedure. Further software repositories containing implementation for different KGE models can be found at[19] and[20].

8 Limitations and Future Work

Currently, all the KGE models available within the KEEN Universe make only use of the triples of a KG. However, several KGs contain additional information such as textual descriptions of entities, images and numerical values which can be used to train multimodal KGE models. Based on multimodal data, KGE models can be developed that are capable of performing inference among different KGs which is currently not possible with models that are trained only based on the entities and relations of a KG [30]. We plan to integrate an additional software package to our ecosystem that contains implementations of multimodal KGE models.

Within PyKEEN, negative samples are created based on the approach described in Bordes *et al.* [7]. However, it has been shown that alternative approaches such as *bern* [27] can yield better performance. Therefore, we aim to implement additional negative sampling approaches.

KGE models are evaluated within our ecosystem based on the widely applied metrics *mean rank* and *hits@k*, but additional metrics such as the *AUC-ROC* and *AUC-PR* curve might be of interest [19]. Furthermore, Sharma *et al.* [24] propose a geometrical analysis of learned embeddings that can provide valuable insights. We plan to implement these additional evaluation metrics within the KEEN Universe.

[19] https://github.com/bookmanhan/Embedding.
[20] https://github.com/TimDettmers/ConvE.

Acknowledgments. This work was partly supported by the KAUST project grant Bio2Vec (grant no. 3454), the European Union's Horizon 2020 funded project BigDataOcean (GA no. 732310), the CLEOPATRA project (GA no. 812997), and the German national funded BmBF project MLwin.

References

1. Abran, A., Khelifi, A., Suryn, W., Seffah, A.: Usability meanings and interpretations in ISO standards. Softw. Qual. J. **11**(4), 325–338 (2003)
2. Akrami, F., Guo, L., Hu, W., Li, C.: Re-evaluating embedding-based knowledge graph completion methods. In: Proceedings of the 27th ACM International Conference on Information and Knowledge Management, CIKM 2018, pp. 1779–1782. ACM, New York (2018). https://doi.org/10.1145/3269206.3269266
3. Ali, M., Hoyt, C.T., Domingo-Fernández, D., Lehmann, J., Jabeen, H.: BioKEEN: a library for learning and evaluating biological knowledge graph embeddings. Bioinformatics (2019). https://doi.org/10.1093/bioinformatics/btz117
4. Belleau, F., et al.: Bio2RDF: towards a mashup to build bioinformatics knowledge systems. J. Biomed. Inform. **41**(5), 706–716 (2008)
5. Bollacker, K., Evans, C., Paritosh, P., Sturge, T., Taylor, J.: Freebase: a collaboratively created graph database for structuring human knowledge. In: Proceedings of the 2008 ACM SIGMOD International Conference on Management of Data, pp. 1247–1250. ACM (2008)
6. Bonatti, P.A., Decker, S., Polleres, A., Presutti, V.: Knowledge graphs: new directions for knowledge representation on the semantic web (dagstuhl seminar 18371). Schloss Dagstuhl-Leibniz-Zentrum fuer Informatik (2019)
7. Bordes, A., et al.: Translating embeddings for modeling multi-relational data. In: Advances in Neural Information Processing Systems, pp. 2787–2795 (2013)
8. Dettmers, T., Minervini, P., Stenetorp, P., Riedel, S.: Convolutional 2D knowledge graph embeddings. arXiv preprint arXiv:1707.01476 (2017)
9. Domingo-Fernandez, D., Hoyt, C.T., Bobis-Álvarez, C., Marin-Llao, J., Hofmann-Apitius, M.: ComPath: an ecosystem for exploring, analyzing, and curating mappings across pathway databases. NPJ Syst. Biol. Appl. **5**(1), 3 (2018)
10. Dong, X., et al.: Knowledge vault: a web-scale approach to probabilistic knowledge fusion. In: Proceedings of the 20th ACM SIGKDD International Conference on Knowledge Discovery and Data Mining, pp. 601–610. ACM (2014)
11. Garofalo, M., Pellegrino, M.A., Altabba, A., Cochez, M.: Leveraging knowledge graph embedding techniques for industry 4.0 use cases. arXiv preprint arXiv:1808.00434 (2018)
12. Goodfellow, I., Bengio, Y., Courville, A.: Deep Learning. MIT Press, Cambridge (2016)
13. Han, X., et al.: OpenKE: an open toolkit for knowledge embedding. In: Proceedings of the 2018 Conference on Empirical Methods in Natural Language Processing: System Demonstrations, pp. 139–144 (2018)
14. Henk, V., Vahdati, S., Nayyeri, M., Ali, M., Yazdi, H.S., Lehmann, J.: Metaresearch recommendations using knowledge graph embeddings. In: AAAI 2019 Workshop on Recommender Systems and Natural Language Processing (RECNLP) (2019)
15. Hildebrandt, M., Sunder, S.S., Mogoreanu, S., Thon, I., Tresp, V., Runkler, T.: Configuration of industrial automation solutions using multi-relational recommender systems. In: Brefeld, U., et al. (eds.) ECML PKDD 2018. LNCS (LNAI),

vol. 11053, pp. 271–287. Springer, Cham (2019). https://doi.org/10.1007/978-3-030-10997-4_17
16. Hoyt, C.T., et al.: Integration of structured biological data sources using biological expression language. BioRxiv, p. 631812 (2019)
17. Kulmanov, M., Liu-Wei, W., Yan, Y., Hoehndorf, R.: EL embeddings: geometric construction of models for the description logic EL++. arXiv preprint arXiv:1902.10499 (2019)
18. Lehmann, J., et al.: DBpedia - a large-scale, multilingual knowledge base extracted from Wikipedia. Semant. Web J. **6**(2), 167–195 (2015). Outstanding Paper Award (Best 2014 SWJ Paper)
19. Nickel, M., Murphy, K., Tresp, V., Gabrilovich, E.: A review of relational machine learning for knowledge graphs. Proc. IEEE **104**(1), 11–33 (2016)
20. Nickel, M., Tresp, V., Kriegel, H.P.: A three-way model for collective learning on multi-relational data. In: Proceedings of the 28th International Conference on Machine Learning (ICML 2011), pp. 809–816 (2011)
21. Paszke, A., et al.: Automatic differentiation in pytorch. In: NIPS-W (2017)
22. Pratt, D., et al.: NDEx, the network data exchange. Cell Syst. **1**(4), 302–305 (2015)
23. Saha, A., Pahuja, V., Khapra, M.M., Sankaranarayanan, K., Chandar, S.: Complex sequential question answering: towards learning to converse over linked question answer pairs with a knowledge graph. arXiv preprint arXiv:1801.10314 (2018)
24. Sharma, A., Talukdar, P., et al.: Towards understanding the geometry of knowledge graph embeddings. In: Proceedings of the 56th Annual Meeting of the Association for Computational Linguistics (Volume 1: Long Papers), vol. 1, pp. 122–131 (2018)
25. Vrandečić, D., Krötzsch, M.: Wikidata: a free collaborative knowledgebase. Commun. ACM **57**(10), 78–85 (2014)
26. Wang, Q., Mao, Z., Wang, B., Guo, L.: Knowledge graph embedding: a survey of approaches and applications. IEEE Trans. Knowl. Data Eng. **29**(12), 2724–2743 (2017)
27. Wang, Z., Zhang, J., Feng, J., Chen, Z.: Knowledge graph embedding by translating on hyperplanes. In: AAAI, pp. 1112–1119. Citeseer (2014)
28. Wilkinson, M.D., et al.: The FAIR guiding principles for scientific data management and stewardship. Sci. Data **3** (2016)
29. Xiao, H., et al.: SSP: semantic space projection for knowledge graph embedding with text descriptions. In: Thirty-First AAAI Conference on Artificial Intelligence (2017)
30. Xie, R., et al.: Representation learning of knowledge graphs with entity descriptions. In: Thirtieth AAAI Conference on Artificial Intelligence (2016)

VLog: A Rule Engine for Knowledge Graphs

David Carral[1], Irina Dragoste[1], Larry González[1], Ceriel Jacobs[2], Markus Krötzsch[1], and Jacopo Urbani[2(✉)]

[1] TU Dresden, Dresden, Germany
{david.carral,irina.dragoste,larry.gonzalez, markus.kroetzsch}@tu-dresden.de
[2] Vrije Universiteit Amsterdam, Amsterdam, The Netherlands
{ceriel,jacopo}@cs.vu.nl

Abstract. Knowledge graphs are crucial assets for tasks like query answering or data integration. These tasks can be viewed as reasoning problems, which in turn require efficient reasoning systems to be implemented. To this end, we present VLog, a rule-based reasoner designed to satisfy the requirements of modern use cases, with a focus on performance and adaptability to different scenarios. We address the former with a novel vertical storage layout, and the latter by abstracting the access to data sources and providing a platform-independent Java API. Features of VLog include fast Datalog materialisation, support for reasoning with existential rules, stratified negation, and data integration from a variety of sources, such as high-performance RDF stores, relational databases, CSV files, OWL ontologies, and remote SPARQL endpoints.

1 Introduction

Semantic web research covers a wide range of topics from knowledge representation, over information integration, to query answering and data analysis. Only a few concepts are important throughout all of these areas. One is the *Knowledge Graph* (KG) concept, that is, a knowledge base that can be represented as an entity-relationship graph. Another one is the *rule* concept, used to derive implicit consequences from given inputs: combinations of rules and (OWL) ontologies have a long tradition [22,28], and recent works introduce rules as ontology languages in their own right [3,12]. Moreover, rules play a key role in many reasoning algorithms [20,21,40]; database dependencies are rules used in data access and information integration [13]; and rules are also the basis of expressive query languages [1] used in graph analysis [34]. It is therefore not surprising that many new rule engines have been created in recent years [4,5,7,14,29,37].

These rule engines are used to solve many different use cases. For instance, the engine Llunatic [14] is tailored to solve data integration issues [13]; that is, to translate data from one or more sources into a single target database. The system RDFox [29] has been used to perform sophisticated data analysis for

C. Ghidini et al. (Eds.): ISWC 2019, LNCS 11779, pp. 19–35, 2019.
https://doi.org/10.1007/978-3-030-30796-7_2

the healthcare provider Kaiser Permanente in [31] (more RDFox use cases are described at https://www.oxfordsemantic.tech/usecases). Furthermore, using acyclicity notions [8,12] or consequence preserving DL-to-Datalog translations in [9–11], one can effectively employ rule engines to solve reasoning tasks over a large subset of OWL ontologies. Note that when it comes to reasoning over ontologies with large amounts of assertions, rule engines are much faster and scalable than state-of-the-art DL reasoners (see the evaluations in [9–11]).

We have recently extended our own rule engine *VLog* [37] with a highly efficient bottom-up computation strategy for existential rules (i.e, rules that allow for existential quantifiers in the head), and showed that it can outperform efficient rule engines such as RDFox [29] in a range of widely common benchmarks [38]. This performance enables rule-based reasoning over KGs with hundreds of millions of facts on a regular laptop, making this system valuable for semantic web applications that involve large KGs such as Wikidata [39].

In spite of these technical achievements, the research prototype used in our previous evaluations was hardly a polished software product, and deployment and practical usage was challenging. Moreover, VLog could originally only be controlled from the command line, making it difficult to interface with it from software applications – arguably one of the main uses of a knowledge representation and data analysis platform. To overcome these obstacles, we have developed VLog from a research prototype into a re-usable software package that bundles many new functionalities:

- Existential rule reasoning support using an optimised version of the *restricted* and *skolem chase* algorithms.
- Support for *stratified negation* [1], allowing negated atoms in rule bodies.
- Translation of OWL and RDFS ontologies into equivalent rule and fact sets.
- Integration with the Graal rule library [4] and its data structures (e.g., existential rules, facts, and queries). This includes support for loading rules in Graal's *DLGP* syntax.
- Methods for *static analysis* of rule sets, e.g., to verify the termination of reasoning over sets of existential rules using *acyclicity notions* [8,12].
- A *data federation layer* to integrate – seamlessly and on demand – data from many sources, including various database management systems, file formats, SPARQL endpoints, and data provided from Java programs.
- All these features are accessible through the Java library *VLog4j*, which provides a full-fledged API for rule representation and reasoning.

VLog (C++) and VLog4j (Java) are free and open source, and use public repositories for development, issue tracking, and continuous integration.[1] This paper is based on VLog v1.2.0 and Vlog4j v0.3.0. Packages for simple installation are distributed via Maven.

We present VLog(4j) through a practical example (Sect. 2) and then give a detailed system overview (Sect. 3). Further sections include a performance evaluation (Sect. 4), a detailed discussion of related tools (Sect. 5), and practical hints on how to obtain VLog (Sect. 6).

[1] https://github.com/karmaresearch/vlog and https://github.com/knowsys/vlog4j.

$$\mathsf{subClHier}(X,Y) \text{ :- } \mathsf{doidRdf}(X, \mathsf{rdfs{:}subClassOf}, Y). \quad (1)$$
$$\mathsf{subClHier}(X,Z) \text{ :- } \mathsf{subClHier}(X,Y), \mathsf{doidRdf}(Y, \mathsf{rdfs{:}subClassOf}, Z). \quad (2)$$
$$\mathsf{doid}(X,Y) \text{ :- } \mathsf{doidRdf}(X, \mathsf{geneon{:}id}, Y). \quad (3)$$
$$\mathsf{cancerDisease}(Z) \text{ :- } \mathsf{subClHier}(X,Y), \mathsf{doid}(Y, \text{"DOID:162"}), \mathsf{doid}(X,Z). \quad (4)$$
$$\mathsf{diedOfCancer}(X) \text{ :- } \mathsf{deathCause}(X,Y), \mathsf{diseaseId}(Y,Z), \mathsf{cancerDisease}(Z). \quad (5)$$
$$\mathsf{diedOfNonCancer}(X) \text{ :- } \mathsf{deathCause}(X,Y), \mathsf{diseaseId}(Y,Z), \sim \mathsf{cancerDisease}(Z). \quad (6)$$
$$\mathsf{hasDoid}(X) \text{ :- } \mathsf{diseaseId}(X,Y). \quad (7)$$
$$\mathsf{diedOfNonCancer}(X) \text{ :- } \mathsf{deathCause}(X,Y), \sim \mathsf{hasDoid}(Y). \quad (8)$$
$$\mathsf{deathCause}(X,Z) \text{ :- } \mathsf{recentDeathsCause}(X,Z). \quad (9)$$
$$\mathsf{deathCause}(X,V) \text{ :- } \mathsf{recentDeaths}(X). \quad (10)$$

Fig. 1. Example for rule reasoning and data integration; geneon:id and rdfs:subClassOf are shortcuts for <http://www.geneontology.org/formats/oboInOwl#id> and <http://www.w3.org/2000/01/rdf-schema#subClassOf>, respectively

2 Functionality Overview

In this section we present an example that illustrates the use of VLog for data integration and reasoning, which allows us to explain VLog's main features in an intuitive way. We use two data sources: the Disease Ontology (DOID),[2] which contains information about human diseases and their relationships, and Wikidata [39], from which we retrieve information about recent fatalities attributed to certain diseases. This data will be integrated and reasoned over using the rules shown in Fig. 1, which we will explain step by step. Rules are written as in logic programming, with premise (body) on the right and conclusion (head) on the left. The overall code for running the example is available as part of VLog4j.[3]

Basic Rule Reasoning. We first configure VLog to use DOID as the only data source. Triples from the RDF serialisation of this ontology are mapped to facts of the form doidRdf(s, p, o). Then we can use rules (1) and (2) to compute the subclass hierarchy of diseases. Rule engines can capture much more complex OWL inferences [9], but RDFS reasoning suffices for this simple example. Rule (3) now extracts a string identifier for each disease IRI, and rule (4) combines this with the disease hierarchy to find all types of cancer (id DOID:162).

Combining Facts from Different Input Sources. VLog can load data from many different sources, including files of various formats and databases. In this example, we add data that is fetched from the live SPARQL endpoint of Wikidata [26]. For example, we can query for humans who died in 2018 as follows:

```
SELECT ?human WHERE { ?human wdt:P31 wd:Q5; wdt:P570 ?deathDate .
                                        FILTER (YEAR(?deathDate)=2018)}
```

[2] More information about the disease ontology at http://disease-ontology.org/.

[3] See file DoidExample.java in the *vlog4j-examples* module (VLog4j repository).

where we use Wikidata IRI such as `wdt:P570` (date of death) or `wd:Q5` (human). The result of this query is mapped to VLog facts recentDeaths(hum). We further define SPARQL-based facts recentDeathsCause(hum, cau) (recent deaths with known cause of death) and diseaseId($dis, doid$) (diseases in Wikidata with a DOID identifier). We can now find all people who died of cancer in 2018, using rule (5). For the moment, let's assume that deathCause in the body holds just the data from recentDeathsCause, as inferred from rule (9). Using VLog, we find 562 cancer-related deaths in 2018.

Negation. VLog supports *stratified* negation, which relies on a simple syntactic check to ensure that no inference can depend recursively on its own negation [1]. Using $\sim$ for negation, rule (6) finds all recently deceased humans who died of a cause that was not cancer. However, there are also people whose cause of death cannot be found in DOID. To include these, we use rule (8), where hasDoid defines Wikidata diseases with a DOID (7). Overall, we thus find 1849 non-cancer casualties in Wikidata.

Existentials and Incomplete Information. These result could lead us to believe that 23% of recent deaths in Wikidata were due to cancer. However, many deceased have no cause of death stated, and are therefore not counted. We can state that every death must have some (possibly unknown) cause using rule existential quantifiers: rule (10) uses a variable Y that occurs only in the head to denote that some such Y must exist, i.e., the rule corresponds to the logical formula $\forall x.\exists y.\mathsf{deathCause}(x, y) \leftarrow \mathsf{recentDeaths}(x)$. This rule allows us to apply (8) even in cases where no cause was specified, leading to a total of 16,173 deaths that are not known to be caused by cancer.

Rule Syntax. Figure 1 uses a common logic programming syntax for illustration. In practice, VLog uses the Graal rule library for Java to read rules from files [4]. This library uses the *DLGP* format, which supports most of Fig. 1 as shown. Only negation is not supported by Graal yet, and our example program therefore constructs rules (6) and (8) directly in Java code.

OWL Support. Another way of defining rules is to load them from OWL ontologies. VLog has built-in methods for converting a (disjunction-free) subset of OWL into rules. In this transformation, OWL classes and properties become unary and binary predicates in VLog, which is different from our example, where classes (diseases) were represented as individual constants to achieve data integration with diseases from Wikidata. In practice, it is important to chose the right perspective on ontological data, and VLog provides this flexibility.

Reasoning Implementation. VLog's main approach for fast inference computation is bottom-up materialisation of consequences. The *standard* (a.k.a. *restricted*) *chase* is used as the main algorithm, but the *skolem* (a.k.a. *semi-oblivious*) *chase* is also supported [38]. In addition, VLog implements some

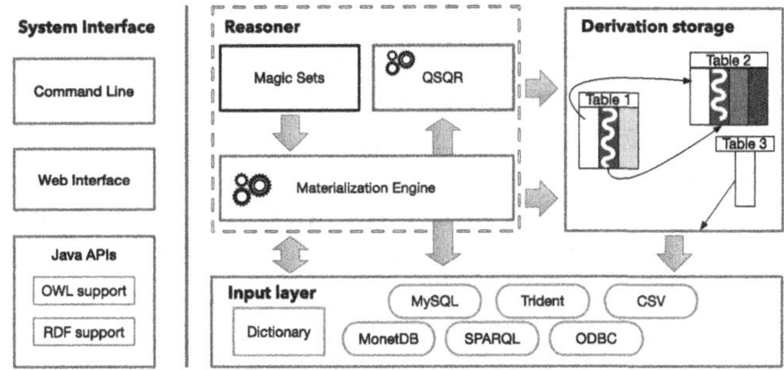

Fig. 2. Overview of the system architecture of VLog

heuristic optimisations based on goal-directed approaches such as *QSQR* and *Magic Sets* [37].

Since existential rules can entail new (unknown) values, reasoning may produce an unbounded number of new facts and thus fail to terminate. Detecting this is undecidable in general, but VLog supports several recently proposed checks that were found to determine chase termination in many practical cases [8].

3 System Overview

In this section we provide a high-level view of our design and overall architecture before elaborating on the details on individual components in the following sections. The design of VLog has been driven by five main requirements: *performance*, *efficiency*, *expressiveness*, *portability*, and the *ability of interfacing with existing technologies*.

Performance and efficiency, i.e., the ability to solve tasks quickly and with a minimum of resources, are obviously central to any reasoner. Performance is important because reasoning can be a time-consuming operation and some use cases introduce time constraints, e.g., to guarantee an interactive usage of the system. Efficiency is crucial to apply our solution also to platforms where the hardware is limited, e.g., IoT devices [35]. Expressiveness broadly refers to the system's ability to use rules that can describe the conceptual relationships of many relevant use cases. There is a well-known trade-off between expressive power and complexity of related computational tasks, so one has to balance this requirement with our considerations for performance.

Portability of a tool refers to its applicability on many different platforms, and as such is well-appreciated in general, and in the particularly diverse application scenarios encountered in the semantic web in particular. It can be challenging to provide portability without compromising performance. Our related requirement of interfacing with existing technologies is a natural consequence of the intention to use our rule engine as a key component for integrating and analysing knowledge from a variety of data sources, including legacy sources and sources that are not under the full control of the user.

In order to achieve good performance and efficiency, VLog takes the distinctive approach of using a *vertical* storage layout that stores derivations column-by-column rather than row-by-row (this approach has been described in more detail in [37]). This strategy is beneficial because it allows memory savings due to data-structure sharing, and is able to avoid much unnecessary computation. Expressiveness is addressed in several ways. Already on the level of the basic Datalog rule language, VLog supports predicates of arbitrary arity. Even in the world of triples, predicates with more than three parameters can be crucial for performing certain computations [21] and they have applications in utilising less strongly normalised data models, as, e.g., in modern knowledge graphs [39]. In addition, VLog supports *existential rules* that extend significantly beyond standard Datalog. Finally, portability and the ability of interfacing to existing sources are addressed at the system level by reducing the external dependencies to the minimum, and by imposing a strict separation between the underlying databases and the set of derivations. This leads to an architecture that can make use of many different data sources during reasoning.

VLog is a complex system where four major components are responsible for different tasks. The components and their interactions are illustrated in Fig. 2. They comprise: the *input layer*, which provides access to the underlying databases; the *derivation storage*, which stores the derivations in main memory; the *reasoner*, which is responsible for the computation of the derivations; and the *system interface*, which provides access to the functionalities to the system.

The components on the right of Fig. 2 are integral parts of the backend of VLog, which is implemented in C++. The system interface involves the Java API VLog4j, which is software project that uses VLog's backend as a dependency and comprises further sub-modules. Each of these components is described in more detail in the following sections.

3.1 Backend Components: Input and Derivation Storage, Reasoning

Input Layer. VLog keeps a strict distinction between data that is available in some external sources and data that is inferred by the rules. To enable a seamless integration with different data structures, we abstracted the access to these sources into a small API. We implemented this API so that our engine can read information from sources like RDF Triple stores, MySQL, ODBC (standard relational database API), remote SPARQL endpoints, and CSV tables. Extending the support to other sources is an operation that does not require a deep knowledge of the system. Note that internally VLog uses numerical IDs to compress the storage of strings. The conversion between strings into IDs (dictionary encoding) is not trivial if the data comes from multiple independent sources. In VLog, we addressed this challenge implementing a sophisticated mechanism to translates on-the-fly terms that are read from multiple sources to shared IDs.

Derivation Storage. A characteristic design choice of VLog is its optimised, "vertical" derivation storage that represents all facts that are computed during reasoning. These are stored in a series of in-memory data structures following the distinctive columnar layout [37]. Moreover, the derivation storage also provides access to derivations in a similar way as the input layer.

Internally, columns of terms can be stored with different data structures. The most commonly used data structure is a plain in-memory array, but other representations are also possible to save memory. For instance, a special representation is used if the column consists of a list of the same repeated term. Another special data structure is used in case the column is a projection of a column of an input predicate. To illustrate this last case, consider as example the Datalog rule $\mathsf{H}(Y, X)$:- $B(X, Y)$ where B is a predicate that maps to an underlying data source. In this case, the column that represents the first field of the H predicate (i.e., Y) is equivalent to the column X in B (assuming that no H-facts have been previously derived, which might require duplicate elimination). To save space, the column Y used in H does not contain a physical copy of all values retrieved from the input layer, but simply stores a query that will allow VLog to retrieve them as needed. This is possible because columns are immutable objects, and in practice results in large memory savings.

Reasoner. VLog supports two types of reasoning: *full materialisation* (i.e., the bottom-up computation of derived facts) and *query-driven reasoning* (i.e., the top-down search for answers to a given conjunctive query). Computing the full materialisation is perhaps the most common reasoning task in the Semantic Web community while query-driven reasoning is useful whenever full materialisation is not possible. The algorithm for performing full materialisation is conceptually simple as it can be seen as a single-threaded loop where all rules are executed one-by-one until saturation. VLog implements the usual "semi-naive" optimisation that largely reduces the amount of duplicates that are inferred, with slight modifications to account for the more fine-grained columnar data structures [37].

When dealing with existential rules, the process becomes significantly more complicated. A blind application of rules would almost always lead to the creation of unbounded numbers of new objects, and the process would not terminate. We therefore implement an additional restriction that checks if existing objects can be re-used to satisfy the conclusion of rules before creating any new objects. In detail, our approach is a variant of the *1-parallel restricted chase* in the terminology of Benedikt et al. [6]. We further refine this approach by ensuring that non-existential (plain Datalog) rules are always saturated before considering an existential rule, which achieves termination in additional cases that occur in real-world knowledge bases [8]. As an optional setting, we also implement the *skolem chase*, which uses a simpler check for deciding on rule applications and terminates in fewer cases. However, experiments suggest that this approach leads to lower performance and higher memory usage across all common benchmarks [38], so this algorithm is not used by default.

In contrast, query-driven reasoning considers an input query and only returns derivations that match it. Two well-known procedures are supported for query-driven reasoning: Magic Sets and QSQR [1]. The first is a rewriting technique which rewrites the rules so that the derivations produced by the rewritten rules are relevant for the input query while the second procedure is a set-based variant of the well-known SLD procedure [1]. Since Magic Sets is a rewriting procedure, it does not perform any reasoning in itself but instead offloads it to the materialisation engine. In contrast, the QSQR algorithm has a dedicated implementation which uses in-memory lightweight data structures to store the intermediate derivations. This makes it suitable for answering queries which do not trigger substantial reasoning due to its small overhead. Magic sets, in contrast, exploits the efficient full materialisation engine so it is able to handle the remaining cases. VLog implements both procedures, and it is the user who can choose the method to use. The query-driven methods can optionally be enabled to heuristically increase reasoning performance even when using materialisation [37]. However, the methods are not applicable to rules with existential quantifiers in their common form, so we do not invoke them in such cases.

3.2 System Interface: Java Integration and Stand-Alone Programs

The system interface component of VLog comprises several independent modules for invoking the reasoner in a variety of application contexts. Concretely, VLog ships with two stand-alone programs – a command-line client and an interactive Web interface –, and is integrated into the Java library VLog4j, which allows the engine to be used within larger applications.

The Java API VLog4j. We have developed a new API for tight integration with Java, which is a popular language in the Semantic Web community. The purpose of this interface is not only to control VLog from Java, but also to provide a complete framework for working with rules and facts. We have therefore designed an object model for representing such data, and provided classes for configuring the reasoning process. Through several extension modules, the Java library can be used to obtain facts from RDF files and to extract rules and facts from OWL. Besides loading facts and rules directly from objects in memory, this library can also configure VLog to use multiple possible data sources, including SPARQL federation, and the results of the materialisation are streamed back using iterators.

This interface also includes some functionalities to simplify the use of the underlying rule engine. In particular, it supports *punning*, i.e., the use of the same predicate name for predicates of different arity. This is not currently allowed in VLog, but it is enabled by the Java interface by renaming predicates before passing them on to the backend. This library also provides methods for transforming rules and sets of rules; more specifically it can ensure that predicates that map to input sources are distinct from all predicates used in rule heads. Further algorithms for transformation and analysis of rule sets are planned for future development.

Conceptually, VLog4j includes some aspects of a data format representation library, making it more similar to Graal [4] than to RDFox in this respect. The successful OWL API [19] is an example of a similar project for OWL ontologies, and indeed has been a model for some of our design. When comparing VLog4j to Graal, we can see that the latter currently provides a larger set of transformation

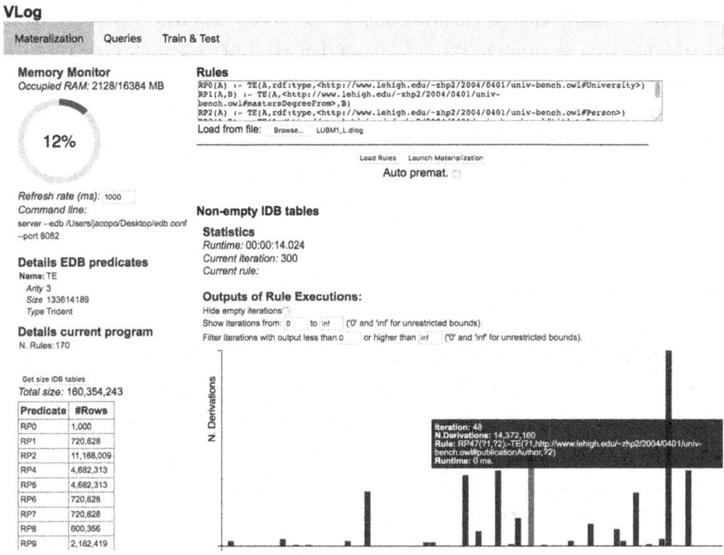

Fig. 3. VLog's Web interface during full materialisation

algorithms, whereas VLog4j comes with a significantly faster reasoning engine [6, 38]. We plan to interface with some components of Graal in upcoming releases so as to establish interoperability between the two projects – unfortunately, no standard for representing rules is widely accepted today, so rule representation APIs often have subtle structural or syntactic differences.

An important goal of VLog4j is to simplify usage, and we take several steps to support this. The online repository includes a Javadoc code documentation and a set of simple example programs to illustrate how to use VLog4j in several scenarios. The Java API is released as a multi-module project through Maven Central to ease its integration into existing projects.

Stand-Alone Programs. Two stand-alone executables are available to run VLog services without the additional Java layer.

Web Interface. We built a web interface to offer the user the ability to specify the rules without using any programming language, and for inspecting the results of the materialisation in a convenient way. The first reason is especially useful for educational purposes, while the second can ease the debugging of the system. A screenshot of the Web interface in action is shown in Fig. 3. On the left side, it reports some useful statistics about the resource consumption and other details about the input layer while the right side allows the user to specify the rules and inspect statistics which are shown as the materialisation progresses. Further information about how to use this interface can be found online[4].

---

4 https://github.com/karmaresearch/vlog/wiki/Web-Interface.

Command Line. From the command line, the user can launch reasoning (both full materialisation and query-driven procedures) and export the results into a number of different formats. For instance, the user can request that all derivations are being exported as RDF triples or simply as CSV files. Moreover, if Trident is used as only input backend, then the reasoner can add back derivations to the original database to enable SPARQL queries on both original and derived triples.

4 Evaluation

A comparison between the performance of VLog and other state-of-the-art systems in computing the materialisation of KBs with large ABoxes is available at [37,38]. In this section, we evaluate the practical feasibility of solving conjunctive query (CQ) answering over data-intensive OWL ontologies using VLog.

Efficient DL reasoning support is highly relevant for our tool, as known rule engines are significantly faster than DL reasoners for solving standard reasoning tasks over ontologies with large data [9–11]. Moreover, (CQ) answering is a non-standard reasoning task that cannot be solved by DL reasoners [15,36].

To solve CQ answering, we use our implementation of the Datalog-first restricted chase (see Sect. 2). All test ontologies, queries, and result tables considered in this section are available online.[5] All experiments were conducted on a Mac Book Pro with 16 GB of RAM, and a 2,2 GHz Intel Core i7 processor.

We consider three real-world OWL ontologies and a benchmark. Each of these ontologies consists of a TBox (a terminological axiom set) and an ABox (a fact set).

- **ChEMBL**, **Reactome**, and **Uniprot** are real-world ontologies available from the European Bioinformatics Institute (EBI) online platform.[6] In order to test scalability on these large datasets, we make use of a data sampling algorithm based on random walks [25], and compute ABox subsets of increasing size. This algorithm was reimplemented for RDF-based data and used in [40].
- **LUBM** is a widely used ontology benchmark [18] modelling universities. The TBox in these ontologies has been manually created and is fixed, whilst an arbitrarily large ABox can be instantiated using an automatic generator.

For simplicity, we filter all axioms containing annotations, data properties, or datatypes. Since VLog does not support non-deterministic rules, we also remove (1) non-Horn axioms that cannot directly be transformed into deterministic existential rules (e.g., "subclass of" axioms containing a disjunction of class names in the superclass). Moreover, we ignore (2) all axioms that, if transformed into rules, would require the use of equality or inequality (e.g., functionality restrictions, or axioms featuring "at most" restrictions or "at least" restrictions with

[5] Evaluation materials at https://github.com/knowsys/eval-2019-ISWC-VLog.

[6] https://www.ebi.ac.uk.

Table 1. Statistics for TBoxes and translated rule sets: the columns report the number of classes and properties in the TBoxes, and the number of existential, Datalog, and non-Datalog rules in the translated rule sets in that order

	#Classes	#Properties	#Rules	#∀-Rules	#∃-Rules
Uniprot	161	52	245	242	3
Reactome	68	55	210	209	1
ChEMBL	134	55	200	200	0
LUBM	43	25	97	89	8

Table 2. Number of atoms and answers per query; in each cell of the table we include the values corresponding to each of the 3 queries considered for each ontology

Ont.	#Atoms	#Answers for samples 1–4			
Chem.	5/7/6	123/738K/60	1K/5.4M/129	7K/26.1M/241	21K/90.2M/339
React.	2/6/6	338K/24/64K	1M/90/123K	2M/319/170K	2.5M/1K/185K
Unip.	2/5/7	9K/5K/15K	20K/10K/32K	30K/16K/50K	39K/23K/68K
LUBM	3/3/2	647K/738K/507K	1.3M/1.5M/1M	2M/2.2M/1.5M	2.6M/2.9M/2M

cardinality strictly larger than (1) because VLog only supports reasoning over equality via axiomatisation and this might be too slow in practice. All axioms removed in steps (1) and (2) were simply commented in the ontology files and can be consulted if desired.

Then, we transform the TBoxes into equivalent rules using the transformation implemented by VLog (see Sect. 2). We include statistics for the ontologies and translated rule sets in Table 1. Finally, we use the acyclicity checks implemented in VLog to determine that the chase does terminate for the translated rule sets (see Sect. 2). Since this is the case, our implementation of the chase can be effectively used to solve CQ answering over the output rules sets (and thus, over the considered ontologies).

For each ontology, we consider three example queries and four ABox samples with an increasing number of facts. The queries are manually designed for each ontology to retrieve significant numbers of answers. Table 2 reports the number of atoms composing each query, and the number of query answers obtained for each of the four samples of facts. Figure 4 reports the execution times of the queries on each of the ontologies. The reported times include performing materialisation and returning all query answers to Java by the C++ reasoner. We exclude time needed to parse the CSV-files that contained the facts.

We find that VLog can efficiently compute answers in all cases, even if the ABox is relatively large. We consider all query answering times to be practically feasible, since they are well within the usual timeouts of, e.g., SPARQL endpoints. When interpreting the times, it must be taken into account that ontological reasoning has a major performance impact in this case as compared to plain query answering on SPARQL.

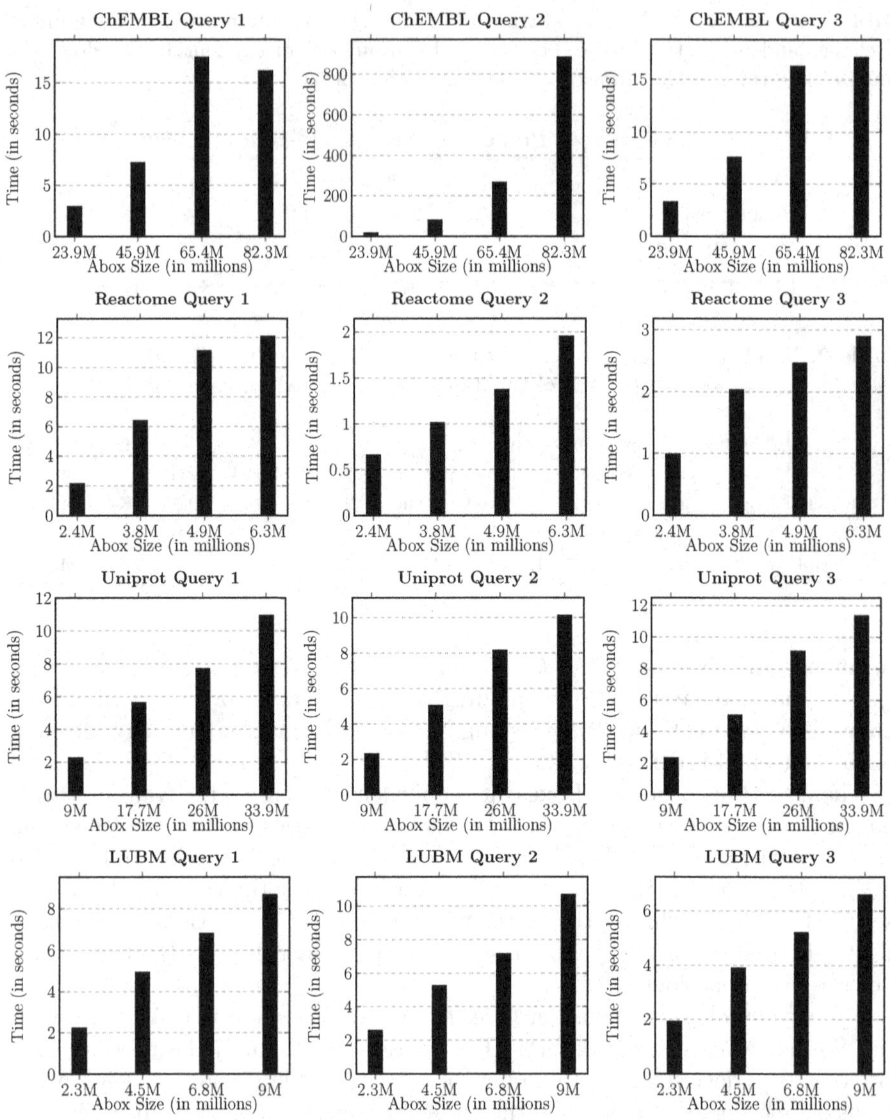

Fig. 4. OWL query answering evaluation results; each table includes results for each of the four different samples considered, one ontology (ChEMBL, Reactome, Uniprot, and LUBM) and one query

We observe an interesting result for answering Query 1 on ChEMBL ontology: the smaller third sample took more than one second longer than the larger fourth sample. This may be due to the fact that VLog uses some heuristics to decide between several join algorithms at runtime, based on cardinalities.

The introduction of an additional Java layer did not seem to hamper performance, and indeed the times needed to convert ontologies to rules and to transfer results back to Java were negligible. Our experiments demonstrate that the use of VLog for CQ answering over data-heavy DL ontologies is feasible.

5 Related Work

To better compare VLog against other state-of-the-art, recursive rule engines, we separate these systems into two broad categories.

1. *RDBMS-based Systems* [7,14,30], which use existing database technologies to implement the chase. This category includes systems such as Demo [30], Llunatic [14], and PDQ [7] which run on top of PostgreSQL.
2. *In-memory Systems*, which rely on the use of RAM memory to compute the chase. This category includes systems such as Graal [4], DLV 2 [2], RDFox [29], and Vadalog [5] as well as our own tool, VLog.

This classification is not perfect. Systems in the second category, such as Graal or VLog, rely on database technologies to store and query input data. Furthermore, systems such as Bash Datalog [33] cannot be categorised as either.

Even if we restrict our focus to "in-memory" tools, it is difficult to compare VLog with the other systems in (2) as these support very distinct features. For instance, DLV 2 supports disjunctions in the head of the rules, Graal can recognise specific logic fragments and use this knowledge to apply specific optimised algorithms, Vadalog can reason over a non-acyclic fragment of existential rules [16], and RDFox is optimised for parallel [27] and even distributed [32] computation. Nevertheless, unlike the other systems, VLog can ingest data from a great variety of heterogenous formats. Furthermore, VLog implements the *Datalog-first restricted chase* [38], a variant of the chase that terminates more often than Skolem and restricted, and has been conjectured to be more computationally powerful [23]. Table 3 compares different features of these Datalog reasoners, based on publications and software released as of June 2019.

In recent work [38], we conduct an extensive evaluation to compare the performance of our tool in comparison with that of RDFox, repeating experiments from [6] and adding several more based on further real-world datasets. We find that, for reasoning with plain existential rules on a reasonably powerful laptop, VLog can often deliver comparable or even better performance than RDFox, while consistently needing much less memory. Note that RDFox greatly outperforms both Graal and DLV [24] in the evaluation presented in [6] (note that DLV is different from DLV 2, which was not considered in [6]). We re-ran our earlier experiments with the current version of VLog, but the results were largely similar (with an average speed-up of 12%), so we do not restate them here.

6 Accessing VLog

VLog is written in C++11, has only very few external dependencies, and compiles with GNU GCC, CLang, and Microsoft's Visual C++ compilers. Binaries

Table 3. Features of in-memory Datalog reasoners: *Inputs* (1: RDBMS, 2: RDF files, 3: CSV files, 4: SPARQL endpoints); *Neg.* (negation semantics); *Eq.* (optimised equality reasoning); *Incr.* (incremental updates); *Mult.* (integrating data from multiple sources)

Engine	Inputs	Neg.	Eq.	Incr.	Mult.	Free license
DLV 2 [2,24]	1	+ (ASP)	+	+	–	–
Graal [4]	1, 2	–	–	–	+	+ (CeCILL)
RDFox [29]	2	–	+	+	–	–
Vadalog [5,17]	1, 2, 3	–	+	–	+	–
VLog	1, 2, 3, 4	+ (strat.)	–	–	+	+ (Apache2)

are available for Linux, MacOS, and Windows. The codebase uses CMake in order to simplify and automate the compilation and in most of the tested scenarios this process reduced to the execution of two commands.

VLog and VLog4j are available on *github* (see Footnote 1). Both projects are free and open-source. They have been released under Apache License 2.0, are available via Maven under artifact id *org.semanticweb.vlog4j*, and their development is monitored by Travis CI to ensure compliance with unit tests.

Furthermore, VLog is also available as Docker image in the Docker repository `karmaresearch/vlog`. Docker images are automatically built when the master branch is updated to ensure the availability of the latest version. The Docker images are useful because they allow the user to either launch the Web interface or use the command line without any prior manual installation. Moreover, they enable a easy deployment of VLog in a cloud environment.

7 Conclusion

We presented VLog, an efficient rule engine that is suitable for scenarios that require expressive reasoning on large KGs. Moreover, the Java API VLog4j allows its usage in complex pipelines, while the ability of the system to interface with existing data sources opens the door to the application of reasoning to novel scenarios (e.g., federated reasoning). VLog and VLog4j support a range of semantic web technologies, including RDF, OWL, and SPARQL, and integrate with other relevant software components, such as Graal. To facilitate the adoption, all the code and documentation is freely available and the development process is open to contributors in the spirit of collaborative open source projects.

The project is under active development and we are considering several new features for implementation. Important directions for extensions of the expressive power will support equality and incremental reasoning, and introduce support for datatypes, especially numbers. We are also considering new optimisations that take advantage of the high level of control that we have on the execution order of rules in VLog. While these are definitely enough to keep us busy, we are also looking forward to inputs from users in the semantic web community, who might encounter completely unforeseen needs in their rule-based applications.

Acknowledgements. This work is partly supported by DFG in projects 389792660 (TRR 248, Center for Perspicuous Systems) and KR 4381/1-1 (DIAMOND).

References

1. Abiteboul, S., Hull, R., Vianu, V.: Foundations of Databases. Addison Wesley, Boston (1994)
2. Alviano, M., et al.: The ASP system DLV2. In: Balduccini, M., Janhunen, T. (eds.) LPNMR 2017. LNCS (LNAI), vol. 10377, pp. 215–221. Springer, Cham (2017). https://doi.org/10.1007/978-3-319-61660-5_19
3. Baget, J.F., Leclère, M., Mugnier, M.L., Salvat, E.: On rules with existential variables: walking the decidability line. J. Artif. Intell. Res. **175**, 1620–1654 (2011)
4. Baget, J.-F., Leclère, M., Mugnier, M.-L., Rocher, S., Sipieter, C.: Graal: a toolkit for query answering with existential rules. In: Bassiliades, N., Gottlob, G., Sadri, F., Paschke, A., Roman, D. (eds.) RuleML 2015. LNCS, vol. 9202, pp. 328–344. Springer, Cham (2015). https://doi.org/10.1007/978-3-319-21542-6_21
5. Bellomarini, L., Sallinger, E., Gottlob, G.: The vadalog system: datalog-based reasoning for knowledge graphs. J. PVLDB **11**(9), 975–987 (2018)
6. Benedikt, M., et al.: Benchmarking the chase. In: Proceedings of the 36th Symposium on Principles of Database Systems (PODS) (2017)
7. Benedikt, M., Leblay, J., Tsamoura, E.: PDQ: proof-driven query answering over web-based data. J. PVLDB **7**, 1553–1556 (2014)
8. Carral, D., Dragoste, I., Krötzsch, M.: Restricted chase (non)termination for existential rules with disjunctions. In: Proceedings of the 26th International Joint Conference on Artificial Intelligence (IJCAI) (2017)
9. Carral, D., Dragoste, I., Krötzsch, M.: The combined approach to query answering in Horn-$\mathcal{ALCHOIQ}$. In: Proceedings of the 16th International Conference on Principles of Knowledge Representation and Reasoning (KR) (2018)
10. Carral, D., Feier, C., Hitzler, P.: A practical acyclicity notion for query answering over Horn-$\mathcal{SRIQ}$ ontologies. In: Groth, P., et al. (eds.) ISWC 2016. LNCS, vol. 9981, pp. 70–85. Springer, Cham (2016). https://doi.org/10.1007/978-3-319-46523-4_5
11. Carral, D., González, L., Koopmann, P.: From Horn-$\mathcal{SRIQ}$ to datalog: a data-independent transformation that preserves assertion entailment. In: Proceedings of the 33rd Conference on Artificial Intelligence (AAAI) (2019)
12. Cuenca Grau, B., et al.: Acyclicity notions for existential rules and their application to query answering in ontologies. J. Artif. Intell. Res. **47**, 741–808 (2013)
13. Fagin, R., Kolaitis, P.G., Miller, R.J., Popa, L.: Data exchange: semantics and query answering. J. Theor. Comput. Sci. **336**, 89–124 (2005)
14. Geerts, F., Mecca, G., Papotti, P., Santoro, D.: That's all folks! LLUNATIC goes open source. J. PVLDB **7**(13), 1565–1568 (2014)
15. Glimm, B., Horrocks, I., Motik, B., Stoilos, G., Wang, Z.: HermiT: an OWL 2 reasoner. J. Autom. Reason. **53**(3), 245–269 (2014)
16. Gottlob, G., Pieris, A.: Beyond SPARQL under OWL 2 QL entailment regime: rules to the rescue. In: Proceedings of the 24th International Joint Conference on Artificial Intelligence (IJCAI) (2015)
17. Gottlob, G., Pieris, A., Sallinger, E.: Vadalog: recent advances and applications. In: Calimeri, F., Leone, N., Manna, M. (eds.) JELIA 2019. LNCS (LNAI), vol. 11468, pp. 21–37. Springer, Cham (2019). https://doi.org/10.1007/978-3-030-19570-0_2

18. Guo, Y., Pan, Z., Heflin, J.: LUBM: a benchmark for OWL knowledge base systems. J. Web Semant. **3**, 158–182 (2005)
19. Horridge, M., Bechhofer, S.: The OWL API: a Java API for OWL ontologies. J. Semant. Web **2**, 11–21 (2011)
20. Kazakov, Y.: Consequence-driven reasoning for Horn-$\mathcal{SHIQ}$ ontologies. In: Proceedings of the 21st International Joint Conferences on Artificial Intelligence (IJCAI) (2009)
21. Krötzsch, M.: Efficient rule-based inferencing for OWL EL. In: Proceedings of the 22nd International Joint Conference on Artificial Intelligence (IJCAI) (2011)
22. Krötzsch, M., Maier, F., Krisnadhi, A.A., Hitzler, P.: A better uncle for OWL: nominal schemas for integrating rules and ontologies. In: Proceedings of the 20th International Conference on World Wide Web (WWW) (2011)
23. Krötzsch, M., Marx, M., Rudolph, S.: The power of the terminating chase (invited talk). In: Proceedings of the 22nd International Conference on Database Theory (ICDT) (2019)
24. Leone, N., et al.: The DLV system for knowledge representation and reasoning. J. ACM Trans. Comput. Log. **7**, 499–562 (2006)
25. Leskovec, J., Faloutsos, C.: Sampling from large graphs. In: Proceedings of the 12th International Conference on Knowledge Discovery and Data Mining (ACM SIGKDD) (2006)
26. Malyshev, S., Krötzsch, M., González, L., Gonsior, J., Bielefeldt, A.: Getting the most out of Wikidata: semantic technology usage in Wikipedia's knowledge graph. In: Vrandečić, D., et al. (eds.) ISWC 2018. LNCS, vol. 11137, pp. 376–394. Springer, Cham (2018). https://doi.org/10.1007/978-3-030-00668-6_23
27. Motik, B., Nenov, Y., Piro, R., Horrocks, I., Olteanu, D.: Parallel materialisation of datalog programs in centralised, main-memory RDF systems. In: Proceedings of the 28th Conference on Artificial Intelligence (AAAI) (2014)
28. Motik, B., Sattler, U., Studer, R.: Query answering for OWL DL with rules. J. Web Semant. **3**, 41–60 (2005)
29. Nenov, Y., Piro, R., Motik, B., Horrocks, I., Wu, Z., Banerjee, J.: RDFox: a highly-scalable RDF store. In: Arenas, M., et al. (eds.) ISWC 2015. LNCS, vol. 9367, pp. 3–20. Springer, Cham (2015). https://doi.org/10.1007/978-3-319-25010-6_1
30. Pichler, R., Savenkov, V.: Demo: data exchange modeling tool. J. PVLDB **2**, 1606–1609 (2009)
31. Piro, R., et al.: Semantic technologies for data analysis in health care. In: Groth, P., et al. (eds.) ISWC 2016. LNCS, vol. 9982, pp. 400–417. Springer, Cham (2016). https://doi.org/10.1007/978-3-319-46547-0_34
32. Potter, A., Motik, B., Nenov, Y., Horrocks, I.: Dynamic data exchange in distributed RDF stores. J. IEEE Trans. Knowl. Data Eng. **30**, 2312–2325 (2018)
33. Rebele, T., Tanon, T.P., Suchanek, F.: Bash datalog: answering datalog queries with unix shell commands. In: Vrandečić, D., et al. (eds.) ISWC 2018. LNCS, vol. 11136, pp. 566–582. Springer, Cham (2018). https://doi.org/10.1007/978-3-030-00671-6_33
34. Seo, J., Guo, S., Lam, M.S.: SociaLite: an efficient graph query language based on datalog. J. IEEE Trans. Knowl. Data Eng. **27**, 1824–1837 (2015)
35. Siow, E., Tiropanis, T., Hall, W.: SPARQL-to-SQL on internet of things databases and streams. In: Groth, P., et al. (eds.) ISWC 2016. LNCS, vol. 9981, pp. 515–531. Springer, Cham (2016). https://doi.org/10.1007/978-3-319-46523-4_31
36. Steigmiller, A., Liebig, T., Glimm, B.: Konclude: system description. J. Web Semant. **27**, 78–85 (2014)

37. Urbani, J., Jacobs, C., Krötzsch, M.: Column-oriented datalog materialization for large knowledge graphs. In: Proceedings of the 30th Conference on Artificial Intelligence (AAAI) (2016)
38. Urbani, J., Krötzsch, M., Jacobs, C., Dragoste, I., Carral, D.: Efficient model construction for horn logic with VLog: system description. In: Galmiche, D., Schulz, S., Sebastiani, R. (eds.) IJCAR 2018. LNCS (LNAI), vol. 10900, pp. 680–688. Springer, Cham (2018). https://doi.org/10.1007/978-3-319-94205-6_44
39. Vrandečić, D., Krötzsch, M.: Wikidata: a free collaborative knowledge base. J. Commun. ACM **57**, 78–85 (2014)
40. Zhou, Y., Cuenca Grau, B., Nenov, Y., Kaminski, M., Horrocks, I.: PAGOdA: pay-as-you-go ontology query answering using a datalog reasoner. J. Artif. Intell. Res. **54**, 309–367 (2015)

ArCo: The Italian Cultural Heritage Knowledge Graph

Valentina Anita Carriero[1(✉)], Aldo Gangemi[1,2], Maria Letizia Mancinelli[3], Ludovica Marinucci[1], Andrea Giovanni Nuzzolese[1], Valentina Presutti[1], and Chiara Veninata[3]

[1] STLab, ISTC-CNR, Rome, Italy
{valentina.carriero,ludovica.marinucci}@istc.cnr.it, {andreagiovanni.nuzzolese,valentina.presutti}@cnr.it
[2] FICLIT, University of Bologna, Bologna, Italy
aldo.gangemi@unibo.it
[3] ICCD, MiBAC, Rome, Italy
{marialetizia.mancinelli,chiara.veninata}@beniculturali.it

Abstract. ArCo is the Italian Cultural Heritage knowledge graph, consisting of a network of seven vocabularies and 169 million triples about 820 thousand cultural entities. It is distributed jointly with a SPARQL endpoint, a software for converting catalogue records to RDF, and a rich suite of documentation material (testing, evaluation, how-to, examples, etc.). ArCo is based on the official General Catalogue of the Italian Ministry of Cultural Heritage and Activities (MiBAC) - and its associated encoding regulations - which collects and validates the catalogue records of (ideally) all Italian Cultural Heritage properties (excluding libraries and archives), contributed by CH administrators from all over Italy. We present its structure, design methods and tools, its growing community, and delineate its importance, quality, and impact.

1 Bringing the Italian Cultural Heritage to LOD

Cultural Heritage (CH) is the legacy of physical artifacts and intangible attributes of a group or society that is inherited from past generations. It carries aesthetical, social, historical, cognitive, as well as economic power. The availability of linked open data (LOD) about CH has already shown its potential in many application areas including tourism, teaching, management, etc. The higher the quality and richness of data and links, the higher the value that society, science and economy can gain from it. As of July 2018, UNESCO has designated a total of 1092 World Heritage sites located in 167 different countries around the world, including cultural (845), natural (209), and hybrid (38) sites. According to UNESCO's list, Italy is the country with the highest number of world heritage sites (54)[1]. UNESCO's list only indexes the tip of the iceberg of Italian CH, which is managed by the Italian Ministry of Cultural Heritage and

[1] 42 additional sites are currently under review.

C. Ghidini et al. (Eds.): ISWC 2019, LNCS 11779, pp. 36–52, 2019.
https://doi.org/10.1007/978-3-030-30796-7_3

Activities (MiBAC). Within MiBAC, ICCD (Institute of the General Catalogue and Documentation) is in charge of maintaining a catalogue of (ideally) every item in the whole Italian CH (excluding libraries and archives), as well as to define standards for encoding catalogue records describing them, and to collect these records from the diverse institutions that administer cultural properties throughout the Italian territory. To date, ICCD has assigned more than 15M unique catalogue numbers to its contributors (cf. Sect. 2 for further details), and has collected and stored ~2.5M records, ~0.8M of which are available for consultation on its official website. This growing, standardised, curated catalogue is the heart of Italian CH data, and a potential *hub* for a highly reliable and rich *knowledge graph* of Italian CH, and beyond.

This paper describes ArCo, a new resource that realises this potential. ArCo is openly released with a CC-BY-SA 4.0 license both on GitHub and on the official MiBAC website. It can be downloaded as a docker container and locally installed, or accessed online. ArCo includes:

- a knowledge graph[2] consisting of:
  - a network of ontologies (and ontology design patterns), modeling the CH domain (with focus on cultural properties) at a fine grained level of detail (cf. Sect. 4);
  - a LOD dataset counting ~169M triples, which describe ~0.8M cultural properties and their catalogue records;
- a software for automatically converting catalogue records compliant to ICCD regulations to ArCo-compliant LOD, which enables automatic and frequent updates, and facilitates reuse;
- a detailed documentation reporting: (i) the ontological requirements, expressed in the form of user stories as well as competency questions (CQs), (ii) the resulting ontological models with diagrams and examples of usage;
- a set of running examples that potential consumers can use as training material. They consist of natural language CQs and their corresponding SPARQL queries, which can be directly tested against ArCo's SPARQL endpoint;
- a test suite, implemented as OWL files and SPARQL queries, used for validating ArCo knowledge graph (KG). It provides a real-case implementation of an ontology testing methodology, which is often overlooked when building Linked Data. This makes the resource especially useful to those who want to build methods for supporting KG design and testing;
- a SPARQL endpoint to explore the resource, run tests, etc.

ArCo data have a highly reliable provenance (cf. Sect. 2). Its ontology network shows high quality, as resulting both from eXtreme Design (XD), an established methodology [4] based on the reuse of ontology design patterns (ODP) (cf. Sect. 3), and from an ex-post evaluation described in Subsect. 5.1.

ArCo ontologies (cf. Sect. 4) address, and are evaluated against, requirements elicited from both the data provider (ICCD), and a community of independent

[2] There is no consensus on a definition for knowledge graph [7], in this context we refer to linked open data including both OWL and RDF entities, and both schema axioms and factual data.

consumer representatives, including private and public organisations working with CH open data. These requirements have raised the need of new ontology models, which have been developed while reusing or aligning to relevant CH ontologies such as CIDOC-CRM [10] and EDM [15]. ArCo data (cf. Subsect. 4.3) links to ~18.7K entities belonging to other LOD datasets, e.g. DBpedia, Wikidata, Geonames.

ArCo is reused in a separate project that involves ICCD and Google Arts & Culture, focused on photographic cultural properties. Indeed, there is evidence of a growing community reusing and interested in ArCo as discussed in Sect. 5. ArCo is published by following FAIR principles (cf. Sect. 6). It is an evolving project, therefore there are many aspects that can and will be improved: they are briefly discussed in Sect. 8.

2 The Official Catalogue of Italian Cultural Heritage

ArCo data derive from the General Catalogue of Italian Cultural Heritage (GC), the official institutional database of Italian CH, maintained and published by ICCD. GC currently contains 2.735.343 catalogue records, 781.902 of which are publicly consultable through the ICCD website. The remaining records may refer to private properties, or to properties being at risk (e.g. items in churches that are not guarded), or to properties that need to be scientifically assessed by accounted institutions, etc. GC is the result of a *collaborative effort* involving many and diverse contributors (currently 487) *formally* authorised by ICCD. These are national or regional, public or private, institutional organisations that administer cultural properties all over the Italian territory. They submit their catalogue records through a collaborative platform named SIGECweb. Submissions undergo an automatic validation phase, aimed to check compliance with cataloguing standards provided by ICCD for all kinds of *cultural properties*. A second scientific validation is performed by appointed experts. The authorisation and validation processes guarantee high standard for quality and provenance reliability of GC data as a source for ArCo.

In addition to GC data, ArCo's input includes requirements deriving from consumers' elicited use cases (cf. Sect. 3), and ICCD cataloguing standards that define many types of *cultural properties*, precisely: archaeological, architectural and landscape, demo-ethno-anthropological, photographic, musical, natural, numismatic, scientific and technological, historical and artistic properties.

Figure 1 depicts a painting by Albert Friscia with some excerpts from its XML catalogue record, from GC. The first issue with XML data is that all information in the records is expressed as strings. In order to build an RDF KG, good practice suggests to produce individuals for every element (or set of elements), whose value (or set of values) refers to anything that may participate as a subject in a triple, or can be linked to, or from, external resources. For example, we want to create an individual for Albert Friscia (the author), as well as an individual for the technical status of this painting. As part of the modeling process (cf. Sect. 4), we define ArCo classes by abstracting from sets of fields and we define rules for creating URIs for their individuals (cf. Sect. 3).

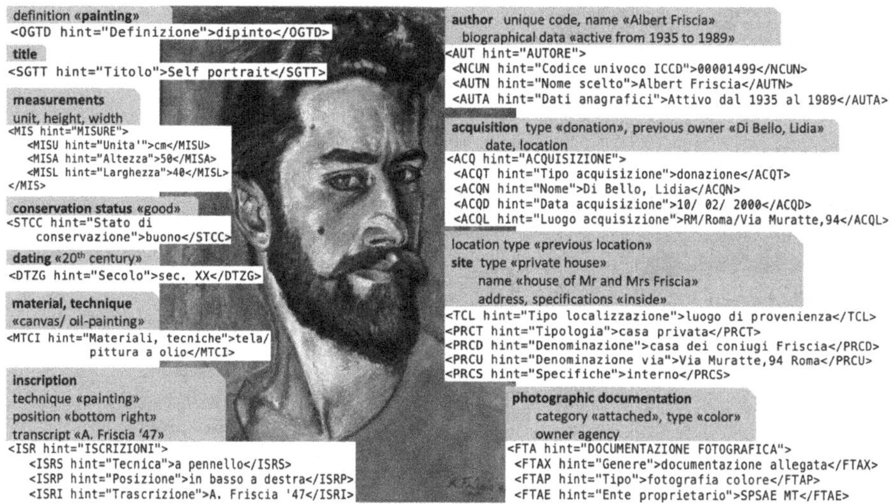

Fig. 1. An example of XML data from ICCD Catalogue. Each snippet is translated to English.

3 Using eXtreme Design for Developing ArCo Knowledge Graph

ArCo knowledge graph (KG) is developed by following eXtreme Design (XD), focused on ontology design patterns (ODPs) reuse [4]. XD is iterative and incremental, implementing a feedback loop cycle by involving different actors: (i) a *design team*, in charge of selecting and implementing suitable ODPs as well as to perform alignments and linking; (ii) a *testing team*, disjoint from the design team, which takes care of testing the ontology; (iii) a *customer team*, who elicits the requirements that are translated by the design team and testing team into ontological commitments (i.e. competency questions and other constraints) that guide the ontology development.

Figure 2 depicts how XD is applied to ArCo, jointly with the tools used in the process, e.g. GitHub, Protégé, etc. The remainder of this section provides a detailed explanation of how each phase is implemented.

Ontology Project Initiation. The design team and the customer team (initially composed of experts from ICCD) have shared their knowledge about the domain, the data and the method, and have agreed on a release plan and on communication means.

Requirements Collection and Continuous Feedback. ArCo's requirements are collected in the form of small stories (according to XD). They are then reformulated as Competency Questions (CQs, cf. [4]), and used for ODP selection by the design team, as well as in the testing phase, by the testing team (more in the remainder of this section). Stories are submitted by the customer team to a

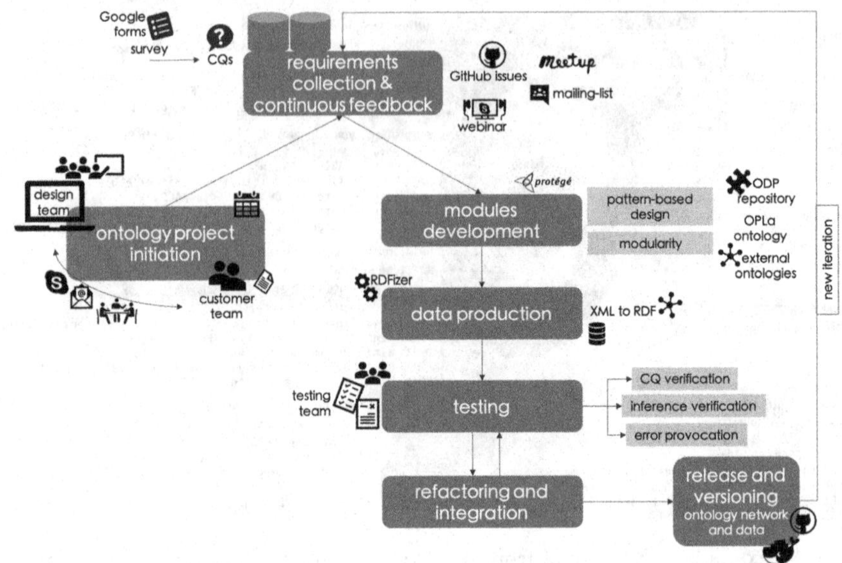

Fig. 2. The XD methodology as implemented for the ArCo knowledge graph.

Google Form. In order to capture a wider perspective on requirements than the institutional and regulatory ones, we extended the customer team by involving a number of representative stakeholders such as private companies and public administrations working with CH data, in addition to the data owner (ICCD).

Improvement proposals and bugs are collected as issues through GitHub. As ArCo is published with incremental releases (cf. Releases and versioning), the customer and the testing teams can contribute continuous and updated feedback, which allows the design team to early detect new emerging requirements and errors, and schedule them for next releases. A growing community, involving interested stakeholders and consumers, interacts *via* a dedicated mailing-list, as well as by participating at meetups and webinars.

Module Design. Ontology design patterns [12] play a central role in ArCo's design as recommended by XD. We adopt both *direct reuse* (i.e. reusing patterns from other ontologies by embedding their implementations in the local ontology) and *indirect reuse* (i.e. reusing patterns from other ontologies as templates, and adding alignment axioms to them). We reuse patterns from online repositories, e.g. ODP portal, and from existing ontologies, e.g. CIDOC-CRM. For details about indirect and direct reuse, the reader is invited to consult [18]. In some cases we have developed new ODPs, as in the case of modeling recurrent events. All (re)used ODPs in ArCo are annotated with OPLa ontology [13], which facilitates future reuse of ArCo as well as matching to other resources. XD encourages and supports a modular design, where each ontology module addresses a subset of requirements and covers a coherent sub-area of the domain. Therefore, ArCo ontology network consists of seven modules, each with its own namespace.

Data Production. ArCo RDF data are produced with RDFizer. Its core component is *XML2RDF Converter*, which takes two inputs: an XML file compliant with ICCD cataloguing standards, and XSLT stylesheets specifying how to map XML tags to RDF. Its output is an RDF dump used to feed a triplestore.

URI Production. Let us consider generating the URI for the author *Albert Friscia*, referring to Fig. 1. ArCo base URI for individuals is https://w3id.org/arco/resource/ with prefix `data:`. Every individual's ID is preceded by the name of its type, e.g. `Agent`. For each type, we manually identify a set of elements that constitute a possible key (e.g. `AUTN`, the author's name). We remove punctuation from the values of these elements (which are strings), convert them in lower case, concatenate them and sort them in alphabetical order, e.g. `albert-friscia`. We compute an MD5 checksum on the resulting string, which is used as the URI's ID e.g, data:Agent/dcd4ca7b54dd3d7dac083dd4c54a9eef. Some types have a unique identifier, e.g. cultural properties. In those cases we directly use it as the URI's ID. In order to minimise duplication, we then perform an entity linking step on the resulting individuals by using LIMES, with the same approach used for linking to external datasets (cf. Subsect. 4.3).

Testing. To detect any incoherence in the ontologies, we regularly run a reasoner, HermiT, during the modeling phase. Then, to evaluate the appropriateness of the ontologies against requirements, we follow the methodology described in [5], which focuses on testing an ontology against its requirements, intended as the ontological commitment expressed by means of CQs and domain constraints. All testing activities and resulting data (OWL files complying to the ontology described in [5]) are documented in a specific section of ArCo's GitHub repository. The testing activity is iterative, and goes in parallel with the modeling activity (XD is test-driven). The testing team performs iterative testing, applying three approaches: *CQ verification, inference verification, error provocation. CQ verification* consists in testing whether the ontology vocabulary allows to convert a CQ, e.g. "When was a cultural property created, and what is the source of its dating?" to a SPARQL query. CQ verification allows to detect any missing concept or gap in the vocabulary (e.g. whether the class for representing the source of a *dating* has been modeled). *Inference verification* focuses on checking expected inferences. For example, if a :`ComplexCulturalProperty` is defined as a `:CulturalProperty` that has one or more `:CulturalPropertyComponents`, an axiom stating that a `:Cultural Property` has a `:CulturalPropertyComponent` would suffice to infer that the property is complex, even if it is not explicitly asserted. But if the reasoner does not infer this information, this means that the appropriate axiom (in this case an equivalence axiom) is missing from the ontology. *Error provocation* is intended to "stress" the knowledge graph by injecting inconsistent data. E.g. when characterising a `:CulturalProperty`, an individual belonging to both a-cd:`AuthorshipAttribution` and `a-cd:Dating` classes, which are supposed to be disjoint, should result as inconsistent. If the reasoner does not detect the injected error, it means that the appropriate (disjointness) axiom is missing.

Refactoring and Integration. Problems spotted during the testing phase are passed back to the design team as issues. The design team refactors the modules and updates the ontology after performing a consistency checking. The result of this step is validated again by the testing team before including the model in the next release.

Releases and Versioning. Incremental versions of ArCo KG are periodically and openly released. Every release has a version number, and each ontology module is marked with its own *version number* and *status*, the latter being one of: (i) *alpha* if the module has partly passed internal testing, (ii) *beta* if internal testing has been thoroughly performed, and testing based on external feedback is ongoing and partly fulfilled, (iii) *stable* when both internal and external testing have been thoroughly done. Releases are published as Docker containers on GitHub and online.

4 ArCo Knowledge Graph

ArCo's main component is a knowledge graph (KG), intended as the union of the ontology network and LOD data. Nevertheless, ArCo KG is released as part of a package including accompanying material (documentation, software, online services) that support its consumption, understanding and reuse. In this Section, we firstly detail what an ArCo release contains, and then we provide details about ArCo KG.

4.1 How to Use ArCo

Each release of ArCo consists of a *docker* container available on GitHub, and its running instance online - both English and Italian versions. Each release contains:

- **User guides** for supporting users in understanding the content of each release, with Graffoo diagrams and narrative explanations of every ontology module.
- **Ontologies**, including their source code and a human-readable HTML documentation created with LODE.
- **A SPARQL endpoint** storing ArCo KG. The SPARQL endpoint also includes LOD data about cultural institutes or sites and cultural events, extracted from "DB Unico 2.0". We use Lodview as RDF viewer.
- **Examples of CQs** (cf. Sect. 3) that ArCo KG can answer, with their corresponding SPARQL queries. This helps users to have a quick understanding of what is in ArCo ontologies and data, and how to use it.
- **A RDFizer tool** converting XML data represented according to ICCD cataloguing standards to RDF complying to ArCo ontologies.

4.2 ArCo Ontology Network

ArCo ontology network consists of 7 ontology modules connected by `owl:imports` axioms (cf. Fig. 3). Two modules – **arco** and **core** – include top-level concepts and cross-module generic relations respectively. The **catalogue** module is dedicated to catalogue records: not only do ArCo ontologies represent cultural properties, but also their ICCD catalogue records, in order to preserve the provenance and dynamics of the data. The remaining four modules (**cultural-event, denotative-description, location, context-description**) focus on cultural properties and their features.

The network base namespace is https://w3id.org/arco/ontology/, which is shared by all modules (for each module we indicate its specific namespace).

ArCo ontologies define 301 classes, 599 object properties, 149 datatype properties, 176 named individuals (at the schema level). ArCo *directly* reuses Cultural-ON and OntoPiA (the ontology network for Italian Public Administrations), while it *indirectly* reuses DOLCE-Zero, DOLCE+DnS, CIDOC-CRM, EDM, BIBFRAME, FRBR, FaBiO, FEntry, OAEntry.

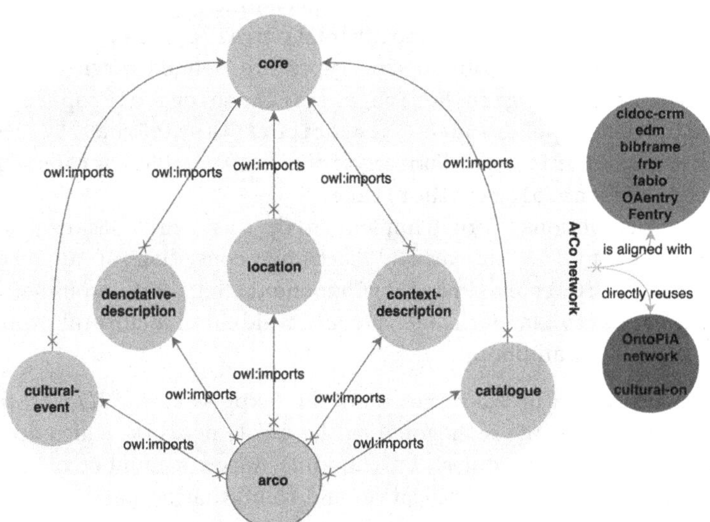

Fig. 3. ArCo ontology network. Blue circles depict ArCo modules, the green circle indicates directly reused ontologies (they are embedded into ArCo), the orange circle indicates indirectly reused ontologies (some of their patterns are reused as templates, and alignment axioms are provided). (Color figure online)

An important requirement that impacted the design of ArCo consists in expressing a same concept both with *n-ary* relation patterns that enable high-level modeling needs such as temporal indexing, state changes, model evolution, meta-classes, etc., and *shortcut* binary relations, which support lightweight modeling and intuitive navigation. With reference to Figs. 4a and b, in order to represent the *material* of a cultural property, ArCo has: (1) a class of (reified) n-ary relations (a-dd:`CulturalEntityTechnicalStatus`) that include the possible `a-dd:Materials`, e.g. `data:carta` (paper), of a `:CulturalProperty`, and (2) an object property `a-dd:hasMaterial` that directly links a `:CulturalProperty` to a `a-dd:Material`, and which is defined as a property chain `[a-dd:hasTechnicalStatus O a-dd:includesTechnical Characteristic]` that makes it a shortcut of the n-ary relation.

In the remainder of this Section we provide details about each of the ArCo modules, with their main concepts, the reused ODPs, and the resulting Description Logic (DL) expressivity.

The arco **module** (prefix : and DL expressivity $\mathcal{SOIQ}(\mathcal{D})$) is the root of the network: it imports all the other modules. It formally represents top-level distinctions from the CH domain, following the definitions given in ICCD cataloguing standards. The top-level class is `:CulturalProperty`, which is modeled as a *partition* of two classes: `:TangibleCulturalProperty`, e.g. a photograph, and `:IntangibleCulturalProperty` e.g. a traditional dance.

`:TangibleCulturalProperty` is further specialized in `:MovableCulturalProperty`, e.g. a painting, and `:ImmovableCulturalProperty`, e.g. an archaeological site. Additional, more specific types are defined down the hierarchy[3]: `:DemoEthnoAnthropologicalHeritage`, `:ArchaeologicalProperty`, `:ArchitecturalOrLandscapeHeritage`, `:HistoricOrArtisticProperty`, `:MusicHeritage`, `:NaturalHeritage`, `:NumismaticProperty`, `:PhotographicHeritage`, `:ScientificOrTechnologicalHeritage`.

Other distinctions are implemented, as in between `:Complex CulturalProperty`, e.g. a carnival costume, consisting of an aggregate of more than one `:CulturalPropertyComponent`, e.g. hat, trousers, etc., and `:CulturalPropertyResidual`, i.e. the only residual of a cultural property, such as the handle of an amphora.

The core **module** (prefix `core:` and DL expressivity $\mathcal{SHI}(\mathcal{D})$) represents general-purpose concepts orthogonal to the whole network, which are imported by all other ontology modules. This module reuses a number of patterns, for example the Part-of, the Classification and the Situation patterns.

The catalogue **module** (prefix `a-cat:` and DL expressivity $\mathcal{SOIF}(\mathcal{D})$) provides means to represent catalogue records, and link them to the cultural properties they are a record of. Different types of `a-cat:CatalogueRecord` are defined, based on the typology of cultural property they describe. `a-cat:CatalogueRecords` have `a-cat:CatalogueRecordVersions`, which are modeled by implementing the Sequence pattern.

The location **module** (prefix `a-loc:` and DL expressivity $\mathcal{SHIF}(\mathcal{D})$) addresses spatial and geometrical information. A cultural property may have multiple locations, motivated by different perspectives: history, storage, finding,

[3] Cf. the diagram on Github.

etc. Sometimes they coincide, sometimes they do not. Those perspectives are represented by the class `a-loc:LocationType`. A certain location type of a cultural property holds during a time interval. This concept is modeled by `a-loc:TimeIndexedTypedLocation`, which implements and specialises the Time-Indexed Situation pattern. This module also defines the concept of `a-loc:CadastralIdentity` of a cultural property, e.g. the cadastral unit, in which the cultural property is located.

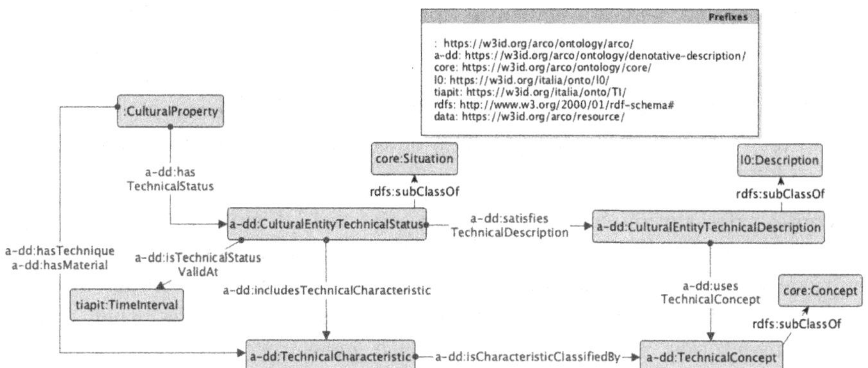

(a) The pattern DnS reused and specialised for modeling technical descriptions and status of a cultural entity.

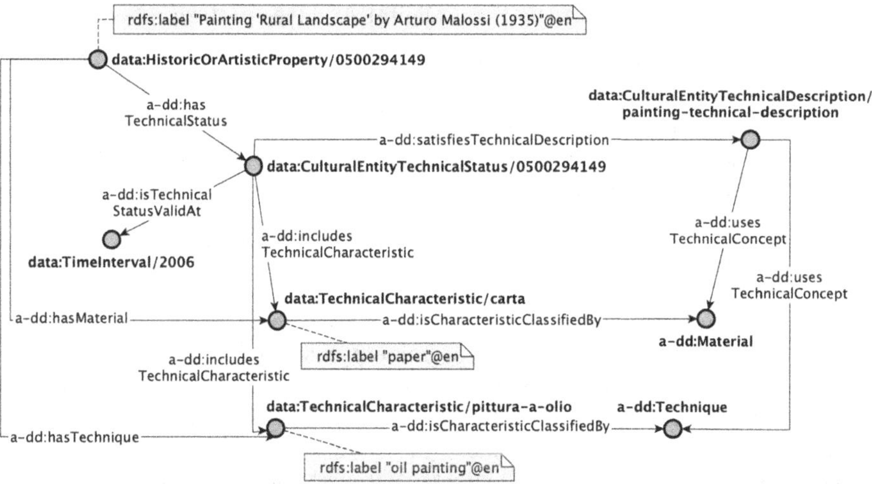

(b) An instance of the model described in Figure 4a, which describes the technical status of a painting made of paper (material) and realised by oil-painting (technique).

Fig. 4. An example (in Graffoo notation) of pattern implementation in ArCo. The *Situation*, *Classification* and *Description* ODPs are reused as templates for modeling technical characteristics of cultural properties.

The denotative description **module** (prefix `a-dd:` and DL expressivity $\mathcal{SOIQ}(\mathcal{D})$) encodes the characteristics of a cultural property, as detectable and/or detected during the cataloguing process and measurable according to a reference system. Examples include measurements e.g. length, constituting materials e.g. clay, employed techniques e.g. melting, conservation status e.g. good, decent, bad.

To represent those characteristics we reuse the Description and Situation and the Classification patterns. Figure 4 shows how we model the `a-dd:CulturalEntityTechnicalStatus`, intended as a situation in which a cultural entity (e.g. a cultural property) has some of these characteristics (e.g. is square-shaped). Each characteristic is *classified* by a `a-dd:TechnicalConcept`, e.g. the `a-dd:Shape`[4]. These concepts are used in the `a-dd:CulturalEntityTechnicalDescription`, that is the conceptualization of the relevant technical characteristics of a cultural entity (see also the beginning of Sect. 4 for more details).

The context description **module** (prefix `a-cd:` and DL expressivity $\mathcal{SOIQ}(\mathcal{D})$) represents attributes that do not result from a measurement of features in a cultural property, but are associated with it. Examples include: information about authors, collectors, copyright holders; relations to other objects such as inventories, bibliography, protective measures, collections; activities such as surveys, conservation interventions; involvement in situations, e.g. commission, coin issuance, estimate, legal proceedings. In order to represent an `a-cd:ArchivalRecordSet`, i.e. fonds, series, subseries, which a cultural property is a member of, we reuse the Born Digital Archives pattern.

The cultural event **module** (prefix `a-ce:` and DL expressivity $\mathcal{SOIQ}(\mathcal{D})$) models cultural events, i.e. events involving cultural properties. It extends, with few classes and properties (e.g. `a-ce:Exhibition`), the Cultural-ON ontology. This module provides an implementation of the `a-ce:RecurrentEvent` ODP, which we have defined based on ArCo's requirements[5].

4.3 ArCo Dataset

ArCo dataset currently counts 169,151,644 triples. Table 1 gives an overview of the dataset, indicating, for the most prominent concepts defined in ArCo, the size of the corresponding extension. ArCo dataset provides 20,838 `owl:sameAs` axioms linking to 20,479 distinct entities in other datasets. Link discovery is limited to authors (11,969 links) and places (8,015 links). Targets of ArCo links are: DBpedia (14,355 linked entities), Deutsche National Bibliothek (152 linked entities) Zeri&LODE (847 linked entities), YAGO (860 linked entities) Europeana (30 linked entities), Linked ISPRA (598 linked entities) Wikidata (2,091 linked entities), Geonames (1,466 linked entities), and from Getty vocabularies: ULAN

[4] For the most common values we provide a controlled vocabulary.

[5] A thorough description of this new ODP is beyond the scope of this paper. It will be described in a dedicated publication, and shared on the ODP portal.

(13 linked entities) and TGN (67 linked entities). Entity linking is performed with LIMES, configured to use a Jaccard distance computed on the `rdfs:label` literals associated with the entities. We use an extremely selective threshold (0.9 on a [0–1] range), below which candidate links are cut off. We tested lower threshold values with manual inspection on 10% of the produced links: 0.9 is the minimum to approximate 100% reliability of results. The LIMES configuration files used in the linking process are available on Zenodo.

Table 1. Size of the extensions for the most representative concepts from ArCo Dataset. Cf. Sect. 4.2 for further details on classes and properties.

Metric	Result	Metric	Result
# instances of CulturalEntity	822,452	# triples of CulturalProperty hasAuthorshipAttribution AuthorshipAttribution	1,428,018
# instances of CulturalProperty	781,902	# instances of agents having role Author	54,204
# instances of TangibleCulturalProperty	781,900	# instances of TimeIndexedTypedLocation	1,085,521
# instances of IntangibleCulturalProperty	2	# instances of LocationType	24
# instances of MovableCulturalProperty	775,148	avg # TimeIndexedTypedLocation per CulturalEntity	1.39
# instances of ImmovableCulturalProperty	6,752	# instances of TechnicalConcept	22
# instances of HistoricOrArtisticProperty	511,733	# instances of TechnicalCharacteristic	22,719
# instances of PhotographicHeritage	20,360	# triples of CulturalEntity hasTechnicalStatus CulturalEntityTechnicalStatus	1,084,548
# instances of ArchaeologicalProperty	149,091	# instances of CatalogueRecord	781,902
# instances of NaturalHeritage	43,964	# instances of CatalogueRecordsVersion	1,767,376
# instances of NumismaticProperty	17,986	# triples of CulturalProperty hasCadastralIdentity CadastralIdentity	14,683
# instances of ArchitecturalOrLandscapeHeritage	6,505	# instances of CulturalEvent	40,331
# instances of ScientificOrTechnologicalHeritage	2,687	# instances of Organization	580
# instances of DemoEthnoAnthropologicalHeritage	29,576	avg # Organization per CulturalProperty	5.2

5 Evaluation and Impact of ArCo

5.1 Evaluation

ArCo KG has been evaluated by following the approach used in [3], along the following dimensions: usability, logical consistency and requirements coverage.

Usability. The numerousness of axioms and annotations, and the use of naming conventions, gives an indication of the easiness to use an ontology and understand its commitment [3,11]. Every ArCo ontology entity has a camel-case ID, at least one label and one comment, both in English and Italian, and is accompanied by a detailed documentation. Many classes are also annotated with examples of usage in Turtle. The ontology network contains 525 restrictions, 175 disjointness axioms, 37 alignments with 7 external ontologies. 23 classes and properties are directly reused from other ontologies.

Semantic Consistency and Requirements Coverage. We refer to Sect. 3 for a description of the testing phase, which allows us to assess semantic consistency and requirements coverage of ArCo. We have performed: 18 tests for inference verification, which raised 3 issues; 29 tests for provoking errors, which detected 14 cases of missing axioms. 53 CQs could be converted into SPARQL queries and provide the expected results. All issues have been fixed by the design team, including 36 issues received on GitHub.

5.2 Potential Impact

ArCo includes a huge high-quality KG of CH entities, which can be used as background knowledge in question answering, entity linking, etc. ArCo first release is dated March 2018. Since then there is evidence of an emerging and growing community around it. A first (of a series of) webinar, attended by 10 participants, has been recently held. ArCo's mailing-list counts 28 subscriptions and 37 threads, so far. Between beginning of January 2019 and end of June 2019, ArCo release site has been accessed 944 times by 329 distinct users. Between June 18th, 2019 and July 2nd, 2019, ArCo SPARQL enpoint has been queried 21,059 times and the GitHub page has had 29 unique visitors and two clones. In the last 12 months, ArCo's official webpage had 1184 unique visitors. We are aware of at least five organisations already using ArCo in their (independent) projects. Google Arts & Culture, in agreement with ICCD, is digitalising its collection of historical photographs (500.000). LOD about these pictures are modelled with ArCo and are ingested by Google Arts & Culture from ICCD SPARQL endpoint. Regesta.exe uses ArCo for publishing LOD about artworks owned by IBC-ER. Synapta reuses ArCo ontologies for representing musical instruments belonging to Sound Archives & Musical Instruments Collection (SAMIC); OnData works on linking data about areas of Italy hit by the earthquakes in 2016 to ArCo's data in the context of the project Ricostruzione Trasparente. InnovaPuglia is extending its ontologies with, and linking its LOD to, ArCo KG.

6 ArCo: Availability, Sustainability and Licensing

Availability. ArCo namespaces are introduced in Sect. 4. We create permanent URIs with the W3C Permanent Identifier Community Group. ArCo KG is available through MiBAC's official portal and SPARQL endpoint, and on GitHub (cf. Subsect. 4.1). Its ontology modules are indexed by, and can be retrieved from, Linked Open Vocabulary (LOV). Additionally, ArCo is published at Datahub and Zenodo, which provides its DOI 10.5281/zenodo.2630447.

ArCo's community channel on Zenodo aggregates all its material (data, experiment configurations, results, etc.).

ArCo sustainability is ensured by MiBAC's commitment to maintain and evolve ArCo[6], by following the XD methodology. In addition, CNR is committed to support and collaborate with MiBAC, based on their long-term and formally established agreement on their shared objectives on this matter. ICCD's experts received guidelines and training for maintaining ArCo KG and using the software for producing LOD. The docker on GitHub and its running instance online will be also maintained. In addition to the institutional commitment, there is an active community growing around ArCo (more information in Sect. 5), which contributes with new requirements, model extensions, alignments, etc.

Versioning and Licensing. ArCo is under version control on a public GitHub repository. ArCo KG license is Attribution-ShareAlike 4.0 International (CC BY-SA 4.0).

7 Cultural Heritage and Knowledge Graphs: Related Work

Semantic technologies, in particular ontologies and LOD, are widely adopted within the CH domain for facilitating researchers, practitioners and generic users to study and consume cultural objects. Notable examples include: the EDM and its datasets, the CIDOC-CRM, the Rijksmuseum collection [9], the Zeri Photo Archive [8], the Getty Vocabularies, the IBC-ER, the Smithsonian Art Museum, the LODLAM, the OpenGLAM, the Google Arts & Culture. ArCo substantially enriches the existing LOD CH cloud with invaluable data on the Italian CH and a network of ontologies addressing many overlooked modelling issues.

Relevant related research discusses good practices for developing ontologies and LOD for CH [1,6,9,14,19]. ArCo draws from the lessons learnt in those projects, as well as from good practices in pattern-based ontology engineering [12].

There are commonalities between CIDOC-CRM, EDM and ArCo. Nevertheless, CIDOC-CRM and EDM resulted insufficient against the requirements that ArCo needs to address. For example, modeling the diagnosis of a paleopathology in anthropological material, the coin issuance, the Hornbostel-Sachs classification of musical instruments, etc., all motivate the need for developing extended ontologies for representing CH properties. To further support this claim we compute the terminological coverage of EDM and CIDOC-CRM against ArCo CQs (cf. Sect. 3), and compare it with ArCo's. We model this task as an ontology matching task between an RDF vocabulary representing ArCo's CQs, and the ontologies being tested. The coverage measure is computed as the percentage of

[6] Moreover, ArCo has been formally included among the datasets of "national interest" in the context of the 3-year plan for Public Administration digitalisation.

matched entities. We use Sketch Engine [16] to extract a reference vocabulary of keywords from ArCo's CQs. The result is an RDF vocabulary of 66 terms. Ontology matching is performed with Silk [20] by using the *substring* metric with 0.5 as threshold. The result shows the following coverage values (0: no coverage, 1: coverage): ArCo 0.68, CIDOC-CRM 0.29, EDM 0.12. However, ArCo ontologies are aligned to (i.e. indirectly reuse) CIDOC-CRM and EDM [15], as well as to BIBFRAME, FRBR and FaBiO (for bibliographic data), and to FEntry and OAEntry (dedicated to photographs and artworks). Directly reused ontologies include: Cultural-ON (Cultural ONtology), which models Italian cultural institutes, sites, and cultural events [17], and is maintained by MiBAC; OntoPiA, a network of ontologies and controlled vocabularies, based on DUL patterns, which model top-level information crossing different domains (e.g. People, Organisation, Location) and recommended as a standard by MiBAC[7].

8 Conclusion and Ongoing Work

This paper presented ArCo: the knowledge graph of Italian Cultural Heritage (CH), encoded and published as linked open data (LOD). ArCo is an evolving creature. As such, it can be further improved and enriched in many ways.

Concerning identity, our URI production strategy might still produce ambiguous identifiers, i.e. a same URI for different entities, typically concerning authors or organisations (contrastingly, cultural properties are uniquely identified, and places have robust keys to make them unique). For this reason, we are currently applying a set of heuristics to detect ambiguous cases, and validating them with the help of experts. We are also experimenting different techniques for improving external linking as well as for discovering possible inconsistencies, including LIMES' machine learning modules, key- and link-key-based interlinking methods [2], and crowdsourcing (involving experts) for both validation and enrichment.

There are aspects that are yet to be modelled: some specific characteristics of naturalistic heritage, e.g. slides and phials associated to an *herbarium*, the optical properties of a stone, etc. ArCo evolution includes associating pictures with cultural entities. Pictures are available, but not yet in the dataset. Additional effort must be put to complete the translation of the data to other languages. At the moment, the data are expressed in Italian as from the Catalogue, and 17,906,639 entities have also an English label. A first step is to complete the English translation. We are considering drafting this task with automatic translation, so that experts can validate or refine it. The MiBAC is also building a new search service that exploits ArCo KG to enrich search results with structured information, including external and internal linking. In order to facilitate the reuse of ArCo ontologies, we plan to develop additional tool support for CH data owners, and to address requirements coming from the library and archive domains.

[7] OntoPia is a *de facto* standard for open data of the Italian Public Administration.

References

1. van Aart, C., Wielinga, B., van Hage, W.R.: Mobile cultural heritage guide: location-aware semantic search. In: Cimiano, P., Pinto, H.S. (eds.) EKAW 2010. LNCS (LNAI), vol. 6317, pp. 257–271. Springer, Heidelberg (2010). https://doi.org/10.1007/978-3-642-16438-5_18
2. Atencia, M., et al.: Data interlinking through robust linkkey extraction. In: Proceedings of ECAI 2014, Prague, Czech Republic, pp. 15–20. IOS Press (2014)
3. Blomqvist, E., et al.: Experiments on pattern-based ontology design. In: K-CAP 2009. ACM (2009)
4. Blomqvist, E., Presutti, V., Daga, E., Gangemi, A.: Experimenting with eXtreme design. In: Cimiano, P., Pinto, H.S. (eds.) EKAW 2010. LNCS (LNAI), vol. 6317, pp. 120–134. Springer, Heidelberg (2010). https://doi.org/10.1007/978-3-642-16438-5_9
5. Blomqvist, E., Seil Sepour, A., Presutti, V.: Ontology testing - methodology and tool. In: ten Teije, A., et al. (eds.) EKAW 2012. LNCS (LNAI), vol. 7603, pp. 216–226. Springer, Heidelberg (2012). https://doi.org/10.1007/978-3-642-33876-2_20
6. de Boer, V., et al.: Amsterdam museum linked open data. Semant. Web **4**(3), 237–243 (2013)
7. Bonatti, P.A., et al.: Knowledge graphs: new directions for knowledge representation on the semantic web (Dagstuhl Seminar 18371). Dagstuhl Rep. **8**(9), 29–111 (2019)
8. Daquino, M., et al.: Enhancing semantic expressivity in the cultural heritage domain: exposing the Zeri photo archive as linked open data. JOCCH **10**(4), 21:1–21:21 (2017)
9. Dijkshoorn, C., et al.: Modeling cultural heritage data for online publication. Appl. Ontol. **13**(4), 255–271 (2018)
10. Doerr, M.: The CIDOC conceptual reference module: an ontological approach to semantic interoperability of metadata. AI Mag. **24**(3), 75–92 (2003)
11. Gangemi, A., Catenacci, C., Ciaramita, M., Lehmann, J.: Modelling ontology evaluation and validation. In: Sure, Y., Domingue, J. (eds.) ESWC 2006. LNCS, vol. 4011, pp. 140–154. Springer, Heidelberg (2006). https://doi.org/10.1007/11762256_13
12. Hitzler, P., et al. (eds.): Ontology Engineering with Ontology Design Patterns - Foundations and Applications. Studies on the Semantic Web, vol. 25. IOS Press, Amsterdam (2016)
13. Hitzler, P., et al.: Towards a simple but useful ontology design pattern representation language. In: Proceedings of WOP 2017, Vienna, Austria (2017)
14. Hyvönen, E.: Semantic portals for cultural heritage. In: Staab, S., Studer, R. (eds.) Handbook on Ontologies. IHIS, pp. 757–778. Springer, Heidelberg (2009). https://doi.org/10.1007/978-3-540-92673-3_34
15. Isaac, A., et al.: Europeana linked open data - data.europeana.eu. Semant. Web **4**(3), 291–297 (2013)
16. Kilgarriff, A., et al.: ITRI-04-08 the sketch engine. Inf. Technol. **105**, 116 (2004)
17. Lodi, G., et al.: Semantic web for cultural heritage valorisation. In: Hai-Jew, S. (ed.) Data Analytics in Digital Humanities. MSA, pp. 3–37. Springer, Cham (2017). https://doi.org/10.1007/978-3-319-54499-1_1

18. Presutti, V., Lodi, G., Nuzzolese, A., Gangemi, A., Peroni, S., Asprino, L.: The role of ontology design patterns in linked data projects. In: Comyn-Wattiau, I., Tanaka, K., Song, I.-Y., Yamamoto, S., Saeki, M. (eds.) ER 2016. LNCS, vol. 9974, pp. 113–121. Springer, Cham (2016). https://doi.org/10.1007/978-3-319-46397-1_9
19. Szekely, P., et al.: Connecting the smithsonian american art museum to the linked data cloud. In: Cimiano, P., Corcho, O., Presutti, V., Hollink, L., Rudolph, S. (eds.) ESWC 2013. LNCS, vol. 7882, pp. 593–607. Springer, Heidelberg (2013). https://doi.org/10.1007/978-3-642-38288-8_40
20. Volz, J., et al.: Silk-a link discovery framework for the web of data. In: LDOW 2009, vol. 538. CEUR-ws (2009)

Making Study Populations Visible Through Knowledge Graphs

Shruthi Chari[1(✉)], Miao Qi[1], Nkechinyere N. Agu[1], Oshani Seneviratne[1], Jamie P. McCusker[1], Kristin P. Bennett[1], Amar K. Das[2], and Deborah L. McGuinness[1]

[1] Rensselaer Polytechnic Institute, Troy, NY 12180, USA
{charis,qim,agun,senevo,mccusj2,bennek}@rpi.edu, dlm@cs.rpi.edu
[2] IBM Research, Cambridge, MA, USA
amardas@us.ibm.com

Abstract. Treatment recommendations within Clinical Practice Guidelines (CPGs) are largely based on findings from clinical trials and case studies, referred to here as research studies, that are often based on highly selective clinical populations, referred to here as study cohorts. When medical practitioners apply CPG recommendations, they need to understand how well their patient population matches the characteristics of those in the study cohort, and thus are confronted with the challenges of locating the study cohort information and making an analytic comparison. To address these challenges, we develop an ontology-enabled prototype system, which exposes the population descriptions in research studies in a declarative manner, with the ultimate goal of allowing medical practitioners to better understand the applicability and generalizability of treatment recommendations. We build a Study Cohort Ontology (SCO) to encode the vocabulary of study population descriptions, that are often reported in the first table in the published work, thus they are often referred to as Table 1. We leverage the well-used Semanticscience Integrated Ontology (SIO) for defining property associations between classes. Further, we model the key components of Table 1s, i.e., collections of study subjects, subject characteristics, and statistical measures in RDF knowledge graphs. We design scenarios for medical practitioners to perform population analysis, and generate cohort similarity visualizations to determine the applicability of a study population to the clinical population of interest. Our semantic approach to make study populations visible, by standardized representations of Table 1s, allows users to quickly derive clinically relevant inferences about study populations.

Resource Website: https://tetherless-world.github.io/study-cohort-ontology/.

Keywords: Scientific Study Data Analysis · Knowledge graphs · Modeling Aggregations and Summary Statistics · Ontology Development

C. Ghidini et al. (Eds.): ISWC 2019, LNCS 11779, pp. 53–68, 2019.
https://doi.org/10.1007/978-3-030-30796-7_4

1 Introduction

Our goal is to build a semantic solution to model the descriptions of study populations and to assist medical practitioners in determining the applicability of a study to their clinical population. Through Fig. 1, we describe the components of a prototype system, that utilizes knowledge representation (KR) techniques to model tabular representations of study population descriptions, often captured in the first table of the scientific publication. We build a Study Cohort Ontology (SCO) (Sect. 4) to support the vocabulary in these Table 1s (plural form) and to model their structure. Further, we encode Table 1s as Resource Description Framework (RDF) knowledge graphs (KGs) [3] (Sect. 5) to expose in a declarative manner[1] these study populations. We demonstrate our ontology and the use of our knowledge graphs with two applications (Sect. 6): one aimed at helping medical practitioners determine the similarity of a patient or a clinical population to the study population, and another aimed at supporting retrospective analysis of a study to expose possible biases or population gaps, such as racial underrepresentations.

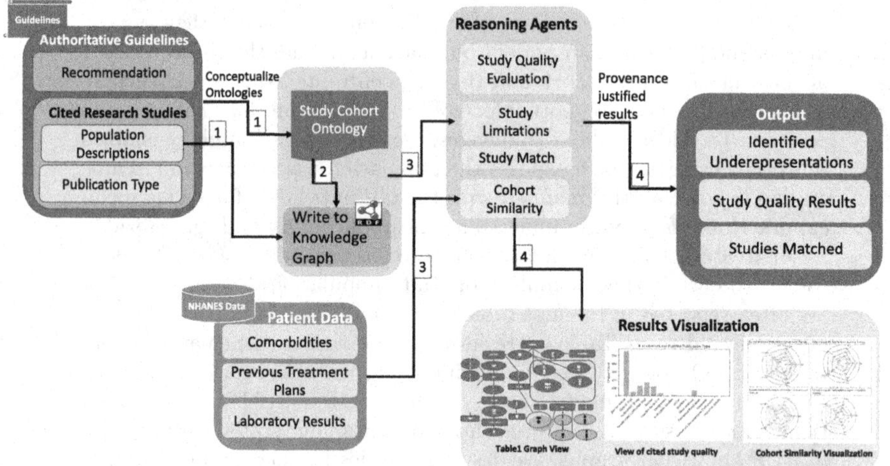

Fig. 1. An overview of the cohort analytics workflow which (1) ingests terms from population descriptions of research studies, (2) standardizes their representations via KR techniques and (3) supports study applicability applications. The numbering is in-line with the figure and is indicative of data flow.

1.1 Use Case

Evidence-based Medicine (EBM) has been gaining popularity, and medical practitioners are using it more often. However, it is challenging to design the CPGs

[1] Declarative manner: in a clear, unambiguous, and computer understandable manner.

to stay current with the growing body of clinical literature. Additionally, medical literature is continuously being revised, e.g., typically, new versions of CPGs are released annually. Treatment recommendations in CPGs are often supported by evidence from cited research studies, i.e. clinical trials and observational case studies, targeting highly selective populations with sociodemographic and comorbid characteristics. In clinical practice, it is well-known that there are biases in clinical evidence that reduce their generalizability. The widely-cited research article, "Trustworthy Clinical Practice Guidelines: Challenges and Potential," [8] states some of the problems in existing guideline practices, such as "Failure to include major population subgroups in the evidence base thwarts our ability to develop clinically relevant, valid guidelines."

Furthermore, when medical practitioners are faced with the treatment of complicated patients who do not wholly align with guideline recommendations, they may want to consult research studies with relevant findings to determine if the study applies to their clinical population. Hence, we are developing a semantic solution to address these challenges, by providing medical practitioners access to high-quality and applicable guideline evidence. We evaluate our solution on the American Diabetes Association's (ADA) Standards of Medical Care 2018 CPG[2] cited research studies, which we will introduce in Sect. 3.

2 Related Work

Existing ontologies for study design and clinical trials are more focused on the study design and methodology aspects of clinical trials, and their vocabulary is insufficient to support cohort descriptions. ProvCaRe [22], an "Ontology for provenance + healthcare research," was developed to assess the scientific rigor and reproducibility of scientific literature. Based on the NIH "Rigor and Reproducibility" guidelines [13], this ontology identifies three components of a study contributing to provenance: study methods (study protocol followed), study instruments (equipment and software used in the study), and study data (metadata about data collection). However, within the ProvCaRe ontology, support for study data is limited to that of inclusion and exclusion criteria, and there is no support for Table 1 terminology, such as subject characteristics and study arms. The Ontology of Clinical Research (OCRE) [20], a widely cited study design ontology used to model the study lifecycle, addresses goals similar to our study applicability scenario. They adopt an Eligibility Rule Grammar and Ontology (ERGO) [21] annotation approach for modeling study eligibility criteria to enable matching a study's phenotype against patient data.

Since we encode a provenance component of guideline evidence, we searched for ontologies for scientific publications. We found that most clinical trial ontologies, e.g., CTO-NDD [24], are domain specific and not directly reusable for a population modeling scenario. Other ontologies, such as the EPOCH suite of clinical trial ontologies [19], that was developed to track patients through their

[2] ADA 2018 CPG at: https://diabetesed.net/wp-content/uploads/2017/12/2018-ADA-Standards-of-Care.pdf.

clinical trial visits, had class hierarchies that were insufficient to represent the types of publications cited in the ADA Standards of Care CPG. Additionally, there is another cohort ontology [11] being developed. However, our modeling of the association of descriptive statistics with subject characteristics differs from their modeling decision to define new properties to represent these associations. Instead, we introduce classes to accommodate new subject characteristic terms upon Table 1 ingestion, and we limit the number of descriptive statistics to a standard set of central tendency measures and boundary values. Hence, we do not leverage their ontology. Further, their ontology is domain specific, including many sleep disorder classes. In SCO we provide a generalized and richer, domain-agnostic Table 1 vocabulary (sufficient to support research studies targeting various diseases).

Clinical trial matching has been attempted multiple times, largely as a Natural Language Processing problem, including a KR approach that improves the quality of the cohort selection process for clinical trials [17]. Clinical trial matching work [17] was carried out with the help of an ontology, and TBOX (knowledge-based) assertions were created from SNOMED-CT for supporting ABOX (real-world) assertions of patient records. However, the focus of their effort was mainly on efficient KR of patient data, and study eligibility criteria was formulated as SPARQL queries on the patient schema. We tackle the converse problem of identifying studies that are applicable to a clinical population based on the study populations reported. We address this problem from the perspective of modeling the study populations.

3 Dataset

Our evaluation dataset is comprised of research studies, cited in the ADA Standards of Medical Care 2018 CPG. We manually reviewed the entire guideline to understand the types of evidence utilized to support treatment recommendations. ADA treatment recommendations are supported through citations within the discussion, which serve as implicit evidence for the recommendation. Further, we used PubMed APIs[3] on the Medline[4] publications, cited in evidence sentences across chapters of the ADA CPG, to retain only those publications that met the qualifications for our definition of research studies. We only considered publications tagged with Pubmed Publication types[5] of: Randomized Controlled Trial, Clinical Trial, and Multicenter Study.

We focused on the pharmaceutical treatments and comorbidities associated with type-2 diabetes, and we filtered our evaluation dataset to contain cited research studies from the Pharmacologic Interventions (Chapter 8) [1] and the Cardiovascular Complications (Chapter 9) [2] of the ADA 2018 CPG. We did a thorough, manual investigation of research studies from these chapters, looking

[3] https://pypi.org/project/pubmed-lookup/.

[4] https://www.nlm.nih.gov/bsd/medline.html.

[5] Find the list of all supported publication types at https://www.ncbi.nlm.nih.gov/books/NBK3827/table/pubmedhelp.T.publication_types/.

for any variance in Table 1s and identifying important study data that explained Table 1 variables. Furthermore, although we were able to gather full-text links for Medline citations through programmatic means, we had to manually follow these links to ensure they are freely available, and, if not, we checked for the availability of the study in other sources. Due to these challenges, we narrowed down the number of research studies to 20 that we list on our resources website.

4 Study Cohort Ontology

As introduced in Sect. 1, we build a Study Cohort Ontology (SCO) to serve as a vocabulary to model the components of a Table 1, the study arms (columns) and their characteristics (rows). We also ensure that the implicit associations exhibited between these components are reflected in SCO. We adopt a bottom-up approach to modeling, that follows, as a by-product of our investigative efforts, the description in Sect. 3. Further, we have attempted to keep our main SCO ontology as domain-agnostic as possible to ensure easy reuse and longevity. In Subsect. 4.1, we introduce the main concepts in our ontology to provide a contextual understanding of the descriptions of populations reported in Table 1s, and walk through our approach to ontology reuse in Subsect. 4.2.

4.1 Primary Classes and Property Associations

The descriptions of study populations that are reported in Table 1s follow a pattern in which columns represent study arms, a group of study subjects who receive an intervention or control regime. The subject characteristics are presented in rows, and are aggregated upon and reported via descriptive statistical measures in the cells of the table. In a conceptual model of SCO as shown in Fig. 2, we depict our modeling of these Table 1 components and the additional details that are necessary to describe a study population in the context of a research study. A more detailed version can be found on our resources website.

As will become evident from a representative Table 1 example shown in Fig. 3, the row and column headers in Table 1s contain specific medical codes and variables that can further be grouped into broad general classifications: Anthropometric Properties (chear:Anthropometry),[6] Demographics (chear:Demographic), Laboratory Results (ncit:C36292), Diseases (doid:0004), and Medical Interventions (provcare:Intervention). Further, we associate all these broad, general classifications we just identified, such as subject characteristics, diseases, interventions etc., via sio:hasAttribute and sio:hasProperty relations to the study subject. More specifically, for properties such as disease and interventions that per-

[6] We use the ontology prefixes: (1) sio: SemanticScience Integrated Ontology (2) uo: The Units of Measurement Ontology (3) chear: Children's Health Exposure Analysis Resource Ontology (4) ncit: National Cancer Institute Thesaurus (5) provcare: ProveCaRe (6) doid: Human Disease Ontology (7) sco: Study Cohort Ontology (8) hasco: Human-Aware Science Ontology (9) prov: The PROV ontology (10) dct: Dublin Core Terms (11) vann: A vocabulary for annotating vocabulary descriptions.

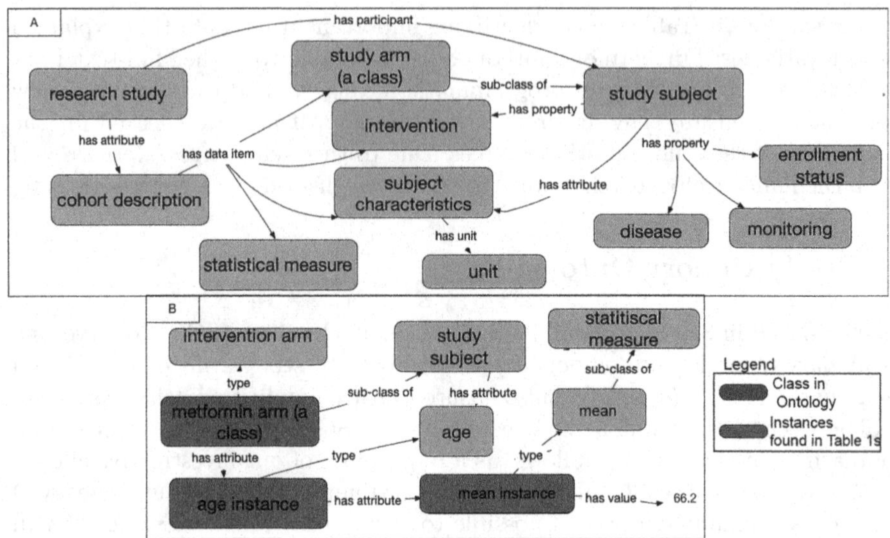

Fig. 2. (A) A high-level overview of SCO that captures the vocabulary and associations needed to model the descriptions of study populations. (B) We depict associations that cannot be realized without actual instantiation of Table 1 data.

sist over time and are characterized by the state the study subject exhibits,[7] we use a sub-property of sio:hasAttribute, i.e. sio:hasProperty, to link them to the study subject. Additionally, we do not maintain certain property associations (e.g. compositional relation between the study arm and study subject) in our ontology and only create them upon the representation of actual Table 1 content in RDF KGs. For the ease of understanding, we depict instances in pink in Fig. 2 to help visualize the realism in our modeling.

To summarize, essentially through SCO, we build a framework to model a set of study subjects, who participate (sio:isParticipantIn) in a research study and belong to a study arm and whose subject characteristics are measured (sio:hasUnit) in units, and are aggregated upon via descriptive statistics. Since we are dealing with the biomedical domain, where multiple definitions may exist for a term, through blank nodes and reification techniques we allow support for this and we maintain provenance for our definitions via prov:wasAttributedTo (person) and dct:source (online source). For example; hasco:ResearchStudy sio:hasAttribute [a skos:definition; sio:hasValue 'A scientific investigation that involves testing a hypothesis'; prov:wasAttributedTo AmarDas]. Additionally, we also provide example usages of our terms via vann:example, to help future users/contributors of our ontology get an idea of the intended usage of the class. Our main SCO ontology, and our accompanying suite of ontologies, Lab Results,

[7] View the definition of sio:hasProperty and sio:hasAttribute relations at: https://raw.githubusercontent.com/micheldumontier/semanticscience/master/ontology/sio/release/sio-subset-labels.owl.

Diseases, Drugs, and Therapies, in which we maintain diabetes specific content, are available as resources. Further, we tested our ontology with the Hermit reasoner.

4.2 Ontology Reuse

We reuse classes and properties from existing biomedical ontologies as much as possible, and only define them ourselves when they do not exist. We primarily reused ontologies available from Bioportal [16] that are regularly maintained and have significant reuse. We have tried to reuse terms from a small set of applicable ontologies to avoid enlarging the ontology when we bring in new classes and additional axioms. We categorize the ontologies, from which we reuse terms, broadly into Study Design ontologies (ProvCaRe, HASCO), Mid-Level ontologies (SIO), Medical ontologies (NCIT, CHEAR, etc.), and Statistical ontologies (STATO, UO). We present a list of our reused ontologies against their groupings on our resources website.

In our approach to ontology reuse, we include minimum information to reference a term (MIREOT) [5] for most of our reused ontologies, such as ProvCare and NCIT, unless we leverage their structure completely. However, we do import a light-weight version of the Child Health Exposure Analysis and Resource (CHEAR) ontology, by applying the MIREOT technique to extract the demographics and anthropometric branches alone. We prefer to import the CHEAR ontology, as it builds off SIO and additionally imports the HAScO human aware science ontology, that we leverage. We utilized an online tool, Ontofox [23], to apply the MIREOT technique to a few ontologies that were supported on this platform. However, for ontologies that were not available on Ontofox, we designed our own SPARQL query to gather subclass and superclass trees for a given ontology class. On our resources website, we make our MIREOT Python script available. This runs the SPARQL query against a Blazegraph endpoint and returns the RDF version of the subset class tree.

5 Knowledge Graph Modeling

We use an annotated example of a Table 1, seen in Fig. 3, to explain our approach of modeling the collections of study subjects, subject characteristics defined on collections, and the descriptive statistics used to summarize these characteristics. We present an RDF snippet in Listing 1.1, and explain smaller sub-portions of our modeling in each subsequent subsection. These snippets form the fundamental pieces of our Table 1 KG. On our resources website, we release the KG representations of the studies in our evaluation dataset, for interested readers to run their analyses.

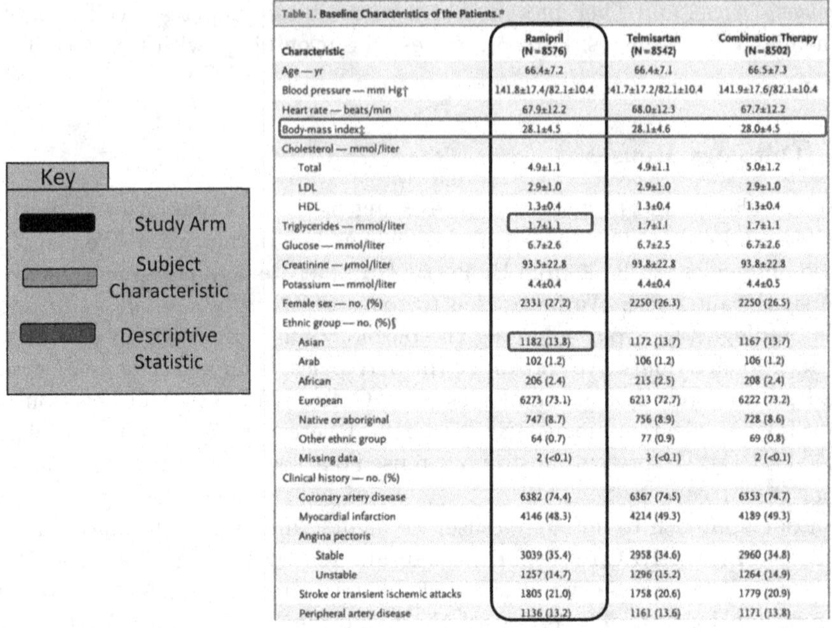

Table 1. **Baseline Characteristics of the Patients.***

Characteristic	Ramipril (N=8576)	Telmisartan (N=8542)	Combination Therapy (N=8502)
Age — yr	66.4±7.2	66.4±7.1	66.5±7.3
Blood pressure — mm Hg†	141.8±17.4/82.1±10.4	141.7±17.2/82.1±10.4	141.9±17.6/82.1±10.4
Heart rate — beats/min	67.9±12.2	68.0±12.3	67.7±12.2
Body-mass index‡	28.1±4.5	28.1±4.6	28.0±4.5
Cholesterol — mmol/liter			
Total	4.9±1.1	4.9±1.1	5.0±1.2
LDL	2.9±1.0	2.9±1.0	2.9±1.0
HDL	1.3±0.4	1.3±0.4	1.3±0.4
Triglycerides — mmol/liter	1.7±1.1	1.7±1.1	1.7±1.1
Glucose — mmol/liter	6.7±2.6	6.7±2.5	6.7±2.6
Creatinine — μmol/liter	93.5±22.8	93.8±22.8	93.8±22.8
Potassium — mmol/liter	4.4±0.4	4.4±0.4	4.4±0.5
Female sex — no. (%)	2331 (27.2)	2250 (26.3)	2250 (26.5)
Ethnic group — no. (%)§			
Asian	1182 (13.8)	1172 (13.7)	1167 (13.7)
Arab	102 (1.2)	106 (1.2)	106 (1.2)
African	206 (2.4)	215 (2.5)	208 (2.4)
European	6273 (73.1)	6213 (72.7)	6222 (73.2)
Native or aboriginal	747 (8.7)	756 (8.9)	728 (8.6)
Other ethnic group	64 (0.7)	77 (0.9)	69 (0.8)
Missing data	2 (<0.1)	3 (<0.1)	2 (<0.1)
Clinical history — no. (%)			
Coronary artery disease	6382 (74.4)	6367 (74.5)	6353 (74.7)
Myocardial infarction	4146 (48.3)	4214 (49.3)	4189 (49.3)
Angina pectoris			
Stable	3039 (35.4)	2958 (34.6)	2960 (34.8)
Unstable	1257 (14.7)	1296 (15.2)	1264 (14.9)
Stroke or transient ischemic attacks	1805 (21.0)	1758 (20.6)	1779 (20.9)
Peripheral artery disease	1136 (13.2)	1161 (13.6)	1171 (13.8)

Fig. 3. An annotated example of Table 1 from a clinical trial "Telmisartan, ramipril, or both in patients at high risk for vascular events" [10] cited in the Cardiovascular Complications (Chapter 9) of the ADA CPG.

Listing 1.1. Representation of a portion of the Ramipril Study Arm

```
sco-i:RamiprilArm
        a     owl:Class, sco:InterventionArm;
        rdfs:subClassOf sio:StudySubject;
        sio:isParticipantIn sco-i:TelmisartanRamiprilStudy;
        sio:hasAttribute
        [ a sco:PopulationSize; sio:hasValue 8576],
        [ a sio:Age; sio:hasUnit sio:Year;
           sio:hasAttribute
           [ a sio:Mean; sio:hasValue 66.4],
           [a sio:StandardDeviation; sio:hasValue 7.2 ]
         ] .
```

5.1 Modeling of Collections of Study Subjects

Study arms are specific subpopulations of study cohorts comprised of a subset of enrolled study subjects. Hence, they are a natural fit for modeling as classes in the OWL web ontology language [4], "Classes provide an abstraction mechanism for grouping resources with similar characteristics. Like RDF classes, every OWL class is associated with a set of individuals, called the class extension.", and model collections as classes.

As discussed earlier in Subsect. 4.1, study arms are represented as columns in Table 1s. Further, the RDF snippet in Listing 1.1 shows a semantic definition of a particular study arm as an instance of the sco:InterventionArm. Study arm definitions are either those of *InterventionArm* or *ControlArm* and they are gathered from the Table 1 columns themselves, if sufficient, if not we consult the study data to find relevant content that describes the arms.

In some Table 1s, there also exist subsets of study arms, created by the presence of categorical row variables (e.g. percentage of Asians), expressed in percentages[8]. Such subsets are expressed as rdfs:subClassOf the main study arm, and have an owl:Restriction defined on them for membership. An example of the representations of these subsets, can be viewed as a part of the KG creation documentation on our resources website.

5.2 Modeling of Characteristics and Descriptive Statistics

As briefly introduced in Subsect. 4.1, subject characteristics are the phenotype properties that are collected for study subjects. In our evaluation dataset, we have observed that all study arms belonging to a study share the same set of characteristics. However, the range of values for these characteristics differ across study arms depending on their composition. Borrowing from our grouping of characteristics from Sect. 4, we reemphasize that characteristics persisting over a period of time are modeled as sio:hasProperty, and the rest are modeled via sio:hasAttribute property. From this discussion it becomes apparent that our modeling of characteristics on study arms is fairly straightforward and we only utilize two SIO property associations. In Listing 1.1, we depict the association of age as a sio:hasAttribute of the *Ramipril study arm*. Further, characteristics can also be classified broadly as categorical, discreet, and continuous. Categorical characteristics are represented in subsets, and their representation is discussed in the previous subsection.

5.3 Modeling of Descriptive Statistics

Another problem we address in this paper is the KR of aggregate statistics on subject characteristics of study populations. Although aggregate statistics are reported in multiple domains, there has been little work on a convention for supporting the modeling of aggregations in RDF. The support for aggregations in Linked Data is presented in [6]. However, their process is more focused on the publishing of statistical data and the metadata than on the representation of statistical data itself.

Descriptive statistics have conventionally been defined, as statistical measures that summarize the data.[9] In Table 1s, they are used to describe summarized values of the characteristics of study subjects, who belong to a study arm.

---

[8] More Table 1 reporting style and composition details at https://prsinfo.clinicaltrials.gov/webinars/module6/resources/BaselineCharacteristics_Handouts.pdf.

[9] Definition adapted from: https://en.wikipedia.org/wiki/Descriptive_statistics.

From our analysis of Table 1s, we have seen a limited set of descriptive statistics measures: mean +/− standard deviation, median +/− interquartile range, and percentages. We model these aggregations and descriptive statistics, seen as reified triples on a property. Reification is an RDF technique developed to "make statements about statements" [18]. As can be seen in the RDF snippet above, we define descriptive statistics as reified triples on an age characteristic. Additionally, since we only reuse SIO object and data properties, we eliminate the need for further punning techniques, to represent these descriptive statistic properties as instances of sio:hasAttribute. In this paper, we only present an example of a mean +/− standard deviation measure. Examples of representing median +/− interquartile via sio:MinimalValue and sio:MaximalValue boundary classes, and percentage association, can be viewed on our resources website.

6 Applications

Our study applicability applications leverage the declarative specifications of study populations in our Table 1 KG. In Subsect. 6.1, we frame three scenarios of clinical relevance that mimic the decision-making of a medical practitioner to determine study applicability. Additionally, we present a cohort similarity visualization strategy in Subsect. 6.2. In Subsect. 6.3, we describe a faceted browser interactive visualization tool aimed at medical practitioners. Moreover, as shown in Fig. 1, we include study details in our application results. Hence, we provide medical practitioners with provenance-justified results that could be used for future analyses and investigation.

6.1 Population Analysis Scenarios

As discussed in Sect. 1.1, there exist challenges with study biases and the varying quality in research studies. Medical practitioners need to be aware of these issues when deciding on applicable studies for their clinical population. Three scenarios of clinical relevance were suggested by our medical expert on the Health Empowerment by Analytics, Learning and Semantics (HEALS) project. Through queries to our Table 1 KG we address a representative competency question for each of these scenarios: (1) Study match: Is there a study that matches this patient on a feature(s)? (2) Study limitation: Is there an absence or an under-representation of population groups in this study? (3) Study quality evaluation: Are there adequate population sizes and is there a heterogeneity of treatment effects among arms? Our declarative representations of Table 1s, allow us to trigger retrospective queries that combine subject characteristics (SPARQL AND clauses), various descriptive statistical representations (limited patterns of modeling as seen in Sect. 5), and aggregate study arms or study cohorts (leveraging SPARQL math constructs such as SUM). Our competency questions and their SPARQL queries[10] can be found on our resources website.

[10] https://tetherless-world.github.io/study-cohort-ontology/application#scenarioquery.

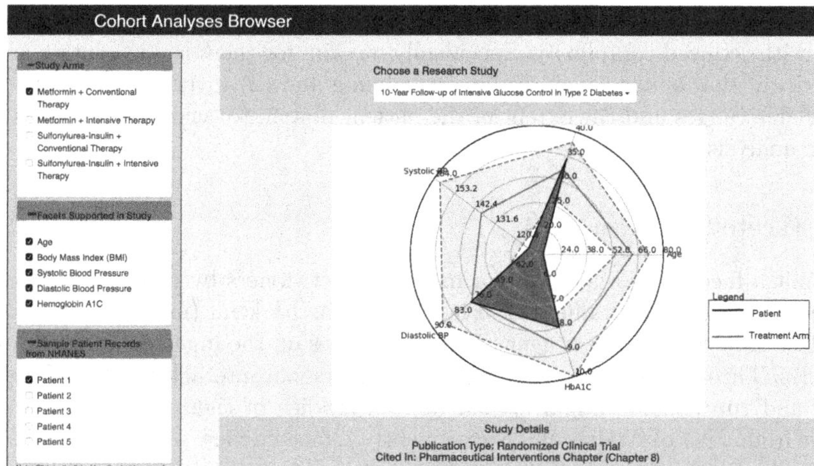

Fig. 4. A snapshot of our faceted browser tool that provides medical practitioners with the ability to customize cohort analyses. Currently, the feature facets are limited to the patient features from NHANES, that overlap with, Table 1 data. If a study doesn't contain some of these 5 features, they will be disabled.

6.2 Cohort Similarity Visualizations

We define cohort similarity as an analytical problem to determine the similarity or closeness of a patient to a given study population. We currently support determination of cohort similarity by generating visualizations, such as a star plot (Fig. 4), by overlaying features of patient records against study arm characteristics. For the purpose of visualization, we select a few sample type-2 diabetes patient records from the National Health and Nutrition Examination Survey (NHANES)[11]. Additionally, we adopt different visual strategies for continuous and categorical variables. In this paper, on the resources website and through our faceted browser we only support star plot visualizations for continuous variables, and we are exploring visualizations such as a pie chart for categorical variables. Visualizations are generated on a per study arm, per patient basis, through results of SPARQL queries triggered to our Table 1 KG. Our visualizations are built by Python plotting modules such as Seaborn[12] and Matplotlib[13], and our visualization code is made available as a resource.

[11] Dataset Information Page. https://wwwn.cdc.gov/nchs/nhanes/continuousnhanes/default.aspx?BeginYear=2015.
[12] https://seaborn.pydata.org/.
[13] https://matplotlib.org/.

Since our visualizations serve the purpose of being quick assessors, we design them with reduced complexity. Specifically, we aim for them to (1) contain sufficient detail that is not considered overwhelming and (2) carry information such as variable ranges and the extent of the patient match, to serve as indicators for future analysis.

6.3 Faceted Browser

We built a faceted browser tool for medical practitioners by utilizing a Python model-view-controller framework, Flask[14]. On the backend (model), we utilized the RDFLib[15] module to trigger SPARQL queries on the ingested ontology and KG files. Through this tool medical practitioners can interact with our Table 1 KGs, and run cohort similarity analyses on studies of their choice. They can choose from a list of studies and, subsequently, a faceted view will be rendered for the study arms of this selected study. As seen in Fig. 4, they can also choose the variables that they would like to visualize. Hence, our prototype faceted browser interface serves as a per-study inspection tool and uses NHANES patient records to illustrate the facets.

7 Results

In the Study Analysis Table 1, shown below, we present a quantitative summarization of the results of each competency question (described in Subsect. 6.1). Some interesting, medically relevant inferences that we output, and that are often spoken about in medical literature, include the lack of a representation of adults above 70,[16] and the lack of heterogeneity in treatment effects.[17] We were surprised that only 6% of the studies in our evaluation dataset were conducted on a large-scale, that their study arms were evenly divided, and all their study subjects were put on the basic, antidiabetes treatment of *guanidines*. We also find that the SCO ontology is epistemologically adequate for representing all Table 1s in our evaluation dataset. We cover 360 ($\approx$ 17 in each study on average) subject characteristics from 20 cited research studies, and 28 study arm definitions. The study arm definitions included terms belonging to classes such as medical interventions, control regimes, and, less commonly occurring, diseases, dosage, year of follow-ups, and titration targets. We found that 19 cohort variables (a term we use to collectively describe interventions and subject characteristics) commonly occur across studies.

---

[14] http://flask.pocoo.org/.

[15] https://rdflib.readthedocs.io/en/stable.

[16] https://www.statnews.com/2019/01/31/nih-rule-make-clinical-research-inclusive/.

[17] NIH Collaboratory run grand-round presentation: https://www.nihcollaboratory.org/Pages/Grand-Rounds-02-28-14.aspx.

Table 1. Percentage of studies meeting the competency question criteria for the population analysis scenarios.

Question	Percentage	Population analysis type
Studies with a representation of Male African American study subjects	75%	Study match
Study Arms with adults below the age of 70	47.6%	Study limitations
Studies with cohort sizes > 1000 and study arm administered drugs of the guanidines family, with sizes 1/3rd those of the cohort size	6%	Study quality evaluation

8 Resource Contributions

We expect the following publicly available artifacts, along with the applicable documentation, to be useful resources for anyone interested in performing analysis on study populations reported in research studies.

1. Ontologies:
   (a) Study Cohort Ontology (SCO)
2. Knowledge Graphs:
   (a) Table 1 Knowledge Graph
3. Source Code:
   (a) MIREOT Script
   (b) Cohort Similarity Visualization
4. Data:
   (a) NHANES Patient Records

9 Future Work

Having demonstrated our ability to apply semantic techniques to make study populations visible, we plan to incorporate interdiscplinary methods to improve on a few aspects of our solution. We have found that there exist variances in Table 1 reporting styles ranging from differences in row and column headers, table formats etc. These variances pose challenges for the scalability and automation aspects of the KG construction. Furthermore, often some subject characteristics and column headers require a contextual understanding for disambiguation, that is present in the unstructured body of the study. Hence, we are exploring a combination of natural language processing and semantic techniques to support an ontology-driven parsing and clean-up of Table 1 data and to develop a contextualized and medical standards compliant Table 1 KG. Further, to ensure longevity and easy reuse of SCO, we plan to develop a set of tools/algorithms to predict the best-fit position for a new term in our SCO suite of ontologies. We also plan to expand and refine our set of competency questions, based on feedback from medical practitioners, and to allow for partial and fuzzy matches using query relaxation [9] and semantically targeted analytics [14].

10 Discussion

We have utilized KR techniques, i.e. OWL encodings of SCO and a knowledge graph of Table 1 content to model and expose descriptions of study populations in an attempt to make scientific data more accessible. Further, we have utilized our semantic modeling to support analytical use cases to determine study applicability. Our evaluation dataset currently is solely comprised of type-2 diabetes research studies. We have kept our descriptions and examples minimally domain specific. We believe that our ontology and KG documentation can serve as resources for researchers interested in the pan-disease analysis of study populations.

Our ontology, SCO, is developed using best-practice ontology principles, some of which are listed at [7]. Specifically, we reuse SIO properties and do not define any new properties. We reuse classes from a limited yet standard set of biomedical ontologies in order to increase the interoperability of SCO.

There have been attempts at improving the reporting of Table 1s in the medical community, such as the Table 1 project [15]. However, they have been confined to the identification of desirable properties for standardization. Our semantic solution presented in this paper, that at its heart utilizes a KR approach, is a step towards achieving this standardization. This can be seen in Listing 1.1 where we have presented an RDF snippet representing fundamental building blocks of our Table 1 KG, i.e. our modeling of collections, subject characteristics, and statistical measures. These identified patterns are reused as templates to realize the association of various variables with study populations reported in Table 1s.

Our Table 1 KGs allows us to address study applicability scenarios motivated from medical literature and to support visualizations that clearly depict cohort similarity. By these capabilities, we demonstrate how our solution addresses our use case of determining study applicability. We believe there is potential for this work to be reused by researchers performing study population analyses. Also in this paper we make assumptions on the content a medical practitioner might want to see, and, from a medical practitioner user survey we are conducting, we will incorporate feedback on their additional requirements.

Our solution does not address or include support for the modeling of study eligibility criteria, i.e. inclusion and exclusion criteria. However, we reuse metadata expression terms from Dublin Core Terms (DCT) to include a link to registries such as ClinicalTrials.gov or International Standard Randomised Controlled Trial Number (ISRCTN),[18] where the criteria is made available as a part of the study data. We expect that the SCO vocabulary is sufficient to express the criteria, but since we are still investigating the merge of the criteria with the Table 1 content, we defer it to future work.

Finally, all the resources that we listed in Sect. 8, are made publicly available in a Github repository and the ontology is hosted on Bioportal. SCO is released

[18] http://www.isrctn.com/page/about.

under the Apache 2.0 license specification. Our resources will be maintained periodically by the authors.

11 Conclusion

We have presented a prototype KR system that can be used to model study populations, to aid in the assessment of study applicability. Our model is tailored around use cases aimed at assisting medical practitioners in the treatment of complex patients and who also often require "efficient-literature searching" [12] capabilities. We presented a solution to make descriptions of study populations more accessible for quick decision-making. We believe that the resources we release, especially SCO, can serve as an extensible schema to represent population descriptions across diseases. We have demonstrated the adequacy of the ontology through a set of what we believe are representative applications supporting a range of use cases contributed by our medical expert. We plan to continue our outreach and ontology reuse in additional diverse evidence-based medicine application settings.

Acknowledgements. This work is partially supported by IBM Research AI through the AI Horizons Network. We thank our colleagues from IBM Research, Dan Gruen, Morgan Foreman and Ching-Hua Chen, and from RPI, John Erickson, Alexander New, and Rebecca Cowan, who greatly assisted the research.

References

1. American Diabetes Association (ADA) et al.: 8. Pharmacologic approaches to glycemic treatment: Standards of medical care in diabetes - 2018. Diabetes Care **41**(Suppl. 1), S73–S85 (2018)
2. American Diabetes Association (ADA) et al.: 9. Cardiovascular disease and risk management: standards of medical care in diabetes - 2018. Diabetes Care **41**(Suppl. 1), S86–S104 (2018)
3. Auer, S., Kovtun, V., Prinz, M., Kasprzik, A., Stocker, M., Vidal, M.E.: Towards a knowledge graph for science. In: Proceedings of the 8th International Conference on Web Intelligence, Mining and Semantics, p. 1. ACM, Novi Sad (2018)
4. Bechhofer, S., et al.: OWL web ontology language reference. OWL Reference Guide. https://www.w3.org/TR/owl-ref/
5. Courtot, M., et al.: MIREOT: The minimum information to reference an external ontology term. Appl. Ontol. **6**(1), 23–33 (2011)
6. Cyganiak, R., Field, S., Gregory, A., Halb, W., Tennison, J.: Semantic statistics: bringing together SDMX and SCOVO. In: Proceedings of the Linked Data on the Web Workshop (LDOW 2010), Raleigh, North Carolina, USA, 27 April 2010 (2010). http://ceur-ws.org/Vol-628/. Accessed 26 Mar 2019
7. Garijo, D., Poveda-VillalÃşn, M.: A checklist for complete vocabulary metadata. List of Desirable Ontology Best-Practices. http://dgarijo.github.io/Widoco/doc/bestPractices/index-en.html
8. Graham, R., et al.: Trustworthy clinical practice guidelines: challenges and potential. In: Clinical Practice Guidelines We Can Trust, pp. 53–75. National Academies Press (US), Washington D.C. (2011)

9. Hurtado, C.A., Poulovassilis, A., Wood, P.T.: Query relaxation in RDF. J. Data Semant. X **4900**, 31–61 (2008)
10. Ontarget Investigators: Telmisartan, ramipril, or both in patients at high risk for vascular events. N. Engl. J. Med. **358**(15), 1547–1559 (2008)
11. Jang, M., Jahanshad, N., Espiritu, R.: The cohort ontology. Enigma Knowledge Capture and Discovery Project. https://knowledgecaptureanddiscovery.github.io/EnigmaOntology/release/cohort/1.0.0/index-en.html
12. Masic, I., Miokovic, M., Muhamedagic, B.: Evidence based medicine-new approaches and challenges. Acta Inform. Med. **16**(4), 219 (2008)
13. National Institute of Health (NIH): Rigor and Reproducibility. Introduction and need for principles. https://www.nih.gov/research-training/rigor-reproducibility
14. New, A., Rashid, S.M., Erickson, J.S., McGuinness, D.L., Bennett, K.P.: Semantically-aware population health risk analyses. Presented as a Poster at Machine Learning for Health (ML4H) Workshop, NeurIPS, Montreal, Canada (2018). https://arxiv.org/abs/1811.11190. Accessed 20 Mar 2019
15. NIH Colloboratory: Table 1 project. Rethinking Clinical Trials. https://sites.duke.edu/rethinkingclinicaltrials/ehr-phenotyping/table-1-project/
16. Noy, N.F., et al.: BioPortal: ontologies and integrated data resources at the click of a mouse. Nucleic Acids Res. **37**($suppl_2$), W170–W173 (2009)
17. Patel, C., et al.: Matching patient records to clinical trials using ontologies. In: Aberer, K., et al. (eds.) ISWC 2007. LNCS, vol. 4825, pp. 816–829. Springer, Heidelberg (2007). https://doi.org/10.1007/978-3-540-76298-0_59
18. Reinhardt, S.: Property reification vocabulary. A Strawman Draft. https://www.w3.org/wiki/PropertyReificationVocabulary
19. Shankar, R.D., Martins, S.B., O'Connor, M.J., Parrish, D.B., Das, A.K.: Epoch: an ontological framework to support clinical trials management. In: Proceedings of the International Workshop on Healthcare Information and Knowledge Management, pp. 25–32. ACM, Arlington (2006)
20. Sim, I., et al.: The ontology of clinical research (OCRe): an informatics foundation for the science of clinical research. J. Biomed. Inform. **52**, 78–91 (2014)
21. Tu, S.W., et al.: A practical method for transforming free-text eligibility criteria into computable criteria. J. Biomed. Inform. **44**(2), 239–250 (2011)
22. Valdez, J., Kim, M., Rueschman, M., Socrates, V., Redline, S., Sahoo, S.S.: Provcare semantic provenance knowledgebase: evaluating scientific reproducibility of research studies. In: AMIA Annual Symposium Proceedings, vol. 2017, p. 1705. American Medical Informatics Association, Washington D.C., USA (2017)
23. Xiang, Z., Courtot, M., Brinkman, R.R., Ruttenberg, A., He, Y.: OntoFox: web-based support for ontology reuse. BMC Res. Notes **3**(1), 175 (2010)
24. Younesi, E.: A knowledge-based integrative modeling approach for in-silico identification of mechanistic targets in neurodegeneration with focus on Alzheimer's disease. Ph.D. thesis, Department of Mathematics and Natural Sciences, Universitäts-und Landesbibliothek Bonn, Bonn, Germany (2014)

LC-QuAD 2.0: A Large Dataset for Complex Question Answering over Wikidata and DBpedia

Mohnish Dubey[1,2](✉), Debayan Banerjee[1,2], Abdelrahman Abdelkawi[2,3], and Jens Lehmann[1,2]

[1] Smart Data Analytics Group (SDA), University of Bonn, Bonn, Germany
{dubey,jens.lehmann}@cs.uni-bonn.de,
debayan@uni-bonn.de
[2] Fraunhofer IAIS, Bonn, Germany
{mohnish.dubey,jens.lehmann}@iais.fraunhofer.de
[3] RWTH Aachen, Aachen, Germany

Abstract. Providing machines with the capability of exploring knowledge graphs and answering natural language questions has been an active area of research over the past decade. In this direction translating natural language questions to formal queries has been one of the key approaches. To advance the research area, several datasets like WebQuestions, QALD and LCQuAD have been published in the past. The biggest data set available for complex questions (LCQuAD) over knowledge graphs contains five thousand questions. We now provide LC-QuAD 2.0 (Large-Scale Complex Question Answering Dataset) with 30,000 questions, their paraphrases and their corresponding SPARQL queries. LC-QuAD 2.0 is compatible with both Wikidata and DBpedia 2018 knowledge graphs. In this article, we explain how the dataset was created and the variety of questions available with examples. We further provide a statistical analysis of the dataset.

Resource Type: Dataset
Website and documentation: http://lc-quad.sda.tech/
Permanent URL: https://figshare.com/projects/LCQuAD_2_0/62270.

1 Introduction

In the past decade knowledge graphs such as DBpedia [8] and Wikidata [14] have emerged as major successes by storing facts in linked data architecture. DBpedia recently decided to incorporate the manually curated knowledge base of Wikidata [7] into its own knowledge graph[1]. Retrieving factual information from these knowledge graphs has been a focal point of research. Question Answering over Knowledge graphs(KGQA) is one of the techniques used to achieve this goal. In KGQA, the focus is generally on translating a natural language question to

[1] We refer this as 'DBpedia2018' further in this article.

C. Ghidini et al. (Eds.): ISWC 2019, LNCS 11779, pp. 69–78, 2019.
https://doi.org/10.1007/978-3-030-30796-7_5

a formal language query. This task has generally been achieved by rule-based systems [6]. However, in the last few years, more systems using machine learning for this task have evolved. QA Systems have achieved impressive results working on simple questions [9] where a system only looks at a single fact consisting of a <subject - predicate - object> triple. On the other hand, for Complex questions (which require retrieval of answers based on more than one triple) there is still ample scope for improvement.

Datasets play an important role in AI research as they motivate the evolution of the current state of the art and the application of machine learning techniques that benefit from large-scale training data. In the area of KGQA, datasets such as WebQuestions, SimpleQuestions and the QALD challenge datasets have been the flag bearers. LCQuAD version 1.0 was an important breakthrough as it was the largest complex question dataset using SPARQL queries at the time of its release. In this work, we present LC-QuAD 2.0 (Large-Scale Complex Question Answering Dataset 2.0) consisting of 30,000 questions with paraphrases and corresponding SPARQL queries required to answer questions over Wikidata and DBpedia2018. This dataset covers several new question type variations compared to the previous release of the dataset or to any other existing KGQA dataset (see comparison in Table 1). Apart from variations in the type of questions, we also paraphrase each question, which allows KGQA machine learning models to escape over-fitting to a particular syntax of questions. This is also the first dataset that utilises qualifier[2] information for a fact in Wikidata, which allows a user to seek more detailed answers (as discussed in Sect. 4).

The following are key contributions of this work:

- Provision of the largest dataset of 30,000 complex questions with corresponding SPARQL queries for Wikidata and DBpedia 2018.
- All questions in LCQuAD 2.0 also consist of paraphrased versions via crowdsourcing tasks. This provide more natural language variations for the question answering system to learn from and avoid over-fitting on a small set of syntactic variations.
- Questions in this dataset have a good variety and complexity levels such as multi-fact questions, temporal questions and questions that utilise qualifier information.
- This is the first KGQA dataset which contains questions with dual user intents and questions that require SPARQL string operations (Sect. 4.2).

This article is organised into the following sections: (Sect. 2) Relevance and significance (Sect. 3) Dataset Creation Workflow (Sect. 4) Dataset Characteristics with comparison (Sect. 5) Availability and Sustainability (Sect. 6) Conclusion and Future Work.

[2] Qualifiers are used in order to further describe or refine the value of a property given in a fact statement: https://www.wikidata.org/wiki/Help:Qualifiers.

2 Relevance

Question Answering: Over the last years, KGQA systems are trying to evolve from a handcrafted rule based system to more robust machine learning (ML) based systems. Such ML approaches require large datasets for training and testing. For simple questions the KGQA community has reached a high level of accuracy but for more complex questions there is scope for much improvement. With a large scale dataset that incorporates a high degree of variety in the formal query expressions, provides a platform for machine learning models to improve the performance of KGQA with complex questions.

Solutions of NLP tasks using machine learning or semantic parsing have proved to be venerable to paraphrases. Moreover, if the system is exposed to paraphrases at the training period, the system could perform better and be more robust [1]. Thus having paraphrases of each original question enlarges the scope of the dataset.

Recently, DBpedia decided to adopt Wikidata's knowledge and mapping it to DBpedia's own ontology [7]. So far no dataset has based itself on this recent development. This work is the first attempt at allowing KGQA over the new DBpedia based on Wikidata[3].

Other Research Areas: *Entity and Predicate Linking:* This dataset may be used as a benchmark for systems which perform entity linking or/and relation linking on short text or on questions only. The previous version of the LCQuAD dataset has been used by such systems [5] and has enabled better performance of these modules.

SPARQL Query Generation: The presented dataset has a high variety of SPARQL query templates which provides a use case for the modules which only focus on generating SPARQL given a candidate set of entities and relations. The SQG system [16] uses tree LSTMs to learn SPARQL generation and used the previous version of LCQuAD.

SPARQL to Natural Language: This dataset may be used for natural language generation over knowledge graphs to generate complex questions at a much larger scale.

3 Dataset Generation Workflow

In this work the aim is to generate different varieties of questions at a large scale. Although different kinds of SPARQLs are used the corresponding natural language questions generated need to appear coherent to humans. Amazon Mechanical Turk (AMT) was used for generating the natural language questions

[3] at the time of writing this article, these updates do not reflect on the public DBpedia end-point. Authors have hosted a local endpoint of their own (using data from http://downloads.dbpedia.org/repo/lts/wikidata/). In future the authors shall release their own endpoint point with the new DBpedia model.

from the system generated templates. A secondary goal is to make sure that the process of verbalisation of SPARQL queries on AMT does not require domain knowledge expertise of SPARQL and knowledge graphs on the part of the human workers (also known as turkers).

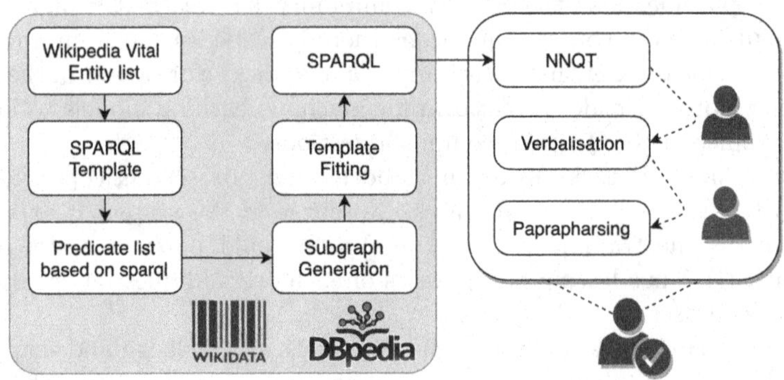

Fig. 1. Workflow for the dataset generation

The core of the methodology is to generate SPARQL queries based on sparql templates, selected entities and suitable predicate. The SPARQLs are then transformed to Template Questions Q_T, which act as an intermediate stage between natural language and formal language. Then a large crowd sourcing experiment (AMT) is conducted where the Q_Ts are verbalised to natural language questions - ie verbalised questions Q_V and then later paraphrase them to the paraphrased questions Q_P. To clarify, a Q_T instance represents SPARQL in a canonical structure which is human understandable. The generation of Q_T is a rule based operation.

The workflow is shown in the Fig. 1. The process starts with identifying a suitable set of entities for creating questions. A large set of entities based on Wikipedia Vital articles[4] is chosen and the corresponding same-as links to Wikidata IDs are found. Page-rank or entity popularity based approaches are avoided as it leads to dis-proportionately high number of entities from certain classes (say person). Instead Wikipedia Vital articles is chosen which provides important entities from a variety of topics such as people, geography, arts and several more, along with sub-topics. As a running example, say "Barack Obama" is selected from the list of entities.

Next a new set of SPARQL query templates are created such that they cover a large variety of question and intentions from a human perspective The template set is curated by observing other QA datasets and the KG architecture. All the templates have a corresponding SPARQL for Wikidata query end point and are valid on a DBpedia 2018 endpoint. The types of questions covered are as follows: simple question (1 fact), multiple fact question, questions that require additional

[4] https://en.wikipedia.org/wiki/Wikipedia:Vital_articles/Level/5.

information over a fact (wikidata qualifiers), temporal information question, two intention question and further discussed in Sect. 4.3. Each class of questions also has multiple variations within the class.

Next, we select a predicate list based on the SPARQL template. For example if we want to make a "Count" question where user intends to know the number of times a particular predicate holds true, certain predicates such as "birthPlace" are disqualified as it will not make a coherent count-question. Thus different predicate white lists for different question types are maintained. Now the sub-graph (Fig. 2) is generated from the KG based on the three factors - entity ("Barack Obama"), SPARQL template (say two intentions with qualifier), and a suitable predicate list. After slotting the predicate and sub-graph into the template the final SPARQL is generated. This SPARQL is then transformed to natural language templates, henceforth known as Q_T (Question Template), and the process is taken over by three step AMT experiments as discussed further.

The First AMT Experiment - Here the aim is to crowd-source the work of verbalising $Q_T \rightarrow Q_V$, where Q_V is the verbalisation of Q_T performed by a turker. Note that Q_T, since system generated, is often grammatically incorrect and semantically incoherrent, hence this step is required. For this we provided clear instruction to the turkers which vary according to the question type. For example: In two intention questions the turkers are instructed to make sure that none of the original intentions are missed in the verbalisation. Sufficient number of examples are provided to turkers so that they understand the task well. Again the examples vary according to the question type in the experiment.

The Second AMT Experiment - The task given to the turkers was to paraphrase the questions which have been generated in experiment 1, $Q_V \rightarrow Q_P$, where Q_P is a paraphrase of Q_V such that Q_P preserves the overall semantic meaning of Q_V while changing the syntactic content and structure. Turkers are encouraged to use synonyms, aliases and further changing the grammar structure of the verbalised question.

The Third AMT Experiment - This experiment performs human verification of experiments 1 and 2 and enforces quality control in the overall work flow. Turkers compare Q_T with Q_V and also Q_V to Q_P, to decide if the two pairs carry the same semantic meaning. The turkers are given a choice between "Yes / No / Can't say".

4 Dataset Characteristics

4.1 Dataset Statistics

In this section we analyse the statistics of our dataset. LCQuAD has 30,000 unique SPARQL - Question pairs. This dataset consists of 21,258 unique entities and 1,310 unique relations. Comparison of LCQuAD 2.0 to other related datasets is shown in the Table 1. There are two datasets which cover simple questions, that is the question only requires one fact to answer. In this case the variation of formal queries is low. ComplexWebQuestion further extends the SPARQL of WebQuestions to generate complex questions. Though the number of questions

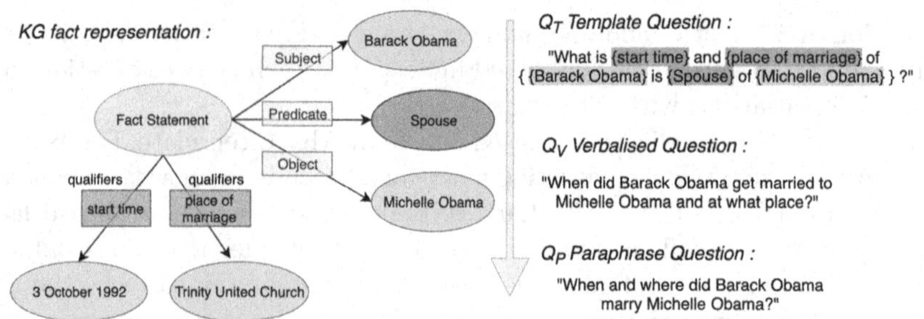

Fig. 2. (left) Representation of a fact with its Qualifiers. (right) Translation of a KG-fact to a verbalised question and then paraphrased question.

in the dataset is in the same range as LCQuAD 2.0, the variation of SPARQLs is higher in LCQuAD 2.0 as it contains question 10 types question (such as boolean, dual intentions, Fact with qualifiers and other - ref 4.3) spread over 22 unique templates.

4.2 Analysis of Verbalisation and Paraphrasing Experiments

To analyze the overall quality of verbalisation and paraphrasing by turkers we also used some automated methods (see Fig. 3). A good verbalisation of a system generated template ($Q_T \rightarrow Q_V$) would mean that Q_V preserves the semantic meaning of Q_T with the addition and removal of certain words. However a good paraphrasing of this verbalisation ($Q_V \rightarrow Q_P$) would mean that while the overall meaning is preserved, the order of words and also the words themselves (syntax) change to a certain degree. To quantify the sense of semantic-meaning vs change-of-word-order we calculate (1) cosine between vectors for each of these sentences pairs using BERT [4] embeddings - denoting "semantic similarity" (2) Levenshtein distance based syntax similarity between sentences showing the change in order of words (Fig. 3).

We observe that the cosine similarities of Q_T, Q_V and Q_P stay high (mean between 0.8–0.9 with standard deviation 0.07) denoting preservation of overall meaning throughout the steps, but syntax similarity stays comparatively low (mean between 0.6–0.75 with standard deviations between 0.14 to 0.16) since during verbalisation several words are added and removed from the imperfect system generated templates, and during paraphrasing the very task is to change the order of words of Q_V.

The last set of histograms shows semantic similarity between Q_T and Q_P directly. Since we have skipped the verbalisation step in between we expect the distances to be farther away than other pairs. As expected the graphs show slightly lower cosine and syntax similarities than other pairs.

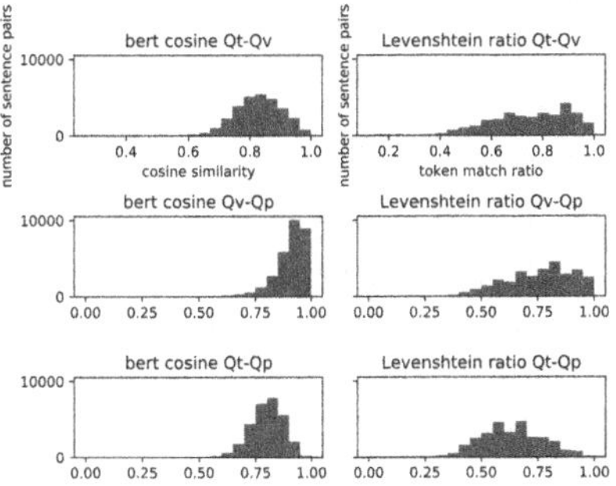

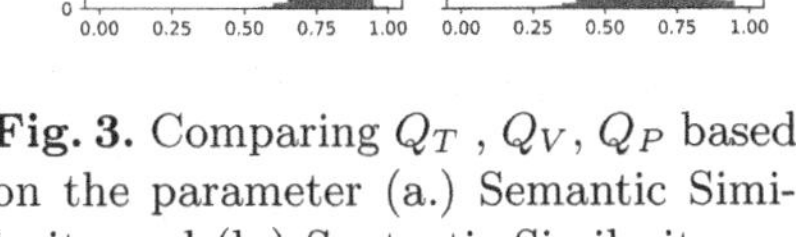

Fig. 3. Comparing Q_T , Q_V, Q_P based on the parameter (a.) Semantic Similarity and (b.) Syntactic Similarity

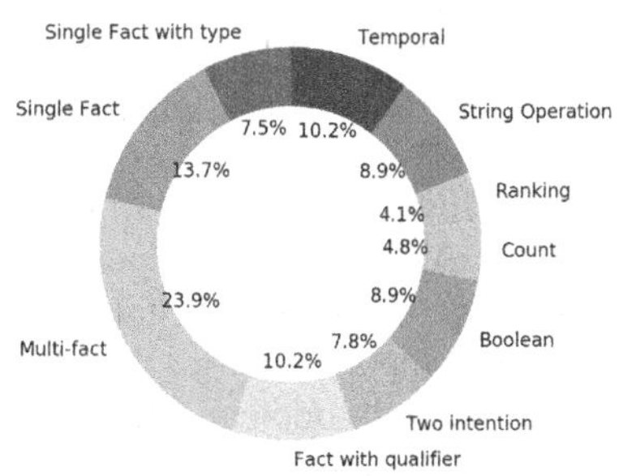

Fig. 4. Distribution of questions across all the question types

Table 1. A comparison of datasets having questions and their corresponding logical forms

Data Set	Size	Variation	Formal Language	Target KG	Paraphrase
Simple Questions [2]	100 K	low	SPARQL	Freebase	No
30M Factoid Question [11]	30 M	low	SPARQL	Freebase	No
QALD-9 [10]	450	high	SPARQL	DBpedia	No
Free917 [3]	917	medium	λ-Calculus	Freebase	No
WebQuestionSP [15]	5 k	medium	SPARQL	Freebase	No
ComplexWebQuestionSP [12]	34 K	medium	SPARQL	Freebase	No
LC-QuAD 1.0 [13]	5 k	medium	SPARQL	DBpedia 2016-04	No
LC-QuAD 2.0	30 K	high	SPARQL	Wikidata & DBpedia2018	Yes

4.3 Types of Questions in LC-QuAD 2.0

1. Single Fact: These queries are over a single fact(S-P-O). The query could return subject or object as answer. Example: "Who is the screenwriter of Mr. Bean?"
2. Single Fact With Type: This template brings type of constraint in single triple query. Example : "Billie Jean was on the tracklist of which studio album?"
3. Multi-fact: These queries are over two connected facts in Wikidata and have six variations to them. Example: "What is the name of the sister city tied to Kansas City, which is located in the county of Seville Province?"
4. Fact with Qualifiers: As shown in the Fig. 2, qualifiers are additional property for a fact stored in KG. LC-QuAD 2.0 utilise qualifiers to make more informative questions. Such as "What is the venue of Barack Obama's marriage ?"
5. Two Intention: This is a new category of query in KGQA, where the user question poses two intentions. This set of questions could also utilise the qual-

ifier information as mentioned above and a two intention question could be generated, such as "Who is the wife of Barack Obama and where did he got married?" or "When and where did Barack Obama get married to Michelle Obama?".

6. Boolean: In boolean question, user intends to know if the given fact is true or false. LC-QuAD 2.0 not only generates questions which returns true by graph matching, but also generate false facts so that boolean question with "false" answers could be generated. We also use predicates that returns a number as an object, so that boolean questions regarding numbers could be generated. Example: "Did Breaking Bad have 5 seasons?"

7. Count: This set of questions uses the keyword "COUNT" in SPARQL, and performs count over the number of times a certain predicate is used with a entity or object. Example "What is the number of Siblings of Edward III of England ?"

8. Ranking: By using aggregates, we generate queries where the user intends an entity with maximum or minimum value of a certain property. We have three variations in this set of questions. Example : "what is the binary star which has the highest color index?"

9. String Operation: By applying string operations in SPARQL we generated questions where the user asks about an entity either at word level or character level. Example : "Give me all the Rock bands that starts with letter R ?"

10. Temporal Aspect: This dataset covers temporal property in the question space and also in the answer space. A lot of the times facts with qualifiers poses temporal information. Example: "With whom did Barack Obama get married in 1992 ?"

5 Availability and Sustainability

To support sustainability we have published the dataset at figshare under CC BY 4.010 license. URL: https://figshare.com/projects/LCQuAD_2_0/62270

The repository of LC-QuAD 2.0 includes following files

–LC-QuAD 2.0 - A JSON dump of the Question Answering Dataset (Test and Train).

–The dataset is available with Template question Q_T, Question Q_V, paraphrased question Q_P and corresponding SPARQLs for Wikidata and DBpedia. Other supplementary material to the dataset can be accessed from our website http://lc-quad.sda.tech/.

6 Conclusion and Future Work

We presented the first large scale data set on Wikidata and upcoming DBpedia, consisting variety of complex questions. The dataset is generated in a semi-automatic setting that further requires crowd sourcing stages without domain knowledge expertise. In future we will maintain a benchmark strategy for KGQA systems on this dataset. We also plan to work towards developing a baseline KGQA system using the dataset LC-QuAD 2.0.

Acknowledgements. This work has mainly been supported by the Fraunhofer-Cluster of Excellence "Cognitive Internet Technologies" (CCIT). It has also partly been supported by the German Federal Ministry of Education and Research (BMBF) in the context of the research project "InclusiveOCW" (grant no. 01PE17004D).

References

1. Berant, J., Liang, P.: Semantic parsing via paraphrasing. In: Proceedings of the 52nd Annual Meeting of the Association for Computational Linguistics (Volume 1: Long Papers), vol. 1, pp. 1415–1425 (2014)
2. Bordes, A., Usunier, N., Chopra, S., Weston, J.: Large-scale simple question answering with memory networks. CoRR, abs/1506.02075 (2015)
3. Cai, Q., Yates, A.: Large-scale semantic parsing via schema matching and lexicon extension. In: ACL, pp.423–433 (2013)
4. Devlin, J., Chang, M., Lee, K., Toutanova, K.: BERT: pre-training of deep bidirectional transformers for language understanding. CoRR, abs/1810.04805 (2018)
5. Dubey, M., Banerjee, D., Chaudhuri, D., Lehmann, J.: EARL: joint entity and relation linking for question answering over knowledge graphs. In: Vrandečić, D., et al. (eds.) ISWC 2018. LNCS, vol. 11136, pp. 108–126. Springer, Cham (2018). https://doi.org/10.1007/978-3-030-00671-6_7
6. Dubey, M., Dasgupta, S., Sharma, A., Höffner, K., Lehmann, J.: AskNow: A framework for natural language query formalization in SPARQL. In: International Semantic Web Conference, pp. 300–316 (2016)
7. Ismayilov, A., Kontokostas, D., Auer, S., Lehmann, J., Hellmann, S., et al.: Wikidata through the eyes of DBpedia. Semant. Web **9**(4), 493–503 (2018)
8. Lehmann, J., et al.: DBpedia-a large-scale, multilingual knowledge base extracted from Wikipedia. The Semantic Web, pp. 167–195 (2015)
9. Lukovnikov, D., Fischer, A., Lehmann, J., Auer, S.: Neural network-based question answering over knowledge graphs on word and character level. In: Proceedings of the 26th International World Wide Web Conference, pp. 1211–1220 (2017)
10. Choi, K.S., et al. (eds.): 9th Question Answering over Linked Data challenge (QALD-9) co-located with 17th International Semantic Web Conference, Monterey, California, United States of America, CEUR Workshop Proceedings, CEUR-WS.org, vol. 2241 (2018). https://dblp.org/rec/bib/conf/semweb/2018semdeep
11. Serban, I.V., et al.: Generating factoid questions with recurrent neural networks: the 30M factoid question-answer corpus. In: 54th Annual Meeting of the Association for Computational Linguistics (2016)
12. Talmor, A., Berant, J.: The web as a knowledge-base for answering complex questions. In: Proceedings of the 2018 Conference of the North American Chapter of the Association for Computational Linguistics: Human Language Technologies, vol. 1 (Long Papers), pp. 641–651 (2018)
13. Trivedi, P., Maheshwari, G., Dubey, M., Lehmann, J.: LC-QuAD: a corpus for complex question answering over knowledge graphs. In: d'Amato, C., et al. (eds.) ISWC 2017. LNCS, vol. 10588, pp. 210–218. Springer, Cham (2017). https://doi.org/10.1007/978-3-319-68204-4_22
14. Vrandečić, D., Krötzsch, M.: Wikidata: a free collaborative knowledge base (2014)

15. Yih, W.-T., Chang, M.-W., He, X., Gao, J.: Semantic parsing via staged query graph generation: question answering with knowledge base. In: Proceedings of the 53rd Annual Meeting of the ACL and the 7th International Joint Conference on NLP (2015)
16. Zafar, H., Napolitano, G., Lehmann, J.: Formal query generation for question answering over knowledge bases. In: Gangemi, A., et al. (eds.) ESWC 2018. LNCS, vol. 10843, pp. 714–728. Springer, Cham (2018). https://doi.org/10.1007/978-3-319-93417-4_46

SEO: A Scientific Events Data Model

Said Fathalla[1,3(✉)], Sahar Vahdati[1,6(✉)], Christoph Lange[2], and Sören Auer[4,5]

[1] Smart Data Analytics (SDA), University of Bonn, Bonn, Germany
{fathalla,vahdati,langec}@cs.uni-bonn.de
[2] Fraunhofer FIT, Sankt Augustin, Germany
[3] Faculty of Science, University of Alexandria, Alexandria, Egypt
[4] Computer Science, Leibniz University of Hannover, Hanover, Germany
[5] TIB Leibniz Information Center for Science and Technology, Hannover, Germany
soeren.auer@tib.eu
[6] Department of Computer Science, University of Oxford, Oxford, UK

Abstract. Scientific events have become a key factor of scholarly communication for many scientific domains. They are considered as the focal point for establishing scientific relations between scholarly objects such as people (e.g., chairs and participants), places (e.g., location), actions (e.g., roles of participants), and artifacts (e.g., proceedings) in the scholarly communication domain. Metadata of scientific events have been made available in unstructured or semi-structured formats, which hides the interconnected and complex relationships between them and prevents transparency. To facilitate the management of such metadata, the representation of event-related information in an interoperable form requires a uniform conceptual modeling. The Scientific Events Ontology (OR-SEO) has been engineered to represent metadata of scientific events. We describe a systematic redesign of the information model that is used as a schema for the event pages of the *OpenResearch.org* community wiki, reusing well-known vocabularies to make OR-SEO interoperable in different contexts. OR-SEO is now in use on thousands of *OpenResearch.org* events pages, which enables users to represent structured knowledge about events without having to deal with technical implementation challenges and ontology development themselves.

Keywords: Scientific events ontology · Knowledge engineering · Scholarly data · Linked data · Knowledge sharing

1 Introduction

Recent years have witnessed a continual growth in scholarly information: at least 114 million English-language scholarly documents are accessible on the Web [33], thanks to the ease of organizing events and of submitting and publishing manuscripts, in both academia and industry. This information, emanating from scientific events, publishing houses and social networks (e.g., *ResearchGate*) is available online in an unstructured format (e.g., call for papers (CfP) emails) or semi-structured format (e.g., event home pages) which limits the visibility and hampers the discovery of interconnected relationships for humans as well as

C. Ghidini et al. (Eds.): ISWC 2019, LNCS 11779, pp. 79–95, 2019.
https://doi.org/10.1007/978-3-030-30796-7_6

machines. This plethora of scientific literature and heterogeneity of the metadata makes it increasingly difficult to keep an overview of the current state of research. Therefore, establishing knowledge-based representation of information in scholarly communication motivates the development of data models, ontologies and knowledge graphs. Semantically enriched representation of such information makes it easier to efficiently query and process the data [1]. Consequently, collecting, integrating and analyzing the metadata of scientific events, such as association with an event series, important dates, submitted and accepted articles, venue, event type, or the field of research, is of paramount importance for tracking scientific progress [9,11]. An important topic in semantic publishing is the development of semantic models related to various scholarly communication elements in order to describe the meaning and the relationships between data, thus enabling machines to interpret meaning, which is crucial for facilitating the information needs of stakeholders including authors and publishers [22]. Given the heterogeneity of event metadata as input, semantic representation of such information involves modeling event metadata covering different types of entities involved, such as persons, organizations, location, roles of persons before/during/after the event, etc. This article tackles the problem of representing scientific events metadata in a semantic way, i.e., integrating existing events vocabularies and making explicit the relationships and interconnections between event data, thus supporting the transformation of from a "Web of documents" into a "Web of data" in the scientific domain. In this paper, we present OR-SEO (with the namespace prefix `seo`), which enables a semantically enriched representation of scholarly event metadata, interlinked with other datasets and knowledge graphs. OR-SEO does not only represent what happened, i.e., time and place of a scholarly event, but also the roles that each agent played, and the time at which this role was held by a particular agent at a particular event. OR-SEO is in use as the schema of the event pages of *OpenResearch* (OR)[1]. OpenResearch is a semantic wiki platform for crowd-sourcing such metadata and generally facilitating scholarly metadata management and exploitation [31]. We publish event metadata in a semantically structured, machine-comprehensible, and reusable way, i.e., as linked data. Standard methodologies and best practices have been considered when designing and publishing the ontology. OR-SEO has been developed using the Simplified Agile Methodology for Ontology Development (SAMOD) [21], an iterative process that aims at building the final model through a series of small steps. OR-SEO has been designed with a minimum of semantic commitment to guarantee maximum applicability for analyzing event metadata from diverse sources, and maximum reusability by datasets using the ontology for modeling different aspects of scientific events. In accordance with best practices, OR-SEO emphasizes the reuse of events-related vocabularies and the alignment with concepts between them as well as the design and visualization patterns. OR-SEO is available using persistent identifiers (https://w3id.org/seo); future versions can be collaboratively revised on a corresponding Git repository, and it is registered

[1] http://openresearch.org.

and indexed by Linked Open Vocabularies (LOV)[2]. To support knowledge discovery by automated reasoning, a set of SWRL rules has been defined. The validation of the ontology is performed on syntactic and semantic levels using the W3C RDF validation service and description logic reasoners respectively. This step is crucial for making OR-SEO reusable. We shed light on what OR-SEO contributes to the existing literature by reviewing the existing event-related models and pointing out their weaknesses. Furthermore, the ontology is aligned with existing event ontologies. A public SPARQL endpoint to query the ontology is available online (cf. Table 1).

The remainder of this paper is structured as follows: we present an overview of related models in Sect. 2. The development of the OR-SEO ontology and its structure are described in Sect. 3. The main entities in OR-SEO are described in Sect. 4. Two real-world use cases of OR-SEO are presented in Sect. 5. The evaluation of the ontology is presented in Sect. 6. We conclude with an outlook on future work in Sect. 7.

2 Related Data Models

In recent years, several data models have been developed for describing events, such as the Event Ontology (EO) [26], Linking Open Descriptions of Events (LODE) [27], the Simple Event Model (SEM) [32], Wikidata[3], and the Semantic Web Dog Food (SWDF) [19]. Typically, these models differ by focus, i.e., event type, size, and level of abstraction, and they focus on the description of event metadata, including time, location, and topical classifications of events. Early efforts towards events metadata modeling include the metadata projects of the ESWC 2006 and ISWC 2006 conferences [19], but they did not yet provide detailed descriptions of the events. The *Semantic Web Conference (SWC) ontology* is an ontology for describing academic conferences [20]. Semantic Web for Research Communities (SWRC) is an ontology for describing entities involved in research communities [29]. Compared with OR-SEO, SWC and SWRC do not cover several entities related to scientific events, such as awards, registration, Sponsorship and travel information. *Semantic Web Dog Food (SWDF)* dataset and its successor *ScholarlyData*[4] are among the pioneers of comprehensive scholarly metadata. The *Event Ontology (EO)*[5] is a simple ontology centered around four classes (Event, Agent, Factor, and Product) and 17 properties. EO has been designed as a general ontology and therefore does not cover the domain knowledge specific to scientific events. Both EO and OR-SEO reflect the domain of events, but OR-SEO describes more aspects related to scientific events and related entities, such as participants' roles, sponsors and publishers. Similarly, the Scholarly Event Description Ontology (SEDE) [17] describes scholarly events in terms of agents (e.g., persons, committees), places (e.g., cities, venues). The

[2] https://lov.linkeddata.es/dataset/lov/vocabs/seo.
[3] https://www.wikidata.org/wiki/Q1656682.
[4] http://www.scholarlydata.org.
[5] http://motools.sourceforge.net/event/event.html.

SEDE ontology provides a basis to represent, collect, and share scholarly event metadata. Compared with OR-SEO, several aspects were not considered, such as the roles of the organizers, types of events, venue, and proceedings. *Linking Open Descriptions of Events (LODE)*[6] is an ontology for describing historical events and for mapping between other event-related vocabularies and ontologies, such as Time, EO and SKOS. In other words, it links people, places, or things to an event. Compared with EO, it has some restrictions and follows a higher level of abstraction. In the latest version (of 2010), it contains one class (`Event`) and only seven properties: `illustrates`, `inSpace`, `circa`, `atPlace`, `involved`, `involvedAgent` and `atTime`. Furthermore, LODE does not model the connection of agents to events through roles. Compared with OR-SEO, LODE also does not cover entities related to scientific events, such as sponsors, publishers and hosting organization. The *Simple Event Model ontology (SEM)*[7] has a defined core, which is relatively close to EO and LODE, but still far from our ontology, in terms of describing aspects related to scientific events, which do not exist in regular events, such as publishers. SEM is formalized purely in RDFS, describing the fundamental constituents of an event, including their types, roles, temporary validity and the view according to which these constraints hold. SEM has four core classes: `Event`, `Actor`, `Place` and `Time` in addition to three types of constraints: `Role` (the role of an individual in a specific event), `Temporary` (defines the temporal boundary within which a property holds, for example, the type of the place) and `View` (defines points of view).

In the context of publishing metadata of scientific events as Linked Data, Fathalla et al. [7] published EVENTSKG, a knowledge graph featuring a comprehensive semantic description of 73 renowned event series belonging to eight computer science communities since 1969. Notably, EVENTSKG uses the updated version of OR-SEO as a reference ontology for modeling event metadata and connecting related data that was not connected in the previous release. In 2018, Gottschalk and Demidova [15] published a multilingual dataset (EVENTKG) about events and temporal relations. It describes general events at a high level of abstraction. On the contrary, we put a particular focus on scientific events and their related entities. Despite these continuous efforts, there is yet no standard, well-formed ontology covering all those aspects related to scientific events that are covered by OR-SEO, such as types of scientific events, sponsors, publishers and proceedings. OR-SEO is an extended version of the OR ontology [10]; in the comprehensive version presented here, it covers further characteristics of scientific events such as acceptance rate, schedule (submission deadline, notification date, etc.), awards, authors registration types, and social media dissemination (e.g., Twitter account).

[6] http://linkedevents.org/ontology/.
[7] https://semanticweb.cs.vu.nl/2009/11/sem/.

3 OR-SEO Development

OR-SEO is developed to be used as a reference ontology for the conceptualization of scholarly event metadata and capturing the corresponding concepts. It follows the best state-of-the-art practices and design principles for relevant and reusable ontologies. We first point out general design principles, then introduce the terms that we defined for representing the metadata of scientific events.

3.1 Design Principles and Requirements

The best practices within the Semantic Web community have been followed from the initial steps of the OR-SEO development [2]. The paramount intention behind our decision to develop an ontology for scholarly events is that, to the best of our knowledge, there is a need for a well-formed ontology in this domain to describe scholarly events. In particular, aspects related particularly to scholarly events are not covered by existing ontologies, such as roles of organizers, e.g., proceedings chair, sponsors, event proceedings, and quality metrics such as acceptance rate and the ranking of the event. Inspired by Linked Data principles [16], the following design decisions have been made while developing OR-SEO:

- *Addressing different stakeholders:* OR-SEO is developed to be used in the OpenResearch platform, supporting, e.g., authors to find high-impact events to submit their work to, and event chairs and proceedings publishers to derive useful facts to assess the impact of their events and the competing ones.
- *Broad coverage of the relevant concepts:* Events, according to OR-SEO, comprise everything that happens, no matter whether there is a specific place or time, or agents involved.
- *Flexibility and ease of changes:* The use of any class and their corresponding properties is optional, i.e., there are no property or cardinality restrictions such as `owl:allValuesFrom`.
- *Reusability:* We only use **`rdfs:domain`** and **`rdfs:range`** to indicate where to use properties. This facilitates the reuse of OR-SEO by other ontologies.
- *Efficient reasoning:* In the development of OR-SEO, several logic rules have been taken into consideration in order to facilitate efficient reasoning.
- *Availability:* The ontology has been published under a persistent URL (cf. Table 1) under the open CC-BY 3.0 license. OR-SEO is published according to the best practices of the Linked Data community [2]; its source is available from a *GitHub* repository (cf. Table 1). The ontology has been made discoverable through LOV, a high-quality catalog of well-documented vocabularies for data on the Web.
- *Validation:* Two types of validation have been performed: *syntactic* and *semantic* validation. We syntactically validated OR-SEO to conform with the W3C RDF standards using the online RDF validation service[8]. The dereferenceability of the URIs of the OR-SEO terms over the HTTP protocol

[8] https://www.w3.org/RDF/Validator/.

(cf. [18]) has been validated using Vapour[9]. We semantically validated OR-SEO using Protégé reasoners such as FaCT++[10] , and the OOPS! Ontology Pitfall Scanner[11], for detecting inconsistencies.
- *Documentation:* The documentation for the ontology is available online through its PURL. Detailed information about entities and properties are also included in the ontology, i.e., as `rdfs:comments`.
- *Adoption and Sustainability:* OR-SEO is maintained and used by the editors of OR to represent metadata of scientific events so far mainly in computer science but also some other fields including physics and chemistry. OR-SEO also has an issue tracker on its GitHub repository in order to make it easier to request new features, e.g., re-using related ontologies that may appear in future, and to report any problems.
- *Metadata completion*: We followed the best practices for completing the vocabulary metadata proposed in [13].

Table 1. OR-SEO-related resources

Resource	URL
PURL	https://w3id.org/seo
Turtle file	http://kddste.sda.tech/SEOontology/SEO.ttl
RDF/XML file	http://kddste.sda.tech/SEOontology/SEO.rdf
GitHub repository	https://github.com/saidfathalla/SEOontology
Issue Tracker	https://github.com/saidfathalla/SEOontology/issues
SPARQL endpoint	http://kddste.sda.tech/SEOontology/sparql
VoID	http://kddste.sda.tech/SEOontology/VoID.nt

3.2 Challenges and Requirements

Towards the development of an ontology for scholarly events, challenges started with identifying the pitfalls in the state-of-the-art model. In addition, the scholarly events domain itself relates entities from diverse information sources including bibliographical information, spatial and temporal data. Therefore, data models necessitates an effective integration of concepts and their semantics. After studying the domain and the state-of-the-art model, the diversity of information representation and large amount of data pose high requirements to be addressed by OR-SEO. The ontology should be maintainable with respect to the evolution of linked data vocabularies and adaptable to other domains of science. A part of these requirements will be represented as a set of competency questions related

[9] http://linkeddata.uriburner.com:8000/vapour?.
[10] https://github.com/ethz-asl/libfactplusplus.
[11] http://oops.linkeddata.es/.

to different use cases that the ontology should be able to answer. Some of these questions are: (1) *Which events related to the target domain X, e.g., "semantic web", took place in country Y over a particular time span, with an acceptance rate less than a value Z*? (2) *What are the top-X countries hosting most of the events belonging to "Security and Privacy" in the past decade?*", and (3) *In which events did person X participate in the organization committee*? More competency questions and the corresponding SPARQL queries are available at OpenResearch.org.[12]

3.3 Reuse of Existing Ontological Knowledge

Techniques for efficient and effective reuse of ontological knowledge are key factors in developing ontology-based systems [28]. A challenging task for ontology engineers is to decide in advance, which of the available vocabularies are the most useful ones for reuse, especially because the Web allows reuse across domains. By its nature, the scientific events domain involves entities from various other domains, including location, agents, time, and scholarly data, as shown in Fig. 1. Therefore, the first step in building our ontology is reusing terms from related ontologies, since, the more vocabularies a model reuses, the higher the value of its semantic data is. We have selected the most closely related ontologies listed in the Linked Open Vocabularies directory (LOV). The reuse of these vocabularies by explicitly linking to them brings OR-SEO its richness. We reuse several well-known ontologies to make OR-SEO interoperable in different contexts:

- The *Semantic Web Conference (SWC) ontology*, one of the vocabularies of choice for describing academic conferences [20], is used to represent, e.g., `Conferences` and `ConferenceSeries`.
- *Time-indexed Value in Context (TVC)*, a standard ontology design pattern to describe a time-indexed situation that expresses a particular role held by an agent at an event [22], is used to represent, e.g., `Duration` and `Interval`.
- *Dublin Core Metadata Initiative (DCMI)* is used to describe metadata of typical entities in scientific events, e.g., of `Agents` or `Proceedings`,
- The *Friend-of-a-Friend (FOAF)* ontology describes involved persons and their social network profiles,
- *Semantically-Interlinked Online Communities (SIOC)* describes information from online communities such as `Role` and `Site` [3]
- SPAR ontologies [23] describe research papers type (fabio), publications identifiers (datacite) and document parts (doco).
- SemSur ontology describes research findings based on an explicit semantic representation of the knowledge contained in scientific publications [8], and
- DBpedia Ontology (dbo)[13] is used to represent geographical data, such as `dbo:Country` and `dbo:City`.

[12] https://www.openresearch.org/wiki/Sparql_endpoint/Examples.
[13] http://dbpedia.org/ontology/.

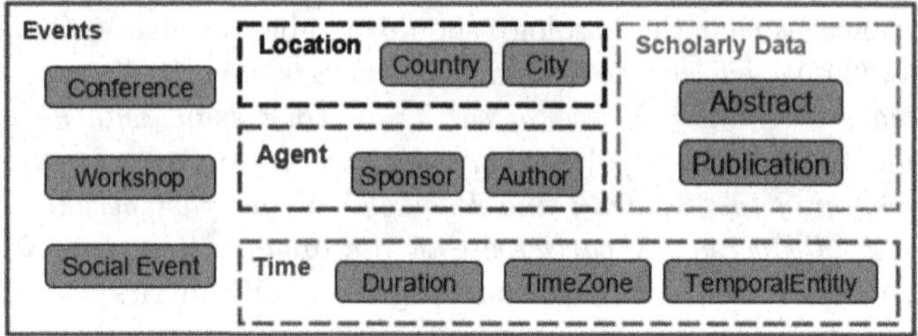

Fig. 1. A layered view of the domains, with corresponding entities of SEO.

4 Ontology Description

The SAMOD agile methodology is used for developing OR-SEO ontology. SAMOD takes into consideration various issues when developing ontologies to achieve a "data-centric" model, such as avoiding inconsistencies, being self-explanatory, and giving examples of usage. This section describes the main entities in the scientific events ontology. We focus on core classes and properties, and reasoning support provided by the ontology. More details can be found in the online documentation of the ontology.

4.1 Core Classes

The OR-SEO ontology imports some of the main classes from the ontologies introduced in Subsect. 3.3. For the ones not explicitly matching with the concepts addressed by OR-SEO, new definitions have been developed. The core entities of the scholarly events in OR-SEO are: (1) *Event*, as the entity of main interest, including metadata such as event type (e.g., conference or workshop), bibliographic and retrospective information (the numbers of submitted and accepted articles, information about the attendees, tracks), (2) *Agents*, including the *Organizations* hosting or sponsoring the event and *Persons* involved in the organization of the events in different roles, (3) *Role during event* of such stakeholders and persons, (4) *Location*, the city and country in which the event was held, (5) *Proceedings*, the proceedings including the publications produced by the event, and (6) *Time*, to describe the duration of events. Concretely, these entities are represented in OR-SEO as follows (see Figs. 2 and 3): `OrganizedEvent` represents the event itself and all the sub-events of those which are about the topic or theme of the main event, such as academic or non-academic events. `Agent` represents a person, group, company or organization, which can be a sponsor or a publisher of the proceedings of the event. `RoleDuringEvent` represents a time indexed situation that expresses a role held by an agent in the context of the event. `Country/City` represents the physical location of the event. `Proceedings` represents proceedings produced by academic events. `TemporalDuration` is a time interval representing the duration of the event. Agents, i.e., persons and organizations, play a key role in the scholarly events domain. Agents hold different roles (`RoleDuringEvent`) in participating in scholarly events, including

Publishing Role During Event, *Organizational Role During Event* and *Chair Role During Event*.

Class Specialization: Because of the complexity and diversity of the concepts, some of the defined or reused classes need more specialization, so we created respective subclasses. For instance, `Symposium` has been added as a subclass of the `AcademicEvent` class, and another subclass to represent the series of such events as `SymposiumSeries` to the super class `EventSeries`. In addition, a set of classes missing from other ontologies, for example, to describe agents and their roles more specifically, such as `Publisher` and `Sponsor`, have been added.

Class Disjointness: We assert pairwise disjointness, where applicable, between any of the classes in the ontology. For instance, the `IrregularRegistration` class is disjoint with `RegularRegistration` and `LateRegistration` is disjoint with `EarlyBirdRegistration`.

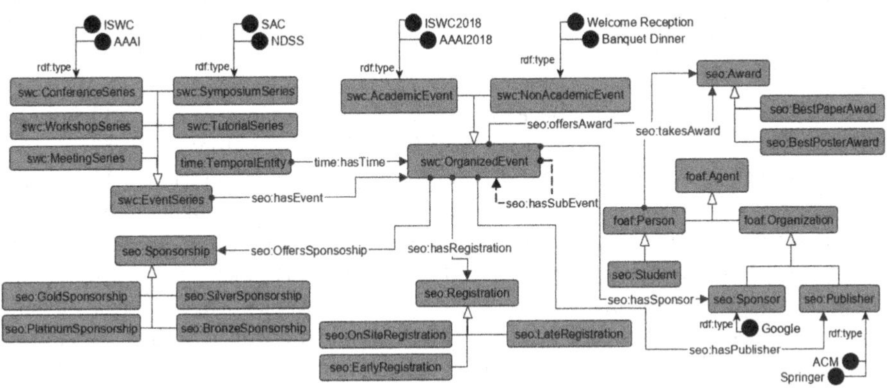

Fig. 2. Core concepts in OR-SEO and their relationships. Arrows with open arrow heads denote `rdfs:subClassOf` properties between the classes.

4.2 Properties

OR-SEO's properties are divided into two categories: newly defined and directly reused properties. We indicate the classes to be used with several data and object properties by defining domain and range using `rdfs:domain` and `rdfs:range` respectively. For instance, we capture the domain of newly-defined data properties for describing abstract and submission deadline, i.e., `seo:abstractDeadline` and `seo:submissionDeadline`, to be `swc:AcademicEvent` and the range to be `xsd:dateTime`. In addition, OR-SEO defines its own object properties, such as `seo:belongsToSeries`, `seo:hasTrack`, `seo:colocatedWith`, `seo:hasPublisher`. Some properties have complex ranges, e.g., `seo:hasRegistrationType` has range (`LateRegistration`

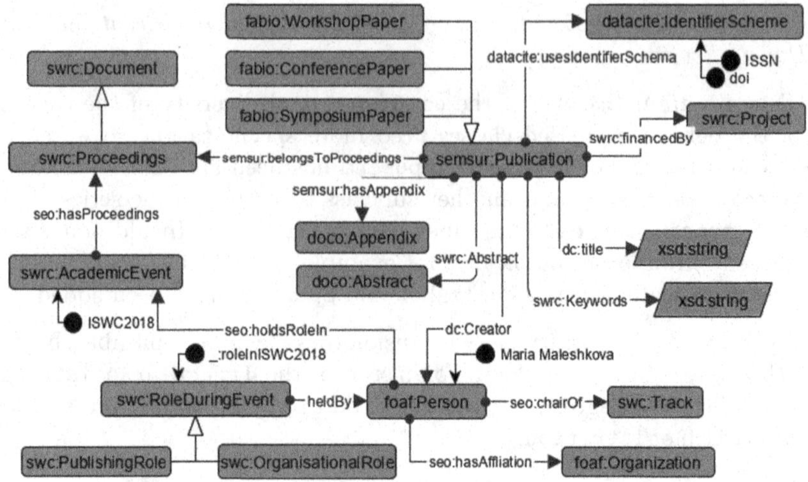

Fig. 3. Publications and roles of Agents during a scientific event.

⊔ `EarlyBirdRegistration`) because these two classes are disjoint. Ontology design patterns are applied, e.g., the OWL patterns of Gangemi [12], to capture notions such as inverse relations and composition of relations. There are some inverse relations, e.g., `seo:isTrackOf` is the inverse of `seo:hasTrack` and `seo:isSponsorOf` is the inverse of `seo:hasSponsor`. Thus, if an event E `seo:hasTrack` T, then it can be inferred that T `seo:isTrackOf` E. Also, some symmetric relations are defined, such as `seo:colocatedWith`, e.g., if an event E_1 is co-located with another one E_2, then it could be inferred that E_2 is also co-located with E_1. Furthermore, it is a property whose domain is the same as its range, which provides the information that an organized event can only be co-located with another organized event, and a reflexive relation, i.e., each event is co-located with itself. Such definitions allow to reveal implicit information and increase the coherence and thus the value of event metadata.

Representation Pattern for n-ary Relations. One common representation of n-ary relations is to represent the relation as a class rather than a property, and using n properties to point to the related entities. Instances of such classes are instances of the n-ary relation and additional properties can provide binary links to each argument of the relation, i.e., an instance of the relation linking the n individuals. For more illustration, consider the case of *Maria Maleshkova*, the sponsorship chair in the ISWC conference in 2018. As shown in Fig. 4, the individual *:roleInISWC2018* represents a single object encapsulating both the event, the person that had a role there, and the type of the role in that event.

4.3 Reasoning

Inference on the Semantic Web is additionally used to improve the quality of data integration in the ontology by combining rules and ontologies to discover new

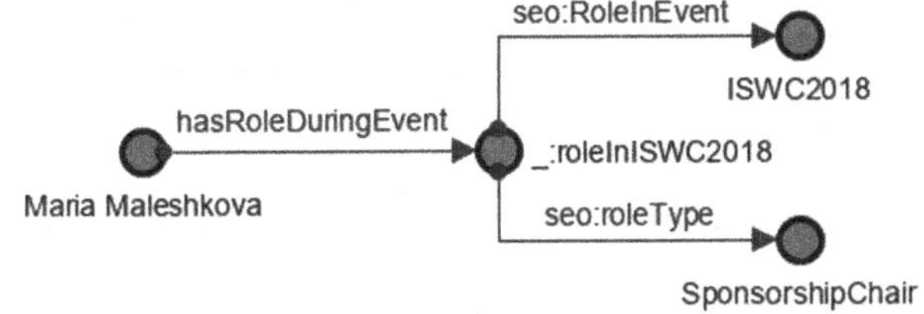

Fig. 4. Representation pattern for n-ary relations in OR-SEO.

relationships, detect possible inconsistencies and infer logical consequences from a set of asserted facts or axioms. Drools reasoner [25] is one of the reasoners that the Protégé ontology development environment uses for performing rule-based inference. Our goal is to define a rule set for discovering new relationships and inferring new knowledge that did not explicitly exist in a knowledge graph. Therefore, a set of rules following the Semantic Web Rule Language (SWRL) [24] has been defined and written using the SWRLtab plugin for Protégé 5.2. SWRL was designed based on a combination of the OWL DL and OWL Lite sub-languages of OWL Full. SWRL allows users to write Horn-like rules expressed in terms of OWL classes and properties to reason about OWL individuals. A set of rules to support the inference in OR-SEO have been defined. These rules have been semantically validated using Drools reasoner. The rule set in OR-SEO includes the following SWRL rules (for readability, we omitted namespaces). Using Formula 1, participants in a specific event can be easily inferred, while using Formula 2, the location of one event can be determined from a co-located event.

$$Agent\ (?a) \wedge holdsRole\ (?a, ?e) \rightarrow participatesIn\ (?a, ?e) \tag{1}$$

$$colocatedWith\ (?e1, ?e2)\ \wedge\ hasLocation\ (?e1, ?l) \rightarrow hasLocation\ (?e2, ?l) \tag{2}$$

5 Real-World Use Cases

This section presents two real-world use cases for the OR-SEO ontology: OpenResearch.org and the EVENTSKG dataset.

Use Case 1. As populating ontologies with instances is a time-consuming and error-prone task, OR-SEO is in use on 6,800+ event pages on *OpenResearch* [31], which facilitates the creation of instances of events and events series as wiki pages, without having to go into the details of the implementation of the ontology. It is an extended version of the original ontology of *OpenResearch*, which has been redesigned and systematically validated. Data acquisition in *OpenResearch* follows an approach that combines manual/crowd-sourced contribution and semi-automated methods. *OpenResearch* provides semantic descriptions of scientific events, publications, tools and organizations using ontologies for each such entity type. Semantic MediaWiki (SMW), a semantically enhanced wiki engine, is the core software for *OpenResearch* that serves as data curation interface employing semantic forms. OpenResearch employs one semantic form per core class of OR-SEO; combined with properties, they enable semantic annotations in the wiki markup. Semantic forms enable users to create and modify the knowledge graph via forms, without the need for actual programming. Listing 1 shows an example of an individual event (ISWC 2018) created on *OpenResearch*[14]. Furthermore, semantically annotated text is found at the bottom of the corresponding wiki page of the ISWC series[15], which represents the metadata of the event using corresponding terms of the ontology, such as chairs, country, or Twitter account. For instance, the *info box* on the right contains the metadata of the events series, including full title, bibliography, CORE 2017 and 2018 ranks, and the average acceptance rate. Semantically annotated metadata can be exported as RDF triples using the *"RDF feed"* feature. Several interesting information can be exposed from OpenResearch, such as a list of upcoming events in a Calendar view[16], and top-ranked events along with their ranking and average acceptance rate[17]. Finally, such ontologies and events metadata added by the community extend *OpenResearch*'s distributed data collection by embedding markup in conference websites aligned with schema.org, and links to other portals and services.

Use Case 2. The second use case of OR-SEO is the representation of a comprehensive dataset (EVENTSKG) of scholarly events sourced from several resources and curated semi-automatically [5–7]. Going beyond existing work (cf. Sect. 2), it comprises metadata of 73 renowned events in eight computer science communities using OR-SEO as its schema. EVENTSKG is not only able to answer quantitative questions, but it also provides qualitative information, such as which countries hosted most events in a particular community.

Listing 1. Use case 1. Representation of metadata on OpenResearch.org in its markup language.

```
{{Event
| Title      = 17th International Semantic Web Conference
| Series     = ISWC             | Type       = Conference
| Field      = Linked Data      | Start date = 2018/10/08
| End date   = 2018/10/12       | Homepage   = iswc2018.semanticweb.org/
| Twitter    = @iswc2018        | City       = Monterey
| Country    = USA
}}
```

[14] http://openresearch.org/wiki/ISWC_2018.

[15] https://www.openresearch.org/wiki/ISWC.

[16] https://www.openresearch.org/mediawiki/index.php?title=Events_Calendar&field=Science.

[17] https://www.openresearch.org/mediawiki/index.php?title=Series&field=Science.

Listing 2. Use case 2. Using OR-SEO in metadata representation for ISWC 2015 in EVENTSKG, in Turtle.

```
### https://w3id.org/seo#ISWC2015
ekg:ISWC2015  rdf:type  owl:NamedIndividual ,
conference-ontology:Conference;
 seo:belongsToSeries      ekg:ISWC ;
 seo:acceptanceRate       "0.22"^^xsd:decimal;
 seo:submittedPapers      "172"^^xsd:int;
 seo:acceptedPapers       "38"^^xsd:int;
 seo:city                 <http://dbpedia.org/page/Bethlehem>;
 seo:country              <http://dbpedia.org/page/United_States>;
 seo:field                seo:InformationSystem ;
 conference-ontology:startDate "2015-10-11"^^xsd:date;
 conference-ontology:endDate  "2015-10-15"^^xsd:date;
 seo:eventWebsite         "http://iswc2015.semanticweb.org/"^^xsd:anyURI.
```

The aim is to transform event metadata, distributed across different sources, to Linked Open Data, which can be interpreted by machines to create innovative event-related services. Listing 2 shows the metadata of ISWC 2015 in EVENTSKG. Three major prefixes are used in metadata representation namely: `ekg`, `seo` and `conference-ontology` according to http://prefix.cc/.

6 Evaluation

Evaluating ontologies is the process of measuring the quality of the ontology content, ensuring that its definitions satisfy the requirements or perform correctly in the real world [14]. In other words, the quality of ontologies can be assessed using metrics that evaluate the success of the ontology in modeling a real-world domain (as illustrated in Sect. 5). Ontologies can be evaluated against a gold standard, or using a criteria-based or task-based evaluation [34]. This is majorly a manual task because it is difficult to construct automated tests to compare ontologies using such criteria [4]. We assess OR-SEO using a criteria-based evaluation as proposed by Tartir et al. [30]. They proposed an ontology evaluation model, called OntoQA, which evaluates the ontology using schema metrics and instance metrics. We evaluate the ontology design by comparing to the related work (with the best coverage of the domain, i.e., SWC, SEDE, and SWRC).

- *Attribute richness (AR)* refers to the average number of attributes per class. Formally, $AR = A/C$, the number of attributes for all classes (A) divided by the number of classes (C). The more attributes are defined, the more knowledge the ontology provides.
- *Relationship richness (RR)* refers to the diversity of relations and the placement of them in the ontology. Formally, $RR = R/(S + R)$, the number of relationships (R) defined in the schema, divided by the sum of the number of sub-classes (S) and the number of relationships. The more relations, except is-a relations, the ontology has, the richer it is.

– *Inheritance richness (IR)* refers to the average number of sub-classes per class. Formally, $IR = S/C$, the number of sub-classes divided by the sum of the number of classes. A high IR means that ontology represents a wide range of general knowledge, i.e., is of a horizontal nature.

Table 2. Evaluation of OR-SEO using OntoQA model

Ontology	Classes	Sub-classes	Attributes	Relations	AR	RR	IR
SWC	390	351	118	189	0.30	0.40	0.90
SEDE	122	46	47	56	0.39	0.60	0.38
SWRC	248	221	51	57	0.21	0.21	0.89
OR-SEO	165	197	93	177	**0.57**	**0.61**	**1.19**

As shown in Table 2, OR-SEO has a moderate size but an overall beneficial knowledge structure. Among similar domain ontologies it has the largest *AR* which enables the provision of more knowledge per instance. Regarding *RR*, OR-SEO has moderate diversity of relations and has much richer relations in comparison with SWC and SWRC, and slightly richer than SEDE. Regarding *IR*, OR-SEO has the highest value of all ontologies (1.19), which means that it represents a wider range of knowledge than the state of the art. In terms of usability evaluation, most of the users of OpenResearch found it easy to populate the ontology via a user-friendly interface, i.e., SMW semantic forms. For instance, event organizers, or even any researcher interested in an event, can add event series or an individual event metadata using "*Add event series*"[18] and "*Add event*"[19] semantic forms, respectively. As mentioned before in Sect. 5, the produced data are wiki pages presenting events metadata in a user-friendly way.

7 Conclusions and Future Work

We presented OR-SEO, a reference ontology for capturing metadata of scientific events. Its real-world instantiation in the OpenResearch platform is discussed with some inference rules to discover new relationships, detect possible inconsistencies and infer logical consequences from a set of asserted facts. We shed light on what OR-SEO contributes to the existing literature by reviewing the existing event-related models, pointing out their weaknesses. Actually, OR-SEO covers issues closely related to scholarly events, which are not covered by other scholarly communication domain ontologies, such as types of scholarly events, sponsor, publisher and proceedings. Furthermore, OR-SEO models scholarly events characteristics, such as acceptance rate, submission deadline, and notification date, and Twitter account. The ontology is publicly available online, following

[18] https://www.openresearch.org/wiki/Special:FormEdit/EventSeries.

[19] https://www.openresearch.org/wiki/Special:FormEdit/Event.

ontology resource publication best practices. We showed that it fits well for a heterogeneous set of existing metadata covered by the OpenResearch platform. The ontology will continue to be maintained and extended in the context of the *OpenResearch* effort, aiming at large scale event data acquisition and analysis through applying semi-automated and crowd-sourcing methods. We hope that OR-SEO will thus contribute to facilitating the representation and analysis of the currently not yet well-structured space of scholarly event information, thus supporting all stakeholders of events, particularly including organizers and potential authors.

Regarding future work in the context of the maintenance plan of OR-SEO we envision to: (1) model event evolution considering property changes such as type, e.g., from symposium to conference, or events re-scheduled, or events whose chairs changed, (2) adapt the ontology to cover events in other research fields, such as Physics, Mathematics, and Engineering, where scholarly events take a different shape, (3) improve the coverage, by including more concepts related to sponsorship, event's program, social events within the event itself and events' calls for papers, (4) model other publishing venues such as journals, and (5) develop a smart data analytics tool in order to assess events' progress and recommend relevant events to potential authors and a SPARQL endpoint and a Linked Data navigator to browse the ontology and its instances.

Acknowledgement. This work is supported by EPSRC grant EP/M025268/1, WWTF grant VRG18-013, EC Horizon 2020 grants LAMBDA (#809965) and the ERC project ScienceGRAPH (#819536).

References

1. Auer, S., Kovtun, V., Prinz, M., Kasprzik, A., Stocker, M., Vidal, M.E.: Towards a knowledge graph for science. In: 8th International Conference on Web Intelligence, Mining and Semantics. ACM (2018)
2. Berrueta, D., Phipps, J., Miles, A., Baker, T., Swick, R.: Best practice recipes for publishing RDF vocabularies. In: Working draft, W3C (2008)
3. Breslin, J.G., Decker, S., Harth, A., Bojars, U.: SIOC: an approach to connect web-based communities. Int. J. Web Based Commun. **2**(2), 133–142 (2006)
4. Brewster, C., Alani, H., Dasmahapatra, S., Wilks, Y.: Data driven ontology evaluation. In: 4th International Conference on Language Resources and Evaluation, LREC 2004 (2004)
5. Fathalla, S., Lange, C.: EVENTS: a dataset on the history of top-prestigious events in five computer science communities. In: González-Beltrán, A., Osborne, F., Peroni, S., Vahdati, S. (eds.) SAVE-SD 2017-2018. LNCS, vol. 10959, pp. 110–120. Springer, Cham (2018). https://doi.org/10.1007/978-3-030-01379-0_8
6. Fathalla, S., Lange, C.: EVENTSKG: a knowledge graph representation for top-prestigious computer science events metadata. In: Nguyen, N.T., Pimenidis, E., Khan, Z., Trawiński, B. (eds.) ICCCI 2018. LNCS (LNAI), vol. 11055, pp. 53–63. Springer, Cham (2018). https://doi.org/10.1007/978-3-319-98443-8_6

7. Fathalla, S., Lange, C., Auer, S.: EVENTSKG: a 5-star dataset of top-ranked events in eight computer science communities. In: Hitzler, P., et al. (eds.) ESWC 2019. LNCS, vol. 11503, pp. 427–442. Springer, Cham (2019). https://doi.org/10.1007/978-3-030-21348-0_28
8. Fathalla, S., Vahdati, S., Auer, S., Lange, C.: SemSur: a core ontology for the semantic representation of research findings. Proc. Comput. Sci. **137**, 151–162 (2018)
9. Fathalla, S., Vahdati, S., Auer, S., Lange, C.: Metadata analysis of scholarly events of computer science, physics, engineering, and mathematics. In: Méndez, E., Crestani, F., Ribeiro, C., David, G., Lopes, J.C. (eds.) TPDL 2018. LNCS, vol. 11057, pp. 116–128. Springer, Cham (2018). https://doi.org/10.1007/978-3-030-00066-0_10
10. Fathalla, S., Vahdati, S., Auer, S., Lange, C.: The scientific events ontology of the openresearch.org curation platform. In: Proceedings of the 34th ACM/SIGAPP Symposium on Applied Computing (2019)
11. Fathalla, S., Vahdati, S., Lange, C., Auer, S.: Analysing scholarly communication metadata of computer science events. In: Kamps, J., Tsakonas, G., Manolopoulos, Y., Iliadis, L., Karydis, I. (eds.) TPDL 2017. LNCS, vol. 10450, pp. 342–354. Springer, Cham (2017). https://doi.org/10.1007/978-3-319-67008-9_27
12. Gangemi, A., Presutti, V.: Ontology design patterns. In: Staab, S., Studer, R. (eds.) Handbook on Ontologies. IHIS, pp. 221–243. Springer, Heidelberg (2009). https://doi.org/10.1007/978-3-540-92673-3_10
13. Garijo, D., Poveda-Villalón, M.: A checklist for complete vocabulary metadata (2017). https://w3id.org/widoco/bestPractices
14. Gómez-Pérez, A.: Evaluation of ontologies. Int. J. Intell. Syst. **16**(3), 391–409 (2001)
15. Gottschalk, S., Demidova, E.: EventKG: a multilingual event-centric temporal knowledge graph. In: Gangemi, A., et al. (eds.) ESWC 2018. LNCS, vol. 10843, pp. 272–287. Springer, Cham (2018). https://doi.org/10.1007/978-3-319-93417-4_18
16. Heath, T., Bizer, C.: Linked data: evolving the web into a global data space. Synth. Lect. Semant. Web Theory Technol. **1**(1), 1–136 (2011)
17. Jeong, S., Kim, H.-G.: SEDE: an ontology for scholarly event description. J. Inf. Sci. **36**(2), 209–227 (2010)
18. Lewis, R.: Dereferencing HTTP URIs. In: Draft Tag Finding (2007). http://www.w3.org/2001/tag/doc/httpRange-14/2007-05-31/HttpRange-14.html
19. Möller, K., Heath, T., Handschuh, S., Domingue, J.: Recipes for semantic web dog food—The ESWC and ISWC metadata projects. In: Aberer, K., et al. (eds.) ASWC/ISWC -2007. LNCS, vol. 4825, pp. 802–815. Springer, Heidelberg (2007). https://doi.org/10.1007/978-3-540-76298-0_58
20. Nuzzolese, A.G., Gentile, A.L., Presutti, V., Gangemi, A.: Semantic web conference ontology - a refactoring solution. In: Sack, H., Rizzo, G., Steinmetz, N., Mladenić, D., Auer, S., Lange, C. (eds.) ESWC 2016. LNCS, vol. 9989, pp. 84–87. Springer, Cham (2016). https://doi.org/10.1007/978-3-319-47602-5_18
21. Peroni, S.: A simplified agile methodology for ontology development. In: Dragoni, M., Poveda-Villalón, M., Jimenez-Ruiz, E. (eds.) OWLED/ORE -2016. LNCS, vol. 10161, pp. 55–69. Springer, Cham (2017). https://doi.org/10.1007/978-3-319-54627-8_5
22. Peroni, S.: The semantic publishing and referencing ontologies. Semantic Web Technologies and Legal Scholarly Publishing. LGTS, vol. 15, pp. 121–193. Springer, Cham (2014). https://doi.org/10.1007/978-3-319-04777-5_5

23. Peroni, S., Shotton, D.: The SPAR ontologies. In: Vrandečić, D., et al. (eds.) ISWC 2018. LNCS, vol. 11137, pp. 119–136. Springer, Cham (2018). https://doi.org/10.1007/978-3-030-00668-6_8
24. Plinere, D., Borisov, A.: SWRL: rule acquisition using ontology. Sci. J. Riga Tech. Univ. Comput. Sci. **40**(1), 117–122 (2009)
25. Proctor, M.: Drools: a rule engine for complex event processing. In: Schürr, A., Varró, D., Varró, G. (eds.) AGTIVE 2011. LNCS, vol. 7233, pp. 2–2. Springer, Heidelberg (2012). https://doi.org/10.1007/978-3-642-34176-2_2
26. Raimond, Y., Abdallah, S.: The event ontology (2007)
27. Shaw, R., Troncy, R., Hardman, L.: LODE: linking open descriptions of events. In: Gómez-Pérez, A., Yu, Y., Ding, Y. (eds.) ASWC 2009. LNCS, vol. 5926, pp. 153–167. Springer, Heidelberg (2009). https://doi.org/10.1007/978-3-642-10871-6_11
28. Simperl, E.: Reusing ontologies on the semantic web: a feasibility study. Data Knowl. Eng. **68**(10), 905–925 (2009)
29. Sure, Y., Bloehdorn, S., Haase, P., Hartmann, J., Oberle, D.: The SWRC ontology – semantic web for research communities. In: Bento, C., Cardoso, A., Dias, G. (eds.) EPIA 2005. LNCS (LNAI), vol. 3808, pp. 218–231. Springer, Heidelberg (2005). https://doi.org/10.1007/11595014_22
30. Tartir, S., Arpinar, I.B., Moore, M., Sheth, A.P., Aleman-Meza, B.: OntoQA: metric-based ontology quality analysis. In: IEEE ICDM Workshop on Knowledge Acquisition from Distributed, Autonomous, Semantically Heterogeneous Data and Knowledge Sources (2005)
31. Vahdati, S., Arndt, N., Auer, S., Lange, C.: OpenResearch: collaborative management of scholarly communication metadata. In: Blomqvist, E., Ciancarini, P., Poggi, F., Vitali, F. (eds.) EKAW 2016. LNCS (LNAI), vol. 10024, pp. 778–793. Springer, Cham (2016). https://doi.org/10.1007/978-3-319-49004-5_50
32. Van Hage, W.R., Malaisé, V., Segers, R., Hollink, L., Schreiber, G.: Design and use of the simple event model (SEM). Web Seman. Sci. Serv. Agents World Wide Web **9**(2), 128–136 (2011)
33. Wu, Z., Wu, J., Khabsa, M., Williams et al.: Towards building a scholarly big data platform: Challenges, lessons and opportunities. In: 14th ACM/IEEE- CS Joint Conference on Digital Libraries. IEEE Press (2014)
34. Yu, J., Thom, J.A., Tam, A.: Ontology evaluation using Wikipedia categories for browsing. In: 16th ACM Conference on Conference on Information and Knowledge Management (2007)

DBpedia FlexiFusion the Best of Wikipedia > Wikidata > Your Data

Johannes Frey[1(✉)], Marvin Hofer[1], Daniel Obraczka[2], Jens Lehmann[1,3], and Sebastian Hellmann[1]

[1] Leipzig University (AKSW/KILT Group) & DBpedia Association, Leipzig, Germany
{frey,hofer,obraczka,lehmann,hellmann}@informatik.uni-leipzig.de
[2] Leipzig University (Database Group), Leipzig, Germany
[3] Smart Data Analytics (SDA) Group, Bonn, Germany & Fraunhofer IAIS, Dresden, Germany
jens.lehmann@iais.fraunhofer.de
http://aksw.org/Groups/KILT
https://dbs.uni-leipzig.de

Abstract. The data quality improvement of DBpedia has been in the focus of many publications in the past years with topics covering both knowledge enrichment techniques such as type learning, taxonomy generation, interlinking as well as error detection strategies such as property or value outlier detection, type checking, ontology constraints, or unit-tests, to name just a few. The concrete innovation of the DBpedia FlexiFusion workflow, leveraging the novel DBpedia PreFusion dataset, which we present in this paper, is to massively cut down the engineering workload to apply any of the vast methods available in shorter time and also make it easier to produce customized knowledge graphs or DBpedias. While FlexiFusion is flexible to accommodate other use cases, our main use case in this paper is the generation of richer, language-specific DBpedias for the 20+ DBpedia chapters, which we demonstrate on the Catalan DBpedia. In this paper, we define a set of quality metrics and evaluate them for Wikidata and DBpedia datasets of several language chapters. Moreover, we show that an implementation of FlexiFusion, performed on the proposed PreFusion dataset, increases data size, richness as well as quality in comparison to the source datasets.

Stable Databus IRI: https://databus.dbpedia.org/dbpedia/prefusion

Keywords: Data fusion · Quality assessment · Provenance

1 Introduction

From ancient history until today, being in possession of the right information at the right moment promised great rewards. From the movable types of the Gutenberg press to the long tail of information delivered by the WWW, we can cite ample examples in history where more adequate information delivery

C. Ghidini et al. (Eds.): ISWC 2019, LNCS 11779, pp. 96–112, 2019.
https://doi.org/10.1007/978-3-030-30796-7_7

had a great effect on society. We certainly do not claim to have discovered such a disruptive technology as the movable types of the Gutenberg Press, which allowed effective production of different kind of books, however, we see our work as a step in the right direction of rapid production of movable knowledge graphs.

The concrete innovation of the DBpedia FlexiFusion approach is to massively cut down engineering workload to produce customized DBpedias. Our main use case here is the generation of richer language-specific DBpedias for the 20+ DBpedia chapters, which we demonstrate on the use case of the Catalan DBpedia[1] (cf. Sect. 5). Regarding further advances in data engineering, we see various additional uses that can benefit from the flexibility provided. In particular this flexibility concerns:

1. Flexibility of source selection via the DBpedia Databus[2]. In this paper, we load 140 DBpedia language-editions and Wikidata from the Databus. Beyond this, we already experimented with the inclusion of data from the Dutch and German national libraries via existing links and mappings in FlexiFusion.
2. A new format, which stores value options for triples including resolvable rich provenance information.
3. A flexible fusion approach to reduce and resolve available options to materialize new knowledge graphs, that are downward-compatible with the RDF standard. We list a short overview of previous fusion approaches that are applicable in Sect. 7.

In the next section, we introduce the DBpedia Databus as background, followed by the PreFusion dataset in Sect. 3. Section 4 describes the details of FlexiFusion. Subsequently, we show two usage scenarios and concrete configurations of FlexiFusion to produce custom fused datasets in Sect. 5 and evaluate our datasets w.r.t. data coverage and data quality in Sect. 6. We finish with related work, conclusions and a final discussion.

2 DBpedia Databus - the Digital Factory Platform

The Databus platform is developed via a use-case driven methodology. FlexiFusion is the first use case that has been realized with the Databus and is described here in the context of the Databus. The platform provides two tools to connect consumers and producers: 1. *for consumers*, the website https://databus.dbpedia.org and the SPARQL API https://databus.dbpedia.org/repo/sparql serve as a user interface to configure data set retrieval and combination in catalogues, 2. *for providers*, the Databus Maven plugin[3] enables systematic upload and release of datasets on the bus.

2.1 FlexiFusion Workflow on the Databus

Data management tasks such as ETL, integration, fusion and quality assurance are hard and repetitive. In the course of developing the new DBpedia

[1] http://ca.dbpedia.org.
[2] https://databus.dbpedia.org/.
[3] http://dev.dbpedia.org/Databus_Maven_Plugin.

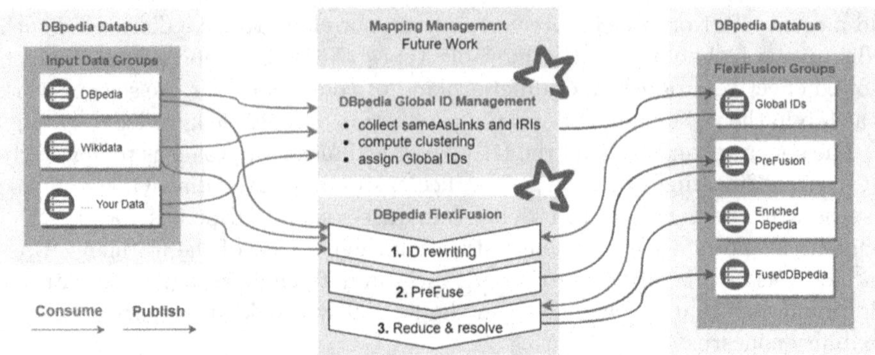

Fig. 1. FlexiFusion on the Databus. (Color figure online)

strategy "Global and Unified Access to Knowledge Graphs", we have intensively studied and discussed the (Linked Open) data network for the past two years and analysed the struggle of stakeholders to collaborate, hindered by technical and organizational barriers. The efforts for the creation and maintenance of mappings and linksets, error detection & correction, to name just a few, are repeated in individual and use case specific data management processes applied both in research, public bodies and corporate environments. With the DBpedia Databus we envision a hub, where users can register various data artifacts of their data management tasks. In that hub, useful operations like versioning, cleaning, transformation, mapping, linking, merging, can be applied and coordinated on a central communication system - the bus - and then again dispersed in a decentralized network to consumers and applications. On the Databus, data flows from data producers through the platform to consumers while errors or feedback can flow in the opposite direction and propagate to the data source to allow a continuous integration and quality improvement.

Figure 1 shows the FlexiFusion workflow, which is an application of medium complexity built on top of the Databus. Data is likewise consumed (green arrows) and published (orange arrows). The image shows a simplified view, describing FlexiFusion as a pipeline, but in fact it is a distributed network model of individual components, which might be better expressed via formalisms such as Petri Nets[4] that enable analysis of circular dependencies and critical paths. An additional layer of complexity is hidden in the data sources and the sinks on the right and left, as these are in fact data artifacts with versioned snapshots. In the future, any component of FlexiFusion can publish additional feedback information to improve e.g. the ID and Mapping Management based on available options found in the fusion process.

2.2 Modular DBpedia Releases on the Databus

The main motivation to develop the Databus was to switch from *one* very complex, highly interdependent, work-intensive release workflow of DBpedia to

[4] https://en.wikipedia.org/wiki/Petri_net.

several agile, frequent and automated modular releases [4] with short cycles which allows a faster delivery of community contributions (mappings, interlinks, extraction framework fixes and Wikipedia/Wikidata updates) to end users.

```
@prefix : <https://downloads.dbpedia.org/repo/lts/mappings/instance-types/2018.12.01/dataid.ttl#> .
@prefix dataid-cv: <http://dataid.dbpedia.org/ns/cv#> . # namespace for content-variants

:Dataset
   a                      dataid:Dataset ;
   dct:title              "DBpedia Ontology instance types"@en ;
   dataid:account          <https://databus.dbpedia.org/dbpedia> ;
   dataid:group            <https://databus.dbpedia.org/dbpedia/mappings> ;
   dataid:artifact         <https://databus.dbpedia.org/dbpedia/mappings/instance-types> ;
   dataid:version          <https://databus.dbpedia.org/dbpedia/mappings/instance-types/2018.12.01> ;
   dct:publisher          <https://webid.dbpedia.org/webid.ttl#this> ;
   dct:license             <http://purl.oclc.org/NET/rdflicense/cc-by3.0> .

:instance-types_transitive_lang=en.ttl.bz2
   a                         dataid:SingleFile ;
   dct:isDistributionOf      :Dataset ;
   dct:title                 "DBpedia Ontology instance types"@en ;
   dct:hasVersion            "2018.12.01" ;
   # language and other variants are encoded here
   dataid:contentVariant    "en" , "transitive" ;
   dataid-cv:lang            "en" ;
   dataid-cv:tag            "transitive" ;
   dcat:downloadURL          :instance-types_transitive_lang=en.ttl.bz2 ;
   dcat:mediaType            dataid-mt:ApplicationNTriples .
```

Listing 1: DBpedia DataID snippet of `https://databus.dbpedia.org/dbpedia/mappings/instance-types/2018.12.01`

Inspired by Maven, datasets are described by `publisher` / `group` / `artifact` / `version`. *Groups* provide a coarse modularization. From a top level view, DBpedia is now separated into 5 different groups, which are produced by separate extraction processes with separated dependencies: *generic* (automatically extracted information from raw infoboxes and other sources), *mappings* (mapping-aided infobox extraction), *text* (article abstracts and textual content), and *wikidata* (Wikidata facts mapped to DBpedia ontology [5]) and the *ontology*. *Artifacts* are the abstract identity of the dataset with a *stable dataset id*, e.g. there is a *geo-coordinates* artifact in generic, mappings and wikidata. Each artifact has *versions*, that usually contain the same set of files for each release. Files within a version are additionally described by content variants (e.g. `lang=en`), mediatype and compression. The overall structure is very flexible as software libraries, but also – once defined – as fixed as software to prevent applications from breaking, if they update on a new dataset version [4]. Further details are described in the user manual[5].

2.3 Data Selection and Retrieval

Once artifacts are established, new versions can be published automatically and the metadata of the published data is machine-comprehensible via the DataID/DCAT vocabulary (an example can be seen in Listing 1). The Databus

[5] http://dev.dbpedia.org/Databus_Upload_User_Manual.

Maven Plugin uses the Maven Lifecycle phases to generate this metadata based on a configuration provided by the publisher via 'mvn databus:metadata' and uploads it to the Databus via 'mvn deploy' at the final stage of the publishing process to the Databus SPARQL endpoint. This endpoint can be queried in order to fetch a custom tailored selection of groups/artifacts/files in specific versions. As the data itself is hosted in the publisher's webspace, queries retrieve metadata in form of `dcat:downloadURLs` for the files.

FlexiFusion is fed by a fine-grained selection of RDF data files (`?files`) via SPARQL queries (see Listing 2) using stable identifiers of the form https://databus.dbpedia.org/<publisher>/<group>/<artifact>. The SPARQL queries are considered as configuration of input data dependencies and can be used to fetch the most recent versions of the dependencies.

```
PREFIX dataid: <http://dataid.dbpedia.org/ns/core#>
PREFIX dcat: <http://www.w3.org/ns/dcat#>
SELECT distinct ?file {
  ?dataid dataid:version ?latest;
          dcat:distribution ?distribution .
  ?distribution dcat:downloadURL ?file;
                dataid:contentVariant "transitive"^^xsd:string .
  { SELECT DISTINCT ( MAX( ?version ) as ?latest ) {
    ?s a dataid:Dataset ;
       dataid:artifact ?artifact;
       dataid:version  ?version .
       FILTER ( ?artifact in (
          <https://databus.dbpedia.org/dbpedia/mappings/instance-types>,
          <https://databus.dbpedia.org/dbpedia/wikidata/instance-types>
        ))
    } GROUP BY ?artifact
}}
```

Listing 2: Example SPARQL query for input dataset selection fetching the download URLs for the latest version of transitive type information from DBpedia and Wikidata instance types artifacts.

3 DBpedia PreFusion Dataset

The *DBpedia **PreFusion*** dataset is a new addition to the modular DBpedia releases combining DBpedia data from over 140 Wikipedia language editions and Wikidata. As an intermediate step in the FlexiFusion workflow, a global and unified preFused view is provided on a core selection of DBpedia dumps extracted by the DBpedia extraction framework [7]. The facts are harvested as RDF triples and aggregated using a new serialization format to track statement-level provenance. Unified access to knowledge from different sources is achieved by exploiting previously existing mappings of the DBpedia Ontology as well as merged, normalized entity identifiers (DBpedia Global IDs). The ontology defines a comprehensive class

```
{ "@id": "fc4ebb0fed3c3171578c299b3ce21f411202ff2afc93568a54b4db7a75",
  "subject": { "@id": "https://global.dbpedia.org/id/12HpzV" },
  "predicate": { "@id": "http://dbpedia.org/ontology/floorCount" },
  "objects": [ {
    "object": {
      "@value": "4",
      "@type": "http://www.w3.org/2001/XMLSchema#positiveInteger" },
    "source": [ {
      "@id": "d0:lang=fr.ttl.bz2",
      "iHash": "cbdcb" } ]
    }, {
    "object": {
      "@value": "3",
      "@type": "http://www.w3.org/2001/XMLSchema#positiveInteger" },
    "source": [ {
      "@id": "d0:lang=en.ttl.bz2",
      "iHash": "1e7d4"
      }, {
      "@id": "d0:lang=es.ttl.bz2",
      "iHash": "eb41e" } ] } ],
  "@context": "sources=dbpw_context.jsonld" }
```


Listing 3: Example PreFusion JSON(-LD) Object for sp-pair *Eiffel tower* and `dbo:floorCount`. The French Wikipedia version reports 3 floors (above ground) in contrast to 4 in English and Spanish.

hierarchy and properties, which are modelling common entities described in Wikipedia and Wikidata, and also reuses prominent vocabularies like FOAF and PROV. The dataset offers knowledge about very broad domains (like persons and organizations) but also for very specific domains (e.g. nutrition facts or animal classifications).

The dataset is published under an open CC-BY license on the DBpedia Databus[6] and there is an experimental web service[7] which allows to browse all triples with their provenance for a given entity id (IRI). The DBpedia Association has drafted a roadmap[8] for automating modular releases and also releases of the PreFusion dataset in a sustainable way. Both the browsable interface and the PreFusion dump are preliminary work for the GlobalFactSync project[9] funded by Wikimedia.

PreFusion Format. The PreFusion dataset is stored as JSON-LD using a custom scheme optimized for an efficient representation of entities with overlapping object values and groups multi-value statement-level provenance. Thus, the dataset can be loaded both into JSON document/NoSQL stores, in case

[6] https://databus.dbpedia.org/dbpedia/prefusion.
[7] https://global.dbpedia.org/.
[8] https://blog.dbpedia.org/2019/07/04/dbpedia-growth-hack.
[9] https://meta.wikimedia.org/wiki/Grants:Project/DBpedia/GlobalFactSyncRE.

Table 1. PreFusion dataset factsheet, `dbpedia/prefusion/$artifact/2019.03.01`

Artifact	Distinct objects	Source triples	Subjects	Sp-pairs	Wikipedias	Size (bz2)
Labels	266,633,208	297,345,045	91,146,077	91,146,077	139+wd	7.2G
Instance-types	191,702,603	293,261,187	25,230,546	25,230,546	40+wd	2.1G
Mappingbased-objects	150,955,259	263,677,844	45,063,398	98,388,770	40+wd	6.1G
Mappingbased-literals	94,111,662	100,049,794	36,500,856	71,427,960	40+wd	4.0G
Geo-coordinates	41,313,484	51,178,574	8,517,009	34,099,723	140+wd	1.8G
Specific-mappingbased	2,198,020	2,548,485	1,083,961	1,568,804	40	82M

simple lookups are required – and triple stores – in case joins are required. Each PreFusion document describes a normalised subject-predicate pair ($sp-pair$) to aggregate all different object and literal values from the input sources as shown in Listing 3. The provenance record(s) are referencing the corresponding input file(s) of the object value and iHash value(s) which can be used to determine the original (non-normalized) IRI(s) of the triple(s) by hashing the result of the Global ID Resolution service[10].

PreFusion Dataset Statistics. The dataset is structured in 6 artifacts[11] shown in Table 1 with similar names to the original structure of the DBpedia and Wikidata extraction dumps. The dataset contains a billion triples and more than 321 million subject-predicate pairs. Mappings are only maintained for 40 Wikipedia languages which explains the lower number of entities for this artifact. We picked 5 essential artifacts with overlapping but also complementary data in the input sources and the `labels` artifact. The latter contains more than 266 million `rdfs:labels` for over 91 million entities covering 139 language (variants). The `instance-types` artifact contains `rdf:type` statements using the DBpedia ontology as foundation but also incorporating other ontology classes (e.g. schema.org, Wikidata, FOAF, etc.). The mapping-based artifacts contain factual knowledge about entities extracted from Wikipedia infoboxes using mappings maintained by the community[12]. The `geo-coordinates` artifact adds a spatial dimension by offering coordinates which have been mapped from the infoboxes but also points which are related to an entity since they have been spotted in the Wikipedia article.

4 FlexiFusion Workflow

4.1 PreFuse: Normalize

ID Management. The Web of Data uses a decentralized approach with `owl:sameAs` relations to interlink different RDF Resources which represent the same thing. However, a lot of effort is required to obtain a global view of this

[10] http://dev.dbpedia.org/Global_IRI_Resolution_Service.
[11] version: https://databus.dbpedia.org/dbpedia/prefusion/$artifact/2019.03.01.
[12] http://mappings.dbpedia.org/index.php/Main_Page.

decentralized knowledge in order to perform a holistic data integration. We developed the DBpedia Global ID Management[13] to create a central curation hub. In a nutshell, it materializes the global view of links formed by several linksets and datasets available in the Web of Data, computes SameAs clusters by deriving connected components, and selects a DBpedia Global ID as a representative for every cluster, which can be used as uniform identifier for all of its equivalent identifiers. Moreover, the ID Management assigns stable Global identifiers for IRIs from a configurable list of data authorities. Current snapshots of the ID Management are accessible as dump or in a resolution service. The ID Management works independent of any link discovery tool. Linking results from any approach can be injected if they are represented as owl:sameAs links.

Mappings. While the ID Management normalizes IRI's of subjects and objects, the normalization of literals and predicates needs to be handled by mappings. For the case of the Wikipedia and Wikidata extraction, the DBpedia ontology is used as global schema. Units (e.g. feet vs. meters) between DBpedia chapters are already normalized and standard RDF datatypes as well as DBpedia Ontology datatypes are used to represent literal values in a normalized form. In order to include other datasets, ontology mappings and value transformations need to be provided. While not developed yet, we can imagine a Mapping Management component which works similar to the ID Management, i.e. connected components over `owl:equivalent(Property|Class)`. In the current workflow, we assume that existing mapping tools are used to provide triple files using normalized predicates and literal values.

4.2 PreFuse: Aggregate

The **PreFuse** operation is fed with the individually tailored combination of *normalized* triple files from Databus artifacts. Every input triple from this collection is extended by a provenance record and then streamed into a sorted queue. A preFused entity e is created by grouping all triples first by same subject and then by their predicate value. We can represent the result of this grouping as a set of predicates for e whereas for each predicate a list of pairs of the form (object, provenance) is stored and then embedded as JSON(-LD) object for its subject-predicate sp-pair. The output of the PreFusion operation is the PreFusion dump with indexed preFused sp-pairs – a global and unified view of its input data. Since this view is persisted on the Databus, it can be used as input for a series of different data fusion approaches without expensive re-computation of the global view. While it can be used for analytical queries as is, we think of it as a predigested version of the input data which can be used to derive custom (fused) datasets from it.

[13] http://dev.dbpedia.org/ID_and_Clustering.

4.3 Fuse: Reduce and Resolve

The PreFusion is followed by two consecutive operations: *reduce* and *resolve*. Different combinations of reduce and resolve realisations can be applied on the PreFusion dump to produce various custom-tailored fused datasets.

The **reduce** operation is a function applied on the subject-predicate pairs to reduce or filter the amount of entities and the amount of information for each entity. Reduce acts as a coarse-grained blocking key that removes irrelevant fusion decisions in resolve. Reduction is based on type, source, predicate or entity, e.g. reducing to `dbo:birthplace` for the five largest language sources or just the 1 millon entities from the Catalan source. Reduce is scalable and can even select just a single subject-predicate pair as in the online service.

The purpose of the **resolve** function is to pick a number of objects from the list of each subject-predicate pair in the reduction and resolve conflicts to improve data quality. Let's consider an example person having multiple contradicting `dbo:birthdates`. The realisation of a resolve function could e.g. be defined to select only one object value if the predicate is a functional property. The candidate to pick could be chosen by heuristics like source-preference, majority-voting, random choice, etc.

In the current resolve prototype (based on Apache Spark), we implemented 2 conflict resolution strategies: a configurable preference list which specifies the priority of input sources and a majority voting approach. The former picks the value from the source which has the highest preference while the latter picks the option which has the highest number of occurrences.

These strategies are further augmented by a cardinality component that limits the number of selected values. Whenever the resolve function resolves an sp-pair with a p declared functional or max-cardinality = 1 in the ontology, it will pick only one value based on the decision of the above conflict resolution strategy. As schema declarations are often missing and to account for misbehaving data, a second approach uses *predicate median out degree (PMOD)* as a heuristic, which is calculated based on the PreFusion Dump for every property. $PMOD(p)$ is defined as the median of the list of all cardinality/out degree values for predicate p from entities with at least one object for p. It triggers, if the $PMOD(p)$ equals one.

5 DBpedia Chapter Use Case

DBpedia is organized in so called chapters. A chapter concentrates and coordinates effort and resources to host and maintain one specific language version of DBpedia. This includes forming a local community to maintain mappings, hosting a SPARQL endpoint and many more. The data quality of the dataset of a specific chapter is influenced by 3 major factors: the richness and freshness of the used Wikipedia version, the language-specific infobox mappings, localization configurations and adaptions in the extraction framework. More importantly, chapter data often contains richer and more accurate information about entities of regional importance which are not covered at all in other prominent chapters or Wikidata. Moreover, every chapter offers some complementary data (e.g. labels of entities in the local language). However, complementing each other via collaboration on the data level has the potential to increase coverage and quality and lessen maintenance workload, thus benefiting primarily chapters, but also the main DBpedia as well as Wikidata and Wikipedia. In the scope of the paper we created two scenarios: a *FusedDBpedia* prototype comprising information of several chapters and an enrichment of the Catalan DBpedia.

For *FusedDBpedia* we reduced to 6 sources, i.e. Wikidata, the English (EN), German (DE), French (FR), Dutch (NL) and Swedish (SV) chapter and resolved via: select 1 object value based on language preference (Wikidata, EN, DE, FR, NL, SV) iff $PMOD(p) = 1$; else take all values. For *EnrichedCatalan* we reduced to *sp*-pairs where s is a subject from the Catalan DBpedia data and resolved via: select all values iff $PMOD > 1$ else Catalan value has preference, if exists, otherwise use preference list of FusedDBpedia. For *FusedDBpedia*, as the earlier evaluation scenario, we used an older version of the PreFusion dataset comprised of DBpedia releases from October 2016, whereas for the *EnrichedCatalan* new releases were available and we used the version from March 2019 presented in Sect. 3. We used the ID Management snapshot from February 2019 which is based on Wikidata Interwiki-Links.

6 Evaluation

6.1 FusedDBpedia Dataset Evaluation

Data Coverage. Table 2 gives an overview on data coverage of the *FusedDBpedia* dataset compared to the 6 source datasets. The fused dataset gained more than 120 million triples and almost 300 million subject-predicate pairs. Entity coverage is improved by 47% with respect to the entity-richest source (Wikidata-DBpedia). Further, the fused data offers on average seven distinct properties per entity compared to around five averaged over all sources with an increased vocabulary usage of 62%.

Table 2. Overall coverage and knowledge gain of fusion.

	Wikidata	English	German	French	Dutch	Swedish	Fusion
Triples	436,808,402	124,994,586	42,630,107	39,438,426	36,924,058	37,942,711	558,597,215
Sp-pairs	179,789,022	77,368,237	26,086,747	26,049,036	24,339,480	29,062,921	465,018,956
Entities	45,649,373	17,576,432	5,020,972	5,429,710	3,638,110	5,862,430	66,822,365
Dist. properties	166	1,412	598	1,052	979	415	2,292
Avg. dist. predicates per entity	3.938	4.402	5.196	4.798	6.690	4.957	6.959

Table 3 shows the distribution of four high frequent entity types. Note that Wikidata refers to the Wikidata-DBpedia extraction [5], which uses several effective methods to discover and clean proper type statements from Wikidata. The

Table 3. Typed entity distribution of the four types person, company, location, organization. Each second line counts the entities that exist in at least one other source, but are only typed in this source. Percentage gain is relative to richest source.

Class	Wikidata	English	German	French	Dutch	Swedish	Fusion
dbo:Person	4,197,564	1.757,100	627,353	491,304	188,025	62,814	4,612,463 (+9,88%)
only typed in source	2,246,879	350,137	26,896	6,498	4,506	316	
dbo:Company	188,107	70,208	25,208	14,889	4,446	3,291	209,433 (+11,34%)
only typed in source	80,443	4,038	834	548	89	121	
dbo:Location	3,952,788	839,987	406,979	276,096	449,750	1,480,627	5,293,969 (+33,93%)
only typed in source	2,451,306	27,430	25,804	14,979	101,422	33,425	
dbo:Animal	8,307	228,319	145	0	675,337	437	784,808 (+16,21%)
only typed in source	2,963	2,302	1	0	2,029	5	

fusion achieved an entity-type gain from ≈10–33% for these types. Furthermore, we observed that one or two datasets significantly contribute to the entity gain, but they vary depending upon the class. Nevertheless, we can see that every (besides French chapter for Animals) dataset contributes knowledge, which is especially indicated by the "only typed in source" values. The value shows how many type statements are uniquely provided by one source and can directly enrich at least one other source, e.g. 2,000 *dbo:Animal* types from Dutch to other sources.

In Table 4, the data coverage and knowledge gain for two frequent properties is shown. We observed violations of the cardinality constraint for the functional *dbo:birthDate* property in every source dataset. This issue is solved in the fused data based on the correct decision of the PMOD-based resolution function to pick only one value. With regard to *dbo:scientificName* the Swedish and Dutch datasets provide a high knowledge gain. In accordance with the findings from Tables 3 and 4 this supports the hypothesis that smaller and therefore less developed and/or chapters with fewer infobox mappings can still contribute valuable information for specific domains. It substantiates the basic idea of FlexiFusion to include all information in the PreFusion dataset and postpone the decision which data to filter and which values to select to the specific use case.

Table 4. Property coverage, gains, and distribution for two high frequent properties.

Property	Wikidata	English	German	French	Dutch	Swedish	Fusion
Triples with dbo:birthDate	3,044,381	1,740,614	639,851	623,055	246,102	606	3,096,767
Distinct entities	3,031,415	1,216,106	639,281	449,742	175,587	606	3,096,767
Only in source	1,376,942	25,272	33,540	4,852	1,330	7	+2,16%
Triples with dbo:scientificName	0	0	241,998	0	890,644	1,329,536	1,691,734
Distinct entities	0	0	43,974	0	890,567	1,329,535	1,691,734
Only in source	0	0	7,171	0	351,990	780,555	+27,24%

Data Quality. Evaluating the correctness of a dataset is a challenging task. To the best of our knowledge no gold standard exists which could be used to automatically evaluate the entire dataset. Therefore, we decided to use RDFUnit [6] as a meter for data quality. RDFUnit performs an automatic generation of test instances based on schema knowledge (ontology) and the used vocabulary. Additionally it contains several manually defined plausibility tests. It supports reporting for the number of failed test instances and prevalence values (how often could the test be applied). The evaluation is based on a simple assumption: a lower number of failures in the data implicates better data quality. Since the number of triples and entities significantly varies between the datasets, we defined the *fail rate* as quality metric. It is determined by normalizing the number of failed test instances by the prevalence value for the test case. In total 12,250 generated and 14 manual tests were used, resulting in 1,833 distinct failed test cases. For the sake of brevity, we have summarized the RDF unit reports in Table 5.

Table 5. Overall failed RDFUnit test case comparison between source and result data.

	Wikidata	English	German	French	Dutch	Swedish	Fusion
Applicable tests (prevalence>0)	531	5,002	1,992	3,560	3,332	1,486	8,060
Overall failed tests	325	1,055	418	722	647	432	1,755
Overall success rate	38.79%	78.91%	79.02%	79.72%	80.58%	70.93%	78.23%
Smaller fail rate in source	86	288	163	221	285	115	-
Equal fail rate in source	5	84	8	74	32	8	-
Greater fail rate in source	214	643	229	406	306	297	-
Not failed in fused data	20	40	18	21	24	12	-
Tendency of data quality improvement	yes	yes	yes	yes	yes	yes	-

To summarize the data quality analysis, the test reports are compared by overall failed tests and also by the fail rate for each test. We classify each test result for the sources based on its fail rate in comparison to the fused fail rate into four categories: *smaller* (fail rate smaller in source than in fusion), *equal*, *greater* and *not failed* (fail rate in fusion = 0) compared to the fusion results. *Smaller* is an indicator that data quality decreased throughout the fusion, while all remaining classes are interpreted as improvement.

About 65,8% of the generated test cases returned a prevalence value greater zero on the fused data. This is the highest prevalence number compared to all sources which in turn reflects data coverage improvements. It was not surprising that the number of failed test cases is the highest, too. However, we did not expect that the success rate would be better than average and close to the best value. The rates on top of Table 5 do not take the number of errors per test (i.e. how badly a test failed) into account. In contrast, the bottom-part classification-based comparison pays tribute to the fail rate of every individual test. Based on this, the fused data shows a tendency of quality improvement compared to each individual source dataset.

6.2 EnrichedCatalan Dataset Evaluation

We defined two binary criteria to study which kind of data is available in the PreFusion dataset for the Catalan enrichment scenario. The *Sole Source Criterion* (SSC) is true for a source s given an sp-pair p iff all values from s in p are only originated in s. The *Alternative Choices Available Criterion* (ACC) is true iff at least one different value from a source other than s is available in p. The distribution is shown in Fig. 2 for 20 sources which contribute the highest number of sp-pairs for Catalan. The combination of SSC and ACC allows to distinguish 4 different categories. The sources are unanimous for `no/no`(blue) and agree on these values, interpretable as more accurate or consensual information. New unique information is contributed by s in case of `yes/no`(light green) and if selected makes the resulting dataset more rich, albeit with unclear accuracy, i.e. just more data. Both `no/yes`(yellow) and `yes/yes`(red) have mixed value in need of more elaborate inspection and resolution, whereas `yes/yes`(red) is more polarized and can be interpreted as either complementary beneficial or an erroneous outlier.

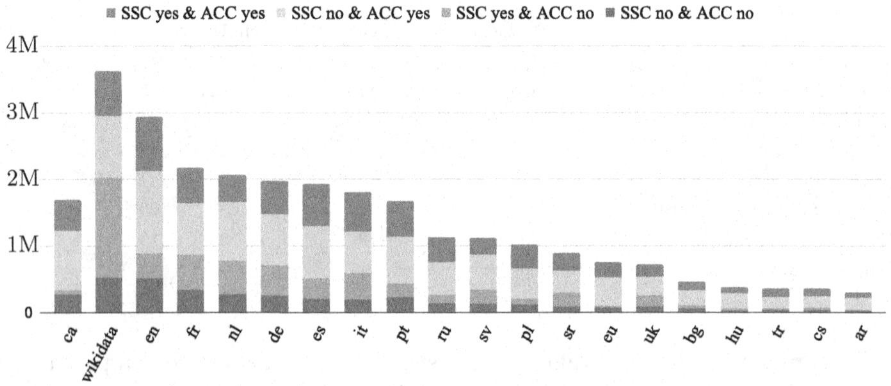

Fig. 2. Information classification in PreFusion reduced for Catalan entities. (Color figure online)

Moreover, we present a few statistics on how the PreFusion dataset was used to boost the Catalan chapter in Table 6. The first part of the table shows the overall boost. In the second part we focus on edges between objects only and show an improvement of both intralinking (indegree) of Catalan entities by factor 11 but also interlinking to resources of external datasets by almost factor 100.

Table 6. Enriched Catalan Statistics

	Original	Enriched	Boost		Original	Enriched	Boost
Overall triples	4,631,162	31,200,104	6.74	Edge to non-Ca IRI	248,685	5,725,446	23.02
Distinct entities	981,795	981,795	1.00	Edge to Global IDs	-	858,551	-
Properties distinct	111	2,275	20.50	Global ID targets	-	254,515	-
Sp-pairs	200,094	4,125,355	20.62	Ext. non-Ca targets	22,464	2,210,614	98.41
Avg pred. outdegree	0.20	4.20	20.62	Ext. non-DBp targets	22,464	1,358,754	60.49
Avg indegree	0.23	2.58	11.20	ext. DBpedia targets	0	597,045	-

7 Related Work

ID Management. An important step in the data integration pipeline is identifying entities that refer to the same real-world thing. In the Semantic Web this is known as *Link Discovery* or *Entity Clustering*, where the latter usually describes the interlinking of entities from multiple sources. A significant amount of research has already been dedicated to this field and an overview can be found in [10]. Dedicated clustering strategies for integrating multiple sources have been developed by Nentwig et al. [9] utlizing existing `owl:sameAs` links to build initial clusters. Saeedi et al. [12] compared different clustering schemes with respect to the suitability and scalability for the entity clustering task. In [11] a scalable approach is presented to integrate new data into existing clusters. To avoid comparing new entities with all members of existing clusters, each cluster creates a cluster representative, that is fused from all the properties of the cluster members. The DBpedia Global ID Management that is used in this approach can be seen as a conservative clustering technique, that makes implicit `owl:sameAs` links that exist in the Web of Data explicit and assigns a global cluster ID.

Fusion Architectures. HumMer [1] is a framework for fusing heterogeneous relational data in three steps: schema mapping (based on (DUMAS) [2]), duplicate detection, and conflict resolution. In addition to the DUMAS algorithm, pairwise similarity measurements are used to detect duplicated entities which are then extended by a uniform *objectID*. The conflict resolution is based on user defined aggregation functions in SQL (e.g. *choose source*, *first or last*, *vote*, *group*, *concatenate*, *most recent value*).

Sieve [8] is a project that aims to fuse Linked Data based on data quality assessments. It is implemented in the JAVA-based Linked Data Integration Framework (LDIF) [13] offering modules for data access, schema mappings, identity resolution, and data output management. Sieve uses scoring functions to rank various content- but also context-based (e.g. release date of the triple) quality indicators to calculate quality metrics. The fusion process relies on a configuration defining one fusion function for each property of a class. A fusion function is able to use the defined quality metrics to select the best value(s).

In comparison to our approach, Sieve - albeit more fine-grained and selective – requires a higher complexity and more configuration effort for every ontology used in the source datasets to tailor the fusion. With respect to the DBpedia ontology this configuration would not be pragmatic due to the large number of different classes and properties.

8 Conclusion

The presented FlexiFusion approach creates the PreFusion dataset as part of future canonical DBpedia releases, which is able to hold all information from the input sources plus additional provenance links on dataset-level and entity-level and enables the comparison of values across datasets.

Based on this PreFusion dump, we have tailored two use-case specific datasets, a fused DBpedia and an enriched version of the Catalan DBpedia based on a datatype-agnostic resolve function, which consists of the computed predicate median out degree and the implementation of the chosen preference or majority value selection.

The first part of the evaluation has shown that the FusedDBpedia has larger coverage, while still containing a higher information density and is overall more consistent regarding RDFUnit test (interpreted as quality improvement). The second part shows that we boost the Catalan source by a factor 7 in size and 10–100 fold in other metrics. The two criteria Sole Source (SSC) and Alternative Choice (ACC) give a high-level insight over all sources about which data is in sync, which data is uniquely gained by new sources and where to expect the most conflicts and quality issues during fusion, thus easing the decision on what to integrate.

9 Discussion and Future Work

As a critical judgement of the DBpedia FlexiFusion approach, we have to admit that while the approach as a workflow is quite advanced and has been evaluated for the Chapter Use Case, the research on best practices of how to configure and evaluate FlexiFusion is still in its early phase. Nevertheless, we decided to publish the dataset resource in its current configuration (140 DBpedia language editions plus Wikidata) as we already see great benefits for further research and applications by the community. Our next steps, will be the automated publication of enriched DBpedia language versions and delivery to Chapters as well as the loading of an enriched English version into the main DBpedia endpoint[14]. For now, we provided one evaluation of Wikidata + 5 large DBpedia language editions, which enabled us to draw the above-described conclusions (cf. Sect. 8), which show the successful application of the Chapter Use Case. However, our evaluation has the following limitations, which create ample opportunities for further research:

- While our work eases the workload to deploy and evaluate fusion approaches (e.g as mentioned [3]), we only implemented three simple methods for the resolve function (median-based, majority, preference), leaving the field wide open for other researchers to experiment with more sophisticated measures.

[14] http://dbpedia.org/sparql.

- We used basic metrics and SHACL shapes in our evaluation. During our development of FlexiFusion, we also saw potential to adjust the fusion algorithm to directly employ the SHACL shapes for selection and resolution, i.e. choosing the option that produces fewest constraint violation. Using SHACL for fusion selection and evaluation at the same time, however, is a weak methodology.
- In our evaluation, we used uniform, rule-based classifiers such as majority or preference, which we expect to be outperformed by deep learning approaches that have shown to produce better fitting results. The main limitation here is the lack of training and test data. The only solace our approach can offer here is that in case a gold standard exists, we can load it alongside the other data into the FlexiFusion format to ease the implementation of further evaluation. Another potential approach is to link, map and load professionally curated data e.g. by libraries to serve as a silver standard.

Moreover we used a simple, but effective method to bootstrap the ID Management to solve the chicken and egg problem: it is hard to automatically derive mappings between two sources without any links for a first clustering, but also hard to compute entity similarities for link discovery without partial mappings. We can imagine to extend the FlexiFusion workflow with feedback loops from the fusion step to the linking and mapping steps. If the fused entity of the cluster has a significant lower similarity to one of its members this is an indicator for an incorrect link. The link in question could be deleted or marked as low confidence link in order to improve the fusion in the next iteration. Similar strategies could be applied to detect mapping errors. Using an automatic quality driven approach linksets and mappings could be refined on every iteration based on the quality reports during the fusion (e.g. high conflict rate for one property).

We also see the potential for a Mapping Management based on analogous concepts to the ID Management. Fed by various (binary) mappings it could form a global mapping view to be able to derive mapping rules to translate classes/properties of a dataset using ontology A into the ones of ontology B, potentially also without the need for a direct mapping from A to B. This could be another step into the direction to reuse mappings, establish synergies and share efforts to cut down engineering costs to create, improve and maintain mappings in a collaborative way.

Acknowledgements. We thank Prof. Rahm for his valuable input during the holistic data integration discussions. We thank Jens Grivolla for providing the Catalan use case and all DBpedia chapters and the community. The work is in preparation to the start of the WMF-funded GlobalFactSync project (https://meta.wikimedia.org/wiki/Grants:Project/DBpedia/GlobalFactSyncRE).

References

1. Bilke, A., Bleiholder, J., Naumann, F., Böhm, C., Draba, K., Weis, M.: Automatic data fusion with hummer. In: Proceedings of the 31st International Conference on Very Large Data Bases, pp. 1251–1254. VLDB Endowment (2005)
2. Bilke, A., Naumann, F.: Schema matching using duplicates. In: Data Engineering, ICDE, pp. 69–80. IEEE (2005)
3. Bleiholder, J., Naumann, F.: Conflict handling strategies in an integrated information system. In: IJCAI Workshop on Information on the Web (IIWeb) (2006)
4. Feeny, K., Davies, J., Welch, J., Hellmann, S., Dirschl, C., Koller, A.: Engineering Agile Big-Data Systems, vol. 1. River Publishers, October 2018
5. Ismayilov, A., Kontokostas, D., Auer, S., Lehmann, J., Hellmann, S.: Wikidata through the eyes of DBpedia. Semant. Web **9**(4), 493–503 (2018)
6. Kontokostas, D., Westphal, P., Auer, S., Hellmann, S., Lehmann, J., Cornelissen, R., Zaveri, A.: Test-driven evaluation of linked data quality. In: WWW, pp. 747–758 (2014). http://svn.aksw.org/papers/2014/WWW_Databugger/public.pdf
7. Lehmann, J., et al.: Dbpedia-a large-scale, multilingual knowledge base extracted from wikipedia. SWJ **6**(2), 167–195 (2015)
8. Mendes, P.N., Mühleisen, H., Bizer, C.: Sieve: linked data quality assessment and fusion. In: EDBT/ICDT, pp. 116–123. ACM, New York (2012). http://doi.acm.org/10.1145/2320765.2320803
9. Nentwig, M., Groß, A., Rahm, E.: Holistic entity clustering for linked data. In: IEEE, ICDMW. IEEE Computer Society (2016)
10. Nentwig, M., Hartung, M., Ngomo, A.C.N., Rahm, E.: A survey of current link discovery frameworks. Semant. Web **8**, 419–436 (2017)
11. Nentwig, M., Rahm, E.: Incremental clustering on linked data. In: 2018 IEEE ICDMW, pp. 531–538 (2018)
12. Saeedi, A., Peukert, E., Rahm, E.: Comparative evaluation of distributed clustering schemes for multi-source entity resolution. In: ADBIS (2017)
13. Schultz, A., Matteini, A., Isele, R., Bizer, C., Becker, C.: LDIF-linked data integration framework. In: COLD, vol. 782, pp. 125–130. CEUR-WS.org (2011)

The Microsoft Academic Knowledge Graph: A Linked Data Source with 8 Billion Triples of Scholarly Data

Michael Färber(✉)

Institute AIFB, Karlsruhe Institute of Technology (KIT), Karlsruhe, Germany
michael.faerber@kit.edu

Abstract. In this paper, we present the *Microsoft Academic Knowledge Graph* (MAKG), a large RDF data set with over eight billion triples with information about scientific publications and related entities, such as authors, institutions, journals, and fields of study. The data set is licensed under the Open Data Commons Attribution License (ODC-By). By providing the data as RDF dump files as well as a data source in the Linked Open Data cloud with resolvable URIs and links to other data sources, we bring a vast amount of scholarly data to the Web of Data. Furthermore, we provide entity embeddings for all 210 million represented publications. We facilitate a number of use case scenarios, particularly in the field of digital libraries, such as (1) entity-centric exploration of papers, researchers, affiliations, etc.; (2) data integration tasks using RDF as a common data model and links to other data sources; and (3) data analysis and knowledge discovery of scholarly data.

Keywords: Scholarly data · Knowledge graph · Digital libraries

1 Introduction

A vast number of scientific publications are published every year. In total, we can count over 81 million scientific journal articles and over 4 million conference papers that have been published across the scientific fields so far.[1] The availability of the metadata about all these publications (and also the publications themselves) enables development of new systems and approaches in the field of digital libraries. For instance, relevant papers can be recommended to users for further reading (i.e., *paper recommendation*) or for citing (i.e., *citation recommendation*). Also, other kinds of entities in the academic field (e.g., venues or reviewers) can be recommended.

However, obtaining large data sets about scientific publications, researchers, institutes, and venues is often nontrivial (see Sect. 2). Only very few data providers provide data according to W3C standards and linked data principles

[1] The values are based on SPARQL queries executed against our data set presented in Sect. 3.

C. Ghidini et al. (Eds.): ISWC 2019, LNCS 11779, pp. 113–129, 2019.
https://doi.org/10.1007/978-3-030-30796-7_8

(i.e., model the data in RDF, enable use of SPARQL as a query language, use resolvable URIs, and link resources to other data sources). The existing RDF data sets are limited in that (1) they are rather small, (2) they cover only a few entity types, (2) they only cover specific scientific domains, (3) they cover data primarily from a single publisher, or (4) they are outdated (see Sect. 2).

In this paper, we present a large RDF data set with over eight billion triples containing information about scientific publications and entities of related entity types, such as authors, institutions, journals, conferences, and fields of study. This data set is based on the *Microsoft Academic Graph* (MAG)[2] [1], which is available with a subscription.[3] Contrarily to what the word "graph" suggests, Microsoft does not provide this data in the form of a (knowledge) graph, although the data is amenable to be modeled in such a structure. Instead, large database dumps (text files, overall about 350 GB in size) are provided every couple of weeks. Although the data seems to be relevant for a variety of disciplines and institutions (e.g., libraries) and various use cases (e.g., evaluating new metrics for the scientific impact of papers and researchers), storing and processing this data set would require overcoming considerable obstacles. In particular, researchers in nontechnical research disciplines, such as digital libraries, digital humanities, and social sciences, might lack the necessary skills and infrastructure to work with the dump files. Going one step further and having the data set available in RDF might appear even more utopian. In addition, IT experts and practitioners might be interested in just using an existing SPARQL endpoint, in getting resource descriptions via URI resolution, or in using pretrained entity embeddings.

By enriching the MAG data and providing this data as an RDF knowledge graph (both in the form of RDF files and as a data source on the Web with HTTP-resolvable URIs) and pretrained entity embeddings of it, potential data consumers of the MAG can get rid of these obstacles. We facilitate a number of scenarios concerning data consumption and data analytics: (1) entity-centric exploration of papers (even time-aware, as we provide updates every few months); (2) easier data integration through the use of RDF and by linking resources to other data sources; and (3) data analysis and knowledge discovery (e.g., measuring the popularity of papers and authors; recommending papers, researchers, and venues; and analyzing the evolution of topics over time).

Overall, we make the following contributions in this paper:

- We transform all data of the MAG, available as text files with a subscription, into RDF, while reusing common vocabularies and serializing the data in the N-Triples format.[4] This leads to a knowledge graph with over 8 billion triples.

[2] See https://www.microsoft.com/en-us/research/project/microsoft-academic-graph/.

[3] Both the initial MAG data set and the MAKG provided by us are licensed under the Open Data Commons Attribution License (ODC-By; https://opendatacommons.org/licenses/by/1-0/index.html; last access: April 9, 2019).

[4] The source code is available online at https://github.com/michaelfaerber/MAG2RDF.

- We link resources to other data sources on the Web, such as DBpedia, Wikidata, OpenCitations [2], and the Global Research Identifier Database (GRID).[5]
- We provide the *Microsoft Academic Knowledge Graph* (MAKG), hosted at http://ma-graph.org,[6] in the following ways:
  1. Every few months, we provide NT-files at http://ma-graph.org, Zenodo,[7] and Amazon S3[8] to the public (1+ TB per version).
  2. We make the URIs of the MAKG resolvable, allowing the MAKG to be part of the Linked Open Data cloud.[9]
  3. We index all MAKG data in a triple store and make it publicly available via a SPARQL endpoint (see http://ma-graph.org/sparql).
- We provide entity embeddings for all 210 million publications represented in the MAKG.

The rest of this paper is structured as follows: First, we discuss related work (see Sect. 2). Then, we describe the process of generating the MAKG RDF data and its characteristics (see Sect. 3), before presenting the MAKG entity embeddings (see Sect. 4). Subsequently, we outline use case scenarios (see Sect. 5), before we conclude the paper (see Sect. 6).

2 Related Work

First of all, the modeling of the computer science bibliography DBLP in RDF [3], Springer's SciGraph,[10] and OpenCitations [2] are noteworthy projects. These projects are restricted to a single discipline (e.g., DBLP), to publications derived from one publisher (e.g., SciGraph), or to the pure modeling of papers and their citation relations without considering other entity types, such as venues and fields of study (e.g., OpenCitations).

Based on initiatives such as WikiCite,[11] Wikidata contains a considerable amount of bibliographic metadata about publications and their authors. Note, however, that the MAKG contains significantly more bibliographic information than Wikidata (e.g., 209,792,741 papers in the MAKG vs. 16,324,110 in Wikidata; see Table 1). The MAKG encompasses 1,380,196,397 references[12] between papers. This is almost eight times the number of references in Wikidata. Note also that in Wikidata, most of the papers are written in English, while in the MAKG, only 65% of the papers are in English.

[5] See https://www.grid.ac/.

[6] The MAKG is also available at the persistent URI https://w3id.org/makg/.

[7] See http://doi.org/10.5281/zenodo.2159723.

[8] See the S3 bucket `arn:aws:s3:::ma-kg`.

[9] See, e.g., `curl -H"Accept:text/n3"` http://ma-graph.org/entity/2826592117 and `curl -H "Accept:text/ttl"` http://ma-graph.org/entity/2826592117.

[10] See https://www.springernature.com/de/researchers/scigraph.

[11] See http://wikicite.org/.

[12] In our paper, the term "citations" refers to in-text citations while "references" refers to links on the document level.

Table 1. Statistical comparison of scholarly RDF data sets (the MAKG as of Nov. 2018, the Open Citations Corpus (OOC) as of Sept. 2017, the OpenCitations Index of Crossref open DOI-to-DOI citations (COCI) as of Nov. 2018, Wikidata as of Dec. 2018 based on http://wikicite.org/, and the AceKG as of 2018).

	MAKG	OOC	COCI	Wikidata	AceKG
# Publications	209,792,741	326,743	46,534,705	21,783,796	61,704,089
# References	1,380,196,397	12,652,601	445,826,118	174,259,894	479,648,000

Among the most similar works to our work is the AceKG [4], a database with 3 billion triples of academic facts about papers, authors, fields of study, venues, and institutes. AceKG data is modeled in RDF. However, contrary to our work, no significant existing vocabularies are reused, and no publicly available triple store or host for resolving URIs via HTTP can be expected. Moreover, all data is gained from the database of the startup Acemap, and no continuous updates of this knowledge graph are provided.

SPedia [5] is a knowledge graph with information about 9 million papers gained from the platform SpringerLink. With over 300 million RDF triples, this data set is a rich source of bibliographic information in the RDF format. Still, it is considerably smaller than the MAKG. Although no SPARQL endpoint or URI-resolving host is available online, data is available upon request. Furthermore, no mappings to other Linked Open Data sources are provided.

Nuzzolese et al. [6] focus on refactoring the Semantic Web Conference ontology. They propose a new ontology [7] and an RDF data set [8] based on it. However, the data set only covers Semantic Web conferences [6]. It is thus only suitable for rather specific usage scenarios compared to our MAKG.

Konstantinou et al. [9] introduce a transformation process for converting an institutional repository into Linked Open Data. This includes the process of creating mappings between domain vocabularies.

3 The Microsoft Academic Knowledge Graph

Based on a push service of Microsoft, we are able to obtain a fresh version of the MAG every few weeks in the form of tab-separated plaintext files. All relevant data to be modeled in RDF takes about 350 GB of disk space. Because the data is in the form of a relational database dump, the data needs to be transformed to obtain the MAKG in the graph structure as outlined in Fig. 1. Furthermore, creating links to other data sources, such as to DBpedia, Wikidata, OpenCitations, and GRID, is another important step to integrating the MAKG into the Linked Open Data cloud.

Overall, we cover 10 entity types in the MAKG, including papers, authors, and affiliations. An overview of the entity types, the object properties, and the data type properties is provided in Fig. 1. Concerning the used knowledge graph properties, our goal was to reuse as much existing vocabulary as possible. Because the data in the MAKG is about publications, researchers, institutions,

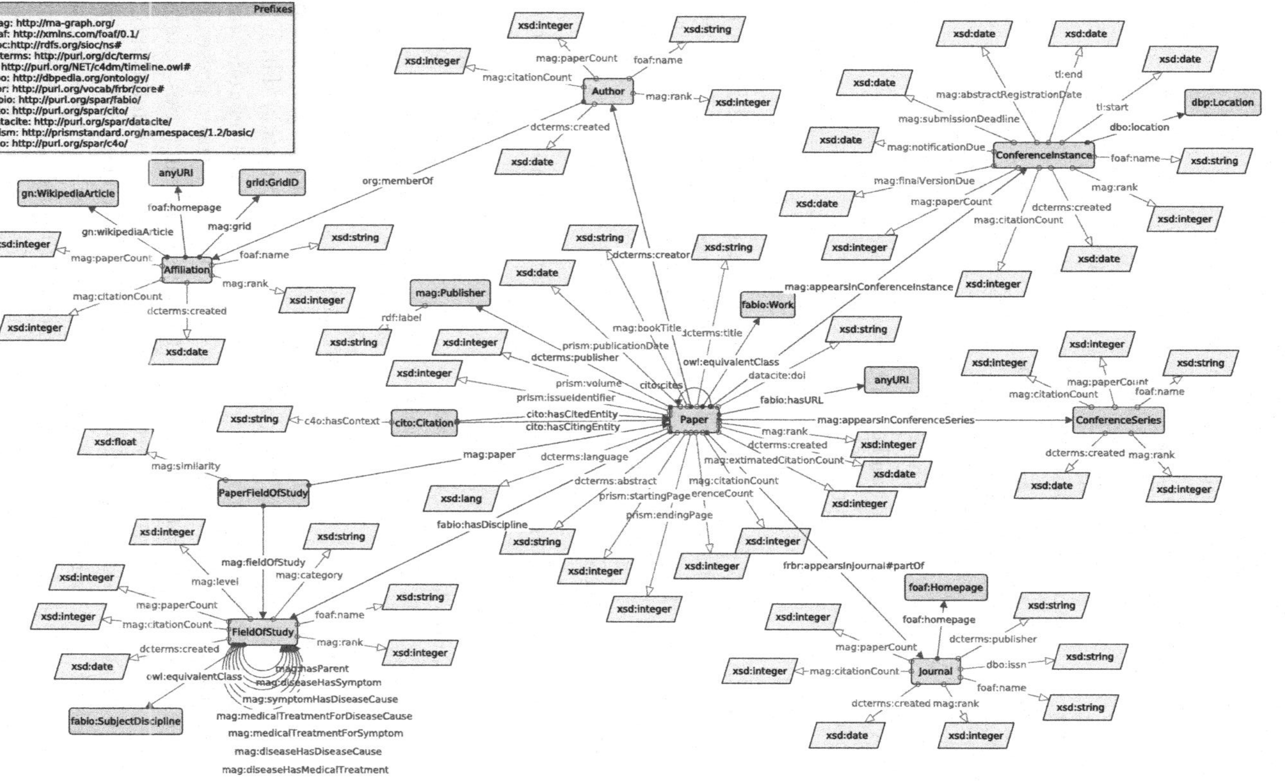

Fig. 1. Schema of the Microsoft Academic Knowledge Graph.

Table 2. Used vocabularies and corresponding prefixes.

Prefix	Associated URI
mag	http://ma-graph.org/
foaf	http://xmlns.com/foaf/0.1/
sioc	http://rdfs.org/sioc/ns
dcterms	http://purl.org/dc/terms/
tl	http://purl.org/NET/c4dm/timeline.owl
dbo	http://dbpedia.org/ontology/
frbr	http://purl.org/vocab/frbr/core
fabio	http://purl.org/spar/fabio/
cito	http://url.org/spar/cito/
datacite	http://purl.org/spar/datacite/
prism	http://prismstandard.org/namespaces/1.2/basic/
c4o	http://purl.org/spar/c4o/

and similar items, we were mainly able to orient ourselves on the existing Semantic Publishing and Referencing (SPAR) ontologies [10], such as FaBiO, CiTo, PRISM, and C4O. In the end, we reused the vocabularies listed in Table 2.

3.1 The Creation Process

The original MAG data dump is presumably designed primarily for data processing (e.g., abstracts are pre-tokenized and not provided as one string). To create an RDF knowledge graph based on these dump files, major changes in the data formatting and the data modeling are necessary. In the following, we outline the most crucial steps of this transformation process.

Papers. The metadata about scientific papers is the core of the MAG data set. The file `Papers.txt` of the initial MAG data dump contains information directly related to papers, such as the paper's title, the publication date, the publisher, the link to the conference at which it appeared, and the reference and citation counts (in total, 21 attributes per paper). We model the represented document type of each publication according to the document types covered in the FaBiO ontology (see Fig. 4). Furthermore, we represent the information about the paper's associated journal, conference series, and conference instance in the form of URIs to provide facts about those entities later on. Note that we skip some information, such as the paper's normalized title (in lower case) and the publication year, from the initial dump for the RDF creation, because this information is already provided in the form of other facts.

Further information about papers represented in the MAKG originate from the following dump files:

- `PaperAbstractInvertedIndex.txt`: For a fraction of the papers stored in the MAG, the abstracts are available. However, the abstracts are only provided as JSON objects in which the key represents the token position and the value the token string (i.e., it is an inverted index). Because our knowledge graph is designed for providing the data in a more natural, non-data mining fashion, we reverted the index and added the papers' abstracts as literal information to the papers in our knowledge graph.
- `PaperLanguages.txt`: Each paper usually has one assigned language in which it is written. We follow the MAG's initial language encoding and use ISO 639-1 for the language code and ISO 3166 for the region code as necessary (e.g., "en" for English and "zh_chs" for simplified Chinese).
- `PaperUrls.txt`: We include the URL at which each paper is available online as an attribute of each paper in our knowledge graph. Note that the URLs provided in the MAG dump often do not link to the papers directly but to the landing pages provided by the papers' publishers.

Authors. Providing information about papers' authors is an obvious next step. Given `PaperAuthorAffiliations.txt`, we can derive which authors wrote which paper (and, in theory, in which author position), and model this information as facts in our knowledge graph, thereby connecting papers with authors. Author entities themselves are enriched by the attribute information provided in `Authors.txt`. Specifically, we store, among other things, the authors' names, their last-known affiliations (linking to affiliation entities using the `memberOf` property), their paper counts, and their citation counts.

Affiliations. In our knowledge graph, we also provide information about the affiliations of the papers' authors based on the `Affiliations.txt` file. Among others, we include the affiliation's name as literal, a link to the institution's GRID identifier, a link to the institution's official homepage, a link to the English Wikipedia article describing this institution, and the number of papers and citations of the institution so far, given the reference and citation information in the MAG. Similar to the other file conversions, we transformed the data into RDF statements using appropriate data types in the case of literals. As far as possible and appropriate, we also transformed string values into URIs in accordance with the linked data principles of having entities represented as URIs. In particular, the links between the affiliations and the Global Research Identifier Database (GRID) identifiers are noteworthy. Because the GRID is part of the Linked Open Data cloud and because GRID URIs of the form http://www.grid.ac/institutes/grid.446382.f are resolvable via HTTP, we transformed the pure GRID identifiers into URIs by adding the URI prefix.

Venues. The MAG data dump provides us with information about conferences (given `ConferenceInstances.txt` and `ConferenceSeries.txt`) and journals (given `Journals.txt`).

- *Conference instances* represent single events at which papers are presented. In addition to the conference name (given in abbreviated form, such as "ECIR 2015"), we represent various attributes of each conference instance in the MAKG, such as the location, the website, temporal information (the start and end date of the conference and deadlines, such as the abstract submission deadline, the paper submission deadline, the notification date, and the final version due date), the number of papers published at this conference, and the number of citations of this conference's papers. For a better integration of the MAKG as a data source into the Linked Open Data cloud, we transform the strings with the conference location (typically city names with their country, such as "Oslo, Norway") into DBpedia URIs. In order to ensure a well performing word-sense-disambiguation, we use the state-of-the-art text annotation tool x-LiSA [11]. Because DBpedia is very rich in terms of cities, we obtained URIs for almost all locations (namely 15,530). Given the conference series identifier, we link each conference instance to the corresponding conference series (e.g., "SIGMOD 2015" to all SIGMOD conferences).
- *Conference series* are represented as URIs with facts about their names (e.g., "SIGMOD"), their paper counts, their citation counts, and their ranks (according to the MAG data set).
- *Journals* are modeled in RDF with facts about the name (e.g., "Scandinavian Journal of Forest Research"), the ISSN number, the publisher, the homepage, the paper count, the citation count, and the rank within the MAKG, among other things.

Taxonomy of Scientific Concepts. Papers in the MAG are assigned to specific research fields and concepts, called the *fields of study* (given in `FieldsOfStudy.txt`). Each field of study is associated with an abstraction level, ranging from 1 to 5. For the MAKG, we model the fields of study as entities of the entity type `FieldOfStudy`. We also store the association of each paper with at least one field of study (given in `PaperFieldsOfStudy.txt`). In this way, the RDF data can be used to categorize papers. We use parent-child relationships between the fields of study (given in `FieldsOfStudyChildren.txt`) to form a taxonomy of scientific concepts within the MAKG. Note, however, that this taxonomy is not a tree. Fields of study can have multiple parents (e.g., "Graph theory" is assigned to computer science and mathematics).

For specific fields of study, the original MAG data contains in addition so-called "main type" information about papers. Main types are primarily given in the field of biology (e.g., "biology.organism_classification"), because this field is well-represented. Relatively few fields of study have such a main type. Nevertheless, we store this additional information if available, along with the general information about the fields of study (e.g., the field of study's name, paper count, citation count, and hierarchy level).

Citations and References. The information about which papers reference which other papers is available as `PaperReferences.txt` and can be directly transformed to RDF triples. Note that if reference information is given, it is ensured that both the referencing paper and the referenced paper are covered by the MAKG. Thus, the issue of various other corpora containing scientific papers (e.g., arXiv CS [12], unarXiv [13], the ACL Anthology Network,[13] and the Scholarly Dataset 2[14]) that reference papers "outside" the data set (i.e., detailed metadata is not available, leading to issues regarding developing approaches for recommending papers, citations, or references) is not a problem.

In addition to the references, which are links on the document level, for a fraction of all papers, the MAG also contains the sentences in which the citations occur, i.e., the so-called *citation contexts* (as a string and with the identifiers of the citing paper and cited paper; see `PaperCitationContexts.txt`). Note that these citation contexts have been automatically extracted by Microsoft. Thus, the citation contexts are to some extent noisy. Because we have to deal with a ternary relationship (which paper cites which other paper in which context) here, we decided to model the citation information separately from the reference information using the class `cito:Citation` from the CiTo ontology as the entity type. Although we do not have the citation context for each reference, it is a valuable information source for tasks such as citation recommendation and citation-based paper summarization.

Summary. Overall, the MAKG, based on the MAG dump of November 2018, contains 8,272,187,245 RDF triples. About 1.2 TB of disk space need to be allocated for the uncompressed RDF files. Indexing the data in Virtuoso requires about 514 GB of disk space and takes about 10 h. Although a lower assignment would be possible, we configured the RDF triple store to use 256 GB of RAM. As a consequence, our SPARQL endpoint can be queried by many users simultaneously and real-world queries can be executed without timeouts.

On the schema level, the MAKG contains 47 properties and 13 entity types (with 8 entity types being in the namespace http://ma-graph.org). As outlined previously, we were able to link 6,706 institute representations to the corresponding DBpedia concepts, 15,530 conference instances to the corresponding Wikipedia articles, and 18,673 affiliations to the corresponding GRID URIs.

3.2 Creating `owl:sameAs` Statements

In addition to the MAKG core data set outlined so far, we linked instances of the MAKG to instances of OpenCitations and Wikidata.[15] The mappings were created by matching the papers' digital object identifiers (DOIs).

[13] See http://clair.eecs.umich.edu/aan/index.php.

[14] See https://www.comp.nus.edu.sg/~sugiyama/Dataset2.html.

[15] The source code is online available at https://github.com/michaelfaerber/makg-linking. The mappings are available as `nt` files with `owl:sameAs` statements on our website.

Table 3. MAKG's entity types and number of instances (as of 2018-11-09).

Entity type	# Instances
Author	253,641,783
Paper	209,792,741
Citation	146,257,535
Field of study	229,716
Journal	48,650
Affiliation	25,431
Conference instance	15,704
Conference series	4,337

1. *OpenCitations.* We were able to create 15,666,233 mappings between papers modeled in the OpenCitations Corpus and papers modeled in the MAKG. This corresponds to 7.5% of all MAKG's papers and 3.5% of OpenCitations' papers. For the mapping, the papers' URIs in OpenCitations were used because they contain the DOI (cf. `http://dx.doi.org/<DOI>`). Of the papers having `owl:sameAs` links to the MAKG, 97.3% are written in English.
2. *Wikidata.* We were able to create 5,472,038 mappings between papers modeled in Wikidata and papers modeled in the MAKG. This corresponds to 2.6% of the MAKG's papers and 33.5% of Wikidata's papers. Note that only those Wikidata's papers were candidates for interlinking that provide DOIs. Of the Wikidata papers having `owl:sameAs` links to the MAKG, 99% are written in English.

3.3 Key Statistics of the Microsoft Academic Knowledge Graph and Example SPARQL Queries

Table 3 shows the distribution of the entities among the different entity types.[16] The MAKG surprisingly contains more authors than papers and more papers than citations. Also, the number of affiliations (25,431) is relatively low given that all research institutions in all fields should be represented. This explains why we have an affiliation in the MAKG only for a fraction of the papers (namely, for 20,928,914 papers). On average, according to this data version, 2.45 authors write a paper together and an author writes 2.94 papers.

Compared to a previous analysis of the MAG [14], the number of instances for all entity types has increased, except for the number of conference instances, which has dropped from 50,202 to 15,704. An obvious reason for this reduction is a data cleaning process. While the number of journals, authors, and papers

[16] Note that only the number of citations is listed and not the number of references, because references are modeled in the MAKG via a relation (`cito:cites`). There are 1,380,196,397 references in the MAKG.

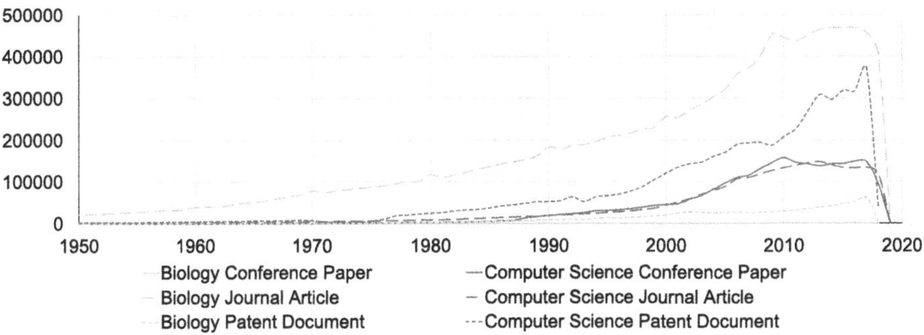

Fig. 2. Number of publications per publication year, per discipline (computer science and biology), and per publication type since 1950.

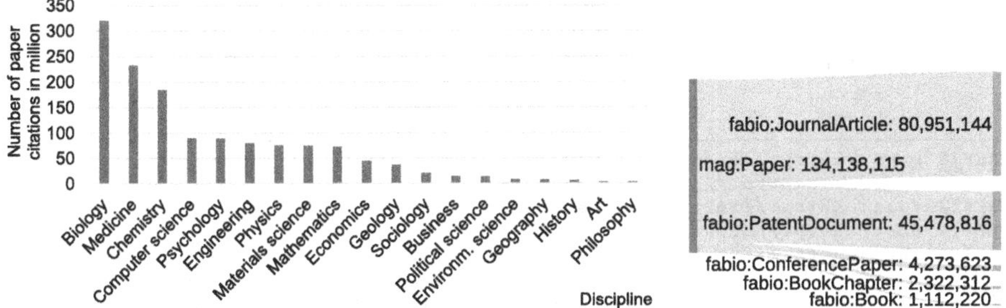

Fig. 3. Number of paper citations per discipline (over all publication types).

Fig. 4. Distribution of `mag:Paper` instances.

have doubled in size compared to the 2016 version [14], the number of conference series and fields of study have increased (almost) four times.

Figure 2 shows how many publications have been published per year in the field of biology and computer science (as example disciplines) according to our data. We can observe that journal articles in biology are published most frequently, followed by patent documents in computer science. Not surprisingly, the number of conference papers in biology is marginal.

Figure 3 displays the number of paper citations per discipline according to the MAKG. As expected, biology, medicine, and chemistry papers are cited the most, while history, art, and philosophy papers are cited the least. Figure 4 shows the frequency of instances per subclass of `mag:Paper`. Note that Figs. 2, 3, and 4 were generated by means of SPARQL queries using our SPARQL endpoint. Listings 1 and 2 show examples of how the MAKG can be queried with SPARQL.

```
PREFIX rdf: <http://www.w3.org/1999/02/22-rdf-syntax-ns#>
PREFIX magp: <http://ma-graph.org/property/>
PREFIX dcterms: <http://purl.org/dc/terms/>
PREFIX foaf: <http://xmlns.com/foaf/0.1/>
PREFIX fabio: <http://purl.org/spar/fabio/>
PREFIX org: <http://www.w3.org/ns/org#>
PREFIX xsd: <http://www.w3.org/2001/XMLSchema#>

SELECT ?affilName ?citCountAffil
WHERE {
?field rdf:type <http://ma-graph.org/class/FieldOfStudy> .
?field foaf:name "Machine␣learning"^^xsd:string .
?paper fabio:hasDiscipline ?field .
?paper dcterms:creator ?author .
?author org:memberOf ?affiliation .
?affiliation foaf:name ?affilName .
?affiliation magp:citationCount ?citCountAffil . }
GROUP BY ?affilName ?citCountAffil
ORDER BY DESC(?citCountAffil)
LIMIT 100
```

List. 1. Querying the top 100 institutions in the area of machine learning according to their overall number of citations.

```
PREFIX magp: <http://ma-graph.org/property/>
PREFIX dcterms: <http://purl.org/dc/terms/>
PREFIX foaf: <http://xmlns.com/foaf/0.1/>
PREFIX dbo: <http://dbpedia.org/ontology/>
PREFIX dbr: <http://dbpedia.org/resource/>

SELECT ?authorName (COUNT(?confInstance) AS ?freq)
WHERE {
 ?paper dcterms:creator ?author .
 ?author foaf:name ?authorName .
 ?paper magp:appearsInConferenceInstance ?confInstance .
 ?confInstance dbo:location dbr:Honolulu . }
GROUP BY ?authorName
ORDER BY DESC(?freq)
LIMIT 100
```

List. 2. Querying the top 100 researchers who have been most frequently to conferences in Honolulu, Hawaii.

3.4 Linked Data Set Descriptions and Ratings

The initial MAG data was provided by Microsoft under the *Open Data Commons license* (ODC-BY),[17] which grants users the right to add values and redistribute the derivatives based on the terms of the Open Data Commons license. All MAKG resources produced by us are published under ODC-BY.

Aside from the MAG RDF documents, we provide the following linked data set descriptions (all available at http://ma-graph.org/):

– *OWL*: We provide our ontology as an OWL file describing the used classes, object properties, and data type properties.

[17] See https://docs.microsoft.com/en-us/academic-services/graph/get-started-setup-provisioning#open-data-license-odc-by.

- *VOAF*: We enrich our ontology with Vocabulary-of-a-Friend (VOAF)[18] descriptors. VOAF is an extension of VoID[19] for linking the ontology to other vocabularies and for introducing the vocabulary to the Linked Open Data community.
- *VoID*: We provide a VoID file to describe our linked data set with an RDF schema vocabulary.

Furthermore, we can categorize the MAKG according to the two kinds of 5-star rating schemes in the Linked Data context:

- *Tim Berners-Lee's 5-star deployment scheme for Open Data:*[20] Our MAKG RDF data set is a 5-star data set according to this scheme, because we provide our data set in RDF (leading to 4 stars) and link (1) entity URIs to DBpedia, Wikidata, OpenCitations, and GRID, and (2) our vocabulary URIs to other vocabularies (leading to 5 stars).
- *Linked Data vocabulary star rating* [15]: This rating is intended to rate the use of vocabulary within Linked (Open) Data. By providing an OWL file, by linking our vocabulary to other vocabularies (see the SPAR ontologies), and by creating a VOAF file, we are able to provide the vocabulary with 4 stars.

Due to our subscription to the Microsoft Academic services, we periodically obtain fresh versions of the MAG dump files. The transformation process described in Sect. 3.1 runs periodically in a semi-automated fashion. Because we are on the mailing list of the Microsoft Academic team, we are notified of any changes to the MAG data and of the data provisioning. In the past, this process has ensured updates of the RDF generation step according to changed data formatting and data provisioning (from Azure Data Lake to Azure Storage).

4 The Microsoft Academic Knowledge Graph Entity Embeddings

Apart from creating and providing the MAKG data set and services (e.g., the SPARQL endpoint), we computed embeddings for the MAKG entities. Entity embeddings have proven to be useful as implicit knowledge representations in a variety of scenarios, as indicated in Sect. 5. Because the MAKG is available in RDF, we applied RDF2Vec [16] to the MAKG using the skip-gram model, a windows size of 5, 128 dimensions, and 10 epochs of training. The training was performed on a machine with 500 GB of RAM and 64 cores. The resulting embedding vectors for all 210 million papers in the MAKG (uncompressed using 310 GB and compressed using 93 GB of storage) are linked on our website.

[18] See http://lov.okfn.org/vocommons/voaf.
[19] See http://www.w3.org/TR/void/.
[20] See http://5stardata.info/.

5 Use Cases of the Microsoft Academic Knowledge Graph

In the past, the MAG has been used in various contexts. This is reflected in the high number of citations of the publication that describes the original data set [1].[21] Also, the MAKG has been recognized and adopted by the community. Considering only Zenodo, the MAKG data has been viewed 1000+ times, downloaded 100+ times, and seen by 75+ Twitter users so far.[22] On average, 50+ unique visitors reach the MAKG website each day.[23] In the following, we outline typical use cases of the original MAG data and of the MAKG.

Using the MAKG as a Linked Data Source in the Linked Open Data Cloud. Because the MAKG is part of the Linked Open Data cloud and contains links to other data sources (see Sect. 3.2), it contributes significantly to the use of linked data in the digital libraries context [17]. Particularly, by using our SPARQL endpoint, users and machines can perform queries that are often associated with fewer burdens than when using the original MAG data dump consisting of raw text files [17] (see also Sect. 3.3). The MAKG can be considered a central data hub for credibility in the linked data context, because it contains metadata about papers (and their authors) that state claims. Claims and crucial concepts mentioned in text documents (e.g., papers' full texts) can be linked to papers and authors in the MAKG to substantiate them [18].

Using the MAKG for Natural Language Processing Tasks. We can mention two examples here:

1. Citation-based tasks, such as citation recommendation, often depend on natural language processing and require implicit or explicit representations of papers, researchers, and institutions. In the case of the MAKG, embeddings for papers and other entities can easily be generated using existing methods for RDF graph embeddings, as demonstrated in Sect. 4.
2. Entity linking describes the task of linking phrases in a text to knowledge graph entities. It has shown several advantages compared to traditional text mining and information retrieval approaches. Consequently, MAKG entities, such as the fields of study and the authors, can be used as the basis for annotating texts (e.g., annotating scientific texts with scientific concepts [19]). Furthermore, using the MAKG, semantic search systems can be developed [20] that are superior to bag-of-words models.

Using the MAKG for Digital Library Tasks. So far, the MAG has been used, among other ways, for citation analysis [21] and for impact analysis of

[21] Sinha et al. [1] have obtained 187 citations as of March 29, 2019, according to Google Scholar.

[22] See https://doi.org/10.5281/zenodo.2159723 (as of April 10, 2019). Note that the data set is also available at http://ma-graph.org/ and on Amazon S3.

[23] See http://ma-graph.org/usage-statistics/ for usage statistics concerning the website and the SPARQL endpoint.

papers and researchers [22,23]. The original MAG data has also been combined with AMiner data to form the Open Citation Graph.[24] In the future, Linked Open Data-based recommender systems that recommend papers or citations can use the MAKG as an underlying database. Furthermore, one can envision that the working style of researchers will considerably change in the next few decades [24,25]. For instance, publications might not be published in PDF format any more, but in either an annotated version of it (with information about the claims, the used methods, the data sets, the evaluation results, and so on) or in the form of a flexible publication form, in which authors can change the content and, in particular, citations, over time. The MAKG can be combined with such new structured data sets easily due to its RDF data format.

Using the MAKG for Benchmarking. Because the MAKG is large in size (over 1 TB in N-Triples format), contains various kinds of information (e.g., papers, authors, institutions, and venues as well as various data types), has uncertainty in the data, and is updated periodically, the MAKG data fulfills the "4 V's" of big data very well. Thus, the MAKG may also be suitable for evaluating methods and benchmarking systems.

6 Conclusions

In this paper, we proposed a large RDF data set with over eight billion triples that covers scholarly data in all scientific disciplines. We described the creation process based on the Microsoft Academic Graph data and the characteristics of our data set. We showed that querying the data set based on SPARQL enables performing complex analyses. By making the SPARQL endpoint publicly available and the URIs resolvable, we enriched the Linked Open Data cloud with a rich data source in the field of digital libraries. We provide RDF dumps, linked data set descriptions, a SPARQL endpoint, and trained entity embeddings online at http://ma-graph.org. In the future, we will use our data set for social analysis studies, because complex information needs can be answered by single SPARQL queries, and for recommending citations in scientific texts.

References

1. Sinha, A., et al.: An overview of Microsoft Academic Service (MAS) and applications. In: Proceedings of the 24th International Conference on World Wide Web Companion, WWW 2015, pp. 243–246 (2015)
2. Peroni, S., Dutton, A., Gray, T., Shotton, D.M.: Setting our bibliographic references free: towards open citation data. J. Doc. **71**(2), 253–277 (2015)
3. Aleman-Meza, B., Hakimpour, F., Arpinar, I.B., Sheth, A.P.: SwetoDblp ontology of computer science publications. J. Web Semant. **5**(3), 151–155 (2007)
4. Wang, R., et al.: AceKG: a large-scale knowledge graph for academic data mining. In: Proceedings of the 27th ACM International Conference on Information and Knowledge Management, CIKM 2018, pp. 1487–1490 (2018)

[24] See https://www.openacademic.ai/oag/.

5. Aslam, M.A., Aljohani, N.R.: SPedia: a central hub for the linked open data of scientific publications. Int. J. Semant. Web Inf. Syst. **13**(1), 128–146 (2017)
6. Nuzzolese, A.G., Gentile, A.L., Presutti, V., Gangemi, A.: Conference linked data: the scholarlydata project. In: Groth, P., et al. (eds.) ISWC 2016. LNCS, vol. 9982, pp. 150–158. Springer, Cham (2016). https://doi.org/10.1007/978-3-319-46547-0_16
7. Nuzzolese, A.G., Gentile, A.L., Presutti, V., Gangemi, A.: Semantic web conference ontology - a refactoring solution. In: Sack, H., Rizzo, G., Steinmetz, N., Mladenić, D., Auer, S., Lange, C. (eds.) ESWC 2016. LNCS, vol. 9989, pp. 84–87. Springer, Cham (2016). https://doi.org/10.1007/978-3-319-47602-5_18
8. Gentile, A.L., Acosta, M., Costabello, L., Nuzzolese, A.G., Presutti, V., Recupero, D.R.: Conference live: accessible and sociable conference semantic data. In: Proceedings of the 24th International Conference on World Wide Web Companion, WWW 2015, pp. 1007–1012 (2015)
9. Konstantinou, N., Spanos, D., Houssos, N., Mitrou, N.: Exposing scholarly information as Linked Open Data: RDFizing DSpace contents. Electron. Libr. **32**(6), 834–851 (2014)
10. Peroni, S., Shotton, D.: The SPAR ontologies. In: Vrandečić, D., et al. (eds.) ISWC 2018. LNCS, vol. 11137, pp. 119–136. Springer, Cham (2018). https://doi.org/10.1007/978-3-030-00668-6_8
11. Zhang, L., Rettinger, A.: X-LiSA: cross-lingual semantic annotation. PVLDB **7**(13), 1693–1696 (2014)
12. Färber, M., Thiemann, A., Jatowt, A.: A high-quality gold standard for citation-based tasks. In: Proceedings of the Eleventh International Conference on Language Resources and Evaluation, LREC 2018, pp. 1885–1889 (2018)
13. Saier, T., Färber, M.: Bibliometric-enhanced arXiv: a data set for paper-based and citation-based tasks. In: Proceedings of the 8th International Workshop on Bibliometric-enhanced Information Retrieval, BIR 2019, pp. 14–26 (2019)
14. Herrmannova, D., Knoth, P.: An analysis of the Microsoft academic graph. D-Lib Mag. **22**(9/10) (2016)
15. Janowicz, K., Hitzler, P., Adams, B., Kolas, D., Vardeman, C.: Five stars of linked data vocabulary use. Semant. Web **5**(3), 173–176 (2014)
16. Ristoski, P., Paulheim, H.: RDF2Vec: RDF graph embeddings for data mining. In: Groth, P., et al. (eds.) ISWC 2016. LNCS, vol. 9981, pp. 498–514. Springer, Cham (2016). https://doi.org/10.1007/978-3-319-46523-4_30
17. Carrasco, M.H., Luján-Mora, S., Maté, A., Trujillo, J.: Current state of linked data in digital libraries. J. Inf. Sci. **42**(2), 117–127 (2016)
18. Fathalla, S., Vahdati, S., Auer, S., Lange, C.: Towards a knowledge graph representing research findings by semantifying survey articles. In: Kamps, J., Tsakonas, G., Manolopoulos, Y., Iliadis, L., Karydis, I. (eds.) TPDL 2017. LNCS, vol. 10450, pp. 315–327. Springer, Cham (2017). https://doi.org/10.1007/978-3-319-67008-9_25
19. Färber, M., Nishioka, C., Jatowt, A.: ScholarSight: visualizing temporal trends of scientific concepts. In: Proceedings of the 19th ACM/IEEE on Joint Conference on Digital Libraries, JCDL 2019, pp. 436–437 (2019)
20. Färber, M., Sampath, A., Jatowt, A.: *PaperHunter*: a system for exploring papers and citation contexts. In: Azzopardi, L., Stein, B., Fuhr, N., Mayr, P., Hauff, C., Hiemstra, D. (eds.) ECIR 2019. LNCS, vol. 11438, pp. 246–250. Springer, Cham (2019). https://doi.org/10.1007/978-3-030-15719-7_33
21. Hug, S.E., Ochsner, M., Brändle, M.P.: Citation analysis with Microsoft academic. Scientometrics **111**(1), 371–378 (2017)

22. Mohapatra, D., Maiti, A., Bhatia, S., Chakraborty, T.: Go wide, go deep: quantifying the impact of scientific papers through influence dispersion trees. In: Proceedings of the 19th ACM/IEEE Joint Conference on Digital Libraries, JCDL 2019, pp. 305–314 (2019)
23. Fire, M., Guestrin, C.: Over-optimization of academic publishing metrics: observing Goodhart's law in action. CoRR abs/1809.07841 (2018)
24. Hoffman, M.R., Ibáñez, L.-D., Fryer, H., Simperl, E.: Smart papers: dynamic publications on the blockchain. In: Gangemi, A., et al. (eds.) ESWC 2018. LNCS, vol. 10843, pp. 304–318. Springer, Cham (2018). https://doi.org/10.1007/978-3-319-93417-4_20
25. Jaradeh, M.Y., Auer, S., Prinz, M., Kovtun, V., Kismihók, G., Stocker, M.: Open research knowledge graph: towards machine actionability in scholarly communication. CoRR abs/1901.10816 (2019)

The RealEstateCore Ontology

Karl Hammar[1(✉)], Erik Oskar Wallin[2], Per Karlberg[2], and David Hälleberg[3]

[1] Department of Computer Science and Informatics, Jönköping University, Jönköping, Sweden
karl.hammar@ju.se

[2] Idun Real Estate Solutions AB, Stockholm, Sweden
{erik,per}@idunrealestate.com

[3] Akademiska Hus AB, Stockholm, Sweden
david.halleberg@akademiskahus.se

Abstract. Recent developments in data analysis and machine learning support novel data-driven operations optimizations in the real estate industry, enabling new services, improved well-being for tenants, and reduced environmental footprints. The real estate industry is, however, fragmented in terms of systems and data formats. This paper introduces RealEstateCore (REC), an OWL 2 ontology which enables data integration for smart buildings. REC is developed by a consortium including some of the largest real estate companies in northern Europe. It is available under the permissive MIT license, is developed and hosted at GitHub, and is seeing adoption among both its creator companies and other product and service companies in the Nordic real estate market. We present and discuss the ontology's development drivers and process, its structure, deployments within several companies, and the organization and plan for maintaining and evolving REC in the future.

Resource Type: Ontology
IRI: https://w3id.org/rec/full/3.0/
DOI: https://doi.org/10.5281/zenodo.2628367

Keywords: Ontology · Smart Buildings · Building automation · IoT · Energy optimization · Space analytics

1 Introduction

Real estate companies today face new data integration demands, driven by both changing customer expectations in an increasingly digital market, and by societal challenges relating to sustainability and resource efficiency. Concretely, customers expect landlords to be able to communicate and interact digitally regarding the leased property and the equipment, furnishings, and systems within it. Increasingly, customers are requesting access to building systems and data streams in order to themselves carry out different types of analytics and optimization. Simultaneously, real estate companies operate on competitive markets and thus need to reduce operating expenditures, e.g., facility management costs,

C. Ghidini et al. (Eds.): ISWC 2019, LNCS 11779, pp. 130–145, 2019.
https://doi.org/10.1007/978-3-030-30796-7_9

inventory management costs, and energy costs. Reducing energy utilization is a particularly important goal since it is both one of the most substantial costs, and one which immediately affects the organisation's environmental footprint.

The use of sensor and actuation systems together with data integration and analytics platforms (augmented by recent advantages in machine learning) show great promise in enabling companies to meet these demands. A building equipped with such systems and platforms is sometimes referred to as a *Smart Building*; future visions of city planners and real estate developers often revolve around *Smart Cities* made up of such Smart Buildings. In this vision, buildings will for instance regulate heating and cooling systems based not only on the number of inhabitants at the present; but also on future numbers anticipated based on historic trends and signals from the surrounding city (e.g., from the public transport system); and on anticipated temperatures and wind speeds from weather forecasts. The building systems will be able to inform the landlord when maintenance is due or when a subsystem breaks; it will inform the tenant when they are using their leased spaces inefficiently, and allow them to integrate physical and digital access control; it will enable external service providers access to parts of the physical and digital building, as required to provide their services.

All of these Smart Building features require that data from and about the building can be exchanged in standardized formats using agreed-upon meaning. Semantic Web ontologies are an obvious technology solution to enable such exchange. There have been several attempts to develop such ontologies for the Smart Buildings domain. However, these ontologies have typically been developed based on the needs of distinct but narrow groups: ontology engineers, building engineers, hardware or systems developers; or for comparatively narrow use cases such as assisted living scenarios. In this paper we present the RealEstateCore[1] (REC) ontology: the first, to our knowledge, ontology developed specifically by real estate companies for their needs. RealEstateCore is developed according to agile Ontology Engineering best practices; it is modular, to avoid ontological over-commitment and enable customization; it is free for anyone to use, licensed under the permissive MIT license; and *it works*, being used in commercial products and being deployed to represent 100.000+ data signals in 12 buildings covering over 220.000 m^2.

The paper is organized as follows: Sect. 2 describes prior work in this field, and positions our contributions against said work; Sect. 3 describes RealEstateCore, how it was developed, and some distinguishing features; Sect. 4 presents the consortium behind RealEstateCore, and some companies and systems that use RealEstateCore today; and finally, Sect. 5 concludes the paper by discussing planned future developments for the ontology and associated API:s and tools.

2 Related Work

The RealEstateCore ontology spans across and draws influences from prior work in three distinct but related domains: digital representations of buildings and

[1] https://realestatecore.io/.

their constituent elements; control and operation of the building and its systems; and emerging IoT ontologies.

Data in the first domain is typically represented using the *Industry Foundation Classes* (IFC) data model, an established and open ISO standard developed in the late 1990s by the buildingSMART industry group. IFC supports interoperability among a variety of BIM and CAD tools [3]. The standard has been evaluated and found to aid in data exchange in building design and planning processes [2,8]. IFC has been translated into and made available as an OWL representation, *ifcOWL*, as described in [4]. IFC/ifcOWL is a very large and comprehensive standard, covering 1300+ classes and 1500+ properties, including a large amount of content that from a sensor data integration perspective is superfluous. The building structure needs that we have revolve primarily around navigating the building parthood hierarchy, which is only a small subset of the functionality provided in ifcOWL. Consequently, the RealEstateCore consortium has elected to not reuse ifcOWL as is, but rather to align REC to IFC concepts as needed, to allow imports of existing IFC models.

There are three major legacy standards in building automation that a Smart Building system would need to be able to interoperate with; *KNX* (commonly used in Europe), *BACnet* (commonly used in the US), and *Modbus* (commonly used in industry factory settings). All three are available in different dialects and versions, some of which can operate over IP networks, others of which use other communications protocols but can be bridged to IP networks using specialized hardware. The Brick Schema [1] is an OWL ontology that models the categories of equipment and measurable properties that might be found in such systems, based on the notion of *tagsets* (roughly comparable to an OWL class and in Brick represented as such) and *points* (roughly comparable to a sensor). The model is elegant, generic, and proven; the RealEstateCore consortium is working on establishing REC-Brick alignments, for increased interoperability between the two models. However, Brick only covers metadata about a building system installation: to this, REC adds features that are required to interact with said installation, e.g., device configuration, observation and actuation messages, etc.

The *Semantic Sensor Networks* (SSN) [10] and *Sensor, Observation, Sample, and Actuator* (SOSA) [12] ontologies are well-established and integrated models covering the sensor/actuator domains. SOSA covers the fundamentals of observations, sensors, features of interests, actuations, processes, results, etc., and SSN extends on this with concepts relating systems of devices, deployments of systems, system capabilities, input and output to procedures, etc. The original SSN model (sans SOSA) was developed for ontology engineers. In developing REC we considered adopting that original SSN model as a foundation, but our intended users (software developers in real estate companies) found the model to be too complex for them to apply; we thus developed a REC-specific device model. However, the more recent editions of SSN cited above, which extend SOSA, have been significantly simplified, and we are looking to integrate REC with SSN/SOSA going forward. SSN/SOSA complements REC with more expressive semantics for processes, sampling, and features; REC complements

SSN/SOSA with domain knowledge relevant to the real estate sector, e.g., the types of devices, communications protocols, and measurements used.

The *Smart Appliances REFerence*(SAREF) ontology [6] is another contender in this space. As the name indicates, SAREF provides a model covering Smart Appliances, e.g., home appliances for residential use. RealEstateCore targets a broader class of systems, typically installed in the building itself, and used for building-wide analytics and optimization.

The reader will note that RealEstateCore does not claim to improve on the modeling state-of-the-art in any of these domains; instead, our value is in providing a comprehensive Semantic Web ontology model that covers and integrates all of them, based on actual real estate owners' needs.

3 The RealEstateCore Ontology

3.1 Initial Use Cases

RealEstateCore was initially developed in support of two specific use cases; energy usage analysis and optimization; and presence analysis.

Energy Usage Analysis and Optimization. Energy costs are a substantial part of the operational costs of running a building. In order to reduce these costs, one needs to reduce both total energy utilization over time and the momentary peak power load. Typically, utilities companies charge by both of these measures, and the tariffs are set by the latter. A reduced operational cost causes an increase in operational net income, which in standard accounting models is immediately linked to the book-keeping value of the property in question; i.e., reducing the energy utilization of a building *immediately* increases its value. Additionally, of course, reducing energy use also reduces environmental impact.

There are numerous examples of how machine learning systems can be used to operate heating/cooling systems in buildings, with energy gains of 40% being reported [7]. However, doing this type of analysis and optimization on a large scale, spanning the full portfolio of a real estate owner, is very difficult. The common case is that real estate owners have several different building automation systems, making the installation of an energy reducing system into a substantial and different project for each real estate and its building automation system[2].

Normalizing data (e.g., using the REC ontology) from different building automation systems makes it possible to apply an energy reducing system on a large scale. In order to reduce energy consumption different data-driven methods can then be applied, such as:

- Finding broken or misaligned equipment (sensors reporting outlier values).

[2] At Vasakronan, a key REC sponsor and user, a September 2018 inventory of the deployed building automation systems identified more than 10 different archetypes (climate control, access control, fire alarm, elevator control, etc.) and up to 30 different vendors and version combinations—it's a mess.

- Adapt the heating/cooling/ventilation/lightning of the rooms in the building after the actual need (i.e., by detecting momentary occupancy and load).
- Anticipating future needs and running systems based accordingly. E.g., *What is the prediction of needed heating/cooling tomorrow/in half a day/in the next hour?* Systems might stop the cooling already by noon on Friday, if historically the office has cleared out by 3 o'clock.
- Utilizing thermo-dynamical effects. Can the characteristics of the building's material be used to store heat or cold? E.g. to use bare concrete walls or ceilings to accumulate energy (when price is lower) to be discharged to achieve the intended climate.

Presence Analysis. As indicated above, a key factor in operating a building system efficiently is the ability to detect to what degree different parts of the building are occupied by people. Important metrics include the number of people present in parts of the building, people flows through the building (i.e., from where and to where are they moving), what activity is being carried out (high- or low-intensity), etc. Presence analysis is also important in optimizing the design of building spaces for better usage, based on people densities, flows, etc. Understanding and adapting to the behavior of tenants and their customers in this manner has started to become vital to the business offering, and for the real estate owner's long term planning of how to manage their portfolio.

Presence can be detected or deduced not only from dedicated infrared sensors or cameras, but also from other types of more commonly deployed sensors (air quality sensors, sound sensors, etc.) and even from infrastructure that has traditionally not been used for such purposes (Wifi usage, coffee machine energy use via electricity meters, bathroom water flows using water meters, etc.). This enables presence analytics in a building using an already installed building automation system's sensors, hence reducing the need to install new dedicated presence sensors, saving costs and time.

3.2 Development Process and Priorities

RealEstateCore has been under development since 2016, by a team of academics and real estate owners in collaboration (see Sect. 4). The development process has been shaped by the need to rapidly reach a state where the ontology can be deployed and used by software developers with limited ontology engineering experience, for the purposes discussed above. A minimum viable product perspective has thus been employed, and when we have needed to balance between different quality aspects, clarity and usability have been given priority over expressiveness, reusability, or metaphysical grounding. Implications of this prioritization include our class and property naming strategies (employing cognitively relevant common-sense terms, avoiding premature generalization), the use of single-domain and single-range properties (the semantics of multiple `rdfs:range` or `rdfs:range` declarations can be unclear to this category of users [11, pp. 127–128]) and our choice not to build on established foundational ontologies (which can be difficult for non-expert users to understand and maintain

[11, pp. 177–181]). To streamline communications with this class of users we have found WIDOCO [9] and WebVOWL [14,16] to be very helpful tools.

The minimum viable product approach marries well to the eXtreme Design [5] (XD) ontology engineering method, which we have employed in an adapted format. Our initial attempts at executing a "pure" XD process, based on composing the ontology from small reusable Ontology Design Patterns (ODPs), was unsuccessful; there simply weren't enough ODPs of sufficient quality, relevant to the domain we were modeling, to support our development process. We considered generalizing our own designs and creating a pattern library out of them, but the overhead costs associated with this process were deemed prohibitive. Instead, we chose to reuse known good solutions as built-in components of our ontology implementation, and to adopt other aspects of the XD method:

Requirements management. XD's recommendation to formalize requirements by way of user stories, competency questions (CQ:s), contextual statements, and reasoning requirements, have helped structure and delimit the modeling problems. Some example CQ:s are given in Table 1; the full set is provided as annotations on the individual ontology modules[3].

Modular development. While ODPs haven't been used, the domain we cover has been split apart into larger modules, enabling flexibility in ontology composition, or the development of custom modules, by a deploying organization.

Pair programming. We have had a minimum of two developers jointly work on the modules under development. These developers have been selected such that they represent both the ontology engineering disciplines and the domain disciplines covered by the modeling challenge at hand.

Release early, release often. Every iteration has been passed to the software developer teams for testing and deployment; on several occasions those developers have pushed back and required changes to simplify system development. We have applied semantic versioning principles such that removal or renaming of ontology content (i.e., breaking changes) have resulted in the ontology and its modules being assigned new major version numbers [13,15]; as a consequence of this the ontology is, at the time of writing, already at version number 3.0, even though all initial use-cases have not yet been fully implemented in the ontology (see Sect. 5).

In accordance with the XD method, the requirements that were prioritized by the customers were developed first. Consequently, several features relating to the presence analysis use case remain in our backlog at the time of writing.

We align REC to existing semantic resources whenever feasible, using established alignment predicates from OWL, RDFS and SKOS[4]. For non-semantic resources we create namespaces and mint IRIs based on identifier values from

---

[3] We have used the `cpannotationschema:coversRequirements` annotation property for this purpose; while it was originally designed to cover CQ requirements on ODPs, we have found no more suitable vocabulary for expressing CQ:s over ontologies.

[4] `owl:equivalentClass`, `owl:equivalentProperty`, `rdfs:seeAlso`, `owl:sameAs`, `skos:related`, etc.

Table 1. RealEstateCore competency questions excerpt.

Question	Module
Which buildings and land make up the real estate Ulvsnaes 1:7?	Core
Where is the real estate Ulvsnaes 1:7 located?	Core
Which parts of Building 1 (e.g., rooms, wings, etc) are covered by electricity meter 3?	Core
What equipment is mounted in server rooms in Building 7?	Building
Are there any labs in Building 7?	Building
Which facade- or roof-mounted sensors are installed in Building 7?	Building
What kind of device is AHU731?	Device
How is device AHU731 connected to the building infrastructure (comms bus, protocol, protocol version, connection parameters, etc)?	Device
What addressable components (sensors, actuators, etc) make up device AHU731?	Device
Which sensor did observation OBS-846294-PID22-88 come from?	Device
What are all the values reported over the past 24 h from temperature sensors in rooms 2, 4, and 7?	Device

those resources (e.g., https://w3id.org/rec/alignments/Haystack/sensor). The alignments are versioned and published in the project GitHub repository[5].

The systems that are used in the real estate business typically have a long lifetime, on the order of 20+ years. It is important that the REC ontology is robust enough to continue working for similar time periods. As we cannot risk link rot over time breaking the ontology, we have chosen to avoid direct dependencies on external resources (i.e., `owl:imports` against non-REC ontologies). Instead, we redefine those external classes and properties that we reuse (GeoSPARQL, Dublin Core, VANN, etc.) within our own ontology modules. While this may be unorthodox it is not formally illegal, and we believe it to be necessary to ensure the longevity and maintainability of the ontology.

3.3 Ontology Description

RealEstateCore is constructed as two base modules (*Metadata* and *Core*), and several domain-specific modules extending this base via `owl:imports` predicates:

- *Metadata:* Includes annotation properties that are used to document the ontology (from Dublin Core[6], CreativeCommons[7], and VANN[8]).
- *Core:* Collects the top-level classes and properties that span over or are reused within multiple REC modules. Imports the Metadata module, and is in turn imported by all other specific child modules.
- *Agents:* Covers basic types of agents (people, organizations, groups), structurally aligned with FOAF[9].

[5] https://github.com/RealEstateCore/rec.
[6] http://purl.org/dc/elements/1.1/.
[7] http://creativecommons.org/ns.
[8] http://purl.org/vocab/vann/.
[9] http://xmlns.com/foaf/spec/.

- *Building:* Covers types of building components and rooms.
- *Device:* Covers different device types (sensors and actuators), device configurations, device actuation, etc.
- *Lease:* Covers lease contracts, types of leasable premises, etc.

The RealEstateCore ontology imports all of these modules. In total, the ontology contains 141 classes, 56 object properties, 63 data properties, and 181 individuals. Visualizing and communicating the design of an ontology of this size is a challenge; Fig. 1 provides a partial schema diagram covering some key classes and Fig. 2 lists the top-level classes and properties. For a detailed specification we refer the reader to the documentation[10]. The ontology and its documentation are both made available via content negotiation at the ontology IRI https://w3id.org/rec/full/3.0/. Additionally, in accordance with community practice, the ontology has been indexed in LOV[11].

Many of the design choices when implementing REC were straight-forward, based on our understanding of the domain and problem space. However, several were not; in particular, the notions of `QuantityKind`, `PlacementContext`, and `DeviceFunctionType`.

QuantityKind. Our use cases deal largely with sensor observations, which are typically grouped by *measurement category* (e.g., *"temperature"*) and quantified into some *measurement units* (e.g., C°). These two attributes are disjoint; there isn't a 1–1 mapping between measurement categories and measurement units, and in fact many measurement units are reused across different measurement categories. Thus both need to be represented and related to sensor observations.

To model this, we considered creating a subclass hierarchy of different types of observations based on the measurement category to which each observation belonged, e.g., `'':obs1 rdf:type :TemperatureObservation; :hasUnit :celsiusUnit . :TemperatureObservation rdfs:subClassOf :Observation''`. However, this design would constrain our ability to use subclass relations for other types of as-yet unforeseen categorization, and it would also require T-box modifications to support new types of observations, which reduces modifiability and reusability. As the name indicates, we instead found a solution in the `QuantityKind` concept from the QUDT ontology[12], which is defined as follows: *"A Quantity Kind is any observable property that can be measured and quantified numerically. Familiar examples include physical properties such as length, mass, time, force, energy, power, electric charge, etc.[...]"*. We standardize on this notion and in the ontology provide a number of named `QuantityKind` instances relevant to our domain, e.g., `Temperature`, `ActiveEnergyL1`, `CurrentL1`, `CO2`, etc. QuantityKind is the "what" that is being measured or acted upon.

10 https://doc.realestatecore.io/3.0/full/.
11 https://lov.linkeddata.es.
12 http://qudt.org/schema/qudt/.

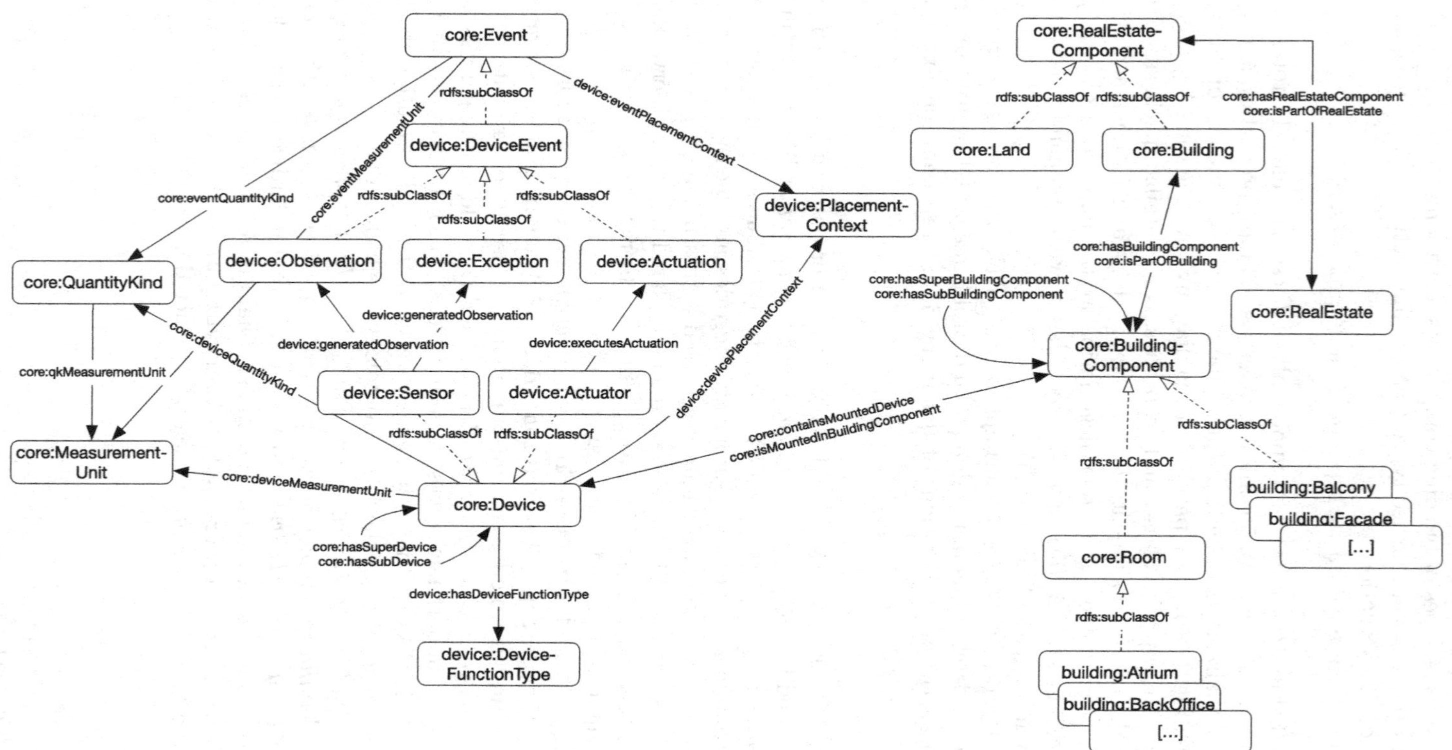

Fig. 1. Partial schema diagram of the RealEstateCore ontology.

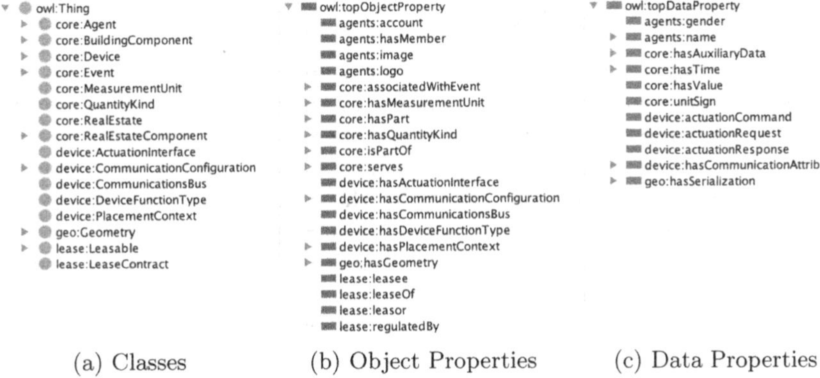

(a) Classes (b) Object Properties (c) Data Properties

Fig. 2. RealEstateCore top-level constructs.

PlacementContext. Sensor and actuator positions in a building are typically described either in terms of spatial placement, or in terms of meronymic placement. Often, both types of placement information are used concurrently. However, in understanding how a sensor or actuator can be analysed or used, a different type of placement information is typically needed, one that describes the *functional placement* of the device (i.e., what part of a process that this sensor or actuator has been placed to measure and/or affect). We attempted to model this type of information using established methods, but found not suitable vocabularies covering our needs. Accordingly, we developed the class `PlacementContext` to cover this need, and provide a set of named instances for it, e.g., `PrimaryCoolingFlow`, `ExhaustAir`, `ElectricalGridIntake`, etc. PlacementContext is the "where" something is being measured or acted upon. The use of QuantityKind and PlacementContext in combination provides a large flexibility to describe different sensing and actuation situations.

DeviceFunctionType. We need to be able to represent a large number of device types in buildings, e.g., boilers, dampers, air diffusers, elevators, escalators, etc. Each of these may contain nested devices: different types of sensors, actuators, control units, etc., which in turn might contain even further nested devices. We thus have diverging granularities for the members of the `Device` subclass hierarchy. Trying to reconcile both type hierarchies under one joint root, we found that this made for a very confusing ontology for our intended users – with concepts in close proximity in the hierarchy that in the real world most considered to be quite far apart. We thus opted to model the top-level device typing via an object property `hasDeviceFunctionType`, a corresponding class `DeviceFunctionType`, and a set of named individuals: `Compressor`, `Fan`, `Pump`, `Elevator`, etc.

4 RealEstateCore Usage

The REC ontology has been under development since mid-2016. In late 2017 the RealEstateCore consortium was founded by the majority developers of the ontology; three real estate companies (Vasakronan, Akademiska Hus, and Willhem), one software development company (Klipsk), and two academic partners (RISE and Jönköping University). Initially the consortium operated under a non-binding membership charter; in early 2019, it initiated processes to become an own legal entity, enabling it to apply for R&D grants from funding agencies.

Participation in the consortium is open to anyone interested in contributing to the project's goals. There is a membership fee for corporations (for 2019 set at 1000 €) but individual personal memberships are free-of-charge. There is no need to be a member in order to use or contribute to the RealEstateCore ontologies – all source is freely available on GitHub and is licensed under MIT license – but in order to hold offices within the project (e.g., on the release engineering team, marketing and communications team, etc.) a membership is required.

In the follow section we describe some known uses of RealEstateCore.

4.1 Vasakronan: The Idun Platform

Vasakronan is the leading property company in Sweden, with a focus on commercial properties in major growth regions. Vasakronan owns and manages 174 properties with a total area of approximately 2.4 million m^2 – the portfolio is valued at ca 13.3 billion €. Vasakronan prioritizes environment and climate work; it is a carbon neutral company and is ISO 14001 certified.

The *Idun* smart building platform started as an internal Vasakronan development project, before being spun out into its own commercial startup. Over the past three years, more than 20 man-years of development have been invested into the platform. Idun converts data inputs from devices in the buildings into REC-compliant messages using edge-based servers, and integrates this data to support consumption by external (telemetry streams, time series analytics, etc.) and internal (state models, actuation facilities, etc.) consumers. The platform is built on the open sourced Microsoft Azure IoT Edge framework, which can run either on physical computers in the buildings or at some cloud service provider. When provisioned as a SaaS offering, Idun by default uses a mixture of dedicated physical servers, a private cloud, and the Azure cloud.

Three interfaces are provided for users/systems to consume data from Idun:

- A streaming API for firehose access to the sensor data streams.
- A REST API that provides telemetry data and enables knowledge graph manipulation and actuation.
- An analysis and reporting interface; provides access to a RealEstateCore-based analysis and reporting environment using Microsoft Power BI.

The telemetry messages that are delivered by edge nodes all adhere to the REC ontology (i.e., `Observation`, `Actuation` and `Exception`), but are comparatively terse. When these messages are passed into the system, they carry an authenticated device identity, provided by the edge node. This device identity is used to look up additional device metadata (position, type, units, etc.) from the building knowledge graph, expressed per REC; this metadata is used to enrich the message for later analysis purposes. For a schematic overview of the Idun platform, see Fig. 3.

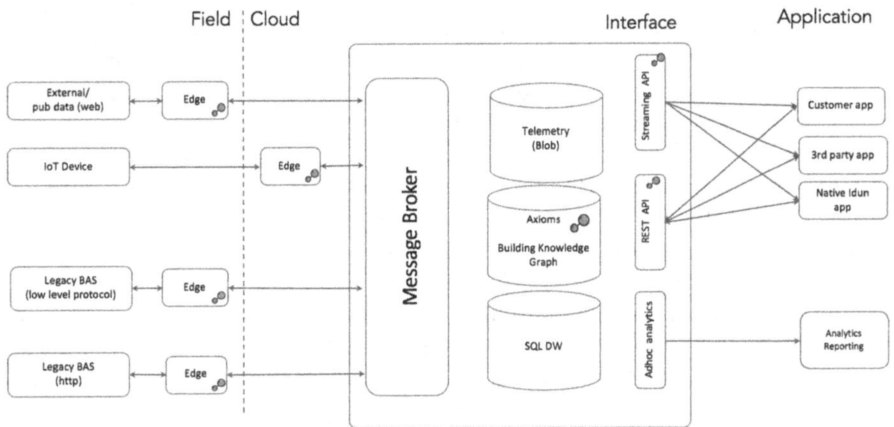

Fig. 3. Idun architecture – the blue overlay icon indicates REC-using components. (Color figure online)

At the time of writing (April 2019) the Idun deployment within Vasakronan covers more than 80.000 physical sensors and actuators (each of which can generate a number of logical signals for consumption by the system) in more than 10 buildings totaling circa 200.000 m^2. In addition another 20.000 signals from external energy reporting systems, weather forecast services, etc. are connected to Idun. Sampling rates depending on the performance capabilities of the underlying systems and necessity – ranging from milliseconds on electricity meters to 15 min for battery powered IoT sensors and once per 24 h for external energy reporting systems. For traditional building automation systems the sample interval is typically once per minute. Idun puts a lot of development effort into streamlining the onboarding of existing buildings; within the next 12 months we expect to have connected 90% of Vasakronan's portfolio.

Presently there are some 15 developed modules that translate building automation system messages into REC semantics for consumption by Idun; and several more are being developed by actors in the REC ecosystem.

4.2 Akademiska Hus

State-owned Akademiska Hus (AH) owns and manages over 3.3 million m^2 of university and college facilities; AH has a market share of 60% of Swedish higher education institutions, with campuses including Sweden's oldest and most prestigious universities (total holdings valued at ca 8.2 billion €). The company has set a goal being carbon neutral in the building operation by 2025. To this end, AH is deploying REC for data integration of and analytics over real-time data streams covering energy performance and indoor climate.

The pilot deployment of REC is at a 13,434 m^2 office building on the KTH campus in Stockholm. The building was constructed in 2005, and it has several modern systems; hi-tech sensors and energy meters throughout, connection to a campus micro-grid for district heating, cooling, and electricity, dedicated systems for energy management, building management, and demand-control ventilation.

The energy management system measures energy utilization for heating-, cooling- and electricity, on subsystem or building level – with 145 sensors exporting data every 60 min. The Building Management System (BMS) measures and controls the installation system within the building. It controls signals, temperatures, pressures, and airflow using both sensors and actuators. Together with the Demand Control Ventilation (DCV) system, energy is distributed within the building to reach a set indoor climate or process. The BMS systems uses a PLC standard and collects 726 signals from sensors and actuators every second minute. The DCV system automatically adjusts supply air-flow to the actual demand (set-points) in the room/spaces that it acclimatizes. It monitors and controls 7,944 signals every minute on a 3,000 m^2 area (typically lecture halls and office- and conference rooms). These signals are all mapped to REC semantics using Azure IoT Edge, before being passed to analytics and infrastructure platforms that can consume REC (e.g., Idun).

In addition to this initial pilot deployment, AH has recently also deployed REC at a second site; the Natural Sciences Building at Umeå University, which generates 3,902 signals (from the DCV system) over 7,800 m^2.

4.3 Willhem

Willhem owns approximately 26,000 rental apartments (1.8 million m^2, worth ca 3.4 billion €) in 13 cities throughout Sweden, with headquarters in Gothenburg. Like Vasakronan and Akademiska Hus, reducing energy utilization is an important driver for Willhem adopting RealEstateCore; the company's long-term goal is to cut their energy use by 50% compared to a 2011 baseline. This will require automating and optimizing energy systems in the buildings, which necessitates data integration. Willhem are at an early stage in their RealEstateCore deployment; they are presently prototyping solutions for how to translate data from an existing sensor infrastructure to REC notation, and how to subsequently consume and analyze that REC-coded data. A candidate technology component in this future workflow is the IoT platform ThingsBoard[13].

[13] https://thingsboard.io/.

4.4 The Building Knowledge Project

The 460'000 € research project *Building Knowledge*, running 2019–2020, develops and evaluates methods for integrating semantic and machine learning technologies, for applications in the real estate sector. The project is closely aligned with the RealEstateCore initiative (five of the six REC founder organisations participate in the project), and it uses the ontology as a test-bed for tooling development, as well as contributes to REC API development.

4.5 Additional Usages

At present more than 10 different partners and suppliers are developing REC-based services or integrations; a subset are presented below.

- *Schneider Electric EcoStruxure integration:* Schneider Electric is a world leader in power management products. They have developed a REC connector for the product EcoStruxure Building Operation[14].
- *Sweco Elements:* Sweco is a leading European architecture and engineering consultancy. The product Sweco Elements is a 3D modeling engine for CAD/BIM planning work that supports REC data consumption for visualization. The internal data sources that drives the Elements product can also expose BIM data in a REC format for ecosystem participants to consume.
- *Flowity:* Flowity is a subsidiary of ÅF, an engineering and design company within the fields of energy, industry and infrastructure, with business and clients all over the world. Their AI-based camera platform analyses the flow of patronage and their behavior, an essential task in real estate based business intelligence. Flowity uses REC to model locations.
- *Metry:* Metry collects and structures consumption data from utility providers, smart meters and offline meters. The company focuses on collection, quality and structure, and manages data points for over a third of Sweden's largest real estate companies, such as Vasakronan, Catena, Rikshem and Kungsleden. Metry has started to implement REC in their data structure and APIs.

5 Future Work

RealEstateCore provides classes and properties that support modeling of devices, their configurations, capabilities, and the values that they report or messages that they receive; modeling of buildings, including components, room types, and locations; and modeling of (rudimentary) contractual situations relating to these buildings. These features enable data integration that supports other systems that provide dashboards and time-series analytics on building, floor, room, or tenant level, which in turn supports the energy optimization use cases discussed

[14] https://web.archive.org/web/20190405122638/https://github.com/BuildingsLabs/EboIoTEdgeConnector.

in Sect. 3. However, we do not yet have classes or properties that cover higher-level concepts (e.g., present energy utilization state, energy-using hardware or processes, target values, prognoses, etc.). A key step in the near future is to increase the expressivity of the ontology to support such higher-level semantics.

As mentioned in Sect. 3.2, the same situation is true for the presence detection and analysis use-case; while we have the semantics in place to support analysis in other systems, we do not yet have first-order representations of detected people, flows, etc. in the RealEstateCore ontology itself. Without such features only device-facing API:s fully utilize the data integration potential afforded by ontology use; when these features are developed (likely using SSN/SOSA as discussed in Sect. 2), higher-order data integration tasks between compliant analytics platforms will be made possible. This is a highly prioritized strategic development for the consortium, as it will enable increased competition among analytics systems suppliers, and prevent vendor lock-in.

We have also identified a number of domains and use cases for which REC modules will need to be adapted or entirely new modules be constructed:

- *Leases and rentals:* The Lease module is rudimentary and needs work to support integration with established facilities and rental management systems.
- *Access control:* Supporting integrated authentication and authorization across both physical (buildings, rooms) and digital (IT systems) assets.
- *Inventory management:* Modeling non-Internet-connected equipment fitted in buildings, including configuration, operations, vendors, protocols, manuals, etc. This could cover everything from PA systems to swing sets.

Finally, while the use of REC as a shared vocabulary has enabled significant data integration gains already, the RealEstateCore consortium has come to realize that standardizing the API:s by which REC-compliant data is exchanged, is an equally important aspect. The Idun platform provides building graph[15] and streaming data[16] API:s for REC 2.3 that have become de-facto standards for REC deployment. These API:s, while fully functional, were not designed to accommodate typical semantic data characteristics, e.g., using IRI identifiers, or using data schemas (ontologies) that can differ from implementer to implementer depending on which modules are loaded. A highly prioritized development over the coming quarters (Q2-Q3 2019) is the development of a standard REC API; we are tentatively looking at GraphQL as potential foundation for that API.

References

1. Balaji, B., et al.: Brick: towards a unified metadata schema for buildings. In: Proceedings of the 3rd ACM International Conference on Systems for Energy-Efficient Built Environments, pp. 41–50. ACM (2016)

[15] https://w3id.org/rec/api/2.3/graph/.
[16] https://w3id.org/rec/api/2.3/streaming/.

2. Bazjanac, V., Crawley, D.: Industry foundation classes and interoperable commercial software in support of design of energy-efficient buildings. In: Proceedings of Building Simulation 1999, vol. 2, pp. 661–667 (1999)
3. Bazjanac, V., Crawley, D.B.: The implementation of industry foundation classes in simulation tools for the building industry. Technical report, Lawrence Berkeley National Laboratory (1997)
4. Beetz, J., Van Leeuwen, J., De Vries, B.: Ifcowl: a case of transforming express schemas into ontologies. Ai Edam **23**(1), 89–101 (2009)
5. Blomqvist, E., Hammar, K., Presutti, V.: Engineering ontologies with patterns - the eXtreme design methodology. In: Hitzler, P., Gangemi, A., Janowicz, K., Krisnadhi, A., Presutti, V. (eds.) Ontology Engineering with Ontology Design Patterns: Foundations and Applications, pp. 23–50. IOS Press, Amsterdam (2016)
6. Daniele, L., den Hartog, F., Roes, J.: Created in close interaction with the industry: the Smart Appliances REFerence (SAREF) ontology. In: Cuel, R., Young, R. (eds.) FOMI 2015. LNBIP, vol. 225, pp. 100–112. Springer, Cham (2015). https://doi.org/10.1007/978-3-319-21545-7_9
7. Evans, R., Gao, J.: DeepMind AI reduces energy used for cooling Google data centers by 40%, July 2016. https://web.archive.org/web/20190322212318/blog.google/outreach-initiatives/environment/deepmind-ai-reduces-energy-used-for/. Accessed 26 Mar 2019
8. Froese, T., et al.: Industry foundation classes for project management-a trial implementation. Electron. J. Inf. Technol. Constr. **4**, 17–36 (1999)
9. Garijo, D.: WIDOCO: a wizard for documenting ontologies. In: d'Amato, C., et al. (eds.) ISWC 2017. LNCS, vol. 10588, pp. 94–102. Springer, Cham (2017). https://doi.org/10.1007/978-3-319-68204-4_9
10. Haller, A., et al.: The modular SSN ontology: a joint W3C and OGC standard specifying the semantics of sensors, observations, sampling, and actuation. Semantic Web **10**(1), 9–32 (2019)
11. Hammar, K.: Content Ontology Design Patterns: Qualities, Methods, and Tools, vol. 1879. Linköping University Electronic Press, Oslo (2017)
12. Janowicz, K., Haller, A., Cox, S.J., Le Phuoc, D., Lefrançois, M.: SOSA: a lightweight ontology for sensors, observations, samples, and actuators. J. Web Semantics **56**, 1–10 (2019)
13. Klein, M.C., Fensel, D.: Ontology versioning on the semantic web. In: SWWS, pp. 75–91 (2001)
14. Lohmann, S., Negru, S., Haag, F., Ertl, T.: Visualizing ontologies with VOWL. Semantic Web **7**(4), 399–419 (2016)
15. Preston-Werner, T.: Semantic versioning 2.0.0. https://web.archive.org/web/20190321081743/semver.org/spec/v2.0.0.html. Accessed 26 Mar 2019
16. Wiens, V., Lohmann, S., Auer, S.: WebVOWL editor: device-independent visual ontology modeling. In: Proceedings of the ISWC 2018 Posters & Demonstrations, Industry and Blue Sky Ideas Tracks. CEUR Workshop Proceedings, vol. 2180. CEUR-WS.org (2018)

FoodKG: A Semantics-Driven Knowledge Graph for Food Recommendation

Steven Haussmann[1], Oshani Seneviratne[1(✉)], Yu Chen[1], Yarden Ne'eman[1], James Codella[2], Ching-Hua Chen[2], Deborah L. McGuinness[1], and Mohammed J. Zaki[1(✉)]

[1] Rensselaer Polytechnic Institute, Troy, NY, USA
{hausss,senevo,cheny39,neemay}@rpi.edu, {dlm,zaki}@cs.rpi.edu
[2] IBM Research, Yorktown Heights, USA
{jvcodell,chinghua}@us.ibm.com

Abstract. The proliferation of recipes and other food information on the Web presents an opportunity for discovering and organizing diet-related knowledge into a knowledge graph. Currently, there are several ontologies related to food, but they are specialized in specific domains, e.g., from an agricultural, production, or specific health condition point-of-view. There is a lack of a unified knowledge graph that is oriented towards consumers who want to eat healthily, and who need an integrated food suggestion service that encompasses food and recipes that they encounter on a day-to-day basis, along with the provenance of the information they receive. Our resource contribution is a software toolkit that can be used to create a unified food knowledge graph that links the various silos related to food while preserving the provenance information. We describe the construction process of our knowledge graph, the plan for its maintenance, and how this knowledge graph has been utilized in several applications. These applications include a SPARQL-based service that lets a user determine what recipe to make based on ingredients at hand while taking constraints such as allergies into account, as well as a cognitive agent that can perform natural language question answering on the knowledge graph.

Resource Website: https://foodkg.github.io

1 Introduction

Chronic diseases such as cardiovascular disease, high blood pressure, type 2 diabetes, some cancers, and poor bone health are linked to poor dietary habits [8]. Although much progress has been made in the development and implementation of evidence-based nutrition recommendations in the past few decades [17], that knowledge has not translated into day-to-day dietary practices. One of the barriers to putting recommended dietary guidelines into practice is that the personalization of the guidelines (e.g., with respect to cultural and lifestyle differences) is largely left to individuals. Much more than just watching one's caloric, fat, salt, and sugar intake, guidelines also advise individuals to eat a

C. Ghidini et al. (Eds.): ISWC 2019, LNCS 11779, pp. 146–162, 2019.
https://doi.org/10.1007/978-3-030-30796-7_10

variety of nutrient-dense foods. Thus, the number of nutritional parameters that need to be considered can become overwhelming.

A natural solution to this problem is to provide an intelligent and automated method for recommending foods. Trattner et al. [23] provide a comprehensive review of the state-of-the-art in food recommender systems. They highlight a recent but growing focus on not only recommending likable foods but going further and ensuring that they are healthful foods as well. The authors note that, despite its importance, food recommendation, in comparison to other domains, is relatively under-researched. Among the several works they reviewed, only [11] involved the use of semantics, motivating the need for methodologies for constructing a food-focused knowledge graph.

Knowledge graphs (KGs) have an important role in organizing the information we encounter on a day-to-day basis and making it more broadly available to both humans and machines. KGs have been used for a variety of tasks, including relationship prediction, searching for similar items, and question answering [6]. While machine learning algorithms can effectively answer questions, they are notorious for producing answers that are hard to explain, especially automatically. Knowledge graphs make it possible to produce automatic explanations of how answers were derived. Interoperability is another important aspect of knowledge graphs, as they enable understanding and reuse. However, the elusiveness of standards and best practices in this area poses a substantial challenge for knowledge engineers who want to maximize KG discovery and reuse, as dictated by the FAIR (Findable, Accessible, Interoperable, Reusable) principles [24].

In this paper, we discuss our methodology for extracting and maintaining publicly available data about food, and for constructing a knowledge graph that can be consumed by both humans and machines, thus providing useful food recommendations that can in turn promote healthier lifestyles. It is important to note that ours is the first extensive FoodKG resource spanning recipes, ingredients, and nutrients that covers over a million recipes and 67 million triples (see https://foodkg.github.io). The novelty and main contribution of our resource is its scope and inclusiveness, not only considering the different datasets it integrates, but the linking with health concepts and the offering of a question-answering service as an application.

1.1 Use Case

Our use case is designed to assist people in personalizing their dietary goals by providing them with information to improve the alignment between their eating behaviors and general nutritional recommendations. For example, consider the American Diabetes Association's (ADA; [1]) recommendation that "Carbohydrate intake from whole grains, vegetables, fruits, legumes, and dairy products, with an emphasis on foods higher in fiber and lower in glycemic load, should be advised over other sources, especially those containing sugars". Unfortunately, translating this into healthful yet palatable food choices can be a daunting task for many individuals, which is partly due to the fact that knowledge is scattered across multiple sources. Thus, our goal is to assist people in exploring how different modifications to their meals can affect their alignment with guidelines by providing a robust system that can be used to construct a Food Knowledge Graph (FoodKG).

Some of the competency questions (i.e., the questions that help capture the scope, content, and the form of evaluation of the knowledge that is modeled) include questions such as: "What are the ingredients and the total calorie count of a piece of a chocolate cake according to USDA[1] nutritional data?". The answer may include butter, eggs, sugar, flour, milk, and cocoa powder for the ingredients, and a calorie count of 424. For a diabetic who is trying to abide by the ADA guidelines, a question like, "How can I increase the fiber content of this cake?" may be a natural follow-up question to ask. Similarly, a person suffering from lactose intolerance may ask "What can I substitute for milk in chocolate cake?". Answering questions like this is not possible from sources such as DBpedia[2] alone, because the information from those sources is not complete. For example, the *dbo:ingredients*[3] for the resource *dbr:Chocolate_cake*[4] contains only *dbr:Cocoa_powder* and *dbr:Chocolate.* FoodKG contains additional information from online recipe sites, along with the corresponding nutrient information from USDA, that has more relevant information than what is available on DBpedia. Therefore, to answer this question, we can use the semantic structure of our knowledge graph to suggest that whole wheat flour be used instead of white flour, or that soy or almond milk be used instead of cow's milk, or that margarine be used instead of butter.

To address questions like those posed above, we present a methodology that can be used to extract publicly available data on food and construct a semantically meaningful knowledge graph that can power applications to help consumers understand their foods and discover substitutions.

2 Related Work

Ontologies representing food are a well-studied topic. The Food Ontology is a universal "farm to fork" food vocabulary [9] that covers the provenance of food contained within the ontology. However, FoodOn lacks nutrition information and recipes, which is our focus. The Personalized Information Platform for Health and Life Services (PIPS) is a large-scale European Union project dedicated to the development of new ways to deliver healthcare [5]. It describes a food ontology that incorporates nutritional information such that it can be applied to help manage different health conditions like diabetes. A similar ontology is described in [7] for use by hypertensive individuals. The Healthy Life Style (HeLiS) Ontology includes a subportion focused on food, including concepts such as 'BasicFood'

[1] USDA refers to US Department of Agriculture. https://www.usda.gov.

[2] DBpedia [2] has structured content from the information created in the Wikipedia.

[3] The *dbo* prefix refers to http://dbpedia.org/ontology and *dbo:ingredient* dereferences to http://dbpedia.org/ontology/ingredient.

[4] The *dbr* prefix refers to http://dbpedia.org/resource and *dbr:Chocolate_cake* dereferences to http://dbpedia.org/resource/Chocolate_cake.

and 'Recipe' [10]. It aligns well with our own goal, although it has a somewhat reduced scope. The Food Product Ontology [16] is designed for business purposes. It includes concepts such as price and brand, which is more suitable for food suppliers than end users. The Cooking Ontology [3] comprises four main classes–actions, foods, recipes, and utensils–with supplementary class units, measures, and equivalencies, and the ontology is integrated into a dialogue system to answer the questions. However, they currently do not support a version in English, and have not mapped to comparable classes in other ontologies, which is essential for reuse. Similarly, the BBC Food Ontology (https://www.bbc.co.uk/ontologies/fo/1.1) only constructs the important concepts and needs to cooperate with other existing ontologies to work better. The SmartProducts Network of Ontologies (http://projects.kmi.open.ac.uk/smartproducts/ontology.html) also contains a food ontology, however our USDA nutrients ontology has more than twice as many food items as in their food_nutrients.owl ontology.

The FOod in Open Data (FOOD) [20] project implements existing ontology designs for foods that are designated as "protected" in the European Union, and then extracts data contained in the Italian agricultural policy documents to produce Linked Open Data (LOD) for public use. However, they focus on characteristics important for policy evaluation and enforcement, rather than for health. Other systems include an information retrieval system that incorporates knowledge from domains of food, health, and nutrition, to recommend food health information based on the users' conditions and preferences is described in [14], and the food search through knowledge graphs [26] focuses on the user's ratings and opinions on tapas/pintxos (small bites/dishes). Finally, the FOODS-Diabetes ontology [22] is meant for medical providers to plan patient meals in terms of caloric intakes, etc., and does not include any recipes or ingredients.

The "internet of food" review [4], and the LOV4iot project [13] (http://lov4iot.appspot.com/?p=lov4iot-food) list a number of other food related ontologies. Different food ontologies focus on different aspects of food, such as chemical compositions, supermarket locations, food sources/packaging, and so on. Our focus is on recommendation in the context of personalized health, i.e., suggesting similar or alternative foods and recipes that are more healthy.

3 Data Acquisition

The resource contribution introduced in this paper aims to bridge the gaps between silos of data. However, gathering and integrating data from many sources leads to several challenges with consistency, accuracy, and completeness:

- *Invalid data* - some textual data contains characters that are illegal in an RDF based knowledge graph, requiring escaping. Escaping itself can pose problems for entity recognition and resolution; it must be applied consistently at all stages of the process.
- *Incomplete data* - recipes may lack quantities for ingredients, or provide non-standard units of measure (e.g. *"to taste"*, *"as needed"*, *"a few shakes"*). Nutrient data might be incomplete, with only some nutrients tabulated.

- *Ambiguous entities* - many ingredients are difficult to tie to a specific food item. This has several root causes, such as local spellings and spelling errors; local names and synonyms; and use of different languages. This can lead to a large number of equivalent names, for example, *corn masa, masa harina, corn flour.*
- *Extraneous information* - ingredients are occasionally listed with complicated units (e.g. *1/3 of a 375 g can of beans*) or unnecessary information (e.g. *black beans from the store*).

Our FoodKG relies on three main sources of data: the recipes themselves, the nutritional content of ingredients, and a food ontology to organize the ingredients. We discuss these sources below.

Recipes. Online recipe sites allow users to browse and share recipes. Some display content from specific commercial sources; others permit users to upload their own recipes. Each website has specific conventions for how data is presented. In some cases, this includes an effort to provide *machine-readable data.*

There also exist large collections of recipe data produced for research and commercial purposes. An example of the former is the Recipe1M dataset[5], provided by the authors of *Im2Recipe* [18], and consists of over 1 million recipes collected from various internet recipe sharing sites.

Nutrients. We chose to use USDA's *National Nutrient Database for Standard Reference* (https://catalog.data.gov/dataset/food-and-nutrient-database-for-dietary-studies-fndds), which contains approximately 8,000 records for a variety of types of food and their nutrients. The majority of the foods are generic, rather than coming from a specific brand. Whilst by no means exhaustive, the dataset provides a large variety of foods with extensive nutritional information.

Food Ontologies. Lists of recipes and nutritional tables provide bulk information about millions and thousands of entities, respectively, but suffer from a lack of meaning - these components form a strong *knowledge graph*, but lack an *ontology*. To resolve this, we incorporate relevant portions of the FoodOn ontology [9]. FoodOn provides an extensive taxonomy for foods, organizing them by source organism, region of origin, and so forth. This provides much-needed connections between related concepts. For example, gala apples are siblings of red apples, but are further removed from apple pie. However, it was not designed as a nutritional reference, and thus FoodOn lacks detailed information about the nutritional content of items. It also does not directly relate to real-world recipes.

Since FoodOn is a very large taxonomy, we opted to use only a small subset of it. To accomplish this, we leveraged Ontofox, a tool that extracts terms and axioms from ontologies [25]. Using the tool, we extracted all children of the ***food***

[5] The Recipe1M dataset is available for download after signing up at: http://im2recipe.csail.mit.edu/dataset.

product by organism node, thus capturing a wide variety of food items in a useful hierarchical form (providing a breakdown by *category of organism*, *group of organism*, and finally a specific *organism of origin*).

4 Knowledge Graph Construction

A knowledge graph includes resources with attributes and entities, relationships between such resources, and annotations to express metadata about the resources. Our complete food knowledge graph contains several key components:

(i) Recipes and their ingredients, (ii) Nutritional data for individual food items, (iii) Additional knowledge about foods, and (iv) Linkages between the above concepts.

Recipes. Each recipe describes the ingredients needed to produce a dish. Each recipe receives a unique identifier, which is accompanied by its name, any provided tags, and a set of ingredients. Each ingredient points to its name, unit, and quantity. An example of the resulting structure is provided in Fig. 1.

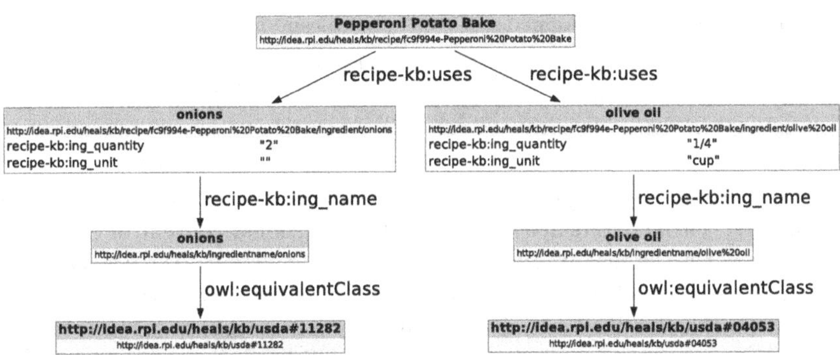

Fig. 1. An example of an imported recipe, pruned to show only two ingredients. The ingredients have been linked to USDA records.

Individual ingredient records usually appear in the form of *(quantity, unit, name)*, such as *2 cups flour* or *1 1/2 lb cabbage, chopped*. Due to the lack of context, parsing these phrases with natural language processors is difficult, and naive parsing methods fail due to minor quirks. To effectively parse such records, we utilize the following steps: (1) Parenthesized statements, such as *(freshly picked)* or *(or chicken)*, are stripped. These provide additional cues to the reader, but are not strictly necessarily to understand components that make up the recipe. Similarly, any text following the first comma is dropped, as it generally describes additional qualities for the ingredient. Whilst these do have meaning, it is less significant than that of the name itself. (2) Numerical values, such as *1/2* or *2.5*, are removed from the start of the string and saved as the *quantity*. The numerical value for an ingredient is, in almost all cases, found before the unit and name of the ingredient. (3) A list of units is compared against the first word in the string; if one matches, it is removed and stored as the *unit*. As when finding the quantity, this almost always succeeds; it is highly uncommon for the unit to be found anywhere but immediately after the quantity. (4) The remaining text is tokenized with the *Natural Language Toolkit* (NLTK; https://www.nltk.org). Adjectives that are not descriptive of color are eliminated. For example, names such as *green bell peppers* and *red onion* are preserved, whilst descriptors like *fresh* are eliminated. Verbs and adverbs are also eliminated, simplifying terms like *diced onion* and *minced garlic*. Text following a conjunction is removed. Finally, NLTK's *WordNetLemmatizer* is used to eliminate plurals. The resulting text is then saved as the *name*. Examples of inputs and results are provided in Table 1. High-quality name recognition significantly improves the quality of later results.

Table 1. Examples of processed ingredient data

Input	Quantity	Unit	Name
1 cup milk	1	Cup	Milk
1 tablespoon parsley, chopped	1	Tablespoon	Parsley
6 tablespoons red currant jelly	6	Tablespoons	Red currant jelly
1 cup butter, softened	1	Cup	Butter

Nutrients. From recipes, we can produce a network of foods and their ingredients. However, without information about the nutritional content of each ingredient, we cannot make meaningful health-related suggestions. We use the USDA public nutrition dataset for this information. The data from USDA exists in a tabular form, describing several dozen nutritional statistics, such as calories, macro-nutrients (protein, carbohydrates, fats), and micro-nutrients (vitamins and minerals). Nutrients are provided per 100 grams of the food item. Two non-mass measurements of the food are also provided, along with the number of grams found in each measure. We make use of the Semantic Data Dictionary approach [21], which produces RDF triples from non-triple data sources. This turns our tabular data into something that can be integrated into our knowledge graph. Some examples of the data converted to the concepts in the knowledge graph can be seen in Table 2.

Table 2. Example USDA data with a few food items and 5/57 nutrients.

Id	Description	Water	Energy	Protein	Lipid	Carbohydrate
1001	Butter, with salt	15.87	717	0.85	81.11	0.06
1009	Cheese, cheddar	37.1	406	24.04	33.82	1.33

Given this data, we can define the shape of the resulting knowledge graph via semantic relationships, as can be seen in Table 3: **Column** represents the column in the raw data, **Attribute/Entity** represents what *rdf:type* this food item is, **Unit** refers to the unit of measurement for that nutrient from community accepted terminologies such as DBpedia and the Units Ontology, and **Label** gives a textual description for the data item that can be used in text mining and auto-completion tasks in applications that use the FoodKG.

Notice the interlinking to other ontologies in then **Attribute/Entity** and the **Unit** columns. The various prefixes[6] in the annotations in Table 3 points to the following ontologies:

- *chebi*: Chemical Entities of Biological Interest Ontology (https://www.ebi.ac.uk/chebi)
- *dbr*: DBpedia Resource Ontology (http://dbpedia.org/resource/)
- *sio*: Semanticscience Integrated Ontology (http://semanticscience.org/resource/)
- *envo*: Environment Ontology (http://purl.obolibrary.org/obo/envo.owl)
- *foodon*: Food Ontology (http://purl.obolibrary.org/obo/foodon.owl)
- *schema*: Schema.org mappings (https://schema.org/)
- *uo*: Units Ontology (http://purl.obolibrary.org/obo/uo.owl)

Table 3. Semantic structural representation of a subset of the USDA data.

Column	Attribute/entity	Unit	Label
Id	chebi:33290, dbr:Food		USDA Id for the food
Description	sio:StatusDescriptor		Short description
Water	envo:00002006, chebi:15377, dbr:Water	dbr:Gram, uo:0000021	Water (g)
Energy	foodon:03510045	dbr:Kcal	Energy (Kcal)
Protein	dbr:Protein	dbr:Gram, uo:0000021	Protein (g)
Lipid	dbr:Lipid	dbr:Gram, uo:0000021	Lipid Total (g)
Carbohydrate	dbr:Carbohydrate, schema:carbohydrateContent	dbr:Gram, uo:0000021	Carbohydrate (g)
Sugar	dbr:Sugar	dbr:Gram, uo:0000021	Sugar Total (g)
Calcium	dbr:Calcium	uo:0000022	Calcium (mg)

After these annotations are completed, the semantic data dictionary conversion script is run to convert the tabular USDA data into quads, which are triples grouped into named graphs. A small piece of the high level structure of the resulting graph can be seen in Fig. 2.

[6] Prefixes can be dereferenced via http://prefix.cc or http://www.ontobee.org.

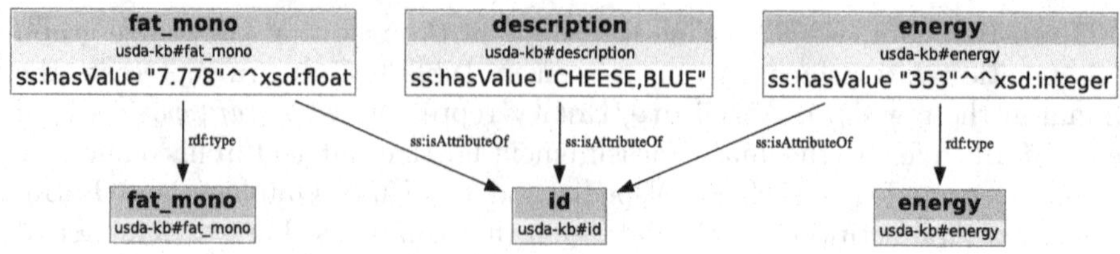

Fig. 2. An example of USDA data, pruned to display a handful of features. The prefixes *usda-kb* and *ss* refers to custom namespaces within our knowledge graph.

5 Knowledge Graph Augmentation

With all of the data imported, we are left with a collection of isolated islands of data. Thus, the second phase of the construction of our knowledge graph is *linkage*. We leverage various entity resolution techniques to automatically connect various concepts together. To ensure that the dataset can be practically expanded and updated, we make use of well-studied linked data techniques to establish provenance of these derived relationships.

Entity Resolution. Names are the most obvious shared attributes between our various domains of recipes, nutrients, and foods. For this reason, we have largely focused on entity resolution techniques that work on strings, such as *cosine similarity*, which performs quite well for matching by name, particularly after normalization. We also examined using word embeddings, such as word2vec [19] and FastText [15], with a pretrained model to resolve names. However, results were poor - likely a product of the embedding capturing only the general meaning of a statement.

Entity Selection. We found it beneficial to limit the domain of concepts to match against, both for the sake of performance (matching is linearly expensive with respect to the number of entities) and to maximize accuracy (more spurious entities to match against cause more false positives). The exact manner in which this is done depends on the datasets being compared.

For instance, many categories of food are rarely seen as ingredients - but, critically, have names that are similar to kinds of food that *are* relevant. The USDA's Standard Reference contains a large number of entries about baby food, with names such as 'Babyfood, juice, apple' and 'Babyfood, meat, lamb, strained'. We remove such entries, since they cause problems with linkage of ingredients. For example, the former will match the 'apple juice' ingredient in a recipe, but is it unlikely that the recipe is referring to babyfood. We similarly remove categories such as fast food and sweets - although even this is not entirely straightforward. For example, "brown sugar" is lumped in with jelly beans and candy bars, but it is desirable to retain it in the FoodKG. We also ignore text beyond the third comma, as we found that the distinctions between entities becomes insignificant at that point; doing so also speeds up the linkage process.

Other sources of data are significantly broader; as an example, we experimented with linking into the DBpedia knowledge graph. Unfortunately, many entities in the DBpedia dataset are incompletely or inaccurately typed; non-foods have the Food type, and many edible items lack it. Therefore, we opted to use heuristics to select for potential ingredients. All DBpedia resources marked as `ingredientOf` were included, as was anything with a *carbohydrate* value. This tended to produce a subset of actual food items, and whilst it resulted in the loss of some entities, it also eliminated a large number of erroneous choices.

Provenance and Publication Information. To provide clear provenance for every claim made in our knowledge graph - including both imported knowledge *and* inferred linkages - we have made extensive and consistent use of the RDF Nanopublication specification [12]. Nanopublications represent atomic units of publishable information, attaching information about *where* it came from and *who/what* published it. They express this knowledge via linked data, using four named graphs:

(i) The *assertions* graph contains the claims being made. For a recipe, this includes a title, tags (if any), and ingredients. Ingredients are described by their name, unit, and quantity. (ii) The *provenance* graph contains information about where the assertions were derived from. For a recipe, this could be the URL from which data was retrieved, or any other reference that points back to the original data. (iii) The *publication info* graph explains who created the nanopublication. For example, the linkages we form are collected into a single nanopublication; the publication info remarks that our linker tool generated the linkages. (iv) The *head* graph ties the prior three graphs together, making it possible to find the three components.

6 Application of the Food Knowledge Graph

6.1 Answering Competency Questions in SPARQL

In order to evaluate the knowledge graph, we establish several competency questions that address its possible applications. Our first competency question is "What recipes contain beef?" which would return a list of all recipes in the knowledge graph that are linked to some entity 'beef' in the knowledge graph. This covers the simple case of understanding what ingredients are found in what recipes in the knowledge graph. The second competency question, "What recipes contain beef, carrots, and potatoes?" takes this a step further by asking for recipes that contain multiple ingredients. This type of question mimics the functionality of traditional recipe sharing websites, where users can look for recipes containing certain types of ingredients. Our third competency question is "What recipes contain bananas that do not contain walnuts?" as can be seen in Listing 1.1. This evaluates the ability of our knowledge graph to return recipes that, in addition to containing certain ingredients, do not contain others. This is especially relevant in cases of allergies or dislikes of certain foods. We can further extend this kind of thinking to nutritional information, based on the knowledge graph's health information from the USDA. This brings us to our fourth competency question, "What recipes that have chicken are low in sugar?" as can be seen in Listing 1.2. This and similar kinds of questions address the application of the knowledge graph to assisting with certain health conditions like diabetes or hypertension that place restrictions on nutritional intake. Currently, this question is answered by using glycemic index information which was manually added by hand to certain ingredients. This approach clearly has its limitations, however, since not all ingredients have a glycemic index and ingredient amounts are not considered in this calculation. Our final competency question is "What recipes are vegan?" Since the knowledge graph structures its knowledge of ingredients in a hierarchical way, it can determine whether certain ingredients fall into certain categories like animal products for vegetarian/vegan diets or pork products for religious restrictions, as a more specific example.

Each of these questions can be answered by querying the underlying ontology using SPARQL, since information like the relationships between recipes and ingredients is encoded directly within the ontology. An example query for the third and fourth competency questions are structured as follows.

```
@PREFIX food: <http://purl.org/heals/food/>
@PREFIX ingredient: <http://purl.org/heals/ingredient/>
SELECT DISTINCT ?recipe
WHERE {
    ?recipe food:hasIngredient ingredient:Banana .
    FILTER NOT EXISTS {
        ?recipe food:hasIngredient ingredient:Walnut .}
}
```

Listing 1.1. SPARQL query for retrieving a food for a person with an allergy

```
@PREFIX food: <http://purl.org/heals/food/>
@PREFIX ingredient: <http://purl.org/heals/ingredient/>
SELECT distinct ?recipe
WHERE {
    ?recipe food:hasIngredient ingredient:Chicken .
    FILTER NOT EXISTS{
        ?recipe food:hasIngredient ?ingredient .
        ?ingredient food:hasGlycemicIndex ?GI .
        FILTER (?GI >= 50)}
}
```

Listing 1.2. SPARQL query for retrieving a food with a low glycemic index

6.2 Answering Competency Questions in Natural Language

We demonstrate another potential use of our FoodKG for answering natural language questions over knowledge graphs, aka, knowledge base question answering

(KBQA). Given questions in natural language, our goal here is to automatically find answers from the underlying knowledge graph.

Since there does not exist a Food Q&A dataset related to ingredients, nutrients and recipes, we choose to create a synthetic Q&A dataset based on our FoodKG using a set of manually designed question templates. We create three types of competency questions with increasing levels of complexity using various templates. Table 4 shows the question templates and data statistics of the created dataset. The simple questions, e.g., "How much sugar is in cheese, cream, fat free?", are created based on the USDA data and require only one hop reasoning. The comparison questions, e.g., "Salt, table or syrups, table blends, pancake, which has less energy?", can be regarded as a composition of two simple questions. The third type of questions we create are those with constraints, e.g., "What Laotian dishes can I make with sugar, water, oranges?"; these queries are based on the Recipe1M data and are similar to those in Sect. 6.1. To create the dataset, we first sample several subgraphs from the FoodKG. For each subgraph, we then randomly sample a question template from our predefined template pool and fill the slots with KG entities and relations.

Table 4. Data statistics of the created synthetic Q&A dataset.

Competency questions	Question template examples	Size	Knowledge source
Simple	How much {nutrient} is in {ingredient}?	12,661	USDA
Comparison	{ingredient1} or {ingredient2}, which has less {nutrient}?	5,565	USDA
Constraint	What {tag} dishes can I make with {ingredient_list}?	6,359	Recipe1M

Experiments. Our Q&A system consists of three components which are the *question type classifier*, *topic entity predictor* and *KBQA model*. Given a natural language question, e.g., "how much sugar is in Cheese, Blue?", the *question type classifier* is intended to determine the question type which is 'simple' in this case. Then the *topic entity predictor* is applied to detect the topic entity mentioned in the question which is 'Cheese, Blue' and links it to the FoodKG. Finally, the *KBQA model* is called to retrieve answers from the KG subgraph surrounding the topic entity 'Cheese, Blue'.

In our experiments, we only evaluate the *KBQA model* which is the most crucial component in our Q&A system. We compare a simple Bag-of-Word vectors based method (BOW) and our state-of-the-art neural network-based method (BAMnet) [6]. In both methods, we encode the question and each candidate answer within the KG subgraph surrounding the topic entity into the same embedding space, and then compute the cosine similarity score between them using a dot product. Candidate answers whose similarity scores are above a certain threshold are returned as predicted answers. The major difference between the two methods is that in BOW, the question and candidate answers are encoded independently as the average of the pretrained word embeddings, while in BAMnet, a more sophisticated neural network module is used to encode them jointly by considering the two-way flow of interactions between them. For more details, please refer to [6]. We split the dataset into training (50%), development (20%) and test set (30%).

Table 5. Experimental results (F1-scores) on the synthetic Q&A test set.

Methods	Simple	Comparison	Constraint	Overall
BOW	13.7	49.6	30.0	26.0
BAMnet	**99.8**	**100.0**	**82.6**	**95.5**

Table 5 shows the results of two methods on the synthetic Q&A test set where we assume that gold topic entities and question types are known beforehand. As we can observe, even though the questions are created using predefined templates and there is no lexical gap between the questions and the KG (i.e., we use the exact entity and relation names to fill the question templates), the BOW method does not perform well. However, our BAMnet method perform very well on this dataset. Moreover, among the three types of questions, those with constraints are the most challenging. Future directions include creating more realistic and complex questions with more diverse templates and lexical gap.

7 Resource

Our FoodKG resource website at **`https://foodkg.github.io`** links to all the resources, which include the FoodKG knowledge graph, the automated scripts to construct the KG, the whattomake application, the natural language querying application, and accompanying documentation. Using the FoodKG, we can answer complex questions related to recipes, ingredients, nutrition and food substitutions that can power applications that target healthy lifestyle behaviors. The SPARQL queries and the source code for the two applications illustrated in Sect. 6 are also made available.

Maintenance: The FoodKG is part of the RPI-IBM Health Empowerment through Analytics Learning and Semantics (HEALS) project (https://idea.tw.rpi.edu/projects/heals), and we expect to support this project actively for the next 3–7 years. We anticipate that these public tools will be useful for anyone aiming to build an integrated knowledge graph for food. As observed in Fig. 3, our resulting FoodKG spans over 67 million triples (obtained by adding all of the triples comprising the USDA, Recipe1M and FoodOn KG subsets, and the linkages between them). Various other statistics are also shown in the figure.

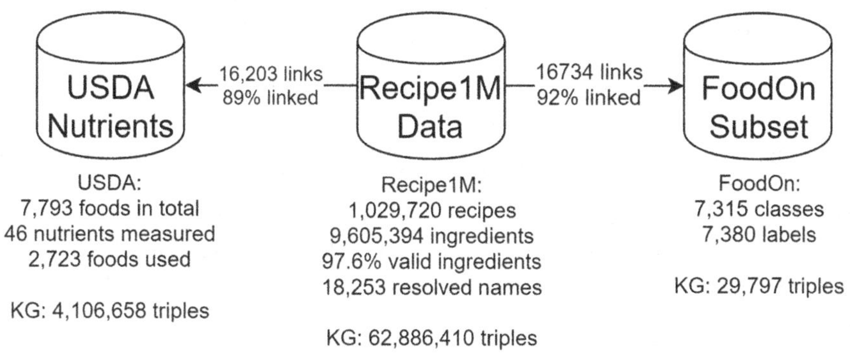

Fig. 3. An overview of the food knowledge graph (FoodKG).

Description: An overview of how to construct the FoodKG with provenance is clearly explained at https://foodkg.github.io/foodkg.html. The FoodKG github repository (https://github.com/foodkg/foodkg.github.io) contains step-by-step instructions to generate the entire FoodKG, resulting in serialized RDF triples. As outlined in Sect. 4, the input data is in various formats (e.g., USDA is in CSV, Recipe1M data is in JSON, and other ontologies in RDF/OWL), which we map to RDF. The output of the KG construction is RDF; more specifically, the output is in the NanoPublications format [12], which includes the corresponding assertion, provenance, and publication information, as outlined in Sect. 5. The output of the scripts include the following serialized RDF files (in .trig format) spanning 67 million triples: (i) usda-links.trig, (ii) foodon-links.trig, (iii) foodkg-core.trig. We do not directly provide the final RDF data, due to the terms of the Recipe1M data. However, our Github code and step-wise instructions can generate the KG exactly as described herein. We believe that generating a KG programmatically for a food knowledge graph has several benefits over supporting a public SPARQL endpoint or a compressed dump of the graph: (1) additional means of enriching the KG programmatically, (2) possibility to tap into various sources of data, (3) clean handling of intellectual property in the ever-changing and complex rights management landscape.

The whattomake app (https://foodkg.github.io/whattomake.html), described in Sect. 6.1, includes comprehensive documentation, sample SPARQL queries, and three food resources: (i) http://purl.org/heals/foodon (a subset of the FoodOn we used in our mappings), (ii) http://purl.org/heals/food, and (iii) http://purl.org/heals/ingredient.

Finally, the KBQA application (https://foodkg.github.io/kbqa.html) includes documentation on how to query the FoodKG using natural language questions. We currently support three types of questions, namely simple, comparison and constraint-based as described in Sect. 6.2.

8 Conclusions and Future Work

It is evident that information on food, while readily available on the Web, requires individuals to combine information from various sources in order to decide what to eat. To address the issue of aggregating all the pertinent information on food in a manner that is consumable by an individual specific to their health and taste preferences, we have created an integrated knowledge graph for food, which can be used to suggest healthier food and restaurant menu item alternatives. We model structured sources in terms of a target ontology, and augment the knowledge graph with other unstructured sources.

More specifically, we extract the relevant data on food from authoritative sources such as the USDA, as well as online recipe sources. We apply a semantics based extract-transform-load procedure to structure the food knowledge using our ontology as well as community accepted terminologies, and link to relevant FoodOn and nutrient resources to support further exploration and augmentation of the FoodKG. The linkages to these resources are done using techniques involving lexical similarity and string matching to find non-perfect matches between sets of data that frequently lack perfect pairings.

Our FoodKG is a valuable resource for the primary task of food recommendation. At the same time, it can also be used as a benchmark dataset to test various entity resolution and semantic linking methods for recipes, ingredients, units, and so on. In the future, we plan to further leverage the food knowledge graph and relationships between ingredients and recipes to develop novel ingredient and recipe embedding models to produce more meaningful representations for food recommendation. Since our ultimate objective is to provide personalized food recommendations to everyday individuals that consider both their health and lifestyle preferences, we see the need for the food knowledge graph to support competency questions that involve more subjective concepts like 'convenient', 'affordable', 'spicy', and 'refreshing'. We also plan to continue to extend our ontology and knowledge sources, as well as explore novel food embeddings that leverage the relationships captured in the food knowledge graph. In conclusion, we have presented a reusable methodology that integrates information on food into a knowledge graph.

Acknowledgements. This work is partially supported by IBM Research AI through the AI Horizons Network.

References

1. American Diabetes Association: 4. lifestyle management: standards of medical care in diabetes—2018. Diab. Care **40**(Suppl. 1), S33–S43 (2017)
2. Auer, S., Bizer, C., Kobilarov, G., Lehmann, J., Cyganiak, R., Ives, Z.: DBpedia: a nucleus for a web of open data. In: Aberer, K., et al. (eds.) ASWC/ISWC -2007. LNCS, vol. 4825, pp. 722–735. Springer, Heidelberg (2007). https://doi.org/10.1007/978-3-540-76298-0_52

3. Batista, F., Pardal, J.P., Mamede, P.V.N., Ribeiro, R.: Ontology construction: cooking domain. Artif. Intell.: Method. Syst. Appl. **41**, 1–30 (2006)
4. Boulos, M., Yassine, A., Shirmohammadi, S., Namahoot, C., Brückner, M.: Towards an "internet of food": food ontologies for the Internet of Things. Future Internet **7**(4), 372–392 (2015)
5. Cantais, J., Dominguez, D., Gigante, V., Laera, L., Tamma, V.: An example of food ontology for diabetes control. In: ISWC workshop on Ontology Patterns for the Semantic Web (2005)
6. Chen, Y., Wu, L., Zaki, M.J.: Bidirectional attentive memory networks for question answering over knowledge bases. In: Annual Conference of the North American Chapter of the Association for Computational Linguistics (2019)
7. Clunis, J.: Designing an ontology for managing the diets of hypertensive individuals. Int. J. Digit. Librar. **20**, 269–284 (2019)
8. DeSalvo, K., Olson, R., Casavale, K.: Dietary guidelines for Americans. JAMA **315**(5), 457–458 (2016)
9. Dooley, D.M., et al.: FoodOn: a harmonized food ontology to increase global food traceability, quality control and data integration. npj Sci. Food **2**(1), 23 (2018)
10. Dragoni, M., Bailoni, T., Maimone, R., Eccher, C.: HeLiS: an ontology for supporting healthy lifestyles. In: Vrandečić, D., et al. (eds.) ISWC 2018. LNCS, vol. 11137, pp. 53–69. Springer, Cham (2018). https://doi.org/10.1007/978-3-030-00668-6_4
11. El-Dosuky, M.A., Rashad, M.Z., Hamza, T.T., EL-Bassiouny, A.H.: Food recommendation using ontology and heuristics. In: Hassanien, A.E., Salem, A.-B.M., Ramadan, R., Kim, T. (eds.) AMLTA 2012. CCIS, vol. 322, pp. 423–429. Springer, Heidelberg (2012). https://doi.org/10.1007/978-3-642-35326-0_42
12. Groth, P., Gibson, A., Velterop, J.: The anatomy of a nanopublication. Inf. Serv. Use **30**, 51–56 (2010)
13. Gyrard, A., Bonnet, C., Boudaoud, K., Serrano, M.: Lov4iot: a second life for ontology-based domain knowledge to build semantic web of things applications. In: 4th IEEE International Conference on Future Internet of Things and Cloud (2016)
14. Helmy, T., Al-Nazer, A., Al-Bukhitan, S., Iqbal, A.: Health, food and user's profile ontologies for personalized information retrieval. Procedia Comput. Sci. **52**, 1071–1076 (2015)
15. Joulin, A., Grave, E., Bojanowski, P., Mikolov, T.: Bag of tricks for efficient text classification. In: 15th Conference of the European Chapter of the Association for Computational Linguistics (2017)
16. Kolchin, M., Zamula, D.: Food product ontology: Initial implementation of a vocabulary for describing food products. In: 14th Conference of Open Innovations Association (2013)
17. Ley, S.H., Hamdy, O., Mohan, V., Hu, F.B.: Prevention and management of type 2 diabetes: dietary components and nutritional strategies. Lancet **383**(9933), 1999–2007 (2014)
18. Marin, J., et al.: Recipe1m: a dataset for learning cross-modal embeddings for cooking recipes and food images. arXiv preprint arXiv:1810.06553 (2018)
19. Mikolov, T., Sutskever, I., Chen, K., Corrado, G.S., Dean, J.: Distributed representations of words and phrases and their compositionality. In: Advances in Neural Information Processing Systems, pp. 3111–3119 (2013)
20. Peroni, S., Lodi, G., Asprino, L., Gangemi, A., Presutti, V.: FOOD: FOod in open data. In: Groth, P., et al. (eds.) ISWC 2016. LNCS, vol. 9982, pp. 168–176. Springer, Cham (2016). https://doi.org/10.1007/978-3-319-46547-0_18

21. Rashid, S.M., Chastain, K., Stingone, J.A., McGuinness, D.L., McCusker, J.P.: The semantic data dictionary approach to data annotation & integration. In: 1st Workshop on Enabling Open Semantic Science (2017)
22. Snae, C., Bruckner, M.: FOODS: a food-oriented ontology-driven system. In: 2nd IEEE International Conference on Digital Ecosystems and Technologies (2008)
23. Trattner, C., Elsweiler, D.: Food recommender systems: important contributions, challenges and future research directions. arXiv preprint arXiv:1711.02760 (2017)
24. Wilkinson, M.D., et al.: The fair guiding principles for scientific data management and stewardship. Scientific Data **3**, 160018 EP - (2016)
25. Xiang, Z., Courtot, M., Brinkman, R.R., Ruttenberg, A., He, Y.: Ontofox: web-based support for ontology reuse. BMC Res. Notes **3**(1), 175 (2010)
26. Zulaika, U., Gutiérrez, A., López-de Ipiña, D.: Enhancing profile and context aware relevant food search through knowledge graphs. In: 12th International Conference on Ubiquitous Computing and Ambient Intelligence (2018)

BTC-2019: The 2019 Billion Triple Challenge Dataset

José-Miguel Herrera[1], Aidan Hogan[1(✉)], and Tobias Käfer[2]

[1] IMFD; DCC, Universidad de Chile, Santiago, Chile
{jherrera,ahogan}@dcc.uchile.cl
[2] Karlsruhe Institute of Technology (KIT), Karlsruhe, Germany
tobias.kaefer@kit.edu

Abstract. Six datasets have been published under the title of Billion Triple Challenge (BTC) since 2008. Each such dataset contains billions of triples extracted from millions of documents crawed from hundreds of domains. While these datasets were originally motivated by the annual ISWC competition from which they take their name, they would become widely used in other contexts, forming a key resource for a variety of research works concerned with managing and/or analysing diverse, real-world RDF data as found natively on the Web. Given that the last BTC dataset was published in 2014, we prepare and publish a new version – BTC-2019 – containing 2.2 billion quads parsed from 2.6 million documents on 394 pay-level-domains. This paper first motivates the BTC datasets with a survey of research works using these datasets. Next we provide details of how the BTC-2019 crawl was configured. We then present and discuss a variety of statistics that aim to gain insights into the content of BTC-2019. We discuss the hosting of the dataset and the ways in which it can be accessed, remixed and used.

Resource DOI: https://doi.org/10.5281/zenodo.2634588
Resource type: Dataset

1 Introduction

The Billion Triple Challenge (BTC) began at ISWC in 2008 [44], where a dataset of approximately one billion RDF triples crawled from millions of documents on the Web was published. As a demonstration of contemporary Semantic Web technologies, contestants were then asked to submit descriptions of systems capable of handling and extracting value from this dataset, be it in terms of data management techniques, analyses, visualisations, or end-user applications. The challenge was motivated by the need for research on consuming RDF data in a Web setting, where the dataset provided not only a large scale, diverse collection of RDF graphs, but also a snapshot of how real-world RDF data were published.

A BTC dataset would be published each year from 2008–2012 for the purposes of organising the eponymous challenge at ISWC [5–7,30,44], with another BTC dataset published in 2014 [3]. These datasets would become used in a wide

C. Ghidini et al. (Eds.): ISWC 2019, LNCS 11779, pp. 163–180, 2019.
https://doi.org/10.1007/978-3-030-30796-7_11

variety of contexts unrelated to challenge submissions, not only for evaluating the performance, scalability and robustness of a variety of systems, but also for analysing Semantic Web adoption in the wild; our survey of how previous BTC datasets have been used (described in more detail in Sect. 2) reveals:

- **Evaluation**: the BTC datasets have been used for evaluating works on a variety of topics relating to querying [25,26,28,35,46,57,62,64,65], graph analytics [11,14,15,33,60], search [8,17,40,47], linking and matching [10,32,49], reasoning [42,52,58], compression [21,59], provenance [1,61], schemas [9,39], visualisation [22,66], high performance computing [24], information extraction [41], ranking [45], services [53], amongst others.
- **Analysis:** The BTC datasets have further been used for works that aim to analyse the adoption of Semantic Web standards on the Web, including analyses of ontologies and vocabularies [23,48,54], links [20,27], temporal information [51], publishing practices [50], amongst others.

We also found that BTC datasets have been used not only for the eponymous challenges [3,5–7,29,30,44], but also for other contests including the TREC Entity Track [2], and the SemSearch Challenge [55].

In summary, the BTC datasets have become a key resource used not only within the Semantic Web community, but also by other communities [11,14,15, 60]. Noting that the last BTC dataset was published in 2014 (five years ago at the time of writing), we thus argue that it is nigh time for the release of another BTC dataset (even if not associated with a challenge of the same name).

In this paper, we thus announce the Billion Triple Challenge 2019 dataset. We first provide a survey of how BTC datasets have been used in research works down through the years as both evaluation and analysis datasets. We then describe other similar collections of RDF data crawled from the Web. We provide details on the crawl used to achieve the BTC-2019 dataset, including parameters, seed list, duration, etc.; we also provide statistics collected during the crawl in terms of response codes, triples crawled per hour, etc. Next we provide detailed statistics of the content of the dataset, analysing various distributions relating to triples, documents, domains, predicates, classes, etc., including a high-level comparison with the BTC-2012 and BTC-2014 predecessors; these results further provide insights as to the current state of adoption of the Semantic Web standards on the Web. We then discuss how the data are published and how they can be accessed. We conclude with a summary and outlook for the future.

2 BTC Dataset Adoption

As previously discussed, we found two main types of usage of BTC datasets: for evaluation of systems, and for analysis of the adoption of Semantic Web technologies in the wild. In order to have a clearer picture of precisely how the BTC datasets have been used in the past for research purposes, we performed a number of searches on Google Scholar for the keywords `btc dataset` and `billion triple challenge` (the latter with a phrase search). Given the large number of results returned, for each search we surveyed the first 50 results, looking for papers that used a BTC dataset for either evaluation or analysis, filtering papers that are later or earlier versions of papers previously found; while this method is incomplete, we already gathered more than enough papers in this sample to get an idea of the past impact of these datasets. We note that Google Scholar uses the number of citations as a ranking measure, such that by considering the first 50 results, we consider the papers with the most impact, but may also bias the sample towards older papers.

In Table 1, we list the research papers found that use a BTC dataset for evaluation purposes; we list a key for the paper, the abbreviation of the venue where it was published, the year it was published, the system, the topic, the year of the BTC dataset used, and the scale of data reported; regarding the latter metric, we consider the figure as reported by the paper itself, where in some cases, samples of a BTC dataset were used, or the BTC dataset was augmented with other sources (the latter cases are marked with '*'). Considering that this is just a sample of papers, we see that BTC datasets have become widely used for evaluation purposes in a diverse range of research topics, in order of popularity: querying (9), graph analytics (5), search (4), linking and matching (3), reasoning (3), compression (2), provenance (2), schemas (2), visualisation (2), high-performance computing (1), information extraction (1), ranking (1), and services (1). While most works consider a Semantic Web setting (dealing with a standard like RDF, RDFS, OWL, SPARQL, etc.), we note that many of the works in the area of graph analytics have no direct connection to the Semantic Web, and rather use the link structure of the dataset to test the performance of network analyses and/or graph algorithms [11,14,15,60]. Furthermore, looking at the venues, we can see that the datasets have been used in works published not only in core Semantic Web venues, but also venues focused on Databases, Information Retrieval, Artificial Intelligence, and so forth. We also remark that some (though not all) works prefer to select a more recent BTC dataset (e.g., from the same year or the year previous).

In Table 2, we instead look at papers that have performed analyses of Semantic Web adoption on the Web based on a BTC dataset. In terms of the types of analysis conducted, most relate to analysis of ontologies/vocabularies (3) or links (2), with temporal meta-data (1) and publishing practices relating to SPARQL endpoint (1) also having been analysed. Though fewer in number, these papers play an important role in terms of Semantic Web research and practice.

Most of the papers discussed were not associated with a challenge (perhaps due to how we conducted our survey). For more information on the challenges using the BTC dataset, we refer to the corresponding descriptions for the TREC [2], SemSearch [55], and Billion Triple Challenges [3,5–7,29,30,44].

We reiterate that this is only a sample of the works that have used these datasets, where a deeper search of papers would likely reveal further research depending on the BTC dataset. Likewise, we have only considered published works, and not other applications that may have benefited from or otherwise

Table 1. Use of BTC datasets as evaluation datasets

Paper	Venue	Year	System	Topic	BTC	Max. scale
Neumann and Weikum [46]	SIGMOD	2009	RDF-3X*	Querying	2008	562,469,278
Urbani et al. [58]	ISWC	2009	–	Reasoning	2008	864,800,000
Delbru et al. [17]	ESWC	2010	SIREN	Search	–	*10,000,000,000
Papadakis et al. [49]	iiWAS	2010	–	Linking	2009	1,150,000,000
Fang et al. [63]	TREC	2010	Purdue	Search	2010	–
Arias et al. [22]	SemSearch	2011	–	Visualisation	2010	13,000,000
Blanco et al. [8]	ISWC	2011	–	Search	2009	1,140,000,000
Böhm et al. [9]	JWS	2011	–	Schema	2010	3,170,000,000
Cheng et al. [14]	ICDE	2011	–	Analytics	2009	673,300,000
Goodman et al. [24]	ESWC	2011	–	HPC	2009	–
Groppe and Groppe [26]	SAC	2011	–	Queries	2009	830,000,000
Mulay and Kumar [45]	COMAD	2011	SPRING	Ranking	2010	10,000,000
Ladwig and Tran [40]	CIKM	2011	–	Search	2009	10,000,000
Speiser and Harth [53]	ESWC	2011	LIDS	Services	2010	3,162,149,151
Cheng et al. [15]	KDD	2012	–	Analytics	2009	773,000,000
Bohm et al. [10]	CIKM	2012	LINDA	Linking	2010	566,200,000
Görlitz et al. [25]	ISWC	2012	SPLODGE	Querying	2011	2,000,000
Neumayer et al. [47]	ECIR	2012	–	Search	2009	1,140,000,000
Wang and Cheng [60]	VLDB	2012	–	Analytics	2010	773,000,000
Shaw et al. [52]	Datalog	2012	–	Reasoning	2010	3,200,000,000
Umbrich et al. [57]	ISWC	2012	–	Querying	2011	2,145,000,000
Fernandez et al. [21]	JWS	2013	HDT	Compression	2010	232,542,405
Hose and Schenkel [35]	DESWEB	2013	WARP	Querying	2008	*562,469,278
Urbani et al. [59]	Concurrency	2013	–	Compression	–	3,180,000,000
Yang et al. [62]	DASFAA	2013	–	Querying	2010	1,280,000,000
Yuan et al. [64]	VLDB	2013	TripleBit	Querying	2012	1,048,920,108
Zeng et al. [65]	VLDB	2013	Trinity	Querying	2010	3,171,793,030
Bu et al. [11]	VLDB	2014	Pregelix	Analytics	2014	*6,177,086,016
Zhang et al. [66]	JWS	2014	–	Visualisation	2014	1,436,500,000
Liu et al. [42]	Cybernetics	2015	IDIM	Reasoning	2012	1,436,545,555
Avgoustaki et al. [1]	ESWC	2016	–	Provenance	2009	500,000
Gurajada et al. [28]	SIGMOD	2014	TriAD	Querying	2012	1,048,920,108
Konrath et al. [39]	JWS	2012	SchemEx	Schema	2011	2,100,000,000
Lehmerg et al. [41]	JWS	2015	MSJ Engine	Inf. Ex	2014	4,000,000
Heflin and Song [32]	AAAI	2016	–	Linking	2012	1,400,000
Hogan [33]	TWEB	2017	BLabel	Analytics	2014	4,000,000
Wylot et al. [61]	TKDE	2017	TripleProv	Provenance	2009	42,944,553

leveraged these datasets. Still however, our survey reveals the considerable impact that BTC datasets have had on research in the Semantic Web community, and indeed in other communities. Though the BTC-2019 dataset has only recently been published, we believe that this analysis indicates the potential impact that the newest edition of the BTC dataset should have.

Table 2. Use of BTC datasets as analysis datasets

Paper	Venue	Year	Analysis	BTC	Max. scale
Rula et al. [51]	ISWC	2012	Temporal	2011	2,100,000
Ding et al. [20]	ISWC	2010	Linking	2010	9,358,227
Gueret et al. [27]	ISWC	2010	Linking	2009	3,200,000,000
Nikolov and Motta [48]	COLD	2010	Ontologies	2009	1,140,000,000
Glimm et al. [23]	LDOW	2012	Ontologies	2011	2,145,000,000
Stadtmüller et al. [54]	CSWS	2012	Ontologies	2011	2,100,000,000
Paulheim and Hertling [50]	ISWC	2013	Publishing	2012	10,000

3 Related Work

The BTC datasets are not the only RDF corpora to have been collected from the Web. In this section we cover some of the other initiatives found in the literature for acquiring such corpora.

Predating the release of the first BTC dataset in 2008 were the corpora collected by a variety of search engines operating over Semantic Web data, including Swoogle [19], SWSE [31], Watson [16], Falcons [13], and Sindice [56]. These works described methods for crawling large volumes of RDF data from the Web. Also predating the first BTC dataset, Ding and Finin [18] collected one of the first large corpora of RDF data from the Web, containing 279,461,895 triples from 1,448,504 documents. They proceeded to analyse a number of aspects of the resulting dataset, including the domains on which RDF documents were found, the age and size of documents, how resources are described, as well as an initial analysis of quality issues relating to `rdfs:domain`. Though these works serve as an important precedent to the BTC datasets, to the best of our knowledge, the corpora were not published and/or were not reused.

On the other hand, since the first BTC dataset, a number of collections of RDF Web data have been published. The Sindice 2011 [12] contains 11 billion statements from 231 million documents, collecting not only RDF but also Microformats, and was used in 2011 for the TREC Entity Track; unfortunately the dataset is no longer available from its original location. The Dynamic Linked Data Observatory (DyLDO) [37] has been collecting RDF data from the Web each week since 2013; compared with the BTC datasets (which are yearly, at best), the DyLDO dataset are much smaller, crawling in the order of 16–100 million quads per week, with emphasis on tracking changes over time. LOD Laudromat [4] is an initiative to collect, clean, archive and republish Linked Datasets, offering a range of services from descriptive metadata to SPARQL endpoints and visualisations; unlike the BTC datasets, the focus is on collecting and republishing datasets in bulk rather than crawling documents from the Web. Meusel et al. [43] have published the WebDataCommons, extracting RDFa, Microdata and Microformats from the massive Common Crawl dataset; the result is a collection of 17,241,313,916 RDF triples, which, to the best of our knowledge, is the largest collection of crawled RDF data to have been published to-date; however, the nature of the WebDataCommons dataset is different from a typical BTC instance since it collects a lot of relatively shallow metadata from HTML pages, where the most common properties instantiated by the data are, for example, Open Graph metadata such as `ogp:type`, `ogp:title`, `ogp:url`, `ogp:site_name`, `ogp:image`, etc.; hence while WebDataCommons is an important resource, it is somewhat orthogonal to the BTC series of datasets.

4 Crawl

We follow a similar procedure for crawling the BTC-2019 dataset as in the most recent years. Our crawl uses the most recent version of the LDspider [36] (version 1.3[1]), which offers a variety of features for configuring crawls of native RDF content, including support for various RDF syntaxes, various traversal strategies, various ways to scope the crawl, and most importantly, components to ensure a "polite" crawl that respects the `robots.txt` exclusion protocol and implements a minimal delay between requests to the same server to avoid DoS-like patterns.

The crawl was executed on a single virtual machine running Ubuntu 18.04 on an Intel Xeon Silver 4110 CPU@2.10 GHz, with 30 G of RAM. The machine was hosted in the University of Chile. Following previous configurations for BTC datasets, LDspider is configured to crawl RDF/XML, Turtle and N-Triples following a breadth-first strategy; the crawler does not yet support JSON-LD, while enabling RDFa currently tends to gather a lot of shallow disconnected metadata from webpages, which we interpret as counter to the goals of BTC datasets. IRIs ending in `.html`, `.xhtml`, `.json`, `.jpg`, `.pdf` are not visited with the assumption that they are unlikely to yield content in one of the desired formats. To enable higher levels of scale, the crawler is configured to use the hard-disk to manage the frontier list (the list of unvisited URLs). Based on initial experiments with the available hardware, 64 threads were chosen for the crawl (adding more threads did not increase performance); implementing a delay between subsequent requests to the same (pay-level) domain is then important to avoid DoS-style polling, where we allow a one second delay. The crawler respects the `robots.txt` exclusion protocol[2] and will not crawl domains or documents that are blacklisted by the respective file. All HTTP(S) IRIs from an RDF document without a blacklisted extension – irrespective of the subject/predicate/object position – are considered candidates for crawling. In each round, IRIs are prioritised in terms of the number of links found, meaning that unvisited IRIs mentioned in more visited documents will be prioritised for crawling. We store the data collected as an N-Quads file, where we use the graph term to indicate the location of the document in which the triple is found; a separate file indicating the redirects

[1] https://github.com/ldspider/ldspider.

[2] One exception is the `Crawl delay` definition, where all websites are configured for a one second delay only irrespective of the `robots.txt` file.

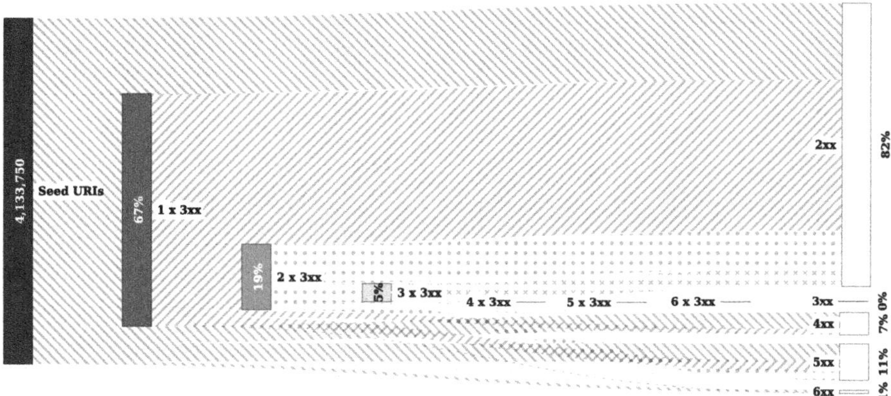

Fig. 1. Sankey diagram showing response codes for the crawled URIs. $n \times 3xx$ indicates n-th redirection.

encountered, as well as various logs, are also maintained.[3] A diverse list of 442 URLs taken from DyDLO [37] were given as input to the crawl.[4]

We ran the crawl with this configuration continuously for one month from 2018/12/12 until 2019/01/11, during which we collect 2,162,129,316 quads. Since we apply streaming parsers to be able to handle large RDF documents, in cases where a document contains duplicated triples, the initial output will contain duplicate quads; when later removed, we were left with 2,155,856,225 unique quads in the dataset from a total of 2,641,253 documents on 394 pay-level-domains (PLDs).[5]

In Fig. 1, we show the crawling behaviour on the HTTP level. As the HTTP status does not cover issues on the networking level, we added a class (`6xx`) for networking issues, which allows us to present the findings on the HTTP and networking levels in a uniform manner. We assigned exceptions that we encountered during crawling to the status code classes, according to whether we consider them a server problem (eg. `SSLException`) or a networking issue (eg. `ConnectionTimeoutException`) as in [38]. The number of seed URIs is composed of all URIs we ever tried to dereference during the crawling, where in total we tried to dereference 4,133,750 URIs. We see that about two thirds of

[3] The script used to run the call – including all arguments passed to LDspider – is available at https://github.com/jotixh/RDFLiteralDefinitions/blob/master/ldspider-runner/bin/crawl.sh.

[4] https://github.com/jotixh/RDFLiteralDefinitions/blob/master/ldspider-runner/seed.txt.

[5] A pay-level domain (PLD) is one that must be paid for to be registered; examples would be dbpedia.org, data.gov, bbc.co.uk, but not en.dbpedia.org, news.bbc.co.uk, etc. Oftentimes datasets will rather report fully-qualified domain names (FQDNs), which we argue is not a good practice since, for example, sub-domains can be used for individual user accounts (as was the case for sites like Livejournal, which had millions of sub-domains: one for each user).

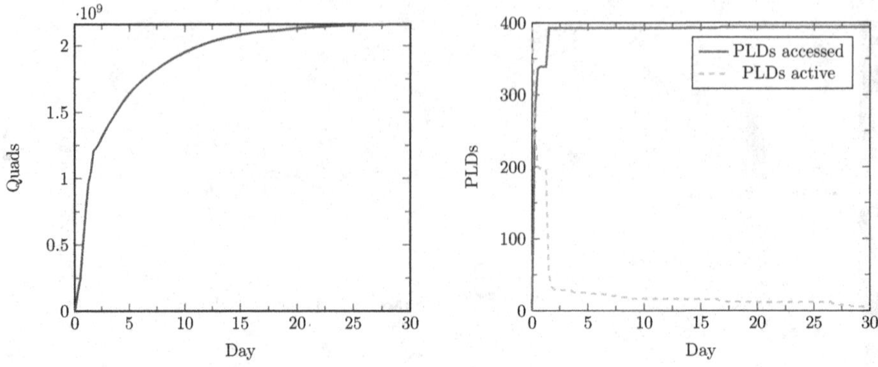

Fig. 2. Quads crawled after each day

Fig. 3. PLDs included after each day

dereferenced URIs responded with an HTTP status code of the Redirection class (3xx), which are about three times as many as the URIs that directly provided a successful response (2xx). A total of 6% of requests immediately fail due to server or network issues (5xx/6xx). In total, 82% of seed URIs eventually yielded a successful response, i.e., about 3.3 million seed URIs, which is considerable more than documents in the final crawl (2.6 million); reasons for this difference include the fact that many seed URIs redirect to the same document, that multiple hash URIs from the same documents are in the seed list, etc.

In Fig. 2, we show the number of (non-distinct) quads crawled as the days progress, where we see that half of the data are crawled after about 1.6 days; the rate at which quads are crawled decays markedly over time. This decay in performance occurs because at the start of the crawl there are more domains to crawl from, where smaller domains are exhausted early in the crawl; this leaves fewer active domains at the end of the crawl. Figure 3 then shows the number of PLDs contributing quads to the crawl as the days progress (accessed), where all but one domain is found after 1.5 days. Figure 3 also shows the number of active PLDs: the PLDs that will contribute quads to the crawl in the future, where for example we see based on the data for day 15 that the last 15 days of the crawl will retrieve RDF successful from 16 PLDs. By the end of the crawl, there are only 6 PLDs active from which the crawler can continue to retrieve RDF data. These results explain the trend in Fig. 2 of the crawl slowing as it progresses: the crawl enters a phase of incrementally crawling a few larger domains, where the crawl delay becomes the limit to performance. For example, at the end of the crawl, with 6 domains active, a delay limit of 1 s means that 6 documents can be crawled per second. Similiar crawls of RDF documents on the Web have encountered this same phenomenon of "PLD starvation" [34].

In summary, we crawl for 30 days collecting a total of 2,155,856,033 unique quads from 2,641,253 RDF documents on 394 pay-level domains. Per Fig. 2, running the crawl for more time would have limited effect on the volume of data.

5 Dataset Statistics

The data are collected from 2,641,253 RDF documents collected from 394 pay-level domains containing a total of 2,155,856,033 unique quads. Surprisingly, the number of unique triples in the dataset is much lower: 256,059,356. This means that on average, each triples is repeated in approximately 8.4 different documents; we will discuss this issue again later. In terms of schema, the data contain 38,156 predicates and instances of 120,037 unique classes; these terms are defined in a total of 1,746 vocabularies (counting unique namespaces).

Next we look at the sources of data for the crawl. RDF content was successfully crawled from a total of 394 different PLDs. In Table 3, we show the top 25 PLDs with respect to the number of documents crawled and the overall percentage of documents sourced from that site; the largest provider of documents is dbpedia.org (6.14%), followed by loc.gov (5.68%), etc. We remark that amongst these top PLDs, the distribution is relatively equal. This is because documents

Table 3. PLDs by docs.

№	PLD	Docs.	%
1	dbpedia.org	162,117	6.14%
2	loc.gov	150,091	5.68%
3	bnf.fr	146,186	5.53%
4	sudoc.fr	144,877	5.49%
5	theses.fr	141,228	5.35%
6	wikidata.org	141,207	5.35%
7	linkeddata.es	130,459	4.94%
8	getty.edu	130,398	4.94%
9	fao.org	92,838	3.51%
10	ontobee.org	92,812	3.51%
11	dbtune.org	91,755	3.47%
12	wals.info	88,786	3.36%
13	lexvo.org	87,584	3.32%
14	ordnancesurvey.co.uk	86,801	3.29%
15	idref.fr	83,670	3.17%
16	glottolog.org	79,365	3.00%
17	l3s.de	77,650	2.94%
18	uba.de	73,648	2.79%
19	uni-mannheim.de	71,883	2.72%
20	pokepedia.fr	70,300	2.66%
21	ontologycentral.com	64,407	2.44%
22	bl.uk	55,951	2.12%
23	d-nb.info	55,731	2.11%
24	cnr.it	47,955	1.82%
25	bne.es	39,437	1.49%

Table 4. PLDs by triples

№	PLD	Triples	%
1	wikidata.org	133,535,555	52.15%
2	dbpedia.org	32,981,420	12.88%
3	idref.fr	16,820,681	6.57%
4	bnf.fr	11,769,268	4.60%
5	getty.edu	6,571,525	2.57%
6	linkeddata.es	5,898,762	2.30%
7	loc.gov	5,362,064	2.09%
8	sudoc.fr	4,972,647	1.94%
9	ontologycentral.com	4,471,962	1.75%
10	theses.fr	4,095,897	1.60%
11	dbtune.org	3,697,811	1.44%
12	l3s.de	2,747,392	1.07%
13	bl.uk	2,575,875	1.01%
14	glottolog.org	1,913,034	0.75%
15	d-nb.info	1,501,742	0.59%
16	wals.info	1,441,392	0.56%
17	uba.de	1,400,424	0.55%
18	fao.org	1,170,742	0.46%
19	pokepedia.fr	1,117,102	0.44%
20	ordnancesurvey.co.uk	822,175	0.32%
21	myexperiment.org	815,221	0.32%
22	bne.es	788,499	0.31%
23	lexvo.org	774,028	0.30%
24	githubusercontent.com	683,901	0.27%
25	kit.edu	641,578	0.25%

Table 5. PLDs by quads

№	PLD	Quads	%
1	wikidata.org	2,006,338,975	93.06%
2	dbpedia.org	36,686,161	1.70%
3	idref.fr	22,013,225	1.02%
4	bnf.fr	12,618,155	0.59%
5	getty.edu	7,453,134	0.35%
6	sudoc.fr	7,176,301	0.33%
7	loc.gov	6,725,390	0.31%
8	linkeddata.es	6,485,114	0.30%
9	theses.fr	4,820,874	0.22%
10	ontologycentral.com	4,633,947	0.21%
11	dbtune.org	3,943,928	0.18%
12	bl.uk	3,348,410	0.16%
13	l3s.de	3,084,744	0.14%
14	pokepedia.fr	3,039,193	0.14%
15	myexperiment.org	2,401,693	0.11%
16	kit.edu	2,361,368	0.11%
17	glottolog.org	1,936,776	0.09%
18	d-nb.info	1,719,665	0.08%
19	uba.de	1,474,952	0.07%
20	wals.info	1,459,402	0.07%
21	ontobee.org	1,332,477	0.06%
22	uni-mannheim.de	1,316,328	0.06%
23	fao.org	1,170,742	0.05%
24	ordnancesurvey.co.uk	1,165,124	0.05%
25	githubusercontent.com	1,015,635	0.05%

Table 6. PLDs per voc.

№	Vocab.	PLDs	%
1	rdf:	389	98.73%
2	rdfs:	224	56.85%
3	foaf:	218	55.33%
4	owl:	170	43.15%
5	dce:	145	36.80%
6	dct:	138	35.03%
7	skos:	76	19.29%
8	geo:	58	14.72%
9	admin:	52	13.20%
10	schema:	43	10.91%
11	rss:	36	9.14%
12	con:	34	8.63%
13	bibo:	33	8.38%
14	cc:	31	7.87%
15	void:	28	7.11%
16	cert:	28	7.11%
17	atom:	26	6.60%
18	vann:	23	5.84%
19	sioc:	23	5.84%
20	vcard:	23	5.84%
21	ldp:	23	5.84%
22	doap:	22	5.58%
23	content:	21	5.33%
24	bio:	20	5.08%
25	wot:	19	4.82%

are crawled from each domain at a maximum rate of 1/s, meaning that typically a document will be polled from each active domain with the same interval. To counter the phenomenon of PLD starvation, we stop the polling of active domains when the number of active domains is below a certain threshold and move to the next hop (the documents in the queues of the domains are ranked by in-links as a measure of importance). The result is that large domains are often among the last active domains, where the polling is stopped before the domain is crawled exhaustively and for all domains after downloading almost the same number of documents. However, looking at Table 4, which displays the top 25 PLDs in terms of unique triples, we start to see some skew, where 52.15% of all unique triples come from Wikidata (despite it accounting for only 5.35% of documents). Even more noticeably, if we look at Table 5, which displays the top-25 PLDs by number of quads, we see that Wikidata accounts for 93.06% of all quads; in fact, if we divide the number of quads for Wikidata by the number of documents, we find that it contains, on average, approximately 14,208

Table 7. PLDs per pred.

№	Predicate	PLDs	%
1	rdf:type	389	98.73%
2	foaf:name	168	42.64%
3	rdfs:label	165	41.88%
4	foaf:homepage	151	38.32%
5	rdfs:seeAlso	146	37.06%
6	foaf:primaryTopic	134	34.01%
7	owl:sameAs	117	29.70%
8	foaf:knows	102	25.89%
9	foaf:maker	102	25.89%
10	dce:title	99	25.13%
11	rdfs:comment	98	24.87%
12	foaf:mbox_sha1sum	98	24.87%
13	foaf:nick	87	22.08%
14	foaf:workplaceHomepage	87	22.08%
15	foaf:depiction	86	21.83%
16	dct:title	79	20.05%
17	rdfs:subClassOf	76	19.29%
18	foaf:title	75	19.04%
19	dct:modified	72	18.27%
20	foaf:mbox	72	18.27%
21	dce:creator	67	17.01%
22	rdfs:range	67	17.01%
23	rdfs:subPropertyOf	67	17.01%
24	rdfs:domain	65	16.50%
25	foaf:family_name	64	16.24%

Table 8. PLDs per class

№	Class	PLDs	%
1	foaf:Person	167	42.39%
2	foaf:PersonalProfileDocument	88	22.34%
3	owl:Class	76	19.29%
4	owl:Ontology	65	16.50%
5	owl:ObjectProperty	61	15.48%
6	foaf:Document	60	15.23%
7	owl:DatatypeProperty	57	14.47%
8	skos:Concept	50	12.69%
9	foaf:Organization	38	9.64%
10	rss:channel	34	8.63%
11	owl:Restriction	34	8.63%
12	rdf:Property	32	8.12%
13	foaf:OnlineAccount	31	7.87%
14	owl:AnnotationProperty	30	7.61%
15	rdf:Seq	27	6.85%
16	rdfs:Class	27	6.85%
17	atom:feed	26	6.60%
18	skos:ConceptScheme	25	6.35%
19	rss:item	24	6.09%
20	geo:Point	24	6.09%
21	foaf:Project	24	6.09%
22	cert:RSAPublicKey	23	5.84%
23	schema:Person	22	5.58%
24	owl:TransitiveProperty	22	5.58%
25	owl:FunctionalProperty	21	5.33%

triples per document! By way of comparison, DBpedia contains 226 triples per document. Hence given that the crawl, by its nature, balances the number of documents polled from each domain, and that Wikidata's RDF documents are orders of magnitude larger than those of other domains, we see why the skew in quads occurs. Further cross referencing quads with unique triples, we see a lot of redundancy in how Wikidata exports RDF, repeating each triple in (on average) 15 documents; by way of comparison, DBpedia repeats each unique triple in (on average) 1.11 documents. This skew occurs as a result of how Wikidata chooses to export its data; while representing how real-world data are published, consumers of the BTC-2019 dataset should keep this skew in mind when using the data, particularly if conducting analyses of adoption; for example, analysing the most popularly-used predicates by counting the number of quads using each predicate would be disproportionately affected by Wikidata.

Turning towards the use of vocabularies in the data, Table 6 presents the most popular vocabularies (extracted from predicate and class terms) in terms of the number of PLDs on which they are used (and the percentage of PLDs). Unsurprisingly core Semantic Webs standards head the list, followed by Friend of a Friend (FOAF), Dublin Core (DC) vocabularies, etc.; almost all of these vocabularies have been established for over a decade, with the exception of the Linked Data Platform (LDP) vocabulary which appears in 21st place. On the other hand, Table 7 presents the number of PLDs per predicate, while Table 8 presents the number of PLDs per class, where again there are few surprises at the top of the list, with most terms corresponding to the most popular namespaces. We conclude that BTC-2019 is a highly diverse dataset featuring hundreds of thousands of vocabulary terms from thousands of vocabularies.

6 Comparison with BTC-2012 and BTC-2014

We now provide a statistical comparison between BTC-2019 and its two most recent predecessors: BTC-2014 and BTC-2012. We downloaded these latter two datasets from their corresponding webpages and ran the same statistical code as used for the BTC-2019 dataset. Noting that BTC-2014 and BTC-2012 included HTTP header meta-data as part of their RDF dump, for the purposes of comparability, we pre-filtered such triples from these crawls as they were not part of the native RDF documents (and thus were not included in the BTC-2019 files).

We begin in Table 9 with a comparison of high-level statistics between the three datasets, where we see that in terms of quads, BTC-2019 is larger

Table 9. Comparison of BTC 2012, 2014, 2019: High-level Statistics

Statistic	BTC-2012	BTC-2014	BTC-2019
Quads	1, 230, 391, 773	3, 974, 427, 819	2, 155, 856, 033
Unique triples	974, 810, 809	3, 168, 111, 983	256, 059, 356
PLDs	829	47, 634	394
Documents	8, 373, 075	43, 598, 858	2, 641, 253
Predicates	57, 235	2, 192, 434	38, 156
Classes	296, 605	2, 700, 640	120, 037
Vocabularies	1, 775	977, 606	1, 746

Table 10. Comparison of BTC 2012, 2014, 2019: Top PLDs per Documents

№	BTC-2012		BTC-2014		BTC-2019	
	PLD	Docs	PLD	Docs	PLD	Docs
1	dbpedia.org	2,714,588	openlinksw.com	1,885,141	dbpedia.org	162,117
2	freebase.com	1,849,859	crossref.org	1,388,354	loc.gov	150,091
3	data.gov.uk	1,328,918	b3kat.de	1,189,744	bnf.fr	146,186
4	kasabi.com	324,769	legislation.gov.uk	1,153,601	sudoc.fr	144,877
5	opera.com	297,657	sysoon.com	1,142,464	theses.fr	141,228
6	loc.gov	192,125	bibsonomy.org	1,118,619	wikidata.org	141,207
7	fu-berlin.de	162,455	dbpedia.org	1,107,836	linkeddata.es	130,459
8	vu.nl	149,920	loc.gov	1,099,278	getty.edu	130,398
9	europa.eu	145,351	linkedct.org	1,052,459	fao.org	92,838
10	lexvo.org	127,924	rdfize.com	1,049,708	ontobee.org	92,812

than BTC-2012 but smaller than BTC-2014; as previously discussed, BTC-2014 extracted a lot of shallow HTML-based metadata from small RDFa documents, which we decided to exclude from BTC-2019: as can be seen by cross-referencing the quads and documents statistics, BTC-2019 had on average 816 quads per document, while BTC-2012 had on average 147 quads per document and BTC-2014 had on average 91 quads per document. Of note is the relatively vast quantity of predicates, classes and vocabularies appearing in the BTC-2014 dataset; upon further analysis, most was noise relating to a bug in the exporter of a single site – `gorodskoyportal.ru` – which linked to nested namespaces of the form:

```
http://gorodskoyportal.ru/moskva/rss/channel/.../channel/*
```

where "..." indicates repetitions of the `channel` sub-path.

We see that BTC-2019 also comes from fewer domains than BTC-2012 and much fewer than BTC-2014; this is largely attributable not only to our decision to not include data embedded in HTML pages, but also to a variety of domains that have ceased publishing RDF data. Regarding the largest contributors of data in terms of PLDs, Table 10 provides a comparison of the domains contributing the most documents to each of the three versions of the BTC datasets, where we see some domains in common across both (e.g., dbpedia.org, loc.gov), some domains appearing in older versions but not in BTC-2019 that have gone offline (freebase.com, kasabi.com, opera.com, etc.), as well as some new domains appearing only in the more recent BTC-2019 version (e.g., wikidata.org).

7 Publication

We publish the files on the Zenodo service, which provides hosting in CERN's data centre and also assigns resources published with DOIs. The DOI of the BTC-2019 dataset is http://doi.org/10.5281/zenodo.2634588. The data are published in N-Triples format using GZip compression. Due to the size of the dataset, rather than publish the data as one large file, we publish the following:

Unique triples (1 file: 3.1 GB) this file stores only the unique triples of the BTC-2019 dataset.

Quads (114 files: 26.1 GB total) given the large volume of quads, we split the data up, creating a separate file for the quads collected from each of the top 100 PLDs, and an additional file containing the quads for the remaining 294 PLDs. Given the size of Wikidata, we split its file into 14 segments, each containing at most 150 million quads each and taking 1.8 GB of space.

Hence we offer consumers a number of options for how they wish to use the BTC-2019 dataset. Consumers who are mostly interested in the graph structure (e.g., for testing graph analytics or queries on a single graph) may choose to download the unique triples file. On the other hand, other consumers can select smaller files from the PLDs of interest, potentially remixing the BTC-2019 into various samples; another possibility, for example, would be to take one file from each PLD (including Wikidata), thus potentially reducing the skew in quads previously discussed. Aside from the data themselves, we also publish a VoID file describing metadata about the crawl, and offer documentation on how to download all of the files at once, potential parsers that can be used, etc.

8 Conclusion

In this paper, we have provided a survey indicating how the BTC datasets have been used down through the years, providing a strong motivation for continuing the tradition of publishing these datasets. Observing that the last BTC crawl was conducted 5 years ago in 2014, we have thus crawled and published the newest edition to the BTC series: BTC-2019. We have provided various details on the crawl used to acquire the dataset, various statistics regarding the resulting dataset, as well as discussion on how the data are published in a sustainable way.

In terms of the statistics, we noted two problematic aspects: a relatively low number of PLDs contributing to the crawl, leading to exhausting the available PLDs relatively quickly, and a large skew in the number of quads sourced from Wikidata. These observations are based on how the data are published on the Web rather than being a particular artifact of the crawl. Still, the resulting dataset is highly diverse, reflects current publishing, and can be used for evaluating methods on real-world data; furthermore, with appropriately designed metrics taking into account the skew on Wikidata, the BTC-2019 dataset contains valuable insights on how data are being published on the Web today.

Acknowledgements. This work was supported by Fondecyt Grant No. 1181896 and by the Millenium Institute for Foundational Research on Data (IMFD).

References

1. Avgoustaki, A., Flouris, G., Fundulaki, I., Plexousakis, D.: Provenance management for evolving RDF datasets. In: Sack, H., Blomqvist, E., d'Aquin, M., Ghidini, C., Ponzetto, S.P., Lange, C. (eds.) ESWC 2016. LNCS, vol. 9678, pp. 575–592. Springer, Cham (2016). https://doi.org/10.1007/978-3-319-34129-3_35
2. Balog, K., Serdyukov, P., de Vries, A.P.: Overview of the TREC 2011 entity track. In: Text REtrieval Conference (TREC). NIST (2011)
3. Bechhofer, S., Harth, A.: The semantic web challenge 2014. J. Web Semant. **35**, 141 (2015)
4. Beek, W., Rietveld, L., Bazoobandi, H.R., Wielemaker, J., Schlobach, S.: LOD laundromat: a uniform way of publishing other people's dirty data. In: Mika, P., et al. (eds.) ISWC 2014. LNCS, vol. 8796, pp. 213–228. Springer, Cham (2014). https://doi.org/10.1007/978-3-319-11964-9_14
5. Bizer, C., Maynard, D.: The semantic web challenge 2010. J. Web Semant. **9**(3), 315 (2011)
6. Bizer, C., Maynard, D.: The semantic web challenge 2011. J. Web Semant. **16**, 32 (2012)
7. Bizer, C., Mika, P.: The semantic web challenge 2009. J. Web Semant. **8**(4), 341 (2010)

8. Blanco, R., Mika, P., Vigna, S.: Effective and efficient entity search in RDF data. In: Aroyo, L., et al. (eds.) ISWC 2011. LNCS, vol. 7031, pp. 83–97. Springer, Heidelberg (2011). https://doi.org/10.1007/978-3-642-25073-6_6
9. Böhm, C., Lorey, J., Naumann, F.: Creating void descriptions for web-scale data. J. Web Semant. **9**(3), 339–345 (2011)
10. Böhm, C., de Melo, G., Naumann, F., Weikum, G.: LINDA: distributed web-of-data-scale entity matching. In: ACM International Conference on Information and Knowledge Management (CIKM), pp. 2104–2108. ACM (2012)
11. Bu, Y., Borkar, V.R., Jia, J., Carey, M.J., Condie, T.: Pregelix: Big(ger) graph analytics on a dataflow engine. PVLDB **8**(2), 161–172 (2014)
12. Campinas, S., Ceccarelli, D., Perry, T.E., Delbru, R., Balog, K., Tummarello, G.: The sindice-2011 dataset for entity-oriented search on the web of data. In: International Workshop on Entity-Oriented Search (EOS), pp. 26–32 (2011)
13. Cheng, G., Ge, W., Qu, Y.: Falcons: searching and browsing entities on the semantic web. In: International Conference on World Wide Web (WWW), pp. 1101–1102. ACM (2008)
14. Cheng, J., Ke, Y., Chu, S., Özsu, M.T.: Efficient core decomposition in massive networks. In: International Conference on Data Engineering (ICDE), pp. 51–62. IEEE (2011)
15. Cheng, J., Zhu, L., Ke, Y., Chu, S.: Fast algorithms for maximal clique enumeration with limited memory. In: SIGKDD International Conference on Knowledge Discovery and Data Mining (KDD), pp. 1240–1248. ACM (2012)
16. d'Aquin, M., Baldassarre, C., Gridinoc, L., Angeletou, S., Sabou, M., Motta, E.: Characterizing knowledge on the semantic web with watson. In: International Workshop on Evaluation of Ontologies (EON), pp. 1–10. CEUR-WS.org (2007)
17. Delbru, R., Toupikov, N., Catasta, M., Tummarello, G.: A node indexing scheme for web entity retrieval. In: Aroyo, L., et al. (eds.) ESWC 2010. LNCS, vol. 6089, pp. 240–256. Springer, Heidelberg (2010). https://doi.org/10.1007/978-3-642-13489-0_17
18. Ding, L., Finin, T.: Characterizing the semantic web on the web. In: Cruz, I., et al. (eds.) ISWC 2006. LNCS, vol. 4273, pp. 242–257. Springer, Heidelberg (2006). https://doi.org/10.1007/11926078_18
19. Ding, L., et al.: Swoogle: a search and metadata engine for the semantic web. In: International Conference on Information and Knowledge Management (CIKM), pp. 652–659. ACM (2004)
20. Ding, L., Shinavier, J., Shangguan, Z., McGuinness, D.L.: SameAs networks and beyond: analyzing deployment status and implications of owl:sameas in linked data. In: Patel-Schneider, P.F., et al. (eds.) ISWC 2010. LNCS, vol. 6496, pp. 145–160. Springer, Heidelberg (2010). https://doi.org/10.1007/978-3-642-17746-0_10
21. Fernández, J.D., Martínez-Prieto, M.A., Gutiérrez, C., Polleres, A., Arias, M.: Binary RDF representation for publication and exchange (HDT). J. Web Semant. **19**, 22–41 (2013)
22. Gallego, M.A., Fernández, J., Martínez-Prieto, M., de la Fuente, P.: RDF visualization using a three-dimensional adjacency matrix. In: Semantic Search Workshop (SEMSEARCH) (2011)
23. Glimm, B., Hogan, A., Krötzsch, M., Polleres, A.: OWL: yet to arrive on the web of data? In: Linked Data on the Web (LDOW). CEUR-WS.org (2012)
24. Goodman, E.L., Jimenez, E., Mizell, D., al-Saffar, S., Adolf, B., Haglin, D.: High-Performance computing applied to semantic databases. In: Antoniou, G., et al. (eds.) ESWC 2011. LNCS, vol. 6644, pp. 31–45. Springer, Heidelberg (2011). https://doi.org/10.1007/978-3-642-21064-8_3

25. Görlitz, O., Thimm, M., Staab, S.: SPLODGE: systematic generation of SPARQL benchmark queries for linked open data. In: Cudré-Mauroux, P., et al. (eds.) ISWC 2012. LNCS, vol. 7649, pp. 116–132. Springer, Heidelberg (2012). https://doi.org/10.1007/978-3-642-35176-1_8
26. Groppe, J., Groppe, S.: Parallelizing join computations of SPARQL queries for large semantic web databases. In: Symposium on Applied Computing (SAC), pp. 1681–1686. ACM (2011)
27. Guéret, C., Groth, P., van Harmelen, F., Schlobach, S.: Finding the achilles heel of the web of data: using network analysis for link-recommendation. In: Patel-Schneider, P.F., et al. (eds.) ISWC 2010. LNCS, vol. 6496, pp. 289–304. Springer, Heidelberg (2010). https://doi.org/10.1007/978-3-642-17746-0_19
28. Gurajada, S., Seufert, S., Miliaraki, I., Theobald, M.: TriAD: a distributed shared-nothing RDF engine based on asynchronous message passing. In: SIGMOD International Conference on Management of Data, pp. 289–300. ACM (2014)
29. Harth, A., Bechhofer, S.: The semantic web challenge 2013. J. Web Semant. **27–28**, 1 (2014)
30. Harth, A., Maynard, D.: The semantic web challenge 2012. J. Web Semant. **24**, 1–2 (2014)
31. Harth, A., Umbrich, J., Decker, S.: MultiCrawler: a pipelined architecture for crawling and indexing semantic web data. In: Cruz, I., et al. (eds.) ISWC 2006. LNCS, vol. 4273, pp. 258–271. Springer, Heidelberg (2006). https://doi.org/10.1007/11926078_19
32. Heflin, J., Song, D.: Ontology instance linking: towards interlinked knowledge graphs. In: AAAI Conference on Artificial Intelligence, pp. 4163–4169. AAAI (2016)
33. Hogan, A.: Canonical forms for isomorphic and equivalent RDF graphs: algorithms for leaning and labelling blank nodes. TWEB **11**(4), 22:1–22:62 (2017)
34. Hogan, A., Harth, A., Umbrich, J., Kinsella, S., Polleres, A., Decker, S.: Searching and browsing linked data with SWSE: the semantic web search engine. J. Web Semant. **9**(4), 365–401 (2011)
35. Hose, K., Schenkel, R.: WARP: workload-aware replication and partitioning for RDF. In: Workshops Proceedings of the International Conference on Data Engineering (ICDE), pp. 1–6. IEEE (2013)
36. Isele, R., Umbrich, J., Bizer, C., Harth, A.: LDspider: an open-source crawling framework for the web of linked data. In: ISWC Posters & Demonstrations. CEUR-WS (2010)
37. Käfer, T., Abdelrahman, A., Umbrich, J., O'Byrne, P., Hogan, A.: Observing linked data dynamics. In: Cimiano, P., Corcho, O., Presutti, V., Hollink, L., Rudolph, S. (eds.) ESWC 2013. LNCS, vol. 7882, pp. 213–227. Springer, Heidelberg (2013). https://doi.org/10.1007/978-3-642-38288-8_15
38. Käfer, T., Wins, A., Acosta, M.: Modelling and analysing dynamic linked data using RDF and SPARQL. In: Workshop on Dataset PROFILing and fEderated Search for Web Data (PROFILES) (2017)
39. Konrath, M., Gottron, T., Staab, S., Scherp, A.: SchemEX - efficient construction of a data catalogue by stream-based indexing of linked data. J. Web Semant. **16**, 52–58 (2012)
40. Ladwig, G., Tran, T.: Index structures and top-k join algorithms for native keyword search databases. In: Conference on Information and Knowledge Management (CIKM), pp. 1505–1514. ACM (2011)
41. Lehmberg, O., Ritze, D., Ristoski, P., Meusel, R., Paulheim, H., Bizer, C.: The mannheim search join engine. J. Web Semant. **35**, 159–166 (2015)

42. Liu, B., Huang, K., Li, J., Zhou, M.: An incremental and distributed inference method for large-scale ontologies based on MapReduce paradigm. IEEE Trans. Cybern. **45**(1), 53–64 (2015)
43. Meusel, R., Petrovski, P., Bizer, C.: The WebDataCommons microdata, RDFa and microformat dataset series. In: Mika, P., et al. (eds.) ISWC 2014. LNCS, vol. 8796, pp. 277–292. Springer, Cham (2014). https://doi.org/10.1007/978-3-319-11964-9_18
44. Mika, P., Hendler, J.: The semantic web challenge 2008. J. Web Semant. **7**(4), 271 (2009)
45. Mulay, K., Kumar, P.S.: SPRING: ranking the results of SPARQL queries on linked data. In: International Conference on Management of Data (COMAD), pp. 47–56. Allied Publishers (2011)
46. Neumann, T., Weikum, G.: Scalable join processing on very large RDF graphs. In: SIGMOD International Conference on Management of Data, pp. 627–640. ACM (2009)
47. Neumayer, R., Balog, K., Nørvåg, K.: When simple is (more than) good enough: effective semantic search with (almost) no semantics. In: Baeza-Yates, R., et al. (eds.) ECIR 2012. LNCS, vol. 7224, pp. 540–543. Springer, Heidelberg (2012). https://doi.org/10.1007/978-3-642-28997-2_59
48. Nikolov, A., Motta, E.: Capturing emerging relations between schema ontologies on the web of data. In: Consuming Linked Data (COLD). CEUR (2010)
49. Papadakis, G., Demartini, G., Fankhauser, P., Kärger, P.: The missing links: discovering hidden same-as links among a billion of triples. In: International Conference on Information Integration and Web-based Applications and Services, pp. 453–460. ACM (2010)
50. Paulheim, H., Hertling, S.: Discoverability of SPARQL endpoints in linked open data. In: ISWC Posters & Demonstrations, pp. 245–248. CEUR-WS.org (2013)
51. Rula, A., Palmonari, M., Harth, A., Stadtmüller, S., Maurino, A.: On the diversity and availability of temporal information in linked open data. In: Cudré-Mauroux, P., et al. (eds.) ISWC 2012. LNCS, vol. 7649, pp. 492–507. Springer, Heidelberg (2012). https://doi.org/10.1007/978-3-642-35176-1_31
52. Shaw, M., Koutris, P., Howe, B., Suciu, D.: Optimizing large-scale semi-naïve datalog evaluation in Hadoop. In: Barceló, P., Pichler, R. (eds.) Datalog 2.0 2012. LNCS, vol. 7494, pp. 165–176. Springer, Heidelberg (2012). https://doi.org/10.1007/978-3-642-32925-8_17
53. Speiser, S., Harth, A.: Integrating linked data and services with linked data services. In: Antoniou, G., et al. (eds.) ESWC 2011. LNCS, vol. 6643, pp. 170–184. Springer, Heidelberg (2011). https://doi.org/10.1007/978-3-642-21034-1_12
54. Stadtmüller, S., Harth, A., Grobelnik, M.: Accessing information about linked data vocabularies with vocab.cc. In: Li, J., Qi, G., Zhao, D., Nejdl, W., Zheng, H.T. (eds.) CSWS 2012. SPCOM, pp. 391–396. (2012). https://doi.org/10.1007/978-1-4614-6880-6_34
55. Tran, T., Mika, P., Wang, H., Grobelnik, M.: SemSearch'11: the 4th semantic search workshop. In: International Conference on World Wide Web (Companion Volume), pp. 315–316. ACM (2011)
56. Tummarello, G., Delbru, R., Oren, E.: Sindice.com: weaving the open linked data. In: Aberer, K., et al. (eds.) ASWC/ISWC -2007. LNCS, vol. 4825, pp. 552–565. Springer, Heidelberg (2007). https://doi.org/10.1007/978-3-540-76298-0_40

57. Umbrich, J., Karnstedt, M., Hogan, A., Parreira, J.X.: Hybrid SPARQL queries: fresh vs. fast results. In: Cudré-Mauroux, P., et al. (eds.) ISWC 2012. LNCS, vol. 7649, pp. 608–624. Springer, Heidelberg (2012). https://doi.org/10.1007/978-3-642-35176-1_38
58. Urbani, J., Kotoulas, S., Oren, E., van Harmelen, F.: Scalable Distributed reasoning using MapReduce. In: Bernstein, A., et al. (eds.) ISWC 2009. LNCS, vol. 5823, pp. 634–649. Springer, Heidelberg (2009). https://doi.org/10.1007/978-3-642-04930-9_40
59. Urbani, J., Maassen, J., Drost, N., Seinstra, F.J., Bal, H.E.: Scalable RDF data compression with MapReduce. Concurrency Comput.: Pract. Experience **25**(1), 24–39 (2013)
60. Wang, J., Cheng, J.: Truss decomposition in massive networks. PVLDB **5**(9), 812–823 (2012)
61. Wylot, M., Cudré-Mauroux, P., Hauswirth, M., Groth, P.T.: Storing, tracking, and querying provenance in linked data. IEEE Trans. Knowl. Data Eng. **29**(8), 1751–1764 (2017)
62. Yang, T., Chen, J., Wang, X., Chen, Y., Du, X.: Efficient SPARQL query evaluation via automatic data partitioning. In: Meng, W., Feng, L., Bressan, S., Winiwarter, W., Song, W. (eds.) DASFAA 2013. LNCS, vol. 7826, pp. 244–258. Springer, Heidelberg (2013). https://doi.org/10.1007/978-3-642-37450-0_18
63. Fang, Y., Si, L., Somasundaram, N., Al-Ansari, S., Yu, Z., Xian, Y.: Purdue at TREC 2010 entity track: a probabilistic framework for matching types between candidate and target entities (2010)
64. Yuan, P., Liu, P., Wu, B., Jin, H., Zhang, W., Liu, L.: TripleBit: a fast and compact system for large scale RDF data. PVLDB **6**(7), 517–528 (2013)
65. Zeng, K., Yang, J., Wang, H., Shao, B., Wang, Z.: A distributed graph engine for web scale RDF data. PVLDB **6**(4), 265–276 (2013)
66. Zhang, X., Song, D., Priya, S., Daniels, Z., Reynolds, K., Heflin, J.: Exploring linked data with contextual tag clouds. J. Web Semant. **24**, 33–39 (2014)

Extending the YAGO2 Knowledge Graph with Precise Geospatial Knowledge

Nikolaos Karalis(✉), Georgios Mandilaras, and Manolis Koubarakis

Department of Informatics and Telecommunications,
National and Kapodistrian University of Athens, Athens, Greece
{nkaralis,gmandi,koubarak}@di.uoa.gr

Abstract. We extend YAGO2 with geospatial information represented by geometries (e.g., lines, polygons, multipolygons, etc.) encoded by Open Geospatial Consortium standards. The new geospatial information comes from official sources such as the administrative divisions of countries but also from volunteered open data of OpenStreetMap. The resulting knowledge graph is currently the richest in terms of geospatial information publicly available, open source, knowledge graph.

Keywords: Knowledge graphs · YAGO · Geospatial knowledge

1 Introduction

Many intelligent applications are driven today by knowledge graphs (KGs) such as the Google KG[1], DBpedia[2] and YAGO [9]. The first version of YAGO was released in 2007 [16,17]. YAGO was created by combining knowledge from WordNet [13] and Wikipedia, and it is one of the first open and free knowledge graphs. The entities of YAGO were created from pages of Wikipedia, whereas WordNet was used to create its classes and their hierarchy. YAGO knowledge is encoded in triples *SPO* where *S* is the subject, *P* is the predicate and *O* is the object.

YAGO2 [6,7], the second version of YAGO, was released in 2011. YAGO2 introduces geospatial and temporal information to the YAGO knowledge graph by introducing *geoentities*. Geopatial information in YAGO2 comes not only from Wikipedia but also from GeoNames[3]. GeoNames is a gazetteer[4], whose data and accuracy have been studied in [1,2,5].

The geospatial information in YAGO2 is represented with the properties `hasLongitude` and `hasLatitude` which give the longitude and latitude of the center of a geoentity. In YAGO2, the coordinates of Greece are represented

[1] https://developers.google.com/knowledge-graph/.
[2] https://wiki.dbpedia.org/develop/getting-started.
[3] https://www.geonames.org/.
[4] A gazetteer is a geographical dictionary that is used, in most cases, together with a map. Given a name (i.e., a city or a river) a gazetteer gives geospatial information about that name.

C. Ghidini et al. (Eds.): ISWC 2019, LNCS 11779, pp. 181–197, 2019.
https://doi.org/10.1007/978-3-030-30796-7_12

with the following triples: `<Greece> <hasLatitude> "39.00"^^<degrees>` and `<Greece> <hasLongitude> "22.00"^^<degrees>`.

Temporal information is introduced in YAGO2 to entities of type `people`, `groups`, `artifacts` or `events`. Temporal information is represented using dates. Dates in YAGO2 follow the ISO 8601 format (YYYY-MM-DD) and represent time points. If we want to model intervals e.g., the lifetime of an entity such as a person, we can use pairs of properties e.g., `wasBornOnDate` and `diedOnDate` which connect an entity with a date.

To represent geospatial and temporal knowledge, YAGO2 uses the *SPOTL* data model, which extends the SPO model for knowledge graph triples discussed above: T stands for time, L stands for location, and S, P and O as defined above. The SPOTL model not only allows temporal and geospatial relations between entities, but also temporal and geospatial relations between facts. For example, the fact that Barack Obama was inaugurated as president of the USA can be associated with a place (Washington D.C.) and a date (2009-01-20).

YAGO3 [12], the latest version of YAGO, came out in 2015. YAGO3 is multilingual since it combines information from Wikipedias in multiple languages.

The main technical contributions of this paper are the following.

We develop a new version of YAGO2, called YAGO2geo, with more precise geospatial information. YAGO2geo contains *640 thousand polygons* and *137 thousand lines*. The line and polygon information introduced in YAGO2geo makes, in many cases, more sense than the coordinate pairs that exist in YAGO2. For example, we do not need to model any more the longitude/latitude center of a stream or another geoentity for which it is not clear what the center is. Also, YAGO2geo can be used to answer questions for which precise geospatial information is required. This has not been possible with YAGO2. For example, such questions are "what is the city of Germany where two streams meet at a lake", or "which are the neighboring municipalities of the municipality of Athens?".

The extension, in combination with the 12 million coordinate pairs of YAGO2, creates a geospatial KG much richer, in terms of geospatial knowledge, compared to DBpedia which contains 1 million coordinate pairs and Wikidata which contains almost 2 million coordinate pairs and only 2 thousand shapes. This makes YAGO2geo the richest, in terms of geospatial information, publicly available, open source, knowledge graph.

We draw the new geospatial information from two sources. First, we utilize administrative data taken from official datasets of three countries: the Greek Administrative Geography (GAG) dataset, the administrative divisions dataset for the United Kingdom obtained from Ordnance Survey (OS)[5] and Ordnance Survey Northern Ireland (OSNI)[6], and the administrative division datasets of the Republic of Ireland obtained from Ordnance Survey Ireland (OSI)[7]. To obtain the geometries of administrative divisions of countries of the whole world, we also utilized the latest (2018) version of the Global Administrative Areas dataset

[5] https://www.ordnancesurvey.co.uk/.

[6] https://www.nidirect.gov.uk/campaigns/ordnance-survey-of-northern-ireland.

[7] https://www.osi.ie/.

(GADM)[8]. We also introduce to YAGO2geo geospatial information from the biggest volunteered, crowdsourced and open dataset with geospatial information, OpenStreetMap (OSM)[9].

While introducing more precise geospatial information to YAGO2, we follow the following methodology. If the geoentity we enrich is already in YAGO2, we augment its geospatial information by defining its geometry more precisely (e.g., by a multipolygon for a city which we take from GADM, as opposed to a latitude/longitude pair that exists in YAGO2). We also keep the existing information (e.g., the old coordinate pair that gave the center of the city). Interested practitioners can use our methodology to enrich YAGO2geo with even more geospatial information (e.g., administrative divisions of their own country from official datasets, the European land cover and land use dataset CORINE[10] etc.).

We make a detailed comparison of the geospatial information available from YAGO2 and the geospatial information in OSM and the administrative datasets GAG, OS, OSNI, OSI and GADM.

We make YAGO2geo available publicly at http://yago2geo.di.uoa.gr. The free and open dataset there includes the extended KG encoded in RDF. The geospatial information follows the standards of the Open Geospatial Consortium, hence YAGO2geo can be queried using GeoSPARQL.

The rest of this paper is structured as follows. Section 2 discusses related works. Section 3 gives detailed information about the data sources that were used in order to extend YAGO2 with geospatial information. Sections 4 and 5 present the methodology that we followed and demonstrate the knowledge in YAGO2geo with examples. Last, in Sect. 6 we summarize our contributions, present our conclusions and discuss future work.

2 Related Work

In this section we discuss in some detail which of the existing well-known KGs contain geospatial and temporal knowledge. In GIS terminology which we often follow in this paper, a *geographic feature* (or simply feature) is an abstraction of a real world phenomenon and can have various attributes that describe its *thematic* and *spatial* characteristics. For example, the country Greece is a feature, its name and population are thematic attributes, while its location on Earth, in terms of polar coordinates, is a spatial attribute. Knowledge about the spatial attributes of a feature can be *quantitative* or *qualitative*. Quantitative geographic knowledge is usually represented using *geometries* (e.g., points, lines and polygons on the Cartesian plane) while qualitative geographic knowledge is captured by *qualitative binary relations* between the geometries of features (e.g., Greece is south of Bulgaria).

DBpedia, like YAGO2, contains latitude and longitude pairs for the center of cities, towns etc. extracted from Wikipedia. There are 1 million coordinate pairs

[8] https://gadm.org/.
[9] https://www.openstreetmap.org/.
[10] https://land.copernicus.eu/pan-european/corine-land-cover.

available in DBpedia. In addition, DBpedia contains knowledge about some thematic attributes that can be used to infer knowledge about spatial attributes of features. For example, for each country, the neighboring countries are given, or for each city, the country to which the city belongs is given. In this way, one can infer knowledge about the corresponding geospatial attributes of features e.g., "the geometry of Greece externally connects with the geometry of Bulgaria" using the vocabulary of Region Connection Calculus RCC-8 [14]. Recently, DBpedia has been attempting to add cardinal direction knowledge (e.g., Athens is north of Crete) via properties `dbp:north`, etc.

Grütter et al. in [5] carried out an extensive evaluation of topological relations found in DBpedia and GeoNames about the administrative divisions of Switzerland and Scotland. The authors present two different approaches for the evaluation of the topological relations: the *single dataset approach* and the *interlinked datasets approach*. In the first case, the topological relations of DBpedia are evaluated. In the second case, the topological relations of GeoNames are evaluated, which can be obtained from the `owl:sameAs` links that exist between the entities of DBpedia and GeoNames. The results of their work show that the values of recall and precision are relatively high when DBpedia is queried via GeoNames (i.e., in the second approach) and the links between these two sources are replaced by manually created links, that the authors created based on their expertise on Swiss and Scottish administrative divisions. In the case of Scotland, these values are really low when only the information of DBpedia is used or DBpedia is queried via the original links of GeoNames.

Wikidata [18], is an open and free knowledge graph and the successor of Freebase [3]. It is an activity of the Wikimedia foundation and it is used to serve many other projects of Wikimedia. Wikidata is developed collaboratively by members of its community. The users of Wikidata are able to add new knowledge to the underlying graph but also modify its schema. Wikidata is a multilingual knowledge base, and unlike DBpedia which has different versions for every language, the information of the entities of Wikidata is translated to multiple languages and is part of the same graph. When it comes to quantitative geospatial information, Wikidata provides two data types: `Globe Coordinate` and `Geographic Shape`. The coordinates of an entity can be obtained using the property `coordinate location` for that entity. There are currently over 7 million triples that contain this property (i.e., over 7 million entities for which Wikidata knows their coordinates). The data type `Geographic Shape` has the property `geoshape` which can be used to associate a knowledge graph entity (e.g., the entity for Athens) with a geometry. Geometries in Wikidata are encoded using the GeoJSON format. Currently, Wikidata contains only 2000 geometries which are mostly polygons and multipolygons. Apart from quantitative geospatial information, Wikidata also contains rich topological information, that is represented with various properties, such as `shares border with` and `country`.

Similarly to YAGO2, both DBpedia and Wikidata provide temporal information in the form of dates. One key difference is the fact that YAGO2 has a specific schema for the representation of temporal knowledge, whereas in DBpedia and especially in Wikidata there is a plethora of properties that are used in temporal facts. On the one hand that makes YAGO2 easier to query and to comprehend, but on the other hand Wikidata provides larger amount of temporal information. Moreover, the dates in YAGO2 follow a specific pattern, which is not the case in DBpedia and in Wikidata. Last, time intervals in DBpedia and Wikidata can be represented just like in YAGO2.

Table 1 summarizes the geospatial and temporal information that is currently available in YAGO2, DBpedia and Wikidata. In order to compare the quantity of temporal knowledge, we show the number of birth and death facts that appear in each knowledge base, because they are the most common date facts. We can observe that YAGO2 contains the most coordinate pairs, because of the facts that come from GeoNames. Wikidata also contains a significant amount of geographic points and is the only knowledge base that contains geographic shapes. In addition, it provides more temporal information than DBpedia and YAGO2. Table 1 also stresses out the importance of YAGO2geo, since detailed geographic information (i.e., lines and polygons) is currently very limited.

Table 1. Geospatial and temporal Information in current knowledge graphs.

	DBpedia	Wikidata	YAGO2	YAGO2geo
Coordinates	1M	7.2M	12M	12M
Lines and polygons (shapes)	–	2K	–	137K Linestrings and 640K Polygons and Multipolygons
Date of birth	1.7M	3.5M	1.6M	1.6M
Date of death	721K	1.7M	797K	797K

3 Data Sources

YAGO2geo is built from YAGO2 and new geospatial knowledge from multiple sources. First, we use geographical administrative data provided by official sources of Greece, the United Kingdom and the Republic of Ireland. We also extract geospatial information about the administrative units of every country from the GADM dataset as well as for other types of features, such as lakes, from OpenStreetMap. Apart from the geometries, each data source provides additional information (e.g., population for cities) that we include in YAGO2geo.

The geospatial information about the administrative divisions of Greece that we introduce in YAGO2geo comes from official sources of the Kallikratis law which defines the administrative divisions of Greece in 2011. The administrative divisions of Greece, according to Kallikratis, consist of *decentralized administrations*, *regions*, *regional units*, *municipalities*, *municipal units* and *municipal communities*. The Kallikratis administrative divisions have been defined as linked data and called *Greek Administrative Geography* (GAG) by our group in the past and has been publicly available[11].

Ordnance Survey is the national mapping agency of the United Kingdom. It provides data about the countries of England, Scotland and Wales that form Great Britain. For our purposes we used the Boundary-Line dataset[12], which contains the administrative boundaries of Great Britain. More specifically, we used the information about the following administative divisions: *European regions*, *counties*, *districts and metropolitan districts*, *unitary authorities*, *boroughs*, *wards*, *parishes*, and *communities*.

Ordnance Survey Northern Ireland is the official cartographic agency of Northern Ireland. Users are able to obtain its data using the ONSI Open Data portal[13]. In this work we use the datasets *NI Outline*, *Local Government Districts 2012*, *Wards 2012* and *Townlands*.

The Ordnance Survey Ireland is the national mapping agency of the Republic of Ireland and it provides multiple products and datasets. The authors of [4] transformed the geospatial data about the boundaries of the administrative areas of Ireland into RDF. For the extension of the geospatial information of entities that belong to the Republic of Ireland, we consider the datasets (i.e., administrative areas) *city and county council*, *county council*, *city council*, *municipal district*, *barony*, *parish*, *townland* and *rural area*.

GADM provides geographic data about the administrative divisions of every country in the world. Administrative units are divided into six different layers (i.e., administrative levels `level-0` to `level-5`) and there are over 386,000 administrative areas in total. GADM does not only provide the boundaries of every administrative area, but it also provides additional useful information about them (e.g., administrative division and the upper administrative units). Version 3.6 of GADM was released in May 2018 and for our purposes we transformed the provided shapefiles into RDF using our tool GeoTriples [10]. GADM is a very useful dataset but its web site reveals little about it. For example, which group of people have constructed it, where did they find their data for various countries (e.g., Greece), etc. To the best of our knowledge there are also no studies that evaluate the quality of GADM. However, our experience with this and a previous version of the dataset since 2012 tells us that GADM has very good quality geospatial information (see also Sect. 4.4).

OpenStreetMap is a volunteer project, whose goal is to provide free geographic data and maps to its users. OSM provides geospatial information about multiple features. Such features are natural features (e.g., beaches, lakes, etc.), land use features (e.g., vineyards, etc.), places (e.g., villages, cities, etc.), points of interest, water bodies, waterways and more. We obtained OSM data from Geofabrik[14], which is a company that provides free, regularly-updated extracts

[11] http://linkedopendata.gr/dataset/greek-administrative-geography.
[12] https://www.ordnancesurvey.co.uk/business-and-government/products/boundaryline.html.
[13] http://osni-spatial-ni.opendata.arcgis.com/.
[14] https://www.geofabrik.de/.

of OSM. Geofabrik provides compressed OSM files (osm.pbf) and free shapefiles. After examining both types of files we came to the realization that there are some classes that are not included in the free shapefiles (e.g., airports)[15]. In addition, the OSM files provide every available name of each entity, which is very important in our work. Last, the free shapefiles do not follow the *key-value* schema of OSM. For these reasons, we obtained the necessary information from the compressed OSM files using the tool TripleGeo[16] extended with a plug-in implemented by the second author of this paper.

Note that we have *not* used the OSM data provided by the LinkedGeoData [15] project which was the first attempt to make OSM data available on the web as linked data. The OSM data currently on the LinkedGeoData web site are *not* the most recent and they are not maintained actively, to the best of our knowledge. Thus, Geofabrik was the best portal available to obtain OSM data.

4 The Knowledge Graph YAGO2geo

The main goal of this work is to extend the YAGO2 knowledge graph with detailed geospatial information without duplicating existing knowledge. To ensure that, we try to match geoentities of YAGO2 with entities of the data sources that we have presented in Sect. 3. For example, the resource `geoentity_Hellenic_Republic_390903` and the entity with identifier `GRC` represent Greece in YAGO2 and GADM respectively. Therefore they should be declared to be identical using an `owl:sameAs` triple. The matching phase for identifying identical entities consists of applying two filters: (i) the label similarity filter and (ii) the geometry distance filter. Our methodology is based on the methodology that was used in YAGO2 when integrating information from GeoNames [7]. A similar approach has been used in LinkedGeoData [15].

The first filter of the matching phase is the *label similarity filter*. It produces matches between the geoentities of YAGO2 and the entities of the specified data source (e.g., GADM) that have similar names. For this purpose we experimented with the Levenshtein distance [11] and also the Jaro-Winkler similarity [8] and found out that, for our task, the latter produces more matches while maintaining high precision. In order for two resources to be matched, the similarity between their labels must be higher than a specific threshold, which we have set at 0.82. We examine every label of each entity, without considering its language tag like in [15]. Here, an entity of YAGO2 can be matched with multiple entities.

After the label similarity fitler is completed, we apply the geometry distance filter. The *geometry distance filter* is applied on the matches that were produced by the first filter and its goal is to eliminate any false matches. Since there are many geographic entities that share the same name (e.g., Athens, Greece and Athens, Alabama), the geometry distance filter is also a disambiguation step. The geometry distance filter checks if the Euclidean distance in the WGS:84

[15] http://www.geofabrik.de/data/geofabrik-osm-gis-standard-0.7.pdf (Sect. 8.3).

[16] https://github.com/SLIPO-EU/TripleGeo.

Table 2. Greece: results of the matching phase

GAG	YAGO2	# Matches	Precision
decentralized administration	administrative_division	6/7	1.000
region	first-order	11/13	1.000
regional unit	administrative_division	21/74	1.000
municipality	third-order	325/325	1.000
municipal unit and community	populated_place and locality	530/1037	0.907

coordinate system[17] between the geometry provided by GADM, OSM, or an official country data source and the point provided by YAGO2 is smaller than a specific threshold, which is set at 0.2°. In case there are multiple entities of YAGO2 that are matched with the same resource, we keep the entity that is closest, in terms of distance, to that resource.

The number of matches produced by the two filters presented above is typically very large and, consequently, it is not possible to manually check if every match is correct. As a solution to this problem, we randomly selected a subset of the matches[18] and manually check if these matches are correct, by checking the label of the matched resources. This methodology has also been used in [7,15].

Let us now apply the matching methodology we just discussed to the problem of matching geoentities from YAGO2 and entities from each data source.

4.1 Greece: GAG Dataset

In this section, we try to find matches between the entities of GAG and the geoentities of YAGO2. To achieve this, we carry out the matching phase on pairs of official administrative divisions (Sect. 3) and classes of YAGO2, as shown in Table 2. More specifically, the decentralized administrations and few regional units are instances of the class `geoclass_administrative_division`. The regions of Greece are matched with the geoentities of YAGO2 that are instances of the class `geoclass_first-order_administrative_division`. The second administrative level of YAGO2 does not appear in the results because it contains *prefectures*. Prefectures are no longer an administrative division in Greece and in the Kallikratis law they are replaced by regional units. Greek municipalities are found in the third administrative level of YAGO2. Last, since municipal units and communities are not found in the administrative levels of YAGO2, we try to match them with `populated places` and `localities`.

Table 2 summarizes our results. The number of administrative units that are found in each division of GAG is shown on the third column. The third column also presents the number of matches we were able to generate, whereas

[17] A *coordinate reference system* (CRS) is a coordinate system that is related to an object (e.g., the Earth, a planar projection of the Earth) through a so-called datum which specifies its origin, scale, and orientation. WGS84 is the latest version of the *World Geodetic System* (WGS) and was established in 1984.

[18] For each matching phase we evaluate $max\{300, \#matches * 0.01\}$ matches.

Table 3. United Kingdom: results of the matching phase

YAGO2, UK	(# Entities)	OS and OSNI	# Matches	Precision
first-order	(4)	euro. region	2	1,000
second-order	(185)	counties, unitary auth. metr. districts and boroughs	182	0,953
third-order	(3852)	unitary auth., districts boroughs,wards and parishes	3718	0,933
fourth-order	(7717)	wards, parishes and communities	7642	0,913
populated_place and locality	(15719)	wards, parishes, communties and townlands	1272	0,897

the fourth column shows the quality of the generated matches (i.e., the recall and precision of the matching phase). For the case of Greece we evaluated every match manually. The results show that our methodology was able to match perfectly the majority of the decentralized administrations and regions, that passed the label similarity filter, and all municipalities of GAG. The class `geoclass_administrative_division` of YAGO2 contains 21 Greek regional units and we matched all of them. Here, we have to mention that we found some regional units in the second level of YAGO2, which however are labeled as prefectures. For this reason, we were not able to match them. Regarding the municipal units and communities, even though the precision is not high, it is very satisfying. As we have explained already, not only we extended matched geoentities of YAGO2, but we also include in YAGO2geo all unmatched entities of GAG.

4.2 United Kingdom: OS and OSNI Datasets

The data that is provided by OS and OSNI is used to enrich the geoentities of YAGO2 that belong to the UK with official geospatial information. The countries of the UK are instances of the class `geoclass_first-order_administrative_division` of YAGO2. Counties, metropolitan districts, unitary authorities and the Greater London authority are found in the second administrative level of YAGO2. The third level of YAGO2 has entities that are communities, civil parishes, districts, London boroughs, metropolitan district wards or unitary authority wards. Communities and civil parishes are also found in the fourth administrative level of YAGO2, which also contains district wards.

The results (Table 3) show that we were able to match most of the geoentities of the UK that are found in the administrative levels of YAGO2. In order to match more entities of OS and OSNI, we carried out the matching phase using the class `geoclass_populated_place` of YAGO2. We can also observe that the quality of the produced matches across all classes of YAGO2 is really high. In the majority of the false matches we have entities of the official datasets that contained words such as *North* and *Lower*, and entities of YAGO2 that did not contain these words in their labels (e.g., Carryduff East of OSNI is matched with Carryduff of YAGO2 and Carryduff West of OSNI remains unmatched). There are many entities of OS and OSNI that are not matched. We extended matched geoentities and introduced unmatched entities to YAGO2.

4.3 Republic of Ireland: OSI Dataset

Even though the provinces of Ireland (i.e., Ulster, Connach, Leinster and Munster) are no longer considered as administrative units, they can be found in the first administrative level of YAGO2. Irish city and county councils, county councils and city councils are instances of the class `geoclass_second_order_administrative_division` of YAGO2. The remaining administrative levels of YAGO2 do not contain any Irish entities. Like in the case of the UK, we try to match entities of OSI with `populated places` and `localities` of YAGO2.

Table 4. Republic of Ireland: results of the matching phase

YAGO2, Ireland	(# Entities)	OSI	# Matches	Precision
first-order	(4)	–	0	–
second-order	(31)	councils	31	1,000
populated_placeand locality	(13175)	baronies, parishes, townlands and rural areas	7193	0,786

Table 5. GADM: results of the matching phase

YAGO2	(# Entities)	GADM	(# entities)	# Matches	Precision
countries	(233)	level-0	(256)	221	1.000
first-order	(3958)	level-1	(3610)	3127	0.987
second-order	(44554)	level-2	(45958)	31632	0.974
third-order	(121648)	level-3	(144608)	47579	0.972
fourth-order	(124729)	level-4	(137983)	46511	0.952
fifth-order	(51112)	level-5	(51427)	14	0.571

Since provinces are no longer administrative units, we have zero matches in the first administrative level of YAGO2. In the second level we were able to match all councils. Regarding the remaining administrative divisions of Ireland (Sect. 3), we were not able to match any municipal districts, but we were able to match almost half of the baronies, parishes and rural areas. There are over 50000 townlands provided by OSI and we matched almost 7000. Table 4 shows the number of geoentities of YAGO2 that were matched.

4.4 GADM

Here we present the results of the matching phase between YAGO2 and GADM. Similalry to the previous cases, we manually align the classes of YAGO2 and the administrative levels of GADM, as shown in Table 5. The classes `geoclass_independent_political_entity`, `geoclass_dependent_political_entity` and `geoclass_semi-independent_political_entity` of YAGO2 contain countries and are combined together in order to be matched with the administrative `level-0` of GADM, that also contains countries.

The results of the matching phase between YAGO2 and GADM (Table 5) show that the precision of the generated matches, in most administrative levels, is really high. We also observe that at higher administrative levels the number of matches is close to the number of geoentities that exist in YAGO2. At lower levels the percentage of the geoentities that were matched drops.

After examining both YAGO2 and GADM and also the results of the matching phase, we see that each data source has its own view of the administrative hierarchies of a country. We also conjecture that these views might not fully reflect the current administrative situation of a country, especially a small one or one where the administrative divisions were reorganized recently. Let us consider the example of Greece with which we are very familiar and for which both properties hold (it is a small country and its latest administrative reorganization was done in 2011). As we have already mentioned in Sect. 4.1, municipal units and communities are not found in the administrative levels of YAGO2. The second level of YAGO2 contains some outdated information (i.e., prefectures) and some regional units that are not labeled properly. GADM does not provide information about the municipal units and communities, like YAGO2. In addition it does not contain the level of the regional units. Moreover, the Greek entities that are instances of *geoclass_first-order_administrative_division* of YAGO2 (i.e., regions), are found in the second administrative level of GADM. The first level of GADM contains (correctly) decentralized administrations.

We also closely examined the information provided by YAGO2 and GADM about German administrative units. We observed that the units that belong in the third administrative level of YAGO2 are found in the second level of GADM. On the other hand, both sources have almost the same German administrative units in the first and fourth levels and we were able to match almost all of them.

The results of the fifth administrative level are not satisfying, due to the fact that GADM contains only French and Rwandan administrative units in this level. That is not the case with YAGO2, which contains only a few entities that belong to France and Rwanda. Furthermore, French entities that are found in both YAGO2 and GADM (e.g., arrondissements of Paris) are not matched because the provided labels are not similar enough.

In YAGO2geo matched geoentities of YAGO2 are extended with information that is provided by GADM. The information GADM provides for Greece and the UK, even though it is missing administrative units, is of high quality. For that reason, we chose to bring into YAGO2geo unmatched entities of GADM.

4.5 OpenStreetMap

OpenStreetMap has geospatial information for many types of features, such as natural features (e.g, rivers, lakes, etc.) and man-made features (e.g., airports, restaurants, bars, etc.). For YAGO2geo, we focus on features that have a *permanent location.* The majority of these entities are features of nature (e.g, water bodies, waterways, etc.), but we also take into consideration other types as well, such as cities and islands. In Table 6 the groups of features, that are used in order to extend YAGO2, are shown. The group `natural` contains types of water bodies (i.e., lakes, reservoirs and lagoons), as well as beaches and bays. Streams and canals are part of the group `waterways`, whereas `landuse and leisure` consists of forests, parks and nature reserves. Last but not least, `places` contains islands, cities, villages and towns. The types of these groups are manually matched with the classes that are available in YAGO2. For example, forests of OSM are matched with forests (e.g., `geoclass_forest`) that are found in YAGO2, whereas cities, towns and villages are matched with populated places.

Table 6. OpenStreetMap: results of the matching phase

OSM groups	# OSM entities	# YAGO2 entities	# Matches	Precision
natural	138640	437209	37447	0.957
waterways	1927776	1132239	137523	0.947
landuse and leisure	527403	131863	37502	0.963
places	189554	4674127	98444	0.952

Regarding the results of the matching phase, Table 6 shows that the quantity of matches is relatively low compared to the number of entities provided by both data sources. There are two reasons that led to this situation. Firstly, as we already mentioned in Sect. 3, OSM is a volunteered, crowdsourced project, which means that it may contain noisy data. Such data ultimately do not contribute to our cause. Secondly, the labels for the majority of the entities of OSM are not available in multiple languages and in most cases they are written in the language of the country that they belong to. This problem affects our results negatively, even though YAGO2 provides the names of many geoentities in multiple languages. We could have produced more matches if we have used looser constraints in our filters but that would have had a negative impact on the quality of our results. Our main goal is to bring information of high quality to the YAGO2 knowledge graph and the results show that, regardless of the groups and the number of produced matches, the quality is always high. Since OSM contains noisy data we chose, unlike the case of GADM, to *only extend matched geoentities* and not bring unmatched entities to the knowledge graph.

4.6 Wikipedia and GeoNames

The geospatial information that already exists in YAGO2, as we have already mentioned, comes from Wikipedia and GeoNames. In this section we present the impact that both sources had during the matching phase. For each individual case, we count the number of matched geoentities of YAGO2 that come from Wikipedia as well as the number of geoentities that come from GeoNames.

The results are shown in Fig. 1. In the case of GADM, we see that both Wikipedia and GeoNames have almost equal contribution to the produced matches. In the case of OpenStreetMap, over 90% of the matched geoentities come from GeoNames. Table 6 shows that most matches come from waterways and places. This means that Wikipedia does not contain enough information about these features. Consequently, information about these features found in YAGO2 was extracted from GeoNames. More specifically, the cities, villages and towns of OpenStreetMap are matched with the populated places of YAGO2. This agrees with the findings of [1] that states that most features of GeoNames are populated places and that streams are one of the most common natural features. This also explains the results we have for OSI and OSNI, since the majority of their entities are matched with populated places. Last, we see that in the cases of GAG and OS, that most entities come from Wikipedia. It seems that Wikipedia provides rich information about the administrative units that belong to higher administrative levels for both Greece and Great Britain.

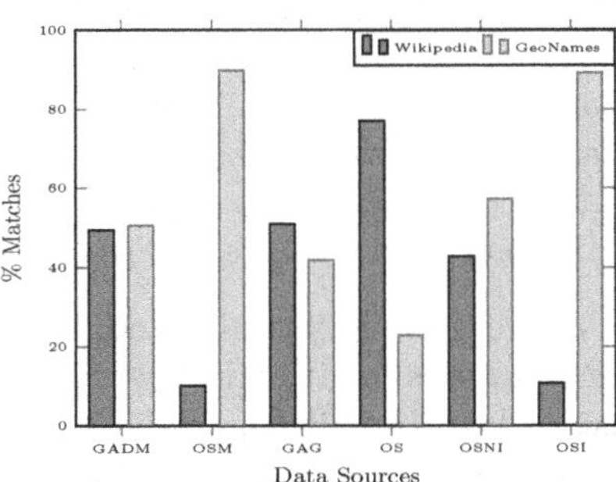

Fig. 1. The comparison between Wikipedia and GeoNames knowledge in YAGO2

5 The Geospatial Knowledge in YAGO2geo

YAGO2geo is publicly available[19] at http://yago2geo.di.uoa.gr and its knowledge can be queried using GeoSPARQL[20] and can be visualised using the linked spatiotemporal data visualization tool Sextant[21]. Currently YAGO2geo is curated and used by our research group only but we expect other groups to use it once this paper is published.

YAGO2geo is structured as follows. For each official data source and GADM, we provide a file that contains the matched geoentities of YAGO2 extended with new knowledge and a file that contains the new entities of YAGO2geo. For the official datasets we also provide the topological relations between the administrative units that can be inferred by the geometric knowledge. For OSM, we only provide a file that contains extended geoentities of YAGO2. Last, for each data source we provide the generated matches and the new ontology.

This section discusses how YAGO2geo is enriched with new geospatial knowledge. We present a detailed example for the case of Greece and the GAG dataset. As we already discussed in Sect. 4, we follow the following uniqueness principle. For every geoentity g of YAGO2, only entities g', which are different than g and are not already in YAGO2 are introduced in YAGO2geo. If a geoentity is already in YAGO2 then its geospatial knowledge is *enriched* in YAGO2geo.

Let us consider the city of Lamia in Central Greece. In YAGO2, we have the following knowledge about Lamia (<geoentity_Dimos_Lamia_8133738>[22]):

1. <geoentity_Dimos_Lamia_8133738> rdfs:label "Dimos Lamia"@eng.
2. <geoentity_Dimos_Lamia_8133738> <hasLatitude> "38.86649"^^<degrees>.
3. <geoentity_Dimos_Lamia_8133738> <hasLongitude> "22.36735"^^<degrees>.
4. <geoentity_Dimos_Lamia_8133738> rdfs:label "Lamia".
5. <geoentity_Dimos_Lamia_8133738> rdfs:label "Lamieon".
6. <geoentity_Dimos_Lamia_8133738> rdfs:label "Λαμιέων".
7. <geoentity_Dimos_Lamia_8133738> <isLocatedIn> <Phthiotis> .
8. <geoentity_Dimos_Lamia_8133738> rdf:type <geoclass_third-order_administrative_division> .

The triples 2 and 3 above give us latitude and longitude of the center of Lamia. Lamia is part of Phthiotis (<Phthiotis>), which is a prefecture of the former administrative divisions law Kapodistrias which preceded Kallikratis. This knowledge is encoded by an isLocatedIn relation, as shown in triple 7. Lamia includes the municipal units of Lamia, Gorgopotamos, Leianokladi, Pavliani and Ypati. In the Kapodistrias law, these units were previously municipalities themselves, but, since 2011, according to the Kallikratis law, they are no longer municipalities and they all belong to the municipality of Lamia. As it is expected,

[19] Published under the license found at https://creativecommons.org/licenses/by/4.0/.
[20] http://test.strabon.di.uoa.gr/yago2geo.
[21] http://test.strabon.di.uoa.gr/SextantOL3/?mapid=m95dp4hsgkafoe40_.
[22] Dimos comes from "Δήμος" which means municipality in Greek.

although YAGO2 contains these toponyms (`<Gorgopotamos>`, `<Leianokladi>`, `<Pavliani>` and `<Ypati>`), we do not have any `isLocatedIn` relations between these four municipal units and Lamia.

Figure 2 shows how the class hierarchy of YAGO2geo is extended with the GeoSPARQL ontology[23] and the ontology of GAG so that the geospatial knowledge extracted from the GAG dataset can be represented. Similar additions to the YAGO2geo class hierarchy have been done for OS, OSNI, OSI, GADM and OSM, but they are not shown here due to space.

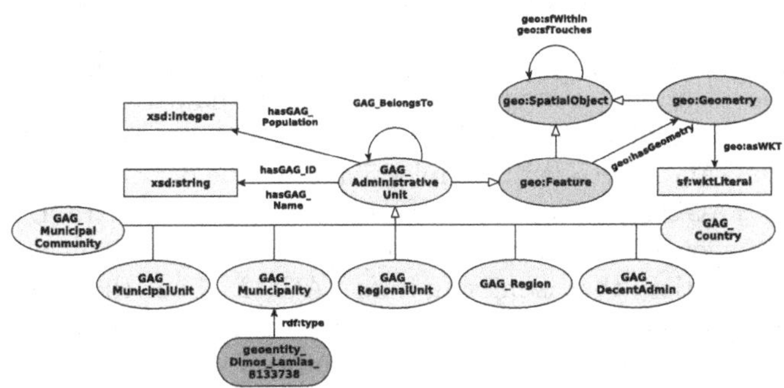

Fig. 2. The ontology of YAGO2geo: GAG part

As shown in Fig. 2, a geoentity, like Lamia, becomes a GeoSPARQL feature (white arrows denote the `rdfs:subclassOf` property) and it is also associated with a geometry (see triples 5 and 6 below). This matched entity is extended with geospatial knowledge and also with additional knowledge provided by the GAG dataset. Here, we enrich the geoentity municipality of Lamia with its population, its identifier in the GAG dataset, its administrative division and its official name. This knowledge is encoded in YAGO2geo with the following triples:

1. `<geoentity_Dimos_Lamia_8133738> y2geo:hasGAG_Populaton "71693"^^xsd:integer.`
2. `<geoentity_Dimos_Lamia_8133738> y2geo:hasGAG_Name "ΔΗΜΟΣ ΛΑΜΙΕΩΝ".`
3. `<geoentity_Dimos_Lamia_8133738> y2geo:hasGAG_ID "9160".`
4. `<geoentity_Dimos_Lamia_8133738> rdf:type y2geo:GAG_Municipality.`
5. `<geoentity_Dimos_Lamia_8133738> geo:hasGeometry y2geo:Geometry_GAG_9160.`
6. `y2geo:Geometry_GAG_9160 geo:asWKT "MULTIPOLYGON(((...)))" .`
7. `<geoentity_Dimos_Lamia_8133738> geo:sfWithin y2geo:gagentity_804.`
8. `<geoentity_Dimos_Lamia_8133738> geo:sfTouches <Amfikleia-Elateia>.`

[23] We do not show the complete GeoSPARQL ontology due to space.

9. <geoentity_Dimos_Lamia_8133738> y2geo:GAG_BelongsTo y2geo:gagsentity_804.
10. y2geo:gagentity_916001 y2geo:GAG_BelongsTo <geoentity_Dimos_Lamia_8133738>.
11. <Gorgopotamos> y2geo:GAG_BelongsTo <geoentity_Dimos_Lamia_8133738>.
12. <Leianokladi> y2geo:GAG_BelongsTo <geoentity_Dimos_Lamia_8133738>.
13. <Pavliani> y2geo:GAG_BelongsTo <geoentity_Dimos_Lamia_8133738>.
14. <Ypati> y2geo:GAG_BelongsTo <geoentity_Dimos_Lamia_8133738>.

Triples 1, 2 and 3 contain thematic attributes (i.e., the population, the official name and the identifier) extracted from the GAG dataset. Triple 4 gives us the administrative division to which Lamia belongs. The geospatial knowledge obtained from GAG is encoded by triples 5 and 6. The detailed geometries that we bring into YAGO2geo allow us to make use of the GeoSPARQL topological vocabulary, as shown in the triples 7 and 8 above. The last four triples above model the information, that is missing from YAGO2, about the municipal units that are part of Lamia. The property GAG_BelongsTo is crucial, because the geometries of the municipal units and communities are not available in GAG, hence we are not able to generate topological relations that involve municipal units and communities. Last, triples 8 and 14 show entities (the regional unit of Pthiotis and the municipal unit of Lamia respectively) that are not part of YAGO2 and are created from unmatched entities of the GAG dataset. Extended and new entities of YAGO2geo follow the same schema.

6 Summary and Future Work

In this work we presented YAGO2geo, an extension of YAGO2 with precise geospatial knowledge. The new geospatial knowledge comes from official sources (e.g., Ordnance Survey), open source projects (e.g., GADM) and volunteer data sources (e.g., OSM). We expect that other users of YAGO2geo will want to add administrative divisions of their countries or other geospatial data (e.g., Natura 2000 areas, etc.) to the KG. Sections 4 and 5 will serve to guide these users.

In future work we plan to show how to model geospatial data that changes over time in YAGO2geo (e.g., evolution of administrative areas). For this purpose, we will extend the temporal dimension of YAGO2 with official data. Last, we will develop a geospatial question answering system on top of YAGO2geo.

Acknowledgments. We acknowledge the comments of G. Weikum, J. Hoffart and F. Suchanek on YAGO2geo. Part of this work was done while the third author was visiting Max Planck Institute for Informatics, Saarbrücken.

References

1. Acheson, E., Sabbata, S.D., Purves, R.S.: A quantitative analysis of global gazetteers: patterns of coverage for common feature types. Comput. Environ. Urban Syst. **64**, 309–320 (2017)
2. Ahlers, D.: Assessment of the accuracy of GeoNames gazetteer data. In: GIR (2013)
3. Bollacker, K., Evans, C., Paritosh, P., Sturge, T., Taylor, J.: Freebase: a collaboratively created graph database for structuring human knowledge. In: SIGMOD (2008)
4. Debruyne, C., et al.: Ireland's authoritative geospatial linked data. In: d'Amato, C., et al. (eds.) ISWC 2017. LNCS, vol. 10588, pp. 66–74. Springer, Cham (2017). https://doi.org/10.1007/978-3-319-68204-4_6
5. Grütter, R., Purves, R.S., Wotruba, L.: Evaluating topological queries in linked data using DBpedia and GeoNames in Switzerland and Scotland. Trans. GIS **21**(1), 114–133 (2017)
6. Hoffart, J., Suchanek, F.M., Berberich, K., Lewis-Kelham, E., de Melo, G., Weikum, G.: YAGO2: exploring and querying world knowledge in time, space, context, and many languages. In: WWW (2011)
7. Hoffart, J., Suchanek, F.M., Berberich, K., Weikum, G.: YAGO2: a spatially and temporally enhanced knowledge base from Wikipedia. Artif. Intell. **194**, 28–61 (2013)
8. Jaro, M.A.: Probabilistic linkage of large public health data files. Stat. Med. **14**(5–7), 491–498 (1995)
9. Jia, Z., Abujabal, A., Roy, R.S., Strötgen, J., Weikum, G.: TEQUILA: temporal question answering over knowledge bases. In: CIKM (2018)
10. Kyzirakos, K., et al.: Geotriples: transforming geospatial data into RDF graphs using R2RML and RML mappings. J. Web Semant. **52–53**, 16–32 (2018)
11. Levenshtein, V.I.: Binary codes capable of correcting deletions, insertions, and reversals. In: Soviet Physics Doklady, vol. 10 (1966)
12. Mahdisoltani, F., Biega, J., Suchanek, F.M.: YAGO3: a knowledge base from multilingual Wikipedias. In: CIDR (2015)
13. Miller, G.A.: WordNet: a lexical database for English. Commun. ACM **38**(11), 39–41 (1995)
14. Randell, D.A., Cui, Z., Cohn, A.G.: A spatial logic based on regions and connection. In: KR (1992)
15. Stadler, C., Lehmann, J., Höffner, K., Auer, S.: LinkedGeoData: a core for a web of spatial open data. Semant. Web J. **3**(4), 333–354 (2012)
16. Suchanek, F.M., Kasneci, G., Weikum, G.: Yago: a core of semantic knowledge. In: WWW (2007)
17. Suchanek, F.M., Kasneci, G., Weikum, G.: YAGO: a large ontology from Wikipedia and WordNet. J. Web Semant. **6**(3), 203–217 (2008)
18. Tanon, T.P., Vrandecic, D., Schaffert, S., Steiner, T., Pintscher, L.: From freebase to Wikidata: the great migration. In: WWW (2016)

The SEPSES Knowledge Graph: An Integrated Resource for Cybersecurity

Elmar Kiesling[1(✉)], Andreas Ekelhart[1,2], Kabul Kurniawan[1,3], and Fajar Ekaputra[1,4]

[1] TU Wien, Favoritenstraße 9-11, Vienna, Austria
elmar.kiesling@tuwien.ac.at
[2] SBA Research, Favoritenstraße 16, Vienna, Austria
[3] University of Vienna, Währingerstraße 29, Vienna, Austria
[4] CDL-SQI - TU Wien, Favoritenstraße 9-11, Vienna, Austria

Abstract. This paper introduces an evolving cybersecurity knowledge graph that integrates and links critical information on real-world vulnerabilities, weaknesses and attack patterns from various publicly available sources. Cybersecurity constitutes a particularly interesting domain for the development of a domain-specific public knowledge graph, particularly due to its highly dynamic landscape characterized by time-critical, dispersed, and heterogeneous information. To build and continually maintain a knowledge graph, we provide and describe an integrated set of resources, including vocabularies derived from well-established standards in the cybersecurity domain, an ETL workflow that updates the knowledge graph as new information becomes available, and a set of services that provide integrated access through multiple interfaces. The resulting semantic resource offers comprehensive and integrated up-to-date instance information to security researchers and professionals alike. Furthermore, it can be easily linked to locally available information, as we demonstrate by means of two use cases in the context of vulnerability assessment and intrusion detection.

Keywords: Knowledge graph · Cybersecurity · Security vocabularies · Security standards · Security analysis · Intrusion detection

1 Introduction

Security and privacy have become key issues in today's modern societies characterized by a strong dependence on Information and Communication Technologies (ICT). Security incidents, such as ransomware and data theft, are widely reported in the media and illustrate the ongoing struggle to protect ICT systems. In their mission to secure systems, security professionals rely on a wealth of information such as known and newly identified vulnerabilities, weaknesses,

C. Ghidini et al. (Eds.): ISWC 2019, LNCS 11779, pp. 198–214, 2019.
https://doi.org/10.1007/978-3-030-30796-7_13

threats, and attack patterns. Such information is collected and published by, e.g., Computer Emergency Response Teams (CERTs), research institutions, government agencies, and industry experts. Whereas a lot of relevant information is still shared informally as text, initiatives to make security information available in well-defined structured formats, largely driven by MITRE[1] and NIST[2], have made significant progress and resulted in a wide range of standards [1]. These standards define high-level schemas for cybersecurity information and have resulted in various structured lists that are available for browsing on the web and for download in heterogeneous structured formats. This wealth of cybersecurity data is highly useful, but the current approach for sharing it is associated with several limitations: First, individual entities and data sets remain isolated and cannot easily be referenced and linked from other data sets. Second, whereas the governed schemas provide a well-defined structure, the semantics are not as well-defined. This limits the potential for integration and automated machine interpretation. Consequently, the resulting abundance of data raises challenges for security analysts and professionals who have to keep track of all the available sources and identify relevant information within them.

In this paper, we propose that integrating cybersecurity information into a regularly updated, public knowledge graph can overcome these limitations and open up exciting opportunities for cybersecurity research and practice. Thereby, it is possible not only to query public cybersecurity information, but also to use it to contextualize local information. As we illustrate with two example use cases in this paper, this facilitates applications such as *(i)* improved vulnerability assessment by automatically determining which new vulnerabilities affect a given infrastructure, and *(ii)* improved incident response through better contextualization of intrusion detection alerts.

Our main contributions can be summarized as follows: For cybersecurity research and practice, we advance the state of the art by providing an integrated up-to-date view on cybersecurity knowledge in a semantically explicit representation. Furthermore, we provide tools and services to query and make use of this interlinked knowledge graph. From a semantic web research perspective, we illustrate how Linked Data principles can be applied to combine local and public knowledge in a highly dynamic environment characterized by fast-changing, dispersed, and heterogeneous information. To this end, we develop an ETL pipeline that integrates newly available structured data from public sources into the knowledge graph, which involves acquisition, extraction, lifting, linking, and validation steps. We provide the following resources[3]: *(i)* vocabularies for the rich representation and interlinking of security-related information based on five well-established standards in the cybersecurity domain. *(ii)* a comprehensive SEPSES Cybersecurity Knowledge Graph (KG)[4] with detailed instance data[5]

[1] https://www.mitre.org.
[2] https://nist.gov.
[3] Available at https://w3id.org/sepses/cyber-kg.
[4] *Semantic Processing of Security Event Streams* is an ongoing research project.
[5] 36,594,388 triples as of July 2, 2019.

accessible through multiple interfaces. *(iii)* an ETL workflow published as open source that updates the knowledge graph as new information becomes available. *(iv)* a website[6] that provides documentation, status information, and pointers to the various access mechanisms provided. *(v)* a set of services to access the data, i.e., a SPARQL endpoint, a triple pattern fragments interface, a Linked Data interface, and download options for the whole data set as well as various subsets.

This semantic approach can provide a foundation for tools and services that support security analysts in applying external security knowledge and efficiently navigating dynamic security information. Ultimately, this should contribute towards improved cybersecurity knowledge sharing and increased situational awareness, both in large organizations that have dedicated security experts who are often overwhelmed by the large amount of information, and in smaller organizations that do not have the resources to invest in specialized tools and experts.

The remainder of this paper is organized as follows: Sect. 2 provides an overview of related work; Sect. 3 covers construction and maintenance of the KG, including vocabularies, data acquisition mechanisms, and updating pipelines; Sect. 4 provides an overview of the provided mechanisms to access the data in the KG and discusses its sustainability, maintenance and extensibility; Sect. 5 illustrates the usefulness of the resource by means of two example use cases; Sect. 6 concludes the paper with an outlook on future work.

2 Related Work

Various information security standards, taxonomies, vocabularies, and ontologies have been developed in academia, industry, and government agencies. In this section, we review these lines of related work, which fall into two broad categories: *(i)* standard data schemas for information sharing in the cybersecurity domain (covered in Sect. 2.1) and *(ii)* higher-level conceptualizations of security knowledge (covered in Sect. 2.2). We conclude the section by identifying the gap between those strands of work.

2.1 Standard Data Schemas

Efficient information exchange requires common standards, particularly in highly diverse and dynamic domains such as cybersecurity. Hence, a set of standards has emerged that define the syntax of description languages for structured cybersecurity information and the semantics associated with those descriptions in natural language. Some of these standards are driven by traditional standardization bodies such as ISO, ITU, IEEE or IETF. The majority, however, are contributed by open source communities or other entities such as MITRE[7], a not-for-profit research and development cooperation.[8]

---

[6] https://sepses.ifs.tuwien.ac.at.

[7] https://www.mitre.org.

[8] For a review of standards for the exchange of security information, cf. [1].

Salient examples for information sharing standards, all of which are integrated in the knowledge graph presented in this paper, include Common Vulnerabilities and Exposures (CVE)[9] for publicly known vulnerabilities, Common Attack Pattern Enumeration and Classification (CAPEC)[10] for known attack patterns used by adversaries, Common Weakness Enumeration (CWE)[11] for software security weaknesses, Common Platform Enumeration (CPE)[12] for encoding names of IT products and platforms, and Common Vulnerability Scoring System (CVSS)[13] for vulnerability scoring. These standards are widely used by security practitioners and integrated into security products and services, but they also serve as an important point of reference for research.

2.2 Security Ontologies

A related line of academic research aims at a high-level conceptualization of information security knowledge, which has resulted in numerous ontologies (e.g., [2,3,6,7,10,11,15]) that typically revolve around core concepts such as *asset*, *threat*, *vulnerability*, and *countermeasure*. The resulting security ontologies are typically scoped for particular application domains (e.g., risk management, incident management). The high-level ontology developed in [8], for instance, mainly focuses on malware and aspects such as *actors*, *victims*, *infrastructure*, and *capabilities*. The authors argue that expressive semantic models are crucial for complex security applications and name Open Vulnerability and Assessment Language (OVAL), CPE, Common Configuration Enumeration (CCE), and CVE as the most promising starting points for the development of a cybersecurity ontology. Inspired by that work, Oltramari et al. [9] introduce an ontological cyber security framework that comprises a top-level ontology based on DOLCE, a mid-level ontology with security concepts (e.g., *threat*, *attacker*, *vulnerability*, *countermeasure*), and a domain ontology of cyber operations including defensive and offensive actions. A comprehensive survey and classification of similar security ontologies can be found in [12].

More recently, various initiatives aimed at developing security ontologies that cover the standard schemas outlined in Sect. 2.1, including an ontology for CVE vulnerabilities [4,16,17] that can be used to identify vulnerable IT products. Ulicny et al. [14] take advantage of existing standards and markup languages such as Structured Threat Information eXpression (STIX), CAPEC, CVE and CybOX and transform their respective XML schemas through XSLT translators and custom code into a Web Ontology Language (OWL) ontology. Furthermore, they integrate external information, e.g., on persons, groups and organizations, IP addresses (WhoIs records), geographic entities (GeoNames), and "killchain" phases. In an application example, the authors illustrate how this can help to

[9] https://cve.mitre.org.
[10] https://capec.mitre.org.
[11] https://cwe.mitre.org.
[12] https://cpe.mitre.org.
[13] https://www.first.org/cvss/.

inspect intrusion detection events, e.g., by mapping events to kill chain stages and obtaining more information about threat actors based on IP addresses.

As part of a research project (STUCCO), Iannacone et al. [5] outline an approach for a cybersecurity knowledge graph and note that they aim to integrate information from both structured and unstructured data sources. Some extraction code and JSON schema data is available on the project website[14] but no integrated knowledge graph has been published. In a similar effort, Syed et al. [13] integrate heterogeneous knowledge schemas from various cybersecurity systems and standards and create a Unified Cybersecurity Ontology (UCO) that aligns CAPEC, CVE, CWE, STIX, Trusted Automated eXchange fo Indicator Information (TAXII)[15] and Att&ck[16]. Whereas most ontologies proposed in the literature are not publicly available, UCO is offered for download[17], including some example instances from industry standard repositories. However, the instance data in the dump is neither complete nor updated, and there is no public endpoint available. Finally, the Cyber Intelligence Ontology[18] is another example of an ontology that is available for download in RDF and offers classes, properties and restrictions on many industry standards, but no instance data.

Overall, a review of related work shows that although basic concepts in the cybersecurity domain have been formalized repeatedly, no model has so far emerged as a standard. Furthermore, the proposed high-level conceptualizations typically lack concrete instance information.

On the other hand, there are many standards for cybersecurity information sharing and the information is published in various structured formats[19], navigable on the web and/or available for download; however, there is no integrated view on this scattered, heterogeneous information. Hence, each application that makes use of the published data has to parse and interpret each source individually, which makes reuse, machine interpretation, and integration with local data difficult. In the following section, we describe how an evolving cybersecurity knowledge graph that provides an integrated perspective on the cybersecurity landscape can fill this gap.

3 Knowledge Graph Construction and Evolution

To construct and regularly update the SEPSES Cybersecurity KG, we define a set of vocabularies, described in Sect. 3.1, and an architecture for initial ingestion and incremental updating of the graph, covered in Sect. 3.2. Publication via Linked Data (LD), Triple Pattern Fragments (TPF), a SPARQL endpoint, and RDF dumps are covered in Sect. 4.

---

[14] https://github.com/stucco.
[15] https://oasis-open.github.io/cti-documentation/.
[16] https://attack.mitre.org.
[17] https://github.com/Ebiquity/Unified-Cybersecurity-Ontology.
[18] https://github.com/daedafusion/cyber-ontology.
[19] Most commonly as XML or JSON files.

3.1 Conceptualization and Vocabularies

To model the domain of interest, we started with a survey and found that the vast majority of conceptualizations described in the literature are not available online. Those that were available did not provide sufficiently detailed classes and properties to represent all the information available in the cybersecurity repositories we target.

Hence, we opted for a bottom-up approach starting from a set of well-established industry data sources. We structured our vocabularies based on the schemas used to publish existing instance data and chose appropriate terms based on the survey of existing conceptualizations. In choosing this approach, our main design goal was to include the complete information from the original data sources and make the resulting knowledge graph self-contained. To facilitate mapping to other existing conceptualizations, we kept the Resource Description Framework (RDF) model structurally similar to the data models of the original sources. This should make it easy for users already familiar with the original data sources to navigate and integrate our semantic resource. Furthermore, we can easily refer to the original documentation and examples in the vocabularies. We then created a schema that covers the following security information repositories (cf. Fig. 1 for a high-level overview).[20]

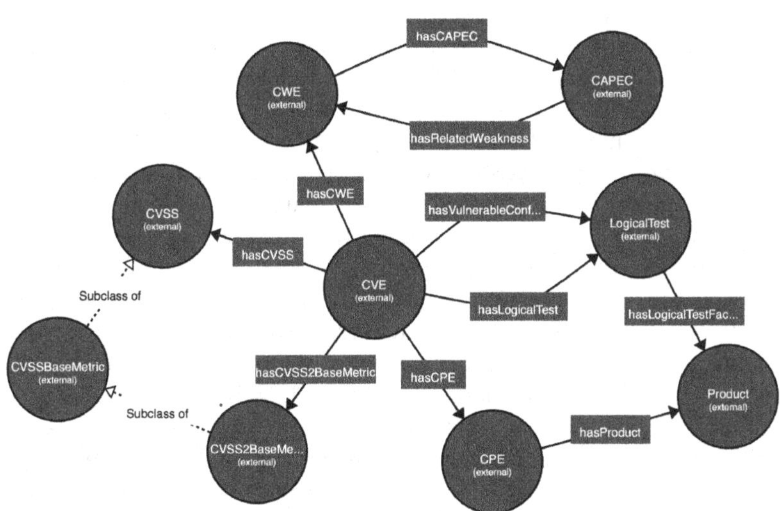

Fig. 1. SEPSES knowledge graph vocabulary high-level overview

CVE is a well-established industry standard that provides a list of identifiers for publicly known cybersecurity vulnerabilities. In addition to CVE, we

[20] The figure omits detailed concepts for the sake of clarity. The complete vocabularies can be found at https://github.com/sepses/vocab.

integrate the National U.S. Vulnerability Database (NVD), which enriches CVEs with additional information, such as security checklist references, security-related software flaws, misconfigurations, product names, and impact metrics. We represent this information in the CVE class, which includes data type properties such as `cve:cveId`, `cve:description`, `cve:issued` and `cve:modified` timestamps. Based on the NVD information, we can link CVE to affected products (`cve:hasCPE`), vulnerable configurations (`cve:hasVulnerableConfiguration`), impact scores (`cve:hasCVSS`), related weaknesses (`cve:hasCWE`), and external references (`cve:hasReference`).

CVSS provides a quantitative model to describe characteristics and impacts of IT vulnerabilities. It is well-established as a standard measurement system for organizations worldwide. We integrate the CVSS scores provided by NVD, and model the CVSS metrics by means of the CVSSBaseMetric, CVSSTemporalMetric, and CVSSEnvironmentalMetric classes to comply with the CVSS specification[21].

CPE provides a structured naming scheme for IT systems, software, and packages based on URIs. NIST hosts and maintains the CPE Dictionary, which currently is based on the CPE 2.3 specification. We represent CPEs with the CPE class and reference product information with `cpe:hasProduct`. Furthermore, we define a set of properties that describe a product, such as product name, version, update, edition, language, etc. The vendor of each product is modeled as a Vendor and referenced by `cpe:hasVendor`.

CWE is a community-developed list of common software security weaknesses that contains information on identification, mitigation, and prevention. NVD vulnerabilities are mapped to CWEs to offer general vulnerability information. This information is modeled using the CWE class and a set of datatype properties such as `cwe:id`, `cwe:name`, `cwe:description`, and `cwe:status`, as well as object properties, to e.g., link applicable platforms (`cwe:hasApplicablePlatform`), attack patterns (`cwe:hasCAPEC`), consequences (`cwe:hasCommonConsequence`), related weaknesses to model the CWE hierarchy (`cwe:hasRelatedWeakness`) and potential mitigations (`cwe:hasPotentialMitigation`).

CAPEC is a dictionary of known attack patterns used by adversaries to exploit known vulnerabilities, and can be used by analysts, developers, testers, and educators to advance community understanding and enhance defenses. We model CAPEC patterns in the CAPEC class with datatype properties such as `capec:id`, `capec:name`, `capec:likelihoodOfAttack`, and `capec:description`. Additional information is linked via object properties such as consequences `capec:hasConsequences`, required skills `capec:hasSkillRequired`, attack prerequisites `capec:prerequisites`, and attack consequences `capec:hasConsequence`.

Most of these data sets define identifiers for key entities such as vulnerabilities, weaknesses, and attack patterns and reuse some concepts from other standards (e.g., CPE names and CVSS scores are used within CVE). In the next section, we will describe how we leverage these references to link the data.

---

[21] https://www.first.org/cvss/specification-document.

3.2 ETL Process

Figure 2 illustrates the overall architecture and the data acquisition, resource extraction, entity linking and validation, storage and publication steps necessary to provide a continuously updated cybersecurity knowledge graph. In the following, we describe the steps in the core Extraction, Transformation, Loading (ETL) process that periodically checks and digest data from the various sources.

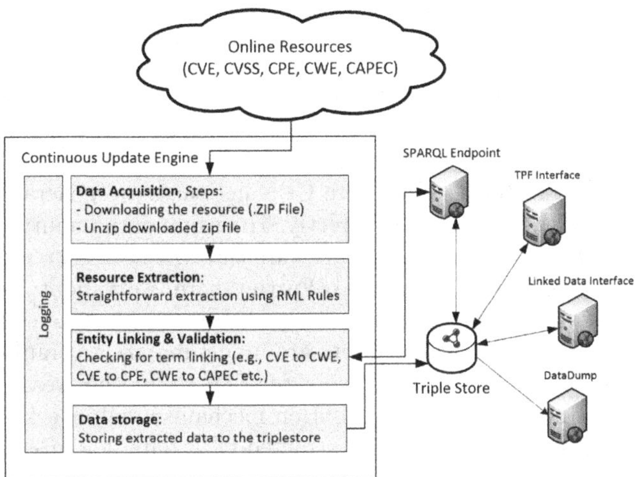

Fig. 2. Architecture: ETL process and publishing

Data Acquisition. We populate our KG using data from various sources that provide data on their respective web sites for download in heterogeneous formats such as CSV, XML, and JSON. These cybersecurity data sources are updated regularly to reflect changes in the real-world. CVE data, for instance, is typically updated once every two hours.[22] In order to capture changes and reflect them in the knowledge graph, our ETL engine will regularly poll for updates and ingest the latest version of the sources.

Resource Extraction. We use the caRML engine[23] to transform the original source files from their various formats. Furthermore, we use Apache Jena[24] to transform the raw RDF data obtained from the RML mappings into the structure of the final ontology. Initially, we developed RDF Mapping Language (RML) transformation mappings that utilized specific features from caRML, such as *carml:multiJoinCondition*. Due address performance issues, however, we decided

[22] cf. https://nvd.nist.gov/vuln/data-feeds.
[23] https://github.com/carml/carml.
[24] https://jena.apache.org.

to restructure the initial mapping into generic RML mappings that do not involve specific constructs from caRML, which improved performance considerably.[25] Because the original data sources have an established ID system, instance ID generation was straightforward for most sources (i.e., CWE, CVE CAPEC, and CVSS). For CPE, however, the instance name is a composite of several naming elements (e.g., product name, part, vendor, version, etc.), separated by special characters. To solve the issue, we use `XPath` functions to clean and produce a unique name for each CPE instance.

Entity Linking and Validation. In this part of the ETL process, we link data from different sources based on common identifiers in the data. Each CWE weakness, for example, typically references several CAPEC attack patterns. Based on these identifiers, we create direct links between associated resources. Specifically for CPE, we deploy the exact same `XPath` functions for its identifier in the two sources (CPE and CVE) where CPE instances are generated, to make sure that these data can be linked correctly. To ensure data quality, we validate the generated RDF with SHACL to make sure that the necessary properties are included for each generated individual. Furthermore, we validate whether the resulting resources are linked correctly, as references to identifiers that are not or no longer available in other data sets are unfortunately a common issue. As an example, a CVE instance may have a relation to another resource such as a CPE identifier. In this case, the validation mechanism will check whether the referenced CPE instance exists in the extracted CPE data, log missing instances and create temporary resources for them.

Data Storage. We store the extracted data in a triple store and generate statistics such as parsing time, parsing status (success or fail), counts of instances, links, and generation time. To make sure that the data is continuously up to date, we wrote a set of bash scripts that are set to be executed in regular intervals to trigger the knowledge generation process and store the result in the triple store. To date, this resulted in more than half a million instances and 36 million triples; Table 1 provides a breakdown of the generated data.

Table 1. SEPSES knowledge graph statistics (As per July 2, 2019.)

	CVE	CVSS	CPE	CWE	CAPEC	SnortRules
Axioms	68	248	111	256	149	486
Class count	7	9	5	10	8	10
Object property Count	6	8	4	9	6	10
Data property count	8	37	18	40	22	103
Individual count	123,005	123,220	393,695	808	516	3,488

[25] In some cases, this reduced processing time from appr. an hour to less than a minute.

4 Knowledge Graph Access

The SEPSES web site[26] provides pointers to the various resources covered in this paper, i.e., the LD resources[27], the SPARQL[28] and TPF query interfaces[29], a download link for the complete RDF snapshots[30], and the ETL engine source code[31]. This allows users to choose the most appropriate access mechanism for their application context.

4.1 Sustainability, Maintenance and Extensibility

The SEPSES KG is being developed jointly by TU Wien and SBA Research, a well-established research center for information security that is embedded within a network of more than 70 companies as well as 15 Universities and research institutions. Endpoints and data sets are hosted at TU Wien and maintained as part of the research project SEPSES, which aims to leverage semantic web technologies for security log interpretation. During this project, we will extend the KG and leverage it as background knowledge in research on semantic monitoring and forensic analysis.

To keep the KG in sync with the evolving cybersecurity landscape, we will continue to automatically poll and process updates of the original raw data sources. We choose our polling strategy according to the varying update intervals of the data sources: CVEs are typically updated once every two hours, CPEs are typically updated daily. CWE and CAPEC are less dynamic and are updated approximately on a yearly schedule.

Furthermore, SBA Research has an active interest in developing and diffusing the KG internally and within its partner network, which will secure long-term maintenance beyond the current research project. We also expect the KG to grow and establish an active external user community during that time. To this end, we publish our vocabularies and the source code under an open source MIT license[32] and encourage community contributions.[33] Adoption success will be measured *(i)* based on access statistics (web page access, SPARQL queries, downloads, etc.), and *(ii)* the emergence of a community around the knowledge graph (code contributions, citations, attractiveness as a linked data target, number of research and community projects that make use of it, etc.).

---

26 https://w3id.org/sepses.
27 e.g., https://w3id.org/sepses/resource/cve/CVE-2014-0160.
28 https://w3id.org/sepses/sparql.
29 https://ldf-server.sepses.ifs.tuwien.ac.at.
30 https://w3id.org/sepses/dumps/.
31 https://github.com/sepses/cyber-kg-converter.
32 https://opensource.org/licenses/MIT.
33 The original raw data are published by MITRE with a no-charge copyright license and by NVD without copyright.

5 Use Cases

In this section, we illustrate the applicability of the cybersecurity knowledge graph by means of two example scenarios.

5.1 Vulnerability Assessment

In security management, identifying, quantifying, and prioritizing vulnerabilities in a system is a key activity and a necessary precondition for threat mitigation and elimination and hence for the successful protection of valuable resources. This Vulnerability Assessment (VA) process can involve both active techniques such as scanning and penetration testing and passive techniques such as monitoring the wealth of public data sources for relevant vulnerabilities and threats. For the latter, keeping track of all the relevant information and determining relevance and implications for the assets in a system is a challenging task for security professionals. In this scenario, we illustrate how the developed knowledge graph can support security analysts by linking organization-specific asset information to a continuously updated stream of known vulnerabilities.

Setting: To illustrate the approach, we modeled a simplified example network comprising of three HOSTs – two workstations, a server – and NETWORKDEVICEs. All hardware components are sub classes of ITASSETs. Furthermore, we model the software installed on each HOST by means of the `hasInstalledProduct` property that links the host to a CPE specification. To determine the potential severity of an impact, we also include DATAASSETs, their `classification` (*public*, *private*, *restricted*), and their storage location (`storedOn` HOST) in the model. In practice, the modeling of a system can be supported by existing IT asset/software discovery and inventory tools.

Query 1: Once a model of the local system has been created, the vulnerability information published in the cybersecurity knowledge graph can be applied and contextualized by means of a federated SPARQL query. Note that we also provide a TPF interface for efficient querying. In particular, a security analyst may be interested in all known vulnerabilities that potentially apply to each host, based on the software that is installed on it (cf. Listing 1). Table 2 shows an example query result. Each resource in the table points to its Linked Data representation, which can serve as a starting point for further exploration. Note that as new vulnerability information becomes available and is automatically integrated into the knowledge graph through the process described in Sect. 3, the query results will automatically reflect newly identified vulnerabilities.

Table 2. Vulnerability assessment query 1 – results

hostName	IP	product	cveIds
DBServer1	192.168.1.3	Windows Server 2016	CVE-2016-3332, ..., CVE-2017-8746
Workstation1	192.168.1.1	Windows 10	CVE-2016-3302, ..., CVE-2015-2554

```
PREFIX rdfs: <http://www.w3.org/2000/01/rdf-schema#>
PREFIX asset: <http://w3id.org/sepses/vocab/bgk/assetKnowledge#>
PREFIX cve: <http://w3id.org/sepses/vocab/ref/cve#>
PREFIX cpe: <http://w3id.org/sepses/vocab/ref/cpe#>
PREFIX cvss: <http://w3id.org/sepses/vocab/ref/cvss#>
PREFIX cwe: <http://w3id.org/sepses/vocab/ref/cwe#>

SELECT  distinct ?hostName str(?ip) as ?IP ?product
(group_concat(?cveId) as ?cveIds)  from
<http://localhost:8890/localdata2>
WHERE {
      ?s a asset:Host.
      ?s rdfs:label ?hostName.
      ?s asset:ipAddress ?ip.
      ?s asset:hasProduct ?p.
SERVICE <http://sepses.ifs.tuwien.ac.at/sparql> {
      ?cve cve:hasCPE ?p .
      ?cve cve:id ?cveId.
          ?p cpe:title ?product .
  }
}
group by ?hostName ?ip ?product
```

Listing 1: Vulnerability Asessment Query 1 – Vulnerable Assets

Query 2: In order to assess the potential impact that a newly identified vulnerability may have, it is critical to asses which data assets might be exposed if an attacker can successfully exploit it. In the next step, we hence take advantage of the modeled data assets and formulate a query (cf. Listing 2)[34] to retrieve the most severe vulnerabilities, i.e., those that affect hosts that store *sensitive private* data (classification value = 1) and have a *complete* confidentiality impact (as specified in CVSS). Table 3 shows the query result and illustrates how such immediate analysis can save time by avoiding manual investigation steps.

Exploration: The query results can serve as a starting point for further exploration of the Linked Data in the knowledge graph[35]. By navigating it, a security analyst can access information from various sources such as, e.g., attack prerequisites and potential mitigations from CAPEC, weakness classifications and potential mitigations from CWE, and scorings from CVSS.

Table 3. Vulnerability assessment query 2 – results

hostName	cveId	conf	score	dataAsset	class	consequence
Workstation2	2016-1646	COMPLETE	9.3	EmpData	Private	Read Memory
Workstation2	2016-1653	COMPLETE	9.3	EmpData	Private	DoS: Crash, Exit...
Workstation2	2016-1583	COMPLETE	7.2	EmpData	Private	DoS: Resource Cons...
Workstation2	2016-1583	COMPLETE	9.3	EmpData	Private	Execute Unauthorized ...

[34] Prefixes identical to Listing 1.
[35] e.g., https://w3id.org/sepses/resource/cve/CVE-2016-1646.

```
SELECT  DISTINCT ?hostName  ?cveId
?confidentiality as ?conf ?cvssScore AS ?score ?dataAsset ?classification AS ?class
↪  ?consequence
FROM <http://localhost:8890/localdata>
WHERE {
    ?s a asset:Host.
    ?s rdfs:label ?hostName.
    ?s asset:hasProduct ?product.
    ?s asset:hasDataAsset ?dt.
    ?dt rdfs:label ?dataAsset.
    ?dt asset:hasClassification ?c.
    ?c rdfs:label ?classification.
    ?c asset:dataClassificationValue ?cv
FILTER (?confidentiality = "COMPLETE")
FILTER (?cv = 1)

SERVICE <http://sepses.ifs.tuwien.ac.at/sparql> {
    ?cve cve:hasCPE ?product .
    ?cve cve:id ?cveId.
    ?cve cve:hasCVSS2BaseMetric ?cvss2.
    ?cvss2 cvss:confidentialityImpact ?confidentiality.
    ?cvss2 cvss:baseScore ?cvssScore.
    ?cve cwe:hasCWE ?cwe.
    ?cwe cwe:hasCommonConsequence ?cc.
    ?cc cwe:consequenceImpact ?consequence
   }
}
```

Listing 2: Vulnerability Assessment Query 2 – Critical Vulnerabilities

5.2 Intrusion Detection

In this scenario, we illustrate how alerts from the Network Intrusion Detection System (NIDS) Snort[36] can be connected to the SEPSES Cybersecurity KG in order to obtain a deeper understanding of potential threats and ongoing attacks. As a first step, we acquired the Snort community rule set[37] and integrated it into our cybersecurity repository using a defined vocabulary[38]. Snort can monitor these rules and trigger alerts once it finds matches to these patterns in the network traffic. We represent SNORTRULEs as a class with two linked concepts SNORTRULEHEADER and SNORTRULEOPTION. For SNORTRULEOPTION we include properties such as `sr:hasClassType` and `sr:hasCVEReference`, which will be used to link incoming alerts to CVEs.

Setting: We use a large data set collected during the MACCDC 2012[39] cybersecurity competition as a realistic set of real-world intrusion detection alerts (cf. Listing 3 for an example). We provide and use a Snort alert log vocabulary[40] to map those alerts into RDF.

---

36 https://www.snort.org.
37 https://www.snort.org/downloads.
38 https://w3id.org/sepses/vocab/rule/snort.
39 https://maccdc.org/2012-agenda/, source: https://www.secrepo.com.
40 https://w3id.org/sepses/vocab/log/snort-alert.

```
[**] [1:1807:12] WEB-MISC Chunked-Encoding transfer attempt [**]
[Classification: Web Application Attack] [Priority: 1]
11/10-11:10:12.321349 10.2.189.248:54208 -> 154.241.88.201:80
TCP TTL:61 TOS:0x0 ID:36462 IpLen:20 DgmLen:1200 DF
***A***** Seq: 0xCFAD1EE0  Ack: 0xB27D1032  Win: 0xB7  TcpLen: 32
TCP Options (3) => NOP NOP TS: 2592976 143157138
```

Listing 3: IDS Alert Example from MACCDC

Query: When a Snort alert is triggered, a security expert typically has to analyze its relevance and decide about potential mitigations. False positives are common in this context. For instance, a particular attack pattern may be detected frequently in a network, but it may not be relevant if the targeted host configuration is not vulnerable. To support security analysts in this time-critical and information-intensive analysis task, we identify the corresponding Snort rule that triggered each particular alert. These rules often include a reference to a CVE, which we can use to query our knowledge graph for detailed CVE information related to an alert. Furthermore, by matching the installed software on the host to the vulnerable product configuration defined in CVE (cf. Scenario 1), we can automatically provide security decision makers a better foundation to estimate the relevance of a Snort alert wrt. to their protected assets. To illustrate this process, Listing 4[41] shows an example query to obtain CVE Ids and vulnerable products from Snort alerts. Based on the result Table 4, a security analyst can query if the attacked host has the vulnerable software installed (similar to Listing 1).

```
PREFIX cve:          <http://w3id.org/sepses/vocab/ref/cve#>
PREFIX cpe:          <http://w3id.org/sepses/vocab/ref/cpe#>
PREFIX snort:        <http://w3id.org/sepses/vocab/ref/snort#>
PREFIX snort-rule:   <http://w3id.org/sepses/vocab/rule/snort#>
PREFIX snort-alert: <http://w3id.org/sepses/vocab/log/snort-alert#>

SELECT DISTINCT ?alert ?message ?sid ?sourceIp ?destinationIp ?cveId ?cpeId
FROM <http://localhost:8890/snortalert>
WHERE {
    ?alert a snort-alert:IDSSnortAlertLogEntry ;
           snort:signatureId ?sid ;
           snort:message ?message ;
           snort:sourceIp ?sourceIp ;
           snort:destinationIp ?destinationIp .

    SERVICE <http://w3id.org/sepses/sparql> {
        ?rule a snort-rule:SnortRule ;
               snort-rule:hasRuleOption ?ruleOption .
        ?ruleOption snort:signatureId ?sid ;
                   snort-rule:hasCveReference ?cve .
        ?cve cve:id ?cveId ;
             cve:hasCPE/cpe:id ?cpeId
    }
}
```

Listing 4: Intrusion Detection query

[41] Prefixes from Listing 1 are reused.

Table 4. Intrusion detection query results

alert	message	sid	sourceIP	targetIP	cveId	cpeId
Alert001	WEB-MISC Chunked...	1807	10.2.190.254	154.241.88.201	2002-0392	cpe:/a:apa...
Alert002	WEB-MISC WebDAV...	1070	10.2.190.254	154.241.88.201	2000-0951	cpe:/a:micr...
Alert003	WEB-MISC TRACE...	2056	10.2.197.241	154.241.88.201	2004-2320	cpe:/a:bea:w...
Alert004	WEB-FRONTPAGE...	1248	10.2.190.254	154.241.88.201	2001-0341	cpe:/o:micr...
Alert005	WEB-MISC Netscape...	1048	10.2.197.241	154.241.88.201	2001-0250	cpe:/a:netsc...

6 Conclusions

In this resource paper, we highlight the need for semantically explicit representations of security knowledge and the current lack of interlinked instance data. To tackle this challenge, we present a cybersecurity knowledge graph that integrates a set of widely adopted, heterogeneous cybersecurity data sources.

To maintain the knowledge graph and integrate newly available information, we developed an ETL process that updates it as new security information becomes available. In order to make this resource publicly available and easy to use, we offer multiple services to access the data, including a SPARQL endpoint, a triple pattern fragments interface, a Linked Data interface, and download options for the complete data set.

We demonstrated the usefulness of the graph by means of two example use cases in vulnerability assessment and semantic interpretation of alerts generated by intrusion detection systems. Given the compelling need for efficient exchange of machine-interpretable cybersecurity knowledge, we expect the KG to be useful for practitioners and researchers, and hope that the resource will ultimately facilitate novel and innovative semantic security tools and services. Future work will focus on disseminating the resource in the security domain, building a community of users and contributors around it, and growing the knowledge graph by integrating additional security standards and information extracted from structured and unstructured sources.

Acknowledgments. This work has been supported by netidee SCIENCE, the Austrian Science Fund (FWF) under grant P30437-N31, and the Christian Doppler Research Association. The competence center SBA Research (SBA-K1) is funded within the framework of COMET—Competence Centers for Excellent Technologies by BMVIT, BMDW, and the federal state of Vienna, managed by the FFG.

References

1. Dandurand, et al.: Standards and tools for exchange and processing of actionable information. European Union Agency for Network and Information Security, Luxembourg (2015)
2. Ekelhart, A., Fenz, S., Neubauer, T.: Aurum: a framework for information security risk management. In: Proceedings of the 42nd Hawaii International Conference on System Sciences (2009). https://doi.org/10.1109/HICSS.2009.82

3. Fenz, S., Ekelhart, A.: Formalizing information security knowledge. In: Proceedings of the 4th International Symposium on Information, Computer, and Communications Security (2009). https://doi.org/10.1145/1533057.1533084
4. Guo, M., Wang, J.: An ontology-based approach to model common vulnerabilities and exposures in information security. In: ASEE Southeastern Section Annual Conference (2009)
5. Iannacone, M., et al.: Developing an ontology for cyber security knowledge graphs (2015). https://doi.org/10.1145/2746266.2746278
6. Kim, A., Luo, J., Kang, M.: Security ontology for annotating resources. In: Meersman, R., Tari, Z. (eds.) OTM 2005. LNCS, vol. 3761, pp. 1483–1499. Springer, Heidelberg (2005). https://doi.org/10.1007/11575801_34
7. Martimiano, A., Moreira, E.S.: An owl-based security incident ontology. In: Proceedings of the Eighth International Protege Conference (2005)
8. Obrst, L., Chase, P., Markeloff, R.: Developing an ontology of the cyber security domain. In: Proceedings of the 7th International Conference on Semantic Technologies for Intelligence, Defense, and Security (2012)
9. Oltramari, A., Cranor, L., Walls, R., McDaniel, P.: Building an ontology of cyber security. In: Proceedings of the 9th Conference on Semantic Technology for Intelligence, Defense, and Security (2014)
10. Raskin, V., Hempelmann, C., Triezenberg, K., Nirenburg, S.: Ontology in information security: a useful theoretical foundation and methodological tool. In: Proceedings of the 2001 Workshop on New Security Paradigms (2001). https://doi.org/10.1145/508171.508180
11. Schumacher, M.: Toward a security core ontology. Security Engineering with Patterns. LNCS, vol. 2754, pp. 87–96. Springer, Heidelberg (2003). https://doi.org/10.1007/978-3-540-45180-8_6
12. Souag, A., Salinesi, C., Comyn-Wattiau, I.: Ontologies for security requirements: a literature survey and classification. In: Bajec, M., Eder, J. (eds.) CAiSE 2012. LNBIP, vol. 112, pp. 61–69. Springer, Heidelberg (2012). https://doi.org/10.1007/978-3-642-31069-0_5
13. Syed, Z., Padia, A., Mathews, M., Finin, T., Joshi, A.: UCO: a unified cybersecurity ontology. In: Proceedings of the AAAI Workshop on Artificial Intelligence for Cyber Security (2016)
14. Ulicny, B., Moskal, J., Kokar, M., Abe, K., Smith, J.: Inference and ontologies (2014). https://doi.org/10.1007/978-3-319-11391-3_9
15. Undercoffer, J., Joshi, A., Pinkston, J.: Modeling computer attacks: an ontology for intrusion detection. In: Vigna, G., Kruegel, C., Jonsson, E. (eds.) RAID 2003. LNCS, vol. 2820, pp. 113–135. Springer, Heidelberg (2003). https://doi.org/10.1007/978-3-540-45248-5_7
16. Wang, J., Guo, M.: Security data mining in an ontology for vulnerability management. In: 2009 International Joint Conference on Bioinformatics, Systems Biology and Intelligent Computing (2009). https://doi.org/10.1109/IJCBS.2009.13
17. Wang, J., Guo, M., Camargo, J.: An ontological approach to computer system security. Inf. Secur. J.: A Global Perspect. **19**(2) (2010). https://doi.org/10.1080/19393550903404902

SemanGit: A Linked Dataset from git

Dennis Oliver Kubitza[1,2], Matthias Böckmann[1,2], and Damien Graux[2,3](✉)

[1] University of Bonn, Bonn, Germany
dennis.oliver.kubitza@iais.fraunhofer.de
[2] Enterprise Information Systems, Fraunhofer IAIS, Sankt Augustin, Germany
{matthias.boeckmann,damien.graux}@iais.fraunhofer.de
[3] ADAPT Centre, Trinity College of Dublin, Dublin, Ireland

Abstract. The growing interest in free and open-source software which occurred over the last decades has accelerated the usage of versioning systems to help developers collaborating together in the same projects. As a consequence, specific tools such as git and specialized open-source on-line platforms gained importance. In this study, we introduce and share SemanGit which provides a resource at the crossroads of both Semantic Web and git web-based version control systems. SemanGit is actually the first collection of linked data extracted from GitHub based on a git ontology we designed and extended to include specific GitHub features. In this article, we present the dataset, describe the extraction process according to the ontology, show some promising analyses of the data and outline how SemanGit could be linked with external datasets or enriched with new sources to allow for more complex analyses.

Resource type: Dataset
Website: http://www.semangit.de/
Permanent URL: https://doi.org/10.5281/zenodo.2176047

1 Introduction

The semantic git (SemanGit), is a novel resource description framework dataset comprising information generated by the git protocol and its protocol extensions. So far, it contains nearly 20×10^9 triples about either native git protocol data or about social interactions on the GitHub platform. While GitHub is currently the only used data-source, we designed the underlying ontology to be easily extensible to other providers, such as SourceForge [4], GitLab [3] and Bitbucket [1].

In itself, git is a protocol for tracking file changes, such as insertions, deletions or alterations of lines of code, additions or deletions of entire files, etc. The largest online provider for remote git repositories is GitHub [2]. Besides providing git repositories, GitHub also implements several social features that are not part of the git protocol, such as following other users, watching project changes, creating release versions of a project and pull requests – a request for the contributors of a repository to adapt provided source code changes.

C. Ghidini et al. (Eds.): ISWC 2019, LNCS 11779, pp. 215–228, 2019.
https://doi.org/10.1007/978-3-030-30796-7_14

Our goal was to add semantics to the git protocol to make use of the strengths of both semantics and graph databases in general, such as interlinkage with other datasets or general graph traversal tasks. Particularly, by using RDF, as recommended by the W3C, we ensure an easy integration with other datasets from the Linked Open Data cloud[1]. The backbone and initial step of our project was the design of an ontology to support the logical inference.

Due to the vast size of GitHub, we chose to extract our data from this provider for creating our resource description framework, our first data source. They provide a REST API [11] as a query point from which one can gather data. With its limitation of 5,000 queries per hour per token, it would take over 2 years to query all 100 million repositories [10] just once, yielding only a fraction of the data.

The GHTorrent project [12] however provides large amounts of data which they have gathered from GitHub using a multitude of tokens over several years, offering us a better input than the rate limited GitHub API. Its data is stored in a relational model and therefore not well suited for analysis of linked data, where a graph dataset is preferred instead. To bypass this issue, we wrote a Converter transforming the relational tables into a RDF. Since our input data is already several hundred gigabytes in size, we were forced to optimize our output as much as possible, while still ensuring valid Turtle syntax [8].

The datasets are subject to the *CC BY-SA 4.0* license (see [9] for more details) and are available under:

www.semangit.de

The latest version of our implementation is available under the following link:

https://doi.org/10.5281/zenodo.2176047

The rest of this article is structured as follows. Firstly, we present background knowledge in Sect. 2 to provide the reader with concepts coming from open Open-Source communities. Then, in Sect. 3, we review the related research efforts close to our approach. Next in Sect. 4, we describe the vocabulary and the ontology we particularly designed to generate the dataset. Afterwards, in Sect. 5, we present the shared resource we developed, before presenting some sample analyses in Sect. 6. In Sect. 7, we collect further interesting use cases. Finally we conclude in Sect. 8 and round everything up by elaborating our sustainability plan and future works.

2 Preliminaries

In this Section, we recall some important concepts and standards which will then be used during the detailed description of the SemanGit.

Developed in 2005, git [16] is a system aiming at tracking changes in a file system while providing several properties such as data integrity or support for distributed and non-linear workflows. As a consequence, it has been adopted

[1] https://lod-cloud.net/.

by the Open-Source developers as a tool to work concurrently on large shared projects. Since the file system represented by a git repository can be distributed, developers embed their changes into a git repository and once they are ready "push" their contributions to the "bare"-repository so that collaborators can then have access to the latest version.

Quickly, the git protocol has evolved to provide more and more features dedicated to large Open-Source communities and projects. These features comprise for example the possibility of creating new branches for a project where a sub-group of contributors can develop additional features independently, which could thereafter be merged back into the "master" branch.

3 Related Work

To the best of our knowledge, SemanGit is the first open attempt to systematically build a linked dataset from a group of git repositories.

Nonetheless, SemanGit is not the first effort that aims towards extracting and grouping information from an open git platform. Indeed, Gousios in [12] introduced the GHTorrent project which aims at providing data dumps extracted from the GitHub public API.

To be precise, the SemanGit project falls within the domain of transforming public data into linked data. So far, numerous projects are already providing such datasets each one tackling a distinct domain. Among this list, we can mention DBpedia [6] which proposes a linked version of Wikipedia, or also [7] which deals with geographical data. For a more exhaustive list, we refer the reader to the Linked Open Data cloud which groups 1,239 distinct datasets as of March 2019.

4 A git Dedicated Vocabulary

The git protocol in itself relies on so-called repositories in which data can be stored. Many online git repository providers add some features of their own that are not part of the git protocol, such as social features. In order to have an extensible ontology, we need to clearly distinguish between what is part of the git protocol and what is provider specific. As an example, according to the git protocol, the author of a commit is simply a pair "Name <email>" whereas on GitHub an author, i.e. a user, is much more complex. It has additional attributes such as a creation date, an avatar, a location and even social-featured ones such as an associated website.

The part of the ontology covering the git protocol features only represents the data that strictly belong to the protocol. The classes in this section mostly form the basis from which platform-specific classes inherit, see Fig. 1 for an example.

This protocol-related part is rather small and comprises of merely four classes: Users, projects (i.e. repositories), commits and pull requests, the user class storing no more than an email address. The projects refer to a URL, a timestamp of creation and the commits that were submitted to it. The other

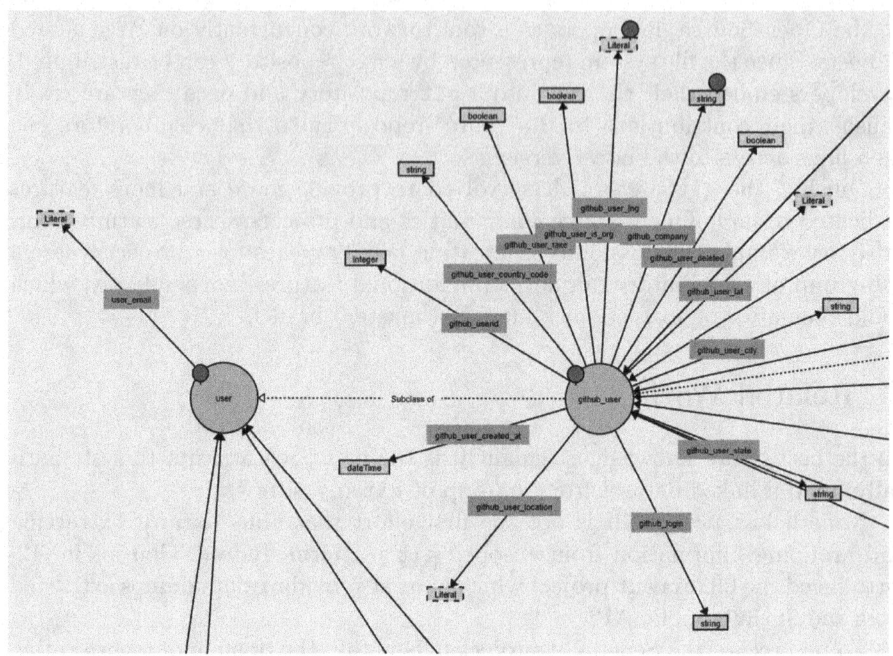

Fig. 1. A visualization with WebVOWL [15] of a small section of the ontology

two classes are slightly more complex, as commits have a hierarchical structure in themselves and pull requests are requests to accept a cross-project commit.

Seeing that all extensions of the `git` protocol are still required to provide the base functionality, we have chosen a hierarchical approach for our ontology, letting extensions inherit from protocol-conform classes to make them take over all properties they are required to have.

These classes corresponding to provider-specific extensions of the protocol are set apart from the original one by putting a prefix such as "github_" to the class name. Large parts of our ontology do not refer to parts of the `git` protocol but try to encompass those features that have been added or extended by providers on top of it. Some of them are purely social relations, such as one user following another, or multiple users forming an organization. Others are actual versioning features, like forking of projects and issue tracking. `GitHub` allows users to leave comments on certain objects, such as commits and pull requests, which is not specified in the `git` protocol, which only allows for an initial commit message. In such a case where an entire feature has been added that is not an extension of an existing `git` protocol feature, the corresponding class in the ontology does not inherit from a class that represents a `git` feature. An example of this is the issue tracking system implemented by `GitHub`, see Fig. 2. The full ontology file can be found on GitHub[2] and an interactive visualization can be found on VisualDataWeb[3].

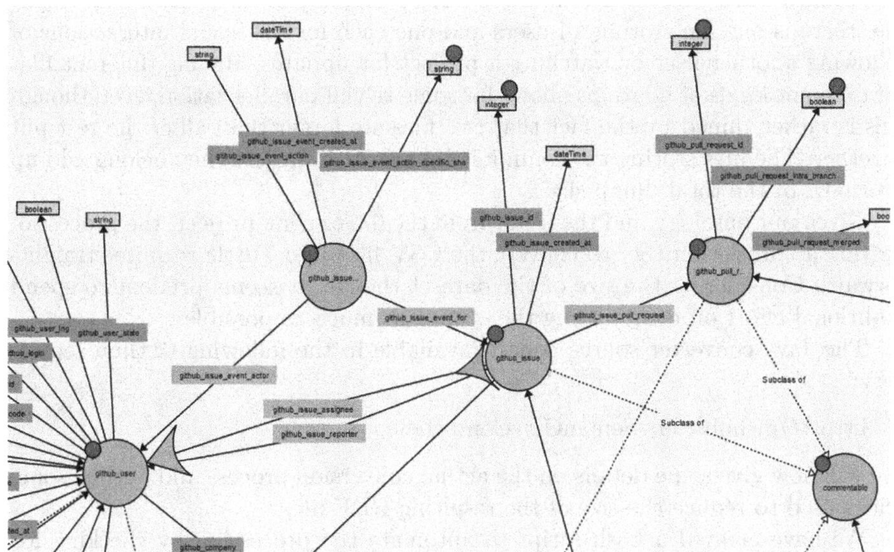

Fig. 2. A visualization with WebVOWL [15] of a provider specific feature

5 Creating the SemanGit Dataset

We will start off this chapter by giving detailed information on how the SemanGit dataset is created. Afterwards, we present statistics on the effectiveness of the steps we have taken to reduce the disk size of the output.

5.1 Data Generation Process

One could now take the most direct path and start querying GitHub via their REST API [11]. This approach faces the drawback of running into limitations regarding the number of queries one can fire at the API per hour, which is currently at 5,000 queries per token per hour. Hence, even with the drastic underestimation of only requiring one query per repository to get all relevant information, it would already require multiple years to query all repositories just once, of which there are more than 100×10^6 as of November 2018 [10]. The GHTorrent project [12] has been mining meta information from GitHub

[2] https://github.com/SemanGit/SemanGit/blob/master/Documentation/ontology/semangitontology.ttl.

[3] http://visualdataweb.de/webvowl/#opts=doc=0;editorMode=true;#iri=https://raw.githubusercontent.com/SemanGit/SemanGit/master/Documentation/ontology/semangitontology.ttl.

since 2013, using several access tokens in parallel. They offer monthly database dumps which we use to get around the query limitations of GitHub's API.

The monthly data dumps are provided in the form of comma separated value (CSV) files which store different objects or certain object relations. As an example, there is one file storing all users and one each for the social interactions of following another user or watching a project for updates. Having different files for different kinds of relations allows for some trivial parallelization, even though this is rather ruined by the fact that two files are larger than all of the rest put together: The files storing the commits and to which project they belong add up over 60% of the total dump size.

Given our ontology and the input from the GHTorrent project, the process of writing a translation tool to convert the CSV files into Turtle is quite straightforward. Considering the size of the dataset though, it seems prudent to spend additional effort on compressing the output as much as possible.

The Java converter source code is available in the following GitHub repository:

https://github.com/SemanGit/Converter

We will now give some details on the actual conversion process and outline some tricks used to reduce the size of the resulting RDF file.

We have created a bash script to automate the processing by checking for new data dumps, managing the download, decompression and ensuring fault-tolerance for the used resources. For each step, we have added error checks and fallback mechanisms to guarantee the integrity of the result. These checks are mainly log files, documenting which tasks have been completed up to which point so that we can restart the process at a suitable point. It is for example not required to re-download the dump if the machine runs out of space while extracting, or to re-extract if an issue is encountered during the conversion.

To keep the size of the output as small as possible, we have made the obvious choice of serializing our data in the Turtle format [8], giving us the ability to use prefixes and to abbreviate parts of triples. Seeing that we are working on a fixed ontology, we have taken it to the extreme of creating one prefix for every URI in our ontology, choosing prefix names no longer than two characters and choosing the shortest ones for the most commonly used URIs, such as the empty prefix for the repository resource, which occurred more than 7.7×10^9 times as subject or object.

```
@prefix semangit: <http://semangit.de/ontology/semangit>.

# Unoptimized Data
semangit:ghissue_123456 a semangit:github_issue;
semangit:github_issue_created_at "2002-05-30T09:00:00"^^xsd:dateTime;
semangit:github_issue_project semangit:ghrepo_234567;
semangit:github_issue_assignee semangit:ghuser_345678.

# With prefixing
u:123456 a x:;
```

```
C: "2002-05-30T09:00:00"^^xsd:dateTime;
y: :234567;
A: m:345678.

# With Base64 like integer representation
u:x3T a x:;
C: "2002-05-30T09:00:00"^^xsd:dateTime;
y: :WR9;
A: m:af93.
```

Additionally, the data from `GHTorrent` is presorted, coming from relational tables, maximizing the number of abbreviations possible. Lastly, we were able to reduce the output size drastically by transforming all integers in resource identifiers from the base 10 representation to a base 64 like representation, that is compatible with Turtle syntax.

After the data generation process is finished, we describe the resulting dataset with the Vocabulary of Interlinked Datasets (VoID) [5]. These triples include a name and description for the dataset, its format, the license under which it is available, links to the associated homepage, modification and creation date, author contact details and more.

5.2 Statistics on the Dataset

At the time of writing this study, the most recent version of SemanGit is from April 2019 and has a size of 353 GB with over 21 billion triples. The input files from GHTorrent use 340 GB of space, which means we create less than 4% overhead by adding semantics, which is owed to the measures we described in the last section. By using prefixing to the extent that the turtle format allows, we achieved to be little more than 25% larger than the input files. By also adding a Base64 like integer representation, this overhead was reduced to the above mentioned 4%. The entire conversion process was completed in less than seven hours.[4] Our dataset contains 31,205,000 users, which is slightly more than the number of users GitHub claims to have had in November 2018 [10].

6 Example Analyses

To emphasize the value of the dataset and its structure, we have created two sample analyses, computed on our previously mentioned server. In the first one, we take a brief look at international cooperation of developers for the countries New Zealand and Germany. In the second analysis, we compute statistics for the internal structure of organizations, by using the `follow` relation. To present the potential for knowledge discovery, we extract the data of some colleagues, who work in different roles for the same organization and compare them to these statistics.

[4] Intel Core i7-5820 CPU @ 6×3.3 GHz, 64 GB DDR3, Ubuntu 18.04.

6.1 Global Cooperation Within Repositories

Many users on `GitHub` state the country they live in or originate from. With this data, we can derive interesting analysis for countries on a global scale, enabling comparison on regional differences for programming languages, coding style, social media behaviour or even business policies. Besides comparing differences regarding those aspects, one can also analyze how well countries cooperate. A repository can have multiple collaborators. The SemanGit dataset represent this information through the class `project_join_event`, linked to a user and a project. For the sake of demonstration, we will analyze which nations New Zealanders collaborate with frequently. In two separate queries, we collect for all countries the absolute number of users $N_{country}$ and the number of users working together with at least one New Zealander in a project $N_{country,NZ}$. The total execution time for both queries was below 9 m. As our triplestore makes use of intermediate results, it is difficult to measure the runtimes of queries independently, without resetting the server after each query.

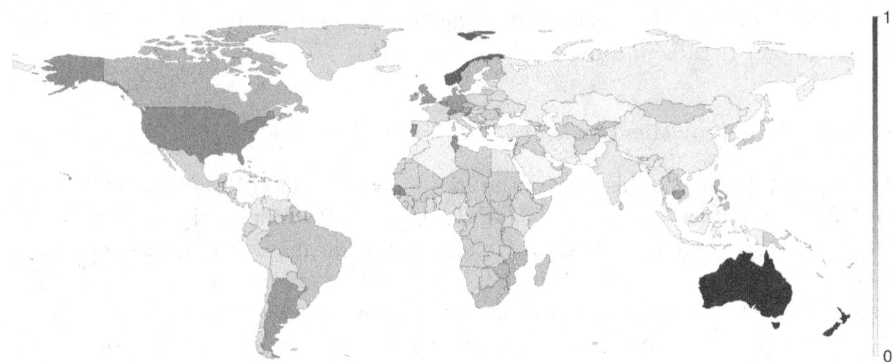

Cooperation Index $I_{country,NZ}$ represented in shades of blue
Excluded countries in gray. New Zealand in red.

Fig. 3. Cooperation with New Zealanders (Color figure online)

From these data, we calculated the share of people per country collaborating with New Zealanders $S_{country,NZ} = \frac{N_{country}}{N_{country,NZ}}$ and normalized the results to form an index.

$$I_{country,NZ} = \frac{S_{country,NZ}}{\max_{c \in Countries}(S_{c,NZ})}$$

Figure 3 contains the results, showing a strong collaboration with New Zealand's neighbour Australia (1.00), but also with countries like Norway (0.75), Senegal (0.54), the United States (0.54), Switzerland (0.53), Portugal (0.53), Tunisia (0.53), Slovenia (0.51) and Cyprus (0.51). For comparison, we applied the same procedure for Germany, revealing that collaboration with other German-speaking countries is more common than with other nations, see Fig. 4.

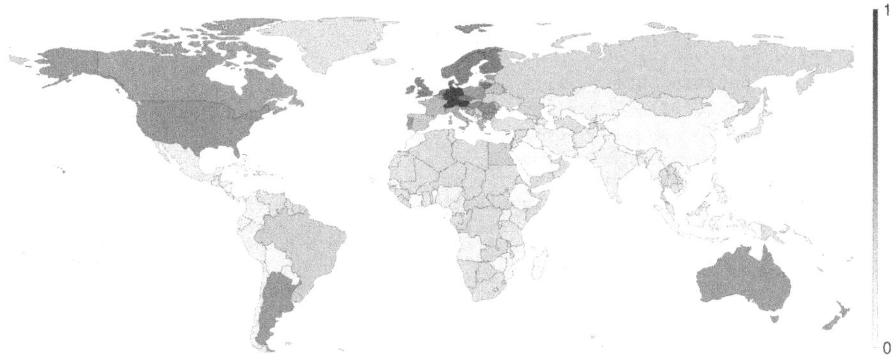

Cooperation Index $I_{country,DE}$ represented in shades of blue
Excluded countries in gray. Germany in red.

Fig. 4. Cooperation with Germans (Color figure online)

6.2 Social Relations for Organizations

To glimpse at possible investigations of social aspects in Open Source collaboration, we analyzed two features: the number of members of an organization and the number of followers a user has. In the SemanGit dataset the class user corresponds either to natural user, or an organization. In the second case, the organization has different members, which are also users. We track the membership with `organization_join_events`. By agglomerating over all these events, it is possible to get the set of all members. Also SemanGit tracks which user follows whom on `GitHub` with the `follow_event`, also linked to two users.

We have the hypothesis, that we can learn something about the internal structure of an organization by looking at the behaviour of their users. Without information about the real structure of these organizations this kind of analysis would fall into the category of unsupervised learning. To avoid the application of machine learning, we investigated an organization for which we know the internal structure and roles of people. This anonymous organization `Org` comprises 19 members and overall 31 follow relations. To obtain an overview about the dataset, we queried all organizations, the cardinality of their members and internal follow events. The Listing 1.1 provides a precise description of how, practically, the results are extracted from SemanGit. Indeed, the query is used to return a sorted list (see line 18) of triplets (lines 2 to 4); the `optional` section is used to collect the internal following relationships.

```
PREFIX sgo: <http://semangit.de/ontology/> .
SELECT ?organization
       (COUNT(DISTINCT ?user1) AS ?users)
       (COUNT(DISTINCT ?follow_event) AS ?follows)
WHERE
{
  ?organization sgo:github_user_is_org true .
  ?join_event_1 sgo:github_organization_is_joined ?organization ;
                sgo:github_organization_joined_by ?user1 .
  # Collect the internal follow relations
  OPTIONAL
  {
    ?join_event_2 sgo:github_organization_is_joined ?organization ;
                  sgo:github_organization_joined_by ?user2 .
    ?follow_event sgo::github_follows  ?user1 ;
                  sgo::github_follower ?user2 .
  }
} GROUP BY ?organization}
```

Listing 1.1. SPARQL query used to extract the needed information from organizations

The resulting data contains almost 300, 000 organizations. From this data we selected all 1, 375 organizations with 17 to 22 members and printed the distribution of internal follow relations compared to `Org`. Figure 5 shows these results, with `Org` being located slightly after the peak, showing it is neither significant low nor high numbers of follow relations.

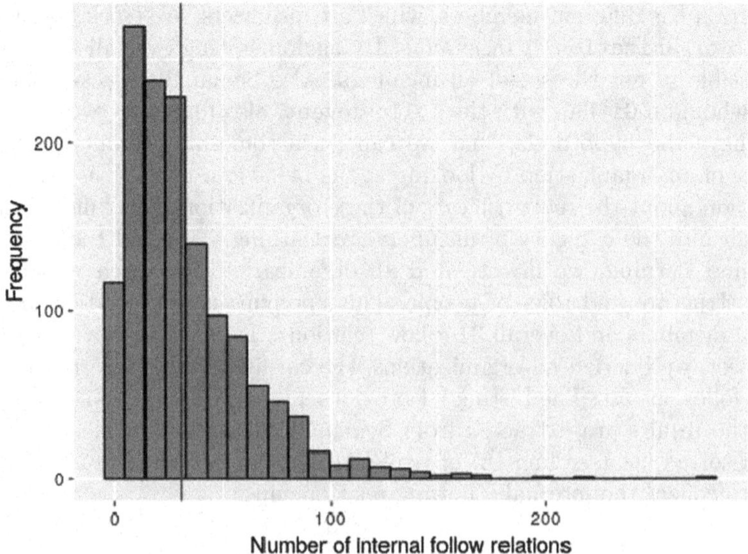

Histogram for organizations with 17 to 22 members.
Observation for a well known organization as vertical-line on $x = 31$.

Fig. 5. Number of follow relations within organizations

An investigation against organizations with a significantly different number of such relations, would be meaningless. Therefore, we picked the 93 organizations with 17 to 23 internal relations to compare against `Org`. For each user affiliated to one of these organizations we now queried for two informations: the number of followers, and the number of people she follows. The outcomes are plotted in Fig. 6. For `Org` we observed two users with 14 and 5 followers, already summing up to 55% of the follow relations. Querying their names revealed, that these are the developer responsible for maintaining the repositories on `GitHub` and the department leader. Overall, six of the colleagues were not followed at all, five of them having assisting positions.

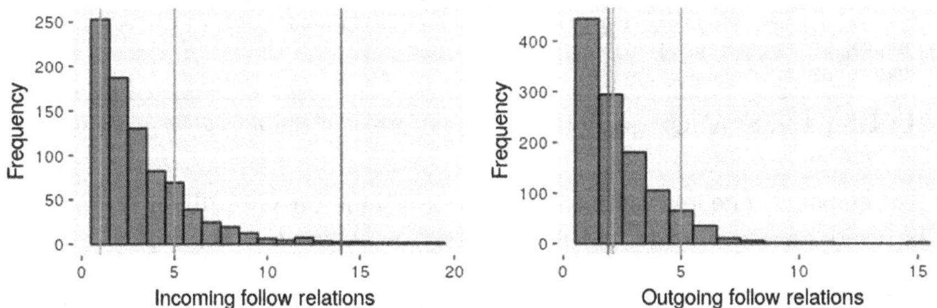

Histogram for organizations with 17 to 22 members and 29 to 33 follow relations. Observation for different roles within the well known organization as vertical lines. Leader of Research Group (green), Post Doctoral Researcher and Main Developer (red), PhD Student (orange)

Fig. 6. Followed within an organization (Color figure online)

We do not claim that our hypothesis is true according to these results, but they provide at least a hindsight about the value of the contained information.

7 Further Use Cases

The sample analyses from Sect. 6 already indicate that the domain of use cases is quite diverse. We will now present a few sample use cases to demonstrate the potential value of the dataset.

The Headhuntress – Finding computer scientists to hire can be quite challenging. Suppose a headhuntress is looking for quality programmers to employ. While it is easy to determine how high-quality programming is reflected on GitHub (no major issues reported, positive comments on projects, no infrequent commits), it is more problematic to actually measure and compare these traits. With SemanGit, she can find a representative subpopulation and generate benchmark results either by doing analysis manually or applying machine-learning. Furthermore, the dataset contains geographical information about many users, which is geocoded from the *location* field on a users profile. With the DBpedia interlinkage [6], one could, for example, look for users inside or close to a given city by using the *nearestCity* relation. She can even attempt to find well socialised, skilled programmers by adopting an analysis as mentioned in Sect. 6.

```
PREFIX sgo: <http://semangit.de/ontology/> .
SELECT  ?other_project
        (COUNT(DISTINCT ?user) AS ?users)
WHERE
{
  ?project sgo:github_repo_name "SemanGit" .
  ?project_watch_event1 sgo:project_is_followed ?project ;
                        sgo:github_project_followed_by ?user .
  ?project_watch_event2 sgo:github_project_followed_by ?user ;
                        sgo:github_project_followed ?other_project .
} GROUP BY ?other_project
  ORDER BY DESC(?users)
```

Listing 1.2. SPARQL query used in the context of the *developer* use case

The Developer – The records of social interactions on GitHub in our dataset can be used for more than just social analysis. Assume a developer has been working with an open-source tool and is looking for an alternative tool. With SemanGit, he could try to find similar projects by taking the set of developers who are watching the tool's repository and evaluating the set of repositories these developers are watching (see e.g. Listing 1.2).

The Economist – One topic of economics is the analysis of driving forces, structures and institutions of an economy. While the behavior of agents in traditional scenarios are well-documented, the analysis of Open-Software-Projects and the motivation behind contribution is subject to notable current research [13]. For such research interests, the use of linked data offers new opportunities as it is tailored for the analysis of local models and offers direct access to empirical data on individual level.

8 Conclusions, Future Work and Sustainability

In this article, we presented and shared the SemanGit dataset which is a linked data version of `GitHub` activities. It already consists of more than 20 billions RDF triples. In addition to the openly available dataset, we also provided the extractor in our GitHub repository, which converts the data from GHTorrent to ontology compliant RDF, and the ontology we designed to represent `git` repositories and `GitHub` activities.

As explained, the SemanGit structure is prone to be extended by considering adding new "social feature" related terms to the already existing ontology in order to include other `git` platforms such as `GitLab` for instance. In addition to this horizontal extension, we are already orienting our next efforts towards the computation of several layers of analysis as presented above. Moreover, in order to offer an even more complete dataset, we are currently exploring directions to link even more the dataset with already well-established data such as e.g., DBpedia [6] or DBLP [14]. SemanGit is currently still lacking a public SparQL endpoint, making the full dataset available. This task is rather challenging due to the size of the data. Currently we commit our computational resources to the inclusion of the vertical extensions and linking with other datasets. After the necessary computational power and storage will be freed, we plan to implement an endpoint on our server.

More generally, even if the regular extraction process is still recent, the SemanGit dataset already has several directions of development. It will be sustained by several European projects on which we are contributing right now e.g. the QualiChain project. As a consequence, we will maintain the project at least until 2022, by providing the most recent datasets in bi-monthly intervals and continuing the development. To ensure that all dumps are recreatable, even if not listed on our homepage, the extraction and converter tools remain in the public repositories on `Github`.

We have built the SemanGit dataset having in mind a large number of possibilities it would offer, thus we do hope it will soon be considered as a bridge between the Open-Source and Semantic Web communities.

Acknowledgment. This work is partly supported by the German Federal Ministry of Education and Research (BMBF) in the context of the research project "Industrial Data Space Plus" (GA 01IS17031) as well as the Fraunhofer Cluster of Excellence "Cognitive Internet Technologies" (CCIT); by the EU H2020 project "QualiChain" (GA 822404); and by the ADAPT Centre for Digital Content Technology funded under the SFI Research Centres Programme (Grant 13/RC/2106) and co-funded under the European Regional Development Fund.

References

1. Bitbucket. https://bitbucket.org/. Accessed 16 Aug 2019
2. Comparison of source code hosting facilities. https://en.wikipedia.org/wiki/Comparison_of_source_code_hosting_facilities. Accessed 16 Aug 2019
3. GitLab. https://about.gitlab.com/. Accessed 16 Aug 2019
4. SourceForge. https://sourceforge.net/. Accessed 16 Aug 2019
5. Alexander, K., Cyganiak, R., Hausenblas, M., Zhao, J.: Void guide—using the vocabulary of interlinked datasets. Community Draft, voiD Working Group (2009)
6. Auer, S., Bizer, C., Kobilarov, G., Lehmann, J., Cyganiak, R., Ives, Z.: DBpedia: a nucleus for a web of open data. In: Aberer, K., et al. (eds.) ASWC/ISWC -2007. LNCS, vol. 4825, pp. 722–735. Springer, Heidelberg (2007). https://doi.org/10.1007/978-3-540-76298-0_52
7. Auer, S., Lehmann, J., Hellmann, S.: LinkedGeoData: adding a spatial dimension to the web of data. In: Bernstein, A., et al. (eds.) ISWC 2009. LNCS, vol. 5823, pp. 731–746. Springer, Heidelberg (2009). https://doi.org/10.1007/978-3-642-04930-9_46
8. Eric Prud'hommeaux, G.C.: RDF 1.1 turtle: terse RDF triple language. http://www.w3.org/TR/2014/REC-turtle-20140225/, The latest edition is available at http://www.w3.org/TR/turtle/

9. Attribution-Sharealike 4.0 International (CC BY-SA 4.0). https://creativecommons.org/licenses/by-sa/4.0/. Accessed 16 Aug 2019
10. GitHub About. https://github.com/about. Accessed 16 Aug 2019
11. GitHub REST API. https://developer.github.com/v3/. Accessed 16 Aug 2019
12. Gousios, G.: The GHTorrent dataset and tool suite. In: Proceedings of the 10th Working Conference on Mining Software Repositories, MSR 2013, pp. 233–236. IEEE Press, Piscataway (2013). http://dl.acm.org/citation.cfm?id=2487085.2487132
13. Lerner, J., Tirole, J.: Some simple economics of open source. J. Ind. Econ. **50**(2), 197–234 (2002)
14. Ley, M.: The DBLP computer science bibliography: evolution, research issues, perspectives. In: Laender, A.H.F., Oliveira, A.L. (eds.) SPIRE 2002. LNCS, vol. 2476, pp. 1–10. Springer, Heidelberg (2002). https://doi.org/10.1007/3-540-45735-6_1
15. Lohmann, S., Link, V., Marbach, E., Negru, S.: WebVOWL: web-based visualization of ontologies. In: Lambrix, P., et al. (eds.) EKAW 2014. LNCS (LNAI), vol. 8982, pp. 154–158. Springer, Cham (2015). https://doi.org/10.1007/978-3-319-17966-7_21
16. Torvalds, L., Hamano, J.: Git: fast version control system (2010). http://git-scm.com

Squerall: Virtual Ontology-Based Access to Heterogeneous and Large Data Sources

Mohamed Nadjib Mami[1,2(✉)], Damien Graux[2,3], Simon Scerri[1,2], Hajira Jabeen[1], Sören Auer[4], and Jens Lehmann[1,2]

[1] Smart Data Analytics (SDA) Group, Bonn University, Bonn, Germany
{mami,scerri,jabeen,jens.lehmann}@cs.uni-bonn.de
[2] Enterprise Information Systems, Fraunhofer IAIS, Sankt Augustin, Germany
damien.graux@iais.fraunhofer.de
[3] ADAPT Centre, Trinity College of Dublin, Dublin, Ireland
[4] TIB, Hannover University, Hannover, Germany
auer@l3s.de

Abstract. The last two decades witnessed a remarkable evolution in terms of data formats, modalities, and storage capabilities. Instead of having to adapt one's application needs to the, earlier limited, available storage options, today there is a wide array of options to choose from to best meet an application's needs. This has resulted in vast amounts of data available in a variety of forms and formats which, if interlinked and jointly queried, can generate valuable knowledge and insights. In this article, we describe Squerall: a framework that builds on the principles of Ontology-Based Data Access (OBDA) to enable the querying of disparate heterogeneous sources using a unique query language, SPARQL. In Squerall, original data is queried on-the-fly without prior data materialization or transformation. In particular, Squerall allows the aggregation and joining of large data in a distributed manner. Squerall supports out-of-the-box five data sources and moreover, it can be programmatically extended to cover more sources and incorporate new query engines. The framework provides user interfaces for the creation of necessary inputs, as well as guiding non-SPARQL experts to write SPARQL queries. Squerall is integrated into the popular SANSA stack and available as open-source software via GitHub and as a Docker image.

Software Framework. https://eis-bonn.github.io/Squerall.

1 Introduction

For over four decades, relational data management remained a dominant paradigm for storing and managing structured data. However, the advent of extremely large-scale applications revealed the weakness of relational data management at dynamically and horizontally scaling the storage and querying of massive amounts of data. This prompted a paradigm shift, calling for a new breed of databases capable of managing large data volumes without jeopardising query performance by reducing query expressivity and consistency requirements. Since 2008 to date, a wide array of so-called *non-relational* or *NoSQL* (Not

C. Ghidini et al. (Eds.): ISWC 2019, LNCS 11779, pp. 229–245, 2019.
https://doi.org/10.1007/978-3-030-30796-7_15

only SQL) databases emerged (e.g., Cassandra, MongoDB, Couchbase, Neo4j). This heterogeneity contributed to one of the main Big Data challenges: variety. The integration of heterogeneous data is the key rational for the development of semantic technologies over the past two decades. Local data schemata are *mapped* to global ontology terms, using *mapping languages* that have been standardized for a number of popular data representations, e.g., relational data, JSON, CSV or XML. Heterogeneous data can then be accessed in a *uniform* manner by means of queries in a standardized query language, SPARQL [15], employing terms from the ontology. Such data access is commonly referred to as Ontology-Based Data Access (OBDA) [23]. The term *Data Lake* [11] refers to the schema-less pool of heterogeneous and large data residing in its original formats on a horizontally-scalable cluster infrastructure. It comprises databases (e.g., NoSQL stores) or scale-out file/block storage infrastructure (e.g., Hadoop Distributed File System), and requires dealing with the original data without *prior physical transformation or pre-processing.* After emerging in industry, the concept has increasingly been discussed in the literature [21,24,32]. The integration of semantic technologies into Data Lakes led to the Semantic Data Lake concept, briefly introduced in our earlier work [2]. By adopting the OBDA paradigm to the NoSQL and Data Lake technology space, we realize the Semantic Data Lake concept and present in this article a comprehensive implementation.

Implementing an OBDA architecture atop Big Data raises three challenges:

1. *Query translation.* SPARQL queries must be translated into the query language of each of the respective data sources. A generic and dynamic translation between data models is challenging (even impossible in some cases e.g., join operations are unsupported in Cassandra and MongoDB [20]).
2. *Federated Query Execution.* In Big Data scenarios it is common to have non-selective queries with large intermediate results, so joining or aggregation cannot be performed on a single node, but only distributed across a cluster.
3. *Data silos.* Data coming from various sources can be connected to generate new insights, but it may not be readily 'joinable' (cf. definition below).

To target the aforementioned challenges we build Squerall [19], an extensible framework for querying Data Lakes.

- It allows *ad hoc* querying of large and heterogeneous data sources *virtually* without any data transformation or materialization.
- It allows the *distributed* query execution, in particular the joining of disparate heterogeneous sources.
- It enables users to declare query-time *transformations* for altering join keys and thus making data *joinable.*
- Squerall integrates the state-of-the-art Big Data engines Apache Spark and Presto with the semantic technologies RML and FnO.

The article is structured as follows. Squerall architecture is presented in Sect. 2 and its implementation in Sect. 3. The performance is evaluated in Sect. 4 and its sustainability, availability and extensibility aspects are discussed in Sect. 5. Related Work is presented in Sects. 6 and 7 concludes with an outlook on possible future work.

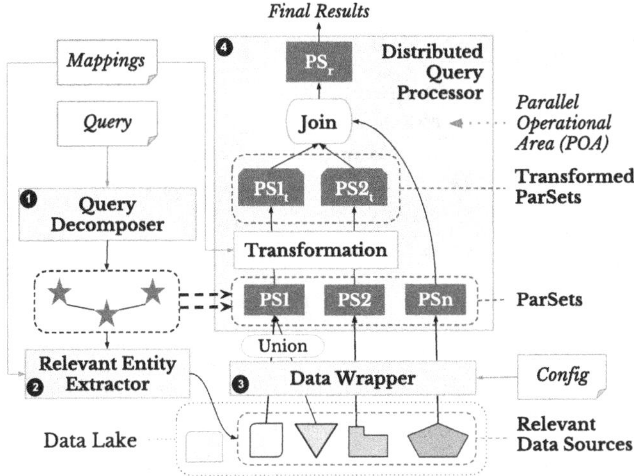

Fig. 1. Squerall architecture (mappings, query and config are user inputs).

2 Architecture

Squerall (Semantically query all) is built following the OBDA principles [23]. The latter were originally devised for accessing relational data but do not impose a restriction on the type or size of data it deals with. We project them to large and heterogeneous data sources contained in a Data Lake.

2.1 Preliminaries

In order to guide the subsequent discussions, we first define the following terms:

Data Attribute represents all concepts used by data sources to characterize a particular stored datum, e.g., a *column* in a tabular database like Cassandra, or a *field* in a document database like MongoDB.

Data Entity and Relevant Entity: an entity represents all concepts that are used by data sources to group together similar data, e.g., a *table* in a tabular database or a *collection* in a document database. An entity has one or multiple data attributes. An entity is relevant to a query if it contains information matching a part of the query (similarly found in federated systems, e.g., [25]).

ParSet and Joinable ParSets: from *Parallel dataSet*, ParSet refers to a data structure that is partitioned and distributed, and that is queried in parallel. ParSet is populated on-the-fly, and not materialized. Joinable ParSets are ParSets that store inter-matching values. For example, if the ParSet has a tabular representation, it has the same meaning as joinable tables in relational algebra, i.e., tables sharing common attribute values.

Parallel Operational Area (POA) is the parallel distributed environment where ParSets are loaded, joined and transformed, in response to a query. It has its internal data structure, which ParSets comply with.

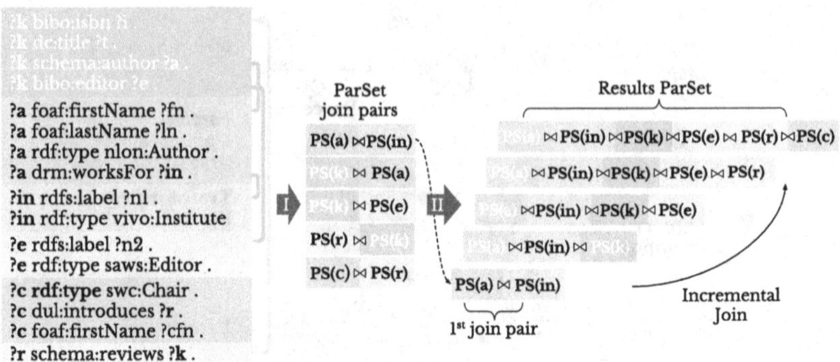

Fig. 2. ParSets extraction and join (for clarity ParSet(x) is shortened to PS(x)).

Data Source refers to any storage medium, e.g., plain file storage or a database.

Data Lake is a repository of multiple data sources where data is stored and accessed directly in its original form and format, without prior transformation.

2.2 OBDA Building Blocks

A typical OBDA system is composed of five main components:

Data. A Data Lake is a collection of multiple heterogeneous data sources, be it raw files (e.g., CSV), structured file formats (e.g., Parquet) or databases (e.g., MongoDB). Currently, Squerall does not support unstructured data but it can be part of the Data Lake.

Schema. A Data Lake is by definition a schema-less repository of data. Schemata exist at the level of the individual data sources.

Ontology. Ontologies are used to define a common domain conceptualization across Data Lake entities. At least class and properties definition is required.

Mappings. Mappings are association links between elements of the data schema and ontology terms (i.e., classes and properties). Three mapping elements need to be provided as input for an entity to be queried:

1. **Class mapping:** associates an entity to an ontology class.
2. **Property mappings:** associate entity attributes to ontology properties.
3. **Entity ID:** specifies an attribute to be used as identifier of the entity.

For example, `Author(AID,first_name,last_name)` is an entity in a table of a Cassandra database. In order to enable finding this entity, the user must provide the three mapping elements. As example, (1) *Class mapping:* (Author, nlon:Author) (2) *Property mappings:* (first_name, foaf:firstName), (last_name, foaf:lastName), and (3) *Entity ID:* AID. `firstName` and `lastName` are properties from the `foaf` ontology (http://xmlns.com/foaf/spec) and `Author` is a class from the `nlon` ontology (http://lod.nl.go.kr/page/ontology).

```
- Input: ParSetJoinsArray // An Array of all join pairs [ParSet,ParSet]
- Output: ResultsParSet // A ParSet joining all ParSets
ResultsParSet = ParSetJoinsArray.head // First join pair
iterate ParSetJoinsArray : current-pair
    if current-pair joinable_with ResultsParSet
        ResultsParSet = ResultsParSet join current-pair
    else add current-pair to PendingJoinsQueue
// Next, iterate through PendingJoinsQueue like ParSetJoinsArray
```

Listing 1.1. ParSet Join.

Query. The purpose of using a top query language, SPARQL in our case, is mainly to *join* data coming from multiple sources. Therefore, we assume that certain query forms and constructs are of less concern to Data Lake users, e.g., multi-level nested queries, queries with variable properties, `CONSTRUCT` queries.

2.3 Architecture Components

Squerall consists of four main components (cf. Fig. 1). Because of Squerall extensible design, also for clarity, we hereafter use the generic ParSets and POA concepts instead of Squerall's underlying equivalent concrete terms, which differ from engine to engine. The latter are presented in Sect. 3.

(1) Query Decomposor. This component is commonly found in OBDA and query federation systems (e.g., [12]). It here decomposes the query's Basic Graph Pattern (BGP, conjunctive set of triple patterns in the `where` clause) into a set of star-shaped sub-BGPs, where each sub-BGP contains all the triple patterns sharing the same *subject variable*. We refer to these sub-BGPs as *stars* for brevity; (see Fig. 2 left, stars are shown in distinct colored boxes). Query decomposition is subject-based (variable subjects), because the focus of query execution is on bringing and joining *entities* from different sources, not to retrieve a specific known entity. Retrieving a specific entity, i.e., subject is constant, requires full-data parsing and creating an index in a pre-processing phase. This defies the Data Lake definition to access original data without a pre-processing phase. A specific entity can be obtained, nonetheless, by filtering on its attributes.

(2) Relevant Entity Extractor. For every extracted star, this component looks in the *Mappings* for entities that have attributes mappings to *each of* the properties of the star. Such entities are *relevant* to the star.

(3) Data Wrapper. In the classical OBDA, SPARQL query has to be translated to the query language of the relevant data sources. This is in practice hard to achieve in the highly heterogeneous Data Lake settings. Therefore, numerous recent publications (e.g., [4,29]) advocated for the use of an intermediate query language. In our case, the intermediate query language is POA's query language, dictated by its internal data structure. The Data Wrapper generates data in POA's data structure at query-time, which allows for the parallel execution

```
<#AuthorMap>
 rml:logicalSource [
  rml:source: "../authors.parquet" ; nosql:store nosql:parquet ] ;
 rr:subjectMap [
   rr:template "http://exam.pl/../{AID}" ; rr:class nlon:Author ] ;
 rr:predicateObjectMap [
   rr:predicate foaf:firstName ; rr:objectMap [rml:reference "Fname"] ] ;
 rr:predicateObjectMap [ rr:predicate drm:worksFor ; rr:objectMap <#FunctionMap>] .
<#FunctionMap>
 fnml:functionValue [ rml:logicalSource "../authors.parquet" ; # Same as above
   rr:predicateObjectMap [ rr:predicate fno:executes ;
    rr:objectMap [rr:constant grel:string_toUppercase] ];
   rr:predicateObjectMap [
     rr:predicate grel:inputString ; rr:objectMap [rr:reference "InID"]
   ] ] . # Transform "InID" attribute using grel:string_toUppercase
```

Listing 1.2. Mapping an entity using RML and FnO.

of expensive operations, e.g., join. There must exist *wrappers* to convert data entities from the source to POA's data structure, either fully, or partially if parts of the data can be pushed down to the original source. Each identified star from step (1) will generate exactly one ParSet. If more than an entity are relevant, the ParSet is formed as a *union*. An auxiliary user input *Config* is used to guide the conversion process, e.g., authentication, or deployment specifications.

(4) Distributed Query Processor. Finally, ParSets are joined together forming the final results. ParSets in the POA can undergo any query operation, e.g., selection, aggregation, ordering, etc. However, since our focus is on querying multiple data sources, the emphasis is on the *join* operation. Joins between stars translate into joins between ParSets (Fig. 2 phase I). Next, ParSet pairs are all iteratively joined to form the *Results ParSet* (Fig. 2 phase II) using Listing 1.1 algorithm. In short, extracted join pairs are initially stored in an array. After the first pair is joined, it iterates through each remaining pair to attempt further joins or, else, add to a queue[1]. Next, the queue is similarly iterated, when a pair is joined, it is unqueued. The algorithm completes when the queue is empty. As the *Results ParSet* is a ParSet, it can also undergo query operations. The join capability of ParSets in the POA replaces the lack of the join common in many NoSQL databases, e.g., Cassandra, MongoDB [20]. Sometimes ParSets cannot be readily joined due to a syntactic mismatch between attribute values. Squerall allows users to declare *Transformations*, which are atomic operations applied to textual or numeral values, details are given in Subsect. 3.2.

3 Implementation

Squerall[2] is written in Scala. It uses *RML* and *FnO* to declare data mappings and transformations, and *Spark* [35] and *Presto*[3] as query engines.

[1] We used queue data structure simply to be able to dynamically pull (unqueue) elements from it iteratively till it has no more elements.

[2] Available at https://github.com/EIS-Bonn/Squerall (Apache-2.0 license).

[3] http://prestodb.io.

3.1 Data Mapping

Squerall accepts entity and attribute mappings declared in RML [10], a mapping language extending the W3C R2RML [7] to allow mapping heterogeneous sources. The following fragment is expected (e.g., `#AuthorMap` in Listing 1.2):

- `rml:logicalsource` used to specify the entity source and type.
- `rr:subjectMap` used (only) to extract the entity ID (in brackets).
- `rr:predicateObjectMap`, used for all entity attributes; maps an attribute using `rml:reference` to an ontology term using `rr:predicate`.

We complement RML with the property `nosql:store` (line 5) from our NoSQL ontology[4], to enable specifying the entity type, e.g., Cassandra, MongoDB, etc.

3.2 Data Transformation

To enable data joinability, Squerall allows users to declare transformations. Two requirements should be met: (1) transformation specification should be decoupled from the technical implementation, (2) transformations should be performed on-the-fly on *query-time*, complying with the Data Lake definition.

We incorporate the Function Ontology (FnO, [8]), which allows to declare machine-processable high-level functions, abstracting from the concrete technology used. We use FnO in conjunction with RML similarly to the approach in [9] applied to the DBpedia Extraction Framework. However, we do not physically generate RDF triples but only apply FnO transformations on-the-fly at query-time. Instead of directly referencing an entity attribute `rml:reference` (e.g., line 7 Listing 1.2), we reference an FnO function that alters the values of the attribute (line 9 Listing 1.2). For example in Listing 1.2, the attribute `InID` (line 18) is indirectly mapped to the ontology term `drm:worksFor` via the `#FunctionMap`. This implies that the attribute values are to be transformed using the function represented by the `#FunctionMap`, `grel:string_toUppercase` (line 16). The latter sets the `InID` attribute values to uppercase.

Squerall visits the mappings at query-time and triggers specific Spark and Presto operations over the query intermediate results whenever a transformation declaration is met. In Spark, a *map()* transformation is used, in Presto corresponding string or numeral SQL operations are used. For the uppercase example, in Spark `upper(DataFrame column)` function inside a *map()* is used, in Presto the SQL `upper()` string function is used.

3.3 Data Wrapping and Querying

We implement Squerall engine using two popular frameworks: Apache Spark and Presto. Spark is a general-purpose processing engine and Presto a distributed SQL query engine for interactive querying, both base their computations primarily in memory. We leverage Spark's and Presto's connector concept,

[4] URL: http://purl.org/db/nosql, details are out of the scope of this article.

which is a wrapper able to load data from an external source into their internal data structure (ParSet), performing *flattening* of any non-tabular representations. Spark's internal data structure is called *DataFrame*, which is a tabular structure *programmatically* queried in SQL. Their schema corresponds to the schema of the ParSet, *a column per star predicate*. As explained with ParSets, DataFrames are created from the relevant entities, and incrementally joined. Other non-join operations found in SPARQL query (e.g., selection, aggregation, ordering) are translated to equivalent SQL operations; they are applied either at the level of individual DataFrames, or the level of the final results DataFrame, whichever is more optimal. As an optimization, in order to reduce the intermediate results and, thus, data to join with, we push the selection and transformation to the level of individual DataFrames. We leave aggregation and ordering to the final results DataFrame, as those have results-wide effect. Presto also loads data into its internal native data structure. However, unlike Spark, it does it transparently; it is not possible to manipulate those data structures. Rather, Presto accepts one self-contained SQL query with references to all the relevant data sources, e.g., `SELECT cassandra.cdb.product C JOIN mongo.mdb.producer M ON C.producerID = M.ID`. ParSets in this case are views (SELECT sub-queries), which we create, join and optimize similarly to DataFrames.

Spark and Presto make using connectors very convenient, users only provide values to a pre-defined list of *options*. Spark DataFrames are created as follows: `spark.read.format(sourceType).options(options).load`. In Presto, options are added to a simple file. Leveraging on this simplicity, Squerall supports out-of-the box five data sources: Cassandra, MongoDB, Parquet, CSV and JDBC (MySQL tested). We chose Spark and Presto as they have a good balance between the number of connectors, ease of use and performance [17,33].

3.4 User Interfaces

Squerall is provided with three user interfaces allowing to generate its three needed input files (config, mappings and query), respectively described as follows:

Connect UI shows and receives from users the required options that enable the connection to a data source, e.g., host, port, password, cluster settings, etc.

Mapping UI uses connection options to extract data schema (entity and attributes). It then allows the users to fill or search existing ontology catalogues for equivalent ontology terms (cf. Fig. 3a).

SPARQL UI guides non-SPARQL experts to build correct SPARQL queries by means of widget offered for different SPARQL constructs (cf. Fig. 3b).

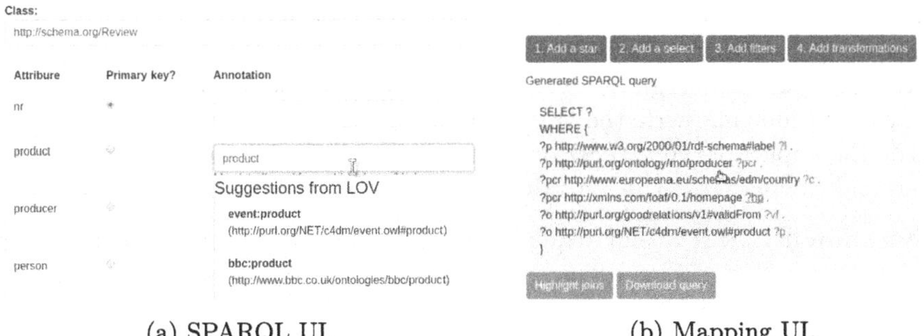

(a) SPARQL UI. (b) Mapping UI.

Fig. 3. Screenshots from Squerall GUIs.

4 Performance Analysis

4.1 Setup

Datasets: As there is no Data Lake dedicated benchmark with SPARQL support, we opt for BSBM [3], a benchmark conceived for comparing the performance of RDF triple stores with SPARQL-to-SQL rewriters. We use its data generator to generate SQL dumps. We pick five tables: Product, Producer, Offer, Review, and Person tables, pre-process them to extract tuples and load them into five different data sources (cf. Table 1). Those were chosen to enable up to 4-chain joins of five different data sources. We generate three scales: 500k, 1.5M and 5M (number of products)[5].

Table 1. Data sources and corresponding number of tuples loaded.

Generated data (BSBM)	Product	Offer	Review	Person	Producer
	Cassandra	MongoDB	Parquet	CSV	MySQL
# of tuples Scale 0.5M	0.5M	10M	5M	26K	10K
# of tuples Scale 1.5M	1.5M	30M	15M	77K	30K
# of tuples Scale 5M	5M	100M	50M	2.6M	100K

Queries: Since we only populate a subset of the generated BSBM tables, we have to alter the initial queries accordingly. We discard joining with tables we do not consider, e.g., Vendors, and replace them with others populated. All queries[6] result in a cross-source join, from 1 (between 2 sources e.g., Q3) to 4 (between 5 sources e.g., Q4). Queries with yet unsupported syntax, e.g., `DESCRIBE`, `CONSTRUCT`, are omitted.

[5] The 1.5M scale factor generates 500M RDF triples, and the 5M factor 1,75B triples.

[6] See https://github.com/EIS-Bonn/Squerall/tree/master/evaluation.

Metrics: We evaluate results *accuracy* and query *performance*. For accuracy, we compare query results against a centralized relational database (MySQL), as it represents data at its highest level of consistency. For performance, we measure query execution time wrt. the three generated scales. A particular emphasis is put on the impact of the *number of joins* on query time. We run each query three times and calculate their mean value. The timeout threshold is set to 3600 s.

Environment: We ran our experiments in a cluster of three machines each having DELL PowerEdge R815, 2x AMD Opteron 6376 (16 cores) CPU and 256 GB RAM. In order to exclude any effect of caching, all queries are run on a cold cache. Also, no optimization techniques from the query engines were used.

4.2 Results and Discussion

We compare the performance of Squerall's two underlying query engines: Spark and Presto, in absence of a similar work allowing to query all five data sources and SPARQL fragment that Squerall supports.

Accuracy. The number of results returned by Squerall was in all queries of scale 0.5 m identical to MySQL, i.e., 100% accuracy. MySQL timed out with data of scale 1.5M, starting from which we compared the performance between the two engines, and results were also identical.

Performance. The results (cf. Fig. 4) suggest that Squerall overall exhibits reasonable performance throughout the various queries, i.e., different number of joins, with and without filtering and ordering. Presto-based Squerall exhibits significantly better performance than Spark-based, up to an order of magnitude. With the 0.5M data scale, query performance is superior across all the queries with an increase of up to 800%. With scales 1.5M and 5M, Presto-based is superior in all queries other than Q1, with an increase of up to 1300%. This superiority is due to a number of factors. Presto is built following the MPP (Massively Parallel Processing) principles specifically to optimize SQL querying. Another factor is that Presto has far less preparation overhead (e.g., mid-query fault-tolerance, resource negotiation) than Spark. Spark, in the other hand, is a general-purpose system, basing its SQL library on its native in-memory tabular data structure not originally conceived for *ad hoc* querying. Also, it incurs overhead to guarantee query resiliency and manage resources.

Query performance was homogeneous across all the scales and between the two engines, except for Q2, which was among the fastest in Presto contrarily to Spark. This query is special in that it projects out most *Product* attributes joining the largest entity, *Offer*, without any filtering, which may indicate that Presto handles intermediate results of unselective queries better. Q3 was the fastest, as it has the lowest number of joins. Followed by Q1 and Q8, which contain more joins, but with significantly filtered number of products. The rest of the queries are notably slower because they join with the large entity *Offer*. The presence of the `LIMIT` clause did not have a direct effect on query time, it is present in Q1–Q5, Q8 and Q10, across which the performance varies significantly.

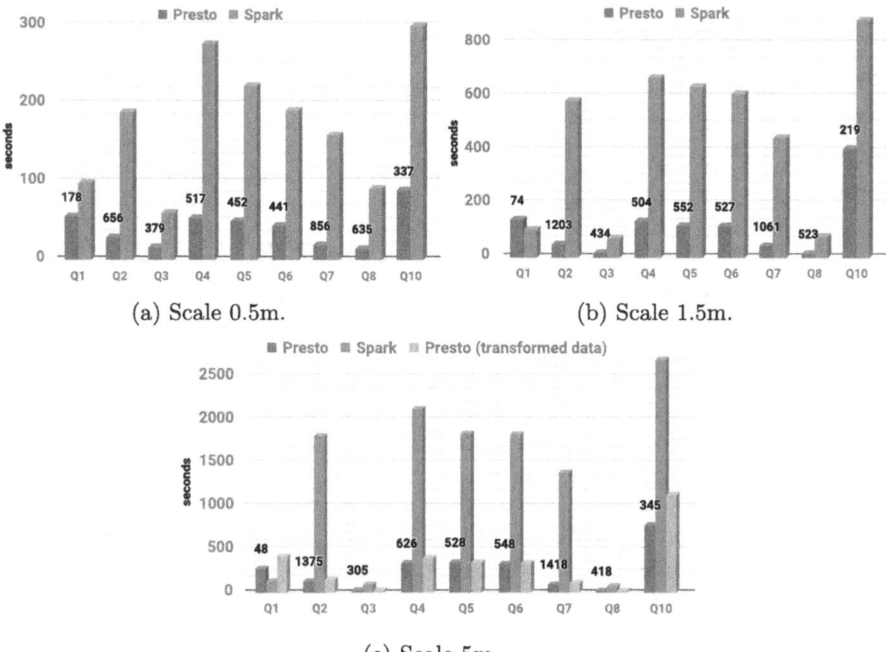

(a) Scale 0.5m.

(b) Scale 1.5m.

(c) Scale 5m.

Fig. 4. Query execution time (seconds). The labels on top of Presto's columns show the percentage between Presto's and Spark's execution times, e.g., in (a) in Q2, 178 means that Presto-based Squerall is 178% faster than Spark-based.

Although the current data distribution does not represent the best-case scenario (e.g., query performance would be better if *Review* data was loaded into Cassandra instead), we intentionally stored the large data into the better performing data sources. Our purpose in this experiment series was to observe Squerall behavior using Spark and Presto across the various scales and queries. For example, we observed that, although the largest data entity was loaded into a very efficient database, MongoDB, the queries implicating this entity were the slowest anyway. This gives an indication of the performance of those queries if the same entity was loaded into a less capable source, e.g., Parquet or CSV.

Increasing data size did not diminish query performance; query times were approximately proportional to the data size (cf. Fig. 5), and remained under the threshold. In order to evaluate the effect of the query-time data transformations, we intentionally introduce variations to the data so it becomes *unjoinable.* In table `Product`, we decrease the column *pr* values by 71, in table `Producer`, we append the string "-A" to all values of column *pr*, and in table *Review* we prefix the values of column *person* with the character "P". We declare the necessary transformations accordingly. The results show that there is a negligible cost in the majority of the cases. This is attributed to the fact that both Spark and Presto base computations in memory. In Spark, those transforma-

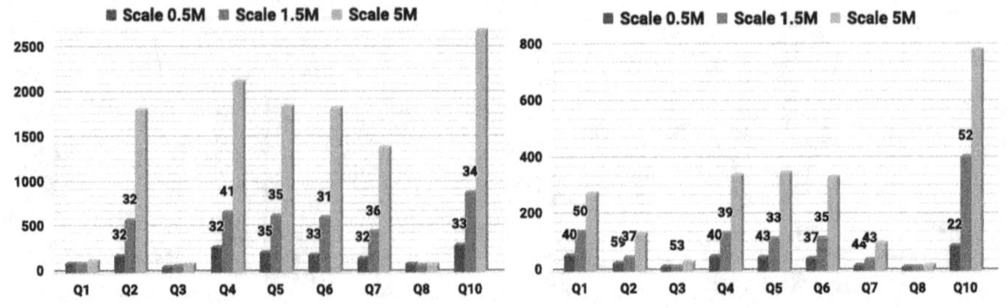

(a) Spark-based Squerall query times. (b) Presto-based Squerall query times.

Fig. 5. Numbers above the bars denote time percentage differences between the scales, e.g., in (a) Q2 execution time in scale 0.5M is 32% of that in scale 1.5M, which is 32% of that in 5M. On average, percentages are ≈30% in all cases (both engines), which is proportional to the data scale (5 m = 30%1.5 m = 30%0.5 m).

tions involve only *map* function, which is executed locally very efficiently, not requiring any data movement. Only few queries in 5M in Presto-based Squerall exhibited noticeable but not significant costs, e.g., Q1 and Q10. Due to the insignificant differences and to improve readability, we only add the results of the transformation cost in the scale 5M Fig. 4c. Our results could be considered as a performance comparison between Spark and Presto, of which few exist [17,33].

5 Availability, Sustainability, Usability and Extensibility

Squerall is integrated[7] into SANSA [18] since version 0.5, a large framework for distributed querying, inference and analytics over knowledge graphs. SANSA has been used across a range of funded projects, such as BigDataEurope, SLIPO, and BETTER. Via the integration into SANSA, Squerall becomes available to a large user base. It benefits from SANSA's various deployment options, e.g., Maven Central integration and runnable notebooks. SANSA has an active developer community (≈20 developers), an active mailing list, issue tracking system, website and social media channels. Prior to its integration, Squerall features were recurrently requested in SANSA, to allow it to also access large non-RDF data. Squerall sustainability is ensured until 2022 thanks to a number of contributing innovation projects including Simple-ML, BETTER, SLIPO, and MLwin. Further, Squerall is being adopted and extended in an internal use-case of a large industrial company; we plan to report this in a separate adequate submission.

The development of Squerall was driven by technical challenges identified by the H2020 BigDataEurope project[8], whose main technical result, the Big Data Integrator platform, retains a significant amount of interest by the open-source community. In the absence of appropriate technical solutions supporting Data

[7] https://github.com/SANSA-Stack/SANSA-DataLake.
[8] www.big-data-europe.eu & https://github.com/big-data-europe.

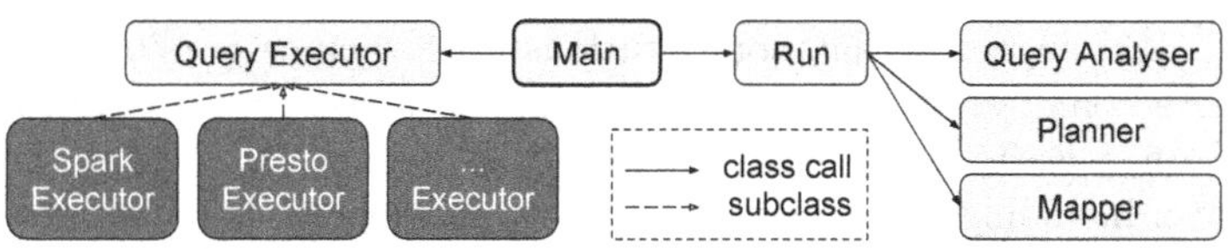

Fig. 6. Squerall class call hierarchy. Engine classes (colored) are decoupled from the rest (grey). A new engine can be added by extending only query executor class (implementing it methods). (Color figure online)

Lake scenarios, the platform development was constrained to transform and centralize most of the data in the use-cases. The need to invest in architectures, tools and methodologies to allow for decentralized Big Data management was highly emphasized by the project. Further, demonstrating the feasibility and effectiveness of OBDA on top of the ever increasing movement of NoSQL has a positive impact on the adoption of Semantic Web principles. This indicates some clear evidence of Squerall's value and role in the community.

Squerall is openly available under *Apache-2.0* terms; it is hosted on GitHub[9] and registered in Zenodo[10] (DOI: *10.5281/zenodo.2636436*). Squerall makes use of open standards and ontologies, including SPARQL, RML, and FnO. It can easily be built and used thanks to its detailed documentation. Its usage is facilitated by the accompanied user interfaces, which are demonstrated in a walkthrough screencast[11]. Further, we provide a Docker image allowing to easily setup Squerall and reproduce the presented evaluation. Squerall was built with extensibility in mind; it can be programmatically extended[12] by (1) adding a new query engine, e.g., Drill, due to its modular code design (cf. Fig. 6), and (2) supporting more data sources with minimal effort by leveraging Spark/Presto connectors. A mailing list and a Gitter community are made available for the users.

6 Related Work

There are several solutions for mapping relational databases to RDF [28], and OBDA over relational databases [34], e.g., Ontop, Morph, Ultrawrap, Mastro, Stardog. Although we share the OBDA concepts, our focus goes to the heterogeneous non-relational and distributed scalable databases. On the non-relational side, there has been a number of efforts, which we can classify into ontology-based and non-ontology-based.

For non-ontology-based access, [6] defines a mapping language to express access links to NoSQL databases. It proposes an intermediate query language to transform SQL to Java methods accessing NoSQL databases. However, query processing is neither elaborated nor evaluated, e.g., cross-database join is not

[9] https://github.com/EIS-Bonn/Squerall.
[10] https://zenodo.org/record/2636436.
[11] https://github.com/EIS-Bonn/Squerall/tree/master/evaluation/screencasts.
[12] https://github.com/EIS-Bonn/Squerall/wiki/Extending-Squerall.

mentioned. [13] suggests that computations performance can be improved if data is shifted on query-time between multiple databases; the suitable database is decided on a case-to-case basis. Although it demonstrates that the overall performance, including the planning and data movement, is higher when using one database, this is not proven to be true with large data. In real large-scale settings, data movement and I/O can dominate the query time. [26] allows to run CRUD operations over NoSQL databases; beyond, the same authors in [27] enable joins as follows. If the join involves entities in the same database, it is performed locally, if not or if the database lacks join capability, data is moved to another capable database. This implies that no intra-source distributed join is possible, and, similarly to [13], moving data can become a bottleneck in large scales. [1] proposes a unifying *programming* model to interface with different NoSQL databases. It allows direct access to individual databases using *get*, *put* and *delete* primitives. Join between databases is not addressed. [16] proposes a SQL-like language containing invocations to the native query interface of relational and NoSQL databases. The learning curve of this query language is higher than other efforts suggesting to query solely using plain (or minimally adapted) SQL, JSONPath or SPARQL. Although its architecture is distributed, it is not explicitly stated whether intra-source join is also distributed. Besides, the code-source is unfortunately not available. A number of efforts, e.g., [4,29,30], aim at bridging the gap between relational and NoSQL databases, but only one database is evaluated. Given the high semantic and structural heterogeneity found across NoSQL databases, a single database cannot be representative of all the family. Among those, [30] adopts JSON as both conceptual and physical data model. This requires physically transforming query's intermediate results, costing the engine transformation price (a limitation also observed in other efforts). Moreover, the prototype is evaluated with only small data on a single machine. [22] presents SQL++, an ambitious general query language that is based on SQL and JSON. It covers a vast portion of the capabilities of query languages found across NoSQL databases. However, the focus is on the query language, and the prototype is only minimally validated using a single database: MongoDB. [31] considers data duplicated in multiple heterogeneous sources, and identifies the best source to send a query to. Thus, joins between sources are not explored. For ontology-based access, Optique [14] is a reference platform with consideration also for dynamic streaming data. Although based on the open-source Ontop, sources of the Big Data instance are not publicly available. Ontario[13] is a very similar (unpublished) work; however, we were not able to run it due to the lack of documentation, and it appears that wrappers are manually created. [5] considers simple query examples, where joins are minimally addressed. Distributed implementation is future work.

In all the surveyed solutions, support for data source variety is limited or faces bottlenecks. Only support for a few data sources (1–3) is observed, and wrappers are manually created or hard-coded. In contrast, Squerall does not reinvent the wheel and makes use of the many wrappers of existing engines. This makes it the

[13] https://github.com/SDM-TIB/Ontario.

solution with the broadest support of the Big Data Variety dimension in terms of data sources. Additionally, Squerall has among the richest query capabilities (see full fragment in[14]), from joining and aggregation to various query modifiers.

7 Conclusion and Future Work

In this article, we presented Squerall—a framework realizing the Semantic Data Lake, i.e., querying heterogeneous and large data sources using Semantic Web techniques. It performs distributed cross-source join operation and allows users to declare transformations that enable joinability on-the-fly at query-time. Squerall is built using state-of-the-art Big Data technologies, Spark and Presto. Relying on the latter's connectors to wrap the data, Squerall relieves users from handcrafting wrappers—a major bottleneck in supporting data variety throughout the literature. It also makes Squerall easily extensible, e.g., in addition to the five sources evaluated here, Couchbase and Elasticsearch were also tested. There are dozens of connectors already available[15]. Furthermore, due to its modular code design, Squerall can also be programmatically extended to use other query engines. In the future, we plan to support more SPARQL operations, e.g., `OPTIONAL` and `UNION`, and also to exploit the query engines' own optimizations to accelerate query performance. Finally, in such a heterogeneous environment, there is a natural need for retaining provenance at data and query results levels.

Acknowledgment. This work is partly supported by the EU H2020 projects BETTER (GA 776280) and QualiChain (GA 822404); and by the ADAPT Centre for Digital Content Technology funded under the SFI Research Centres Programme (Grant 13/RC/2106) and co-funded under the European Regional Development Fund.

References

1. Atzeni, P., Bugiotti, F., Rossi, L.: Uniform access to non-relational database systems: the SOS platform. In: Ralyté, J., Franch, X., Brinkkemper, S., Wrycza, S. (eds.) CAiSE 2012. LNCS, vol. 7328, pp. 160–174. Springer, Heidelberg (2012). https://doi.org/10.1007/978-3-642-31095-9_11
2. Auer, S., et al.: The BigDataEurope platform – supporting the variety dimension of big data. In: Cabot, J., De Virgilio, R., Torlone, R. (eds.) ICWE 2017. LNCS, vol. 10360, pp. 41–59. Springer, Cham (2017). https://doi.org/10.1007/978-3-319-60131-1_3
3. Bizer, C., Schultz, A.: The Berlin SPARQL benchmark. Int. J. Semant. Web Inf. Syst. (IJSWIS) **5**(2), 1–24 (2009)
4. Botoeva, E., Calvanese, D., Cogrel, B., Corman, J., Xiao, G.: A generalized framework for ontology-based data access. In: Ghidini, C., Magnini, B., Passerini, A., Traverso, P. (eds.) AI*IA 2018. LNCS (LNAI), vol. 11298, pp. 166–180. Springer, Cham (2018). https://doi.org/10.1007/978-3-030-03840-3_13

[14] https://github.com/EIS-Bonn/Squerall/tree/master/evaluation.

[15] https://spark-packages.org https://prestodb.io/docs/current/connector.

5. Curé, O., Kerdjoudj, F., Faye, D., Le Duc, C., Lamolle, M.: On the potential integration of an ontology-based data access approach in NoSQL stores. Int. J. Distrib. Syst. Technol. (IJDST) **4**(3), 17–30 (2013)
6. Curé, O., Hecht, R., Le Duc, C., Lamolle, M.: Data integration over NoSQL stores using access path based mappings. In: Hameurlain, A., Liddle, S.W., Schewe, K.-D., Zhou, X. (eds.) DEXA 2011. LNCS, vol. 6860, pp. 481–495. Springer, Heidelberg (2011). https://doi.org/10.1007/978-3-642-23088-2_36
7. Das, S., Sundara, S., Cyganiak, R.: R2RML: RDB to RDF mapping language. Working Group Recommendation, W3C, September 2012
8. De Meester, B., Dimou, A., Verborgh, R., Mannens, E.: An ontology to semantically declare and describe functions. In: Sack, H., Rizzo, G., Steinmetz, N., Mladenić, D., Auer, S., Lange, C. (eds.) ESWC 2016. LNCS, vol. 9989, pp. 46–49. Springer, Cham (2016). https://doi.org/10.1007/978-3-319-47602-5_10
9. De Meester, B., Maroy, W., Dimou, A., Verborgh, R., Mannens, E.: Declarative data transformations for linked data generation: the case of DBpedia. In: Blomqvist, E., Maynard, D., Gangemi, A., Hoekstra, R., Hitzler, P., Hartig, O. (eds.) ESWC 2017. LNCS, vol. 10250, pp. 33–48. Springer, Cham (2017). https://doi.org/10.1007/978-3-319-58451-5_3
10. Dimou, A., Vander Sande, M., Colpaert, P., Verborgh, R., Mannens, E., Van de Walle, R.: RML: a generic language for integrated RDF mappings of heterogeneous data. In: LDOW (2014)
11. Dixon, J.: Pentaho, Hadoop, and Data Lakes (2010). https://jamesdixon.wordpress.com/2010/10/14/pentaho-hadoop-and-data-lakes. Accessed 27 Jan 2019
12. Endris, K.M., Galkin, M., Lytra, I., Mami, M.N., Vidal, M.-E., Auer, S.: MULDER: querying the linked data web by bridging RDF molecule templates. In: Benslimane, D., Damiani, E., Grosky, W.I., Hameurlain, A., Sheth, A., Wagner, R.R. (eds.) DEXA 2017. LNCS, vol. 10438, pp. 3–18. Springer, Cham (2017). https://doi.org/10.1007/978-3-319-64468-4_1
13. Gadepally, V., et al.: The BigDAWG polystore system and architecture. In: High Performance Extreme Computing Conference, pp. 1–6. IEEE (2016)
14. Giese, M., et al.: Optique: zooming in on big data. Computer **48**(3), 60–67 (2015)
15. Harris, S., Seaborne, A., Prud'hommeaux, E.: SPARQL 1.1 query language. W3C Recommendation **21**(10) (2013)
16. Kolev, B., Valduriez, P., Bondiombouy, C., Jiménez-Peris, R., Pau, R., Pereira, J.: CloudMdsQL: querying heterogeneous cloud data stores with a common language. Distrib. Parallel Databases **34**(4), 463–503 (2016)
17. Kolychev, A., Zaytsev, K.: Research of the effectiveness of SQL engines working in HDFS. J. Theor. Appl. Inf. Technol. **95**(20), 5360–5368 (2017)
18. Lehmann, J., et al.: Distributed semantic analytics using the SANSA stack. In: d'Amato, C., et al. (eds.) ISWC 2017. LNCS, vol. 10588, pp. 147–155. Springer, Cham (2017). https://doi.org/10.1007/978-3-319-68204-4_15
19. Mami, M.N., Graux, D., Scerri, S., Jabeen, H., Auer, S.: Querying data lakes using spark and presto (2019, To appear in The WebConf - Demonstrations)
20. Michel, F., Faron-Zucker, C., Montagnat, J.: A mapping-based method to query MongoDB documents with SPARQL. In: Hartmann, S., Ma, H. (eds.) DEXA 2016. LNCS, vol. 9828, pp. 52–67. Springer, Cham (2016). https://doi.org/10.1007/978-3-319-44406-2_6
21. Miloslavskaya, N., Tolstoy, A.: Application of big data, fast data, and data lake concepts to information security issues. In: International Conference on Future Internet of Things and Cloud Workshops, pp. 148–153. IEEE (2016)

22. Ong, K.W., Papakonstantinou, Y., Vernoux, R.: The SQL++ unifying semi-structured query language, and an expressiveness benchmark of SQL-on-Hadoop, NoSQL and NewSQL databases. CoRR, abs/1405.3631 (2014)
23. Poggi, A., Lembo, D., Calvanese, D., De Giacomo, G., Lenzerini, M., Rosati, R.: Linking data to ontologies. In: Spaccapietra, S. (ed.) Journal on Data Semantics X. LNCS, vol. 4900, pp. 133–173. Springer, Heidelberg (2008). https://doi.org/10.1007/978-3-540-77688-8_5
24. Quix, C., Hai, R., Vatov, I.: GEMMS: a generic and extensible metadata management system for data lakes. In: CAiSE Forum, pp. 129–136 (2016)
25. Saleem, M., Ngonga Ngomo, A.-C.: HiBISCuS: hypergraph-based source selection for SPARQL endpoint federation. In: Presutti, V., d'Amato, C., Gandon, F., d'Aquin, M., Staab, S., Tordai, A. (eds.) ESWC 2014. LNCS, vol. 8465, pp. 176–191. Springer, Cham (2014). https://doi.org/10.1007/978-3-319-07443-6_13
26. Sellami, R., Bhiri, S., Defude, B.: Supporting multi data stores applications in cloud environments. IEEE Trans. Serv. Comput. **9**(1), 59–71 (2016)
27. Sellami, R., Defude, B.: Complex queries optimization and evaluation over relational and NoSQL data stores in cloud environments. IEEE Trans. Big Data **4**(2), 217–230 (2018)
28. Spanos, D., Stavrou, P., Mitrou, N.: Bringing relational databases into the semantic web: a survey. Semant. Web 1–41 (2010)
29. Unbehauen, J., Martin, M.: Executing SPARQL queries over mapped document stores with SparqlMap-M. In: 12th International Conference on Semantic Systems (2016)
30. Vathy-Fogarassy, Á., Hugyák, T.: Uniform data access platform for SQL and NoSQL database systems. Inf. Syst. **69**, 93–105 (2017)
31. Vogt, M., Stiemer, A., Schuldt, H.: Icarus: towards a multistore database system. In: 2017 IEEE International Conference on Big Data (Big Data), pp. 2490–2499 (2017)
32. Walker, C., Alrehamy, H.: Personal data lake with data gravity pull. In: 5th International Conference on Big Data and Cloud Computing, pp. 160–167. IEEE (2015)
33. Wiewiórka, M.S., Wysakowicz, D.P., Okoniewski, M.J., Gambin, T.: Benchmarking distributed data warehouse solutions for storing genomic variant information. Database **2017** (2017)
34. Xiao, G., et al.: Ontology-based data access: a survey. In: IJCAI (2018)
35. Zaharia, M., Chowdhury, M., Franklin, M.J., Shenker, S., Stoica, I.: Spark: cluster computing with working sets. HotCloud **10**(10–10), 95 (2010)

List.MID: A MIDI-Based Benchmark for Evaluating RDF Lists

Albert Meroño-Peñuela[1](✉) and Enrico Daga[2]

[1] Computer Science Department, Vrije Universiteit Amsterdam, Amsterdam, The Netherlands
albert.merono@vu.nl

[2] Knowledge Media Institute, The Open University, Milton Keynes, UK
enrico.daga@open.ac.uk

Abstract. Linked lists represent *a countable number of ordered values*, and are among the most important abstract data types in computer science. With the advent of RDF as a highly expressive knowledge representation language for the Web, various implementations for RDF lists have been proposed. Yet, there is no benchmark so far dedicated to evaluate the performance of triple stores and SPARQL query engines on dealing with ordered linked data. Moreover, essential tasks for evaluating RDF lists, like generating datasets containing RDF lists of various sizes, or generating the same RDF list using different modelling choices, are cumbersome and unprincipled. In this paper, we propose `List.MID`, a systematic benchmark for evaluating systems serving RDF lists. `List.MID` consists of a dataset generator, which creates RDF list data in various models and of different sizes; and a set of SPARQL queries. The RDF list data is coherently generated from a large, community-curated base collection of Web MIDI files, rich in lists of musical events of arbitrary length. We describe the `List.MID` benchmark, and discuss its impact and adoption, reusability, design, and availability.

Keywords: Linked lists · RDF · Benchmarks

1 Introduction

Linked lists are data structures that represent *a countable number of ordered values*, and are one of the fundamental abstract data types in computer science [15]. They are at least basically supported, with a variety of implementations, in the core libraries of all major programming languages [20].

With the advent of the Semantic Web [4], the Resource Description Framework [23] (RDF) becomes the standard for knowledge representation on the Web. As an expressive data format designed for enabling semantic interoperability, data integration, and data modeling in all sorts of domains, many use cases demand standard ways of representing classic data structures; linked lists are among them. Consequently, Semantic Web standards such as RDF itself [23],

C. Ghidini et al. (Eds.): ISWC 2019, LNCS 11779, pp. 246–260, 2019.
https://doi.org/10.1007/978-3-030-30796-7_16

RDF Schema [6], and more recently JSON-LD [24] propose various implementations for RDF lists: `rdf:Seq`, based on list ordering properties; `rdf:List`, based on LISP-like `rdf:first` and `rdf:rest` pointers; or the `"@list": []` JSON-LD attribute. Moreover, the community itself has developed its own ontology design patterns [10] to implement list-like ontological structures.

With this variety of alternatives, many questions arise on practical and performance issues with respect to RDF lists. For example, it is hard to choose one such implementation in large-scale, list-based RDF datasets [18] without knowing the impact of such choice in query performance. Differently, other users may be interested in favoring list readability over performance. In order to address this, some remarkable users have reported ways to query such RDF lists.[1] However, no standard benchmark has been so far proposed in the Semantic Web in order to generate RDF list data, in all its possible modeling alternatives, in a systematic and principled way. Such a benchmark could contribute to clarify many of the open questions about RDF list modeling and publishing on the Web, such as query performance, list readability, triplestore reproducible evaluations, and so forth.

In this paper, we introduce the `List.MID` benchmark, an RDF list data generator and query template set specifically designed for the evaluation of RDF lists. The benchmark has two focus points: (a) to cover as many RDF list implementations as possible, following a systematic study that surveys and summarizes different RDF list modeling practices into *6 different RDF list modeling templates* [8]; and (b) to create such multi-model RDF lists *out of real-world data*, through the large-scale, list-rich symbolic music notation dataset of the MIDI Linked Data cloud [18]. Specifically, the contributions of the paper are:

- We list and describe 6 abstract RDF list modeling patterns recently surveyed [8] (Sect. 3.1)
- We describe the `List.MID` data generator (Sect. 3.2), which generates RDF list data according to these patterns from the MIDI Linked Data cloud dataset [18]; and a set of SPARQL query templates for retrieval (Sect. 3.3)
- We show evidence of use and potential adoption for our proposed benchmark (Sect. 4)

The rest of the paper is organized as follows: Sect. 2 covers the related work; Sect. 3 describes the `List.MID` benchmark, data generator, and queries; Sect. 4 shows evidence of use and potential adoption for the benchmark; and Sect. 5 draws our conclusions.

2 Related Work

Multiple ways of modelling RDF lists have been proposed. The RDF Schema (RDFS) recommendation [6] defines several container classes to represent

[1] See e.g. https://stackoverflow.com/questions/16223095/sparql-queries-over-collection-and-rdfcontainers and http://www.snee.com/bobdc.blog/2014/04/rdf-lists-and-sparql.html.

collections: `rdf:Bag` to contain unordered elements; `rdf:Alt` for "alternative" containers whose typical processing will be to select one of its members; and `rdf:Seq` to contain elements ordered by the numerical order of the container membership properties. [6] also defines a collection vocabulary to describe closed collection that can have no more members, through the class `rdf:List` and the properties `rdf:first`, `rdf:rest`, and `rdf:nil`. In the more recent JSON-LD [24], ordered lists like `"@list": [ "bob", "alice", "carol" ]` have equivalent representations as `rdf:List`. Similarly, the RDF 1.1 Turtle [2] syntax allows for the specification of `rdf:List` instances, e.g. `:a :b ( "bob" "alice" "carol")`. Besides W3C standards, various ontology design patterns [10], like the Sequence Ontology Pattern[2] (SOP), address the task of representing RDF lists. About relevant previous work on benchmarks, the Semantic Web community has developed a number of them for evaluating the performance of SPARQL engines. The Berlin SPARQL Benchmark (BSBM) [5] generates benchmark data about exploring products and analyzing consumer reviews. The Lehigh University Benchmark (LUBM) [13] does so on data about universities, departments, professors and students. SP^{2}Bench [22] enables comparison of SPARQL optimization strategies, an estimation of their generality, and the prediction of their benefits in real-world scenarios; it includes a benchmark data generator based on the DBLP bibliographic database [16]. Similarly, the DBpedia SPARQL benchmark [19] proposes human-written queries that execute against non-relational schemas. The Waterloo SPARQL Diversity Test Suite (WatDiv) focuses on measuring "how an RDF data management system performs across a wide spectrum of SPARQL queries with varying structural characteristics and selectivity classes" [1]. Other approaches like Linked SPARQL queries (LSQ) [21] focus specifically on benchmark queries from SPARQL query logs, but typically do not generate data to run these queries on. More recently, frameworks to integrate and compare various benchmarks, such as IGUANA [7][3], have emerged. Other, more pragmatic approaches propose ad-hoc benchmarks supporting specific applications [25] or SPARQL features, like federation [12]. To the best of our knowledge, none of these benchmarks address specifically the evaluation of RDF lists.

3 The `List.MID` Benchmark

In this Section we describe the `List.MID` benchmark. First, we summarize the various modeling alternatives for lists in RDF (Sect. 3.1); for a complete survey, see [8]). Second, we implement these modeling alternatives in a benchmark data generator that creates RDF datasets rich in lists from a large MIDI data collection (Sect. 3.2). Finally, we propose a set of SPARQL queries to retrieve RDF list data according to the different modeling alternatives (Sect. 3.3).

All the `List.MID` benchmark resources are available online in a GitHub repository at https://github.com/midi-ld/List.MID. The benchmark is licensed under

[2] http://ontologydesignpatterns.org/wiki/Submissions:Sequence.

[3] See also https://github.com/dice-group/triplestore-benchmarks.

Table 1. Links to key resources of the `List.MID` benchmark.

Meroño-Peñuela, A. and Daga, E. (2019). *List.MID: A MIDI-based benchmark for evaluating RDF lists.* https://doi.org/10.5281/zenodo.3265139	
Resource	Link
GitHub repository	https://github.com/midi-ld/List.MID
Benchmark queries	https://github.com/midi-ld/List.MID/tree/master/queries
Benchmark example data	https://github.com/midi-ld/List.MID/tree/master/data
Benchmark generation data	https://github.com/midi-ld/sources
	https://github.com/albertmeronyo/awesome-midi-sources
Full dump download	https://github.com/midi-ld/List.MID/archive/master.zip
Zenodo	https://zenodo.org/record/3265139#.XRoYXXUzaV4
Figshare	https://figshare.com/articles/List_MID_A_MIDI-Based_Benchmark_for_Evaluating_RDF_Lists/8426912
Datahub	https://datahub.ckan.io/dataset/list-mid-a-midi-based-benchmark-for-evaluating-rdf-lists

the Creative Commons Attribution-ShareAlike 4.0 International[4] (CC CY-SA 4.0) license. The benchmark is deposited in Zenodo, Figshare, and Datahub. The open availability of the benchmark in these platforms allows for fast and frictionless contributions from other parties. All relevant URLs and canonical citation are shown in Table 1.

3.1 Modeling Lists in RDF

There are various models for representing a sequence, a *finite collection of ordered elements*, in RDF. In this section we offer a summary of such models and their properties, recalling the research in [8]. These models were surveyed by selecting them from the following sources, including W3C standards[5] ontology design patterns [10], resource track papers in ISWC (e.g. [3,18]), and lookups of relevant terms in Linked Open Vocabularies [28]. For a further detail and a description of the surveying methodology, see [8].

RDF Sequences. The RDF Schema (RDFS) recommendation [6] defines the container classes `rdf:Bag`, `rdf:Alt`, `rdf:Seq` to represent collections. Since `rdf:Bag` is intended for unordered elements, and `rdf:Alt` for "alternative" containers whose typical processing will be to select one of its members, these two models do not fit our sequence definition, and thus we do not include them among our candidates. Conversely, we do consider *RDF Sequences*: collections represented by `rdf:Seq` and ordered by the properties `rdf:_1`, `rdf:_2`, `rdf:_3`, ... instances of the class `rdfs:ContainerMembershipProperty` (see Fig. 1).

Properties. RDF Sequences indicate membership through various *properties*, which are used in triples in *predicate position*. Ordering of elements is *absolute* in such predicates through an integer index after an underscore ("_").

[4] https://creativecommons.org/licenses/by-sa/4.0/.
[5] https://www.w3.org/standards/.

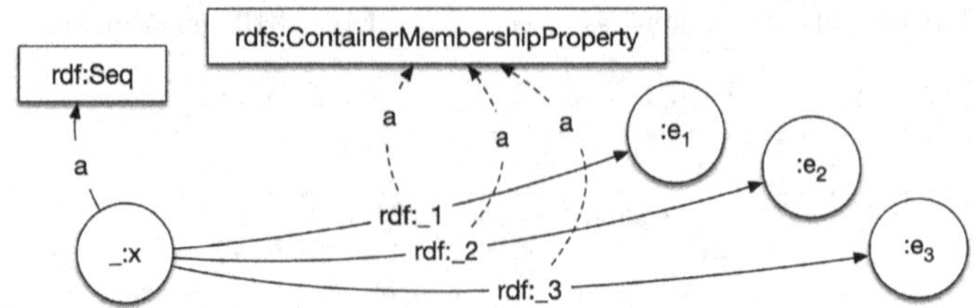

Fig. 1. The RDF Sequence model.

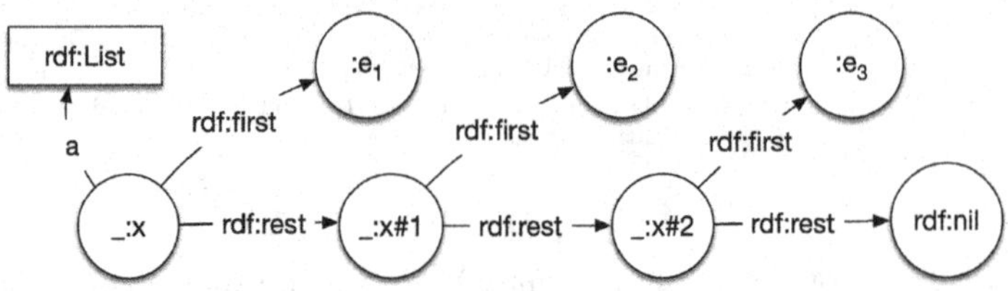

Fig. 2. The RDF List model.

RDF Lists. The RDFS recommendation [6] also defines a vocabulary to describe closed collections or *RDF Lists*. Such lists are members of the class `rdf:List`. Resembling LISP lists, every element of an RDF List is represented by two triples: `<L_k rdf:first E_k>`, where E_k is the k-th element of the list; and `<L_k rdf:rest L_k+1>`, representing the rest of the list (in particular, `rdf:nil` to end the list) (see Fig. 2).

Properties. RDF Lists indicate membership through the use of a *unique property* `rdf:first` in *predicate position*. Ordering of elements is *relative* to the use of the `rdf:rest` property, and given by the sequential forward traversal of the list.

URI-Based Lists. A more practical approach followed by many RDF datasets [3,18] consists of establishing list membership through an explicit property or class membership, and assigning order by a unique identifier embedded in the element's URI. For instance, the triple `<http://ld.zdb-services.de/resource/1480923-0> a <http://purl.org/ontology/bibo/Periodical>` indicates that the subject belongs to a list of periodicals with list order 14809234; the triple `<http://purl.org/midi-ld/piece/8cf9897/track00> midi:hasEvent <http: //purl.org/midi-ld/piece/8cf9897/track00/event0006>` identifies the 7th event in a MIDI track [18] (see Fig. 3).

Properties. URI-based lists indicate membership through the use of *class membership* or through *properties*. Order is *absolute* and given by URI-embedded sequential identifiers.

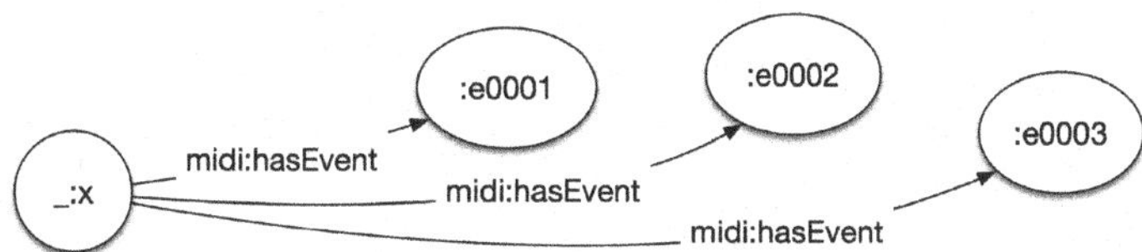

Fig. 3. The URI-based list model.

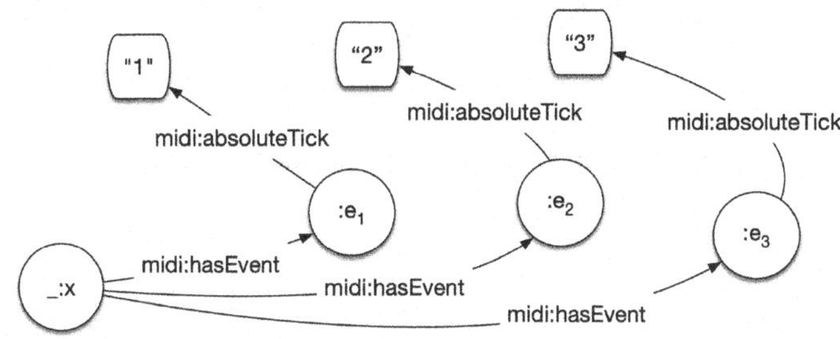

Fig. 4. The Number-based list model.

Number-Based Lists. Another practical model, used e.g. in the Sequence Ontology/Molecular Sequence Ontology (MSO) [9],[6] also uses class membership or object properties to specify the elements that belong to a list, but use a *literal value* in a separate property to indicate order. For instance, the triple `<http://purl.org/midi-ld/piece/8cf9897/track00>` `midi:hasEvent` `<http://purl.org/midi-ld/piece/8cf9897/track00/event0006>` indicates that the object belongs to a list of events; and the additional triple `<http://purl.org/midi-ld/piece/8cf9897/track00/event0006>` `midi:absoluteTick 6` indicates that the event has index 6 (see Fig. 4).

Properties. Number-based lists indicate membership through the use of *class membership* or through *properties*. Order is *absolute* and given by an integer index in a literal as an object of an additional property.

Timestamp-Based Lists. Similarly to Number-based lists, other lists modeled by e.g. the Simple Event Model (SEM) [27], use timestamp markers instead of integer indexes to indicate the time in which the element of the list occurs. This is particularly useful in event-based applications, in which order clashes in the list are of lesser importance, as long as the timestamp order is preserved. For instance, the triple `<http://purl.org/midi-ld/piece/8cf9897535d79e68c33a3076aa06d073/track00/event0006>` `midi:absoluteTime 0e+00` indicates that the 7th event occurs at the start of the list, possibly simultaneously with other events (see Fig. 5).

[6] https://github.com/The-Sequence-Ontology/Specifications/blob/master/gff3.md.

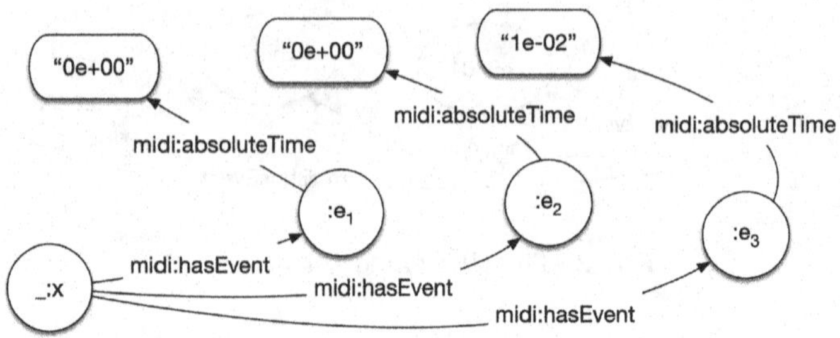

Fig. 5. The Timestamp-based list model.

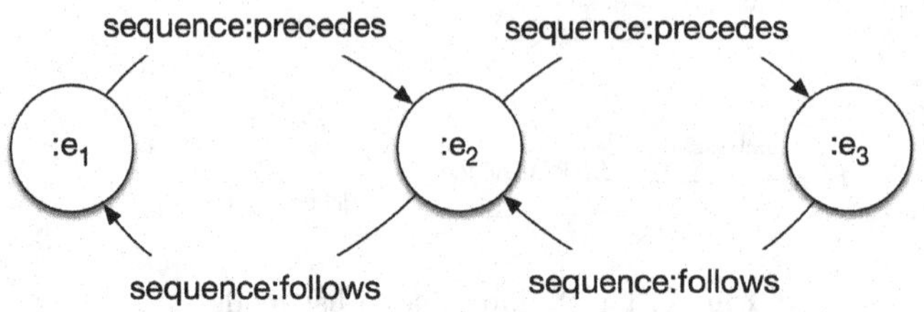

Fig. 6. The Sequence Ontology Pattern model.

Properties. Timestamp-based lists indicate membership through the use of *class membership* or through *properties*. Order is *absolute* and given by a timestamp in a literal as an object of an additional property.

Sequence Ontology Pattern. A number of models use RDF, RDFS and OWL to model sequences in domain specific ways. For example, the Time Ontology [14] and the Timeline Ontology[7] offer a number of classes and properties to model temporality and order, including timestamps (see Sect. 3.1), but importantly also before/after relations. The *Sequence Ontology Pattern*[8] (SOP) is an ontology design pattern [10] that "represents the 'path' cognitive schema, which underlies many different conceptualizations: spatial paths, time lines, event sequences, organizational hierarchies, graph paths, etc.". We select SOP as an abstract model representing this group of list models (see Fig. 6).

Properties. SOP lists indicate list membership through *properties*. Order is *relative* and given by the sequential forward or backward traversal of the sequence.

3.2 Data Generator

The first component of the `List.MID` benchmark is an algorithm to generate RDF datasets with lists according to the modeling patterns discussed above.

[7] http://motools.sourceforge.net/timeline/timeline.html.
[8] http://ontologydesignpatterns.org/wiki/Submissions:Sequence.

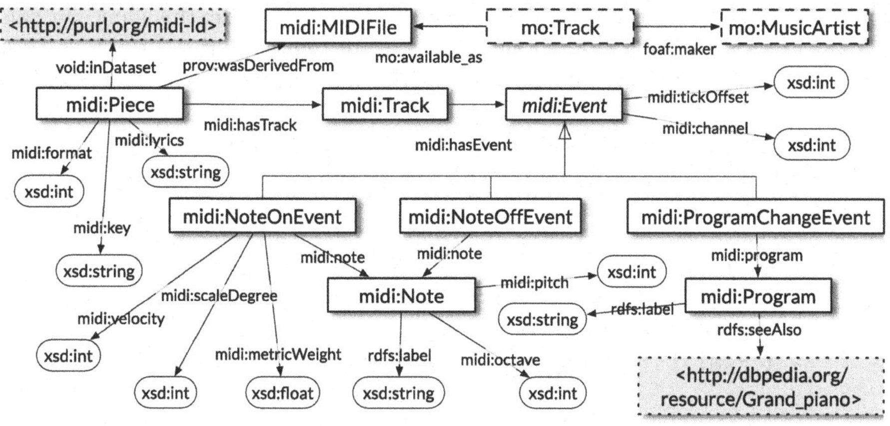

Fig. 7. Excerpt of the MIDI ontology. Tracks contain lists of sequential MIDI events.

The source code and all documentation are available on GitHub at https://github.com/midi-ld/List.MID.

In order to root our benchmark within real-world data, we propose to generate data using MIDI files [26], a symbolic music encoding, as a basis. The reason for this is that MIDI files, and symbolic music notations in general, must encode musical events (the start of a note, the end of a note, the switching of one instrument for another, etc.) in strict sequential order to preserve musical coherence. Consequently, we use the `midi2rdf` algorithm proposed in [17] to generate RDF graphs from MIDI files; and we extend this algorithm here in order to encode RDF lists of musical events supporting the list data models discussed in Sect. 3.1.

Figure 7 shows an excerpt of the MIDI ontology used by the original `midi2rdf` algorithm. The relevant elements here are `midi:Track`, each containing a sequence of related musical events (e.g. notes played by one single instrument); and `midi:Event`, each representing a musical event that happens in a strict order within the track (e.g. the start of a note, the end of a note). For more details on MIDI event encoding see [17,18,26].

The original `midi2rdf` algorithm generates *implicit* lists of events by encoding their order in the URI of the event (e.g. `ex:track00/event02` happens immediately before `ex:track00/event01` and immediately after `ex:track00/event01`), and hence adhering to the *URI-based Lists* pattern discussed in Sect. 3.1. We extend this generation to the remaining patterns.

Usage. The first step is to find a MIDI file with the desired *list size*. The MIDI Linked Data cloud API[9] incorporates a query[10] to retrieve all track sizes in number of events in descending order from the dataset [18]. Since this query is expensive, we include a resulting dump in the benchmark. An inspection of this

[9] See http://grlc.io/api/midi-ld/queries/.

[10] http://grlc.io/api/midi-ld/queries/#/default/get_events_count_per_track_piece.

result allows users to select a MIDI identifier of the chosen size; this identifier can be used in a second query[11] to download an RDF dump for the MIDI file. This dump can be transformed into an input MIDI file with the included `rdf2midi` command [17].

Once the chosen input MIDI file has been generated, the `midi2rdf` CLI tool of the `List.MID` benchmark can be used to generate its RDF graph according to the requested list pattern. The syntax is:

```
midi2rdf [-h]
         [--format [{xml,n3,turtle,nt,pretty-xml,trix,trig,nquads,
                     json-ld}]]
         [--gz] [--order [{uri,prop_number,prop_time,seq,list,
                           sop}]]
         [--version]
         filename [outfile]
```

The relevant introduced argument is `order`, which lets the user select the RDF list modeling to use for data generation. The mapping for the values of this argument with the patterns of Sect. 3.1 is: *RDF Sequences* → `seq`, *RDF Lists* → `list`, *URI-based Lists* → `uri`, *Number-based Lists* → `prop_number`, *Timestamp-based Lists* → `prop_time`, *Sequence Ontology Pattern* → `sop`. For example, to generate benchmark data of a preselected http://purl.org/midi-ld/pattern/bc7d9c25f81a4d90c000c30b6efc887d MIDI with 16,638 list elements using the RDF List pattern, we do:

```
midi2rdf --format turtle --order list
         bc7d9c25f81a4d90c000c30b6efc887d.mid benchmark.ttl
```

The output `benchmark.ttl` file is ready to be used in a standard compliant RDF store. As shown in the syntax above, the benchmark is agnostic with respect to serialization formats, and the most frequent (including JSON-LD) are supported.

3.3 Queries

In this section we propose a set of SPARQL query templates for retrieval of elements of lists, according to the patterns described in Sect. 3.1. Since the full coverage of list operations in SPARQL is cumbersome, here we restrict ourselves to typical *data publishing* functionality. Therefore, we consider minimal and atomic *read* operations; and we do not consider *management* operations (edit, merge, split of lists, etc.). The implementation of management operations is possible, but depend on implementations of read operations; thus, we focus here on read operations, and leave management operations for future work.

Therefore, the currently supported operations in `List.MID` consist of (a) orderly retrieve all elements of the list; and (b) access the n-th element of the list.

[11] http://grlc.io/api/midi-ld/queries/#/default/get_pattern_graph.

In order to systematically do this in datasets following one of the RDF list modeling patterns (Sect. 3.1), we include corresponding SPARQL query templates in the benchmark. The queries can be found online in the GitHub repository of the benchmark,[12] and are summarized in Table 2.

Table 2. SPARQL query templates of the benchmark.

ID	RDF list model	Access	SPARQL
Q1	RDF Sequences	Full list	`WHERE {[] a midi:Track ; midi:hasEvents [ ?seq ?event ] . BIND (xsd:integer(SUBSTR(str(?seq), 45)) AS ?index) } ORDER BY ?index`
Q2	RDF Sequences	n-th item	`WHERE {[] a midi:Track ; midi:hasEvents [ ?seq ?event ] . BIND (xsd:integer(SUBSTR(str(?seq), 45)) AS ?index)} ORDER BY ?index OFFSET n LIMIT 1`
Q3	RDF Lists	Full list	`WHERE {[] a midi:Track ; midi:hasEvents ?events . ?events rdf:rest*/rdf:first ?event . BIND (xsd:integer(SUBSTR(str(?event), 77)) AS ?id) } ORDER BY ?id`
Q4	RDF Lists	n-th item	`WHERE {[] a midi:Track ; midi:hasEvents ?events . ?events rdf:rest*/rdf:first ?event . BIND (xsd:integer(SUBSTR(str(?event), 77)) AS ?id) } ORDER BY ?id OFFSET n LIMIT 1`
Q5	URI-based	Full list	`WHERE { [] a midi:Track ; midi:hasEvent ?event . BIND (xsd:integer(SUBSTR(str(?event), 77)) AS ?id) } ORDER BY ?id`
Q6	URI-based	n-th item	`WHERE { [] a midi:Track ; midi:hasEvent ?event . BIND (xsd:integer(SUBSTR(str(?event), 77)) AS ?id) } ORDER BY ?id OFFSET n LIMIT 1`
Q7	Number-based	Full list	`WHERE { [] a midi:Track ; midi:hasEvent ?event . ?event midi:absoluteTick ?tick . } ORDER BY ?tick`
Q8	Number-based	n-th item	`WHERE { [] a midi:Track ; midi:hasEvent ?event . ?event midi:absoluteTick ?tick . } ORDER BY ?tick OFFSET n LIMIT 1`
Q9	Timestamp-based	Full list	`WHERE { [] a midi:Track ; midi:hasEvent ?event . ?event midi:absoluteTick ?tick . } ORDER BY ?tick`
Q10	Timestamp-based	n-th item	`WHERE { [] a midi:Track ; midi:hasEvent ?event . ?event midi:absoluteTick ?tick . } ORDER BY ?tick OFFSET n LIMIT 1`
Q11	Sequence Ontology Pattern	Full list	`WHERE { [] a midi:Track ; midi:hasEvent ?event . ?event sequence:precedes? ?next_event . ?next_event sequence:follows? ?event . BIND (xsd:integer(SUBSTR(str(?event), 77)) AS ?id) } ORDER BY ?time`
Q12	Sequence Ontology Pattern	n-th item	`WHERE { [] a midi:Track ; midi:hasEvent ?event . ?event sequence:precedes? ?next_event . ?next_event sequence:follows? ?event . BIND (xsd:integer(SUBSTR(str(?event), 77)) AS ?id) } ORDER BY ?time OFFSET n LIMIT 1`

4 Experiments and Reuse

In this Section we discuss current use and potential for reuse of our proposed benchmark in research.

4.1 First Experiment

The `List.MID` benchmark has been used in a first Semantic Web research experiment [8]. The purpose of this work is to understand the impact of different

[12] See https://github.com/midi-ld/List.MID.

RDF list modeling patterns (see Sect. 3.1) in the performance and availability of sequential retrieval of Linked Data. This crucially includes basic list operations such as orderly getting all elements of the list; randomly accessing one element of the list; and randomly accessing a sublist contained in a list. The most important findings quantify the impact of different list modeling choices in retrieval; and show that this impact is triplestore-invariant to a great degree. For a full report on such experiments, see [8]. These experiments demonstrate the applicability and usefulness of the benchmark, and can be easily reproduced with `List.MID` and the supplementary materials at https://www.dropbox.com/sh/m98115y7ah2nqcv/AAAxkGsWuiPaLf6X7c_uM0yWa.

4.2 Online Survey

Since the `List.MID` benchmark is a *new resource* for the Semantic Web community, we discuss here evidence for potential adoption. To gather such evidence, we perform an **online survey** in which we directly ask the community of potential adopters 8 questions regarding their background, relevance, and interest in benchmarking RDF lists. The online survey was distributed in the `semantic-web` and `public-lod` public mailing lists of the W3C; and in the internal mailing lists of the affiliation labs of the authors. In total we gathered $N = 24$ responses. The survey can be found online.[13] Fig. 8 shows the results.

Except for question 3 (Fig. 8c), all questions ask the respondents to quantify the agreement with the statement made from 1 (absolutely disagree) to 5 (absolutely agree), being 3 a neutral response (no agree nor disagree). In the first two questions (Fig. 8a, 8b) we assess the background of the respondents, finding that 75% of them have experience in modeling and publishing RDF, and 54.2% have experience or interest in RDF benchmarking; and thus proving adequacy of the population sample. Among the various RDF list modeling practices (Fig. 8c), `rdf:List` is the most popular, known by 2/3 of the respondents. Other practices like `rdf:Seq` (37.5%), implicit RDF elements as proxies (URIs, properties, etc.; 25%) and ontology design patterns (20.8%) are also familiar. Some respondents express here other less known approaches that could fit the broader categories (e.g. using a `xyz:nextitem`). Figure 8d shows that the community is divided in whether expressing lists in RDF is a real need; conversely, Fig. 8e shows that the impact of list modeling choices in query performance is a real concern (0% disagree; 83.3% agree or strongly agree). Figure 8f signals that current benchmarks might be missing coverage for RDF lists (only 8.3% find them somewhat covered). Most importantly, the community feels the **need of new benchmarks specifically designed for the evaluation of RDF lists** (Fig. 8g, 70.9%). Asking directly on their interest as potential users of a new RDF list benchmark, the community seems divided (Fig. 8h), although this could be attributed to different research interests. **29.1% of the respondents would be interested in reusing an RDF list benchmark like the one here proposed.**

[13] See https://forms.gle/SwkCdFFFVGXWCgCp7.

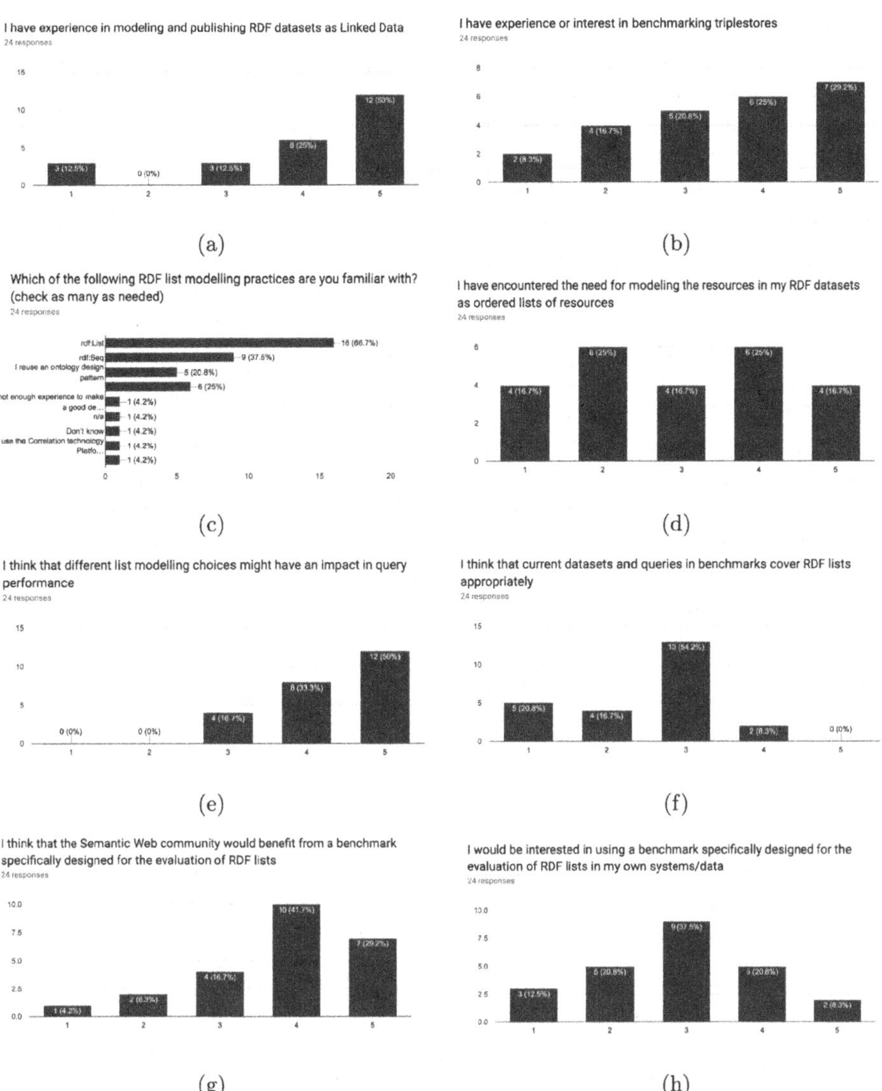

Fig. 8. Results of the online survey

5 Conclusions

Lists are fundamental data structures in computer science, and various models implementing them in the Semantic Web —using RDF, standards, and community best practices— have been proposed. So far, studying the differences, and trade-offs, in features and performance of these RDF list models has been done only in a superficial and exploratory manner. To address this, in this paper we contribute two important findings. First, we show evidence that the Semantic

Web community feels the need for a benchmark specifically designed for the evaluation of RDF lists; and that a number of researchers would be interested in reusing such a benchmark. Second, we propose the benchmark to precisely address this issue, enabling a systematic and principled way of generating, and querying, RDF list data from real-world datasets according to dominant RDF list models in the Semantic Web. We feel that, by adopting this benchmark, researchers will be able to understand better the implications of different list-modeling practices; and developers will find a first building block to construct more varied and performant solutions for RDF lists. We expect both researchers and developers to fundamentally contribute, through their research and software, in making the `List.MID` benchmark better.

This room for improvement can be observed from various prisms. First, in next iterations we will include more real-world use cases and base datasets from which to generate the benchmark data. Similarly, we will include additional list operations regarding list management, such as inserting a new element, and swapping two elements, taking inspiration from array operations in programming [11]. If more, alternative models for modeling RDF lists become a need for our users, we will support them too. Finally, we will continue working to deploy a more automated and usable infrastructure and tools for RDF list benchmarking.

Acknowledgements. This work was partially funded by the CLARIAH project of the Dutch Science Foundation (NWO). We are grateful to all participants of the online survey.

References

1. Aluç, G., Hartig, O., Özsu, M.T., Daudjee, K.: Diversified stress testing of RDF data management systems. In: Mika, P., et al. (eds.) ISWC 2014. LNCS, vol. 8796, pp. 197–212. Springer, Cham (2014). https://doi.org/10.1007/978-3-319-11964-9_13
2. Beckett, D., Berners-Lee, T., Prud'hommeaux, E., Carothers, G.: RDF 1.1 turtle - terse RDF triple language. Technical report, World Wide Web Consrotium (2014). https://www.w3.org/TR/turtle/
3. Beek, W., Rietveld, L., Bazoobandi, H.R., Wielemaker, J., Schlobach, S.: LOD laundromat: a uniform way of publishing other people's dirty data. In: Mika, P., et al. (eds.) ISWC 2014. LNCS, vol. 8796, pp. 213–228. Springer, Cham (2014). https://doi.org/10.1007/978-3-319-11964-9_14
4. Berners-Lee, T., Hendler, J., Lassila, O., et al.: The semantic web. Sci. Am. **284**(5), 28–37 (2001)
5. Bizer, C., Schultz, A.: The Berlin SPARQL benchmark. Int. J. Semant. Web Inf. Syst. **5**(2), 1–24 (2009)
6. Brickley, D., Guha, R.: RDF schema 1.1. Technical report, World Wide Web Consrotium (2014). https://www.w3.org/TR/rdf-schema/
7. Conrads, F., Lehmann, J., Saleem, M., Morsey, M., Ngonga Ngomo, A.-C.: Iguana: a generic framework for benchmarking the read-write performance of triple stores. In: d'Amato, C., et al. (eds.) ISWC 2017. LNCS, vol. 10588, pp. 48–65. Springer, Cham (2017). https://doi.org/10.1007/978-3-319-68204-4_5

8. Daga, E., Meroño-Peñuela, A., Motta, E.: Modelling and querying lists in RDF. A pragmatic study. In: 3rd Workshop on Querying and Benchmarking the Web of Data (QuWeDa 2019), ISWC 2019 (2019)
9. Eilbeck, K., et al.: The sequence ontology: a tool for the unification of genome annotations. Genome Biol. **6**(5), R44 (2005)
10. Gangemi, A.: Ontology design patterns for semantic web content. In: Gil, Y., Motta, E., Benjamins, V.R., Musen, M.A. (eds.) ISWC 2005. LNCS, vol. 3729, pp. 262–276. Springer, Heidelberg (2005). https://doi.org/10.1007/11574620_21
11. Gopan, D., Reps, T., Sagiv, M.: A framework for numeric analysis of array operations. SIGPLAN Not. **40**(1), 338–350 (2005). http://doi.acm.org.vu-nl.idm.oclc.org/10.1145/1047659.1040333
12. Görlitz, O., Thimm, M., Staab, S.: SPLODGE: systematic generation of SPARQL benchmark queries for linked open data. In: Cudré-Mauroux, P., et al. (eds.) ISWC 2012. LNCS, vol. 7649, pp. 116–132. Springer, Heidelberg (2012). https://doi.org/10.1007/978-3-642-35176-1_8
13. Guo, Y., Pan, Z., Heflin, J.: LUBM: a benchmark for OWL knowledge base systems. J. Web Semant. Sci. Serv. Agents World Wide Web **3**(2), 158–182 (2005)
14. Hobbs, J.R., Pan, F.: Time ontology in OWL. W3C working draft **27**, 133 (2006)
15. Hopcroft, J.E., Ullman, J.D.: Data structures and algorithms (1983)
16. Ley, M.: The DBLP computer science bibliography: evolution, research issues, perspectives. In: Laender, A.H.F., Oliveira, A.L. (eds.) SPIRE 2002. LNCS, vol. 2476, pp. 1–10. Springer, Heidelberg (2002). https://doi.org/10.1007/3-540-45735-6_1
17. Meroño-Peñuela, A., Hoekstra, R.: The song remains the same: lossless conversion and streaming of MIDI to RDF and back. In: Sack, H., Rizzo, G., Steinmetz, N., Mladenić, D., Auer, S., Lange, C. (eds.) ESWC 2016. LNCS, vol. 9989, pp. 194–199. Springer, Cham (2016). https://doi.org/10.1007/978-3-319-47602-5_38
18. Meroño-Peñuela, A., et al.: The MIDI linked data cloud. In: d'Amato, C., et al. (eds.) ISWC 2017. LNCS, vol. 10588, pp. 156–164. Springer, Cham (2017). https://doi.org/10.1007/978-3-319-68204-4_16
19. Morsey, M., Lehmann, J., Auer, S., Ngonga Ngomo, A.-C.: DBpedia SPARQL benchmark – performance assessment with real queries on real data. In: Aroyo, L., et al. (eds.) ISWC 2011. LNCS, vol. 7031, pp. 454–469. Springer, Heidelberg (2011). https://doi.org/10.1007/978-3-642-25073-6_29
20. Reingold, E.M., Nievergelt, J., Deo, N.: Combinatorial Algorithms: Theory and Practice. Prentice Hall College Div, Englewood Cliffs (1977)
21. Saleem, M., Ali, M.I., Hogan, A., Mehmood, Q., Ngomo, A.-C.N.: LSQ: the linked SPARQL queries dataset. In: Arenas, M., et al. (eds.) ISWC 2015. LNCS, vol. 9367, pp. 261–269. Springer, Cham (2015). https://doi.org/10.1007/978-3-319-25010-6_15
22. Schmidt, M., Hornung, T., Lausen, G., Pinkel, C.: SP^{2}Bench: a SPARQL performance benchmark. In: 2009 IEEE 25th International Conference on Data Engineering, ICDE 2009, pp. 222–233. IEEE (2009)
23. Schreiber, G., Raimond, Y.: RDF 1.1 primer. Technical report, World Wide Web Consrotium (2014). https://www.w3.org/TR/rdf11-primer/
24. Sporny, M., Kellogg, G., Lanthaler, M.: JSON-LD 1.0. Technical report, World Wide Web Consrotium (2014). https://www.w3.org/TR/2014/REC-json-ld-20140116/
25. Thakker, D., Osman, T., Gohil, S., Lakin, P.: A pragmatic approach to semantic repositories benchmarking. In: Aroyo, L., et al. (eds.) ESWC 2010. LNCS, vol. 6088, pp. 379–393. Springer, Heidelberg (2010). https://doi.org/10.1007/978-3-642-13486-9_26

26. The MIDI Manufacturers Association: MIDI 1.0 detailed specification. Technical report, Los Angeles, CA (1996–2014). https://www.midi.org/specifications
27. Van Hage, W.R., Malaisé, V., Segers, R., Hollink, L., Schreiber, G.: Design and use of the simple event model (SEM). Web Semant. Sci. Serv. Agents World Wide Web **9**(2), 128–136 (2011)
28. Vandenbussche, P.Y., Atemezing, G.A., Poveda-Villalón, M., Vatant, B.: Linked open vocabularies (LOV): a gateway to reusable semantic vocabularies on the web. Semant. Web **8**(3), 437–452 (2017)

A Scalable Framework for Quality Assessment of RDF Datasets

Gezim Sejdiu[1(✉)], Anisa Rula[1,2], Jens Lehmann[1,3], and Hajira Jabeen[1]

[1] Smart Data Analytics, University of Bonn, Bonn, Germany
{sejdiu,rula,jens.lehmann,jabeen}@cs.uni-bonn.de
[2] Department of Computer Science, Systems and Communication (DISCo), University of Milano-Bicocca, Milan, Italy
anisa.rula@disco.unimib.it
[3] Fraunhofer IAIS, Sankt Augustin, Germany
jens.lehmann@iais.fraunhofer.de

Abstract. Over the last years, Linked Data has grown continuously. Today, we count more than 10,000 datasets being available online following Linked Data standards. These standards allow data to be machine readable and inter-operable. Nevertheless, many applications, such as data integration, search, and interlinking, cannot take full advantage of Linked Data if it is of low quality. There exist a few approaches for the quality assessment of Linked Data, but their performance degrades with the increase in data size and quickly grows beyond the capabilities of a single machine. In this paper, we present DistQualityAssessment – an open source implementation of quality assessment of large RDF datasets that can scale out to a cluster of machines. This is the first distributed, in-memory approach for computing different quality metrics for large RDF datasets using Apache Spark. We also provide a quality assessment pattern that can be used to generate new scalable metrics that can be applied to big data. The work presented here is integrated with the SANSA framework and has been applied to at least three use cases beyond the SANSA community. The results show that our approach is more generic, efficient, and scalable as compared to previously proposed approaches.

Resource type Software Framework
Website http://sansa-stack.net/distqualityassessment/
Permanent URL https://doi.org/10.6084/m9.figshare.7930139

1 Introduction

Large amounts of data are being published openly to Linked Data by different data providers. A multitude of applications such as semantic search, query answering, and machine reading [18] depend on these large-scale[1] RDF datasets. The quality of underlying RDF data plays a fundamental role in large-scale data consuming applications. Measuring the quality of linked data spans a number of dimensions including but not limited to: accessibility, interlinking, performance, syntactic validity or completeness [22]. Each of these dimensions can be expressed through one or more quality

[1] http://lodstats.aksw.org/.

C. Ghidini et al. (Eds.): ISWC 2019, LNCS 11779, pp. 261–276, 2019.
https://doi.org/10.1007/978-3-030-30796-7_17

metrics. Considering that each quality metric tries to capture a particular aspect of the underlying data, numerous metrics are usually provided against the given data that may or may not be processed simultaneously.

On the other hand, the limited number of existing techniques of quality assessment for RDF datasets are not adequate to assess data quality at large-scale and these approaches mostly fail to capture the increasing volume of big data. To date, a limited number of solutions have been conceived to offer quality assessment of RDF datasets [4, 10, 11, 13]. But, these methods can either be used on a small portion of large datasets [13] or narrow down to specific problems e.g., syntactic accuracy of literal values [4], or accessibility of resources [17]. In general, these existing efforts show severe deficiencies in terms of performance when data grows beyond the capabilities of a single machine. This limits the applicability of existing solutions to medium-sized datasets only, in turn, paralyzing the role of applications in embracing the increasing volumes of the available datasets.

To deal with big data, tools like Apache Spark[2] have recently gained a lot of interest. Apache Spark provides scalability, resilience, and efficiency for dealing with large-scale data. Spark uses the concepts of Resilient Distributed Datasets (RDDs) [21] and performs operations like transformations and actions on this data in order to effectively deal with large-scale data.

To handle large-scale RDF data, it is important to develop flexible and extensible methods that can assess the quality of data at scale. At the same time, due to the broadness and variety of quality assessment domain and resulting metrics, there is a strong need to provide a generic pattern to characterize the quality assessment of RDF data in terms of scalability and applicability to big data.

In this paper, we borrow the concepts of data *transformation* and *action* from Spark and present a pattern for designing quality assessment metrics over large RDF datasets, which is inspired by design patterns. In software engineering, design patterns are general and reusable solutions to common problems. Akin to design pattern, where each pattern acts like a blueprint that can be customized to solve a particular design problem, the introduced concept of Quality Assessment Pattern ($\mathcal{QAP}$) represents a generalized blueprint of scalable quality assessment metrics. In this way, the quality metrics designed following $\mathcal{QAP}$ can exhibit the ability to achieve scalability to large-scale data and work in a distributed manner. In addition, we also provide an open source implementation and assessment of these quality metrics in Apache Spark following the proposed $\mathcal{QAP}$.

Our contributions can be summarized in the following points:

- We present a Quality Assessment Pattern $\mathcal{QAP}$ to characterize scalable quality metrics.
- We provide DistQualityAssessment[3] – a distributed (open source) implementation of quality metrics using Apache Spark.
- We perform an analysis of the complexity of the metric evaluation in the cluster.

---

[2] https://spark.apache.org/.

[3] https://github.com/SANSA-Stack/SANSA-RDF/tree/develop/sansa-rdf-spark/src/main/scala/net/sansa_stack/rdf/spark/qualityassessment.

- We evaluate our approach and demonstrate empirically its superiority over a previous centralized approach.
- We integrated the approach into the SANSA[4] framework. SANSA is actively maintained and uses the community ecosystem (mailing list, issues trackers, continues integration, web-site etc.).
- We briefly present three use cases where DistQualityAssessment has been used.

The paper is structured as follows: Our approach for the computation of RDF dataset quality metrics is detailed in Sect. 2 and evaluated in Sect. 3. Related work on the computation of quality metrics for RDF datasets is discussed in Sect. 5. Finally, we conclude and suggest planned extensions of our approach in Sect. 6.

2 Approach

In this section, we first introduce basic notions used in our approach, the formal definition of the proposed quality assessment pattern and then describe the workflow.

2.1 Quality Assessment Pattern

Data quality is commonly conceived as a multi-dimensional construct [2] with a popular notion of 'fitness for use' and can be measured along many dimensions $\mathcal{D}$ such as accuracy ($d_{accu} \in \mathcal{D}$), completeness ($d_{comp} \in \mathcal{D}$) and timeliness ($d_{tmls} \in \mathcal{D}$). The assessment of a quality dimensions d is based on quality metrics $\mathcal{QM} = m_1, m_2 \ldots \ldots m_k$ where m_i is a heuristic that is designed to fit a specific assessment dimension. The following definitions form the basis of $\mathcal{QAP}$.

Definition 1 (Filter). *Let $\mathcal{F} = f_1, f_2 \ldots \ldots f_l$ be a set of filters where each filter f_i sets a criteria for extracting predicates, objects, subjects, or their combination. A filter f_i takes a set of RDF triples as input and returns a subgraph that satisfies the filtering criteria.*

Definition 2 (Rule). *Let $\mathcal{R} = r_1, r_2 \ldots \ldots r_j$ be a set of rules where each rule r_i sets a conditional criteria. A rule takes a subgraph as input and returns a new subgraph that satisfies the conditions posed by the rule r_i.*

Definition 3 (Transformation). *A transformation $\tau : \mathcal{G} \to \mathcal{G}'$ is an operation that applies rules defined by $\mathcal{R}$ on the RDF graph $\mathcal{G}$ and returns an RDF subgraph $\mathcal{G}'$. A transformation τ can be a union $\cup$ or intersection $\cap$ of other transformations.*

Definition 4 (Action). *An action $\alpha : \mathcal{G} \to \mathbb{R}$ is an operation that triggers the transformation of rules on the filtered RDF graph $\mathcal{G}'$ and generates a numerical value. Action α is the count of elements obtained after performing a τ operation.*

Definition 5 (Quality Assessment Pattern $\mathcal{QAP}$). *The Quality Assessment Pattern $\mathcal{QAP}$ is a reusable template to implement and design scalable quality metrics. The $\mathcal{QAP}$ is composed of transformations and actions. The output of a $\mathcal{QAP}$ is the outcome of an action returning a numeric value against the particular metric.*

[4] http://sansa-stack.net/.

$\mathcal{QAP}$ is inspired by Apache Spark operations and designed to fit different data quality metrics (for more details see Table 1). Each data *quality metric* can be defined following the $\mathcal{QAP}$. Any given data quality metric m_i that is represented through the $\mathcal{QAP}$ using transformation τ and action α operations can be easily transformed into Spark code to achieve scalability.

Table 1. Quality assessment pattern

Quality Metric	:= Action |(Action $\mathcal{OP}$ Action)
$\mathcal{OP}$	:= $*$ |- |/ |+
Action	:= Count(Transformation)
Transformation	:= Rule(Filter) |(Transformation BOP Transformation)
Filter	:= getPredicates ~?p |getSubjects ~?s |getObjects ~?o |getDistinct(Filter) |Filter or Filter |Filter && Filter)
Rule	:= isURI(Filter) |isIRI(Filter) |isInternal(Filter) |isLiteral(Filter) |!isBroken(Filter) |hasPredicateP |hasLicenceAssociated(Filter) |hasLicenceIndications(Filter) |isExternal(Filter) |hasType((Filter) |isLabeled(Filter)
BOP	:= ∩ — ∪

Table 2 demonstrates a few selected quality metrics defined against proposed $\mathcal{QAP}$. As shown in Table 2, each quality metric can contain multiple rules, filters or actions. It is worth mentioning that action count(triples) returns the total number of triples in the given data. This can also be seen that the action can be an arithmetic combination of multiple actions i.e. ratio, sum etc. We illustrate our proposed approach on some metrics selected from [10,22]. Given that the aim of this paper is to show the applicability of the proposed approach and comparison with existing methods, we have only selected those which are already provided out-of-box in Luzzu.

2.2 System Overview

In this section, we give an overall description of the data model and the architecture of DistQualityAssessment. We model and store RDF graphs $\mathcal{G}$ based on the basic building block of the Spark framework, RDDs. RDDs are in-memory collections of records that can be operated in parallel on a large distributed cluster. RDDs provide an interface based on *coarse-grained* transformations (e.g *map*, *filter* and *reduce*): operations applied on an entire RDD. A *map* function transforms each value from an input RDD into another value while applying τ rules. A *filter* transforms an input RDD to an output RDD, which contains only the elements that satisfy a given condition. *Reduce* aggregates the RDD elements using a specific function from τ.

The computation of the set of quality metrics $\mathcal{QM}$ is performed using Spark as depicted in Fig. 1. Our approach consists of four steps:

Defining Quality Metrics Parameters (Step 1). The metric definitions are kept in a dedicated file which contains most of the configurations needed for the system to evaluate quality metrics and gather result sets.

Table 2. Definition of selected metrics following $\mathcal{QAP}$.

	Metric	Transformation τ	Action α
L1	Detection of a Machine Readable License	r = hasLicenceAssociated(?p)	α = count(r) α > 0 ? 1 : 0
L2	Detection of a Human Readable License	r = isURI(?s) ∩ hasLicenceIndications(?p) ∩ isLiteral(?o) ∩ isLicenseStatement(?o)	α = count(r) α > 0 ? 1 : 0
I2	Linkage Degree of Linked External Data Providers	r_1 = isIRI(?s) ∩ internal(?s) ∩ isIRI(?o) ∩ external(?o) r_2 = isIRI(?s) ∩ external(?s) ∩ isIRI(?o) ∩ internal(?o) r_3 = r_1 ∪ r_2	α_1 = count(r_3) α_2 = count(triples) α = a_1/a_2
U1	Detection of a Human Readable Labels	r_1 = isURI(?s) ∩ isInternal(?s) ∩ isLabeled(?p) r_2 = isInternal(?p) ∩ isLabeled(?p) r_3 = isURI(?o) ∩ isInternal(?o) ∩ isLabeled(?p)	α_1 = count(r_1) + count(r_2) + count(r_3) α_2 = count(triples) α_1/ α_2
RC1	Short URIs	r_1 = isURI(?s) ∪ isURI(?p) ∪ isURI(?o) r_2 = resTooLong(?s, ?p, ?o)	α_1 =count(r_2) α_1/count(triples)
SV3	Identification of Literals with Malformed Datatypes	r = isLiteral(?o) ∩ getDatatype(?o) ∩ isLexicalFormCompatibleWithDatatype(?o)	α = count(r)
CN2	Extensional Conciseness	r = isURI(?s) ∩ isURI(?o)	α_1 = count(r) α_2 = count(triples) (α_2- α_1)/ α_2

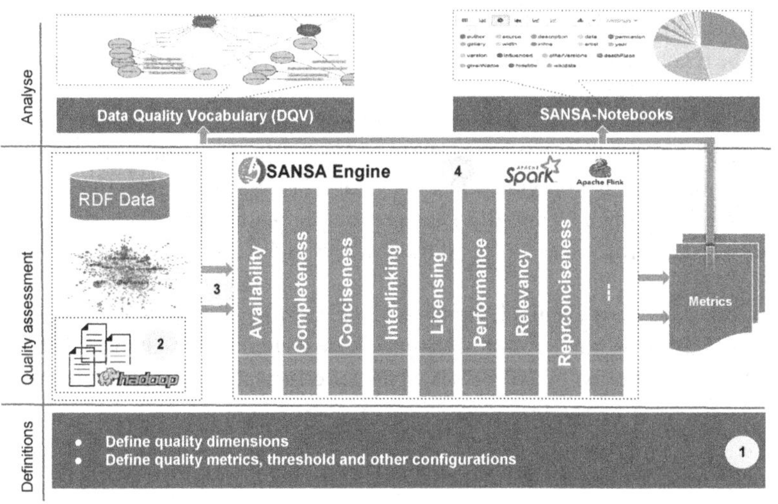

Fig. 1. Overview of distributed quality assessment's abstract architecture.

Retrieving the RDF Data (Step 2). RDF data first needs to be loaded into a large-scale storage that Spark can efficiently read from. We use Hadoop Distributed File-System[5] (HDFS). HDFS is able to fit and stores any type of data in its Hadoop-native format and parallelizes them across a cluster while replicating them for fault tolerance. In such a distributed environment, Spark automatically adopts different data locality strategies to perform computations as close to the needed data as possible in HDFS and thus avoids data transfer overhead.

Parsing and Mapping RDF into the Main Dataset (Step 3). We first create a distributed dataset called *main dataset* that represent the HDFS file as a collection of triples. In Spark, this dataset is parsed and loaded into an RDD of triples having the format *Triple<(s, p, o)>*.

Quality Metric Evaluation (Step 4). Considering the particular quality metric, Spark generates an execution plan, which is composed of one or more τ transformations and α actions. The numerical output of the final action is the quality of the input RDF corresponding to the given metric.

2.3 Implementation

We have used the Scala[6] programming language API in Apache Spark to provide the distributed implementation of the proposed approach.

The DistQualityAssessment (see Algorithm 1) constructs the *main dataset* (line 1) while reading RDF data (e.g. NTriples file or any other RDF serialization format) and converts it into an RDD of triples. This latter undergoes the transformation operation of applying the filtering through rules in R and producing a new *filtered* RDD ($\mathcal{G}'$) (line 5). At the end, $\mathcal{G}'$ will serve as an input to the next step which applies a set of α actions (line 8). The output of this step is the metric output represented as a numerical value (line 8). The result set of different quality metrics (line 12) can be further visualized and monitored using SANSA-Notebooks [12].

The user can also choose to extract the output in a machine-readable format (line 10). We have used the data quality vocabulary[7] (DQV) to represent the quality metrics.

Furthermore, we also provide a Docker image of the system integrated within the BDE platform[8] - an open source Big Data processing platform allowing users to install numerous big data processing tools and frameworks and create working data flow applications.

The work done here (available under *Apache License 2.0*) has been integrated into SANSA [16], an open source[9] *data flow processing engine* for scalable processing of large-scale RDF datasets. SANSA uses Spark offering fault-tolerant, highly available

[5] https://hadoop.apache.org/docs/r1.2.1/hdfs_design.html.
[6] https://www.scala-lang.org/.
[7] https://www.w3.org/TR/vocab-dqv/.
[8] https://github.com/big-data-europe.
[9] https://github.com/SANSA-Stack.

Algorithm 1. Spark-based parallel quality assessment algorithm.

```
input  : RDF: an RDF dataset, param: quality metrics parameters.
output: dqv description or metric numerical value
triples = spark.rdf(lang)(input)
triples.persist()
dqv ← ∅
foreach m ∈ param.getListOfMetrics do
    triples ← triples.Tranform { t =>
        rule ← m.Rule
        t.apply(rule) }
    metric ← triples.apply(m.Action)
    if m.hasDQVdescription then
        dqvify ← metric.dqvify()
    dqv.add(dqvify)
return (dqv, metric)
```

and scalable approaches to process massive sized datasets efficiently. SANSA provides the facilities for semantic data representation, querying, inference, and analytics at scale. Being part of this integration, DistQualityAssessment can take advantage of having the same user community as well as infrastructure build via SANSA project. Doing so, it can also ensure the sustainability of the tool given that SANSA is supported by several grants until at least 2021.

Complexity Analysis. We deem that the overall time complexity of the distributed quality assessment evaluation is $O(n)$. The performance of metrics computation depends on data shuffling (while filtering using rules in R) and data scanning. Our approach performs a direct mapping of any quality metric designed using $\mathcal{QAP}$ into a sequence of Spark-compliant Scala-commands, as a consequence, most of the operators used are a series of transformations like *map*, $filter$ and *reduce*. The complexity of *map* and $filter$ is considered to be linear with respect to the number of triples associated with it. The complexity of a metric then depends on the α operation that returns the count of the filtered output. This later step works on the distributed RDD between p nodes which imply that the complexity of each node then becomes $O(n/p)$, where n is number of input triples. Let be $O(\tau)$ a complexity of τ, then the complexity of the metric will be $O(n/p * O(\tau))$. This indicates that the runtime increases linearly when the size of an RDD increases and decreases linearly when more nodes p are added to the cluster.

3 Evaluation

The main aim of DistQualityAssessment is to serve massive large-scale real-life RDF datasets. We are interested in addressing the following additional questions.

- **Flexibility:** How fast our approach processes different types of metrics?
- **Scalability:** How large are the RDF datasets that DistQualityAssessment can scale to? What is the system speedup w.r.t the number of nodes in a cluster mode?

– **Efficiency:** How well our approach performs compared with other state-of-the-art systems on real-world datasets?

In the following, we present our experimental setup including the datasets used. Thereafter, we give an overview of our results.

3.1 Experimental Setup

We chose two real-world and one synthetic datasets for our experiments:

1. *DBpedia* [15] (v 3.9) – a cross domain dataset. DBpedia is a knowledge base with a large ontology. We build a set of 3 pipelines of increasing complexity: (i) $M^{en}_{DBpedia}$ (≈813M triples); (ii) $M^{de}_{DBpedia}$ (≈337M triples); (iii) $M^{fr}_{DBpedia}$ (≈341M triples). DBpedia has been chosen because of its popularity in the Semantic Web community.
2. *LinkedGeoData* [20] – a spatial RDF knowledge base derived from OpenStreetMap.
3. *Berlin SPARQL Benchmark (BSBM)* [6] – a synthetic dataset based on an e-commerce use case containing a set of products that are offered by different vendors and reviews posted by consumers about products. The benchmark provides a data generator, which can be used to create sets of connected triples of any particular size.

Properties of the considered datasets are given in Table 3.

Table 3. Dataset summary information (nt format).

⟶	LinkedGeoData	DBpedia			BSBM		
		en	de	fr	2 GB	20 GB	200 GB
#nr. of triples	1,292,933,812	812,545,486	336,714,883	340,849,556	8,289,484	81,980,472	817,774,057
Size (GB)	191.17	114.4	48.6	49.77	2	20	200

We implemented DistQualityAssessment using Spark-2.4.0, Scala 2.11.11 and Java 8, and all the data were stored on the HDFS cluster using Hadoop 2.8.0. The experiments in local mode are all performed on a single instance of the cluster. Specifically, we compare our approach with Luzzu [10] v4.0.0, a state-of-the-art quality assessment system[10]. All distributed experiments were carried out on a small cluster of 7 nodes (1 master, 6 workers): Intel(R) Xeon(R) CPU E5-2620 v4 @ 2.10 GHz (32 Cores), 128 GB RAM, 12 TB SATA RAID-5. The machines were connected via a Gigabit network. All experiments have been executed three times and the average value is reported in the results.

[10] https://github.com/Luzzu/Framework.

3.2 Results

We evaluate the proposed approach using the above datasets to compare it against Luzzu [10]. We carry out two sets of experiments. First, we evaluate the runtime of our distributed approach in contrast to Luzzu. Second, we evaluate the horizontal scalability via increasing nodes in the cluster. Results of the experiments are presented in Table 4, Figs. 2 and 3. Based on the metric definition, some metrics make use of external access (e.g. Dereferenceability of Forward Links) which leads to a significant increase in Spark processing due to network latency. For the sake of the evaluation we have suspended such metrics. As of that, we choose seven metrics (see Table 2 for more details) where the level of difficulty vary from simple to complex according to combination of transformation/action operations involved.

Performance Evaluation on Large-Scale RDF Datasets. We started our experiments by evaluating the *speedup* gained by adopting a distributed implementation of quality assessment metrics using our approach, and compare it against Luzzu. We run the experiments on five datasets ($DBpedia_{en}$, $DBpedia_{de}$, $DBpedia_{fr}$, *LinkedGeoData* and $BSBM_{200GB}$). Local mode represent a single instance of the cluster without any tuning of Spark configuration and the cluster mode includes further tuning. Luzzu was run in a local environment on a single machine with two strategies: (1) streaming the data for each metric separately, and (2) one stream/load – all metrics evaluated just once.

Table 4. Performance evaluation on large-scale RDF datasets.

	⟶	Runtime (m) (mean/std)				
		Luzzu		**DistQualityAssessment**		
		a) single	b) joint	c) local	d) cluster	e) speedup ratio w.r.t Luzzu |DistQualityAssessment[c)]
Large-scale	*LinkedGeoData*	Fail	Fail	446.9/63.34	7.79/0.54	n/a|56.4x
	$DBpedia_{en}$	Fail	Fail	274.31/38.17	1.99/0.04	n/a|136.8x
	$DBpedia_{de}$	Fail	Fail	161.4/24.18	0.46/0.04	n/a|349.9x
	$DBpedia_{fr}$	Fail	Fail	195.3/26.16	0.38/0.04	n/a|512.9x
	$BSBM_{200GB}$	Fail	Fail	454.46/78.04	7.27/0.64	n/a|61.5x
Small to medium	$BSBM_{0.01GB}$	2.64/0.02	2.65/0.01	0.04/0.0	0.42/0.04	65x|(-0.9x)
	$BSBM_{0.02GB}$	5.9/0.16	5.66/0.02	0.04/0.0	0.43/0.03	146.5x|(-0.9x)
	$BSBM_{0.05GB}$	16.38/0.44	15.39/0.21	0.05/0.0	0.46/0.02	326.6x|(-0.9x)
	$BSBM_{0.1GB}$	40.59/0.56	37.94/0.28	0.06/0.0	0.44/0.05	675.5x|(-0.9x)
	$BSBM_{0.2GB}$	101.8/0.72	101.78/0.64	0.07/0.0	0.4/0.03	1453.3|(-0.8x)
	$BSBM_{0.5GB}$	459.19/18.72	468.64/21.7	0.15/0.01	0.48/0.03	3060.3x|(-0.7x)
	$BSBM_{1GB}$	1454.16/10.55	1532.95/51.6	0.4/0.02	0.56/0.02	3634.4x|(-0.3x)
	$BSBM_{2GB}$	Timeout	Timeout	3.19/0.16	0.62/0.04	n/a|4.1x
	$BSBM_{10GB}$	Timeout	Timeout	29.44/0.14	0.52/0.01	n/a|55.6x
	$BSBM_{20GB}$	Fail	Fail	34.32/9.22	0.75/0.29	n/a|44.8x

Table 4 shows the performance of two approaches applied to five datasets. In Table 4 we indicate "Timeout" whenever the process did not complete within a certain amount of time[11] and "Fail" when the system crashed before this timeout delay. Column Luzzu$^{(a)}$ represents the performance of Luzzu on bulk load – considering each metric as a sequence of the execution, on the other hand, the column Luzzu$^{(b)}$ reports on the performance of Luzzu using a joint load by evaluating each metric using one load. The last columns reports on the performance of DistQualityAssessment run on a local mode (*c*), cluster mode (*d*) and speedup ratio of our approach compared to Luzzu$^{(b)}$ $(d)/b) - 1)$ and itself evaluated on local mode $(d)/c) - 1)$ is reported on the column (*e*). We observe that the execution of our approach finishes with all the datasets whereas this is not the case with Luzzu which either timeout or fail at some point.

Unfortunately, Luzzu was not capable of evaluating the metrics over large-scale RDF datasets from Table 4 (part one). For that reason we run yet another set of experiments on very small datasets which Luzzu was able to handle. Second part of the Table 4 shows a performance evaluation of our approach compared with Luzzu on very small RDF datasets. In some cases (e.g. RC1, SV3) for a very small dataset Luzzu performs better than our approach with a small margin of runtime in the local mode. It is due to the fact that in the streaming mode, when Luzzu$^{(a)}$ finds the first statement which fulfills the condition (e.g.finding the shortest URIs), it stops the evaluation and return the results. On the contrary, our approach evaluates the metrics over the whole dataset exploiting the fault-tolerance and resilient features build in Spark. In other cases Luzzu suffers from significant slowdowns, which are several orders of magnitude slower. Therefore, its average runtime over all metrics is worst as compared to our approach. It is important to note that our approach on these very small datasets degrades while running on the cluster mode. This is because of the network overhead while shuffling the data, but it outperforms Luzzu$^{(a),(b)}$ when considering "average runtime" over all the metrics (even for very small datasets).

Findings shown in Table 4 depict that our approach starts outperforming when the size of the dataset grows (e.g. $BSBM_{2GB}$). The runtime in the cluster mode stays constant when the size of the data fits into the main memory of the cluster. On other hand, Luzzu is not able to evaluate the metrics when the size of data starts increasing, the time taken lasts beyond the delay we set for small datasets. Because of the large differences, we have used a logarithmic scale to better visualize these results.

Scalability Performance Analysis. In this experiment we evaluate the efficiency of our approach. Figures 2 and 3 illustrates the results of the comparative efficiency analysis.

Data Scalability. To measure the performance of *size-up* scalability of our approach, we run experiments on five different sizes. We fix the number of nodes to 6 and grow the size of datasets to measure whether DistQualityAssessment can deal with larger datasets. For this set of experiments we consider BSBM benchmark tool to generate synthetic datasets of different sizes, since the real-world dataset are considered to be unique in their size and attributes.

We start by generating a dataset of 2 GB. Then, we iteratively increase the size of datasets. On each dataset, we run our approach and the runtime is reported on Fig. 2. The *x*-axis shows the size of BSBM dataset with an increasing order of 10x magnitude.

[11] We set the timeout delay to 24 hours of the quality assessment evaluation stage.

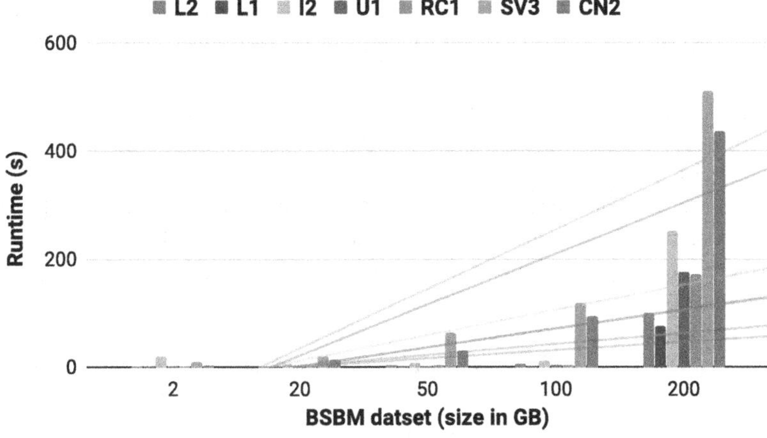

Fig. 2. Sizeup performance evaluation.

By comparing the runtime (see Fig. 2), we note that the execution time increases linearly and is near-constant when the size of the dataset increases. As expected, it stays near-constant as long as the data fits in memory. This demonstrates one of the advantages of utilizing the in-memory approach for performing the quality assessment computation. The overall time spent in data read/write and network communication found in disk-based approaches is saved. However, when the data overflows the memory, and it is spilled to disk, the performance degrades. These results show the scalability of our algorithm in the context of size-up.

Node Scalability. In order to measure node scalability, we vary the number of the workers on our cluster. The number of workers have varied from 1, 2, 3, 4 and 5 to 6.

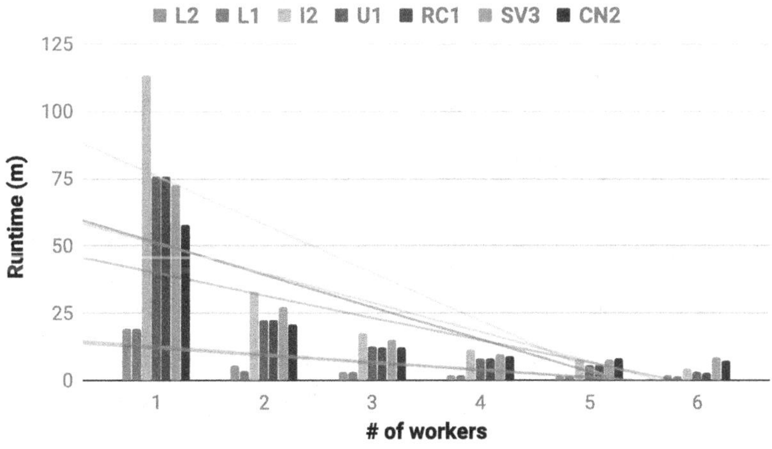

Fig. 3. Node scalability performance evaluation.

Figure 3 shows the speedup for $BSBM_{200GB}$ with the various number of worker nodes. We can see that as the number of workers increases, the execution time cost-decrease is almost linear. The execution time decreases about 14 times (from 433.31 min down to 28.8 min) as cluster nodes increase from one to six worker nodes. The results shown here imply that our approach can achieve near linear scalability in performance in the context of speedup.

Furthermore, we conduct the effectiveness evaluation of our approach. Speedup S is an important metric to evaluate a parallel algorithm. It is defined as a ratio $S = T_s/T_n$, where T_s represents the execution time of the algorithm run on a single node and T_n represents the execution time required for the same algorithm on n nodes with the same configuration and resources. Efficiency is defined as a ratio $E = S/n = T_s/nT_n$ which measures the processing power being used, in our case the speedup per node. The speedup and efficiency curves of DistQualityAssessment are shown in Fig. 5. The trend shows that it achieves almost linearly speedup and even super linear in some cases. The upper curve in the Fig. 5 indicates super linear speedup. The speedup grows faster than the number of worker nodes. This is due to the computation task for the metric being computationally intensive, and the data does not fit in the cache when executed on a single node. But it fits into the caches of several machines when the workload is divided amongst the cluster for parallel evaluation. While using Spark, the super linear speedup is an outcome of the improved complexity and runtime, in addition to efficient memory management behavior of the parallel execution environment.

Correctness of Metrics. In order to test the correctness of implemented metrics, we assess the numerical values for metrics like L1, L2, and RC1 on very small datasets and the results are found correct w.r.t Luzzu. For metrics like I2 and CN2, Luzzu uses approximate values for faster performance, and that is not the same as getting the exact number as in the case of our implementation.

Overall Analysis by Metrics. We analyze the overall run-time of the metric evaluation. Figure 4 reports on the run-time of each metric considered in this paper (see Table 2) on both $BSBM_{20GB}$ and $BSBM_{200GB}$ datasets.

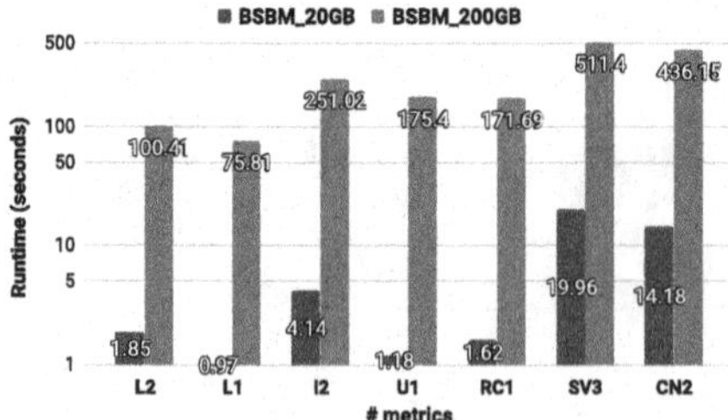

Fig. 4. Overall analysis by metric in the cluster mode (log scale).

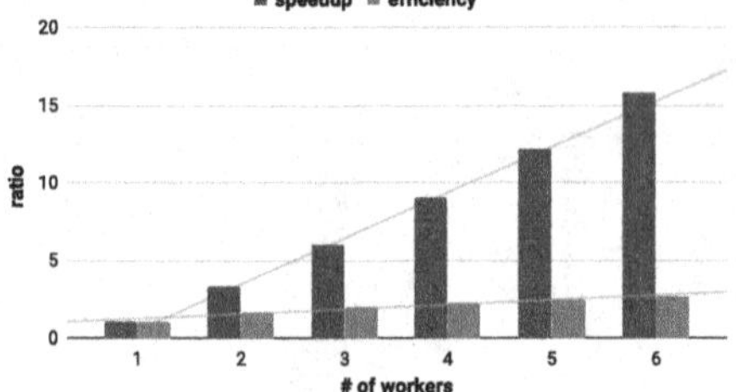

Fig. 5. Effectiveness of DistQualityAssessment.

DistQualityAssessment implements predefined quality assessment metrics from [22]. We have implemented these metrics in a distributed manner such that most of them have a run-time complexity of $O(n)$ where n is the number of input triples. The overall performance of analysis for BSBM dataset with two instances is shown in Fig. 4. The results obtained show that the execution is sometimes a little longer when there is a shuffling involved in the cluster compared to when data is processed without movement e.g. Metric L2 and L1. Metric SV3 and CN2 are the most expensive ones in terms of runtime. This is due to the extra overhead caused by extracting the literals for objects, and checking the lexical form of its datatype.

Overall, the evaluation study carried out in this paper demonstrates that distributed computation of different quality measures is scalable and the execution ends in reasonable time given the large volume of data.

4 Use Cases

The proposed quality assessment tool is being used in many use cases. These includes the projects QROWD, SLIPO, and an industrial application by Alethio[12].

QROWD – Crowdsourcing Streaming Big Data Quality Assessment Use Case. QROWD[13] is a cross-sectoral streaming Big Data integration project including geographic, transport, meteorological, cross domain and news data, aiming to capitalize on hybrid Big Data integration and analytics methods. One of the major challenges faced in QROWD, is to investigate options for effective and scalable data quality assessment on integrated (RDF) datasets using their crowdsourcing platform. In order to perform this task efficiently and effectively, QROWD uses DistQualityAssessment as an underlying quality assessment framework.

Blockchain – Alethio Use Case. Alethio[14] has build an Ethereum analytics platform that strives to provide transparency over the transaction pool of the whole Ethereum ecosystem. Their 18 billion triple data set[15] contains large scale blockchain transaction data modelled as RDF according to the structure of the Ethereum ontology[16]. Alethio is using SANSA in general and DistQualityAssesment in particular, for performing large-scale batch quality checks, e.g. analysing the quality while merging new data, computing attack pattern frequencies and fraud detection. Alethio uses DistQualityAssesment on a cluster of 100 worker nodes to assess the quality of their ≈7 TB of data.

SLIPO – Scalable Integration and Quality Assured Fusion of Big POI Data. SLIPO[17] is a project which leverages semantic web technologies for scalable and quality assured integration of large Point of Interest (POI) datasets. One of the key features of the project is the fusion process. SLIPO-fusion receives two different RDF datasets containing POIs and their properties, as well as a set of links between POI entities of

12 https://goo.gl/mJTkPp.

13 http://qrowd-project.eu/.

14 https://aleth.io/.

15 https://medium.com/alethio/ethereum-linked-data-b72e6283812f.

16 https://github.com/ConsenSys/EthOn.

17 http://slipo.eu/.

the two datasets. SLIPO is using DistQualityAssessment to assess the quality of both input datasets. The SLIPO-fusion produces a third, final dataset, containing consolidated descriptions of the linked POIs. This process is often data and processing intensive, therefore, it requires a scalable mechanism for data quality check. SLIPO uses DistQualityAssessment for fusion validation and quality statistics/assessment to facilitate and assure the quality of the fusion process.

5 Related Work

Even though quality assessment of big datasets is an important research area, it is still largely under-explored. There have been a few works discussing the challenges and issues of big data quality [3,8,19]. Only recently, a few of them have started to address the problem from a practical point of view [10], which is the focus of our work as stated in Sect. 1. In the following, we divide the section between conceptual and practical approaches proposed in the state of the art for big data quality assessment. In [9] the authors propose a big data processing pipeline and a big data quality pipeline. For each of the phases of the processing pipeline they discuss the corresponding phase of the big data quality pipeline. Relevant quality dimensions such as accuracy, consistency and completeness are discussed for the quality assessment of RDF datasets as part of an integration scenario. Given that the quality dimensions and metrics have somehow evolved from relational to Linked Data, it is relevant to understand the evolution of quality dimensions according to the differences between the structural characteristics of the two data models [1]. This allows to manage the huge variability of methods and techniques needed to manage data quality and understand which are the quality dimensions that prevail when assessing large-scale RDF datasets.

Most of the existing approaches can be applied to small/medium scale datasets and do not horizontally scale [10,14]. The work in [14] presents a methodology for assessing the quality of Linked Data based on a test case generation analogy used for software testing. The idea of this approach is to generate templates of the SPARQL queries (i.e., quality test case patterns) and then instantiate them by using the vocabulary or schema information, thus producing quality test case queries. Luzzu [10] is similar in spirit with our approach in that its objective is to provide a framework for quality assessment. In contrast to our approach, where data is distributed and also the evaluation of metrics is distributed, Luzzu does not provide any large-scale processing of the data. It only uses Spark streaming for loading the data which is not part of the core framework. Another approach proposed for assessing the quality of large-scale medical data implements Hadoop Map/Reduce [7]. It takes advantage of query optimization and join strategies which are tailored to the structure of the data and the SPARQL queries for that particular dataset. In addition, this work, differently from our approach, does not assess any data quality metric defined in [22]. The work in [5] propose a reasoning approach to derive inconsistency rules and implements a Spark-based implementation of the inference algorithm for capturing and cleaning inconsistencies in RDF datasets. The inference generally incurs higher complexity. Our approach is designed for scalability, and we also use Spark-based implementation for capturing inconsistencies in the data. While the approach in [5] needs manual definitions of the inconsistency rules, our approach runs automatically, not only for consistency metrics but also for other quality metrics. In addition, we test the performance of our approach on large-scale RDF datasets while their approach is not experimentally evaluated. LD-Sniffer [17], is a tool for assessing the accessibility of Linked Data resources according to the metrics defined in the Linked Data Quality Model. The limitation of this tool, besides that it is a centralized version, is that it does not provide most of the quality assessment metrics defined in [22]. In addition to above, there is a lack of unified structure to propose and develop new quality metrics that are scalable and less computationally expensive.

Based on the identified limitations of these aforementioned approaches, we have introduced DistQualityAssessment which bases its computation and evaluations mainly in-memory. As a result the computation of the quality metrics show a high performance for large-scale datasets.

6 Conclusions and Future Work

The data quality assessment becomes challenging with the increasing sizes of data. Many existing tools mostly contain a customized data quality functionality to detect and analyze data quality issues within their own domain. However, this process is both data-intensive and computing-intensive and it is a challenge to develop fast and efficient algorithms that can handle large scale RDF datasets.

In this paper, we have introduced DistQualityAssessment, a novel approach for distributed in-memory evaluation of RDF quality assessment metrics implemented on top of the Spark framework. The presented approach offers generic features to solve common data quality checks. As a consequence, this can enable further applications to build trusted data utilities.

We have demonstrated empirically that our approach improves upon previous centralized approach that we have compared against. The benefit of using Spark is that its core concepts (RDDs) are designed to scale horizontally. Users can adapt the cluster sizes corresponding to the data sizes, by dropping when it is not needed and adding more when there is a need for it.

Although we have achieved reasonable results in terms of scalability, we plan to further improve time efficiency by applying intelligent partitioning strategies and persist the data to an even higher extent in memory and perform dependency analysis in order to evaluate multiple metrics simultaneously. We also plan to explore near real-time interactive quality assessment of large-scale RDF data using Spark Streaming. Finally, in the future we intend to develop a declarative plugin for the current work using Quality Metric Language (QML) [10], which gives users the ability to express, customize and enhance quality metrics.

Acknowledgment. This work was partly supported by the EU Horizon2020 projects BigDataOcean (GA no. 732310), Boost4.0 (GA no. 780732), QROWD (GA no. 723088) and CLEOPATRA (GA no. 812997).

References

1. Batini, C., Rula, A., Scannapieco, M., Viscusi, G.: From data quality to big data quality. J. Database Manag. **26**(1), 60–82 (2015)

2. Batini, C., Scannapieco, M.: Data and Information Quality - Dimensions Principles and Techniques. Data-Centric Systems and Applications. Springer, Cham (2016). https://doi.org/10.1007/978-3-319-24106-7
3. Becker, D., King, T.D., McMullen, B.: Big data, big data quality problem. In: International Conference on Big Data, pp. 2644–2653. IEEE (2015)
4. Beek, W., Ilievski, F., Debattista, J., Schlobach, S., Wielemaker, J.: Literally better: analyzing and improving the quality of literals. Semant. Web **9**(1), 131–150 (2018)
5. Benbernou, S., Ouziri, M.: Enhancing data quality by cleaning inconsistent big RDF data. In: International Conference on Big Data, pp. 74–79. IEEE (2017)
6. Bizer, C., Schultz, A.: The Berlin SPARQL benchmark. Int. J. Semant. Web Inf. Syst. **5**, 1–24 (2009)
7. Bonner, S., et al.: Data quality assessment and anomaly detection via map/reduce and linked data: a case study in the medical domain. In: International Conference on Big Data. IEEE (2015)
8. Cai, L., Zhu, Y.: The challenges of data quality and data quality assessment in the big data era. Data Sci. J. **14**, 2 (2015)
9. Catarci, T., Scannapieco, M., Console, M., Demetrescu, C.: My (fair) big data. In: International Conference on Big Data, pp. 2974–2979. IEEE (2017)
10. Debattista, J., Auer, S., Lange, C.: Luzzu-a methodology and framework for linked data quality assessment. J. Data Inf. Qual. (JDIQ) **8**(1), 4 (2016)
11. Debattista, J., Lange, C., Auer, S., Cortis, D.: Evaluating the quality of the LOD cloud: an empirical investigation. Semant. Web **9**(6), 859–901 (2018)
12. Ermilov, I., et al.: The tale of sansa spark. In: 16th International Semantic Web Conference, Poster & Demos (2017)
13. Färber, M., Bartscherer, F., Menne, C., Rettinger, A.: Linked data quality of DBpedia, Freebase, OpenCyc, Wikidata, and YAGO. Semant. Web **9**(1), 77–129 (2018)
14. Kontokostas, D., et al.: Test-driven evaluation of linked data quality. In: 23rd International World Wide Web Conference, WWW 2014, Seoul, Republic of Korea, 7–11 April 2014, pp. 747–758 (2014)
15. Lehmann, J., et al.: DBpedia - a large-scale, multilingual knowledge base extracted from Wikipedia. Semant. Web J. **6**(2), 167–195 (2015)
16. Lehmann, J., et al.: Distributed semantic analytics using the SANSA stack. In: Proceedings of 16th International Semantic Web Conference - Resources Track (ISWC 2017) (2017)
17. Mihindukulasooriya, N., García-Castro, R., Gómez-Pérez, A.: LD sniffer: a quality assessment tool for measuring the accessibility of linked data. In: Ciancarini, P., et al. (eds.) EKAW 2016. LNCS (LNAI), vol. 10180, pp. 149–152. Springer, Cham (2017). https://doi.org/10.1007/978-3-319-58694-6_20
18. Ngomo, A.-C.N., Auer, S., Lehmann, J., Zaveri, A.: Introduction to linked data and its lifecycle on the web. In: Koubarakis, M., et al. (eds.) Reasoning Web 2014. LNCS, vol. 8714, pp. 1–99. Springer, Cham (2014). https://doi.org/10.1007/978-3-319-10587-1_1
19. Rao, D., Gudivada, V.N., Raghavan, V.V.: Data quality issues in big data. In: International Conference on Big Data, pp. 2654–2660. IEEE (2015)
20. Stadler, C., Lehmann, J., Höffner, K., Auer, S.: Linkedgeodata: a core for a web of spatial open data. Semant. Web J. **3**(4), 333–354 (2012)
21. Zaharia, M., et al.:. Resilient distributed datasets: a fault-tolerant abstraction for in-memory cluster computing. In: Proceedings of the 9th USENIX Conference on Networked Systems Design and Implementation. USENIX (2012)
22. Zaveri, A., Rula, A., Maurino, A., Pietrobon, R., Lehmann, J., Auer, S.: Quality assessment for linked data: a survey. Semant. Web **7**(1), 63–93 (2015)

QaldGen: Towards Microbenchmarking of Question Answering Systems over Knowledge Graphs

Kuldeep Singh[1(✉)], Muhammad Saleem[2], Abhishek Nadgeri[3], Felix Conrads[2], Jeff Z. Pan[5,6], Axel-Cyrille Ngonga Ngomo[4], and Jens Lehmann[7]

[1] Nuance Communications Deutschland GmbH, Aachen, Germany
kuldeep.singh1@nuance.com
[2] University of Leipzig, Leipzig, Germany
saleem@informatik.uni-leipzig.de
[3] Service Lee Technologies, Mumbai, India
abhishek.n@servify.in
[4] University of Paderborn, Paderborn, Germany
axel.ngonga@upb.de
[5] Edinburgh Research Centre, Huawei, Edinburgh, UK
[6] University of Aberdeen, Aberdeen, UK
jeff.z.pan@abdn.ac.uk
[7] Fraunhofer IAIS, Sankt Augustin, Germany
jens.lehmann@iais.fraunhofer.de

Abstract. Over the last years, a number of Knowledge Graph (KG) based Question Answering (QA) systems have been developed. Consequently, the series of Question Answering Over Linked Data (QALD1–QALD9) challenges and other datasets have been proposed to evaluate these systems. However, the QA datasets contain a fixed number of natural language questions and do not allow users to select micro benchmarking samples of the questions tailored towards specific use-cases. We propose `QaldGen`, a framework for microbenchmarking of QA systems over KGs which is able to select customised question samples from existing QA datasets. The framework is flexible enough to select question samples of varying sizes and according to the user-defined criteria on the most important features to be considered for QA benchmarking. This is achieved using different clustering algorithms. We compare state-of-the-art QA systems over knowledge graphs by using different QA benchmarking samples. The observed results show that specialised micro-benchmarking is important to pinpoint the limitations of the various QA systems and its components.

Resource Type: *Evaluation benchmarks or Methods*
Repository: https://github.com/dice-group/qald-generator
License: *GNU General Public License v3.0*

K. Singh and M. Saleem—These two authors contributed equally as first author.

C. Ghidini et al. (Eds.): ISWC 2019, LNCS 11779, pp. 277–292, 2019.
https://doi.org/10.1007/978-3-030-30796-7_18

1 Introduction

Question answering (QA) systems provide users with an interactive way to extract useful information from various sources such as documents, knowledge graphs, relational tables, etc. by posing questions in natural language or as voice input. Since the initial stages of TREC challenge for QA over Web data in the year 1999 [33], researchers have developed several novel approaches that include question answering over structured and unstructured data sources [10,11]. Publicly available Knowledge Graphs (KGs) provide a rich source of structured information. Since 2010 more than 62 QA systems have been developed over KGs including DBpedia [1], Freebase [3] and Wikidata [34] as underlying knowledge source [9]. The question answering approaches over KGs can be broadly categorised into three categories based on their implementation [24]: the first category is *semantic parsing based QA systems* that heavily use linguistic principles such as POS tagging, dependency parsing, and entity recognition for extracting answers of the input question. It is often the case that there is no (or little) training data. The second category is *end-to-end machine learning based QA systems* that require large amounts of training data (e.g., [10]). Lastly, a recently introduced *collaborative QA systems* development focuses on building QA systems by reusing several existing QA systems and components (e.g. OKBQA [4]). Several independent components (e.g. EARL [7], Falcon [18], SQG [36]) perform tasks such as named entity disambiguation, relation linking, and SPARQL query generator for building QA systems in collaborative efforts have also been released by the semantic web research community.

Research Gap: Irrespective of the approaches opted for by researchers for the implementation, QA systems and components over knowledge graphs have been evaluated using several standard datasets such as LC-QuAD [28], QALD [29], and WebQuestion [2]. Nearly all report the results using the global metrics of precision, recall, and F-score as performance indicators [33]. Benchmarking Frameworks such as Gerbil [32] or leader boards[1] also follow the same principle and outline the final results based on the global performance metric. The results are calculated as ***average over all the (test) questions of the dataset*** and indicates the overall gain/loss in the performance w.r.t state of the art. However, it does not shed any light on the strength or weakness of a particular QA system and component. This allows the same issue to persist over time causing performance limitation of the QA system. For example, Muldoven et al. [16] pointed out in the year 2003 that answer type (boolean, count, list) and Wh-type questions (what, who, etc.) have an impact on the performance of the open domain QA systems. Saleem et al. [20] recently raised similar issues pertaining to QA systems over DBpedia. For instance, the overall winner of the 6th edition of the Question Answering over Linked Data Challenge (QALD6) was CANALI, which suffered limitations when the question started with `"Give me"`. CANALI is outperformed by another QA systems UTQA for such type of questions [20]. Similarly, the capitalisation of entity labels (surface forms) in a sentence is an

[1] http://qa.mpi-inf.mpg.de/comqa/.

issue reported by Derczynski et al. [5] by performing an in-depth analysis of entity linking tools. Sakor et al. [18] and Singh et al. [26,27] again reported this issue in state of the art entity linking tools evaluated over standard QA datasets. Therefore, it is evident that the common practice of reporting results average over all the questions of the dataset (often referred as macro evaluation) does not always reveal details on state-of-the-art pitfalls, limitations, strengths, and potentials for further QA research.

Motivation and Contributions. There are concrete pieces of evidence in the literature that question features such as "headword", "answer type", number of triples in SPARQL queries, explicit (exact string match between the entity candidate and KG mention) and implicit (no exact match i.e. mapping `NYC` to `dbr:New_York_City`[2]) nature of entities, etc. have an impact on the performance of the QA systems and the QA components [9,18,20,26,27]. Furthermore, question classification has been a long-standing field of research where researchers have focused on identifying several such features [12]. This motivates our work and in this article, we provide a reusable resource `QaldGen` for the community to select personalised question samples for microbenchmarking QA systems over the DBpedia knowledge graph. `QaldGen` uses state-of-the-art clustering algorithms to cluster most prominent questions by using distance metrics. `QaldGen` further allows researchers to select personalised question samples based on specific question features that evidently impact the performance of a QA system or component. We not only provide `QaldGen` for the QA system but also to evaluate several QA components that can be reused in collaborative QA frameworks for tasks such as named entity disambiguation (NED), relation linking (RL) (for mapping natural language relations to KG), and SPARQL query generator (Query Builder). Our contributions are two-fold:

- R1 `QaldGenData` - **An RDF Dataset for Personalised Microbenchmarking:** We automatically annotated a total 5408 questions from QALD9 and LC-QuAD datasets with 51 features and converted it into RDF format. This dataset can be reused in training machine learning approaches related to question answering.
- R2 `QaldGen` **-A Personalised Question Sample Generator:** We collected 51 question features from existing literature that impact the performance of the QA systems and components. A user can choose one or multiple question features to be included in the customised question sample for microbenchmarking. `QaldGen` selects personalised question samples of variable sizes using clustering algorithms from two standard datasets over DBpedia: QALD9 [17], containing 408 questions consolidating previous QALD editions and LC-QuAD [28], having 5000 questions. A user can customise questions (in terms of the number of question and the number of diverse features) using `QaldGen` to evaluate their QA system or the component either independently or using benchmarking frameworks such as Gerbil [32] or the Frankenstein platform [25].

[2] Prefix `dbr` is bound to http://dbpedia.org/resource/.

The rest of this paper is organised as follows: the next section describes our two resources and approach to build QaldGen. Section 4 presents the importance and impact of this work for the research community. Section 5 presents our plan for availability and sustainability of resources. Section 6 reviews the state of the art and we close with the conclusion and future work in Sect. 7.

2 QaldGen Question Sample Generator

In this section, we present the question sampling process in the QaldGen. We first discuss the R1 dataset that we use as input for the QaldGen question sample generation framework. We then discuss the question sampling process along with the personalised micro benchmark generation.

2.1 QaldGen Dataset

Our framework takes a set of natural language questions as input and selects the required sample of questions according to the user-defined criteria. We use our R1 dataset as input to QaldGen where customised question samples will be selected from. As mentioned before, this RDF dataset of QA is selected from QALD9 and LC-QuAD which contains a total of 5408 questions. A QA benchmark should be comprising of questions/tests of varying question features. To this end, we have attached a total of 51 important QA related features summarised in Fig. 1. We divide these features according to the question and the corresponding answer. The features attached to the question are related to the entities, relations and classes used in the SPARQL query, along with the natural language features such as headword, POS tags, etc. In addition, we store the number of words in the question and the origin (QALD9 or LC-QuAD) of the question. Each question has a SPARQL query to be executed to get the

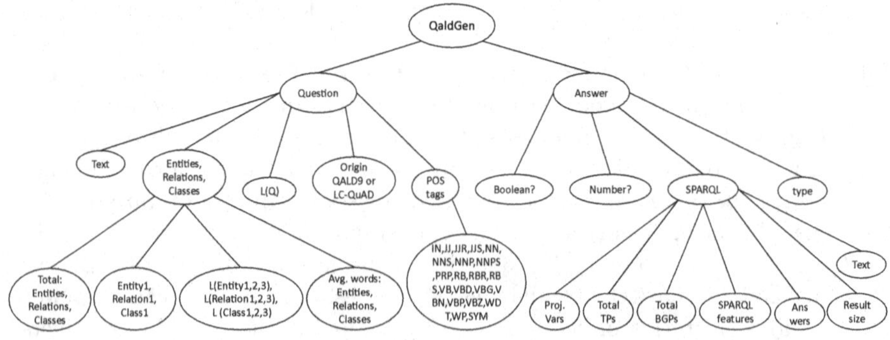

Fig. 1. A tree of features attached to QaldGen dataset questions. L(X) stands for number of words in X.TPs = number of triple patterns, Proj. Vars = number of projection variables

correct answers. We store SPARQL related features such as the number of projection variables, number of triple patterns, number of BGPs, filters, regex etc. A sample RDF representation of a `QaldGen` question is available in the listing 1.1. We re-used the Linked SPARQL Queries (LSQ) [19] vocabulary to represent the SPARQL query related features. In addition, we re-used properties from the QALD JSON datasets.

The benefit of this dataset is that it can be directly queried using SPARQL and easily can be used in wide range of Linked Data and Semantic Web applications. In addition, each question has more features attached as compared to the original QALD9 and LC-QuAD datasets.

2.2 Question Sample Generation for Microbenchmarking

First, we define our question sampling generation problem and then explain the generation process. Our Question Sampling problem is defined as follows:

Definition 1 (Question Sampling Problem). *Let L represent the set of input natural language questions. Our goal is to select the N questions that best represent L as well as being more diverse in features, with $N \ll |L|$.*

Figure 2 shows the general steps involved in the `QaldGen` question sample generation process. The user provides the input R1 RDF dataset, the required number N of questions and the selection criteria (as SPARQL query) to be considered in the question sampling for microbenchmarking. Then, the sampling is carried out in the following four main steps: (1) Select all the questions along with the required features from the input `QaldGenData` RDF dataset. (2) Generate feature vectors and their normalisation for the selected questions. (3) Generate N number of clusters from the questions. (4) Select single most representative questions from each cluster to be included in the final question sample requested by the user.

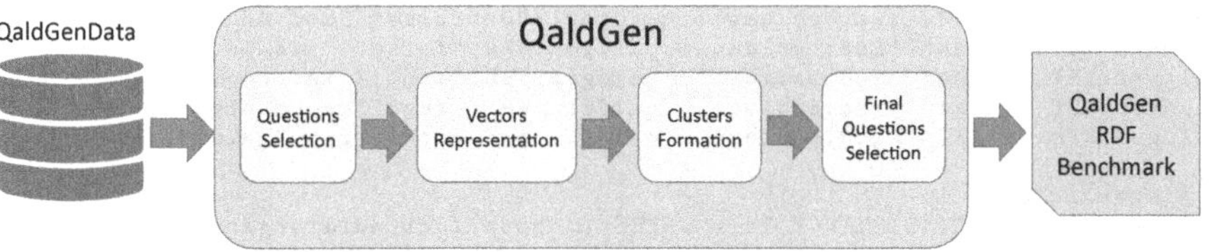

Fig. 2. QaldGen Sampling process.

Selection of Questions. We can select questions along with the required features by simply using SPARQL queries over `QaldGenData` RDF dataset. The `QaldGen` sampling framework retrieves the set of questions along with the required important features (can be any of the 51 features attached to each question) by using a single SPARQL query. For example, the SPARQL query given in Listing 1.2 retrieves all the questions from `QaldGen` RDF dataset along with

```
@prefix lsq: <http://lsq.aksw.org/vocab#> .
@prefix qaldgen: <http://qald-gen.aksw.org/vocab#> .
@prefix qaldgen-res: <http://qald-gen.aksw.org/> .

#Question related
qaldgen-res:question#0 qaldgen:text "What is the time zone of Salt Lake City
    ?" ;
qaldgen:length "9"^^xsd:int ;

 # Entities
qaldgen:totalEntities "1"^^xsd:int ; qaldgen:entity1 "Salt_Lake_City, " ;
qaldgen:totalWordsEntity1 "1"^^xsd:int ; qaldgen:entity2 "" ;
qaldgen:totalWordsEntity2 "0"^^xsd:int ; qaldgen:entity3 "" ;
qaldgen:totalWordsEntity3 "0"^^xsd:int ; qaldgen:avgEntitiesWords "1.0"^^
    xsd:double ;

 # Relations
qaldgen:totalRelations "1"^^xsd:int ;
qaldgen:relation1 "timeZone" ;
qaldgen:totalWordsRelation1 "1"^^xsd:int ;
qaldgen:relation2 "" ;
qaldgen:totalWordsRelation2 "0"^^xsd:int ;
qaldgen:relation3 "" ;
qaldgen:totalWordsRelation3 "0"^^xsd:int ;
qaldgen:avgRelationsWords "1.0"^^xsd:double ;

 # Classes
qaldgen:totalClasses "0"^^xsd:int ;
qaldgen:class1 "" ;
qaldgen:totalWordsClass1 "0"^^xsd:int ;
qaldgen:class2 "" ;
qaldgen:totalWordsClass2 "0"^^xsd:int ;
qaldgen:class3 "" ;
qaldgen:totalWordsClass3 "0"^^xsd:int ;
qaldgen:avgClassesWords "0.0"^^xsd:double ;
qaldgen:answerType "resource" ;
qaldgen:isNumberAnswer "0" ;
qaldgen:isBooleanAnswer "0" ;

 # POS tags
qaldgen:IN "true"^^xsd:boolean ; qaldgen:JJ "false"^^xsd:boolean ;
qaldgen:JJR "false"^^xsd:boolean ; qaldgen:JJS "false"^^xsd:boolean ;
qaldgen:NN "true"^^xsd:boolean ; qaldgen:NNS "false"^^xsd:boolean ;
qaldgen:NNP "true"^^xsd:boolean ; qaldgen:NNPS "false"^^xsd:boolean ;
qaldgen:PRP "false"^^xsd:boolean ; qaldgen:RB "false"^^xsd:boolean ;
qaldgen:RBR "false"^^xsd:boolean ; qaldgen:RBS "false"^^xsd:boolean ;
qaldgen:VB "false"^^xsd:boolean ; qaldgen:VBD "false"^^xsd:boolean ;
qaldgen:VBG "false"^^xsd:boolean ; qaldgen:VBN "false"^^xsd:boolean ;
qaldgen:VBP "false"^^xsd:boolean ; qaldgen:VBZ "true"^^xsd:boolean ;
qaldgen:WDT "false"^^xsd:boolean ; qaldgen:WP "true"^^xsd:boolean ;
qaldgen:SYM "false"^^xsd:boolean ; qaldgen:questionOrigin "qald9" ;

# Answer related
lsq:text """SELECT DISTINCT ?uri WHERE { <http://dbpedia.org/resource/
    Salt_Lake_City> <http://dbpedia.org/ontology/timeZone ?uri }""" ;
lsq:tps "1"^^xsd:int ;
lsq:bgps "1"^^xsd:int ;
lsq:usesFeature lsq:Select , lsq:Distinct ;
lsq:projectVars "1"^^xsd:int ;
lsq:answers "( ?uri = <http://dbpedia.org/resource/Mountain_Time_Zone ), " ;
lsq:resultSize "1"^^xsd:int .
```

Listing 1.1. An example QaldGenData RDF representation of a question

```
Prefix qaldGen: <http://qald-gen.aksw.org/vocab#>
Prefix lsq: <http://lsq.aksw.org/vocab#>
SELECT  DISTINCT ?qId ?totalWords ?totalEntities ?
    totalRelations ?totalClasses ?avgEntitiesWords ?tps ?
    rs ?bgps ?pvars
{
?qId  qaldGen:length ?totalWords .
?qId  qaldGen:totalEntities ?totalEntities .
?qId  qaldGen:totalRelations ?totalRelations .
?qId  qaldGen:totalClasses ?totalClasses .
?qId  qaldGen:avgEntitiesWords ?avgEntitiesWords .
?qId  lsq:tps ?tps .
?qId  lsq:resultSize  ?rs .
?qId  lsq:bgps  ?bgps .
?qId  lsq:projectVars ?pvars .
}
```

Listing 1.2. Natural language questions selection along with required features from QaldGenData RDF dataset

the features: the total number of words, entities, relations, classes along with average words per entity in the question. In addition, it considers the number of triple patterns, the number of answers, the number of BGPs, and the number of projection variables. In other words, the user can select any number of features that are considered important for microbenchmarking. The result of this query execution is stored in a map that is used in the subsequent sampling steps. In Sect. 2.3, we show how this query can be modified to select customised samples for microbenchmarking.

Normalised Feature Vectors. The cluster generation algorithms (explained in the next section) require distances between questions to be computed. Each question (that was retrieved in the previous step) from the input `QaldGenData` dataset is mapped to a vector of length equal to the number of retrieved features. The vector stores the corresponding *question features* that were retrieved along with the input questions. To ensure that dimensions with high values do not bias the selection of questions for benchmarking, we normalise the question feature vectors with values between 0 and 1. This is to ensure that all questions are located in a unit hypercube. At this point, each of the individual values in every feature vector is divided by the overall maximal value (across all the vectors) for that question feature.

Generation of Clusters. As a next step, we generate N clusters from the given input QaldGen question represented as normalised feature vectors. For this step we used 5 existing well-known algorithms – FEASIBLE [21], FEASIBLE-Exemplars [21], KMeans++, DBSCAN+KMeans++, Random selection – which allow the generation of the required fixed number of clusters. Note DBSCAN+KMeans++ means that we applied DBSCAN first to remove the outlier queries and then applied KMeans++ to generate the required number of clusters. Please also consider that we need an additional normalisation of the remaining vectors after outliers are removed. Moreover, our framework is flexible enough to integrate any other clustering algorithm and allows the generation of a fixed number of clusters.

Selection of Most Representative Questions. Finally, we perform the selection of a single prototypical question from each cluster. This step is exactly the same as performed in FEASIBLE [21]: For each cluster S, compute the centroid c which is the average of the feature vectors of all the queries in S. Following this, compute the distance of each query in S with c and select the query of minimum distance to include in the resulting benchmark. The final output of the QaldGen sampling generator is an RDF file containing the finally selected natural language questions along with the complete list of attached features. Thus the RDF output can be directly queried using SPARQL. Current QA benchmark execution frameworks such as GERBIL [32] require the benchmark to be represented in JSON format. Thus, `QaldGen` is also able to select GERBIL compatible QA benchmarks.

Our framework also allows the generation of question samples using random selection. In addition, it allows the generation of samples using Agglomerative clustering [21]. However, Agglomerative clustering does not allow the creation of fixed size samples. The QaldGen website contains the CLI options for the generation of benchmarks.

2.3 Question Sample Personalisation

As mentioned before, our framework allows customised question sample generation according to the criteria specified by the user. This can be done by simply specialising the query given in Listing 1.2. For example, imagine the user wants to select customised samples with the following features: The question sample should only be selected from QALD9 and hence skipping LC-QuAD questions. The personalised sample should only contain "what"-type questions, and the number of triple patterns should be greater than 1 and there should be at least one answer of this question. The query for the selection of such a personalised benchmark is given in Listing 1.3. Users can use such personalised question samples to micro benchmark the QA system.

2.4 Diversity of Question Samples

The selected sample should not be mostly comprised of a similar type of natural language question. To ensure the overall quality of the selected sample, sufficient diversity in the micro benchmarking questions is important, which `QaldGen` is able to select using different clustering algorithms. We define their diversity as follows:

```
Prefix qaldGen: <http://qald-gen.aksw.org/vocab#>
Prefix lsq: <http://lsq.aksw.org/vocab#>
SELECT  DISTINCT ?qId ?totalWords ?totalEntities ?totalRelations ?totalClasses ?avgEntitiesWords ?tps ?rs ?bgps ?pvars
{
?qId  qaldGen:length ?totalWords .
?qId  qaldGen:totalEntities ?totalEntities .
?qId  qaldGen:totalRelations ?totalRelations .
?qId  qaldGen:totalClasses ?totalClasses .
?qId  qaldGen:avgEntitiesWords ?avgEntitiesWords .
?qId  lsq:tps ?tps .
?qId  lsq:resultSize  ?rs .
?qId  lsq:bgps    ?bgps .
?qId  lsq:projectVars ?pvars .

# Options for Personalisation
?qId  qaldGen:questionOrigin "qald9" .
?qId  qaldGen:questionType  ?qType .
Filter Regex (?qType, "What")
Filter (?tps > 1 && ?rs>0)
}
```

Listing 1.3. Benchmark Personalisation

Definition 2 (Question Sample Diversity). *Let μ_i mean and σ_i the standard deviation of a given distribution w.r.t. the ith feature of the said distribution. Let B be a question sample extracted from a set of queries L. The diversity score D is the average standard deviation of the query features k included in the sample B:*

$$D = \frac{1}{k}\sum_{i=1}^{k}(\sigma_i(B)).$$

The command line tool provided on the project website will report the diversity score after the generation of the desired QA benchmark.

3 Evaluation and Results

In this section, we describe our evaluation setup and the results.

3.1 Experiment Setup

Micro Benchmarking: We used three personalised question samples in our evaluation at a micro level: (1) a 200 question sample was used to compare the

QA systems. We used the FEASIBLE-Exemplars clustering method because it had the highest diversity score. We used the query given in Listing 1.2 to select the input questions for `QaldGen`. (2) a 100 question sample was selected using FEASIBLE-Exemplars to test the named entity disambiguation (NED) tools. In this benchmark we only consider features related to the named entities like the number of entities, the number of words in entities etc. (3) a 100 question sample was generated using FEASIBLE-Exemplars to test the relation linking (RL) tools. In this sample, we only considered features related to the relations used in the questions like number relations, number of words in relations, etc.

QA Systems: We compared all the systems which took part in the QALD9 challenge [17] and which are currently part of Gerbil framework. However, only ganswer2 and QUEPY were online and returned answers. We used `QaldGen` extension integrated in Gerbil to calculate the results. This also illustrates the adaptability and compatibility of R2 into a generic benchmarking framework. The results can be also found at persistent URI provided by Gerbil[3].

NED and RL Tools: We also extended our evaluation study at component level. We evaluated the top-2 components over LC-QuAD[4] performing NED (DBpedia Spotlight [15] and TagMe [8]) and RL tasks (RNLIWOD[5] and EARL [7]), respectively. For this study, we utilised the Frankenstein framework because these tools are already part of the framework[6]. The customised questions selected by `QaldGen` are uploaded in Frankenstein to calculate the final results.

3.2 Experiment Results

Table 1 summarises our evaluation results and we employ the performance metric of Precision (P), Recall (R), and F-Score (F) for reporting the results[7]. It is clearly observable in the table that the performance of QA systems and components fluctuate when customised question samples were selected using `QaldGen`. For instance, ganswer2 is the overall winner of QALD9, however, for a diverse set of 200 questions selected by `QaldGen`, QUEPY is the winner. This clearly show that performance of QA systems vary with the diversity of questions used in the evaluation. It is highly possible that a QA system is tuned for a particular type of question and may not perform well when exposed to question samples of varying diversity while performing microbenchmarking. In addition, a QA system designed for a particular use-case should only be tested with a use-case specific micro benchmark. Such systems will likely not perform well when tested with general QA benchmarks. For NED tools, TagMe remains the overall winner for macro and micro evaluation but its F-score drops sharply over customised

[3] http://gerbil-qa.aksw.org/gerbil/experiment?id=201903190000.
[4] As reported by [27] and [7].
[5] https://github.com/dice-group/NLIWOD.
[6] http://frankenstein.qanary-qa.com.
[7] https://github.com/dice-group/gerbil/wiki/Precision,-Recall-and-F1-measure.

Table 1. Performance of QA systems and components. We can observe fluctuation of P, R, F values when customised question samples have been selected using R2. For instance, QUEPY is the new baseline outperforming ganswer2 (overall baseline of QALD9 dataset) on the customised benchmark selected by `QaldGen`. Similar performance variation has been observed in the tools performing NED and RL tasks.

Systems	Dataset	P	R	F
baseline QA system (ganswer2) [17]	QALD9	0.29	0.33	0.30
ganswer2	QaldGen	0.24	0.24	0.24
QUEPY	QaldGen	**0.27**	**0.27**	**0.27**
baseline NED (TagMe) [27]	LCQuAD	0.69	0.67	0.68
TagMe	QaldGen	**0.44**	**0.40**	**0.41**
DBpedia Spotlight	QaldGen	0.37	0.38	0.36
baseline RL (RNLIWOD) [27]	LCQuAD	0.25	0.22	0.23
RNLIWOD	QaldGen	0.23	0.19	0.20
EARL	QaldGen	**0.38**	**0.39**	**0.37**

sampling questions. When we consider specific question features (total number of entities as two and more than two words in the entity label) for generating a personalised question sample, the performance of TagMe is limited. In the case of RL tools, EARL outperforms RNLIWOD when we selected a personalised question sample with particular question features (explicit relations, number of relations = 1). It provides a clear indication of the strength of the EARL tool for a particular type of questions. Please note that in the scope of this paper, we are not analysing the architecture of the QA systems and components to understand the performance variation for specific question features. Our aim is to illustrate with empirical results that the term "baseline or state of the art" solely depends on the type of questions and considered features. Therefore, using our reusable resources, developers can better understand the strength or weaknesses of their tools by evaluating their tools at micro level.

4 Impact

38 QA systems from over 40 research groups in the semantic web community have participated in nine editions of QALD [17]. The LC-QuAD dataset has also gained recognition and is already cited 25 times since its release in October 2018 [28]. However the same issues of question ambiguity, capitalisation of entity labels, complex questions, implicit/explicit nature of entity and relation label, etc. are reported repeatedly in the evaluation studies [9,20,26].

In this article, we provide the semantic web community with two reusable resources for micro benchmarking of QA components and systems. Please note that we are **not** proposing any new benchmarking dataset or a benchmarking framework such as Frankenstein [25] or Gerbil [31]. We reuse the existing QA datasets (QALD9 and LC-QuAD) over DBpedia and in addition have developed R2 that can be reused by QA developers to select personalised question samples for micro benchmarking their systems and components. This is the first step towards a more fine grained evaluation of QA systems and we expect the QA community to utilise R2 to dig deeper into the strength and weaknesses of their systems. Similar effort has also been started towards micro-benchmarking entity linking tools [35], however micro benchmarking of QA components and systems is a major research gap. Our second resource R1 can be reused by developers as a rich source of questions represented in RDF format with its features. Furthermore, we hope fine grained benchmarking of QA systems will trigger discussion within the community to release datasets with diverse question features.

5 Adoption and Reusability

The resources R2 and R1 are licensed under the GNU General Public License v3.0 and publicly available for reuse. Detailed instructions are provided for the easy adaptability of the resources. Developers can either use the proposed resources independently or can select personalised benchmarking questions using R2 and adapt it for benchmarking frameworks. For community adaptation, both resources are made compatible with Gerbil [31] and Frankenstein framework [25]. Furthermore, Gerbil supports an easy extension of its core architecture and it is a widely used platform for calculating global performance metrics of QA systems and entity linking components. The maven version of R2 has already been integrated with Gerbil. Therefore, researchers can choose customised benchmarking questions based on their needs, and use Gerbil to calculate the global performance metric for a sub-set of customised questions selected by R2. The extension of Gerbil with `QaldGen` is already completed and it is available for public reuse in official Github repository of Gerbil[8].

6 Related Work

QA Systems and Macro Benchmarking: TREC QA series [33] for evaluating open domain question answering was one of the earlier attempts in the direction of providing researchers with standard datasets and a performance metric for benchmarking QA systems. Question answering over KG gained momentum in the last decade after the inception of publicly available KGs such as DBpedia and Freebase. Datasets such as SimpleQuestions[9] and WebQuestions [2] are commonly used for evaluating QA systems that employ Freebase as the underlying KG. For benchmarking QA systems over DBpedia, the QALD series was launched in 2011[10] and is currently running its 9th edition. In the last 8 years,

[8] https://github.com/dice-group/gerbil/wiki/QALD-Generation.
[9] https://research.fb.com/downloads/babi/.
[10] http://qald.aksw.org/index.php?x=home&q=1.

over 38 QA systems using DBpedia as the underlying KG have been evaluated using QALD [9]. However, the maximum number of questions in QALD is 408 which hinders the development of machine learning based approaches. In contrast with QALD, LC-QuAD dataset provides a rich and diverse set of 5000 complex questions for DBpedia [28]. Recently developed QA systems and frameworks also report results on LC-QuAD [6,13,27]. However, the reported results across these datasets are on **macro level** i.e. an average on all questions of the dataset.

Question Classification and Micro Benchmarking: Question classification techniques aim to classify questions based on several features that may impact the overall performance of the QA system [12]. In the semantic web community, Usbeck et al. [30] first attempted to use question classification and question features such as headword, answer type, entity type, etc were extracted to provide a labelled representation of each question. Classifiers were trained using these features to choose a QA system among six that can potentially answer an input question. This approach resulted in an increase in the overall performance of the proposed hybrid QA system. Saleem et al. [20] used question classification to **micro benchmark** (i.e. reporting results based on the type of the questions containing specific features) QA systems to understand the strengths and the weaknesses. The authors conclude that a QA system which is the overall winner for all questions of the QALD-6 dataset is not always the winner for the questions with particular features. This empirical study also revealed that macro F-score (average on all questions) varies a lot based on the type of questions. For example, the highest reported F-score for all questions is 0.89 (CANALI QA system [14]). However, for a specific type of questions starting with "Give me" (e.g. Give me all cosmonauts.), F-score sharply drops to 0.34 and the UTQA QA system outperforms CANALI. Singh et al. [26,27] extended the concept of micro-benchmarking to QA component level where exhaustive evaluations of 28 QA components including 20 named entity disambiguation, five relation linking, two class linking, and two SPARQL query generator have been performed using over 3000 questions from LC-QuAD. The authors observe significant fluctuation of the F-score even at the component level published in the extended study of Frankenstein framework [26]. For example, SINA [23] generates SPARQL queries which requires DBpedia URIs of entities and predicates present in the question as input. SINA is the baseline (F-Score 0.80) for the subset of 729 questions from LC-QuAD having SPARQL queries with two triples compared to the overall winner (F-score 0.48 reported by NLIWOD component) on all the questions of LC-QuAD dataset considered by authors. However, when the number of triples in SPARQL queries is four, SINA reports F-score 0.0 for a subset of 1256 questions. The above-mentioned micro-benchmarking studies provide a foundation to our work. We reuse all the question features reported by [20,27] in `QaldGen` for micro benchmarking.

The work by Waitelonis et al. [35] proposes fine-grained benchmarking of entity linking tools using the Gerbil framework [32] based on the features of entity type (person, organisation, place). This work is most closely related to our approach. Unlike QaldGen, the above-mentioned work is limited to the entity linking tools whereas the novelty of QaldGen is to provide a reusable resource for the fine-grained micro-benchmarking study of the QA systems and reusable components for QA frameworks performing various tasks (e.g. NED, RL, Query Builder).

Finally, there are benchmark generators available for SPARQL queries [21] to test the runtime performances of triplestores, and SPARQL query containments [22] to test the query containments solvers. However, to the best of our knowledge, there was no QA over Linked Data benchmark generator available to generator customised benchmarks.

7 Conclusion and Future Work

In this paper, we present two reusable resources for generating personalised question samples for micro benchmarking question answering systems over knowledge graphs, more specifically DBpedia. Our first offered resource R2 is QaldGen. QaldGen uses state of the art clustering algorithms to cluster the most diverse or similar questions based on the features that impact the overall performance of QA systems. QaldGen is compatible with Gerbil and Frankenstein framework. Hence developers can directly use these frameworks to compare their system with state of the art on specific questions selected by QaldGen for personalised micro benchmarking.

The second resource R1 is a collection of 5408 questions from two standard datasets with a diverse representation of 51 features in each question. In the previous works [21,27,30], QA developers extracted such features multiple times for different research studies. Using R1, researchers can now select question features they would like to consider for training machine learning algorithms rather than extracting the features again from scratch. We believe that using our resources, researchers can now evaluate their systems on their specific needs. We also hope that our work will trigger discussion in the QA community to come up with a dataset containing more diverse question features and start reporting performance at the micro level. We plan to extend this work in three directions (1) extend questions to other knowledge graphs such as Wikidata (2) include more datasets in the R1 and (3) develop a similar micro-benchmarking approach for open domain question answering datasets such as reading comprehension.

Acknowledgments. This work has been supported by the project LIMBO (Grant no. 19F2029I), OPAL (no. 19F2028A), KnowGraphs (no. 860801), and SOLIDE (no. 13N14456)

References

1. Auer, S., Bizer, C., Kobilarov, G., Lehmann, J., Cyganiak, R., Ives, Z.: DBpedia: a nucleus for a web of open data. In: Aberer, K., et al. (eds.) ASWC/ISWC -2007. LNCS, vol. 4825, pp. 722–735. Springer, Heidelberg (2007). https://doi.org/10.1007/978-3-540-76298-0_52

2. Berant, J., Chou, A., Frostig, R., Liang, P.: Semantic parsing on freebase from question-answer pairs. In: Proceedings of the 2013 Conference on Empirical Methods in Natural Language Processing, EMNLP 2013, pp. 1533–1544. ACL (2013)
3. Bollacker, K.D., Evans, C., Paritosh, P., Sturge, T., Taylor, J.: Freebase: a collaboratively created graph database for structuring human knowledge. In: ACM SIGMOD, pp. 1247–1250 (2008)
4. Choi, K.-S., Mitamura, T., Vossen, P., Kim, J.-D., Ngomo, A.-C.N.: SIGIR 2017 workshop on open knowledge base and question answering (OKBQA 2017). In: Proceedings of the ACM SIGIR, pp. 1433–1434 (2017)
5. Derczynski, L., et al.: Analysis of named entity recognition and linking for tweets. Inf. Process. Manag. **51**(2), 32–49 (2015)
6. Diefenbach, D., Both, A., Singh, K., Maret, P.: Towards a question answering system over the semantic web. arXiv preprint arXiv:1803.00832 (2018)
7. Dubey, M., Banerjee, D., Chaudhuri, D., Lehmann, J.: EARL: joint entity and relation linking for question answering over knowledge graphs. In: Vrandečić, D., et al. (eds.) ISWC 2018. LNCS, vol. 11136, pp. 108–126. Springer, Cham (2018). https://doi.org/10.1007/978-3-030-00671-6_7
8. Ferragina, P., Scaiella, U.: TAGME: on-the-fly annotation of short text fragments (by Wikipedia entities). In: Proceedings of the 19th ACM Conference on Information and Knowledge Management, CIKM 2010, Toronto, Ontario, Canada, 26–30 October 2010, pp. 1625–1628. ACM (2010)
9. Höffner, K., Walter, S., Marx, E., Usbeck, R., Lehmann, J., Ngomo, A.N.: Survey on challenges of question answering in the semantic web. Semant. Web **8**(6), 895–920 (2017)
10. Huang, X., Zhang, J., Li, D., Li, P.: Knowledge graph embedding based question answering. In: Proceedings of the Twelfth ACM International Conference on Web Search and Data Mining, pp. 105–113. ACM (2019)
11. Li, F., Jagadish, H.V.: Constructing an interactive natural language interface for relational databases. PVLDB **8**(1), 73–84 (2014)
12. Loni, B.: A survey of state-of-the-art methods on question classification (2011)
13. Maheshwari, G., Trivedi, P., Lukovnikov, D., Chakraborty, N., Fischer, A., Lehmann, J.: Learning to rank query graphs for complex question answering over knowledge graphs. arXiv preprint arXiv:1811.01118 (2018)
14. Mazzeo, G.M., Zaniolo, C.: Answering controlled natural language questions on RDF knowledge bases. In: EDBT, pp. 608–611 (2016)
15. Mendes, P.N., Jakob, M., García-Silva, A., Bizer, C.: DBpedia spotlight: shedding light on the web of documents. In: Proceedings the 7th International Conference on Semantic Systems, I-SEMANTICS 2011, Graz, Austria, 7–9 September 2011, pp. 1–8. ACM (2011)
16. Moldovan, D., Paşca, M., Harabagiu, S., Surdeanu, M.: Performance issues and error analysis in an open-domain question answering system. ACM Trans. Inf. Syst. (TOIS) **21**(2), 133–154 (2003)
17. Ngomo, N.: 9th challenge on question answering over linked data (QALD-9). Language 7:1
18. Sakor, A., et al.: Old is gold: linguistic driven approach for entity and relation linking of short text. In: NAACL 2019. ACL (2019, to appear)
19. Saleem, M., Ali, M.I., Hogan, A., Mehmood, Q., Ngomo, A.-C.N.: LSQ: the linked SPARQL queries dataset. In: Arenas, M., et al. (eds.) ISWC 2015. LNCS, vol. 9367, pp. 261–269. Springer, Cham (2015). https://doi.org/10.1007/978-3-319-25010-6_15

20. Saleem, M., Dastjerdi, S.N., Usbeck, R., Ngomo, A.N.: Question answering over linked data: what is difficult to answer? What affects the F scores? In: Joint Proceedings of BLINK 2017: Co-Located with (ISWC 2017), Austria (2017)
21. Saleem, M., Mehmood, Q., Ngonga Ngomo, A.-C.: FEASIBLE: a feature-based SPARQL benchmark generation framework. In: Arenas, M., et al. (eds.) ISWC 2015. LNCS, vol. 9366, pp. 52–69. Springer, Cham (2015). https://doi.org/10.1007/978-3-319-25007-6_4
22. Saleem, M., Stadler, C., Mehmood, Q., Lehmann, J., Ngomo, A.-C.N.: SQCFramework: SPARQL query containment benchmark generation framework. In: Proceedings of the Knowledge Capture Conference, p. 28. ACM (2017)
23. Shekarpour, S., Marx, E., Ngomo, A.N., Auer, S.: SINA: semantic interpretation of user queries for question answering on interlinked data. J. Web Sem. **30**, 39–51 (2015)
24. Singh, K.: Towards dynamic composition of question answering pipelines. Ph.D. thesis, University of Bonn, Germany (2019)
25. Singh, K., Both, A., Sethupat, A., Shekarpour, S.: Frankenstein: a platform enabling reuse of question answering components. In: Gangemi, A., et al. (eds.) ESWC 2018. LNCS, vol. 10843, pp. 624–638. Springer, Cham (2018). https://doi.org/10.1007/978-3-319-93417-4_40
26. Singh, K., Lytra, I., Radhakrishna, A.S., Shekarpour, S., Vidal, M.-E., Lehmann, J.: No one is perfect: Analysing the performance of question answering components over the DBpedia knowledge graph. arXiv:1809.10044 (2018)
27. Singh, K., et al.: Why reinvent the wheel: let's build question answering systems together. In: Web Conference, pp. 1247–1256 (2018)
28. Trivedi, P., Maheshwari, G., Dubey, M., Lehmann, J.: LC-QuAD: a corpus for complex question answering over knowledge graphs. In: d'Amato, C., et al. (eds.) ISWC 2017. LNCS, vol. 10588, pp. 210–218. Springer, Cham (2017). https://doi.org/10.1007/978-3-319-68204-4_22
29. Unger, C., et al.: Question answering over linked data (QALD-5). In: Working Notes of CLEF 2015 - Conference and Labs of the Evaluation forum, Toulouse, France, 8–11 September 2015. CEUR-WS.org (2015)
30. Usbeck, R., Hoffmann, M., Röder, M., Lehmann, J., Ngomo, A.N.: Using multi-label classification for improved question answering. CoRR (2017)
31. Usbeck, R., et al.: Benchmarking question answering systems. Semant. Web J. (2019)
32. Usbeck, R., et al.: GERBIL: general entity annotator benchmarking framework. In: WWW 2015, pp. 1133–1143 (2015)
33. Voorhees, E.M., Harman, D.K. (eds.): Proceedings of The Eighth Text REtrieval Conference, TREC 1999, Gaithersburg, Maryland, USA, 17–19 November 1999, volume Special Publication, 500-246. National Institute of Standards and Technology (NIST) (1999)
34. Vrandecic, D.: Wikidata: a new platform for collaborative data collection. In: Proceedings of the 21st World Wide Web Conference, WWW 2012, Lyon, France, 16–20 April 2012 (Companion Volume), pp. 1063–1064. ACM (2012)
35. Waitelonis, J., Jürges, H., Sack, H.: Remixing entity linking evaluation datasets for focused benchmarking. Semant. Web **10**(2), 385–412 (2019)
36. Zafar, H., Napolitano, G., Lehmann, J.: Formal query generation for question answering over knowledge bases. In: Gangemi, A., et al. (eds.) ESWC 2018. LNCS, vol. 10843, pp. 714–728. Springer, Cham (2018). https://doi.org/10.1007/978-3-319-93417-4_46

Sparklify: A Scalable Software Component for Efficient Evaluation of SPARQL Queries over Distributed RDF Datasets

Claus Stadler[1(✉)], Gezim Sejdiu[2], Damien Graux[3,4], and Jens Lehmann[2,3]

[1] Institute for Applied Informatics (InfAI), University of Leipzig, Leipzig, Germany
cstadler@informatik.uni-leipzig.de

[2] Smart Data Analytics, University of Bonn, Bonn, Germany
{sejdiu,jens.lehmann}@cs.uni-bonn.de

[3] Enterprise Information Systems, Fraunhofer IAIS, Sankt Augustin, Germany
{damien.graux,jens.lehmann}@iais.fraunhofer.de

[4] ADAPT Centre, Trinity College of Dublin, Dublin, Ireland

Abstract. One of the key traits of Big Data is its complexity in terms of representation, structure, or formats. One existing way to deal with it is offered by Semantic Web standards. Among them, RDF – which proposes to model data with triples representing edges in a graph – has received a large success and the semantically annotated data has grown steadily towards a massive scale. Therefore, there is a need for scalable and efficient query engines capable of retrieving such information. In this paper, we propose *Sparklify*: a scalable software component for efficient evaluation of SPARQL queries over distributed RDF datasets. It uses Sparqlify as a SPARQL-to-SQL rewriter for translating SPARQL queries into Spark executable code. Our preliminary results demonstrate that our approach is more extensible, efficient, and scalable as compared to state-of-the-art approaches. Sparklify is integrated into a larger SANSA framework and it serves as a default query engine and has been used by at least three external use scenarios.

Resource type Software Framework
Website http://sansa-stack.net/sparklify/
Permanent URL https://doi.org/10.6084/m9.figshare.7963193

1 Introduction

In the recent years, our information society has reached the stage where it produces billions of data records, amounting to multiple quintillion of bytes[1], on a daily basis. Extraction, cleansing, enrichment and refinement of information are key to fuel value-adding processes, such as analytics as a premise for decision making. Devising appropriate (ideally uniform) representations and facilitating efficient querying of data, metadata and provenance arising from such

[1] https://www.domo.com/learn/data-never-sleeps-5.

C. Ghidini et al. (Eds.): ISWC 2019, LNCS 11779, pp. 293–308, 2019.
https://doi.org/10.1007/978-3-030-30796-7_19

phases constantly poses challenges, especially when data volumes are vast. The most prominent and promising effort is the W3C consortium with encouraging Resource Description Framework (RDF)[2] as a common data representation and vocabularies (e.g. RDFS, OWL) as a way to include meta-information about the data. These data and meta-data can be further processed and analyzed using the de-facto query language for RDF data, SPARQL[3].

SPARQL serves as a standard query language for manipulating and retrieving RDF data. Querying RDF data becomes challenging when the size of the data increases. Recently, many distributed RDF systems capable of evaluating SPARQL queries have been proposed and developed ([7,17]). Nevertheless, these engines lack one important information derived from the knowledge, *RDF terms*. RDF terms includes information about a statement such as *language*, *typed literals* and *blank nodes* which are omitted from most of the engines.

To cover this spectrum requires a specialized system which is capable of constructing an efficient SPARQL query engine. Doing so comes with several challenges. First and foremost, recently the RDF data is increasing drastically. Just as a record, today we count more than 10,0000 datasets[4] available online represented using the Semantic Web standards. This number is increasing daily including many other (e.g. Ethereum[5] dataset) datasets available at the organization premises. In addition, being able to query this large amount of data in an efficient and faster way is a requirement from most of the SPARQL evaluators.

To overcome these challenges, in this paper, we propose *Sparklify*[6]: a scalable software component for efficient evaluation of SPARQL queries over distributed RDF datasets. The conceptual foundation is the application of *ontology-based data access* (OBDA) tooling, specifically SPARQL-to-SQL rewriting, for translating SPARQL queries into Spark executable code. We demonstrate our approach using Sparqlify, which has been used in the LinkedGeoData[7] community project to serve more than 30 billion triples on-the-fly from a relational OpenStreetMap database. Our contributions are:

- We present a novel approach for vertical partitioning including RDF terms using the distributed computing framework, Apache Spark.
- We developed a scalable query engine using Sparqlify – a SPARQL-to-SQL rewriter on top of Apache Spark (under the *Apache Licence 2.0*).
- We evaluate our approach with state-of-the-art engines and demonstrate it empirically.
- We integrated the approach into the SANSA [11][8] larger framework. Sparklify serves as a default query engine in SANSA. SANSA is an active project and maintained, including issue tracker, mailing list, changelogs, website, etc.

[2] https://www.w3.org/TR/rdf11-primer/.

[3] https://www.w3.org/TR/sparql11-overview/.

[4] http://lodstats.aksw.org/.

[5] https://goo.gl/mJTkPp.

[6] https://github.com/SANSA-Stack/SANSA-Query/tree/develop/sansa-query-spark/src/main/scala/net/sansa_stack/query/spark/sparqlify.

[7] http://linkedgeodata.org.

[8] http://sansa-stack.net/.

The paper is structured as follows: Our approach for data modeling and query translation using a distributed framework is detailed in Sect. 3 and evaluated in Sect. 4. Related work on the SPARQL query engines is discussed in Sect. 6. Finally, we conclude and suggest planned extensions of our approach in Sect. 7.

2 Preliminaries

In this section, we first introduce the basic notions used in throughout the paper.

2.1 Sparqlify

Sparqlify[9] is a SPARQL-to-SQL rewriter that enables answering SPARQL queries on relational databases via a set of view definitions. R2RML[10] and the more intuitive *Sparqlification Mapping Language (SML)*[11] [18] are supported. In general, the rewriter compiles every SPARQL query into two related artifacts: A SQL query and set of SPARQL result variable definitions by means of expressions over the SQL query's result set. Sparqlify first converts the query into an algebra expression. Subsequently, algebraic optimizations and normalizations are applied, such as filter placement and constant folding. Given a query pattern, the view selection component identifies for every triple pattern the set of candidate view definitions together with the renaming of their variables to those of the requesting pattern. This is the base for obtaining the final algebra expression. In general, this involves a cartesian product between triple patterns and views definitions, which leads to a union of joins between the candidate views. Pruning is performed based on RDF term types and IRI prefixes: Choosing a view that binds variables to certain term types or prefixes will constrain subsequent loops only to those candidates with compatible bindings for these variables. Finally, this algebra expression are transformed into an SQL algebra expression using the general relational algebra for RDB-to-RDF mappings. The SQL query, which has been obtained, is used further (e.g. in our case for executing it over Spark SQL engine).

2.2 Apache Spark

Apache Spark is a fast and generic-purpose cluster computing engine which is built over Hadoop ecosystem. Its core data structure are Resilient Distributed Dataset (RDD) [19] which are a fault-tolerant and immutable collections of records that can be operated in a parallel setting. Spark also provides high-level APIs, and tools, including Spark SQL [2] for SQL and structured data processing which allows querying structured data inside Spark programs. In this work, we make use of the above libraries from the Apache Spark stack.

9 https://github.com/SmartDataAnalytics/Sparqlify.
10 https://www.w3.org/TR/r2rml/.
11 http://sml.aksw.org/.

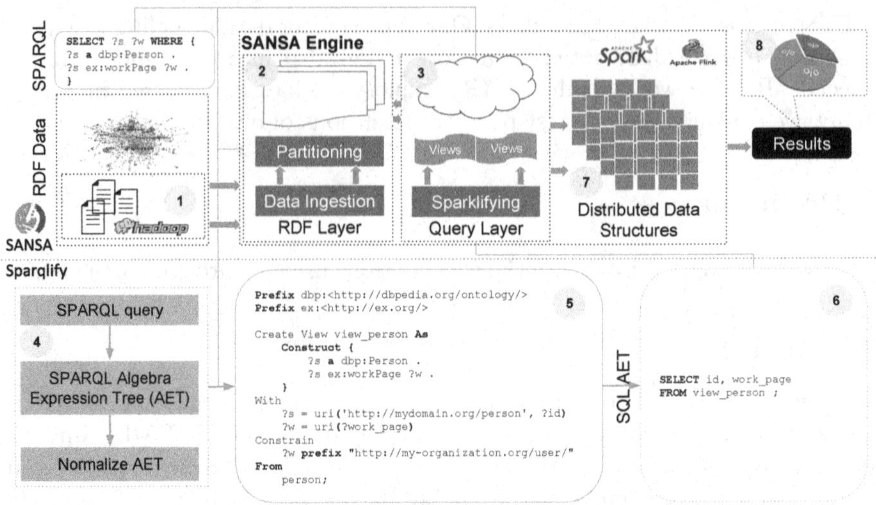

Fig. 1. Sparklify architecture overview.

3 Sparklify

In this section, we present the overall architecture of our proposed approach, the SPARQL-to-SQL rewriter, and mapping to Spark Scala-compliant code.

3.1 System Architecture

The overall system architecture is shown in Fig. 1. It consists of four main components: Data Model, Mappings, Query Translator and Query Evaluator. In the following, each component is discussed in details.

Data Model. SANSA [11] comes with different data structures and different partitioning strategies. We model and store RDF graph following the concept of RDDs – a basic building blocks of the Spark Framework. RDDs are in-memory collections of records which are capable of operating in parallel overall larger cluster. Sparklify makes use of SANSA bottom layer which corresponds with the extended vertical partitioning (VP) including RDF terms. This partition model is the most convenient storage model for fast processing of RDF datasets on top of HDFS.

Data Ingestion (Step 1). RDF data first needs to be loaded into a large-scale storage that Spark can efficiently read from. We use Hadoop Distributed File-System (HDFS)[12]. Spark employ different data locality scheme in order to accomplish computations nearest to the desired data in HDFS, as a result avoiding i/o overhead.

[12] https://hadoop.apache.org/docs/r1.2.1/hdfs_design.html.

Data Partition (Step 2). VP approach in SANSA is designed to support extensible partitioning of RDF data. Instead of dealing with a single three-column table (s, p, o), data is partitioned into multiple tables based on the used RDF predicates, RDF term types and literal datatypes. The first column of these tables is always a string representing the subject. The second column always represents the literal value as a Scala/Java datatype. Tables for storing literals with language tags have an additional third string column for the language tag.

Mappings/Views. After the RDF data has been partitioned using the extensible VP (as it has been described on *step 2*) the relational-to-RDF mapping is performed. Sparqlify supports both the W3C standard R2RML sparqlification [18].

The main entities defined with SML are *view definitions*. See *step 5* in the Fig. 1 as an example. The actual view definition is declared by the *Create View* ... *As* in the first line. The remainder of the view contains these parts: (1) the *From* directive defines the logical table based on the partitioned table (see *step 2*). (2) an RDF template is defined in the *Construct* block containing, URI, blank node or literals constants (e.g. *ex:worksAt*) and variables (e.g. *?emp*, *?institute*). The *With* block defines the variables used in the template by means of RDF term constructor expressions whose arguments refer to columns of the logical table.

Query Translation. This process generates a SQL query from the SPARQL query using the bindings determined in the mapping/view construction phases. It walks through the SPARQL query (*step 4*) using Jena ARQ[13] and generates the SPARQL Algebra Expression Tree (AET). Essentially, rewriting SPARQL basic graph patterns and filters over views yields AETs that are UNIONS of JOINS. Further, these AETs are normalized and pruned in order to remove UNION members that are known to yield empty results, such as joins based on IRIs with disjoint sets of known namespaces, or joins between different RDF term types (e.g. literal and IRI). Finally, the SQL is generated (*step 6*) using the bindings corresponding to the views (*step 5*).

Query Evaluator. The SQL query created as described in the previous section can now be evaluated directly into the Spark SQL engine. The result set of this SQL query is distributed data structure of Spark (e.g. DataFrame) (*step 7*) which then is mapped into a SPARQL bindings. The result set can further used for analysis and visualization using the SANSA-Notebooks (*step 8*) [5].

3.2 Algorithm Description

The algorithm described in this paper has been implemented using the Apache Spark framework (see Algorithm 1). It constructs the graph (line 1) while reading RDF data and converts it into RDD of triples. After, it partitions the data (line

[13] https://jena.apache.org/documentation/query/.

Algorithm 1. Sparklify algorithm.

```
  input : q: a SPARQL query, input: an RDF dataset
  output: df list of result set
1 graph = spark.rdf(lang)(input)
2 graph.persist()
3 partitionGraph ← graph.partitionGraph()
4 result ← partitionGraph.sparql(q)
5 return result
```

Algorithm 2. PartitionGraph algorithm.

```
   input : graph: an RDD[Triple] dataset
   output: views a mapped views
1  foreach triple ∈ graph do
2      s ← triple.getSubject; o ← triple.getObject
3      subjectType ← getRDFTermType(s); objectType ←
       getRDFTermType(o)
4      predicate ← triple.getPredicate.getURI
5      if o.isLiteral then
6          if isPlainLiteral(o) then
7              datatype ← XSD.xstring.getURI
8          else
9              datatype ← o.getLiteralDatatypeURI
10     else
11         datatype ← string.Empty
12     langTagPresent ← isPlainLiteral(o)
13     views.add(partitioner(subjectType, predicate, objectType, datatype,
14                langTagPresent))
15 return views
```

3, for more details see Algorithm 2) using the vertical partitioning (VP) strategy. Finally, the query evaluator is constructed (line 4) which is described into more details in Algorithm 3 for consistency.

Partitioning the Graph. The partitioning algorithm (see Algorithm 2) transforms the RDF graph into a convenient VP including RDF terms (line 13). For each triple in the graph in a distributed fashion, it does the following: It gets the RDF terms about subjects and objects (line 3). In case of a literal it assigns the data type for a given column while partitioning the data to: *String* (line 7) when is plain literal, otherwise gets the data type of a given literal (e.g. *Integer*, *Double*) (line 9). The remaining block is the language tag (line 12) which is required for an extra column on the partitioned table containing the language tag value. After all this information is populated, the partitioned block is performed using the *map* transformation function of Spark splitting the tables based on the above information.

Algorithm 3. sparql algorithm.

```
   input  : views: a Map[partition, RDD[Row]] views, q: a SPARQL query
   output: df a data frame with the rewritten SPARQL query's result set
1  vds ← emptyList()
2  foreach (v, rdd) ∈ views do
3      vd ← Sparqlify.createViewDefinition(v)
4      tableName ← vd.logicalTableName
5      scalaSchema ← v.layout.schema
6      sparkSchema ← ScalaReflection.schemaFor(scalaSchema).dataType
7      df ← spark.createDataFrame(rdd, sparkSchema)
8      df.createOrReplaceTempView(vd.logicalTableName)
9      vds.add(vd)
10 rewriter ← Sparkqlify.createDefaultSparqlSqlStringRewriter(vds)
11 rewrite ← rewriter.rewrite(q)
12 sqlQueryStr ← rewrite.sqlQueryString
13 df ← spark.sql(sqlQueryStr)
14 return df
```

Querying the Graph. Given a SPARQL query and a set of partitions together with associated RDDs, Sparklify first has to create OBDA view definitions from the partitions (line 3) and register their corresponding RDDs with names that can be referenced from Spark SQL (line 8). Hence, the algorithm collects the schema (line 6) and constructs a logical table name (line 4) based on the partitions. The final step is to create a Spark data frame (line 13) from the SQL query that is part of the rewrite object generated by Sparqlify (line 12).

4 Evaluation

The goal of our evaluation is to observe the impact of the extensible VP as well as analyzing its scalability when the size of the datset increases. At the same time, we also want to measure the effect of using Sparqlify optimizer for improving the query performance. Especially, we want to verify and answer the following questions:

(Q1) : Is the runtime affected when more nodes are added in the cluster?
(Q2) : Does it scale to a larger dataset?
(Q3) : How does it scale when adding a larger number of datasets?

In the following, we present our experiments setting including the benchmarks used and server configurations. Afterword, we elaborate on our findings.

4.1 Experimental Setup

We used two well-known SPARQL benchmarks for our evaluation. The *Lehight University Benchmak (LUBM)* v3.1 [9] and *Waterloo SPARQL Diversity Test Suite (WatDiv)* v0.6 [1]. Characteristics of the considered datasets are given in Table 1.

LUBM comes with a *Data Generator (UBA)* which generates synthetic data over the *Univ-Bench* ontology in the unit of a university. Our *LUBM* datasets consist of 1000, 5000, and 10000 universities. The number of triples varies from 138M for 1000 universities, to 1.4B triples for 10000 universities. *LUBM*'s test suite is comprised of 14 queries.

We have used *WatDiv* datasets with approximate 10K to 1B triples with scale factors 10, 100 and 1000, respectively. *WatDiv* provides a test suite with different query shapes, therefore, it allows us to compare the performance of Sparklify and the other approach we compare with in a more compact way. We have generated these queries using the *WatDiv Query Generator* and report the average mean runtime in the overall results presented below. It comes with a set of 20 predefined query templates so-called *Basic Testing Use Case* which is grouped into four categories, based on the query shape: *star (QS)*, *linear (QL)*, *snowflake (QF)*, and *complex (QC)*.

Table 1. Summary information of used datasets (nt format).

⟶	LUBM			Watdiv		
	1K	5K	10K	10M	100M	1B
#nr. of triples	138,280,374	690,895,862	1,381,692,508	10,916,457	108,997,714	1,099,208,068
Size (GB)	24	116	232	1.5	15	149

We implemented Sparklify using Spark-2.4.0, Scala 2.11.11, Java 8, and Sparqlify 0.8.3 and all the data were stored on the HDFS cluster using Hadoop 2.8.0. All experiments were carried out on a commodity cluster of 7 nodes (1 master, 6 workers): Intel(R) Xeon(R) CPU E5-2620 v4 @ 2.10 GHz (32 Cores), 128 GB RAM, 12 TB SATA RAID-5, connected via a Gigabit network. The experiments have been executed three times and the average runtime has been reported into the results.

4.2 Results

We evaluate Sparklify using the above datasets and compare it with the chosen state-of-the-art distributed SPARQL query evaluator. Since our approach does not involve any pre-processing of the RDF data before being able to evaluate SPARQL queries on it, Sparklify is thereby closer to the so-called direct evaluators. Indeed, Sparklify only needs to virtually partition the data prior. As a consequence, we omit other distributed evaluators (such as e.g. S2RDF [17]) and compare it with SPARQGX [7] as it outperforms other approaches as noted by Graux et al. [7]. We compare our approach with *SPARQLGX*'s direct evaluator named SDE and report the loading time for partitioning and query execution time, see Table 2. We specify "fail" whenever the system fails to complete the task and "n/a" when the task could not be completed due to a failure in one of the intermediate phase. In some cases e.g. in Table 2, *QC in Watdiv-1B* dataset, we define "partial fail" due to the failure of one of the queries, therefore the sum-up is not possible.

Findings of the experiments are depicted in Table 2, Figs. 2, 3, and 4.

To verify Q1, we analyze the *speedup* and compare it with SPARQLGX. We run the experiments on three datasets, *Watdiv-10M*, *Watdiv-1B* and *LUBM-10K*.

Table 2. Performance analysis on large-scale RDF datasets.

		Runtime (s) (mean)			
→		**SPARQLGX-SDE**	**Sparklify**		
		a) total	b) paritioning	c) querying	d) total
Watdiv-10M	*QC*	103.24	134.81	61	195.84
	QF	157.8	241.24	107.33	349.51
	QL	102.51	236.06	134	370.3
	QS	131.16	237.12	108.56	346
Watdiv-1B	*QC*	partial fail	778.62	2043.66	2829.56
	QF	6734.68	1295.31	2576.52	3871.97
	QL	2575.72	1275.22	610.66	1886.73
	QS	4841.85	1290.72	1552.05	2845.3
LUBM-10K	*Q*1	1056.83	627.72	718.11	1346.8
	*Q*2	fail	595.76	fail	n/a
	*Q*3	1038.62	615.95	648.63	1267.37
	*Q*4	2761.11	632.93	1670.18	2303.18
	*Q*5	1026.94	641.53	564.13	1206.67
	*Q*6	537.65	695.74	267.48	963.62
	*Q*7	2080.67	630.44	1331.13	1967.25
	*Q*8	2636.12	639.93	1647.57	2288.48
	*Q*9	3124.52	583.86	2126.03	2711.24
	*Q*10	1002.56	593.68	693.73	1287.71
	*Q*11	1023.32	594.41	522.24	1118.58
	*Q*12	2027.59	576.31	1088.25	1665.87
	*Q*13	1007.39	626.57	6.66	633.26
	*Q*14	526.15	633.39	258.32	891.89

Table 2 shows the performance analysis of two approaches run on three different datasets. Column SPARQLGX-SDE[a] reports on the performance of

SPARQLGX-SDE considering the total runtime to evaluate the given queries. Column Sparklify^b lists the times required for Sparklify to perform the VP and then the query execution time is reported on the Sparklify^c. Total runtime for Sparklify is shown in the last column, Sparklify^d.

We observe that the execution of both approaches fails for the *Q2* in the *LUBM-10K* dataset while evaluating the query. We believe that it is due to the reason that *LUBM Q2* involves a triangular pattern which is often resource consuming. As a consequence, in both cases, Spark performs the shuffling (e.g. data scanning) while reducing the result set. It is interesting to note that for the *Watdiv-1B* dataset, SPARQLGX-SDE fails for the query *C3* when data scanning is performed. Sparklify is capable of evaluating it successfully. Due to the Spark SQL optimizer in conjunction with Sparqlify's approach of rewriting a SPARQL query typically into only a single SQL query – effectively offloading all query planning to Spark – Sparklify performs better than SPARQLGX-SDE when the size of the dataset increases (see *Watdiv-1B results* in the Table 2) and when there are more joins involved (see *Watdiv-1B* and *LUBM-10K* results in the Table 2). SPARQLGX-SDE evaluates the queries faster when the size of the datasets is smaller, but it degrades when the size of the dataset increases. The likely reason for Sparklify's worse performance on smaller datasets is its higher partitioning overhead. Figure 2 shows that Sparklify starts outperforming when the size of the datasets grows (e.g. *Watdiv-100M*).

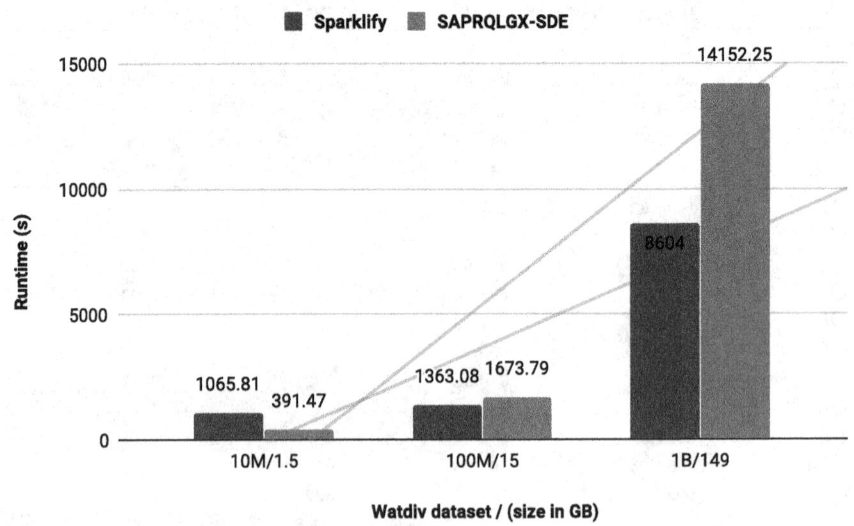

Fig. 2. Sizeup analysis (on Watdiv dataset).

Size-up Scalability Analysis. To measure the performance of the data scalability (e.g. size-up) of both approaches, we run experiments on three different sizes of *Watdiv* (see Fig. 2). We keep the number of nodes constant i.e 6 worker nodes and grow the size of the datasets to measure whether both approaches can deal with larger datasets. We see that the execution time for Sparklify grows linearly compared with SPARQLGX-SDE, which keeps staying as near-linear when the size of the datasets increases. The results presented show scalability of Sparklify in context of the sizeup, which addresses the question Q2.

Node Scalability Analysis. To measure the node scalability of Sparklify, we vary the number of worker nodes. We vary them from 1, 3 to 6 worker nodes. Figure 3 depict the speedup performance of both approaches run on *Watdiv-100M* dataset when the number of worker nodes varies. We can see that as the number of nodes increases, the runtime cost for the Sparklify decrease linearly. The execution time for Sparklify decreases about 0.6 times (from 2547.26 s down to 1588.4 s) as worker nodes increase from one to three nodes. We see that the speedup stays constant when more worker nodes are added since the size of the data is not that large and the network overhead increases a little the runtime when it runs over six worker nodes. This imply that our approach is efficient up to three worker nodes for the *Watdiv-100M* (15GB) dataset. In another hand, SPARQLGX-SDE takes longer to evaluate the queries when running on one worker node but it improves when the number of worker nodes increases.

Result presented here shows that Sparklify can achieve linear scalability in the performance, which addresses Q3.

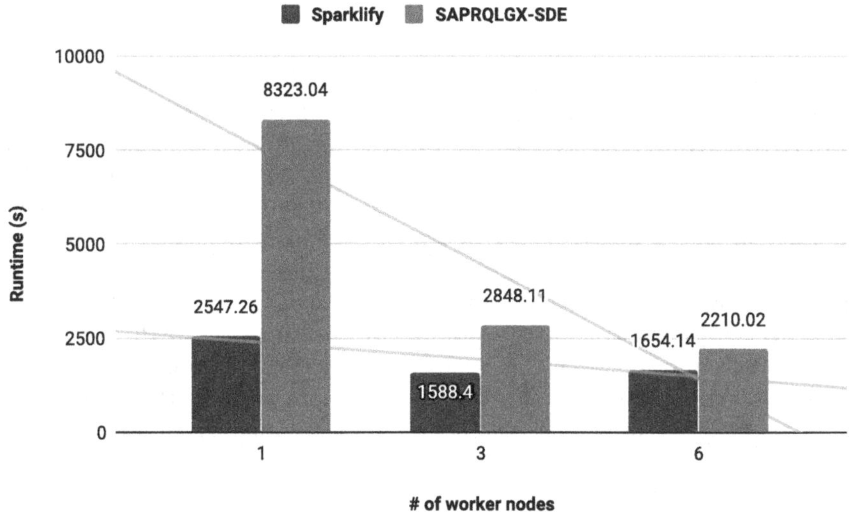

Fig. 3. Node scalability (on Watdiv-100M).

Correctness of the Result Set. In order to assess the correctness of the result set, we computed the count of the result set for the given queries and compare it within both approaches. We conclude that both approaches return exactly the same result set which implies the correctness of the results.

Overall Analysis by SPARQL Queries. Here we analyze Watdiv queries run on *Watdiv-100M* dataset in a cluster mode on both approaches.

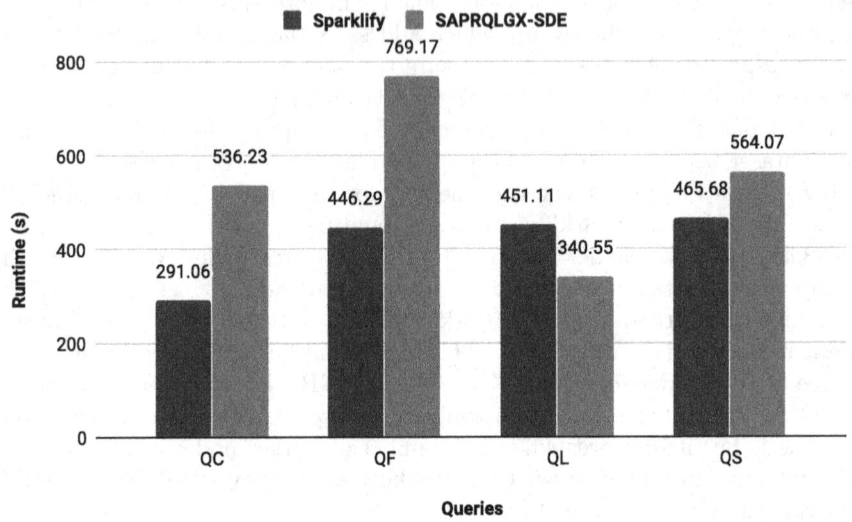

Fig. 4. Overall analysis of queries on Watdiv-100M dataset (cluster mode).

According to Fig. 4, SPARQLGX-SDE performance decreases as the number of triple patterns involved in the query increase. This might be due to the fact that SPARQLGX-SDE has to read the whole triple file each time. In contrast to SPARQLGX-SDE, Sparklify seems to perform well when there are more triple pattern involved (see queries *QC*, *QF* and *QS* in the Fig. 4) but slightly worst when there are linear queries (see *QL*) evaluated. This may be due to the reason that Sparqlify typically rewrites a SPARQL query into a single SQL query, thus maximizing the opportunities given to the Spark SQL optimizer. Conversely, SPARQLGX-SDE constructs the workflow by chaining Scala API calls, which may restrict the possibilities e.g. in regard to join ordering. Based on our findings and the evaluation study carried out in this paper, we show that Sparklify is scalable and the execution time ends in a reasonable time given the size of the dataset.

5 Use Cases

Sparklify, as a default query engine for SANSA has been used in different major use cases. Below, we list some of them that we are aware of using Sparklify:
Blockchain – Alethio Use Case. Alethio[14] try to present the big picture of the whole Ethereum ecosystem. It is a powerful blockchain data, analytics, and

[14] https://aleth.io/.

visualisation platform. It contains more than 18 Billion triples datasets "rdfized" using the structure of the Ethereum ontology[15]. They are taking advantage of the SANSA stack by querying this amount of data at scale e.g. analyzing the Hubs & Authorities in the Ethereum Transaction Network[16] and other analytics.
SPECIAL – A Semantic Transparency and Compliance Use Case. SPECIAL[17] is a Scalable Policy-aware Linked Data platform for privacy, transparency, and compliance. Within the project, they introduce SPIRIT – a transparency and compliance checking implementation of the SANSA stack. SPECIAL uses SANSA engine in order to analyze the log information concerning personal data processing and sharing that as an output from line of business applications on a continuous basis, and to present the information to the user via the SPIRIT dashboard. The SPIRIT transaction log processing allows users to: (1) define the set of policies rules, (2) initialize the query engine with the log and schema/ontology data, here is where Sparklify is used in specific, (3) create a reasoner set reasoning profile, and (4) apply these rules to the given query in order be compliant with the policy rules.
SLIPO – Categorizing Areas of Interests (AOI) Use Case. SLIPO[18] take advantage of the Semantic Web Technologies for the scalable and efficient integration of Big Point of Interest (POI) datasets. In particular, the project focuses on designing efficient pipelines dealing with large semantic datasets of POIs: a wide range of features are available inter alia fusion & cleaning distinct datasets or detection of future "hot" AOIs where businesses should be created. In this project, Sparklify is used through the SANSA query layer to refine, filter and select the relevant POIs which are needed by the pipelines.

6 Related Work

As our main focus is on the area of distributed computing, we omit the centralized systems e.g. RDF-3X [12] or Virtuoso [4] (see [6] for a survey) and we review the distributed ones only (see [10] for a recent survey). Further, this set of tools is divided into: *MapReduce-based* systems and *In-Memory* systems e.g. on top of Apache Spark.

MapReduce systems – SHARD [14] is one approach which groups RDF data into a dedicated partition so-called semantic-based partition. It groups these RDF data by subject and implements a query engine which iterates through each of the clauses used on the query and performs a query processing. A MapReduce job is created while scanning each of the triple patterns and generates a single plan for each of the triple pattern which leads to a larger query plan, therefore, it contains too many Map and Reduces jobs. PigSPARQL [15] is yet another approach which uses Hadoop based implementation of vertical partitioning for data representation. It translated the SPARQL queries into Pig[19] LATIN queries

[15] https://github.com/ConsenSys/EthOn.
[16] https://bit.ly/2YX7CXG.
[17] https://www.specialprivacy.eu.
[18] http://slipo.eu/.
[19] https://pig.apache.org/.

and uses Pig as an intermediate engine. Another approach which is based on the MapReduce is Sempala [16] – as SPARQL-to-SQL approach on top of Hadoop. It uses Impala[20] as a distributed SQL processing engine. Sempala uses a so-called unified vertical partitioning (single property table) in order to boost the star-shaped queries by excluding the joins. Hence, its limitation is that it is designed only to that particular shape of the queries. RYA [13] is a Hadoop based scalable RDF store that uses Accumulo[21] as a distributed key-value store for indexing the RDF triples. RYA indexes triples into three tables and replicate them across the cluster for leveraging the indexes over all the possible records. It has the mechanism of performing join reorder, but it lacks of the in-memory computation, which makes it not comparable with other systems. While the MapReduce paradigm has been realized for disk-based as well as in-memory processing, the concept is not concerned with controlling aspects of general distributed workflows, such as which intermediate results to cache. As a consequence, high level frameworks were devised which may use MapReduce as a building block. Apache Spark is one of them [19]. Below, we will list some of the approaches which make use of the Apache Spark (in-memory computation) framework.

In-Memory systems – SPARQLGX [7] and S2RDF [17] approaches are considered the most recent distributed SPARQL evaluators over large-scale RDF datasets. SPARQLGX is a scalable query engine which is capable of evaluating efficiently the SPARQL queries over distributed RDF datasets [8]. It provides a mechanism for translating SPARQL queries into Spark executable code for better leveraging the advantage of the Spark framework. It uses a simplified VP approach, where each predicate is assigned with a specific parquet file. As an addition, it is able to assign RDF statistics for further query optimization while also providing the possibility of directly query files on the HDFS using SDE. S2RDF is similar to SPARQLGX, but instead of dealing with direct Spark code (aka RDDs), it translates SPARQL queries into SQL ones run by Spark-SQL. It introduces a data partitioning strategy that extends VP with additional statistics, containing pre-computed semi-joins for query optimization.

7 Conclusions and Future Work

Querying RDF data becomes challenging when the size of the data increases. Existing Spark-based SPARQL systems mostly do not retain all RDF term information consistently while transforming them to a dedicated storage model such as using vertical partitioning. Often, this process is both data and computing intensive and raises the need for a scalable, efficient and comprehensive query engine which can handle large scale RDF datasets.

In this paper, we propose *Sparklify*: a scalable software component for efficient evaluation of SPARQL queries over distributed RDF datasets. It uses Sparqify as a SPARQL-to-SQL rewriter for translating SPARQL queries into Spark executable code. By doing so, it leverages the advantages of the Spark framework.

[20] https://impala.apache.org/.

[21] https://accumulo.apache.org.

SANSA features methods to execute SPARQL queries directly as part of Spark workflows instead of writing the code corresponding to those queries (sorting, filtering, etc.). It also provides a command-line interface and a W3C standard compliant SPARQL endpoint for externally querying data that has been loaded using the SANSA framework. We have shown empirically that our approach can scale horizontally and perform well w.r.t to the state-of-the-art approaches.

With this work, we showed that the application of OBDA tooling to Big Data frameworks achieves promising results in terms of scalability. We present a working prototype implementation that can serve as a baseline for further research. Our next steps include evaluating other tools, such as Ontop [3], and analyze how their performance in the Big Data setting can be improved further. For example, we intend to investigate how OBDA tools can be combined with dictionary encoding of RDF terms as integers and evaluate the effects.

Acknowledgment. This work was partly supported by the EU Horizon2020 projects BigDataOcean (GA no. 732310), Boost4.0 (GA no. 780732), SLIPO (GA no. 731581) and QROWD (GA no. 723088); and by the ADAPT Centre for Digital Content Technology funded under the SFI Research Centres Programme (Grant 13/RC/2106) and co-funded under the European Regional Development Fund.

References

1. Aluç, G., Hartig, O., Özsu, M.T., Daudjee, K.: Diversified stress testing of RDF data management systems. In: Mika, R., et al. (eds.) ISWC 2014. LNCS, vol. 8796, pp. 197–212. Springer, Cham (2014). https://doi.org/10.1007/978-3-319-11964-9_13
2. Armbrust, M., et al.: Spark SQL: relational data processing in Spark. In: Proceedings of the 2015 ACM SIGMOD International Conference on Management of Data, SIGMOD 2015, pp. 1383–1394. ACM, New York (2015)
3. Calvanese, D., et al.: Ontop: answering SPARQL queries over relational databases. Semant. Web **8**, 471–487 (2017)
4. Erling, O., Mikhailov, I.: Virtuoso: RDF support in a native RDBMS. In: de Virgilio, R., Giunchiglia, F., Tanca, L. (eds.) Semantic Web Information Management, pp. 501–519. Springer, Heidelberg (2010). https://doi.org/10.1007/978-3-642-04329-1_21
5. Ermilov, I., et al.: The Tale of Sansa Spark. In 16th International Semantic Web Conference, Poster & Demos (2017)
6. Faye, D.C., Curé, O., Blin, G.: A survey of RDF storage approaches. Revue Africaine de la Recherche en Informatique et Mathématiques Appliquées **15**, 11–35 (2012)
7. Graux, D., Jachiet, L., Genevès, P., Layaïda, N.: SPARQLGX: efficient distributed evaluation of SPARQL with Apache Spark. In: Groth, P., et al. (eds.) The Semantic Web - ISWC 2016. LNCS, pp. 80–87. Springer International Publishing, Cham (2016). https://doi.org/10.1007/978-3-319-46547-0_9
8. Graux, D., Jachiet, L., Geneves, P., Layaïda, N.: A multi-criteria experimental ranking of distributed SPARQL evaluators. In: 2018 IEEE International Conference on Big Data (Big Data), pp. 693–702. IEEE (2018)

9. Guo, Y., Pan, Z., Heflin, J.: LUBM: a benchmark for owl knowledge base systems. J. Web Semant. **3**, 158–182 (2005)
10. Kaoudi, Z., Manolescu, I.: RDF in the clouds: a survey. VLDB J.-Int. J. Very Large Data Bases **24**(1), 67–91 (2015)
11. Lehmann, J., et al.: Distributed semantic analytics using the SANSA stack. In: d'Amato, C., et al. (eds.) ISWC 2017. LNCS, vol. 10588, pp. 147–155. Springer, Cham (2017). https://doi.org/10.1007/978-3-319-68204-4_15
12. Neumann, T., Weikum, G.: RDF-3X: a RISC-style engine for RDF. Proc. VLDB Endow. **1**(1), 647–659 (2008)
13. Punnoose, R., Crainiceanu, A., Rapp, D.: Rya: a scalable RDF triple store for the clouds. In: Proceedings of the 1st International Workshop on Cloud Intelligence, Cloud-I 2012, pp. 4:1–4:8. ACM, New York (2012)
14. Rohloff, K., Schantz, R.E.: High-performance, massively scalable distributed systems using the MapReduce software framework: the SHARD triple-store. In: Programming Support Innovations for Emerging Distributed Applications, PSI EtA 2010, pp. 4:1–4:5. ACM, New York (2010)
15. Schätzle, A., Przyjaciel-Zablocki, M., Lausen, G.: PigSPARQL: mapping SPARQL to Pig Latin. In: Proceedings of the International Workshop on Semantic Web Information Management, SWIM 2011, pp. 4:1–4:8. ACM, New York (2011)
16. Schätzle, A., Przyjaciel-Zablocki, M., Neu, A., Lausen, G.: Sempala: interactive SPARQL query processing on Hadoop. In: Mika, P., et al. (eds.) ISWC 2014. LNCS, vol. 8796, pp. 164–179. Springer, Cham (2014). https://doi.org/10.1007/978-3-319-11964-9_11
17. Schätzle, A., Przyjaciel-Zablocki, M., Skilevic, S., Lausen, G.: S2RDF: RDF querying with SPARQL on Spark. Proc. VLDB Endow. **9**(10), 804–815 (2016)
18. Stadler, C., Unbehauen, J., Westphal, P., Sherif, M.A., Lehmann, J.: Simplified RDB2RDF mapping. In: Proceedings of the 8th Workshop on Linked Data on the Web, LDOW 2015, Florence, Italy (2015)
19. Zaharia, M., et al.: Resilient distributed datasets: a fault-tolerant abstraction for in-memory cluster computing. In: Proceedings of the 9th USENIX conference on Networked Systems Design and Implementation. USENIX (2012)

ClaimsKG: A Knowledge Graph of Fact-Checked Claims

Andon Tchechmedjiev[1], Pavlos Fafalios[2(✉)], Katarina Boland[3], Malo Gasquet[5], Matthäus Zloch[3], Benjamin Zapilko[3], Stefan Dietze[3,4], and Konstantin Todorov[5]

[1] LGI2P, IMT Mines-Ales, Alès, France
andon.tchechmedjiev@mines-ales.fr
[2] L3S Research Center, Leibniz University of Hanover, Hanover, Germany
fafalios@L3S.de
[3] GESIS - Leibniz Institute for the Social Sciences, Cologne, Germany
{katarina.boland,matthaeus.zloch,benjamin.zapilko, stefan.dietze}@gesis.org
[4] Heinrich-Heine-University Düsseldorf, Düsseldorf, Germany
[5] LIRMM/University of Montpellier/CNRS, Montpellier, France
malo.gasquet@etu.umontpellier.fr, konstantin.todorov@lirmm.fr

Abstract. Various research areas at the intersection of computer and social sciences require a ground truth of contextualized claims labelled with their truth values in order to facilitate supervision, validation or reproducibility of approaches dealing, for example, with fact-checking or analysis of societal debates. So far, no reasonably large, up-to-date and queryable corpus of structured information about claims and related metadata is publicly available. In an attempt to fill this gap, we introduce ClaimsKG, a knowledge graph of fact-checked claims, which facilitates structured queries about their truth values, authors, dates, journalistic reviews and other kinds of metadata. ClaimsKG is generated through a semi-automated pipeline, which harvests data from popular fact-checking websites on a regular basis, annotates claims with related entities from DBpedia, and lifts the data to RDF using an RDF/S model that makes use of established vocabularies. In order to harmonise data originating from diverse fact-checking sites, we introduce normalised ratings as well as a simple claims coreference resolution strategy. The current knowledge graph, extensible to new information, consists of 28,383 claims published since 1996, amounting to 6,606,032 triples.

Keywords: Claims · Fact-checking · Societal debates · Knowledge graphs

1 Introduction

The spread of controversies, biased discourse and falsehoods on the Web has become an increasingly important issue, from both a societal as well as a research

C. Ghidini et al. (Eds.): ISWC 2019, LNCS 11779, pp. 309–324, 2019.
https://doi.org/10.1007/978-3-030-30796-7_20

perspective [1,30]. Recently, a wide range of interdisciplinary research directions are being explored in this broad area, which often rely on a ground truth of labelled claims. Such works include investigations into the spreading pattern of false claims on Twitter [30], pipelines for discovering the stance of claim-relevant (Web) documents [33], approaches for classifying sources of news, such as Web pages, domains, users or posts [7,20], or research into fake news detection [27] and automatic fact-checking [12]. In all these cases, the availability of a labelled ground truth, consisting of claims, their corresponding metadata and, in particular, their truth values (or ratings), is essential in order to enable supervision of machine learning methods, reproduction and explainability of the results, and to facilitate fair evaluation and follow-up work. In addition, as documented by the aforementioned works, claims are usually not considered in isolation, but in a context. Thus, reproducing such research requires not only archiving claims and their truth values, but also their related documents, such as journalistic claim reviews, the associated entities and time-frames that can be linked to particular events, accounting in that way for the continuous evolution of Web content.

To our knowledge, no reasonably large and up-to-date corpus of structured information about claims and their context has been made publicly available. We attempt to fill this gap by introducing ClaimsKG, a knowledge graph (KG) of fact-checked claims, which facilitates structured queries about their truth values and other kinds of metadata, constructed and published following the W3C recommendations and best practices. In our context, we define a claim as a *statement which has been reviewed by a fact-checking organisation in order to assess its truthfulness.* ClaimsKG is generated through a semi-automated pipeline, which periodically harvests data from popular fact-checking websites. The *claims* and their *reviews* (articles written by fact-checkers that accompany a claim and explain its context and veracity judgement) are annotated with related *entities* from DBpedia, and all data are lifted into RDF using a dedicated RDF/S model (dubbed *Claims*), which is based on established vocabularies such as schema.org and NIF. In order to harmonise data originating from diverse fact-checking sites, we introduce a normalised truth ratings scheme, as well as a simple claim matching strategy. ClaimsKG enables advanced exploration and information discovery, e.g., via queries such as *"find all false claims by D. Trump in 2017 that also mention the FBI"*, or *"find the top 5 politicians per month involved in false claims"*, as well as exploitation of data from various sources via federated SPARQL queries, e.g., *"retrieve all claims mentioning journalists"*. We also provide a Web interface for exploring the graph, enabling users from outside of the computer science community to retrieve information or sample data from our resource. The dataset, as of April 2019, consists of 28,383 claims published since 1996, amounting to 6,606,032 triples in our KG.

In summary, we provide (1) the *Claims* data model for representing fact-checked claims and associated information, (2) an open-source pipeline for crawling and extracting data from fact-checking websites, and for lifting these data following the *Claims* model, (3) an openly available dynamic large-scale KG of claims and associated metadata, and (4) a Web interface for search and exploration of the resource. In the following section, we provide general information about the resource and links for access. We detail the KG generation process in Sect. 3. We introduce our *Claims* model in Sect. 4, while use-cases and queries are discussed in Sect. 5 along with an overview of the exploratory user interface. We review related work in Sect. 6 before concluding.

2 Claims KG in a Nutshell

ClaimsKG consists of data extracted from a number of fact-checking websites. To select the fact-checking websites, we relied on the International Fact-Checking Network's (IFCN) signatories list,[1] admitting only sources considered by the fact-checking community as highly reputable. At this stage, we only consider information in English from six sources: *africacheck.org, factscan.ca, politifact.com, snopes.com, checkyourfact.com, truthorfiction.com*. Note that ClaimsKG is extensible to new websites, however, the information extraction process may vary from one website to another due to structural specificities of the sources (cf. Sect. 3). Each fact-checking article from these sources is parsed for extracting the text of the claim under review as well as useful related (meta)data including the author of the claim, the date the claim was uttered, its veracity label as well as keywords (tags describing topics) and links to related resources. Moreover, the text of the claim and of its review is annotated with Wikipedia/DBpedia entities mentioned in it. Key links related to ClaimsKG are given in Table 1. The KG is currently accessible from a Virtuoso triplestore with a SPARQL endpoint and downloadable as a Zenodo dump. All represented entities (claims, authors, etc.) are assigned resolvable identifiers following the W3C best practices (see Sect. 3 for an example). The dataset has a DCAT description and is released for free distribution under a Creative Commons Attribution-NonCommercial-ShareAlike 4.0 licence.[2] The graph can be also accessed through ClaimsKG's official webpage, which displays detailed up-to-date statistics and a set of example SPARQL queries. All tools developed for the KG's creation are made available as open source on GitHub. Table 2 offers some general and per-source coverage statistics for the data, in particular the coverage of key properties. In order to account for emerging claims, the dataset is updated regularly (every 3–6 months).

3 Generating Claims KG

ClaimsKG is built through a pipeline, which periodically crawls popular fact-checking sites, normalises ratings and entity mentions, reconciles identical claims, and lifts the data onto the specifically developed *Claims* model, described in Sect. 4. Hereafter, we detail the technical steps of the pipeline, summarised in Fig. 1. Links to its open-source components are given in Table 1.

[1] https://ifcncodeofprinciples.poynter.org/signatories.
[2] https://creativecommons.org/licenses/by-nc-sa/4.0/.

Table 1. Key links to ClaimsKG's data and tools.

ClaimsKG website	https://data.gesis.org/claimskg/site
Dataset DOI	https://doi.org/10.5281/zenodo.2628745
DCAT description	Included in the KG
Zenodo dump	https://zenodo.org/record/2628745
SPARQL endpoint	https://data.gesis.org/claimskg/sparql
The *Claims* ontology	https://data.gesis.org/claimskg/site#model
Exploratory interface	https://data.gesis.org/claimskg/explorer
ClaimsKG pipeline source code	https://github.com/claimskg

Table 2. Claim metadata coverage and statistics (as of April 2019)

Property\Fact-checking website	Global	Snopes	Politifact	AfricaCheck	TruthOrFiction	CheckYourFact	FactScan
Number of claims	28,383	10,685	15,743	560	778	492	125
Claim text	100%	100%	100%	100%	100%	100%	100%
Claim author	93.6%	100%	100%	0.0%	0.0%	0.0%	100%
Claim date published	92.1%	96.3%	100%	0.0%	0.0%	0.0%	98.4%
Claim with references (≥1)	86.5%	99.8%	75.9%	97.0%	100%	99.6%	100%
Claim with keywords (≥1)	93.8%	95.4%	100%	99.5%	0%	0.0%	100%
Claim with entities (≥1)	99.7%	99.9%	100%	98.2%	99.6%	92.9%	100%
Claim review URL	100%	100%	100%	100%	100%	100%	100%
Claim review title	100%	100%	100%	100%	100%	100%	100%
Claim review author	100%	100%	100%	100%	100%	100%	100%
Claim review date published	100%	100%	100%	100%	0%	100%	100%
Claim review language	100%	100%	100%	100%	100%	100%	100%
Claim review with entities (≥1)	66.9%	74.1%	58.7%	80.2%	76.0%	97.0%	96.0%
Claim rating	100%	100%	100%	100%	100%	100%	100%
Exact claim matches	87	38	49	0	0	0	0
True claims	3,725	1,311	2,255	60	97	0	2
False claims	11,068	6,002	4,663	209	191	0	3
Mixture claims	10,420	1,798	8,564	0	56	2	0
Other claims	3,170	1,574	261	291	434	490	120

Extracting Claims and Metadata. The *Claims extractor* crawls the identified fact-checking websites and collects the information in a JSON or Microdata format to consolidate a large multi-sourced data set (as a CSV file). The collected data consist mainly of: (a) the textual statement of the claim; (b) its truth-value or rating (both the normalised and the original one); (c) a link to the claim review from the fact-checking website; (d) the references cited in the claim reviews; (e) the entities extracted from the text of the claim and from the review body; (f) the author of the claim and the author of the review; (g) the date of publication of the claim and that of the review; (h) the title of the review article; (i) a set of keywords extracted from the websites acting as topics (e.g. "abortion").

Fig. 1. Overall architecture of the ClaimsKG pipeline.

Note that the extraction process is tailored individually to the structure of each of the different fact-checking websites, resulting in a set of website-specific extractors. The statistics generated at each run of the pipeline (globally and per domain) allow to monitor the "health" of the extracted data by detecting potential issues that may be related to changes of the structures of the respective fact-checking websites that may have occurred between two runs of the pipeline.

Entity Annotation of the Claims. We annotate the entities (e.g., names of persons, organisations, locations, etc.) mentioned in the texts of the claims and their reviews using the TagMe tool [8]. TagMe allows the automatic identification of entities in a text and their linking to a Wikipedia page and a DBpedia URI. It is known to achieve particularly good results when annotating short texts, which is the case for the statements in this domain, although we also annotate the body of the claim reviews. We run a local version of TagMe, allowing us to update the database regularly, using the latest available dump of Wikipedia (October 2018). We performed all the annotations using the optimal parameters described in [8]. We evaluated our updated TagMe model on the YAGO CONLL-TestB ground truth dataset [14] and obtained an accuracy of 75.5%, which is in line with state of the art performance reported for TagMe.[3]

Normalization of Ratings. Each of the fact-checking websites has its own labels describing the truthfulness of the claims, with different discrete textual values of ratings. While some sites have a controlled vocabulary of possible truth values, others apply an open-ended rating schema. For example, *Truth or Fiction* has a large number of non-uniform labels, such as "truth & misleading" or "reported as fiction". In order to harmonize our dataset, alongside the original ratings, we also provide a normalized rating score, applied across all claims contained in the dataset. For each of the sources, we summarised the distribution of rating values and then assigned them to a conservative and coarser-grained set of labels that correspond to the least common denominator between all the classifications of the individual sites. Given the varied rating schemes, where individual labels often are hard to objectively apply or interpret, we opted for a simple rating scheme consisting of four basic categories (`TRUE`, `FALSE`, `MIXTURE`, `OTHER`) that can be mapped to existing rating schemes.[4] The two extreme cases of a claim being proven true or false are captured by `TRUE` and `FALSE`, while `MIXTURE` characterises something on a truth scale or that holds both a degree of truth and a degree of falsehood. For anything that does not fall into this spectrum,

---
[3] http://nlpprogress.com/english/entity_linking.html.
[4] We provide full correspondence tables here: https://goo.gl/Ykus98.

we chose `OTHER` as a fallback. While the `TRUE/FALSE` ratings are straightforward, `MIXTURE` conflates a very large number of possible truth values, as diverse as "downplayed" or "mostly true". For `OTHER`, we have rating names such as "half-flip", "scam" or "research in progress".

Lifting and Serialisation. We created a Python 3.6 script to read the extracted claims as a CSV file in the extraction step, and then create the corresponding KG following the data model described in Sect. 4. We used the `rdflib` library to create the model and an abstract RDF graph to then serialize it in one of the many supported formats. All the caching needs of the generation process are met with a Redis server. We generate unique URI identifiers as UUIDs based on an one-way hash of key attributes for each instance. For example, the dereferenceable URI http://data.gesis.org/claimskg/creative_work/5f7e8c65-3d8b-57da-bab9-eb3a373bd2ab is created for the claim in https://www.snopes.com/fact-check/was-megyn-kelly-fired-from-nbc/. The triplification package is made available under an open-source licence on GitHub (along with documentation and usage examples) and will be updated regularly with the latest improvements (link given in Table 1).

Handling Simple Claim Coreferences. A certain number of identical claims is present within the websites, published at different dates, with possibly varying reviews. For example, the same claim published at a later date than the original publication will have an updated review. For this reason, instead of fusing these claims, we have opted for establishing `owl:sameAs` links among them. We implemented a simple approach to identify these claims, which aims to ensure 100% precision of the discovered links (exact matches). We normalise the text of the claims and the text of the claim titles only (lowercase; remove all quote characters and certain stop-words, such as "said" and "claimed") and then apply an identity string similarity measure on these texts. This resulted in 38 `owl:sameAs` links on claims from Snopes and 49 from Politifact.

4 The Claims Data Model

Our data model, depicted in Fig. 2, exploits terms from established vocabularies, specifically schema.org, NLP Interchange Format (NIF),[5] and Internationalization Tag Set (ITS).[6] The selection of the vocabularies was based on the following objectives: (i) avoiding schema violations, (ii) enabling data interoperability through term reuse, (iii) having stable identifiers, persistent hosting and open license, (iv) being supported by a community, (v) being extensible (ability to easily extend ClaimsKG with more data).

The core elements of our model are the *claim* and the *claim review*. To represent them, we make use of schema.org. Following Google's suggestion for Web markup of claims,[7] a claim is of type `schema:CreativeWork` and a claim review of type `schema:ClaimReview`. An instance of `schema:ClaimReview` is

[5] https://persistence.uni-leipzig.org/nlp2rdf/ontologies/nif-core/nif-core.html.
[6] https://www.w3.org/TR/its20/.
[7] https://developers.google.com/search/docs/data-types/factcheck.

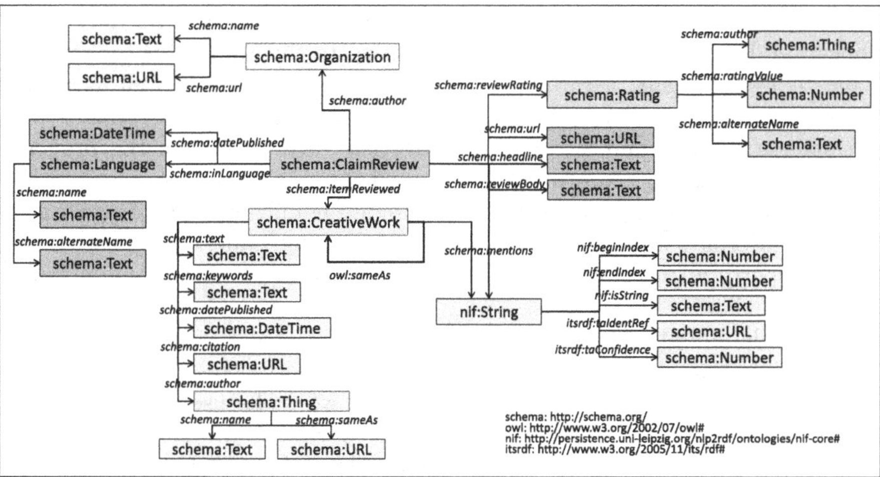

Fig. 2. The *Claims* data model.

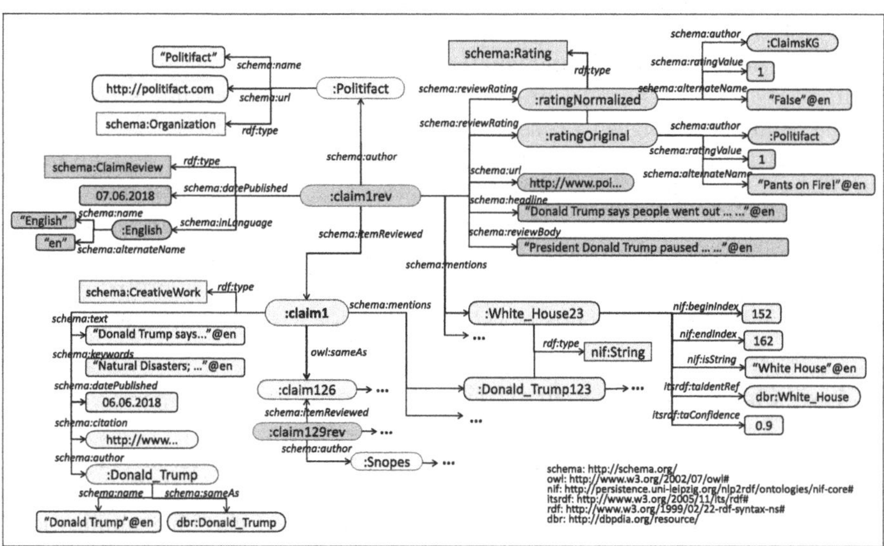

Fig. 3. Instantiation of the *Claims* model for a claim sourced from Politifact made by Donald Trump on June 6, 2018.

connected to an instance of `schema:CreativeWork` through the property `schema:itemReviewed`. A claim is associated with the actual text of the claim, a date (when the claim was uttered), an author (who uttered the claim), as well as with keywords (tags related to the claim acting as topics) and one or more citations (URLs of related resources, e.g., a tweet or a video). Since there might be many instances of the same claim coming from the same or different fact-checking sites, two claims can be connected through a `owl:sameAs` property.

A claim review is associated with metadata, in particular its author, its publication date, its language, its URL (pointing to the full text of the review), its full text (optionally, according to copyright restrictions), as well as with a title and one or more truthfulness assessments (ratings). The assessment is of type `schema:Rating` and is connected with the review through the property `schema:reviewRating`. A rating is represented through three properties: author (who provides the rating), rating value (a number in a pre-specified range, e.g., 1 to 5), and alternate name (a textual label of the rating value, e.g., "false"). The *author* property allows to provide more than one ratings for the same instance of a claim review.

Both a claim and a claim review can be associated with one or more *entity mentions*, i.e., names of entities mentioned in the short text of the claim or in the claim review. To describe this information, we make use of the NIF and ITS vocabularies, which provide classes and properties to describe the result of natural language processing tools applied on texts or documents. An instance of an entity mention is described through five properties: `nif:beginIndex` (starting position in the text), `nif:endIndex` (ending position in the text), `nif:isString` (a word or sequence of words representing the entity), `itsrdf:taIdentRef` (the identity of the mentioned entity), and `itsrdf:taConfidence` (the confidence that the entity has been disambiguated correctly). Depending on the specific requirements with respect to precision and recall, data consumers can select suitable confidence ranges to consider when querying the data.

Figure 3 depicts an example of a claim review by Politifact for a claim made by Donald Trump on June 6, 2018.[8] We notice that there are two instances of `schema:Rating`, one for the original rating by Politifact and one for the normalized rating provided by our KG. Apart from metadata information, we also see that the review mentions the entity name "White House", which probably (with confidence 0.9/1.0) corresponds to the official residence of the US President.

5 Use Cases and Exploitation

Use-Cases and Queries. The publication of structured data about a large collection of claims allows the uncovering of explicit and implicit relations between claims, entities, and sources. A number of existing fact-checking applications rely on linking claims to fact-checked statements in a database (e.g. https://fullfact.org/automated/, [31,34]). By combining claims and ratings from multiple portals and providing a unified structure, ClaimsKG facilitates these efforts. Moreover, the data can be used to enable supervision of machine learning models to support the advancement of automatic fact-checking algorithms [13,20]. In addition to supplying a large number of claims, ClaimsKG enables advanced, entity-centric search, exploration and information discovery, by exploiting data from various sources via federated SPARQL queries. This allows us, for example, to query entities belonging to a specific group (e.g., politicians or journalists)

[8] http://www.politifact.com/texas/statements/2018/jun/07/donald-trump/donald-trump-says-people-went-out-their-boats-watc/.

and create complex queries using both the claims metadata and the extracted entities. We provide different examples on our website (see Table 1 for a link). By exploiting the claim metadata and extracted entities, we can run complex queries that combine different types of information. The query in Fig. 4 requests all *false* claims of *2017* mentioning *Donald Trump* and *Climate change*. For each claim, the query returns its *text*, *date*, as well as the URL of its *review* by a fact-checking site. The query returns the following claim: *Donald Trump signed an executive order naming climate change as a threat 'both to the economy and national security'* (2017-02-01). In a similar way, we can generate a sample of claims based on certain criteria and use it in other tasks, e.g., for evaluation or training by automated fact-checking approaches [13,20]. Such a sample can be easily produced through a concise SPARQL query over ClaimsKG.

```
SELECT ?text ?date ?reviewurl WHERE {
 ?claim a schema:CreativeWork ; schema:datePublished ?date FILTER(year(?date)=2017)
 ?claim schema:author ?author ; schema:text ?text ; schema:mentions ?entity1, ?entity2 .
 ?entity1 itsrdf:taIdentRef dbr:Climate_change .
 ?entity2 itsrdf:taIdentRef dbr:Donald_Trump .
 ?claimReview schema:itemReviewed ?claim ; schema:reviewRating ?rating ; schema:url ?reviewurl .
 ?rating schema:author <http://data.gesis.org/claimskg/organization/claimskg> ;
         schema:alternateName ?ratingName ;
         schema:ratingValue ?ratingValue FILTER (?ratingValue = 1) }
```

Fig. 4. SPARQL query requesting *false* claims of 2017 mentioning both *Donald Trump* and *Climate change*.

Going beyond the computer science domain, ClaimsKG can be a valuable resource supporting (computational) social scientific research investigating, for example, societal debates and agenda-setting. Agenda-setting theory refers to the influence of mass media on the public's focus of attention [22]. While first-level agenda-setting relates to inserting topics, events or entities into the public discourse, thereby regulating societal priorities, second-level agenda-setting is about increasing the salience of specific features or attributes of entities in the discourse. This is also referred to as frame-setting. With the web evolving into a platform where every citizen may become a publisher, express their views and reach out to a large audience, citizens are now able to play a more active role in influencing the public discourse [3]. Online debates about political issues typically exhibit the pattern of a few dominant ideological positions emerging, with different groups expressing different viewpoints and often referring to a disparate set of information sources [24] which, in turn, may focus on different attributes and frames for a given topic. Using ClaimsKG, an exploratory search on a topic and related entities may be performed in order to gain insights on relevant viewpoints, attributes and actors. Also, the KG allows the tracking of differences over time and in relation to specific events, and the relation of views of specific actors to ideological positions.

To illustrate, consider the 2012 incident of the neighbourhood watch coordinator George Zimmerman shooting 17-year-old African-American high school student Trayvon Martin, the incident that later gave rise to the Black Lives Matter movement [15]. The query given in Fig. 5 retrieves all claims mentioning Trayvon Martin or George Zimmerman, yielding 68 claims in total with 8 claims rated true, 33 false, and 24 mixture. The distribution of truth values hints at this being a highly controversial topic with potentially highly polarized viewpoints. Central to the debate is the aspect of racism; some framing the incident as an example of racist violence against black people,[9] some seeing race as an overemphasized point in the Zimmerman trial[10], and others framing the Black Lives Matter debate as racist against white people.[11] An entity frequently mentioned in these claims is the *"stand your ground" law*. The query in Fig. 6 retrieves other entities connected to it revealing a strong association to the *Trayvon Martin* case.

```
SELECT ?text ?reviewurl ?rating WHERE {
  ?claim a schema:CreativeWork ; schema:text ?text ; schema:mentions ?entity1 .
  ?entity1 itsrdf:taIdentRef ?entity2Uri
       FILTER (?entity2Uri IN (dbr:Trayvon_Martin, dbr:George_Zimmerman))
  ?claimReview schema:itemReviewed ?claim ; schema:reviewRating ?rating ; schema:url ?reviewurl }
```

Fig. 5. SPARQL query requesting all claims mentioning *Trayvon Martin or George Zimmerman.*

```
SELECT ?entityUri WHERE {
  ?claim a schema:CreativeWork ; schema:mentions ?entity1, ?entity2 .
  ?entity1 itsrdf:taIdentRef dbr:Stand-your-ground_law .
  ?entity2 itsrdf:taIdentRef ?entityUri FILTER (?entityUri != dbr:Stand-your-ground_law) }
```

Fig. 6. SPARQL query requesting entities mentioned in claims together with *Stand your ground law.*

```
SELECT year(?date) as ?year count(?claim) as ?num WHERE {
  ?claim a schema:CreativeWork ; schema:datePublished ?date FILTER(year(?date)>=2012)
  ?claim schema:author ?author ; schema:text ?text ; schema:mentions ?entity .
  ?entity itsrdf:taIdentRef dbr:Black_Lives_Matter } GROUP BY year(?date) ORDER BY year(?date)
```

Fig. 7. SPARQL query requesting the number of claims mentioning *Black Lives Matter* by year.

The query in Fig. 7 illustrates the tracking of changes over time and the discovery of important events. While for 2015, 2017, 2018 and 2019 maximum three claims per year mentioning the entity *Black Lives Matter* are found, there

[9] https://www.politifact.com/florida/statements/2013/jul/24/jesse-jackson/homicides-blacks-have-tripled-stand-your-ground-wa/.

[10] https://www.politifact.com/florida/statements/2013/jul/17/tweets/look-statistic-blacks-and-murder/.

[11] https://www.snopes.com/fact-check/keith-passmore-murder/.

is a striking peak in 2016 with 17 mentions. This aligns with the incident of law enforcement officers being shot during a Black Lives Matter protest march in July 2016 which reopened a heated debate about the movement. In fact, analysis of the respective claims reveals the emergence of frames attributing violent and disruptive behaviour to the Black Lives Matter movement.[12] Note that the discussed scenarios represent only starting points for initiating further analyses.

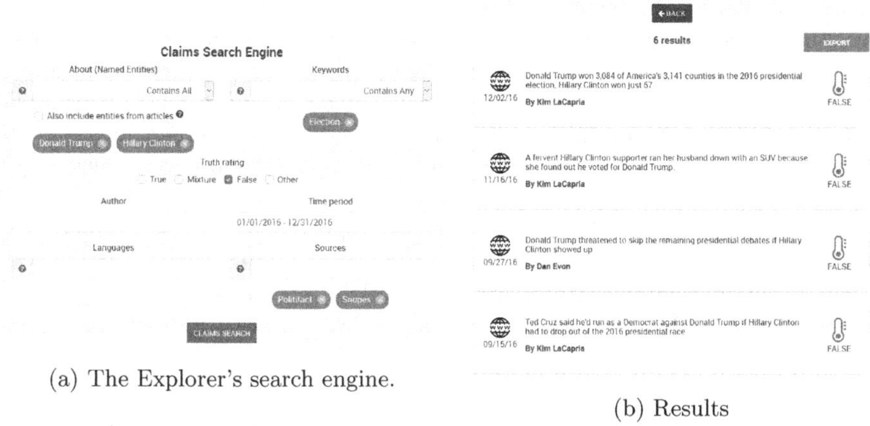

(a) The Explorer's search engine.

(b) Results

Fig. 8. The ClaimsKG Explorer user interface

ClaimsKG Explorer. In order to facilitate data access for researchers from outside of the computer science domain, like journalists and sociologists, we provide ClaimsKG Explorer (link in Table 1), a user-friendly, Web-based interface to query and explore ClaimsKG. The application sends HTTP requests to the ClaimsKG SPARQL endpoint and provides information through a Web user interface. The users are given the possibility to filter their search space with respect to a number of facets (Fig. 8a): *entities* contained in the text of the claim or its review, *keywords* (topics related to the claims), *truth ratings* (the normalised ones), *time frame* of interest, *authors* of claims, *sources* (fact-checking websites), and *languages* (currently only English; work in progress will incorporate non-English websites). After clicking on the CLAIMS SEARCH button, the user is provided a list of clickable claims ordered by their date of publication (most recent ones on top), as shown in Fig. 8b. The search result corresponding to the selected criteria can be exported as a CSV or an RDF file and reused in a particular scenario by clicking on the EXPORT button on the results page.

[12] https://www.politifact.com/wisconsin/statements/2016/dec/02/sean-duffy/donald-trump-backer-sean-duffy-links-attacks-polic/, https://www.politifact.com/wisconsin/statements/2017/apr/17/sheriff-david-clarke-us-senate/pro-sheriff-david-clarke-group-says-clarke-called-/.

Finally, cicking on a particular claim, the user can access all the information related to that claim, like the review article, the entities mentioned in the claim or the review text, the references, and the keywords.

6 Related Work

As outlined above, ground truth data in the form of labelled and contextualised claims is necessary for a number of interdisciplinary research problems. Among the most prominent use-case scenarios is the task of automatic fact-checking, which has been of growing interest for the AI community. A number of approaches have been proposed to extract check-worthy pieces of information from text [12] and to further assess their veracity automatically [30]. The majority of these approaches can be classified either as *reference* or *machine learning approaches*. The former model claims computationally to achieve structured representations [4,23,29,31,34], allowing for their comparison to certified facts contained in knowledge bases or for the application of graph mining techniques on these bases. The latter rely on data in the form of labelled claims in order to train and apply machine learning models. The current section provides an overview of *datasets* for training and/or evaluation covering these two families of approaches. We categorise these datasets according to the process of their collection.

Extracting Gold Standard from Web Sources. Alongside ClaimsKG, a number of approaches rely on extracting data from fact-checking websites, allowing the collection of large number of claims together with veracity annotations of high quality that stem from serious journalistic work. One of the first initiatives in that field is introduced in [28]. The data extraction process is manual, resulting in merely 221 statements collected from Channel 4 and PolitiFact. Since the two sources do not apply the same rating scale, similarly to our approach, the authors map the two respective sets of labels to a common scale consisting of five categories: "true", "mostly true", "half true", "mostly false" and "false". The *Liar* benchmark [32] collects 12.8K Politifact claims over 10 years. Additional information is stored regarding the *speaker*, the *context*, the *label* and the *justification*. The fact-checking approach presented in [21] relies on a data set of approximately 10 K claims, also crawled from Politifact in 2016, while [16] and [20] have collected, respectively, 1K and 5 K claims from Snopes. Wikipedia's lists of proven hoaxes[13] and fictitious people[14] have been used in [19,20] in order to generate ground truth labels, resulting in 157 claims labelled as "fake". In parallel, the authors also collect around 4.8 K labelled claims from Snopes, published before Faburary 2016. The Clef-2018 challenge includes the fact-checking task *Check that!* [2]. The benchmark data (150 claims) consists of sentences collected from debates from the 2016 US Presidential Election Campaign, as well as from other political speeches during and after the campaign.

[13] https://en.wikipedia.org/wiki/Listofhoaxes#Provenhoaxes.

[14] https://en.wikipedia.org/wiki/List_of_fictitious_people.

Evaluations are obtained from FactCheck.org articles resulting in labels of the kind "factually true", "half-true", or "false".

The *Emergent* data set[15] results from collecting claims from various web sources, such as Politifact, Snopes and Twitter accounts such as @Hoaxalizer, particularly dedicated to rumors and hoaxes [9]. The data set contains 300 claims with three types of annotations ("true", "false", "unverified") provided by journalists. A large scale collection of tweet news (126K stories) labelled on the basis of significant degree of agreement among several fact-checking sites (Snopes, Politifact, Factcheck, Truth-or-Fiction, Hoax-slayer and Urbanlegends) is used in [30]. As a result, a sample of news stories assigned one of three possible labels ("true", "false" or "mixed") is created. However, the data is only available upon request for the purposes of reproducing the reported experiments.

Crowdsourced or Manually Annotated Data Sets. Crowdsourcing techniques allow for the extraction and labelling of relatively large sets of claims, although some care should be taken to ensure the reliability of the data harvested. The Open Domain Deception Dataset contains "freely contributed truths and lies" [18]. By using the Amazon Mechanical Turk, each worker has been asked to freely formulate seven one-sentence truths and lies. After cleansing the collection, the final dataset consists of 7.2 K sentences provided by 512 unique contributors, for whom demographic data is also collected and made available. The SemEval'17 challenge dataset contains 5.5 K crowdsourced annotated claims [11], while the FEVER dataset, with 185 K entries, extracts claims from Wikipedia. Semantics-preserving sentence altering techniques are then applied and the resulting claims are annotated by the crowd [25]. Finally, the approach in [17] relies on a dataset of 250 manually annotated claims.

Automatic Annotations. Fact verification methods can be applied in order to construct automatically ground truth datasets for fact-checking. An example is the fake-news dataset,[16] containing text and metadata scraped from 244 websites that have been identified as untrustworthy by the BS Detector Chrome Extension tool.[17] This approach has the risk that the imperfections of the verification system are propagated onto the annotated data.

Knowledge Graphs for Fact-Checking. Finally, we focus on KGs that have been used in a number of fact verification approaches from the *reference* group. Usually, a statement is modelled as a triple and is verified on the basis of properties of the paths involving elements of that triple in existing KGs, considered as ground truth, such as DBpedia [4,10,23]. The Knowledge Vault [6] and the KnowMore [36] resources, or the Voldemort KG [26], rely on structured markup annotations in order to match them to established KGs or perform graph completion. This process implies the verification of the truthfulness of statements and the production of reliable factual information that can be used as ground truth.

---

[15] http://www.emergent.info.

[16] https://www.kaggle.com/mrisdal/fake-news.

[17] http://bsdetector.tech.

Positioning. ClaimsKG is entirely based on data from a number of established fact-checking websites and therefore falls into the first category of datasets presented above. With its more than 28 K claims, it is, to our knowledge, the largest resource of structured fact-checking information so far made available but also one archiving the largest spectrum of metadata categories. The open-source tools for its regeneration and update that we provide will allow for it to grow in size over time. In contrast to existing approaches, we model claims by the help of an RDF/S data model specifically designed for that purpose, fostering re-usability and extensibility. As compared to KG-based *reference* approaches, by dynamically collecting data from fact-checking websites, we focus on information of particular interest for the verification of newly emerging statements that are not available in Wikipedia or established KGs. ClaimsKG can be used as both training and evaluation data, allowing users (researchers in computer science or computational sociology, for example) to compile thematic samples of it with the help of structured queries, or by using the web application (cf. Sect. 5). Beyond the purposes of fact-checking, this is expected to foster research and data-driven studies in different areas of social and computational social science, as discussed in our use-case scenarios.

7 Conclusion and Future Work

We have introduced ClaimsKG, a knowledge graph of fact-checked claims, which facilitates structured queries of related metadata, such as their truth values, authors or time of release. ClaimsKG is generated through a semi-automated pipeline, which harvests data from popular fact-checking sites on a regular basis, lifts data into a specifically developed for that purpose model, and annotates claims with related entities from DBpedia. The KG is expected to provide support to research in the areas of fact-checking, stance detection and multiple topics related to the analysis of societal debates, where a quality ground truth of labelled claims is required in order to facilitate supervision, validation or reproducibility of research methods.

There are several limitations of the current KG that are the focus of ongoing and short-term efforts. The development of an advanced claim matching approach and its evaluation is among them. We are working on building a gold-standard dataset of claim-pairs, annotated with respect to different relatedness categories, in order to evaluate the process and to provide training data to fine-tune state-of-the-art deep language modelling approaches such as BERT [5] to our matching task. We also intend to extend the content of our graph to other fact-checking websites and languages, enabling multi- and cross-lingual information retrieval and approaches for fact verification. With respect to augmenting ClaimsKG with additional claims, we also intend to harvest semi-structured schema.org markup of claims from Web pages by exploiting data fusion pipelines developed as part of prior work [35]. Regarding the exploratory Web interface, in the future we aim to support the execution of federated queries that integrate information from external KGs like DBpedia, as well as the inclusion of a statistical observatory allowing us to extract distributions and correlations of different entities, topics and claims.

Acknowledgments. We thank Vinicius Woloszyn for providing support on the first step of the pipeline (claim extraction), as well as Josselin Alezot, Imran Meghazi and Elisa Gueneau for their work on the Web interface. We thank all fact-checking sites and the fact-checkers community for the laborious work of manual claim verification.

References

1. Allcott, H., Gentzkow, M.: Social media and fake news in the 2016 election. J. Econ. Persp. **31**(2), 211–236 (2017)
2. Barrón-Cedeño, A., et al.: Overview of the CLEF-2018 checkThat! Lab on automatic identification and verification of political claims, task 2: factuality. In: CLEF. CEUR-WS (2018)
3. Bennett, W.L., Pfetsch, B.: Rethinking political communication in a time of disrupted public spheres. J. Commun. **68**(2), 243–253 (2018). https://doi.org/10.1093/joc/jqx017
4. Ciampaglia, G.L., Shiralkar, P., Rocha, L.M., Bollen, J., Menczer, F., Flammini, A.: Computational fact checking from knowledge networks. PloS one **10**, e0128193 (2015)
5. Devlin, J., Chang, M.W., Lee, K., Toutanova, K.: BERT: Pre-training of Deep Bidirectional Transformers for Language Understanding. ArXiv e-prints arXiv:1810.04805 [cs.CL] (2018)
6. Dong, X., et al.: Knowledge vault: a web-scale approach to probabilistic knowledge fusion. In: ACM SIGKDD, pp. 601–610. ACM (2014)
7. Esteves, D., Reddy, A.J., Chawla, P., Lehmann, J.: Belittling the source: trustworthiness indicators to obfuscate fake news on the web. In: 1st Workshop on Fact Extraction and VERification (FEVER), pp. 50–59 (2018)
8. Ferragina, P., Scaiella, U.: TAGME: on-the-fly annotation of short text fragments (by Wikipedia entities). In: ACM ICIKM, pp. 1625–1628. ACM (2010)
9. Ferreira, W., Vlachos, A.: Emergent: a novel data-set for stance classification. In: NAACL-HLT, pp. 1163–1168 (2016)
10. Gerber, D., et al.: Defacto–temporal and multilingual deep fact validation. Web Semant.: Sci. Serv. Agents World Wide Web **35**, 85–101 (2015)
11. Gorrell, G., Bontcheva, K., Derczynski, L., Kochkina, E., Liakata, M., Zubiaga, A.: RumourEval 2019: determining rumour veracity and support for rumours. In: Semantic Evaluation, pp. 60–67 (2017)
12. Hassan, N., et al.: The quest to automate fact-checking. World (2015)
13. Hassan, N., Arslan, F., Li, C., Tremayne, M.: Toward automated fact-checking: detecting check-worthy factual claims by claimbuster. In: ACM SIGKDD, pp. 1803–1812. ACM (2017)
14. Hoffart, J., et al.: Robust disambiguation of named entities in text. In: EMNLP, pp. 782–792. ACL, Stroudsburg (2011). http://dl.acm.org/citation.cfm?id=2145432.2145521
15. Hon, L.: Social media framing within the million hoodies movement for justice. Public Relat. Rev. **42**, 9–19 (2015). https://doi.org/10.1016/j.pubrev.2015.11.013
16. Ma, J., et al.: Detecting rumors from microblogs with recurrent neural networks. In: IJCAI, pp. 3818–3824 (2016)

17. Mihaylova, T., et al.: Fact checking in community forums. In: AAAI, pp. 879–886 (2018)
18. Pérez-Rosas, V., Mihalcea, R.: Experiments in open domain deception detection. In: CEMNLP, pp. 1120–1125 (2015)
19. Popat, K., Mukherjee, S., Strötgen, J., Weikum, G.: Credibility assessment of textual claims on the web. In: ACM ICIKM, pp. 2173–2178. ACM (2016)
20. Popat, K., Mukherjee, S., Strötgen, J., Weikum, G.: Where the truth lies: explaining the credibility of emerging claims on the web and social media. In: WWW, pp. 1003–1012 (2017)
21. Rashkin, H., Choi, E., Jang, J.Y., Volkova, S., Choi, Y.: Truth of varying shades: analyzing language in fake news and political fact-checking. In: EMNLP, pp. 2931–2937 (2017)
22. Scheufele, D.A.: Agenda-setting, priming, and framing revisited: another look at cognitive effects of political communication. Mass Commun. Soc. **3**(2–3), 297–316 (2000). https://doi.org/10.1207/S15327825MCS0323_07
23. Shiralkar, P., Flammini, A., Menczer, F., Ciampaglia, G.L.: Finding streams in knowledge graphs to support fact checking. In: ICDM, pp. 859–864. IEEE (2017)
24. Smith, M., Shneiderman, B., Rainie, L., Himelboim, I.: Mapping Twitter topic networks: from polarized crowds to community clusters, February 2014
25. Thorne, J., Vlachos, A., Christodoulopoulos, C., Mittal, A.: Fever: a large-scale dataset for fact extraction and verification. In: NAACL-HLT, pp. 809–819 (2018)
26. Tonon, A., Felder, V., Difallah, D.E., Cudré-Mauroux, P.: VoldemortKG: mapping schema.org and web entities to linked open data. In: Groth, P., et al. (eds.) ISWC 2016. LNCS, vol. 9982, pp. 220–228. Springer, Cham (2016). https://doi.org/10.1007/978-3-319-46547-0_23
27. Tschiatschek, S., Singla, A., Gomez Rodriguez, M., Merchant, A., Krause, A.: Fake news detection in social networks via crowd signals. In: WWW, pp. 517–524 (2018)
28. Vlachos, A., Riedel, S.: Fact checking: task definition and dataset construction. In: Language Technologies and Computational Social Science, pp. 18–22 (2014)
29. Vlachos, A., Riedel, S.: Identification and verification of simple claims about statistical properties. In: CEMNLP, pp. 2596–2601. ACL (2015)
30. Vosoughi, S., Roy, D., Aral, S.: The spread of true and false news online. Science **359**(6380), 1146–1151 (2018)
31. Walenz, B., et al.: Finding, monitoring, and checking claims computationally based on structured data. In: Computation+Journalism (2014)
32. Wang, W.Y.: Liar, liar pants on fire: a new benchmark dataset for fake news detection. In: AMACL, pp. 422–426 (2017)
33. Wang, X., Yu, C., Baumgartner, S., Korn, F.: Relevant document discovery for fact-checking articles. In: WWW, pp. 525–533 (2018)
34. Wu, Y., Agarwal, P.K., Li, C., Yang, J., Yu, C.: Toward computational fact-checking. Proc. VLDB Endow. **7**(7), 589–600 (2014)
35. Yu, R., Gadiraju, U., Fetahu, B., Lehmberg, O., Ritze, D., Dietze, S.: KnowMore - knowledge base augmentation with structured web markup. Semant. Web J. (2019). http://www.semantic-web-journal.net/content/knowmore-knowledge-base-augmentation-structured-web-markup-1. IOS Press
36. Yua, R., Gadirajua, U., Fetahua, B., Lehmbergb, O., Ritzeb, D., Dietzea, S.: KnowMore-knowledge base augmentation with structured web markup. Semant. Web J. (2017). IOS Press

CoCoOn: Cloud Computing Ontology for IaaS Price and Performance Comparison

Qian Zhang(✉), Armin Haller, and Qing Wang

Australian National University, Canberra 2601, Australia
{miranda.zhang,armin.haller,qing.wang}@anu.edu.au
https://cecs.anu.edu.au/

Abstract. In this paper, we present an OWL-based ontology, the Cloud Computing Ontology (CoCoOn), that defines concepts, features, attributes and relations to describe Cloud infrastructure services. We also present datasets that are built using CoCoOn and scripts (i.e. SPARQL template queries and web applications) that demonstrate the real-world applicability of the ontology. We also describe the design of the ontology and the architecture of related services developed with it.

Keywords: Ontology · Cloud-computing · Semantic-web

1 Introduction

Consumers of Cloud services often face the challenge of selecting the right services for a given use case from a large set of heterogeneous offers. For example, a 2013 survey from Burstorm[1] shows that there are over 426 Compute and Storage service providers with deployments in over 11,072 locations. This problem is further aggregated by the non-standardized naming conventions on heterogeneous types of services (CPU, Storage, Network etc.) and features (Virtualisation technology, SLA model, billing model, Cloud location, cost, etc.)

A unified model is needed as the foundation for data collection, reasoning and analytics to fulfil the goal of a smart Cloud service recommendation To this end, this paper presents our work on the Cloud Computing Ontology (CoCoOn) version 1.0.1, which consolidates Cloud computing concepts: https://w3id.org/cocoon/v1.0.1. The relevant code, data and ontology are made available online as a Github project. Figure 1 depicts the IaaS related parts of CoCoOn v1.0.1. The major additions of CoCoOn v1.0.1 compared to its previous version [18,19] are the Cloud service pricing and QoS modelling features. The datasets presented in this paper are completely new, along with all the tools and code we used to produce the data. When CoCoOn was first developed, there were little existing domain ontologies to reuse, e.g. CoCoOn predated the development of

[1] https://www.burstorm.com/platform/.

C. Ghidini et al. (Eds.): ISWC 2019, LNCS 11779, pp. 325–341, 2019.
https://doi.org/10.1007/978-3-030-30796-7_21

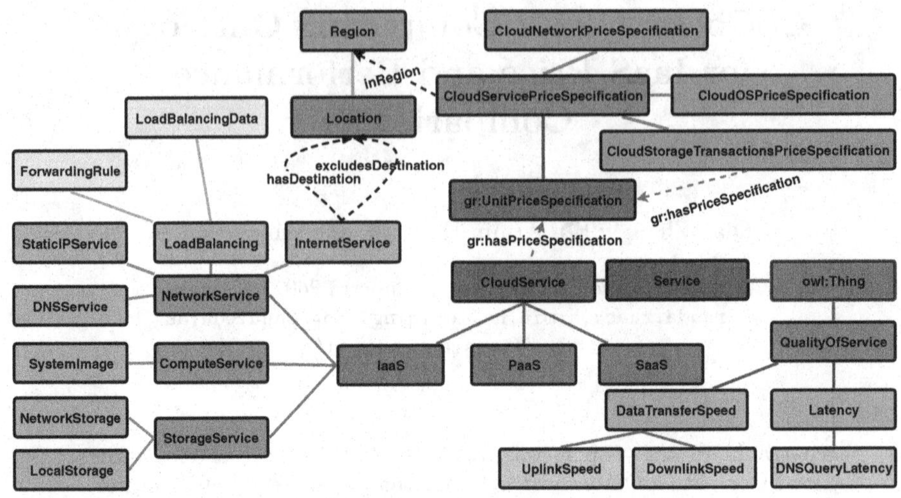

Fig. 1. CoCoOn v1.0.1: IaaS related parts

PROV-O[2], schema.org, Unit of Measure Ontology (QUDT)[3], SSN [6] and Wikidata [16]. The new CoCoOn makes use of those now popular existing ontologies. Consequently, we also removed parts from the old CoCoOn ontology, which are now covered by those standardised/popular domain ontologies. Also, to improve the reusability, we added more rdfs:comments, metadata, documentation, and use cases. Because our old site on purl.org is hard to maintain and update, we moved the ontology and the documentation to GitHub. Also, we are using w3id.org as the permanent URL service instead, which should lead to better sustainability. More specifically, our model aims to facilitate the publication, discovery and comparison of IaaS, by: (i) Providing a schema for constructing and executing complex queries; (ii) Defining frequently referenced data as named individuals; (iii) Providing a unified machine-readable specification, as opposed to provider-specific APIs and documentation. In addition to these, we demonstrate the capabilities of our model by providing real-life usage datasets. Those datasets include services from the Google Cloud and the Microsoft Azure Cloud, which is detailed in Sect. 4.

2 Related Work

There are existing ontologies and models that focus on Web Services [12,14] and their architectures [5] in general. Unlike these works, our model focuses on Cloud computing Infrastructure as a Service (IaaS), i.e. its features and price models.

Previously, Parra-Royon and J.M. Benítez[4] have developed two small Cloud ontologies. The set of concepts and features they cover are limited and, as a

[2] https://www.w3.org/TR/prov-o/.
[3] http://qudt.org/.
[4] http://cookingbigdata.com/linkeddata/dmservices.

result, their examples are limited to some simple cases. For instance, the examples presented in Sect. 3.4.1 cannot be modelled with their ontologies. Furthermore, the main reason why we did not use their "ccpricing", "ccinstances", and "ccregions" ontologies is because they used global scope constraints (i.e. rdfs:domain and rdfs:range) on most (if not all) of the classes and object properties, which we believe are too restrictive and can cause unintended inferences.

Boukadi et al. have developed a Cloud Service Description Ontology (CSO) [1], primarily for the modelling of Cloud service brokerage. Their price model is rather simple and cannot model real-world scenarios. Their model and data are also not available online anymore to be evaluated further or to be reused in other contexts.

In the mOSAIC project [13], researchers proposed an OWL ontology for Cloud services negotiation (i.e. between customers and providers) and composition (i.e. by an administrator). Their ontology is different in scope to ours.

Joshi et al. have developed an OWL Ontology for the Lifecycle of IT Services in the Cloud [9]. This ontology provides models for the steps involved in the phases of discovery, negotiation, composition, and consumption of Cloud services. The modelling of Cloud service features is minimal, and their link to an example of a storage service[5] is no longer accessible.

In the area of Quality of Service (QoS) modelling, some papers have proposed QoS ontologies (i.e. QoSOnt [2] and OWL-QoS [20]). However, they did not publish the actual specifications, and only figures/graphs were given. In this paper, we provide formal modelling of QoS parameters and make it readily available for general use (see Sect. 3.5).

Overall, all the models above have a different scope compared to our ontology. Our focus is on modelling concepts, features, attributes and relations of Cloud infrastructure services. We do not consider models for orchestration [9,13] nor brokerage processes [1] in this paper. Nonetheless, our ontology could be extended in this regard using the models proposed in these works mentioned above. Furthermore, we have also developed tools for automatically adding semantics to information from providers' APIs. We have used existing ontologies whenever fits, such as QUDT for defining price with currency values. For the full list of ontologies we have referenced, see the online documentation.[6]

3 Concepts and Design of CoCoOn v1.0.1

3.1 New Features

In our previous work [17,18], we proposed a simpler model describing concepts of Cloud infrastructure services (IaaS).[7] In this paper we have significantly

5 https://www.csee.umbc.edu/~kjoshi1/storage_ontology.owl.

6 https://github.com/miranda-zhang/cloud-computing-schema/blob/master/vocabularies.md.

7 https://github.com/miranda-zhang/cloud-computing-schema/blob/master/revision_history.md.

extended the capabilities of our initial model, i.e. changes have been made to classes, properties, relationships and axioms, with a strong focus on flexibility and extensibility.

In Sect. 3.3, we describe the syntax, semantics, design and formalisation of CoCoOn v1.0.1, and the rationale behind such design, and some usages. In Sect. 4, we illustrate tools for mapping CoCoOn v1.0.1 to Google Cloud and the Microsoft Azure Cloud services. These tools demonstrate the usability and strength of the ontology we developed.

3.2 Design Rationale

The classes and properties are arranged according to subsumption hierarchies, which represent the skeleton of the model and establish the basic relationships between the components. Following the principle of minimal commitment [3], we use guarded restrictions (i.e. owl:someValuesFrom) instead of domain range restrictions (rdfs:domain, rdfs:range). As such, the domain and ranges are more permissive, keeping the model more flexible and extensible. We also use qualified cardinality restrictions (e.g., exactly, owl:qualifiedCardinality; max, owl:maxQualifiedCardinality) when there is a known cardinality restriction.

Most building blocks of IaaS services naturally correspond to OWL2 classes (e.g., cocoon:CloudService, cocoon:ComputeService, and cocoon:StorageService), object properties (e.g., cocoon:hasMemory, :hasStorage, and cocoon:inRegion) and data properties (e.g., cocoon:numberOfCores). The more challenging part is to capture constraints posed by the possible combination of services in IaaS in the models using ontological axioms. We next describe how this can be accomplished using a combination of OWL 2 axioms and integrity constraints.

We use Turtle syntax throughout our examples, and use Manchester OWL Syntax when explaining the ontology specifications.

3.3 Cloud Service

The class cocoon:CloudService is the main class hosting our Cloud feature vocabularies. We define a top level class cocoon:Service to be its parent, and make it the union of schema:Service and sosa:FeatureOfInterest. So our Cloud service definitions are compatible with the schema.org vocabulary [4] and the SOSA ontology [8] from which we reuse terms.

Cloud services are usually classified into three categories: cocoon:IaaS, cocoon:PaaS and cocoon:SaaS. Some examples of cocoon:SaaS are *database as a service*, *machine learning as a service*, Google Cloud Composer, etc. Some examples of cocoon:PaaS are the Google App Engine, Heroku, etc.

We use gr:UnitPriceSpecification and its associated object property gr:hasPriceSpecification to model price (see Sect. 3.4.1 for more details about price specification). Existential quantifiers (i.e., some, owl:someValuesFrom) are used on gr:hasPriceSpecification.

Note that, although some is the same as min 1, it is not the same as database integrity constraints. We can still define valid Cloud services individuals without a price specification. Under the open world assumption, missing information is just not known but may exist, whereas, in databases (closed world assumption), absence of information often assumes that information does not exist. This open world assumption serves us well because we cannot guarantee that every service will have a price specification. There are services available upon requests, but the price is negotiated later. For example, we may want to specify that secure data centres for governmental use are available, but detailed price information is probably not disclosed publicly.

We assume each service can belong to exactly one provider. A qualified cardinality restriction exactly (owl:qualifiedCardinality) is used to define this type of assumption. We reuse gr:BusinessEntity to define a provider (see Sect. 3.7 for more details).

Infrastructure as a Service can be classified into 3 categories: cocoon:ComputeService (see Sect. 3.3.1), cocoon:StorageService (see Sect. 3.3.2), and cocoon:NetworkService (see Sect. 3.3.3).

3.3.1 Compute Service

The number of cores available on a virtual machine (VM) is defined by the data property cocoon:numberOfCores. Because it can have a non-integer value, we define its datatype as xsd:decimal. For Google Cloud, cores and vCPU refer to the same thing. The performance power of the CPU can be described by cocoon:hasCPUcapacity. The memory size of a VM is specified by cocoon:hasMemory.

The cocoon:LocalStorage available on a VM can be specified with cocoon:hasStorage. We use an existential quantification (i.e. some) on this property, so that it is possible to define more cocoon:NetworkStorage later. Google has a limit for the maximum number of disks that can be attached to a VM, which we model with the object property cocoon:hasMaxNumberOfDisks. Additionally, Google also has a limit for the maximum total disk size that can be attached to a VM, which is modelled with cocoon:hasMaxStorageSize.

We use schema:TypeAndQuantityNode to describe the quantity of things. So value, unit, and type of an object can all be captured (see Sect. 3.7 for more details).

Note that cocoon:ComputeService also inherits properties from its super classes, e.g. the following property is inherited from cocoon:CloudService:

gr:hasPriceSpecification some gr:UnitPriceSpecification

There are data access fees on local disks of the Azure VM.[8] To model this we use gr:hasPriceSpecification max 1 cocoon:StorageTransactionsPriceSpecification. For a short example of cocoon:ComputeService, see Listing 1.1.

[8] https://www.rhipe.com/azure-storage-transactions/.

Listing 1.1. Virtual Machine

```
@prefix schema: <<https://schema.org/>> .
@prefix unit: <<http://qudt.org/vocab/unit#>> .
@prefix xsd: <<http://www.w3.org/2001/XMLSchema#>> .
@prefix rdfs: <<http://www.w3.org/2000/01/rdf-schema#>> .
@prefix gr: <<http://purl.org/goodrelations/v1#>> .
@prefix cocoon: <<https://w3id.org/cocoon/v1.0.1#>> .
@base <<https://w3id.org/cocoon/data/v1.0.1/>> .
<2019-02-12/ComputeService/Gcloud/CP-COMPUTEENGINE-VMIMAGE-N1-HIGHCPU-96-PREEMPTIBLE>
       a cocoon:ComputeService ;
       rdfs:label "CP-COMPUTEENGINE-VMIMAGE-N1-HIGHCPU-96-PREEMPTIBLE" ;
       gr:hasPriceSpecification [ a cocoon:CloudServicePriceSpecification ;
                                  gr:hasCurrency "USD" ;
                                  gr:hasCurrencyValue 0.72 ;
                                  gr:hasUnitOfMeasurement unit:Hour ;
                                  cocoon:inRegion <Region/Gcloud/us-east1>
                                ] ;
       cocoon:hasMemory [ a schema:TypeAndQuantityNode ;
                                  schema:amountOfThisGood 86.4 ;
                                  schema:unitCode cocoon:GB
                                ] ;
       cocoon:hasProvider cocoon:Gcloud ;
       cocoon:numberOfCores "96"^^xsd:decimal ;
       schema:dateModified "2019-02-12"^^xsd:date .
```

3.3.2 Storage Service

Two subclasses for cocoon:StorageService have been defined: cocoon:LocalStorage and cocoon:NetworkStorage.

On the Azure Cloud, snapshot options are available for storage, which is modelled with the object property cocoon:canHaveSnapshot. This information is manually interpreted from the documentation.[9] There are also caps on input/output operations per sec (IOPS) and throughput, which are modeled with cocoon:hasStorageIOMax and cocoon:hasStorageThroughputMax. We have also defined corresponding units, which is explained in Sect. 3.7.

In Listing 1.2, we show a cocoon:NetworkStorage service from cocoon:Azure, which is a Cloud provider we have pre-defined as a named instance. More details on its corresponding storage transaction prices can be found in Sect. 3.4.3.

Next, an example of the Azure provisional Ultra SSD storage service is presented. It has configurable IOPS and throughput. Prices are based on provisioned storage size, IOPS and throughput. There is also a reservation charge imposed if you enable Ultra SSD capability on the VM without connecting an Ultra SSD disk, whose rate is provisioned at per vcpu/hour.

Listing 1.2. Storage

```
@base <<https://w3id.org/cocoon/data/v1.0.1/>> .
<2019-03-07/NetworkStorage/Azure/premiumssd-p30>
       a cocoon:NetworkStorage ;
       rdfs:label "premiumssd-p30" ;
       gr:hasPriceSpecification <CloudStorageTransactionsPriceSpecification/Azure/
            ↪ managed_disk/transactions-ssd> ;
       gr:hasPriceSpecification [ a gr:CloudServicePriceSpecification ;
                                        gr:hasCurrency "USD" ;
                                        gr:hasCurrencyValue 0.13200195133686066 ;
```

[9] https://github.com/miranda-zhang/cloud-computing-schema/blob/master/example/azure/storage.md#disk-snapshots.

```
                                    gr:hasUnitOfMeasurement cocoon:GBPerMonth ;
                                    cocoon:inRegion <Region/Azure/australia-east>
                                  ] ;
      cocoon:canHaveSnapshot <NetworkStorage/Azure/standardssd-snapshot> , <NetworkStorage/
          ↪ Azure/standardhdd-snapshot-zrs> , <NetworkStorage/Azure/premiumssd-snapshot>
          ↪ , </NetworkStorage/Azure/standardhdd-snapshot-lrs> ;
      cocoon:hasProvider cocoon:Azure ;
      cocoon:hasStorageIOMax [ a schema:TypeAndQuantityNode ;
                               schema:amountOfThisGood "5000"^^xsd:nonNegativeInteger ;
                               schema:unitCode cocoon:IOPs
                                 ] ;
      cocoon:hasStorageSize [ a schema:TypeAndQuantityNode ;
                               schema:amountOfThisGood "1024"^^xsd:nonNegativeInteger ;
                               schema:unitCode cocoon:GB
                                 ] ;
      cocoon:hasStorageThroughputMax [ a schema:TypeAndQuantityNode ;
                               schema:amountOfThisGood "200"^^xsd:nonNegativeInteger ;
                               schema:unitCode unit:MegabitsPerSecond
                                 ].

<2019-03-07/NetworkStorage/Azure/ultrassd>
      a cocoon:NetworkStorage ;
      rdfs:label "ultrassd" ;
      gr:hasPriceSpecification [ a gr:CloudServicePriceSpecification ;
                             rdfs:label "vcpu" ;
                             gr:hasCurrency "USD" ;
                             gr:hasCurrencyValue 0.003 ;
                             gr:hasUnitOfMeasurement cocoon:VcpuPerHour ;
                             cocoon:inRegion <Region/Azure/us-east-2>
                           ] ;
      gr:hasPriceSpecification [ a gr:CloudServicePriceSpecification ;
                             rdfs:label "throughput" ;
                             gr:hasCurrency "USD" ;
                             gr:hasCurrencyValue 0.000685 ;
                             gr:hasUnitOfMeasurement cocoon:MegabitsPerSecondPerHour ;
                             cocoon:inRegion <Region/Azure/us-east-2>
                           ] ;
      gr:hasPriceSpecification [ a gr:CloudServicePriceSpecification ;
                             rdfs:label "stored" ;
                             gr:hasCurrency "USD" ;
                             gr:hasCurrencyValue 0.000082 ;
                             gr:hasUnitOfMeasurement cocoon:GBPerHour ;
                             cocoon:inRegion <Region/Azure/us-east-2>
                           ] ;
      gr:hasPriceSpecification [ a gr:CloudServicePriceSpecification ;
                             rdfs:label "iops" ;
                             gr:hasCurrency "USD" ;
                             gr:hasCurrencyValue 0.000034 ;
                             gr:hasUnitOfMeasurement cocoon:IOPsPerHour ;
                             cocoon:inRegion <Region/Azure/us-east-2>
                           ] .
```

3.3.3 Network Service

We classify network services into the following categories: cocoon:InternetService, cocoon:LoadBalancing, cocoon:StaticIPService and cocoon:DNSService.

Internet Service. There is generally no charge to ingress cocoon:InternetService, unless there is a load balancer used. We use the cocoon:hasDirection object property to indicate the direction of traffic. A class cocoon:TrafficDirection is also defined with two disjoint subclasses, cocoon:Egress and cocoon:Ingress. Those can be used to indicate the direction of traffic.

Internet egress rates are based on usage and destination. For example, Google Cloud has three destination categories[10]: Australia, China (excluding Hong Kong) and Worldwide (excluding China and Australia, but including Hong Kong). In this case, the object properties cocoon:hasDestination and cocoon:excludesDestination can be used to specify destination ranges. Because traffic destinations are not constrained by Cloud service regions, cocoon:Location is used, which has more explanations in Sect. 3.6.

The internet egress traffic rates can be modelled by cocoon:CloudNetworkPriceSpecification. For more details, see Sect. 3.4.4.[11]

Load Balancing. Both hardware and software-based load balancing solutions exist. Here we consider load balancing as a hardware feature unless it is known otherwise. We create a class cocoon:LoadBalancing to represent such a service. It is further broken down into two subclasses: cocoon:LoadBalancingData and cocoon:ForwardingRule.

Ingress data processed by a load balancer is charged (per GB) based on its region. Listing 1.3 models such cases with cocoon:LoadBalancingData.

Listing 1.3. Load Balancing Data Price Specification

```
@base <<https://w3id.org/cocoon/data/v1.0.1/2019-02-12/>> .
<LoadBalancingData/Gcloud>
      a cocoon:LoadBalancingData ;
      gr:hasPriceSpecification [ a gr:CloudServicePriceSpecification ;
                                 gr:hasCurrency "USD" ;
                                 gr:hasCurrencyValue 0.008 ;
                                 gr:hasUnitOfMeasurement cocoon:GB ;
                                 cocoon:inRegion <Region/Gcloud/us>
                               ] ;
      cocoon:hasDirection cocoon:Ingress ;
      cocoon:hasProvider cocoon:Gcloud ;
      schema:dateModified "2019-02-12"^^xsd:date .
```

Forwarding rules that are created for load balancing are also charged on an hourly base, regardless of how many forwards. This can be modelled by cocoon:ForwardingRule and cocoon:CloudNetworkPriceSpecification.[12]

Static IP Address. The IP address of a VM instance usually is not guaranteed to stay the same between reboots/resets. So you may want to reserve a static external IP address for your customers or users to have reliable access. It can be modelled with cocoon:StaticIPService and cocoon:CloudServicePriceSpecification.

3.4 Cloud Service Price

For price modelling, we extend the GoodRelations vocabulary [7]. GoodRelations is a Web Ontology Language-compliant ontology for Semantic Web online

[10] Effective until end of June 2019, when this paper has been submitted, after that new pricing takes effect based on not only the destination but also the sources.

[11] https://github.com/miranda-zhang/cloud-computing-schema/blob/master/example/quickstart.md#internet-service.

[12] https://github.com/miranda-zhang/cloud-computing-schema/blob/master/example/quickstart.md#forwarding-rule.

data, dealing with business-related goods and services. In November 2012, it was integrated into the schema.org ontology.

3.4.1 Cloud Service Price Specification

We define cocoon:CloudServicePriceSpecification as a subclass of gr:UnitPrice Specification. As one service can be offered in multiple regions, we extend our specialized class with: cocoon:inRegion some cocoon:Region. For more details on region, see Sect. 3.6.

In GoodRelations, there is a gr:hasCurrencyValue property taking a xsd:float as range. However, floats can introduce cumulative rounding errors. So we extend the existing class to allow xsd:decimal, which can represent exact monetary values: cocoon:hasCurrencyValue exactly 1 xsd:decimal.[13] For more usages, see Sect. 3.3.1.

We also define specialized subclasses to handle the following scenarios: price of a VM image (cocoon:CloudOSPriceSpecification), price of storage transactions (cocoon:CloudStorageTransactionsPriceSpecification), and price of network services (cocoon:CloudNetworkPriceSpecification). These sub-classes are owl:disjointWith each other. Because each case has very different requirements, it is clearer to model them with different subclasses rather than define all properties in the base class cocoon:CloudServicePriceSpecification.

3.4.2 Price of Virtual Machine Images

Under the class cocoon:CloudOSPriceSpecification, the data property cocoon:chargedPerCore specifies if the price is charged per core. For instance, Windows Server images on some machine types from Google Cloud are charged based on the number of CPUs available, i.e., n1-standard-4, n1-highcpu-4, and n1-highmem-4 are machine-types with four vCPUs, and are charged at \$0.16 USD/h (4 × \$0.04 USD/h).

The data property cocoon:forCoresMoreThan is used to describe a price for machines with more than the specified number of cores. Similarly, cocoon:forCoresLessEqual is used to describe a price for machines with less than or equal to the specified number of cores. They can be used together to quantify a range. Listing 1.4 presents an example for OS Price Specification.

Listing 1.4. OS Price Specification

```
@base <<https://w3id.org/cocoon/data/v1.0.1/2019-02-12/>> .
<SystemImage/Gcloud/suse-sap>
        a cocoon:SystemImage ;
        rdfs:label "suse-sap" ;
        gr:hasPriceSpecification [ a cocoon:CloudOSPriceSpecification ;
                                   gr:hasCurrency "USD" ;
                                   gr:hasCurrencyValue 0.41 ;
                                   cocoon:chargedPerCore false ;
                                   cocoon:forCoresMoreThan "4"^^xsd:decimal
                                 ] ;
```

[13] https://github.com/miranda-zhang/cloud-computing-schema/blob/master/example/quickstart.md#cloud-service-price-specification.

```
gr:hasPriceSpecification [ a cocoon:CloudOSPriceSpecification ;
                           gr:hasCurrency "USD" ;
                           gr:hasCurrencyValue 0.34 ;
                           cocoon:chargedPerCore false ;
                           cocoon:forCoresLessEqual "4"^^xsd:decimal ;
                           cocoon:forCoresMoreThan "2"^^xsd:decimal
                         ] ;
gr:hasPriceSpecification [ a cocoon:CloudOSPriceSpecification ;
                           gr:hasCurrency "USD" ;
                           gr:hasCurrencyValue 0.17 ;
                           cocoon:chargedPerCore false ;
                           cocoon:forCoresLessEqual "2"^^xsd:decimal
                         ] .
```

3.4.3 Price of Storage Transactions

For storage transactions, we use the class cocoon:CloudStorageTransactionsPrice Specification to define the price. There are different prices in different regions, but there is a common transaction price specification for a group of cloud storage offers.[14]

3.4.4 Price of Network Services

cocoon:CloudNetworkPriceSpecification can be used to model network services prices, including internet egress traffic and load balancing forwarding rules.

For instance, there are three (monthly) usage tiers for Google Internet egress traffic price: 0–1 TB, 1–10 TB and 10+ TB. Properties cocoon:forUsageLessEqual and cocoon:forUsageMoreThan can be used to specify the upper/lower usage limits. We combine this with schema:TypeAndQuantityNode to define the values with their units.

There are also some special rates, e.g., for Google Cloud Internet Traffic: Egress between zones in the same region (per GB) is 0.01; egress between regions within the US (per GB) is 0.01; egress to Google products (such as YouTube, Maps, and Drive), whether from a VM in GCP with an external or internal IP address is no charge. The property cocoon:specialRateType can be used to model those situations. See an online example for price of Google internet egress between zones in the same region.[15]

3.5 Cloud Service Performance

We use terms from a number of ontologies when modeling QoS, such as SSN [6] and SOSA [8]. The Semantic Sensor Network (SSN) ontology is an ontology for describing sensors and their observations, involved procedures, studied features of interest, samples, and observed properties, as well as actuators. SSN includes a lightweight but self-contained core ontology called SOSA (Sensor, Observation, Sample, and Actuator) for its elementary classes and properties. "SSN System"

[14] https://github.com/miranda-zhang/cloud-computing-schema/blob/master/example/quickstart.md#cloud-storage-transactions-price-specification.

[15] https://github.com/miranda-zhang/cloud-computing-schema/blob/master/example/quickstart.md#cloud-network-price-specification.

contains the terms defined for system capabilities, operating ranges, and survival ranges.

3.5.1 Quality of Service Property

QoS parameters are grouped under cocoon:QualityOfService. We define cocoon:QualityOfService to be an equivalent class of ssn-system:SystemProperty. Then we extend it with the subclass cocoon:DataTransferSpeed.

Data Transfer Speed. cocoon:DataTransferSpeed is measured multiple times with different file sizes, for both the uplink and downlink, which are represented by subclasses cocoon:DownlinkSpeed and cocoon:UplinkSpeed. See an example online.[16]

Latency. There is an existing ssn-system:Latency class, which we can use. We extend this class with a specialized subclass cocoon:DNSQueryLatency, which is the latency for completing the DNS query. The term latency is most commonly referred to as the round-trip delay time, which is the one-way latency for the request to travel from a source to a destination plus the one-way latency for the response to travel back.

3.5.2 Measurement

QoS measurements are modeled with cocoon:Measurement, which is an equivalent class to sosa:Observation. The cocoon:Measurement can use sosa:hasFeatureOfInterest to specify which feature it measures. Since cocoon:Service is equivalent to sosa:FeatureOfInterest, all its subclasses can be used to describe features, and we have some examples can be viewed online.[17]

3.5.3 Device

We extend sosa:Sensor with a subclass cocoon:Device to describe computers used to measure QoS. Listing 1.5 shows an example for device.

Listing 1.5. Device

```
@base <<https://w3id.org/cocoon/data/v1.0.1/>> .
<Device/150.203.213.249/lat=-35.271475/long=149.121434>
        a cocoon:Device ;
        rdfs:comment "The computer used to conduct the tests, belongs to Australian National
             ↪ University College of Engineering & Computer Science."@en ;
        rdfs:label "CECS-030929"@en ;
        cocoon:inPhysicalLocation [ a schema:Place ;
                                    schema:geo [ a schema:GeoCoordinates ;
                                                 schema:address "Hanna Neumann Building #145,
                                                      ↪ Science Road, Canberra ACT 2601" ;
                                                 schema:latitude -35.271475 ;
                                                 schema:longitude 149.121434
                                               ]
                                  ] ;
        cocoon:ipv4 "150.203.213.249" .
```

[16] https://github.com/miranda-zhang/cloud-computing-schema/blob/master/example/quickstart.md#downlink-speed.

[17] https://github.com/miranda-zhang/cloud-computing-schema/blob/master/example/quickstart.md#measurement.

3.6 Location and Region

cocoon:Location is a permissible class that can be used to represent any kind of location, i.e. Worldwide, Australia and Hong Kong. In comparison, cocoon:Region, the subclass of cocoon:Location, is more specialized to represent known/predefined cloud service regions. We link regions from each Cloud provider to GeoNames data[18], and at the same time make it compatible with schema.org. So we define it as the union of gn:Feature and schema:Place. If a specific location or address is known, a physical location can be set with cocoon:inPhysicalLocation. Otherwise, we only describe the approximate location with cocoon:inJurisdiction. Some regions can be in multiple jurisdictions, i.e. nam-eur-asia1 belongs to North America, Europe, and Asia. Usually, a region cannot be in more than one physical location. Each region can also specify which cocoon:continent it is in, which provider it belongs to (with cocoon:hasProvider), and a human readable name with rdfs:label. Currently, there is a simple script written for matching a region to a gn:Feature, but it can be further optimised in future work. We have also obtained some geographic coordinates from the QoS measurements, and modelled such information with schema:geo and schema:GeoCoordinates. Some examples for Location and Region are available online.[19]

3.7 Named Individuals

We define several useful named individuals to be included in this ontology.

Unit: We define cocoon:UnitOfMeasure as an owl:equivalentClass of qudt:Unit, and then use the instances from the unit vocabulary, i.e. unit:Hour and unit:MegabitsPerSecond. We also define a number of custom units with reference to qudt:InformationEntropyUnit and qudt:DataRateUnit, i.e., cocoon:GB, cocoon:GBPerHour, cocoon:GBPerMonth, cocoon:GCEU (which is the Google Compute Engine Unit), cocoon:IOPs, cocoon:IOPsPerHour, cocoon:Megabits PerSecondPerHour, cocoon:TB, and cocoon:VcpuPerHour.

Provider: We define providers as a gr:BusinessEntity, i.e. cocoon:Gcloud and cocoon:Azure.

Quantity and Type: We define some frequently used quantities as named individuals, using schema:TypeAndQuantityNode, i.e. cocoon:1TB. This will save us from redefining each value every time it is used. Since schema:unitCode can take schema:URL, it means we can pass in any external defined units, i.e. cocoon:UnitOfMeasure.

---

18 https://www.geonames.org/.

19 https://github.com/miranda-zhang/cloud-computing-schema/blob/master/example/quickstart.md#location-and-region.

4 Usage Cases

CoCoOn's intended usage is illustrated in Fig. 2. A possible visualisation of Azure's Compute service offers and regions is shown in Fig. 3, with offers in green and regions in purple. Regions with more offers have a bigger size.

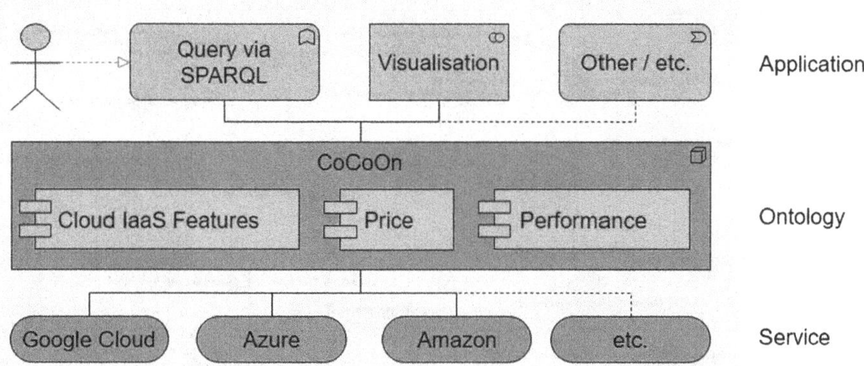

Fig. 2. CoCoOn data integration workflow

4.1 Mapping Service Info to Ontology

Data can be obtained from a provider's API, either in JSON or JS format. We first clean up/transform such data with jq. Next, we map the cleaned data to our ontology.[20] Additional information is added both in `jq` and SPARQL-Generate scripts. Listing 1.6 shows a jq script example which transforms json data from Google API. In this script, we add the number of cores obtained from the vendor's documentation.

Listing 1.6. Script in jq that transforms data from Google API

```
.gcp_price_list | . |=with_entries(select(.key| contains("VMIMAGE") )) |
[ to_entries[] |
    {
      "name": .key,
      "cores":(
        if (.key|contains("F1-MICRO")) then
          0.2
        elif (.key|contains("G1-SMALL")) then
          0.5
        else .value.cores end
      ),
      "memory": .value.memory,
      "gceu": (
        if .value.gceu == "Shared CPU, not guaranteed" then
          null
```

[20] The complete process with input and output for each step is documented online.

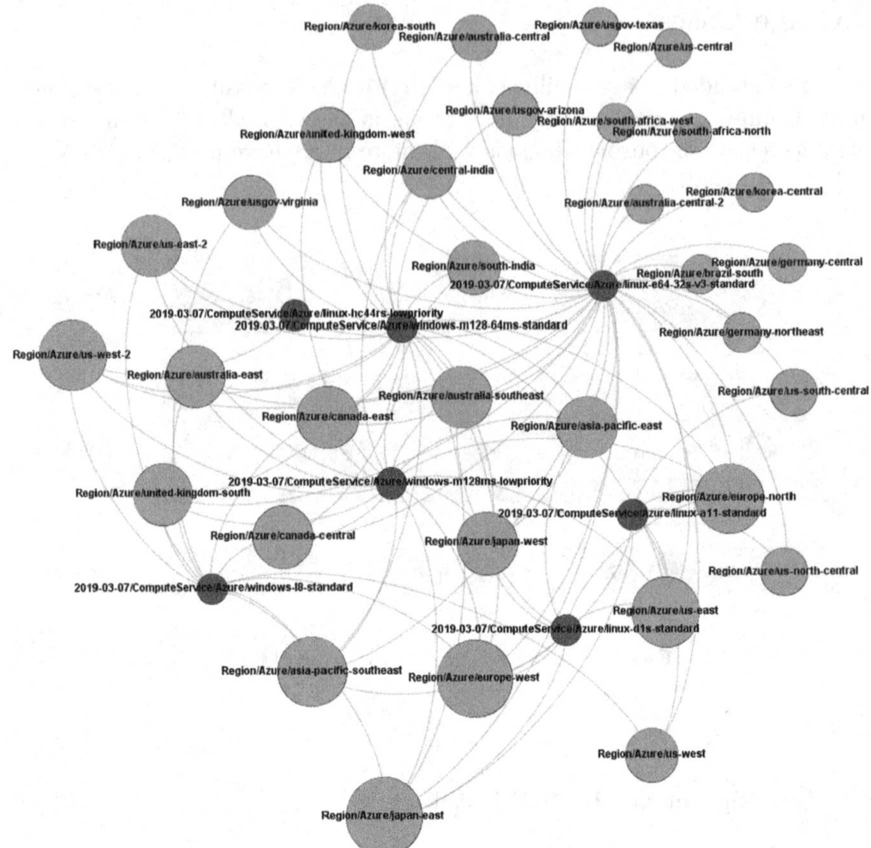

Fig. 3. Azure services regions (Color figure online)

```
        else .value.gceu end
     ),
     "maxNumberOfPd": .value.maxNumberOfPd,
     "maxPdSize": .value.maxPdSize,
     "price":
      [
        .value | del(
            .cores, .memory, .gceu,
            .fixed, .maxNumberOfPd, .maxPdSize, .ssd)
        | to_entries[] | { "region": .key, "price": .value }
      ]
  }
]
```

For converting data from various sources to semantic data, we used SPARQL-Generate [11,15] for defining the mappings. We developed many SPARQL-Generate scripts for this process. For example, a script can map json data from Azure API to CoCoOn v1.0.1, and produce annotated RDF data.

4.2 Gathering QoS Stats

We provided live demos of QoS tests, e.g. Downlink Speed and Latency tests for Google Cloud Services. Uplink tests scripts are written in Python as selenium is required. Additional details on using cloudharmony for measuring QoS are documented online.[21]

4.3 Result Datasets

We have also made the complete datasets (132,282 triples) available at https://w3id.org/cocoon/data. It is hosted with a Linked Data Fragments Server on the Google Cloud. This server can be slow to access as we only used an always free micro instance. It is recommended to download the data and investigate with a triplestore. For example, you can run a query as shown in Listing 1.7, and the results are shown in Table 1.

Table 1. Instance counts of the classes

Class	Count
cocoon:NetworkStorage	45
cocoon:ComputeService	1021
cocoon:Region	55
cocoon:StorageService	161
cocoon:Location	5
cocoon:InternetService	6
cocoon:SystemImage	10

Listing 1.7. A SPARQL query

```
PREFIX cocoon: <<https://w3id.org/cocoon/
    ↪ v1.0.1#>>
PREFIX gr: <<http://purl.org/
    ↪ goodrelations/v1#>>
SELECT ?cls (COUNT(?s) AS ?count)
{
    VALUES ?cls {cocoon:ComputeService
          ↪ cocoon:SystemImage cocoon:
          ↪ StorageService cocoon:
          ↪ NetworkStorage cocoon:
          ↪ NetworkService cocoon:
          ↪ InternetService cocoon:
          ↪ Region cocoon:Location gr:
          ↪ BusinessEntity
    } ?s a ?cls
} GROUP BY ?cls
```

5 Conclusion

This work presents CoCoOn v1.0.1, which captures Cloud service characteristics, including the price and QoS of public cloud service offers. We also presented several semantic datasets developed using this ontology and a range of solutions for different use-case scenarios of our ontology and datasets.

For future work, several possible extensions can be made: More providers should be included to verify the completeness of our model further; Units can be improved with Custom Datatypes (`cdt:ucum` [10]), so composite units do not need to be defined specifically, i.e. instead of cocoon:MegabitsPerSecondPerHour, something like "MB/s/h" could be used; Improve mapping regions to Geonames dataset; and modelling various discounts.

[21] https://github.com/miranda-zhang/cloud-computing-schema/tree/master/example/cloudharmony.

References

1. Boukadi, K., Rekik, M., Ben-Abdallah, H., Gaaloul, W.: Cloud service description ontology: construction, evaluation and interrogation. In: Cloud Service Description Ontology: Construction, Evaluation and Interrogation (2016)
2. Dobson, G., Lock, R., Sommerville, I.: QoSOnt: a QoS ontology for service-centric systems. In: SEAA, pp. 80–87 (2005)
3. Gruber, T.R.: Toward principles for the design of ontologies used for knowledge sharing. Int. J. Hum.-Comput. Stud. **43**(5–6), 907–928 (1995)
4. Guha, R.V., Brickley, D., MacBeth, S.: Schema.org: evolution of structured data on the web. Queue **13**(9), 10:10–10:37 (2015)
5. Haller, A., Cimpian, E., Mocan, A., Oren, E., Bussler, C.: WSMX - a semantic service-oriented architecture. In: ICWS, pp. 321–328 (2005)
6. Haller, A., et al.: The modular SSN ontology: a joint W3C and OGC standard specifying the semantics of sensors, observations, sampling, and actuation. Semant. Web **10**(1), 9–32 (2019)
7. Hepp, M.: GoodRelations: an ontology for describing products and services offers on the web. In: Gangemi, A., Euzenat, J. (eds.) EKAW 2008. LNCS (LNAI), vol. 5268, pp. 329–346. Springer, Heidelberg (2008). https://doi.org/10.1007/978-3-540-87696-0_29
8. Janowicz, K., Haller, A., Cox, S.J., Phuoc, D.L., Lefrançois, M.: SOSA: a lightweight ontology for sensors, observations, samples, and actuators. J. Web Semant. **56**, 1–10 (2019)
9. Joshi, K.P., Yesha, Y., Finin, T.W.: Automating cloud services life cycle through semantic technologies. IEEE Trans. Serv. Comput. **7**, 109–122 (2014)
10. Lefrançois, M., Zimmermann, A.: The unified code for units of measure in RDF: `cdt:ucum` and other UCUM datatypes. In: Gangemi, A., et al. (eds.) ESWC 2018. LNCS, vol. 11155, pp. 196–201. Springer, Cham (2018). https://doi.org/10.1007/978-3-319-98192-5_37
11. Lefrançois, M., Zimmermann, A., Bakerally, N.: A SPARQL extension for generating rdf from heterogeneous formats. In: Blomqvist, E., Maynard, D., Gangemi, A., Hoekstra, R., Hitzler, P., Hartig, O. (eds.) ESWC 2017. LNCS, vol. 10249, pp. 35–50. Springer, Cham (2017). https://doi.org/10.1007/978-3-319-58068-5_3
12. Martin, D.L., et al.: Bringing semantics to web services with OWL-S. World Wide Web **10**(3), 243–277 (2007)
13. Moscato, F., Aversa, R., Martino, B.D., Fortis, T.F., Munteanu, V.I.: An analysis of mOSAIC ontology for cloud resources annotation. In: FedCSIS, pp. 973–980 (2011)
14. Roman, D., et al.: Web service modeling ontology. Appl. Ontol. **1**(1), 77–106 (2005)
15. SPARQL-generate. http://w3id.org/sparql-generate/
16. Wikidata. https://www.wikidata.org/wiki/Wikidata:WikiProject_Ontology
17. Zhang, M., Ranjan, R., Georgakopoulos, D., Strazdins, P., Khan, S.U., Haller, A.: Investigating techniques for automating the selection of cloud infrastructure services. Int. J. Next-Gener. Comput. **4**(3), 1–18 (2013)
18. Zhang, M., Ranjan, R., Haller, A., Georgakopoulos, D., Menzel, M., Nepal, S.: An ontology-based system for cloud infrastructure services' discovery. In: CollaborateCom (2012)

19. Zhang, M., Ranjan, R., Nepal, S., Menzel, M., Haller, A.: A declarative recommender system for cloud infrastructure services selection. In: Vanmechelen, K., Altmann, J., Rana, O.F. (eds.) GECON 2012. LNCS, vol. 7714, pp. 102–113. Springer, Heidelberg (2012). https://doi.org/10.1007/978-3-642-35194-5_8
20. Zhang, Y., Teng, J., He, H., Wang, Z.: On P2P-based semantic service discovery with QoS measurements for pervasive services in the universal network. J. Comput. **9**, 1915 (2014)

In-Use Track

Semantically-Enabled Optimization of Digital Marketing Campaigns

Vincenzo Cutrona[1], Flavio De Paoli[1], Aljaž Košmerlj[2], Nikolay Nikolov[3], Matteo Palmonari[1(✉)], Fernando Perales[4], and Dumitru Roman[3(✉)]

[1] University of Milan-Bicocca, Milano, Italy
{cutrona,depaoli,palmonari}@disco.unimib.it
[2] JSI, Ljubljana, Slovenia
aljaz.kosmerlj@ijs.si
[3] SINTEF AS, Oslo, Norway
{nikolay.nikolov,dumitru.roman}@sintef.no
[4] JOT Internet Media, Madrid, Spain
fernando.perales@jot-im.com

Abstract. Digital marketing is a domain where data analytics are a key factor to gaining competitive advantage and return of investment for companies running and monetizing digital marketing campaigns on, e.g., search engines and social media. In this paper, we propose an end-to-end approach to enrich marketing campaigns performance data with third-party event data (e.g., weather events data) and to analyze the enriched data in order to predict the effect of such events on campaigns' performance, with the final goal of enabling advanced optimization of the impact of digital marketing campaigns. The use of semantic technologies is central to the proposed approach: event data are made available in a format more amenable to enrichment and analytics, and the actual data enrichment technique is based on semantic data reconciliation. The enriched data are represented as Linked Data and managed in a NoSQL database to enable processing of large amounts of data. We report on the development of a pilot to build a weather-aware digital marketing campaign scheduler for JOT Internet Media—a world leading company in the digital marketing domain that has amassed a huge amount of data on campaigns performance over the years—which predicts the best date and region to launch a marketing campaign within a seven-day timespan. Additionally, we discuss benefits and limitations of applying semantic technologies to deliver better optimization strategies and competitive advantage.

Keywords: Semantic enrichment · Big data analytics · Digital marketing · Data linking · Data reconciliation

The work in this paper is partly funded by the EC H2020 projects EW-Shopp (732590) and euBusinessGraph (732003). Authors are listed in alphabetical order.

C. Ghidini et al. (Eds.): ISWC 2019, LNCS 11779, pp. 345–362, 2019.
https://doi.org/10.1007/978-3-030-30796-7_22

1 Introduction

Digital Marketing is a growing industry[1] where the engagement strategy has evolved from non-personalized to highly personalized user targeting, with the aim of reaching the target users with relevant content and promoting user actions (clicks, sales, leads, etc.) on service delivery platforms. In this strategy shift, marketing agencies and marketing departments of large companies need to collect and process large amounts of marketing-related data, and implement new management strategies to optimize the use of marketing budgets in the most profitable campaigns. This requires technical knowledge for managing data for service delivery (e.g., campaigns optimization, programmatic buying, content generation and delivery, organic positioning) and analytical skills to process the existing raw data, analyse actions performance, and generate insights motivating future marketing strategies. Such knowledge and skills are often not available to digital marketing agencies, especially small and medium in size.

In this paper we report on a pilot implementation that uses cutting-edge data semantics and analytics technologies in the context of the rather technology-conservative digital marketing domain. The pilot was facilitated by JOT Internet Media[2] – a Spanish SME operating in the digital marketing domain. JOT is specialized in Web traffic generation by means of investing in sponsored ads in the main search and display platforms (e.g., Google, Bing, Facebook). The massive implementation of its digital marketing campaigns enables daily collection of huge amounts of data related to campaigns' performance. Performance indicators (clicks, impressions, CTR, location, date, time, identifiers, keywords, device, ad platform, etc.) are collected and analyzed daily. Currently, this activity is based on account managers' experience to optimize both the campaign management and bidding strategy to engage the audience and generate actions in service delivery platforms' landing pages, which generates JOT's revenue streams. JOT aims to create a new data-driven campaign management service based on the integration and enrichment of its performance datasets with weather forecasts to predict campaign impact and optimize the budget distribution in marketing campaigns.

Semantic technologies (for enriching the data) and machine learning (for analytics of the enriched data) were identified as promising technologies by JOT to support the creation of its new data monetization service. Together with R&D and technology providers, JOT created a pilot to assess benefits and limitations of semantic technologies and machine learning. In this paper we present and discuss experiences in the design and implementation of this pilot. Contributions of this paper include the definition of a pilot for the use of semantic technologies in the digital marketing domain, a generic approach for marketing campaigns performance data enrichment and analytics, as well as an implementation of the approach using cutting-edge tools, together with experimental insights.

[1] Revenue in the Digital Advertising market amounts to US $63,469m in 2019, according to https://www.statista.com/outlook/216/100/digital-advertising/worldwide.

[2] https://www.jot-im.com.

The rest of this paper is organized as follows. Section 2 provides the necessary background for the developed pilot. Section 3 presents the pilot together with its requirements. Section 4 outlines the developed approach for semantic enrichment and data analytics and reports on experimental insights. Section 5 presents related work and discusses the advantages and limitations of the used technologies and the overall approach. Finally, Sect. 6 summarizes the paper and outlines avenues for potential future work.

2 Background and Motivation

JOT's digital marketing focus is on advertising platforms such as Google Ads[3], where advertisements are placed using Real-time Bidding (RTB). As background for understanding the developed pilot, we give a brief overview of how digital marketing campaigns are executed on such platforms and discuss the opportunities and motivation for semantic data enrichment and analytics in this context.

Upon a user search, platforms such as Google Ads run a bid, where different marketing campaigns compete to display an ad (e.g., an ad linking to a landing Web page). A digital marketing campaign defines, in principle, a set of keywords and for each keyword the maximum cost per click (MaxCPC) paid in a bid for that keyword. The term *impressions* for a keyword refers to the number of times some ad has been displayed on the sponsored ads space in Google Search when users search for that keyword and a campaign wins a bid on that keyword. Therefore, a keyword can generate (and be associated with) impressions only if at least one digital marketing campaign is active for that keyword, and someone searches for that keyword. The number of impressions is considered a key performance indicator (the higher the better), hence a primary goal for a campaign is maximizing the amount of impressions. In this way, the advertised landing page has potentially more visitors and opportunities to increase its brand awareness and sales, which is the ultimate goal of a campaign. For each day, impressions can be counted and visualized to let strategy experts evaluate the performance and define the strategy for the next campaigns.

Performance indicators are influenced by a variety of factors, some related to the marketing domain and campaign implementation (e.g., maximum bid, number of competitors and degree of matching between the landing page and user search), and some related to external factors which are out of control by the companies running the campaign. For example, JOT found evidence that weather events can affect the performance of campaigns in a sensible way. Exploratory analyses found examples where the number of impressions of some specific keywords or keyword categories showed abnormal increase due to the weather. For example, analyzing data from February 2016 revealed that depending on the day and the rain forecast, population in the Madrid region had more interest in "burger at home" or in keywords related to the "DiningNightLife" category. This effect can be replicated to other less obvious keywords, making it extremely

[3] https://adwords.google.com.

useful for marketers and accounts to adjust campaign launch and bidding strategy so they can optimize budget consumption and increase their impact in terms of impressions and ad clicks.

The enrichment of digital marketing campaigns with third-party event-related data and their subsequent analysis can provide several benefits to companies running such campaigns:

Advanced data insights: (i) correlation between marketing performance indicators and external variables such as temperature, probability of rain, light hours; (ii) identification of new trends and patterns; (iii) information useful for bid adjustment for the affected keywords.

New services for campaign scheduling: (i) define campaign launch scheduling according to the influence of external factors to optimize the impact; (ii) consultancy services, such as the identification of key keywords enabling higher impact depending on external factors; (iii) evaluation of impact depending on campaign properties (country, topic, and timing).

3 Pilot: The Weather-Aware Campaign Scheduling Service

The developed pilot – a weather-based campaign scheduling service – was motivated by marketing experts observations about the weather-sensitiveness of certain keywords. This triggered the need for a systematic approach to detect dependencies between weather variables and ads impressions for certain keywords. The assumption was that if a keyword depends on a set of weather variables, then a predictive model to estimate the number of impressions (or at least peaks in impressions) can be defined. Using such a model, a new service can be devised to collect weather forecasts for the geographical regions involved in a given campaign for seven days and to estimate the best date to launch the campaign in each region in that time frame. The service is meant to be used by campaign managers at JOT to schedule marketing campaigns.

The data processing workflow designed as part of this service is depicted in Fig. 1 and explained as follows.

Performance data time-series collection. Time series about campaign performance are collected as historical data aggregated by location (to support weather forecasts) for a period of time long enough to train a predictive model; an example is the top-left-hand table in Fig. 1 ($\#im$ stands for number of impressions).

Enrichment of campaign performance data. Performance data time-series are enriched with weather variables relevant to train predictive models; an example of enriched table is the top-right-hand one in Fig. 1 ($^{\circ}C$ represents temperature in Celsius; mm precipitation in millimeters; and $x/{+y}$ forecasts for the day x plus y days).

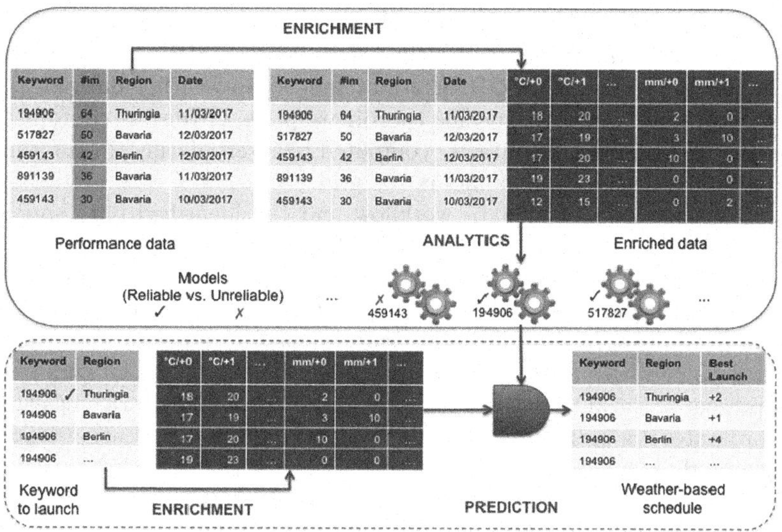

Fig. 1. Data processing for weather-based campaign scheduling.

Analysis of enriched data. Enriched performance time series are used to build predictive models that, based on location and a 7-day weather forecast, can estimate the number of expected daily impressions; notice that the model may not be developed for each keyword, e.g., when accuracy of prediction is too low to provide a reliable model.

Run-time execution of predictive models. When we want to activate a campaign for a keyword and a model exist, that model can be applied using weather forecasts to return a weather-based schedule to campaign managers (as shown in the dashed line box at the bottom of Fig. 1).

Two main **data sources** were identified as relevant for the pilot, as follows. *Marketing Campaign Statistics from JOT.* For the pilot, we consider campaigns run in Germany and Spain for a total of ~22 million keywords, which are associated with (all) Google categories and span over 2016 and 2017. Row data are associated with spatial references based on Google GeoTargets (*location identifiers used by Google*), at city and region level. Data were provisioned in CSV format (~100 GB and ~500M rows). The dataset includes 21 columns that cover: keyword ids (unique identifiers of the keywords in Google), keywords (the keyword tokens), several variables describing *matches* for the ads, i.e., indicators of their performance (e.g., clicks, impressions, ad position) measured in a specific location (a city and its region), specification of campaign data, (country, language, category, listing and match type), and a category associated with the keyword (first level category in the Google taxonomy).

Weather Forecast Data from ECMWF. Data provided via APIs by the European Centre for Medium-Range Weather Forecasts (ECMWF)[4], amounting to 85PB in GRIB[5] format. The GRIB format represents weather data on a grid, where intersection points are specific coordinate pairs. Given the coordinates of a city, the city-level weather data are computed by interpolating the information available for the nearest four points in the grid.

Based on the envisioned data workflow and the identified data sources, a number of **challenges** were identified, as follows.

Data Enrichment. Weather forecast data are in GRIB format, which is very space-efficient, but not time-efficient to support queries due to its binary nature (Fig. 1 reports weather data in an intuitive format to simplify the example). Weather data can be queried using coordinates (longitude and latitude), which are not present in the JOT dataset or in Google location data. Enriching each row with coordinates is a prerequisite to fetch weather data, hence location toponyms in Google need to be reconciled with a geospatial knowledge base where locations have such coordinates in their descriptions. Moreover, data managers at JOT are used to work with tabular data and prefer to design these transformations (reconciliation and extension) leveraging a tabular view over their data.

Data Analytics. Performance data provide signals that are often scattered (because a keyword may be active for a limited number of weeks or days), weak (because of few impressions) and noisy (because of other parameters may affect the campaign performance, e.g., competing bids over a time span). Thus, building models that are accurate-enough to be exploited in a production service is difficult and not possible for a large number of keywords.

Scalability. The size of the datasets is a challenge, even the analysis of campaigns for a single country requires managing roughly ∼1TB of data. JOT runs campaigns targeted to more than 70 countries worldwide, hence the size of the data in the scope of the analysis may become huge, which means that enrichment should be based on flexible technologies to cover more countries upon request (e.g., minimal changes on the schema of the data should be required when adding countries, and coordinates should be fetched only for the new locations). Therefore, simplifying and making the enrichment tasks more scalable is a key requirement to support the analysis of campaign performance data at full scale.

4 Approach for Semantic Enrichment and Analytics

In order to address the main challenges identified above, we devised an approach guided by the following principles.

UI-based design of data transformations. Data transformations should be designed using a UI that supports users in establishing how to transform the

[4] Meteorological Archival and Retrieval System. https://software.ecmwf.int/wiki/display/UDOC/MARS+user+documentation.

[5] General Regularly-distributed Information in Binary form. http://www.wmo.int/pages/prog/www/DPS/FM92-GRIB2-11-2003.pdf.

original data (i.e., tables of data they are familiar with), and in displaying the results in an understandable way (i.e., readable by non-experts in semantics). Moreover, since datasets can be huge, we need to adopt a strategy of working on samples to manage Big Data.

Batch execution of data transformations. The transformations resulting from the UI-based design will be applied to the whole dataset using a scalable platform in batch mode.

Transparent use of semantic technologies. Data enrichment can be broken down into two tasks: *data reconciliation*, where identifiers in the source data are reconciled against a *knowledge base* (KB), and *data extension*, where the identifiers in the KB are used to fetch additional data from third-party sources. Semantics, KBs and Linked Data, are used to support these tasks in a way that is as much as possible transparent to generic users.

Replicability and adaptation of transformations. The transformations resulting from the UI-based design should be repeatable to new datasets that hold the same structure and content (e.g., performance of the campaign in the same country for a different time period), and adaptable (e.g., performance of a campaign with different countries, which may require just an adaptation of the configuration for the reconciliation transformation).

Following these principles our approach is composed of the following steps.

UI-Based Data Transformation Design. The user uploads a data sample and designs transformations to clean the data (e.g., date formatting) after which she enriches them with third-party data. Working on a sample, the user can immediately view the effect of the transformations to tune them.

Knowledge bases (KBs) are used to bridge across different systems of identifiers used in the corporate and in the third-party data sources. An example is GeoNames, which provides a convenient reference KB in our case due to complete coverage, multilingualism and information quality. However, other cross-domain KBs such as WikiData and DBpedia may be useful to access other kinds of information associated with locations.

The user reconciles the values, e.g., spatial references, against shared KBs by using *reconciliation services* for these KBs from the UI. By using a reconciliation service on the sample data the user configures the reconciliation service in such a way that it can be applied later on top of the unseen data processed in batch mode. An example of this configuration is setting a similarity threshold for the algorithm after having explored its impact on the data. Once values are reconciled on the sample data, the user can use a *data extension service* provided by a third-party source, e.g., GeoNames or a weather API, to specify the values to add to each row. This specification includes setting the join conditions on single or multiple values in a row from a widget. For example, given the GeoNames identifier of a location, longitude and latitude can be fetched from GeoNames; given longitude, latitude and a date, weather variables can be fetched from a weather data source. Similarly, if the user needs to normalize impressions by the population density of the region where they have been measured, the population can be fetched form GeoNames, while area can be fetched from Wikidata after

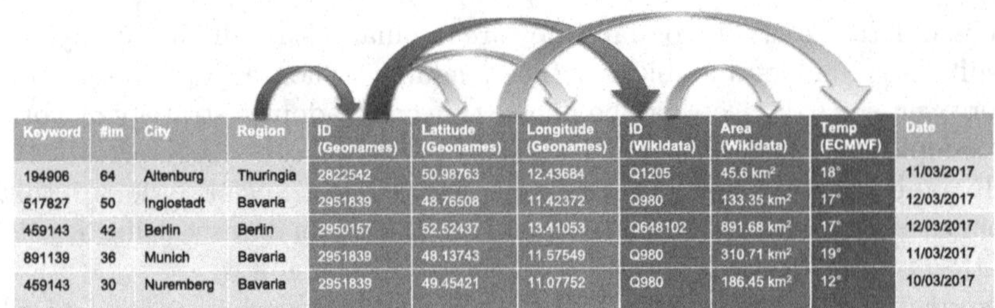

Keyword	#im	City	Region	ID (Geonames)	Latitude (Geonames)	Longitude (Geonames)	ID (Wikidata)	Area (Wikidata)	Temp (ECMWF)	Date
194906	64	Altenburg	Thuringia	2822542	50.98763	12.43684	Q1205	45.6 km²	18°	11/03/2017
517827	50	Inglostadt	Bavaria	2951839	48.76508	11.42372	Q980	133.35 km²	17°	12/03/2017
459143	42	Berlin	Berlin	2950157	52.52437	13.41053	Q648102	891.68 km²	17°	12/03/2017
891139	36	Munich	Bavaria	2951839	48.13743	11.57549	Q980	310.71 km²	19°	11/03/2017
459143	30	Nuremberg	Bavaria	2951839	49.45421	11.07752	Q980	186.45 km²	12°	10/03/2017

Fig. 2. An example of data enrichment.

reconciling the GeoNames identifiers to Wikidata identifiers (using *same-as* links if available, or full-fledged reconciliation). Multiple reconciliation and extension steps can be applied to the data, as depicted in Fig. 2.

Once the table has been extended, data can still be used in tabular format or *mapped to a graph schema*, e.g., an ontology, using schema-level enrichment services from the UI. During the enrichment process, algorithms similar to the ones developed for automatic *semantic table annotation* [10] support the user by providing suggestions on reconciliation and mapping to a schema. Data enrichment is in fact an interesting new application field for semantic table annotation approaches with human-in-the-loop. All the transformations designed by the user with the UI are transformed into code that can be executed in batch mode.

Data Enrichment: Batch Execution of Data Transformations on a Scalable Infrastructure. Data transformations are executed in batch mode in order to support the enrichment of data that are too big to be controlled interactively from a UI. For very large datasets, like JOT's data about campaign performance, using a single host is not sufficient. We employ a scalable infrastructure that can be operated on the cloud and scaled based on performance needs and available budget.

Analytics: Building the Models. Once data are enriched, a data analyst will define useful aggregation functions over the data and test training of different models using standard machine learning methodology. The level of aggregation is often defined by the data analyst also based on an evaluation of the accuracy of the predictions for different levels of aggregation (e.g., signals of impressions at the city level may turn to be too weak to be used, so that data need to be aggregated at the region level).

Preliminary Data Pre-processing to Meet Performance Constraints. While we could apply the above mentioned tool-supported approach to the input data, the large amount of data to be processed, the tight requirements on the reconciliation steps, and the scattered distribution of performance data required the following data processing steps before the design of the data transformation pipelines:

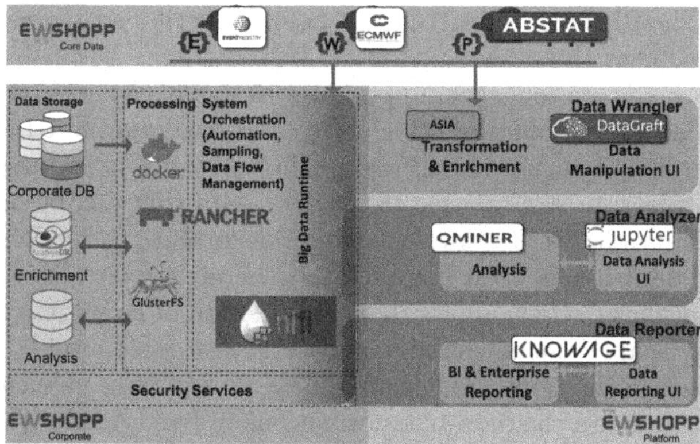

Fig. 3. EW-Shopp toolkit.

- Pre-processing of third-party data downloaded in advance (e.g., weather forecasts for a country considered in the analysis);
- Data linking between systems of identifiers used in the corporate data source (e.g., Google GeoTargets and GeoNames);
- Filtering of campaign performance data based on temporal continuity and signal strength; because signals provided by performance indicators may be too discontinuous or too weak to train a reliable model, performance data should be filtered by strength and continuity in order to analyze the performance of keywords where patterns are more likely to be found.

We built and extended a set of software components to implement the above described approach. The components are organized in a toolkit depicted in Fig. 3, referred to as the EW-Shopp toolkit, to support event-based data enrichment and analytics across a number of related business cases.

The toolkit consists of: *the data wrangler layer*, with **Grafterizer** and **ASIA**, two tightly integrated components for the design and execution of data cleaning and enrichment transformations in DataGraft [11]; *the data analyzer layer* with **QMiner**, one library for efficient data analytics, with a set of scripts to support weather and event-based analyses; *the reporting layer* with **Knowage**, a tool for data visualization whose use is not discussed in this paper. In addition, **APIs** are used to simplify the access to third-party data, including, e.g., the ECMWF weather data source, the Event Registry[6] (the usage of which is not discussed in this paper) and ABSTAT (a knowledge graph profiling tool that is used by ASIA). Grafterizer and ASIA are deployed on the cloud. Data transformations as well as Grafterizer and ASIA backends are enclosed into containers to be run on the company's private cloud infrastructure, where they can be executed using a distributed **Big Data infrastructure** that supports parallel execution. We briefly describe the main features of Grafterizer, ASIA, QMiner and the

[6] http://www.eventregistry.org.

deployment of the Big Data infrastructure, before describing the processing steps applied to implement the pilot.

Grafterizer [13] is a tool that supports the design of data transformations to clean and manipulate tabular data (including transformation to RDF) through a UI. In addition, it provides profiling and quality assessment features to support the process. Grafterizer can be used to produce data that can be onboarded on top of different databases. To develop data transformations for large-scale digital marketing data it has been modified to generate imports to ArangoDB, a multi-model database, which allows the manipulation of large data sources with its support for graph, document and key-value storage/querying capabilities. Grafterizer's transformations are encoded in Clojure scripts in such a way that its backend can execute the data transformations in batch mode. Data transformations can be saved and replicated on new data sources. The main challenge addressed to support transformations on large-scale data was the deployment of the transformations on a Big Data infrastructure that supports parallelization.

ASIA[7] (Assisted Semantic Interpretation and Annotation of tables) is a new tool to help users annotate and enrich a table using semantics in the process. ASIA supports schema-level annotations to map the table schema to existing vocabularies and ontologies by using vocabulary suggestions powered by the ABSTAT profiling tool [12], and instance-level annotations by using reconciliation services. Finally, it supports data extension services to enrich a table with third-party data sources. The ASIA front-end supports these features through a UI encapsulated in the Grafterizer tool. The transformations implicitly encoded into users' annotations can be also replicated and natively executed by ASIA's backend in batch mode on large datasets. To support enrichment of large scale data we addressed the challenge of making data reconciliation and extension services executable in a scalable and efficient manner on a parallel architecture deployed in the Cloud via containerization. The latter is a novel feature compared to existing tools that provide some support for enrichment-related tasks.

QMiner[8] [4] provides fast modeling and execution of analytics on large-scale data providing a large number of machine learning techniques. It is designed to efficiently process both structured and unstructured data, storing and indexing, in a way that makes machine learning algorithms scalable. The algorithms themselves are implemented in a C++ library, which is wrapped in a JavaScript API for ease of use and flexibility, making the deployment of the models in production environments simple without sacrificing performance.

The **Big Data infrastructure** for the scalable execution of data transformations – including semantic enrichment – on the cloud is designed to be deployable on heterogeneous infrastructures that may be managed by a platform user. It consists of a container system, a container orchestration system and a distributed file system. The container system (Docker) is used to encapsulate data workflow steps, which are used to pre-process, transform, semantically

[7] http://inside.disco.unimib.it/index.php/asia.
[8] http://qminer.ijs.si.

enrich, and onboard data. The container orchestration system (Rancher[9]) is used to manage and scale up the data workflows by enabling their deployment across a managed set of hosts provisioned for data workflow execution. The distributed file system (GlusterFS[10]) is the data communication medium through which data are passed between steps and is also used for storage of intermediate results during processing.

The above discussed toolkit has been applied to support the end-to-end data processing as following.

Data Enrichment. Data enrichment includes the following steps.
Data Ingestion. For the pilot, we chose the country of Germany and data about keyword activity during 2017 for four high-level categories: Business, Travel, Health, and Vehicles. Data are structured as described in Sect. 3. The dataset consists of a total of 15 million keywords with all of their matches during 2017 (matches make up most of the data). Data are uploaded to an FTP server (hosted on Amazon Cloud). Weather data are collected from ECMWF using a new weather API (the one depicted in Fig. 3), which was built to support time-efficient queries on the data, solving the problems caused by the space-efficient GRIB format used in the original APIs. Seven days weather forecasts as predicted daily along 2017 for the whole Germany are downloaded in advance. The data are also further processed to make enrichment more efficient at large scale, in particular, data are transformed into JSON using Grafterizer and uploaded to ArangoDB. This step implements pre-fetching of third-party data mentioned in Sect. 4 but also adds an additional processing step using a library that complements the new weather API. Weather forecasts are organized into documents where each document presents a weather forecast made at a given date (the one to be matched against the match date), a given region, and a given offset (e.g., $x/+y/+z$, where x represents the date, $+y$ represents the day offset, and $+z$ represents the hour offset). The region is specified by its GeoNames identifier, after interpolating the grid points in the raw data using region bounding boxes provided in GeoNames. This semantic-enriched graph-based representation of weather data supports more efficient enrichment in batch mode.
UI-Based Data Transformation Design. A sample is extracted from the ingested data and uploaded to Grafterizer. Data transformations are designed using the UI of Grafterizer and ASIA, the first one to clean the data and a reconciliation service of the second one to reconcile Google GeoTarget spatial identifiers against GeoNames. Thanks to the semantic-enriched graph-based representation of weather data the user does not need to add longitude and latitude to the data and can proceed to specify the desired weather variables and the columns used to join data using a weather extension widget in ASIA. For UI-based reconciliation and extension specification in ASIA we refer to online documentation[11].

[9] https://rancher.com.

[10] https://www.gluster.org.

[11] See video at https://youtu.be/4amLd4biYcs and the *Semantic Data Enrichment for Data Scientists* tutorial at https://ew-shopp.github.io/eswc2019-tutorial.

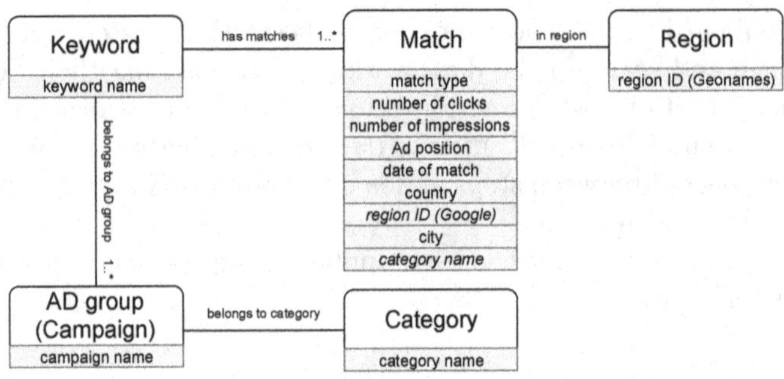

Fig. 4. The pilot data schema.

Data are then mapped to a graph model using Grafterizer's UI to support their transformation in JSON and upload into ArangoDB. In this process, identifiers are associated with performance statistics using triples consisting of the region, the date (of forecast) and the offset, similarly to the identifiers associated with weather documents. In this way it is possible to naturally join performance data and weather data upon upload in the database. The specification of the transformations is extracted as Clojure code. Although ASIA supports interactive reconciliation, in order to make the reconciliation process faster and more reliable we computed links between Google GeoTargets in Spain and Germany and GeoNames using the Silk data linking tool [9] and manually validated them. As a result, the resulting reconciliation service used a identifier-to-identifier dummy reconciliation system. Caching and other strategies are used in batch enrichment to speed up the process (a detailed explanation of these strategies is beyond the scope of this paper).

Batch Execution of Data Transformations on the Big Data Infrastructure. Clojure code and ASIA backend are packaged into containers and executed on the scalable Big Data infrastructure. Enriched performance data are uploaded to ArangoDB (according with a schema depicted in Fig. 4), where they are integrated with weather data through shared identifiers generated during the transformation to the graph model. From this step on, data are available to the data analyst. The graph database here reduces disk usage and the amount of data generated in the transformation by avoiding redundant information that would be contained into a big integrated table. Our implementation can be easily adapted to work only with tabular data, if a user prefers to use a redundant tabular data model instead of a graph database. We tested different configurations and evaluated their impact on the scalability of the solution.

Data Analytics. The goal of the analytics is to build a model that predicts keyword behaviour from weather data. If the model predicts a spike in the level of impressions of a keyword, that is a good time to run a campaign using that keyword.

For modelling, all impressions were aggregated at the region level. As mentioned before, useful keyword impression data is limited to times when the keyword was part of an active campaign. As the information on when the individual keywords are active was not available, this selection process had to be performed manually. As this limits the capacity of the analytics considerably, a better solution is considered as part of future work (see discussion in Sect. 5). The keywords were ranked by the overall volume of impressions and the ones with the highest volume were selected for analysis. The impressions were standardized by region to make them comparable. One region was excluded as the validation sample, the rest were split randomly into a training and test set (70%–30%). To simplify analysis we ignored all weather features with zero variance. In the pilot we applied the Random Forest [1] model which outperformed other models in our tests. The model returns the number of impressions expected in a day. We used Root Mean Square Error (RMSE) to evaluate the goodness of fit of the model.

As explained before, we were only able to run the analytics testing for a limited number of keywords due to manual work in the process. Here we report the results for a single keyword, "deutsche bahn fahrplanauskunft" ("German railways timetable" in English), as an illustrative example. We trained the model over the period from 15.5.2017 to 15.7.2017 where the keyword had the most activity. The Random Forest model achieved RMSE of 0.77 on the test set and RMSE of 0.87 on the validation set. Figure 5 shows the predicted values and the actual values for the validation set (Region 20226 in Google GeoTargets)[12].

The result of the analyses conducted on ∼40 keywords were provided to the weather-based campaign scheduler service (the interface of which is depicted in Fig. 6) that is offered to campaign managers.

5 Related Work and Discussions

From JOT's commercial perspective, there is no similar solution on the market enabling the access to a predictive model identifying the most affected keywords and the time when it is more profitable to launch a campaign.

Our review of related work shows that the field of digital marketing has been aware of semantic technologies for some time, with books in the field dedicating entire chapters to the topic of semantic Web [5,14]. However, semantics are mostly used for content organization with the goal of optimization of website ranking on search engines, though marketing research recognizes their wider potential [3]. According to our review, most of the applications of semantic technologies in digital marketing have been for user profile modelling. In [7] and [8] an approach is described for using semantic annotations of users' browsing behaviour (i.e., the content they interact with) to model them and predict the

[12] The line comparison in Fig. 5 shows a comparison of the actual and predicted level of impressions for an anecdotal example. Its purpose is more illustrative as it does not reflect global performance of the approach, though it does suggest what level of possible deviation a marketing professional has to take into account when using the model.

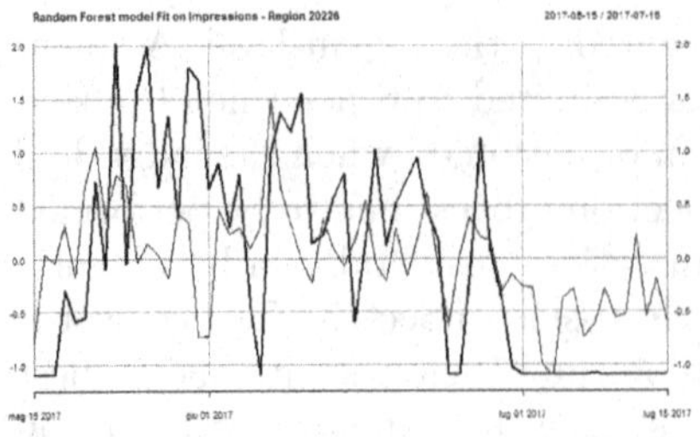

Fig. 5. Actual (black) and predicted (blue) values for standardized number of impressions in a region. (Color figure online)

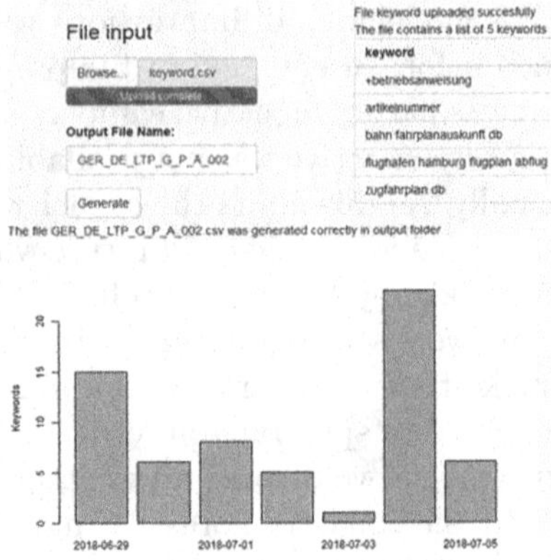

Fig. 6. Service interface.

best marketing content for their preferences. Similar approaches have been proposed for support of organization and management of user interactions in social media, such as the SEMO platform for customer social network analysis based on semantics and emotion mining [6].

We support the data enrichment process with interactive semantic table annotation techniques. Several methods have been proposed to automatically interpret the semantics of tables but they have been usually tailored to many but small tables. For these methods we refer to related work reported in a recent paper [2], comparing our work to (the few) full-fledged interactive table annotation tools. Karma[13] [10] and Odalic[14] provide sophisticated schema-level annotation suggestions, but, to the best of our knowledge, they lack UI-powered services for the reconciliation and extension of column values. OpenRefine has been an important source of inspiration, as it provides a neat user interface and enrichment services, which are used by a relatively large community of end users[15]. We aim at generalizing and improving on the OpenRefine data enrichment features (e.g., more extension services than Wikidata and replicability of transformations) and make them applicable to large amount of data by executing reconciliation and extension services on a scalable infrastructure (batch versions of OpenRefine seem not to support enrichment features, which call external services).

Tools such as Silk[16] and LIMES[17] provide capabilities for data interlinking, however such tools do not perform linking of values occurring in tables. A user would need to use such interlinking tools first (which requires good knowledge of RDF) and then would need to upload links to a triple store and do enrichment via

---

[13] http://usc-isi-i2.github.io/karma.

[14] https://www.adequate.at/odalic.

[15] http://openrefine.org/my%20category/2018/07/16/2018-survey-results.html.

[16] http://silkframework.org.

[17] http://aksw.org/Projects/LIMES.html.

SPARQL queries, switching from one tool to another. Here we support linking within the tabular manipulation tool itself. Furthermore, no approach has worked on linking Google GeoTargets, a crucial dataset to work with in the digital marketing domain (used also in GoogleAnalytics). The novelty in this context is the relevant, high-impact problem domain and the semantics-based solution we devised to successfully address the problem.

Discussion on the Relevance of the Results to JOT. The enrichment pipeline was used to process data for 2016 and 2017 for ~22 million keywords from ~47 thousand campaigns and is now in use to collect and enrich data for 2018 and 2019 analyses. The enriched data were handed over to a data scientist who filtered the most promising keywords to produce predictions to be evaluated by JOT experts. The predictions were tested on a smaller number of keywords, with best results judged valuable for usage in production by the JOT team. RMSE scores were judged valuable for usage in production by JOT experts for the following reasons: (1) the prediction is used to find peaks to determine the launch date (limited accuracy in curve prediction is acceptable for monetization purposes, which is eventually ground on exploiting the peaks); (2) the launch will involve many keywords when the analyses are scaled up. Thus, the JOT team believes that micro-improvements on many individual keywords, even with some errors, will lead to monetization at scale. The pipeline is compliant with JOT cloud infrastructure (that was a big challenge) and is intended for tech staff (not plain marketeers). It is also replicable, as the CSV schema will not change. Thus, the enrichment pipeline is now mature, while the analytics have to be scaled up to go in production.

Discussion on the Use of Semantic Technologies. We briefly discuss here some lessons we learned about the role of semantics for enriching data in industry-driven data science projects, discussing (Pros) and (Cons), with the latter referring to limitations and open issues.

(Pros). The approach and its implementation described in this paper successfully supported the enrichment of large amount of marketing campaign statistics with a large amount of third-party sources, for subsequent analysis. For a set of manually selected keywords weather-based predictions are in fact reliable and usable to support campaign managers of a digital marketing company. Effective enrichment technology can bring much value in the digital marketing domain, where in-depth analytics are key to success and the variables available in the source data is limited by reporting tools provided off-the-shelf by digital marketing platforms (e.g., Google AdWords). **(Cons).** So far we considered weather-based enrichment and many more challenges are ahead - e.g., understanding which data in the LOD cloud can be useful in this domain, and using media coverage signals, extracted from semantic event engines like the Event Registry. In addition, scaling up the analysis requires overcoming the manual selection of promising keywords and the weakness and discontinuity of performance signals over long periods of time (e.g., impressions). To solve this issue we are currently experimenting keyword clustering methods based on multi-lingual word embeddings.

(Pros). Semantics revealed to be a key enabler to support and scale up the enrichment process: reconciliation against reference KBs (e.g., GeoNames) and data interlinking (Google GeoTargets vs. GeoNames) are key pillars for designing enrichment pipelines and for enabling strategies to execute these pipelines in a more efficient way (e.g., by using graph-based databases). **(Cons).** Little work has been done to interlink data, e.g., Google GeoTargets or Google Categories, used in digital marketing platforms that serve millions of companies. Coverage of interlinks between these sources and other sources in the LOD cloud must be improved.
(Pros). Semantic enrichment is a promising yet underinvestigated application of semantic table annotation techniques to facilitate a variety of business analytics. Our contribution targeted mainly engineering problems related to their application for large scale enrichment, thus complementing previous work that focused on intelligent table interpretation. **(Cons).** A better integration of these aspects is a key challenge we are currently addressing.
(Pros). Inspired by tools used by a large user base such as OpenRefine, we developed an approach where semantics are used in a way that is maximally transparent to the user, who uses reconciliation and extension as services from a user interface. We have then shown that annotations can be made with transformations that can be executed in settings that meet the key business requirements (scalability, cloud-based deployment). **(Cons).** Some (semantic) pre-processing steps, in particular for weather data, had to be used, which slightly change our vision, for which integration of corporate data with external sources can be solved by applying a sequence of reconciliation and extension steps. To further optimize the enrichment process and validate the table extension approach, we need to better understand trade-offs between using a big denormalized table and using graph-based representations (which we used to limit space usage and disk writing time).

Finally, we mention that weather-based enrichment (with an external large data source) shows that our approach can be applied in complex and large-scale scenarios. However, there are plenty of LOD sources that are underused despite their potential value, also because of users' limited knowledge of their content and of semantic technologies. Building extension services on top of LOD sources is straightforward, but better support for reconciliation against these sources is needed. The availability of tools to support semantic enrichment in business contexts in the era of analytics may also foster the consumption of LOD beyond the semantic Web enthusiasts.

6 Summary and Outlook

Digital marketing is a domain that has traditionally been rather conservative in adapting new technologies. At the same time, it is moving more and more towards exploitation of data in new ways. With this paper we presented an experiment in using semantic technologies for enriching marketing campaigns data and machine learning to analyze the enriched data, with the final purpose of implementing a new campaign management methodology optimizing the impact of campaigns for a digital marketing company (JOT). In this process, an end-to-end process was devised, from enrichment of data about digital marketing campaigns performance with third-party event data, through the analysis of the enriched information asset using machine learning techniques, to development of value-added services on top of the analytics results. This paper demonstrated the potential use of semantic technologies (with focus on semantic enrichment) for digital marketing—an application domain that has received relatively little attention in the semantic Web community in comparison with other application domains.

As part of future work we consider integrating the pilot into the production systems at JOT and increasing the number of the analytics tasks on the enriched data. Another direction for future work could be the use of OpenWeatherMap (OWM)[18] data as an alternative to weather data from ECMWF[19].

References

1. Breiman, L.: Random forests. Mach. Learn. **45**(1), 5–32 (2001)
2. Chen, J., Jimenez-Ruiz, E., Horrocks, I., Sutton, C.: ColNet: embedding the semantics of web tables for column type prediction. In: AAAI (2019)
3. Erragcha, N., Romdhane, R.: New faces of marketing in the era of the web: from marketing 1.0 to marketing 3.0. J. Res. Mark. **2**(2), 137–142 (2014)
4. Fortuna, B., et al.: QMiner: data analytics platform for processing streams of structured and unstructured data (2014)
5. Frick, T.: Return on Engagement: Content, Strategy and Design Techniques for Digital Marketing. Routledge, Abingdon (2013)
6. Garcia-Crespo, A., Colomo-Palacios, R., Gomez-Berbis, J.M., Ruiz-Mezcua, B.: SEMO: a framework for customer social networks analysis based on semantics. J. Inf. Technol. **25**(2), 178–188 (2010)
7. Hoppe, A., Nicolle, C., Roxin, A.: Automatic ontology-based user profile learning from heterogeneous web resources in a big data context. Proc. VLDB Endow. **6**(12), 1428–1433 (2013)
8. Hoppe, A., Roxin, A., Nicolle, C.: Customizing semantic profiling for digital advertising. In: Meersman, R., et al. (eds.) OTM 2014. LNCS, vol. 8842, pp. 469–478. Springer, Heidelberg (2014). https://doi.org/10.1007/978-3-662-45550-0_47
9. Isele, R., Bizer, C.: Active learning of expressive linkage rules using genetic programming. Web Semant.: Sci. Serv. Agents World Wide Web **23**, 2–15 (2013)
10. Pham, M., Alse, S., Knoblock, C.A., Szekely, P.: Semantic labeling: a domain-independent approach. In: Groth, P., et al. (eds.) ISWC 2016. LNCS, vol. 9981, pp. 446–462. Springer, Cham (2016). https://doi.org/10.1007/978-3-319-46523-4_27
11. Roman, D., et al.: DataGraft: one-stop-shop for open data management. Semant. Web **9**(4), 393–411 (2018)

[18] https://openweathermap.org.

[19] OWM explicitly recommends to call OWM API by city ID to get unambiguous result for cities. In our pilot we need weather for regions (not available in OWM). In fact, obtaining an ID and hence coordinates from an (ambiguous) toponym is the enrichment problem addressed in our pipeline.

12. Spahiu, B., Porrini, R., Palmonari, M., Rula, A., Maurino, A.: ABSTAT: ontology-driven linked data summaries with pattern minimalization. In: Sack, H., Rizzo, G., Steinmetz, N., Mladenić, D., Auer, S., Lange, C. (eds.) ESWC 2016. LNCS, vol. 9989, pp. 381–395. Springer, Cham (2016). https://doi.org/10.1007/978-3-319-47602-5_51
13. Sukhobok, D., et al.: Tabular data cleaning and linked data generation with grafterizer. In: Sack, H., Rizzo, G., Steinmetz, N., Mladenić, D., Auer, S., Lange, C. (eds.) ESWC 2016. LNCS, vol. 9989, pp. 134–139. Springer, Cham (2016). https://doi.org/10.1007/978-3-319-47602-5_27
14. Wertime, K., Fenwick, I.: DigiMarketing: The Essential Guide to New Media and Digital Marketing. Wiley, Hoboken (2011)

An End-to-End Semantic Platform for Nutritional Diseases Management

Ivan Donadello and Mauro Dragoni(✉)

Fondazione Bruno Kessler, Via Sommarive 18, 38123 Trento, Italy
{donadello,dragoni}@fbk.eu

Abstract. The self-management of nutritional diseases requires a system that combines food tracking with the potential risks of food categories on people's health based on their personal health records (PHRs). The challenges range from the design of an effective food image classification strategy to the development of a full-fledged knowledge-based system. This maps the results of the classification strategy into semantic information that can be exploited for reasoning. However, current works mainly address the single challenges separately without their integration into a whole pipeline. In this paper, we propose a new end-to-end semantic platform where: (i) the classification strategy aims to extract food categories from food pictures; (ii) an ontology is used for detecting the risk factors of food categories for specific diseases; (iii) the Linked Open Data (LOD) Cloud is queried for extracting information concerning related diseases and comorbidities; and, (iv) information from the users' PHRs are exploited for generating proper personal feedback. Experiments are conducted on a new publicly released dataset. Quantitative and qualitative evaluations, from two living labs, demonstrate the effectiveness and the suitability of the proposed approach.

1 Introduction

Nutritional diseases can lead to heart diseases, cancer, or type-2 diabetes and are responsible for approximately 678,000 annual deaths in the U.S. They also have a huge impact on the healthcare spending[1]: the annual cost of diabetes associated with diet and inactivity in the U.S. is 245 billions of dollars. Prevention would help people to stay healthy, to lead productive lives, to avoid/delay the onset of diseases and keep diseases far from becoming worse or debilitating. It would also reduce the costs of public health.

Dietary tracking is fundamental for the self-management of nutritional diseases. A common modality for tracking eaten food is to keep a diary of food pictures. This opens the challenge of recognizing all the taken food from users' pictures. However, for an effective management of nutritional diseases, the dietary tracking should be coupled with a reasoning system that (i) checks if the user diet is compliant with some dietary restrictions or with his/her clinical history

[1] https://cspinet.org/eating-healthy/why-good-nutrition-important.

C. Ghidini et al. (Eds.): ISWC 2019, LNCS 11779, pp. 363–381, 2019.
https://doi.org/10.1007/978-3-030-30796-7_23

and (ii) eventually provides useful feedback [16]. This integration requires the mapping of the visual food categories (e.g., cold cuts) into diseases to pay attention (e.g., cardiovascular diseases). However, current approaches are limited to the single image food detection [7,18] or to the nutritional diseases management with logical rules [17]. In addition, image food detection approaches classify meal images according to the whole recipe. Hence, they do not infer the contained food categories. The detection of these categories is fundamental for people affected by particular diseases, such as, diabetes, hypertension, or obesity.

In this paper, we propose an end-to-end semantic platform that supports the management of nutritional diseases. The system covers the whole pipeline from data acquisition (meal pictures taken with a smartphone) to tailored messages to users in order to correct wrong dietary habits within a behavior change context. Here, we focus on the following aspects originally presented in this contribution:

- A multi-label classification of food pictures according to the food categories contained in a specific food recipe of the Mediterranean diet. The classification is performed with a Convolutional Neural Network (CNN).
- An extension of a state-of-the-art ontology (i.e., the HeLiS ontology [9]) about the dietary and physical activity domains with knowledge about the risk level of food categories with respect to a set of diseases.
- A strategy for navigating over the Linked Open Data (LOD) Cloud to infer matches between the user clinical history and the potential risks of diseases and comorbidities induced by an excessive intake of some food categories.
- A new dataset of food pictures, the classification models and the source code of the classification tool. These are released in order to support the reproducibility of the results and to foster further research in this direction.

The significance of our work relies on the integration of deep learning in a Semantic Web (SW) platform for healthcare. Indeed, Computer Vision (CV) methods have no mapping in the semantic space of an ontology, thus they are rarely used as input providers for reasoning systems. SW systems (for healthcare) instead deal with a clean input. This can be time consuming and could affect the scalability. The proposed SW platform allows us to investigate the right balance between effort and effectiveness. We evaluated the proposed platform from three perspectives: (i) the effectiveness of the food categories classification, (ii) the usability of the mobile application adopted by users, and (iii) the effectiveness of the generated messages. In all cases, the obtained results confirm the soundness of the proposed end-to-end semantic platform.

2 Related Work

The end-to-end platform proposed in this paper conjugates two research areas: the classification of food images and the effective navigation of the LOD Cloud for gathering and exploiting knowledge for the realization of intelligent systems.

The recognition of foods from images is the first step for dietary tracking. This task has been studied by the Computer Vision community with techniques of image classification/segmentation and volume estimation. The first works rely on the extraction of visual features from the images and the consequent use of classifiers. The main features used are local/global features and local binary patterns [3,14]. The classifiers are k-NN classifiers, Support Vector or Kernel Machines. Successively, CNNs became the standard technique for food classification [18], thus avoiding the use of engineered features. The Food524DB dataset is used in [7] for food recognition with CNNs and gathers the Food50, Food-101, UEC FOOD-256 and VIREO Food-172 datasets.

Other works estimate the quantity of food in the dish and thus the intake calories. The semantic segmentation of the food dish is performed, then techniques of volume estimation compute the food quantity. However, this requires a database of foods with relatives densities [6,8]. Other works exploit a reference object (e.g., a thumb [23] or a wallet [22]) for the volume computation. Im2Calories [20] uses a CNN to predict a depth map of the image that is used to build the 3D model of the meal. Quantity estimation can be addressed with multi-task learning by training CNNs that learns both the food classification and the relative calories/volume. However, this technique requires a dataset with the annotated calories [11] or the depth information in the images [15].

Few works among those mentioned above predict food categories and match them with some nutritional facts in a database [8,11]. They predict only one food category (e.g., pasta) for each detected food and this can be inaccurate. Indeed, a pasta dish should be avoided by a person suffering of diabetes. However, a pasta dish might have carbonara sauce, containing cold cuts that are not suitable for people suffer from cardiovascular diseases. Therefore, it is important to perform a multi-label classification of the several food categories in the dish.

The promotion of healthy lifestyle through dietary counseling is a recent topic with few available working systems. Nevertheless, some SW-based approaches have been previously proposed. The Medical Decision Support System in [2] supports (i) the collection of patients' relevant information via a mobile application prompting questions related to the patient's medical background, and (ii) the creation of customized advices based on the information collected and on the changes of patient's lifestyle.

In [19] the authors present an approach for designing a semantic reasoning engine to support coaching profiles. This system uses a web-based interface for collecting user data and an ontology for analyzing and processing them. This way, created profiles can be used to optimize the coaching activities of professionals. The work presented in [5] aims to integrate multiple knowledge sources for the development of a dietary consultation system for chronic kidney diseases. The system demonstrates how a knowledge-based approach can achieve sound problem solving modeling and effective knowledge inference. The evaluation involved 84 case patients about recommending appropriate food serving amounts from different food groups for balanced key nutrient ingestion. Finally, in [10] the authors discussed the use of SW technologies to build a system for supporting and motivating people in following healthy lifestyles. SW technologies are used for modeling domain knowledge, and for performing reasoning activities by combining real-time user-generated data and domain expert knowledge.

To the best of our knowledge, our platform innovates the state-of-the-art as it integrates multiple modalities (images, reasoning, LOD Cloud and Personal Health Records) of managing information. Indeed, current CV approaches classify food images according to their recipe label with very poor reasoning about the food intake and related diseases. On the other hand, SW systems do not deal with a noisy input. Our full-fledged solution supports the transformation of food images content into semantic information. This is used for gathering from the LOD Cloud the knowledge of the nutritional diseases associated with the detected food categories. This knowledge is exploited in a fine-grained reasoning process for generating proper personalized feedback.

3 Architecture

Here, we discuss the pipeline modules developed (or reused from existing platforms) for supporting the detection and processing of food categories from users' pictures, see Fig. 1. Such food categories are exploited for (i) detecting the risk level with respect to specific diseases; (ii) navigating the LOD cloud for extracting related diseases and possible comorbidities; and, (iii) linking all collected information with the user's Personal Health Record (PHRs) in order to generate proper feedback.

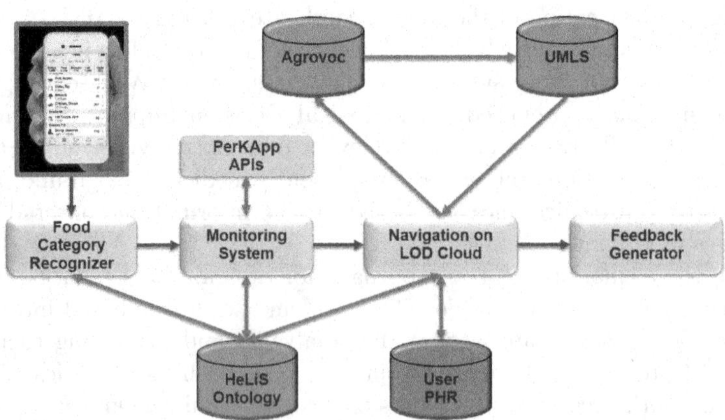

Fig. 1. Architecture of the end-to-end system. Green boxes are external resources, i.e., ontologies. Orange boxes are input data (pictures or PHRs). Light blue boxes are the modules of the system. (Color figure online)

The input module of the pipeline is a mobile application allowing users of taking pictures of consumed food. This kind of input represents the best trade-off between efficiency and effectiveness. On the one hand, the efficiency is supported by the low effort required for providing data. Taking a picture requires less time than providing the complete list of the consumed food. Hence, the reduced effort implies a lower abandonment rate. On the other hand, the effectiveness is given by the fact that it is unfeasible to have a knowledge base with the description of all possible variants for a recipe. Thus, a recipe-based classification system could fail in recognizing all the eaten food categories whereas a food-category-based classification system can be more accurate, see Sect. 8. A correct detection of food categories impacts the consequent reasoning over medical knowledge bases, the inference of risk levels for specific diseases, the alignment of such diseases with users' PHRs and the generation of personalized feedback.

Before detailing the modules of our end-to-end semantic platform, we describe the adopted state-of-the-art components: the HeLiS ontology [9] and the PerKApp platform [16]. The HeLiS ontology is the most updated ontology covering the dietary and physical activity domains. It also defines a model for describing the Mediterranean diet rules that can be associated with user profiles. We extended HeLiS with the risk level of each food category with respect to some diseases, see Sect. 4. The PerKApp platform is a behavior change persuasive platform designed for generating persuasive messages to support people in healthy lifestyles adoption. PerKApp exposes APIs that give access to a subset of its reasoning facilities. This allows the development of applications that monitor users dietary behaviors. Our system exploits the PerKApp APIs to reason about the consumed food categories and trigger the navigation of the LOD Cloud.

The task of recognizing food categories is performed by the **Food Category Recognizer** module (Sect. 5). Such a module uses a CNN trained with recipe images annotated with the contained food categories. During the classification the CNN receives as input the picture taken by the user and it predicts the detected food categories.

Once consumed food categories have been recognized, they are passed to the **Monitoring System** module (i.e., an interface for the PerKApp platform). As mentioned above, this module verifies, through reasoning operations, if the user violated one of the assigned rules defined within the HeLiS ontology.

In case an undesired behavior is detected, information about the involved food categories are sent to the **Navigation on the LOD Cloud** module. This module acquires from nutritional and medical knowledge bases (available in the LOD Cloud) disease information linked with the received food categories. This process is performed through the following activities:

1. The module looks up into the HeLiS extension for the risk level of the detected food categories with respect to the modeled diseases. Such information have been provided by domain experts only for a subset of possible nutritional diseases. Currently the HeLiS extension contains knowledge for five nutritional diseases, see Sect. 4. The rationale behind the limited number is: (i) we want to limit the effort of the domain experts in providing all the knowledge, and (ii) missing information (other nutritional diseases of the literature) are acquired through the second step.

2. The HeLiS ontology is connected to the LOD Cloud due to the alignments with AGROVOC[2], see the *equivalentClass* annotation property in HeLiS. In this step, the module exploits the diseases modeled in HeLiS for accessing to the related nutritional diseases defined within AGROVOC (i.e., children and sibling diseases).
3. PHRs have a very specific medical terminology and they contain detailed information that do not match with the AGROVOC diseases. Hence, the module navigates the LOD Cloud from AGROVOC to the UMLS Knowledge Base[3] to collect information about comorbities associated with the diseases extracted from AGROVOC. Indeed, comorbidities are not directly associated with food categories, thus only the navigation of the LOD Cloud enables the finding of the ones that a user already had in his/her PHR. The UMLS is a medical knowledge base containing both a taxonomy of diseases and properties concerning associated diseases, comorbidities, recidivity degree, etc. Such low-level information increases the likelihood to find an alignment between the content of a PHR and the knowledge collected from the LOD Cloud. For reaching UMLS from AGROVOC, the module exploits the path AGROVOC → Bio2RDF → LinkedCT → Pubmed → UMLS as described in [26].
4. The last step consists in matching all the information extracted from both AGROVOC and UMLS with the information contained in the PHR of the user. The result of this match is provided to the last module of the pipeline.

To perform the LOD Cloud navigation we use the LOD-a-lot [12] service, i.e., a dump of the LOD Cloud that can be queried by using a single SPARQL endpoint for all the involved resources. This prevents us from the possible unreliability of some SW resources, e.g., a fault in the path from AGROVOC to UMLS.

Finally, once the system has computed (i) the intake food categories, (ii) the risk levels of associated diseases, (iii) the related diseases and possible comorbidities, and (iv) the alignments with the user's PHR, it generates a proper feedback that is returned to the user mobile application. The **Feedback Generator** module relies on a template-based engine where the structured information of above is realized into natural language sentences. More details on how templates are populated are in [16].

4 Background Knowledge

The role of background knowledge in our platform is two-fold. First, background knowledge allows our semantic platform to go beyond the sole classification of food images. Indeed, background knowledge enables the possibility of exploiting logic relationships and inference capabilities for reusing the food classification results to support users for more complex goals. For example, the prediction of

[2] http://aims.fao.org/vest-registry/vocabularies/agrovoc.
[3] https://www.nlm.nih.gov/research/umls/.

some food categories might represent a warning for people affected by specific diseases, e.g., pasta for people affected by diabetes. Moreover, background knowledge can contains conceptual models about specific dietary patterns that can be used to improve users' lifestyle, avoiding the rise or sharpening of chronic diseases, and to support a behavioral changing. Second, the exploitation of knowledge resources enables the access to the LOD Cloud. This focuses the modelling only on extending HeLiS since all other semantic information exploited by the system are available through the LOD Cloud.

The background knowledge exploited here is HeLiS [9]: a state-of-the-art ontology for supporting healthy lifestyles. It defines the dietary and physical activity domains together with entities that model concepts concerning users' profiles and the monitoring of their activities. Details about the conceptual model and the methodology for building it are in [9]. The HeLiS ontology has been extended by adding, to the dietary domain, information concerning the risk level of food categories with respect to specific diseases[4]. We discuss the main concepts involved into the food category classification together with the ones modeled within the HeLiS ontology extension, see Fig. 2.

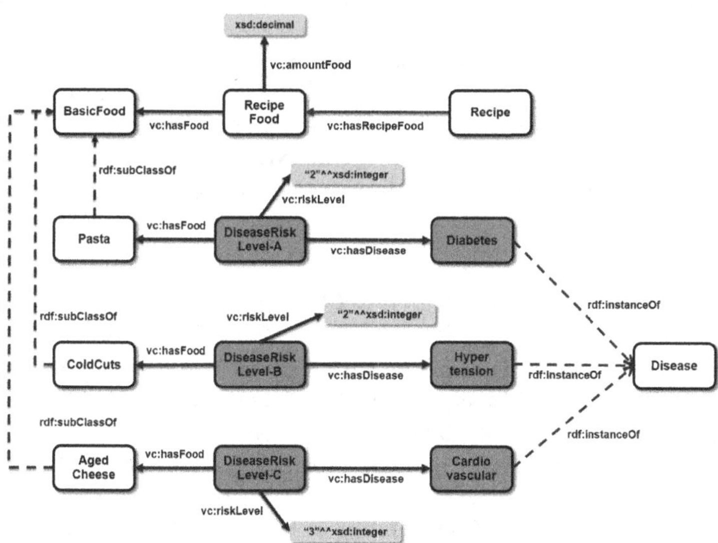

Fig. 2. Excerpt of the HeLiS ontology including the main concepts (white boxes) and instances (blue boxes) exploited by our semantic platform. Solid lines are object properties, dashed lines are RDF core properties (Color figure online)

Instances of the *BasicFood* concept describe foods for which micro-information of nutrients (carbohydrates, lipids, proteins, minerals, and vitamins)

[4] The HeLiS extension is available on the HeLiS website http://w3id.org/helis.

are available. Moreover, these instances belong also to subclasses of the *BasicFood* concept, such as *Pasta*, *Aged Cheese*, *Eggs*, *Cold Cuts* and *Vegetal Oils*. On the other hand, instances of the *Recipe* concept, describe the composition of complex dishes (such as *Pasta with Carbonara Sauce*) by expressing them as a list of instances of the *RecipeFood* concepts. This concept reifies the relationships between each *Recipe* individual, the list of *BasicFood* it contains and the amount of each *BasicFood*. Besides this dual classification, instances of both *BasicFood* and *Recipe* concepts are categorized under a more fine-grained structure. With respect to the number of individuals, currently, HeLiS contains 986 individuals of type *BasicFood* and 4408 individuals of type *Recipe*.

The *Disease* concept defines the diseases supported by the system such that information about the risk level relationship with specific *BasicFood* is available. Currently, we instantiate the *Disease* concept for diabetes, kidney diseases, cardiovascular diseases, hypertension and obesity. Diseases are defined as single individuals instead of concepts for avoiding the creation of a new individual for each specific disease for each user. Instances of the *DiseaseRiskLevel* concept reifies the relationships between each *Disease* and *BasicFood* individuals and with the risk level of a *BasicFood* for that *Disease*. The risk level is represented by a value ranging from 0 (no risk) to 3 (high risk). For readability we report in Fig. 2 only some instances of the *DiseaseRiskLevel* concept, e.g., *DiseaseRiskLevel-A*, *DiseaseRiskLevel-B*, and *DiseasesRiskLevel-C*.

The HeLiS ontology is used by the **Food Category Recognizer module** for getting the list of available food categories, by the **Monitoring System** for supporting the reasoning process, and by the **Navigation on LOD Cloud** as starting point for getting the list of diseases associated with the detected food categories.

5 Multi-label Food Category Classification

Our goal is to assign every food image with a set of food category labels. These categories compose the food recipe in the image and are provided by HeLiS. We address this problem as a multi-label image classification task where $\mathcal{X} \in \mathbb{R}^d$ is the input domain of our images and the subclasses of *BasicFood* are the possible food category labels. Given an image $\boldsymbol{x} \in \mathcal{X}$, we need to predict a vector $\boldsymbol{y} = \{y_1, y_2, \dots, y_K\} \subseteq$ *BasicFood* where y_i is the i-th food category label associated to $\boldsymbol{x}$. State-of-the-art methods in food image recognition mostly classify images according to only one single label taken from *Recipe* without multi-label classification. Here, we exploit two strategies for food-categories classification: (i) a direct multi-label classification of the food categories with a CNN and (ii) a single-label image classification of the food recipes (e.g., *Pasta with Carbonara Sauce*) with a CNN and then the logical inference of all its food categories (i.e., *Pasta*, *Eggs*, etc) through the *RecipeFood* concept.

5.1 Methods

Current methods in image classification use supervised deep learning techniques based on CNNs [13]. These are able to learn the salient features of an image in order to classify it according to some training examples. CNNs exploit several combinations of the hidden layers (convolutions, poolings, activations) in order to improve their performance. In both methods (i) and (ii) we separately train (on the dataset in Sect. 8.1) one of the most performing CNN, the Inception-V3 [25]. This network presents convolutional filters of multiple sizes operating at the same level. This makes the network "wider" and able to better detect the salient parts of an image. Finally, the network has a standard fully-connected layer for predicting the classes. Moreover, this networks does not present some redundant connections between neurons that affect the efficiency of the other CNNs. Further details and performance results can be found in [25].

Direct Multi-label Classification. We train the Inception-V3 for directly learning the vector $\boldsymbol{y}$ of the food categories in *BasicFood*. We use a sigmoid as activation function of the last fully-connected layer and binary cross entropy as loss function. This is a standard setting for multi-label classification.

Single-Label Classification and Inference. Another method to classify food categories consists in: firstly, to classify an input image with a CNN according to the food label (in *Recipe*) it contains (e.g., *Pasta with Carbonara Sauce*). This is the standard multiclass classification where one image is classified with only one food label among many classes. Secondly, to infer the food category labels from the food label by using the *RecipeFood* reification. The detection of *Pasta with Carbonara Sauce* implies the presence of the food categories: *Pasta*, *Eggs*, *Aged cheese*, *Vegetal Oils* and *Cold cuts*. Let CNN be an Inception-V3 trained to multiclassify food labels in *Recipe*. We use a softmax as activation function of the last fully-connected layer and categorical cross entropy as loss function. Thus $CNN(\boldsymbol{x}) = \langle s_1, s_2, \ldots, s_n \rangle$ with $s_i \in \mathbb{R}$ is the classification score of the network for the label $l_i \in Recipe$. Let $l^* \in Recipe$ be the label with highest score in $CNN(\boldsymbol{x})$, then the food category labels vector $\boldsymbol{y}$ is defined as:

$$\boldsymbol{y} = \{y_i \in \mathit{BasicFood} \mid \exists w \in \mathit{RecipeFood} : \mathit{hasFood}(w, y_i) \wedge \mathit{hasRecipeFood}(l^*, w)\}$$

6 From Image Classification to LOD Cloud Navigation

Here we show how the system works through a concrete example. Let us consider a user suffered from anomalies of blood pressure and with a nasal polyps surgery five years before the use of the platform. Her electronic PHR contains all these information related to her clinical history. Then, let us assume that she is going to eat a pasta with carbonara sauce and she sends to the system the meal picture taken with her smartphone. The **Food Category Recognizer** detects the presence of these food categories: *Pasta*, *Eggs*, *AgedCheese*, *VegetalOils* and *ColdCuts*. These are sent to the **Monitoring System**.

As first action, this module adds into the dietary diary of the user, represented as a set of individuals within HeLiS, the consumed food categories. Then, through logical reasoning, the **Monitoring System** checks if the intake food categories follow the rules associated with the user's profile encoded in HeLiS. According with the user's dietary diary and the rules of his profile, the system detects an undesired behavior: in the last 7 days the user has consumed the *ColdCuts* food category four times while the associated rules limits the consumption of *ColdCuts* three times per week.

These undesired food categories are passed to the **Navigation on LOD Cloud** module and trigger the retrieval of possible diseases to pay attention if the user exceeds with *ColdCuts* food consumption. The module queries the HeLiS extension for all instances of type *DiseaseRiskLevel* having an *hasFood* object property instantiated with the concept *ColdCuts*. By looking in Fig. 2, the module finds the *DiseaseRiskLevel-2* individual and from it, retrieves the individual *Hypertension* of type *Disease*. From the *DiseaseRiskLevel-2* individual, the module looks for the *riskLevel* data property for retrieving the risk level associated with the pair $<Hypertension, ColdCuts>$. If the value is greater than 1, the module starts to navigate through the LOD Cloud for finding all related information. Indeed, HeLiS mainly focuses on healthy lifestyles and it is not a medical ontology. Hence, the acquisition of further medical information concerning the diseases associated with the consumed food categories has to be performed from the LOD Cloud. The navigation starts from the alignment between HeLiS and AGROVOC. Here, the system retrieves the children and sibling diseases of *Hypertension* provided by the diseases taxonomy of AGROVOC. Examples of children diseases of *Hypertension* are *Embolism*, *HeartAttack* and *Phlebitis*. However, the specific medical terminology in PHRs do not always match with the diseases in AGROVOC. Hence, the system continues the navigation through the LOD Cloud to refine the list of AGROVOC diseases by extracting information from the UMLS Knowledge Base. In our example, from the *Hypertension* concept, extracted from HeLiS, the platform reaches the *BloodPressureAnomalies* associated disease and *NasalPolyps* possible comorbidity within the UMLS Knowledge Base. The latter contains also the *recidivity* attribute. Every retrieved disease and their attributes are searched in the electronic PHR to provide a more accurate user feedback. In our case, the module finds alignments with *BloodPressureAnomalies* and with *NasalPolyps* that are two diseases that the patient suffered from.

The gathered information (*ColdCuts*, *Hypertension*, *NasalPolyps*, *BloodPressureAnomalies*, *riskLevel(BloodPressureAnomalies, High)*, and *hasAttribute(NasalPolyps, Recidivity)*) are processed by the **Feedback Generation Module**. Its language generation engine fills message templates to realize tailored motivational messages. Concerning our scenario, a sample message is the following: *"This week you have eaten too much cold cuts. Do yo know that an excessive intake of cold cuts could cause the recidivity of nasal polyps and significantly increases the probability of having anomalies in your blood pressure? Next time you can try a meal with some fresh fish."*.

7 Use Cases: The *Key to Health* and *Salute Plus* Living Labs

As specific case studies, we validated our platform within two living labs: *Key To Health* and *Salute Plus*. The *Key To Health* living lab promotes healthy lifestyles in workplaces with the aim of preventing the onset of chronic diseases through organizational interventions directed to workers. Actions can concern the promotion of a correct diet, physical activity, social and individual well-being, or the discouragement of bad habits, such as smoking and alcohol consumption. Within the *Key To Health* living lab, our platform has been used by 120 workers of our institution (both researchers and employers) as a tool to persuade them to follow healthy recommendations. The *Salute Plus* living lab is part of *Trentino Salute 4.0*[5], a digital health initiative promoted by the local healthcare department. Such an initiative aims at proving innovative technological solutions to citizens to promote healthy lifestyles. Table 1 shows the main demographic information concerning the users involved in the two living labs. Whereas Table 2 provides statistics about the usage of the platform. Even if the *Salute Plus* living lab runs from a longer period (it is still active), we consider for the evaluation the data acquired during the first 49 days in order to provide a fair comparison with the *Key To Health* living lab.

Table 1. Demographic information of the users involved in the evaluation campaign.

Dimension	Property	Value	
		Key to health	Salute plus
Gender	Male	57%	48%
	Female	43%	52%
Age	25–35	12%	27%
	36–45	58%	45%
	46–55	30%	28%
Education	High school	0%	56%
	Master degree	42%	43 %
	Ph.D. degree	58%	1 %
Occupation	Ph.D. student	8%	n.a
	Administration	28%	n.a
	Researcher	64%	n.a

The *Key To Health* and *Salute Plus* use cases allowed us to deploy our platform into two different scenarios. The former is a controlled environment in which we performed a complete evaluation both from the quantitative and qualitative perspectives. Whereas, the latter is a real-world environment that allowed us to

[5] http://www.trentinosalutedigitale.it/#primo.

Table 2. Usage statistics during the living labs. We report the number of users involved, the number of days since each living lab started, the number of meals introduced by the users (each meal can be composed by several pictures), and the number of RDF triples currently stored.

Living lab	# Users	Days running	Meals provided	Triples
Key To Health	120	49	18,816	470,400
Salute Plus	2,870	112	902,944	16,704,464

observe (i) the engineering suitability of our platform, and (ii) the effectiveness of our solution within a more open context for comparing the results obtained in the controlled environment. For each living lab, users were equipped with a mobile application[6] based on the services provided by our platform. We analyzed the usage of the mobile application for seven weeks by monitoring the users' input and the associated undesired behaviors (hereafter called "violations"). Results and discussions are in Sect. 8.

8 Experiments

Within the living labs, we validated our platform from both quantitative and qualitative perspectives. The former focuses on the performance of the food category recognizer (Sect. 8.1). The latter regards the whole platform: (i) the user experience with the mobile application and (ii) the effectiveness of the generated messages (Sect. 8.2). Concerning the second point, we compared the impact of the messages generated by using only the reasoning results (a.k.a. the *control group*) with the messages generated by exploiting the knowledge extracted from the LOD Cloud combined with the information in the PHRs. Finally, lessons learnt from this experience are provided (Sect. 8.3).

8.1 Quantitative Evaluation

Good performance of the food category recognizer are important as the misclassification of a meal could generate wrong messages or even no message. In the example of Sect. 6, we noticed that the single-label classification and inference method could wrongly classifies some Carbonara images as *Tomato and Ricotta Cheese Pasta*, thus containing *FreshCheese* instead of *Eggs* and *TomatoSauces* instead of *ColdCuts*. In this case no message will be generated and the user could

[6] The mobile applications are available on the stores and they are compliant, as the whole platform, with the GDPR rules. However, since PHRs from the Trentino Healthcare Department are used, the mobile applications cannot be used by people living outside our province. For informative purposes, here the Google Play Store links: https://play.google.com/store/apps/details?id=eu.fbk.trec.saluteplus https://play.google.com/store/apps/details?id=eu.fbk.trec.lifestyle.

consume another meal with *ColdCuts* next time. Here, we compare the multi-label method against the (more standard) single-label classification of the food recipe and the inference of the food categories. Our claim is that a classification error in a single food recipe affects the majority of the inferred food categories leading to inaccurate results.

The Food and Food Categories (FFoCat) Dataset.[7] We leverage the food and food category concepts in HeLiS extension for the multi-label classification. However, current food image datasets are not built with these concepts as labels, so it is necessary to build a new dataset (named FFoCat) with these concepts. We start by sampling some of the most common recipes in *Recipe* and use them as food labels. The food categories are then automatically retrieved from *BasicFood* with a SPARQL query. Examples of food labels are *Pasta with Carbonara Sauce* and *Baked Sea Bream*. Their associated food categories are *Pasta, AgedCheese, VegetalOils, Eggs, ColdCuts* and *FreshFish, VegetalOils*, respectively. We collect 156 labels for foods (*Recipe* concept) and 51 for food categories (*BasicFood* concept). We scrape the Web, using Google Images as search engine, to automatically download all the images related to the food labels. Then, we manually clean the dataset by checking if the images are compliant with the related labels. This results in 58,962 images with 47,108 images for the training set and 11,854 images for the test set (80-20 ratio of splitting). Then, by leveraging HeLiS properties, we enrich the image annotations with the corresponding food category labels to perform multi-label classification. The dataset is affected by some natural imbalance, indeed the food categories present a long-tail distribution: only few food categories labels have the majority of the examples. On the contrary, many food categories labels have few examples. This makes the food classification challenging.

Experimental Settings and Metrics. For both multi and single-label classification we separately train the Inception-V3 network from scratch on the FFoCat training set to find the best set of weights. The fine tuning using pre-trained ImageNet weights did not perform sufficiently. We run 100 epochs of training with a batch size of 16 and a learning rate of 10^{-6}. At each epoch images are resized to 299 × 299 pixels and are augmented by using rotations, width and height shifts, shearing, zooming and horizontal flipping. This results in a training set 100 times bigger than the initial one. We use early stopping to prevent overfitting. The training has been performed with the Keras framework (TensorFlow as backend) on a PC equipped with a NVIDIA GeForce GTX 1080.

As performance metric we use the mean average precision (MAP) that summarizes the classifier precision-recall curve: $MAP = \sum_{i=1}^{n}(R_n - R_{n-1})P_n$, i.e., the weighted mean of precision P_n achieved at each threshold level n. The weight is the increase of the recall in the previous threshold: $R_n - R_{n-1}$. The macro AP is the average of the AP over the classes, the micro instead considers each entry of the predictions as a label. We prefer MAP instead of accuracy as the latter for sparse vectors can give misleading results: high results for output vectors with all zeros.

[7] The dataset, its comparison and the code are available at https://bit.ly/2Y7zSWZ.

Results of the Multi-label Classification. Given an (set of) input image(s) $\boldsymbol{x}$, the computing of the precision-recall curve requires the predicted vector(s) $\boldsymbol{y}$ of food category labels and a score associated to each label in $\boldsymbol{y}$. In the multi-label method this score is directly returned by the Inception-V3 network. In the single-label and inference method this score needs to be computed. We test two strategies: (i) we perform *exact inference* of the food categories from HeLiS and assign the value 1 to the scores of each $y_i \in \boldsymbol{y}$; (ii) the food categories labels inherit the *uncertainty* returned the CNN: the score of each y_i is the value s_i returned by $CNN(\boldsymbol{x})$. Results are in Table 3. The direct multi-label has very good performance (both in micro and macro AP) in comparison with the single-label models. The micro-AP is always better than the macro-AP as it is sensible to the mentioned imbalance of the data. This confirms our claim that errors in the single recipe classification propagate to the majority of the food categories the recipe contains. That is, the inferred food categories will be wrong because the recipe classification is wrong. On the other hand, errors in the direct multi-label classification will affect only few food categories. With these good results, we use the direct multi-label classification method in our platform. We also performed a qualitative analysis. The single-label method misclassifies an image with *Backed Potatoes* as *Backed Pumpkin* thus missing the category of *FreshStarchyVegetables*. Another image contains a *Vegetable Pie* but the single-label method infers the wrong category of *PizzaBread*. In another image, this method mistakes *Pasta with Garlic, Oil and Chili Peppers* with *Pasta with Carbonara Sauce*, thus inferring wrong *Eggs* and *ColdCuts*. Here the multi-label method classifies all the categories correctly. Therefore, the multi-label method allows a more fine grained classification of the food categories w.r.t. the single-label method. The latter has better results if the score returned by the CNN is propagated to the food categories labels w.r.t. the exact inference. Good performance on food categories classification are important as they reduce the noise for the following modules of the platform.

Table 3. The multi-label classification of food categories outperforms in average precision (AP) the methods based on single-label classification and logical inference.

Method	Micro-AP (%)	Macro-AP (%)
Multi-label	**76.24**	**50.12**
Single-class exact	50.53	31.79
Single-class uncert	60.21	42.51

8.2 Qualitative Evaluation of the System

We present here the validation performed by involving users from the living labs concerning (i) the overall usability of the mobile application and (ii) the effectiveness of the generated messages, i.e. how the number of detected violations changed through time.

Usability Evaluation. The usability of the mobile application has been evaluated through the System Usability Scale (SUS), analyzing the intuitiveness and simplicity of the system. Only the users involved in the *Key To Health* living lab participated to this validation. The evaluation protocol consists in multiple use sessions and follows these steps:

1. Training meetings with the 120 involved users for an introductory explanation of the functionalities available in the mobile application.
2. Four days of usage of the mobile application by the users.
3. Meetings with the users for collecting questions about functionalities. Release of a new version of the mobile application integrating bug fixes reported by the users.
4. Four days of usage of the mobile application by the users.
5. Final meetings with the users and distribution of evaluation questionnaires.

According to the usability test requirements provided by [21], the number of users involved in the test granted the discovery of 100% of the usability problems. The average score obtained from the SUS was 83.1 out of 100, that, according to the adjective rating scale proposed by [1], corresponds to "excellent". Further interviews were conducted to evaluate the impact of the mobile application in their daily life at the end of the seven weeks of pilot study. Users appreciated the system and considered the mobile application a useful tool, especially for increasing the awareness about their eating habits.

Effectiveness of Generated Messages. The last validation we performed concerned the analysis of explanations effectiveness on the users involved within the *Key to Health* and *Salute Plus* living labs. Our goal was to measure the effectiveness of the explanations generated by our platform by observing the evolution of the number of detected violations. The *Key To Health* living lab allowed to plan a more rigorous evaluation thanks to the exploitation of a close environment. The 120 users involved were split in two groups. The first one (92 users) received messages generated by using the whole system: from the results of the reasoning process to the navigation of the LOD Cloud with exploitation of PHRs. Whereas the second group (28 users working as control group) received feedback, as canned text messages, exploiting only the reasoner's results. We expect to find a higher decrease in the number of violations through the time by the users receiving persuasive messages. Concerning, the *Salute Plus* living lab, we did not have the control group since the agreement with our Local Healthcare Department foreseen that all citizens were able to access the complete set of services of the platform. However, we could check if results on both living labs converged or not. Results concerning the evolution of the violation numbers are presented in Fig. 3. We considered two different kinds of rules: (i) DAY-Rules: these rules define the maximum (or minimum) number of portions of a specific food category that can be consumed during a day, and (ii) WEEK-Rules: these rules define the maximum (or minimum) number of portions of a specific food category that can be consumed during a week. DAY-Rules are verified at the end of each day, while WEEK-Rules are verified at the end of each week. The blue and the purple lines represent the average number of violations observed for the *Key To Health* and *Salute Plus* users, respectively. The red and the azure lines are the standard deviations. Observations related to the control group are reported by the green (average number of violations) and the orange line (standard deviation). The increasing trend of the gap between the blue/purple and green lines (for both the DAY and WEEK-Rules) demonstrates the positive impact of the messages sent by the whole platform. In particular, concerning DAY-Rules, the average number of violations per user at the end of the observed period is acceptable as it drops of about 67%. For the WEEK-Rules, however, the drop remained limited. Notice that for both living labs we have a confident decrease of detected violations. Hence, we can conclude that the whole platform was effective within both living labs. The standard deviation is higher for the *Salute Plus* living lab: this is due to the high number of involved people that, unavoidable, led to a marked variance of their behaviors. Notice that both standard deviation lines remain contained within low bounds. In addition, we did not detect the presence of outliers.

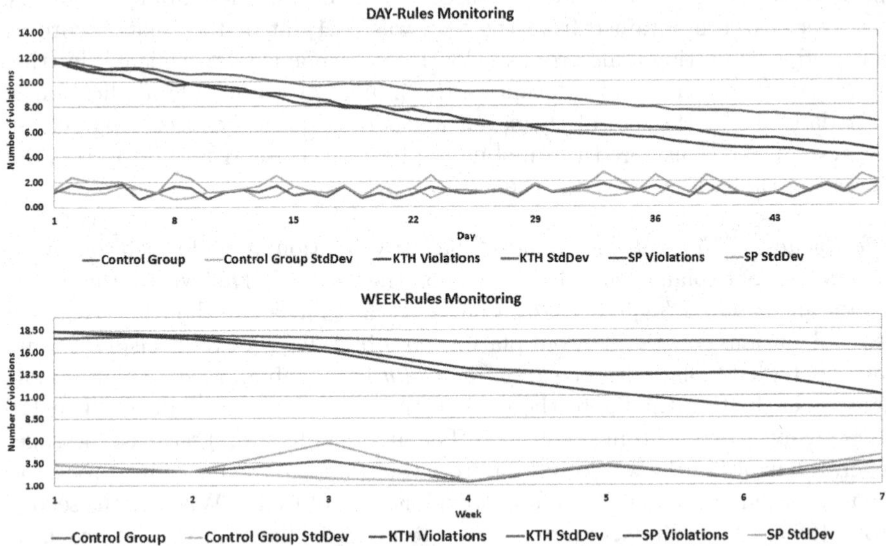

Fig. 3. Evolution of the average number of detected violations (per user), for the DAY and WEEK-Rules, during the *Key To Health* and *Salute Plus* observation period. (Color figure online)

8.3 Lessons Learnt

Both the *Key to Health* and *Salute Plus* experiences allowed us to collect some lessons that will improve the effectiveness of our platform and the design of future living labs.

Real-Time Suitability. The proposed system aims to be deployed into a real-time context. Personalized feedback and recommendations have to be provided timely to users based on the evolution of their behaviors and of the surrounding environment. Hence, we observed the performance of the whole reasoning process implemented into our platform. Therefore, we focus on the optimization process brought us to the deployment of a solution able to support an efficient real-time generation of personalized messages. Our results derived from the optimization of rules design and rules evaluation schedule. In a first stage, we designed few complex rules for covering all possible monitoring activities. On the one hand, we were able to cover several constraints with one rule. On the other hand, the computational time required for evaluating these rules was too high leading to a personalized tracking of users' behavior that was neither effective nor efficient. Hence, in a second stage, we split the rules in simpler ones and schedule their evaluation depending on their timing property (DAY and WEEK). This strategy improved of the reasoning performance by making the platform deployable within a real-time environment and allowed us to have an easier control on the overall reasoning process. A future improvement of personal tracking capabilities will be the investigation of stream reasoning for monitoring a continuous flow of information as well as to exploit learning strategies for suggesting new rules or adaptations of existing ones. An example in the health domain is the real-time monitoring of the glycemic index.

User Perception About Personalization. We consider the actual perception that the users had about the personalization capabilities of the proposed platform. During the focus group organized at the end of the *Key to Health* use case, we collected feedback about such perception by asking to users when the system can be improved concerning personalized interactions. Overall, the users appreciated the system responsiveness and message tailoring capabilities when data about food consumption were provided. However, a common request was related to the possibility of exploiting the geographical information that can be acquired through the smartphones. This information was relevant for motivating people in changing habits within some real-life situations, e.g., to not stop at a vendor machine during a walk. Suggested examples include the possibility of sending alerts, based on the current user location, about close healthy nutrition shops, restaurants cooking recipes that are compliant with users goals and users' habits. These suggestions will lead the next version of the personalization component of our platform in order to improve the perception that the system is providing a real-time support.

9 Conclusions

This paper discusses an end-to-end semantic platform that maps food categories detected from meal images into semantic information of an ontology. The goal is alerting people about the potential risks of food with respect to their PHRs. The platform integrates (i) deep learning for classifying food categories from images; (ii) an ontology associating food categories with possible nutritional diseases; (iii) the navigation of the LOD Cloud for extracting further diseases' knowledge; (iv) the use of PHRs for the generation of proper feedback. We provided a new dataset of annotated images useful for fostering the research. Concerning the image classification, the multi-label food classification outperforms a more standard method based on single-image classification and inference of the food categories. Regarding the feedback generation, the user-based evaluation demonstrated the efficacy of our semantic platform into real-world scenarios.

Future work will focus on exploiting the combination of deep learning with ontologies (in a multi-task learning setting) by using constraints-based methods, such as, Logic Tensor Networks [24], already applied to image classification tasks. This direction will be tested on bigger and standard image datasets, such as, VIREO FOOD-172 [4]. On the semantic part, the HeLiS ontology will be extended with further diseases in order to improve the overall capability of the system. Stream reasoning algorithms will be studied to support the generation of feedback by considering the wider dietary behavior of a user instead of a single recipe. Finally, the proposed semantic platform opens the possibility of an integration into intelligent systems implementing behavior change policies for supporting users in adopting healthy lifestyles.

References

1. Bangor, A., Kortum, P., Miller, J.: Determining what individual SUS scores mean: adding an adjective rating scale. J. Usability Stud. **4**, 114–123 (2009)
2. Benmimoune, L., Hajjam, A., Ghodous, P., Andres, E., Talha, S., Hajjam, M.: Ontology-based medical decision support system to enhance chronic patients' lifestyle within e-care telemonitoring platform. Stud. Health Technol. Inform. **213**, 279–282 (2015)
3. Bossard, L., Guillaumin, M., Van Gool, L.: Food-101 – mining discriminative components with random forests. In: Fleet, D., Pajdla, T., Schiele, B., Tuytelaars, T. (eds.) ECCV 2014. LNCS, vol. 8694, pp. 446–461. Springer, Cham (2014). https://doi.org/10.1007/978-3-319-10599-4_29
4. Chen, J., Ngo, C.: Deep-based ingredient recognition for cooking recipe retrieval. In: ACM Multimedia, pp. 32–41. ACM (2016)
5. Chi, Y., Chen, T., Tsai, W.: A chronic disease dietary consultation system using OWL-based ontologies and semantic rules. J. Biomed. Inform. **53**, 208–219 (2015)
6. Ciocca, G., Napoletano, P., Schettini, R.: Food recognition: a new dataset, experiments, and results. IEEE J. Biomed. Health Inform. **21**(3), 588–598 (2017)
7. Ciocca, G., Napoletano, P., Schettini, R.: Learning CNN-based features for retrieval of food images. In: Battiato, S., Farinella, G.M., Leo, M., Gallo, G. (eds.) ICIAP 2017. LNCS, vol. 10590, pp. 426–434. Springer, Cham (2017). https://doi.org/10.1007/978-3-319-70742-6_41
8. Dehais, J., Anthimopoulos, M., Shevchik, S., Mougiakakou, S.G.: Two-view 3D reconstruction for food volume estimation. IEEE Trans. Multimed. **19**(5), 1090–1099 (2017)
9. Dragoni, M., Bailoni, T., Maimone, R., Eccher, C.: HeLiS: an ontology for supporting healthy lifestyles. In: Vrandečić, D., et al. (eds.) ISWC 2018. LNCS, vol. 11137, pp. 53–69. Springer, Cham (2018). https://doi.org/10.1007/978-3-030-00668-6_4

10. Dragoni, M., Rospocher, M., Bailoni, T., Maimone, R., Eccher, C.: Semantic technologies for healthy lifestyle monitoring. In: Vrandečić, D., et al. (eds.) ISWC 2018. LNCS, vol. 11137, pp. 307–324. Springer, Cham (2018). https://doi.org/10.1007/978-3-030-00668-6_19
11. Ege, T., Yanai, K.: Image-based food calorie estimation using knowledge on food categories, ingredients and cooking directions. In: ACM Multimedia (Thematic Workshops), pp. 367–375. ACM (2017)
12. Fernández, J.D., Beek, W., Martínez-Prieto, M.A., Arias, M.: LOD-a-lot - a queryable dump of the LOD cloud. In: d'Amato, C., et al. (eds.) ISWC 2017. LNCS, vol. 10588, pp. 75–83. Springer, Cham (2017). https://doi.org/10.1007/978-3-319-68204-4_7
13. Kawano, Y., Yanai, K.: Food image recognition with deep convolutional features. In: UbiComp Adjunct, pp. 589–593. ACM (2014)
14. Kawano, Y., Yanai, K.: Foodcam-256: a large-scale real-time mobile food recognition system employing high-dimensional features and compression of classifier weights. In: ACM Multimedia, pp. 761–762. ACM (2014)
15. Lu, Y., Allegra, D., Anthimopoulos, M., Stanco, F., Farinella, G.M., Mougiakakou, S.G.: A multi-task learning approach for meal assessment. In: MADiMa@IJCAI, pp. 46–52. ACM (2018)
16. Maimone, R., Guerini, M., Dragoni, M., Bailoni, T., Eccher, C.: Perkapp: a general purpose persuasion architecture for healthy lifestyles. J. Biomed. Inform. **82**, 70–87 (2018)
17. Mamykina, L., Levine, M.E., Davidson, P.G., Smaldone, A.M., Elhadad, N., Albers, D.J.: Data-driven health management: reasoning about personally generated data in diabetes with information technologies. JAMIA **23**(3), 526–531 (2016)
18. Mezgec, S., Koroušić Seljak, B.: Nutrinet: a deep learning food and drink image recognition system for dietary assessment. Nutrients **9**(7), 657 (2017)
19. Mikolajczak, S., Ruette, T., Tsiporkova, E., Angelova, M., Boeva, V.: A semantic reasoning engine for lifestyle profiling in support of personalised coaching. In: International Conference on Global Health Challenges, pp. 79–83 (2015)
20. Myers, A., et al.: Im2Calories: towards an automated mobile vision food diary. In: ICCV, pp. 1233–1241. IEEE Computer Society (2015)
21. Nielsen, J., Landauer, T.K.: A mathematical model of the finding of usability problems. In: Proceedings of ACM INTERCHI 1993 Conference, pp. 24–29 (1993)
22. Okamoto, K., Yanai, K.: An automatic calorie estimation system of food images on a smartphone. In: MADiMa @ ACM Multimedia, pp. 63–70. ACM (2016)
23. Pouladzadeh, P., Shirmohammadi, S., Almaghrabi, R.: Measuring calorie and nutrition from food image. IEEE Trans. Instrum. Measur. **63**(8), 1947–1956 (2014)
24. Serafini, L., Donadello, I., d'Avila Garcez, A.S.: Learning and reasoning in logic tensor networks: theory and application to semantic image interpretation. In: SAC, pp. 125–130. ACM (2017)
25. Szegedy, C., Vanhoucke, V., Ioffe, S., Shlens, J., Wojna, Z.: Rethinking the inception architecture for computer vision. In: CVPR, pp. 2818–2826. IEEE Computer Society (2016)
26. Tilahun, B., Kauppinen, T., Keßler, C., Fritz, F.: Design and developmentof a linked open data-based health information representation andvisualization system: potentials and preliminary evaluation. JMIR Med. Inform. **2**(2), e31 (2014)

VLX-Stories: Building an Online Event Knowledge Base with Emerging Entity Detection

Dèlia Fernàndez-Cañellas[1,2(✉)], Joan Espadaler[1], David Rodriguez[1], Blai Garolera[1], Gemma Canet[1], Aleix Colom[1], Joan Marco Rimmek[1], Xavier Giro-i-Nieto[2], Elisenda Bou[1], and Juan Carlos Riveiro[1]

[1] Vilynx, Inc., Barcelona, Spain
delia@vilynx.com
[2] Universitat Politecnica de Catalunya (UPC), Barcelona, Spain

Abstract. We present an online multilingual system for event detection and comprehension from media feeds. The system retrieves information from news sites, aggregates them into events (event detection), and summarizes them by extracting semantic labels of its most relevant entities (event representation) in order to answer the journalism Ws: who, what, when and where. The generated events populate VLX-Stories -an event ontology- transforming unstructured text data to a structured knowledge base representation. Our system exploits an external entity Knowledge Graph (VKG) to help populate VLX-Stories. At the same time, this external knowledge graph can also be extended with a Dynamic Entity Linking (DEL) module, which detects emerging entities (EE) on unstructured data. The system is currently deployed in production and used by media producers in the editorial process, providing real-time access to breaking news. Each month, VLX-Stories detects over 9000 events from over 4000 news feeds from seven different countries and in three different languages. At the same time, it detects over 1300 EE per month, which populate VKG.

Keywords: Knowledge base population · Knowledge graph · Event encoding · Entity linking · Emerging entities · Topic detection

1 Introduction

An increasing amount of news documents are published daily on the Web to cover important world events. News aggregators like *Google News*[1] or *Yahoo! News*[2] help users navigate by grouping this overwhelming amount of materials in event clusters. Such systems facilitate users to stay informed on current events and allow them to follow a news story as it evolves over time. This clustering

[1] http://news.google.com.
[2] http://news.yahoo.com.

C. Ghidini et al. (Eds.): ISWC 2019, LNCS 11779, pp. 382–399, 2019.
https://doi.org/10.1007/978-3-030-30796-7_24

task falls on the field of Topic Detection and Tracking (TDT), which aims to develop technologies that organize and structure news materials from a variety of broadcast news media. However, media professionals are in need of more advanced tools to describe, navigate and search specific pieces of information before writing their own piece of news. Semantic Web and Information Extraction (IE) technologies provide high level structured representations of information, which can help solving the mentioned problems. *Knowledge Graphs* (KGs), which store general knowledge represented by world entities and their relations, are currently seen as one of the most essential components of semantic technologies. They allow to generate linked data spaces and structuring information by linking entity mentions to KG entities. The most popular ones are Freebase [4], DBpedia [3], YAGO [36] or Wikidata [39]. Nevertheless, most of these existing KGs focus on traditionally encyclopedic facts like names of popular people, their birth date and place, job, etc. Dynamic information, such as events reported in the news, often involve short term relations and unknown people that are not captured by these resources, and are therefore missed by most KGs. Detecting these out-of-knowledge-base (OOKB) events and its related Emerging Entities (EE) is crucial for any KG maintenance process [14,25,30]. In particular, when willing to provide efficient tools for news description, search and analysis.

In this work, we describe VLX-Stories, a system under exploitation that alleviates the aforementioned issues from journalists teams. It consists of a unified online workflow of event detection, tracking, pattern extraction and Dynamic Entity Linking (DEL), with the aim of building an event-based KB. At the same time, the new EEs detected by VLX-Stories populate an external KG, called *Vilynx Knowledge Graph* (VKG), with background encyclopedic knowledge. In VLX-Stories, events are represented by means of an ontology inspired on the journalist Ws [33]: *what* is happening, *who* is involved, *where* and *when* it took place, and the general *topic* under discussion. The system is characterized by the adoption of semantic technologies, combined with Information Extraction techniques for event encoding. The extraction of mentions and its linkage to entities from an external multilingual KG generates an event linked space. This allows the multilingual linkage across stories, semantic search, and the linkage to customer contents by matching entities.

The goals and contributions of this work are: (a) the generation of an event KB from news stories, (b) the detection of EE from them and (c) the large-scale deployment of the system, which is currently consumed by several media companies to gather information more efficiently. To the best of our knowledge, this is the first system that uses the redundancy of aggregated news articles for a robust detection of EE, in an online manner. Performance statistics are given and evaluation is carried out on the two main contributions addressed (event KB construction and EE detection).

This work is structured as follows. Section 2 describes the industrial context in which this system was built. Section 3 presents the techniques used to detect events on news articles, and Sect. 4 describes how we use pattern mining and entity linking techniques to structure event information. Section 5 includes performance statistics, and Sect. 6 demonstrates the quality of our system by evaluating the distinct modules of our pipeline. Finally, Sect. 7 presents the related work and Sect. 8 the final conclusions and future work.

Fig. 1. Example of the resulting event information displayed on Vilynx Dashboard. In the top we display the article category, the title summarizing *what* happens, and the other properties: *when*, *topic*, *where* and *who*. Titles from articles clustered give context and additional information on the story. At the bottom the entities in the event semantic pattern are displayed as related tags and sorted according to their relevance describing the event.

2 Industrial Use of VLX-Stories

VLX-Stories is a product developed and commercialized by Vilynx[3], an AI company specialized in analyzing media contents. The system is deployed in production worldwide and is currently used by US networks and expanding to Europe and South America. Journalists and editorial teams consume the rich structured news data offered by VLX-Stories to explore how a story relates to other news and detect about which topics they should be writing. This information is served through API calls and a dashboard, providing a general view of what is happening in the world. In Fig. 1, we present an example of a detected event displayed on our dashboard. Notice how the different Ws are addressed and additional context on the news story is given through clustered articles and the related tags (entities). Customers' contents are also linked to detected events using entities, complementing their content information. Thanks to the entities linkage, it is possible to offer a practical interface for navigation and exploring

[3] https://www.vilynx.com.

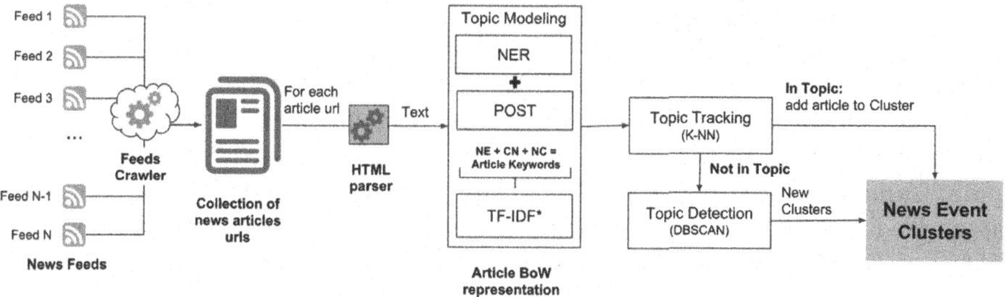

Fig. 2. Schema of the news event detection pipeline.

news. Moreover, VLX-Stories extracts temporal relations and information on temporal trends, which are internally used for other products, e.g. recommendations, trends detection and disambiguation.

Apart from the customer services which can be offered through VLX-Stories, the contributions from this work are also an essential internal tool in Vilynx. The core of Vilynx's technology is the *Vilynx Knowledge Graph* (*VKG*) [8], which is used as a semantic base for indexing media documents. This KG is constructed by merging different public knowledge resources: Freebase, Wikidata and Wikipedia. It provides multilingual aliases for over 3M entities, and 5M relations between entities based on properties. VKG is required to be dynamic because it must support real-time indexation of media documents. Is thus in need of an online detection and population of EE. To provide new knowledge to VKG we use structured data, which is updated periodically by querying the three mentioned public KBs. However, media news often talk about unknown people, who are not indexed on these public knowledge resources or that have not yet been updated [30]. Indexing these novel entities requires extracting EE from non-structured data, e.g. news articles. The VLX-Stories system, presented in this article, will provide the information and dynamics required for VKG maintenance with OOKB entities, while detecting events.

3 Event Detection

This section describes the three parts of the News Event Detection pipeline, outlined in Fig. 2. First, a collection of news articles is built by crawling RSS feeds and parsed (Sect. 3.1). Afterwards, in the topic modeling block (Sect. 3.2), articles are represented with bag-of-words (BoW). Finally, in the topic tracking module, each article vector is compared with articles grouped in event clusters: if matching the event, it is assigned to the cluster; if not, it is added to a pool of articles that will be processed in the topic detection module (Sect. 3.3) in order to detect newly emerging events.

3.1 News Feeds Crawler

News articles are collected by an RSS feeds crawler, which processes 1500 news feeds every 30 min. The RSS feeds come from a manually generated list of 4162 feeds from the main media sources of seven countries: United States, Australia, Spain, Canada, United Kingdom, Portugal and Ireland. Feeds are also manually categorized in seven category groups: *politics*, *sports*, *general news*, *lifestyle and hobbies*, *science and technology*, *business and finance*, and *entertainment*. The feeds crawler visits each feed, crawls it, and stores in the DB each article URL, publication date, title and description if provided. In a second step, whenever a new article is detected in a feed, we crawl the URL and parse the article using a customized HTML parser to extract all its text data and images.

3.2 Topic Modeling

Topic modeling (TM) consists of representing the abstract matter that occurs in a collection of documents. To do this, we will rely on a BoW representation of the articles. As news stories typically revolve around people, places and other named entities (NE), some works [12,32] use mentions of NE instead of all words in the document. However, some news do not turn around NE, e.g. weather news or events related to anonymous people. Therefore, other information, such as common nouns (CN) or noun chunks (NC), is needed to distinguish this kind of events [27]. Combining these three works, we will use named entities, common nouns and noun chunks in the BoW representation, instead of all words in the text corpus. We will call this collection of mentions and nouns *article keywords*. These keywords are extracted from the article's text by a Named Entity Recognition (NER) module and Part of Speech Tagger (POST). We use the Spacy's[4] library and multilingual models for these tasks. For performance reasons, we constraint the articles to be represented for at least 8 keywords, and a maximum of 80 keywords.

BoW keyword's frequencies are weighted by a slightly modified TF-IDF (term frequency - inverse document frequency), which reflects how important a word is to a document in a collection or corpus. TF-IDF is computed as the product of the term frequency (f_k) by the inverse document frequency (idf_k). However, we bias the TF with a weight to give more relevance to those keywords appearing on the title (α), description (α), or that are NE (β). Finally, inspired by [12], we apply a time factor with a linear function, which favors news documents to be assigned to more recent events.

3.3 Topic Detection and Tracking

Once a new article is ingested by the system, we must detect if it is associated to an already detected event (topic tracking) or it describes a new event (topic detection). For the topic tracking, we will use the *k-Nearest Neighbours* (k-NN)

[4] https://spacy.io/.

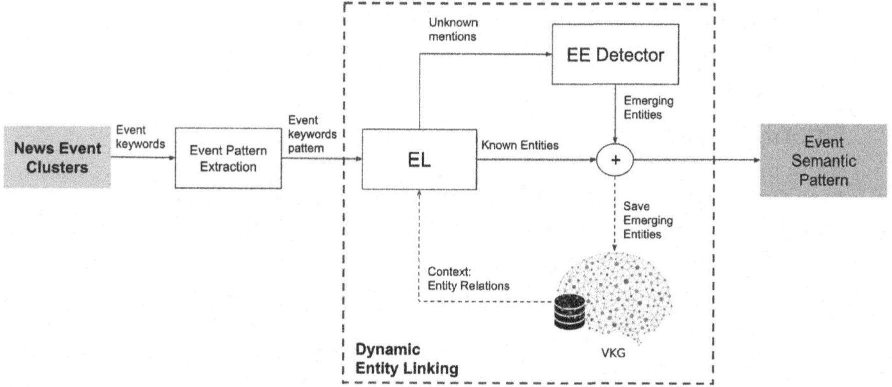

Fig. 3. Pipeline schema of the Event Semantic Pattern extraction module, composed by the Event Pattern Extraction and the Dynamic Entity Linking modules.

algorithm. Thus, a_i being a new article, we will associate the article with an event cluster if there are more than k articles in the cluster with a similarity higher than a given threshold γ. If the incoming article is not associated to any event cluster, we will try to build a new cluster with other articles not yet related to any event. This is the task of topic detection. The chosen clustering technique for topic detection is DBSCAN [7], which is an unsupervised density-based algorithm that provides robustness against the presence of noise. This method requires the estimation of two hyper-parameters: *min samples*, which is the minimum number of samples needed to generate a new cluster, and *eps*, the maximum distance allowed within its samples. We decided to fix the $minsamples = 5$, thus all events will be represented with at least five articles, and we optimize *eps* in order to have high precision without missing many events. We use *cosine similarity* as the distance metric for both tasks.

Moreover, some design decisions were made in order to compensate some of the problems of dealing with an online and large-scale deployment application with noisy Web data. In order to prevent wrong event detections due to web parser errors, we added two extra conditions on the cluster generation: the clustered articles need to be from at least three different news publishers, and one media publisher can not own over 50% of the articles in a cluster. Values were chose after manually analyzing several detection errors. Also, speed issues had to be considered to provide real-time trackin on news events, as the amount of comparisons between articles grows quadratically with the number of articles, slowing the whole article comparison. We decided to cluster articles by country, and for those countries with more feeds, we use a category-based comparison between articles. The category of the feed is used for this split, and in case the feed provides general news from any category, we trained a deep classifier based on a one layer LSTM [13] to predict the article category from its title. The training dataset was constructed by merging the category titles from the

UCI-ML News Aggregator Dataset [6] and titles from the manually labeled RSS news feeds.

4 Event Representation

Event representation tries to synthesize the agents, locations and actions involved in an event in a formal machine understandable way, but still natural for humans. This is achieved by extracting semantics from the event articles and structuring the knowledge. Our approach provides an event semantic pattern by combining pattern mining with a Dynamic Entity Linking module (Sect. 4.1). This module uses VKG for the entity disambiguation, which will also be populated with EE found in the process. Finally, this semantic pattern is post-processed to structure the entities into our event ontology (Sect. 4.2).

4.1 Event Semantic Pattern

The extraction of the event semantic pattern is achieved thanks to the two modules depicted in Fig. 3: Event Pattern Extraction (EPE) and Dynamic Entity Linking (DEL). The EPE module finds the keywords pattern describing the event, and the DEL links these keywords to entities from VKG, while detecting candidates of new entities which populate VKG. The details follow.

Pattern Mining: Data mining techniques search for patterns in data that are representative and discriminative. We define our pattern mining task with an *association rule* approach [2], such that our pattern corresponds to a set of association rules, $t^* \rightarrow y$, that optimize the *support* and *confidence* constraints for each event. Let n be the set of all keywords in the corpus $C = \{k_1, k_2, ..., k_n\}$; and a *transaction* A be the set of keywords from a given article, such that $A \subseteq C$. Given a set of m transactions belonging to the same event $T = \{A_1, A_2, ..., A_m\}$, we want to find the subset of C, say t^*, which can accurately predict the belonging to a target event $y \in E$. The *support* of t^* is an indicator of how often t^* appears in T, and it is defined as the proportion of transactions in the transaction set T that contain the itemset t^*:

$$s(t^*) = \frac{|\{A_a | t^* \subseteq A_a, A_a \in T\}|}{m} \quad (1)$$

Our goal is to find association rules that accurately predict the belonging to an event, given a set of keywords. Therefore, we want to find a pattern such that if t^* appears in a transaction, there is a high likelihood that y, which represents an event category, appears in that transaction as well. We define the *confidence* as the likelihood that if $t^* \subseteq A$ then $y \in A$, which can be expressed as:

$$c(t^* \rightarrow y) = \frac{s(t^* \cup y)}{s(t^*)} \quad (2)$$

Inspired by [22] we use the popular apriori algorithm [1] to find patterns within the transactions. We only keep the association rules with confidence $c_{min} \geq 0.8$ and calculate the support threshold (s_{min}) that ensures at least 10 keywords in the rule. Finally, we select the rule t^* with more keywords associated. This keywords are the ones that will be linked to VKG entities.

Dynamic Entity Linking: The event keywords in the pattern will be mapped to entities in VKG. This task is called Entity Linking (EL) or disambiguation. Our EL module gets entity candidates from VKG for each incoming mention. Entities are retrieved based on similarity matching between the text mention and the entities alias. Then, disambiguation is applied by scoring each candidate. Following the work in [8], an *intra-score* and an *inter-score* are computed for each candidate. On one hand the intra-score is computed by using the information of the mention and entity itself, combining the following metrics: word similarity, entity usability and entity type. On the other hand, the inter-score exploits the contextual information between entities by using distances between entities in a concept embedding space. The combination of all these metrics gives a confidence score for a given mention to be disambiguated to an entity. If this score is higher than a predefined threshold, the mention and entities are linked.

However, news often refer to people that has never been mentioned before, and thus, are not indexed in VKG. In order to populate VKG we added dynamics into the EL module, calling it a Dynamic Entity Linking (DEL). This module maintains EE that refer to unknown people as they appear on the news, and integrates it into VKG. This EE detector filters the unknown mentions, keeping only those that have been recognized as *persons* by the NER module and that are at least composed by two words (name and surname). The detection is highly robust because the EE come from the previously extracted event pattern, which means the entity has appeared in a high amount of articles from different publishers, in the same context, and is thus relevant when describing the event. Once an EE is detected, the system starts being capable of using it for tagging and linking documents, and it is already used to describe new events. However, it will require for a human validation in order to become a proper concept in the KG. This validation is needed because sometimes the names detected are spelling variations of entities already in the KG, or mistakes from the NER module. An independent system takes care of the EEs by searching for entity matching suggestions in external KBs (Google Knowledge Graph, Wikipedia and Wikidata), as well as entities in VKG. Suggestion results are displayed in an internal dashboard, together with context from the sentences where the EE has been seen, where a human makes the final decision. Thanks to previous process and autocomplete tools, the human intervention is minimal and very fast decisions can be made.

Multi-regional Event Matching: Before the final event modeling, the semantic pattern of the events detected for each country are compared and merged in case of match. To do that, we first rank the entities in the Event Semantic

Pattern by relevancy describing the event. The ranking is based on re-scoring entities based on its original keywords appearance frequency and origin (title, description or text body). As we solved the entity disambiguation we recompute the entity frequency taking into account co-references. Origins are taken into account by weighting the frequency of appearance by the origin. Afterwards, country-events are represented with a bag of concepts BoC where entity relevancies are the weights. Cosine similarity is computed between country-events and these events are merged into worldwide-events if its similarity is higher than a manually defined threshold.

4.2 Event Model

Both semantic and contextual event information extracted on previous steps are processed in order to represent the collected data in an ontological manner. This ontological information is stored in VLX-Stories KB, which keeps growing with the multiregional news information provided by the feeds. In this section, we first motivate the modeling decisions we took designing the ontology and we continue by describing the information extraction process.

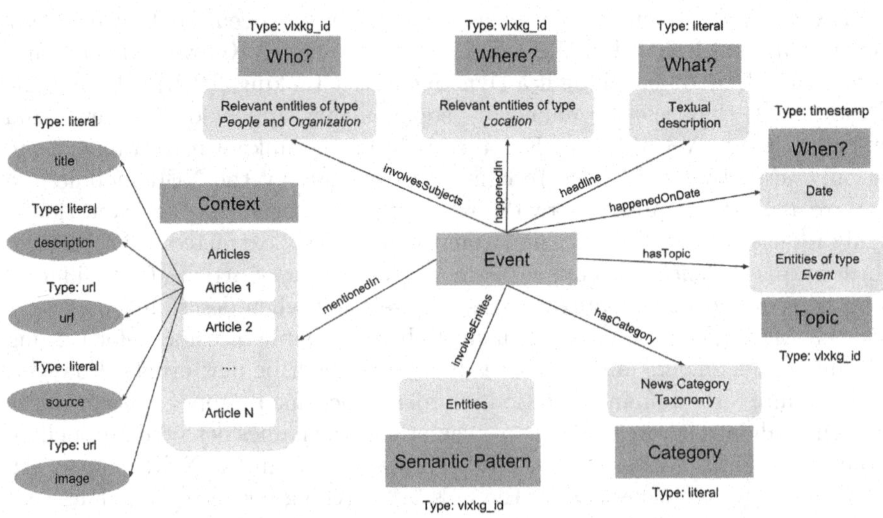

Fig. 4. Event ontology schema.

Modeling the Event Ontology: The main requirement of our event ontology is that it has to synthesize in a both machine and human readable way the unstructured semantic pattern extracted. Events are usually defined by its agents, locations and actions occurring and the moment when the event takes place. Journalistic articles are typically structured to answer four of the journalist 5W-questions: e.g. *what* happened, *who* is involved, *where* and *when* did it happen. These questions should be addressed within the first few sentences of an article to quickly inform readers. The fifth W, *Why* it happened, is often addressed in opinion columns or post-event coverage [16]. Moreover, news stories often fall into bigger topics which are composed by several events, like *Brexit*, *Academy Awards*, *Olympic Games*, etc. This information, if present, offers the possibility of tracking long story lines and to provide a complete context on the development of an event in a point in time.

Considering the above mentioned 4Ws and the topic, we defined our ontology with the next *properties* or *core classes* for each event: Who, What, When, Where and Topic. This properties will be extracted from the event semantic pattern and the titles and descriptions from the event articles. Moreover, as shown in the ontology schema in Fig. 4, all entities in the semantic pattern, answering or not the 4Ws or topic, will be included in the ontology within the Semantic Pattern class. The event Category, e.g. sports, politics, entertainment, etc.; is also included as a property. Additional context on the event is given by the clustered articles, from which we store the title, description, URL, news source and image, if present.

Event Properties Extraction: The Who, Where and Topic are extracted from the Event Semantic Pattern using a set of filters based on entity types. Entities in VKG have a schema[5] type associated, which denotes if the entity is a person, place, organization, etc. These types will be used to classify the entities in the pattern together with the type of metadata field from which they were extracted. For this task only the entities from the title and description are used. Moreover, the same entity relevance scores computed for multi-regional event matching will be used to pick those most relevant entities. The Who property needs to be an entity of type *Person*, *Organization* or *CreativeWork*; the Where is a property of type *Place* and the topic of type *Event*. We define the What of an event with a sentence (literal) summarizing the main event occurring. As news article's titles should give this information, we answer the What with the most descriptive title between the clustered articles. This is selected using a voting algorithm where each word in the title sums its given score in the semantic entities ranking. This approach favors longer titles, which also tend to be semantically richer. To answer When, we take the date of the first article published related to an event. We plan on improving it on next versions by analyzing time expressions in the text. Finally, we complete the ontology by adding the event Category. Categories come from our pre-defined set of categories, e.g. *Sport*, *Entertainment*, *Finances*, *Politics*, etc. The categories assigned to the RSS feeds are used to extract this information. One event may belong to more than one category.

[5] https://schema.org/.

5 System Analytics

VLX-Stories was first deployed on July 2018 for its use in the United States. Since then, the system has been growing, adding new world regions and languages. Table 1 contains the activation date of VLX-Stories for each country, the language it processes, the number of feeds activated on each country, the average number of events detected each day and the daily number of articles processed and associated to events. Results are provided country by country and also on the worldwide event aggregation. According to these statistics, VLX-Stories grows in a speed average above 300 news events/day, classifying an average of over 17k multilingual articles from seven different countries. Since we activated the multi-regional event aggregation module on November 2018, the system includes the option of analyzing how an event is reported in different world regions and in different languages. Semantic disambiguation is essential for this multilingual aggregation task.

Table 1. Statistics on VLX-stories population.

Country	Activation date	Language	#Feeds	Events/Day	Articles/day
USA	07/2018	English	952	96.70	4,745.59
SP	08/2018	Spanish	918	90.61	4,929.01
CA	09/2018	English	551	27.15	990.04
AU	09/2018	English	893	53.19	3,223.09
IR	09/2018	English	121	20.46	654.25
UK	09/2018	English	442	38.57	1,518.63
PT	09/2018	Portuguese	285	35.80	1,235.76
Total	-	-	**4,162**	**362.48**	**17,296.37**
World Wide	11/2018	Multilingual	4,162	301.84	17,296.37

6 Evaluation

VLX-Stories was evaluated by considering each block separately. This approach provides a detailed analysis and facilitates the identification of bottlenecks.

6.1 News Event Detection

Regarding news aggregator or event detection evaluation, we used a subset of the UCI-ML News Aggregator Dataset [6]. This dataset consists of 7,231 news stories, constructed from the aggregation of news web pages collected from March 10 to August 10 of 2014. The resources are grouped into clusters that represent pages discussing the same news story or event. Events are categorized into four different categories: entertainment, health, business and technology. For each news article, its title, URL, news story id and category are given. However, we had to discard a 13% of the events on the dataset because of the following reasons: 36% of the URL link's were broken, our system could not extract enough keywords from 17% of the articles, and finally, we had to discard some of the remaining news stories because they were not represented by enough articles to be detected by our system (each of our events needs to be represented by at least 5 news articles). The final dataset subset consists on 6,289 events constructed by 91,728 news articles. For our experiments the DBSCAN parameters were set to $eps = 0.65$ and $minsamples = 5$. Table 2 presents the news event detection results on the dataset. Most of the events are correctly detected (81.58%), however a lot of articles are not associated to any event. This is reflected by the high average precision (94.57%) but a poor recall (58.548%). This is mostly because of the restrictive parameters set in the system in order to make sure that aggregated news served are correct. Quality of aggregated news is similar across news categories. The lowest quality is found in the business category, because most of the business news share financial terms which are repeated in many articles, even not related ones. Best results are for entertainment, the type of news with more named entities, which improves the representation.

Table 2. Results of the news event detection on UCI Dataset subset

	#articles	#events	Event P.	Article P.	Article R.	F1
Business	21,535	1,796	78.28%	91.44%	51.76%	66.11%
Entertainment	36,790	1,673	88.76%	96.43%	64.44%	77.26%
Technology	23,921	1,811	85.69%	94.38%	57.37%	71.36%
Health	9,482	1,009	68.18%	94.86%	56.85%	71.09%
GLOBAL	**91,72**	**6,28**	**81.58%**	**94.57%**	**58.54%**	**72.32%**

6.2 Dynamic Entity Linking

The mapping of event keyword patterns to event semantic patterns includes the EL task and the EE detection. However, this tasks also depends on the quality of the NER and POS modules from Spacy. According to Spacy's documentation[6] the quality of these modules is state of the art performance, with accuracies close to the 90%. To evaluate the quality on the EL and EE detection we ran two experiments.

Entity Linking: The first experiment evaluated EL of the keywords on the event pattern to semantic labels. The experiments were conducted over a corpus of 100 semantic event patterns randomly selected from the United States

[6] https://spacy.io/usage/facts-figures.

events, detected by our news aggregator module during the week from the 1st of January to the 7th of January 2019. The keywords from the patterns were mapped to entities from VKG using the dynamic EL module. The correctness of the mapping was evaluated with TP when the semantic entity related to the keyword was correct, FP when the semantic entity related was wrong, TN when no entity was related and it is not an existing entity or it is an error from NER, and FN if no entity was mapped but there is an entity in VKG for it. Results are shown in Table 3, with a total accuracy of the 86%. However some mentions do not disambiguate to its correct entities. This is specially common when finding homonym words or unknown contexts. Further research should be developed to improve these ambiguous cases.

Table 3. Results on entity linking

#Event patterns	TP	TN	FP	FN	Precision	Recall	F1	Accuracy
100	966	329	52	156	0.86	0.94	0.90	0.86

Emerging Entities: The capacity of detecting EE was evaluated by deleting existing entities from our VKG and testing the capacity of the system to create them again. We initially built a dataset of 648 news events detected during the week from the 1st to the 7th of January 2019. The multilingual capabilities of the system was tested by choosing events from three regions with different languages: the United States, Spain and Portugal. The dataset was generated by running the Event Semantic Pattern module, removing the corresponding person's entities from VKG, and extracting again the Event Semantic Pattern, expecting for the EE detector to re-generate the deleted entities. As shown in Table 4, an average of 78.86% of the deleted entities were recovered. Some of the missing entities were composed by just one word, like *Rhianna* or *Shakira.* Our system did not detect them because it constrains person entities to be described with two words (name and surname). Other errors were caused by the similarity between entities, which are wrongly disambiguate to existing entities; e.g. when deleting the *Donald Trump* entity, the EL disambiguated to *Donald Trump Jr.* because of a perfect match between the alias and the similar usage context.

Finally, a statistical study of the created entities and their quality is done by analyzing data between 12th December 2018 and 15th March 2019. Table 5 presents the average number of EE detected every day in each language. However, not all the detected EE become new entities in VKG. After the human supervision we extracted the next metrics: 75.45% of the detected EE become new entities, 22.15% are alias of already existing entities and 9.7% are wrong candidates because of NER errors.

Table 4. Results on emerging entities detection

Country	Language	#Stories	#Deleted entities	%EE Recovered
United States	en	282	373	80.16%
Spain	es	251	299	74.91%
Portugal	pt	115	104	85.57%
Total	-	**648**	**776**	**78.86%**

Table 5. Statistics on emerging entities detection by VLX-stories

	EN	ES	PT	Total
Avg. EE detected/day	41.18	20.08	9.27	67.88

7 Related Work

The system presented in this work tries to solve the *semantic gap* between the coverage of structured and unstructured data available on the Web [28], in order to provide journalistic tools for event analyzing. In the past decades, a great amount of research efforts has been devoted to text understanding and Information Extraction (IE). Many research projects have entangled with the different problems described in this work, i.e. news aggregation [5,9,12,20,35], event pattern extraction [15,43], entity linking [12,19,20,23], emerging entity detection [14,17,25,30,34], event ontology population [29,42] and automatically answering journalist Ws [10,11]. However, only a few big projects are comparable to our system as end-to-end online pipelines for event detection and encoding. In this section we will focus on reviewing these large-scale systems.

Two well-known event-encoding systems are the *Integrated Crisis Early Warning Systems*[7] (ICEWS) and the *Global Database of Events, Language and Tone*[8] (GDELT). This two projects have been developed to automatically extract international political incidents such as protests, assaults and mass violence from news media. These datasets are updated online, making them useful for real-time conflict analysis. ICEWS is a project supported by the Defense Advanced Research Projects Agency (DARPA), to be used for US analyst. Its data has recently been made public thought Harvard's Dataverse[9], however events are posted with a 1 year delay and the techniques and code utilized are not open source. GDELT was build as a public and more transparent version of ICEWS. Its data is freely available and includes over 200 million events since 1979, with daily updates. However, legal controversies over how data resources were obtained distanced it from research. It is currently incorporated into Google's services and its data is utilized for analysis of international events [18,21]. As the two more spread news databases, several comparison studies have been made

[7] https://www.icews.com/.
[8] https://www.gdeltproject.org/.
[9] https://dataverse.harvard.edu/dataverse/icews.

between ICEWS and GDELT. Even though no conclusion could be extracted on the superiority of any system, GDELT overstates the number of events by a substantial margin, but ICEWS misses some events as well [40,41].

A more recent event data program is the *Open Event Data Alliance*[10] (OEDA). This organization provides public multi-sourced political event datasets, which are weekly updated [31]. All the data is transparent and they provide open code of the ontologies supported. They use Standford CoreNLP tools [24] and WordNet [26] dictionaries. However, OEDA's efforts still have not reached the scale of the other two mentioned projects.

Another well-known project is the *NewsReader*[11] [38]. This system is a big collaborative research project, which constructs an Event-Centric Knowledge Base (ECKB) based on financial and economic news articles. They take advantage of several public knowledge resources to provide multilingual understanding and use DBpedia [3] as KG for EL. They define their own event ontology, the Simple Event Model (SEM) [37], which is designed to be versatile in different event domains allowing cross-source interoperability. To deal with entities not properly represented in the knowledge resources, they introduce the concept of *dark entities*. Although these detected dark entities are used for event representation, they are not used to populate the background KG.

From the works presented, ICEWS, GDELT and OEDA are focused on political data for the analysis of conflicts, and NewsReader generates an ECKB from financial data. Notice there is still a big coverage gap when it comes to media event encoding. In this sense, VLX-Stories offers a wider service for journalistic purposes, as it covers, as well as politics and finances, many other categories, like sports, entertainment, lifestyle, science and technology.

8 Conclusions

We presented an online event encoding system which aggregates news articles from RSS feeds, and encodes this information using semantic entities from an external KG. These entities populate an event ontology which answers the journalistic Ws. On the process, discovered EE complete the external KG (VKG) with OOKB entities. VLX-Stories realizes thus a twofold functionality: (a) generating an event KB, and (b) maintaining a KG with EEs. The detected events are served through API calls and a dashboard to media producers and other global media companies. These companies use VLX-Stories in the editorial process to identify which topics are gaining momentum, find news related to their contents, and searching for background information on trending stories.

The system matches unstructured text with Semantic Web resources, by exploiting Information Extraction techniques and external knowledge resources. This makes possible the multilingual linkage across events, semantic search, and the linkage to customer contents by matching entities. Moreover the ontological structure behind it facilitates event comprehension, search and navigation. Our

[10] http://openeventdata.org/.
[11] http://www.newsreader-project.eu/.

engine processes an average of 17,000 articles/day, and detects an average 300 worldwide events/day from seven different countries and three languages. Our experimental results show an F-1 score of 72.32% for event detection, and a high capacity of detecting EE of people, with an average of 78.86% of the deleted entities being detected again. EE detection statistics show that the system detects an average of almost 68 EE/day, the 75.45% of which become new entities, and 22.15% are used to populate VKG entities with new alias.

We plan to continue this work by adding more countries, and improving the event representation by extracting semantic triplets that would describe the relations between the entities on the event. Regarding the KG maintenance process we will include the detection of other types of EE.

Acknowledgments. Dèlia Fernàndez-Cañellas is funded by contract 2017-DI-011 of the Industrial Doctorate Program of the Government of Catalonia.

References

1. Agrawal, R.S., Srikant, P.: Fast algorithms for mining association rules in large databases. In: Proceedings of the 20th International Conference on Very Large Data Bases, pp. 487–499 (1994)
2. Agrawal, R., Imieliński, T., Swami, A.: Mining association rules between sets of items in large databases. In: ACM SIGMOD Record, vol. 22, pp. 207–216. ACM (1993)
3. Auer, S., Bizer, C., Kobilarov, G., Lehmann, J., Cyganiak, R., Ives, Z.: DBpedia: a nucleus for a web of open data. In: Aberer, K., et al. (eds.) ASWC/ISWC-2007. LNCS, vol. 4825, pp. 722–735. Springer, Heidelberg (2007). https://doi.org/10.1007/978-3-540-76298-0_52
4. Bollacker, K., Evans, C., Paritosh, P., Sturge, T., Taylor, J.: Freebase: a collaboratively created graph database for structuring human knowledge. In: Proceedings of the 2008 ACM SIGMOD International Conference on Management of Data, pp. 1247–1250. ACM (2008)
5. Conrad, J.G., Bender, M.: Semi-supervised events clustering in news retrieval. In: NewsIR@ ECIR, pp. 21–26 (2016)
6. Dheeru, D., Karra Taniskidou, E.: UCI machine learning repository (2017). http://archive.ics.uci.edu/ml
7. Ester, M., Kriegel, H.P., Sander, J., Xu, X., et al.: A density-based algorithm for discovering clusters in large spatial databases with noise. In: KDD, vol. 96, pp. 226–231 (1996)
8. Fernández, D., et al.: Vits: video tagging system from massive web multimedia collections. In: Proceedings of the 5th Workshop on Web-scale Vision and Social Media (VSM), pp. 337–346. IEEE Press (2017)
9. Guo, X., Gao, L., Liu, X., Yin, J.: Improved deep embedded clustering with local structure preservation. In: IJCAI, pp. 1753–1759 (2017)
10. Hamborg, F., Breitinger, C., Schubotz, M., Lachnit, S., Gipp, B.: Extraction of main event descriptors from news articles by answering the journalistic five W and one H questions. In: JCDL, pp. 339–340 (2018)
11. Hamborg, F., Lachnit, S., Schubotz, M., Hepp, T., Gipp, B.: Giveme5W: main event retrieval from news articles by extraction of the five journalistic W questions.

In: Chowdhury, G., McLeod, J., Gillet, V., Willett, P. (eds.) iConference 2018. LNCS, vol. 10766, pp. 356–366. Springer, Cham (2018). https://doi.org/10.1007/978-3-319-78105-1_39
12. Hennig, L., et al.: SPIGA-a multilingual news aggregator. In: Proceedings of GSCL 2011 (2011)
13. Hochreiter, S., Schmidhuber, J.: Long short-term memory. Neural Comput. **9**(8), 1735–1780 (1997)
14. Hoffart, J., Milchevski, D., Weikum, G., Anand, A., Singh, J.: The knowledge awakens: keeping knowledge bases fresh with emerging entities. In: Proceedings of the 25th International Conference Companion on World Wide Web, pp. 203–206. International World Wide Web Conferences Steering Committee (2016)
15. Ji, H., Grishman, R.: Refining event extraction through cross-document inference. In: Proceedings of ACL 2008: HLT, pp. 254–262 (2008)
16. Jou, B., Li, H., Ellis, J.G., Morozoff-Abegauz, D., Chang, S.F.: Structured exploration of who, what, when, and where in heterogeneous multimedia news sources. In: Proceedings of the 21st ACM International Conference on Multimedia, pp. 357–360. ACM (2013)
17. Kuzey, E., Vreeken, J., Weikum, G.: A fresh look on knowledge bases: distilling named events from news. In: Proceedings of the 23rd ACM International Conference on Conference on Information and Knowledge Management, pp. 1689–1698. ACM (2014)
18. Kwak, H., An, J.: A first look at global news coverage of disasters by using the GDELT dataset. In: Aiello, L.M., McFarland, D. (eds.) SocInfo 2014. LNCS, vol. 8851, pp. 300–308. Springer, Cham (2014). https://doi.org/10.1007/978-3-319-13734-6_22
19. Le, P., Titov, I.: Improving entity linking by modeling latent relations between mentions. arXiv preprint arXiv:1804.10637 (2018)
20. Leban, G., Fortuna, B., Grobelnik, M.: Using news articles for real-time cross-lingual event detection and filtering. In: NewsIR@ ECIR, pp. 33–38 (2016)
21. Leetaru, K., Schrodt, P.A.: GDELT: global data on events, location, and tone, 1979–2012. In: ISA Annual Convention, vol. 2, pp. 1–49. Citeseer (2013)
22. Li, H., Ellis, J.G., Ji, H., Chang, S.F.: Event specific multimodal pattern mining for knowledge base construction. In: Proceedings of the 2016 ACM on Multimedia Conference, pp. 821–830. ACM (2016)
23. Luo, G., Huang, X., Lin, C.Y., Nie, Z.: Joint entity recognition and disambiguation. In: Proceedings of the 2015 Conference on Empirical Methods in Natural Language Processing, pp. 879–888 (2015)
24. Manning, C., Surdeanu, M., Bauer, J., Finkel, J., Bethard, S., McClosky, D.: The Stanford CoreNLP natural language processing toolkit. In: Proceedings of 52nd Annual Meeting of the Association for Computational Linguistics: System Demonstrations, pp. 55–60 (2014)
25. Martinez-Rodriguez, J.L., Hogan, A., Lopez-Arevalo, I.: Information extraction-meets the semantic web: a survey. Semant. Web (Preprint), 1–81 (2018)
26. Miller, G.A.: WordNet: a lexical database for English. Commun. ACM **38**(11), 39–41 (1995)
27. Ng, K.W., Tsai, F.S., Chen, L., Goh, K.C.: Novelty detection for text documents using named entity recognition. In: 2007 6th International Conference on Information, Communications & Signal Processing, pp. 1–5. IEEE (2007)
28. Polleres, A., Hogan, A., Harth, A., Decker, S.: Can we ever catch up with the web? Semant. Web **1**(1, 2), 45–52 (2010)

29. Rospocher, M., et al.: Building event-centric knowledge graphs from news. J. Web Semant. **37**, 132–151 (2016)
30. Sagi, T., Wolf, Y., Hose, K.: How new is the (RDF) news? In: Companion Proceedings of The 2019 World Wide Web Conference, pp. 714–721. ACM (2019)
31. Schrodt, P.A., Beieler, J., Idris, M.: Three'sa charm?: open event data coding with EL: DIABLO, PETRARCH, and the open event data alliance. In: ISA Annual Convention (2014)
32. Shah, C., Croft, W.B., Jensen, D.: Representing documents with named entities for story link detection (SLD). In: Proceedings of the 15th ACM International Conference on Information and Knowledge Management, pp. 868–869. ACM (2006)
33. Singer, J.B.: Five Ws and an H: digital challenges in newspaper newsrooms and boardrooms. Int. J. Media Manag. **10**, 122–129 (2008)
34. Singh, J., Hoffart, J., Anand, A.: Discovering entities with just a little help from you. In: Proceedings of the 25th ACM International on Conference on Information and Knowledge Management, pp. 1331–1340. ACM (2016)
35. Steinberger, J.: MediaGist: a cross-lingual analyser of aggregated news and commentaries. In: Proceedings of ACL-2016 System Demonstrations, pp. 145–150 (2016)
36. Suchanek, F.M., Kasneci, G., Weikum, G.: Yago: a core of semantic knowledge. In: Proceedings of the 16th International Conference on World Wide Web, pp. 697–706. ACM (2007)
37. Van Hage, W.R., Malaisé, V., Segers, R., Hollink, L., Schreiber, G.: Design and use of the simple event model (SEM). Web Semant.: Sci. Serv. Agents World Wide Web **9**(2), 128–136 (2011)
38. Vossen, P., et al.: Newsreader: using knowledge resources in a cross-lingual reading machine to generate more knowledge from massive streams of news. Knowl.-Based Syst. **110**, 60–85 (2016)
39. Vrandečić, D., Krötzsch, M.: Wikidata: a free collaborative knowledgebase. Commun. ACM **57**(10), 78–85 (2014)
40. Wang, W.: Event detection and extraction from news articles. Ph.D. thesis, Virginia Tech (2018)
41. Ward, M.D., Beger, A., Cutler, J., Dickenson, M., Dorff, C., Radford, B.: Comparing GDELT and ICEWS event data. Analysis **21**(1), 267–297 (2013)
42. Wu, Z., Liang, C., Giles, C.L.: Storybase: towards building a knowledge base for news events. In: Proceedings of ACL-IJCNLP 2015 System Demonstrations, pp. 133–138 (2015)
43. Zhang, T., et al.: Improving event extraction via multimodal integration. In: Proceedings of the 25th ACM International Conference on Multimedia, pp. 270–278. ACM (2017)

Personalized Knowledge Graphs for the Pharmaceutical Domain

Anna Lisa Gentile(✉), Daniel Gruhl, Petar Ristoski, and Steve Welch

IBM Research Almaden, San Jose, CA, USA
{annalisa.gentile,petar.ristoski}@ibm.com,
{dgruhl,welchs}@us.ibm.com

Abstract. A considerable amount of scientific and technical content is still locked behind data formats which are not machine readable, especially PDF files - and this is particularly true in the healthcare domain. While the Semantic Web has nourished the shift to more accessible formats, in business scenarios it is critical to be able to tap into this type of content, both to extract as well as embed machine readable semantic information.

We present our solution in the pharmaceutical domain and describe a fully functional pipeline to maintain up-to-date knowledge resources extracted from medication Package Inserts. We showcase how subject matter expert(s) can have their own view on the available documents, served by a personalized Knowledge Graph - or rather a view on the graph which is specific to them. We share lessons learned from our initial pilot study with a team of medical professionals. Our solution is fully integrated within the standard PDF data format and does not require the use of any external software - nor to be aware of the underlying graph.

1 Introduction

The Semantic Web community is constantly pushing the barrier on processing and producing knowledge that is understandable by both humans and machines. Nonetheless when it comes to technical and scientific content, much of the information is locked behind formats which are not directly machine readable. In the healthcare domain much information is exchanged via PDF files, especially when the communication is across different organizations or when it is directed to the public. In this work we focus on the specific task of building and maintaining consistent and updated knowledge about pharmaceutical drugs. Typically this task requires subject matter experts and it is complex enough that it takes multiple editorial units, each focusing on different aspects of the domain, to make sure that important information from such documents is extracted, categorized and retained in structured knowledge internal to the organization.

Despite the plethora of available Information Extraction (IE) tools that ease the transition from unstructured data to organized knowledge, many IE

C. Ghidini et al. (Eds.): ISWC 2019, LNCS 11779, pp. 400–417, 2019.
https://doi.org/10.1007/978-3-030-30796-7_25

approaches are based on many underlying assumptions: (i) that raw text is available, i.e. the task of obtaining such text from diverse sources (Web pages, text documents, PDF documents, etc.) is neglected; (ii) that a certain loss in accuracy is expected and tolerated; (iii) that agreement exists, i.e. there is a universal truth about what constitutes correct knowledge; (iv) that examples are ready available - or easily obtainable - to train the models. The reality is that the bootstrapping cost of having such IE tools in place is often too high, especially in business engagements with a short life span, where introducing format transformations, new tooling, new training data introduces disruptions for the end users. In our specific use case of collecting drug information, it is important to retain knowledge in the original format (i.e. the PDF document) but at the same time to be able to identify semantic content within the documents and identify relevant changes with respect to previous version of the same document. This aspect is often neglected by Knowledge Graph construction approaches, where the end product is the populated graph itself rather than the graph in combination with the enriched source documents.

We propose a strategy to perform such IE tasks directly on the input documents, so as to be completely transparent for the end user. As our focus is on PDF documents, we add task-specific semantic annotators directly into the PDF files (which are thus viewable with a standard PDF reader). We offer a combination of ontology based annotators as well as the possibility to add new semantic annotators trained on demand, within the PDF itself, with a human-in-the-loop methodology. Transparently to the end user we collect all information from all versions of the documents in a consolidated Knowledge Graph, which is used to keep track of information changes about each drug.

The novelty of this work is that we perform semantic enrichment directly into PDF files. This is not simply a technical contribution but a methodological one, because to build any human-in-the-loop system, the interaction needs to be continuous and non-disruptive for the subject matter expert. In the proposed use case we let the user continue their knowledge curation task exactly as they were used to - by manually reading and analyzing documents - but we enrich the same exact documents with highlights and comments - which are the result of semantic enrichment. The Knowledge Graph in the backstage is the result of the annotations obtained from standard ontology-based annotators, as well as those obtained by any new annotators that the user wants to train on the fly - we will concretely show how we obtain "salient sentences", as defined and trained by the editorial unit curating Adverse Drug Reaction, and Drug-Drug interaction relations. Lastly we can maintain a *personalized* Knowledge Graph for each editorial unit, where only the results of selected annotators are used to maintain their consolidated knowledge.

The advantage of our proposed solution is its ability to unlock semantic information from proprietary documents - especially PDF - seamlessly, and allowing new annotators to be added modularly on demand, after a training interaction with the end user. The direct integration with the users' current workflow and the transparent use of semantic technologies eases the acceptance of the solution by the users. The personalized knowledge views - which are built for each individual editing unit - ensure that the users are not overwhelmed with annotations. Instead they only visualize the annotations they are interested in.

The rest of the paper is structured as follows: after exploring available state of the art (Sect. 2) we describe in detail our use case (Sect. 6), our system (Sect. 4) and present results on a sample of real documents (Sect. 5). We conclude with lesson learned and future work (Sect. 7).

2 State of the Art

Much of today's scientific and technical content is locked behind proprietary document formats, making it difficult to consume for analytic systems. There has been much positive shifting especially in the context of scientific publishing, where many publishers have been showcasing the benefit of augmenting scholarly content with semantic information. Examples are the SciGraph project[1] by Springer-Nature, the Dynamic Knowledge Platforms (DKP) by Elsevier[2] among others. Academic projects such as Biotea [8] pursue the same goal of creating machine readable and sharable knowledge extracted from scientific content in proprietary format (specifically XML files). Academic initiatives have been encouraging the idea of "semantic publishing" [17] where the authors themselves augment their scientific papers with semantic annotations, instead of relying on post-processing information extraction performed by third parties. Other initiatives aim at maintaining sharable knowledge about the metadata of scientific publication [13].

While significant effort has been put into extracting and maintaining semantic information from scientific publications, much of the content is still locked inside PDF files. This is even more true for technical documents that are not necessarily scientific papers, but which still contain extremely valuable information. The use case that we present in this paper specifically focuses on a particular type of technical documents, the medication Package Insert (PI) [12], which provide physicians with information about the proper use and risks of a prescription drug.

There are several efforts in the literature which explore extracting information from PDFs directly. Early examples [19,20] focus on parsing textual content and extracting structured information. They do so without maintaining the user interaction with the original files. This is undesirable, especially in cases where the layout of the text (e.g., tables) or ancillary information (e.g., chemical structures or other illustrations) are critical context to the understanding of the text. More recent examples exploit the specific structure of certain PDF files, therefore also using specific visual clues of the documents to train the extraction models [1,2,18].

On the other hand we propose a solution that is agnostic of any specific structure of the input file and that is fully integrated within a PDF, and thus can

[1] https://www.springernature.com/scigraph.
[2] http://data.elsevier.com/documentation/index.html.

be viewed with the PDF reader the subject matter expert is already using. Our solution allows the user to visually identify the information which is semantically relevant for their business case. Such information is used by the system to train semantic annotators, which are then integrated directly in the PDF viewer tool that the subject matter expert is already using.

In the healthcare and pharmaceutical domains there are numerous proposals to extract semantic information from available data [5,14–16] but the underlying assumption is that they either operate within a proprietary system or that the semantic annotations are performed offline, in a pipeline fashion, where the SMEs cannot tune the models, nor correct or personalize the results. The major methodological advantage in our proposed solution is that we integrate IE tools - based on ontological annotators and on models which are trained on the fly with human-in-the-loop - directly within the PDF data format, fostering acceptance by the subject matter experts.

3 Use Case Description: Extracting Knowledge from Medical Package Inserts

The use case that we address in this work is the following: given a set of drugs of interest, an internal team of knowledge curators (also referred as subject matter experts) has the task to maintain updated knowledge about each drug. The knowledge curators are organized in editorial units, where each unit is tasked with curating specific portion of the knowledge, e.g. one unit may be tasked to identify all adverse drug reactions for a drug, another unit to deal with all dosages information etc. The source documents from where this information need to be extracted are the medication Package Inserts. A Package Insert (PI) is a document included in the package of a medication that provides information about that drug and its use. In U.S.A., annually all pharmaceutical companies must provide updated information about all their drugs to the U.S. Food and Drug Administration (FDA),[3] including the PIs. All this information is then made publicly available on the FDA Web site. *DAILYMED*[4] provides access to 106,938 drug listings including daily updates. Such daily updates can be very useful to monitor the changes in the Package Inserts. For example, new adverse drug reactions could be added, the dosage of the drug is changed, new drug interactions are discovered, etc. Such information is highly valuable to patients and medical practitioners.

The editorial units are tasked to extract relevant information as well as to identify changes in those information every time an updated Package Insert is released for a certain medication. Their workflow involves manually reading the PDF file of a newly released Package Insert, comparing it to the latest previously available version and identifying all relevant new information to be added to the current knowledge base. The tooling they use is mainly based on standard diff

[3] https://www.fda.gov/.

[4] https://dailymed.nlm.nih.gov/dailymed.

tools available within PDF viewer software and then each knowledge curator manually identifies relevant information to be added, changed or deleted from the knowledge base.

Without disrupting their habitual workflow, we perform standard information extraction tasks directly on the PDF documents and embed the results in the PDF format, so that they can decide to visualize additional semantic information to aid their task. Having such semantic annotations - e.g., drug names mentions, adverse drug reactions, dosage terms, and important textual changes - can speed up the process of identifying the most relevant information in the updated documents. The user can still decide to toggle those annotations off, in the same fashion they toggle on/off the display of changes between different versions of the PDFs.

For the particular use case of analyzing PIs, it is important to retain the documents in their exact same form, as in many cases it is crucial to have in situ analysis by a human. Let's take the examples of tables. The table in Fig. 1 lists some potential side effects for a particular drug, which are important to retain in the curated knowledge. Nonetheless, despite the advance of table interpretation techniques [10,22], none of them can guarantee perfect accuracy, especially for tables like the one in Fig. 1 where the schema is particularly complicated to identify and where the caption text is integral for the understanding. Moreover, even for a human in this case it would be difficult to get a complete view of what the risks are with this drug, including the organ systems affected, the symptoms produced by the drug in each organ system, and the relative size of the risk for each symptom unless the table and the accompanying text are read contextually.

Table 1 **Adverse Reactions Occurring at an Incidence of ≥2% in Patients Treated with Telmisartan/Hydrochlorothiazide and at a Greater Rate Than in Patients Treated with Placebo***

	Telmisartan/ Hydrochlorothiazide (n = 414)	Placebo (n = 74)	Telmisartan (n = 209)	Hydrochlorothiazide (n = 121)
Body as a whole				
Fatigue	3%	1%	3%	3%
Influenza-like symptoms	2%	1%	2%	3%
Central/Peripheral nervous system Dizziness	5%	1%	4%	6%
Gastrointestinal system				
Diarrhea	3%	0%	5%	2%
Nausea	2%	0%	1%	2%
Respiratory system disorder Sinusitis	4%	3%	3%	6%
Upper respiratory tract infection	8%	7%	7%	10%

* includes all doses of telmisartan (20 to 160 mg), hydrochlorothiazide (6.25 to 25 mg), and combinations thereof

Fig. 1. A table of adverse reactions from a medication Package Insert.

It is for this reason that *in situ* presentation of the results is so critical in this particular use case, where the editorial units are required to guarantee perfect accuracy and completeness of the produced knowledge. We therefore do not replace the manual annotation process - which is a requirement to guarantee perfect results - but rather enrich the documents with multiple semantic annotations, that can be approved or disapproved by the SMEs and aid the annotation process.

We offer a combination of ontology based annotators as well as the possibility to add new semantic annotators which are trained on demand, within the PDF itself, with a human-in-the-loop methodology, and modularly added to the document. In Sects. 4 and 5 we give all the details of the implemented annotators as well as quantitative indications of how they contribute to the enrichment of the documents.

4 System Overview

In the following we will focus on the specific instantiation of the system for analyzing PI documents and discuss the specific implemented annotators. Nonetheless the architecture and the methodology is general and can be replicated for different use cases and domains.

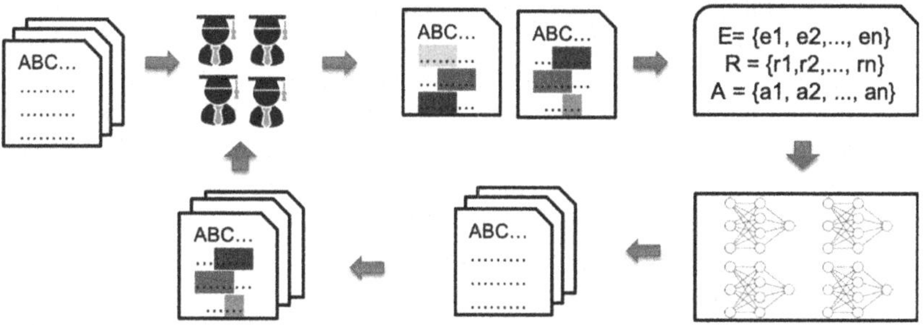

Fig. 2. Document annotation system workflow.

The system takes as input a collection of PI documents $D = \{d_1, d_2, \ldots, d_n\}$ and enriches each document d_i with semantic annotations. The implemented semantic annotators include a set of entity types $E = \{e_1, e_2, ..., e_n\}$, relations between entities $R = \{r_1, r_2, ..., r_n\}$ and textual annotations $A = \{a_1, a_2, \ldots, a_n\}$.

Figure 2 shows the overall workflow of the system. In essence the annotation process runs in two phases, i.e., (i) initialization and (ii) adjudication.

Initialization. The subject matter experts (SMEs) upload the desired collection of PI documents to the system. The system prompts any readily available semantic annotators, which results can be immediately added within the documents. Using existing knowledge based annotators gives us a fast access to readily available knowledge, which can improve the efficiency of the SMEs in their work. For example, for this specific use case we rely on BioPortal,[5] which provides a text annotator based on several hundreds bio-medical ontologies which are extensively used in applications in the pharmaceutical domain. After those annotations are added, the SMEs start annotating the documents, i.e. marking the entities, relations and textual annotations of interest, and by doing so populating the sets of entities E, relations between entities R and textual annotations A. Once a small number of semantic annotation have been added, the system builds state-of-the-art machine learning models for each type of semantic annotations.

Entity Extraction. For identifying entities of interest, the system offers two co-existing options: (i) standard knowledge based annotators as well as (ii) allowing the users to build custom named entity recognition systems. While the selected knowledge based annotators can already provide extensive coverage, in many cases the SMEs require the identification of custom types of entities, for which there is no existing knowledge, or it cannot be trivially obtained. Therefore, the system allow the SMEs to define entity types, and provide models for rapid identification of such entities. For this purpose we use our internal dictionary expansion approach, the *Domain Learning Assistant* (DLA). The SMEs start by manually annotating a few entities of each type, which are then used by *DLA* to propose new candidate entities. DLA currently employs two set expansion engines: Explore and Exploit (EnE) [4,9] and Glimpse [3,6]. *EnE* builds a neural language model on the input text corpus, word2vec and BiLSTM, and given a few initial seeds, identifies new potential dictionary entries. EnE operates in two phases: (i) the Explore phase identifies instances in the input text corpus which are similar to existing dictionary entries, where the similarity is based on the term vectors from the neural language model, using cosine similarity; (ii) the Exploit phase constructs more complex multi-term phrases based on the instances currently in the dictionary, based on a relatedness function. EnE uses the input documents D to generate a single neural language model which is used for generating the dictionaries for all the types of entities. EnE proposes novel additional entities in an incremental fashion: the more the SME accepts proposed entities, the more are suggested. The full description of the EnE algorithm can be found in [9] and the evaluation shows that the EnE approach outperforms the related work approaches on 5 different dictionaries in 3 different tasks. *Glimpse* on the other hand explores the pattern space. It generates patterns of words that occur on either side of seed terms and scans the corpus for other words that match those patterns[6]. Patterns are scored as a function of their produced matches. The peculiarity of *Glimpse* is that it generates all potential patterns (typically tens of millions) and then retrospectively scores them after searching

[5] https://bioportal.bioontology.org/.

[6] As an example, if we consider "apple" as a seed term, Glimpse looks for all occurrences of "apple" in the underlying corpus and generates patterns using wildcards, such as "I like to eat * for breakfast" and "I invest in * stock". Further details can be found in [3,6].

their occurrence in the text. A very high speed pattern matcher allows it to scan gigabytes of text with millions of patterns in just a couple minutes. The two engines are complementary to each other. EnE is quite fast, but does better on entities that are a 1–3 tokens long. Glimpse is slower, but works well on longer token entities (3+). Their combination allows the SMEs to build large lexicons in a short time [4,9].

Relation Extraction. We employ a state-of-the-art neural network architecture for relation classification [21]. The input of the neural network is a text with two marked entities, i.e., the entities for which the system tries to extract a relation, and it doesn't require complicated syntactic or semantic preprocessing of the text. The first layer of the network is a word embeddings layer, where each token in the input text is replaced with an n-dimensional embedding vector. In the second layer of the network a feature vector is generated, which is a concatenation of lexical and sentence level features. As lexical features we use the marked entities and the surrounding tokens, i.e. one token on the left and one on the right of the target entity. The sentence level features include word contexts with window size of 3 and positional features, i.e., the distance between the entities in the text, which are then passed through a convolutional layer and one non linear layer to get the final sentence level feature vector. The lexical feature vector and the sentence level vector are concatenated in one single vector and fed into a fully connected softmax layer, where the output is the confidence score for each of the relations in the domain. The system builds a separate model for each type of entities, i.e., each model processes one type of entities, and N possible relations between the entities.

Textual Annotations. We offer the option to identify full sentences which are of particular interest for the SMEs, e.g. all sentences which as a whole express potential adverse drug events. We use a Convolutional Neural Network (CNN) text classifier and we train it to classify sentences and paragraphs. The architecture of our CNN is inspired by Collobert et al. [7] and Kim et al. [11], which have shown high performance in many NLP tasks. We selected the following parameters for the CNN model: an input embedding layer, 4 convolutional layers followed by max-pooling layers, a fully connected softmax layer, rectified linear units, filter windows of 2, 3, 4, 5 with 100 feature maps each, dropout rate of 0.2 and mini-batch size of 50. For the embedding layer we use word2vec embeddings trained on 20,000 package inserts, with size 300. We train 100 epochs with early stopping.

In conclusion, for all the annotations, the SMEs provide some seed examples of the information they want to extract and specify external Knowledge Resources to be used, if any. The learning models for each type of annotations are learnt and updated as the user interacts with the system.

Adjudication. The initial models are applied to the whole document collection. The SME performs the adjudication of the produced semantic annotations and can (i) correct the mistakes made by the automatic annotation system and (ii) identify and add missing annotations. The adjudication is done directly in the document, and all the collected information is transferred to the system. After each batch of corrections (where the batch size can be adjusted), the models are retrained and reapplied on the rest of the documents. New semantic annotations can be added at any time, i.e., once a new item is added the models are retrained and are able to identify the new item, being entity or textual annotation.

With such a system the SME has full control of what types of semantic annotations will be identified, and they can enforce that the accuracy of the system is always above a certain threshold (even 100% if they are willing or required to manually review the whole collection). The system simply assists the user to improve their efficiency in identifying the semantic annotations of interest, and reducing the human error.

5 System in Action: Document Annotation and Knowledge Graph Generation

In this section we show how we use the system for annotating a set of PDF medication Package Inserts and generating a knowledge graph from them (Sect. 5.1). We then go into quantitative details of our experiments (Sect. 5.2). The experiments are performed with an internal team of healthcare professionals on 300 random drugs, for which we retrieved the last 5 versions of their package insert, totaling to a set of 1,500 documents.[7] The backend system is deployed on a machine with 100 cores and 1TB of RAM. The time to update the models is within couple of seconds, which is not noticeable for the users.

5.1 Processing the Documents

The processing of the documents is done in 3 steps: (i) document parsing; (ii) document annotation and (iii) knowledge graph population.

PDF Parsing. To keep our system independent of the input data format, we transform each document to an internal JSON representation model, thus enabling the processing of any type of document, as long as a parser is implemented. As for processing PDF files we use the Apache PDFBox library,[8] which provides functionalities for creating new PDF files, manipulating existing documents and the ability to extract content from documents. Furthermore, it allows injecting JavaScript code directly in the PDF document, which we use to implement the full human-in-the-loop interaction - accepting, correcting, rejecting or adding new annotations. In the JSON file we keep all content, structural and meta-data information to produce the exact same PDF file when needed. For

[7] We make sure that all selected drugs have at least 5 versions, obtained from DAILYMED.

[8] https://pdfbox.apache.org/.

example, we preserve each token with the information for the bounding box of the token, the style and the token's id. Furthermore, we have implemented a set of rules for identifying sentences, sections, titles and tables, which are also stored in our internal data model. Many of the PDF files in our internal use case are available as images (i.e. they are older scanned documents), but it is still very important to include them in the knowledge base. For those files we use optical character recognition system Tesseract OCR,[9] to first convert the images into machine-encoded text, which is then converted to our internal data model.

All the JSON files are stored in a non-SQL MongoDB database,[10] for fast retrieval and text search.

Document Annotation. As explained in Sect. 4, our system is able to generate models on the fly for various semantic annotations. In our experiment, we use the following semantic annotators:

- *Entities:* We use the BioPortal API[11] for annotating the documents with existing entities from different types. BioPortal offers 764 biomedical ontologies, which contain valuable information for annotating Medication Package Inserts. In this particular case we matched the documents against all the ontologies and ranked them by their utility (number of returned matches) and let the user decide which ones to retain. Besides the external Knowledge Base, the team of SMEs built 6 internal entity extraction models using the DLA approach, i.e., "Symptoms", "Dosage", "Frequency", "Body Part", "Route" and "Clinician". The models were generated iteratively, as the SMEs were making progress through the document collection.
- *Relations:* In this experiment, we build one model for identifying drug-drug interactions (DDI) between drugs. The DDI relation extraction model achieved F-score of 76.92% on our set of documents.
- *Textual annotations:* In this experiment, we build one model for identifying sentences that express Adverse Drug Reactions (ADE). The ADE sentence classification model achieved F-score of 83.2% on our set of documents. We compare this approach to two baseline text classification approaches, i.e., Random Forest and Support Vector Machines, using bag of words with TF-IDF representation, achieving 76.63% and 69.81% F-Score, respectively.
- *Structural annotations:* As the Medication Package Inserts files can significantly change over different versions, it is of paramount value for the SMEs to quickly identify those changes. As we are storing all the content and structural information of the documents, we can easily identify content and structural changes in each version, including content relocation.

All these annotations are added to the JSON representation of the document and stored internally. Furthermore, we preserve the provenance of the editorial

[9] https://github.com/tesseract-ocr/tesseract.
[10] https://www.mongodb.com/.
[11] http://data.bioontology.org/documentation.

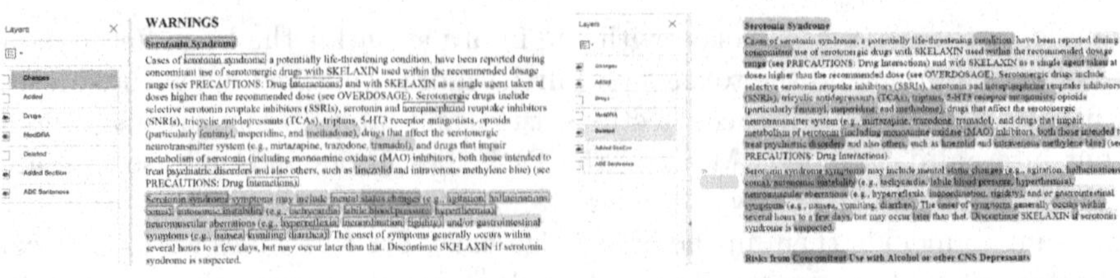

a) *Example of semantically annotated Medication Package Insert.*
b) *Example of content and structural annotations of a Medication Package Insert.*

Fig. 3. Examples of annotated Medication Package Insert.

Layers

Changes
Added
Drugs
MedDRA
Deleted
Added Section
ADE Sentences

Nervous System				
Dizziness	53	(16.5)	42	(12.9)
Headache	80	(24.8)	78	(24.0)
Respiratory System				
Pharyngitis	10	(3.1)	19	(5.8)
Sinusitis	17	(5.3)	18	(5.5)
Upper Respiratory Tract Infection	40	(12.4)	35	(10.8)
Skin and Appendages				
Alopecia	17	(5.3)	8	(2.5)
Urogenital System				
Dysmenorrhea	18	(5.6)	19	(5.8)

OVERDOSAGE
Neither accidental nor intentional overdosing with Actigall has been reported. Doses of Actigall in the range of 16-20 mg/kg/day have been tolerated for 6-37 months without symptoms by 7 patients. The LD_{50} for ursodiol in rats is over 5000 mg/kg given over 7-10 days and over 7500 mg/kg for mice. The most likely manifestation of severe overdose with Actigall would probably be diarrhea, which should be treated symptomatically.

Fig. 4. Example of annotated Medication Package Insert saved in an Image PDF format

unit that applied the changes to the documents. After each annotation we recreate the PDF and present to the SMEs, where each editorial units will be presented documents with the "personalized" annotations. The produced semantic annotations enrich the initial document, without altering its layout (and potentially obscuring the context needed to understand the text). To realize that, we add semantic layers on top of the original document, where each layer contains the information for a specific semantic annotation. Figure 3 shows an example of an annotated PI, as depicted in Adobe Acrobat Reader.[12] The results of the semantic annotators can be toggled on and off at will. For annotators that implement entity resolution (those produced by knowledge based annotators), the recognized entities are linkable and refer to the external sources. Figure 4 shows an example of annotated image PDF file.

Knowledge Graph Population. To generate the knowledge graph, for each drug we maintain a unique ID. For each drug we then maintain the set of different versions, including meta-data, e.g., date of publishing. For each version we store all the semantic annotations. For the entity types, we store the links to the corresponding ontologies or DLA models. We use the relation extraction models to set links between the drugs in the graph, e.g., DDI links. An excerpt of the

[12] https://get.adobe.com/reader/.

resulting knowledge graph for the collection of 300 drugs, is given in Fig. 5. The example shows the different versions of the drugs "Exparel" and "Betadine". For each drug we have a set of different semantic annotations, which are linked to the corresponding ontologies and DLA models. Furthermore, as the DDI relation extraction model identified that there is a relation between the two drugs, we add a link between them in the graph (labeled as "DDI").

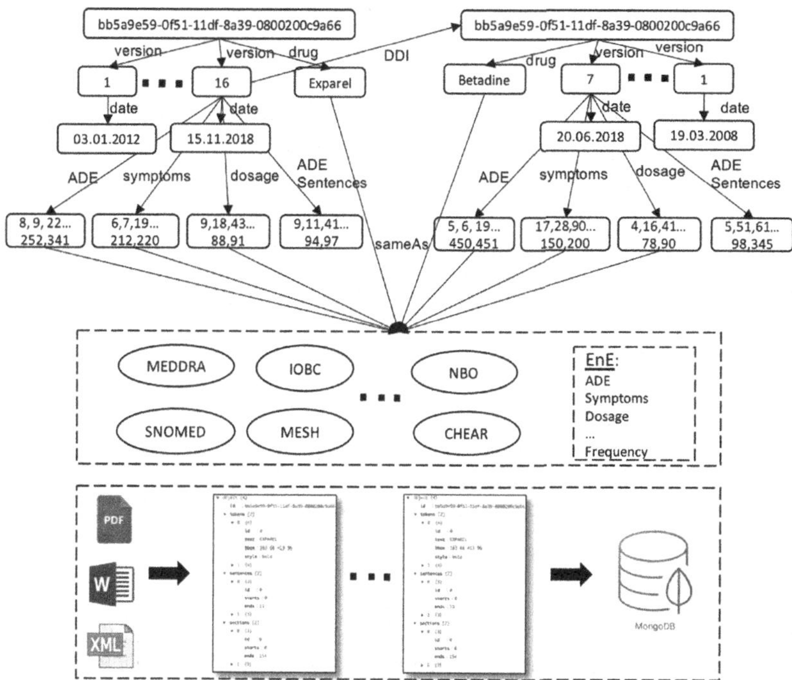

Fig. 5. Architecture of the linked Knowledge Graph generation pipeline.

5.2 Quantitative Results and Data Profiling

In this section, we give insights of the resulting knowledge graph for the selected 300 drugs. First, we show the importance of preserving and linking different versions of the Medication Package Inserts for each drug. Second, we show the importance of involving human-in-the-loop for identifying the correct semantic annotations.

In the first experiment, we capture how the documents evolve over time with each new version. As a proxy of the document changes we use the number of semantic annotations as a measure for comparison between the different versions. We divide all the documents in 5 bins, where bin number 5 contains all

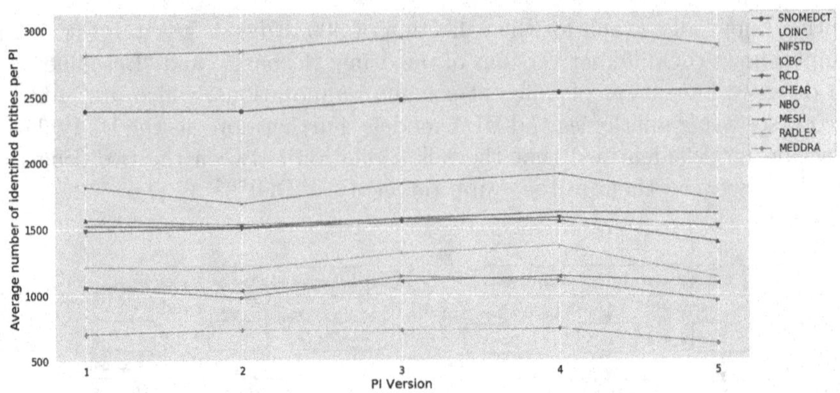

Fig. 6. Average number of identified entities per PI, over 5 different versions.

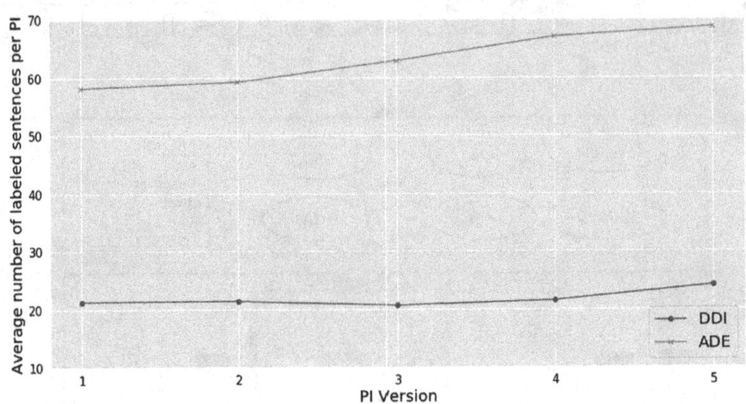

Fig. 7. Average number of identified drug-drug interaction relations (DDI) and Adverse Drug Reactions textual annotations (ADE), over 5 different versions.

the latest versions of the 300 PIs and each other bin contain their previous versions respectively. We count the number of identified semantic annotations for each bin. Figure 6 shows the identified entities per PI for the top 10 ontologies from BioPortal.[13] Figure 7 shows the average number of (i) sentenced labeled as expressing relevant Adverse Drug Reaction (ADE) and (ii) identified drug-drug interactions (DDI). In both charts we can observe that there is significant fluctuation between the different versions of PIs. While in Fig. 6 there is no apparent trend, in Fig. 7 we can observe a strongly increasing trend of discovered ADE textual annotations and DDI relations. This confirms that there are significant changes between different versions of the PIs, and it is important to identify those changes.

[13] Top 10 as for this use case, i.e. those 10 ontologies producing the bigger number of annotations in total.

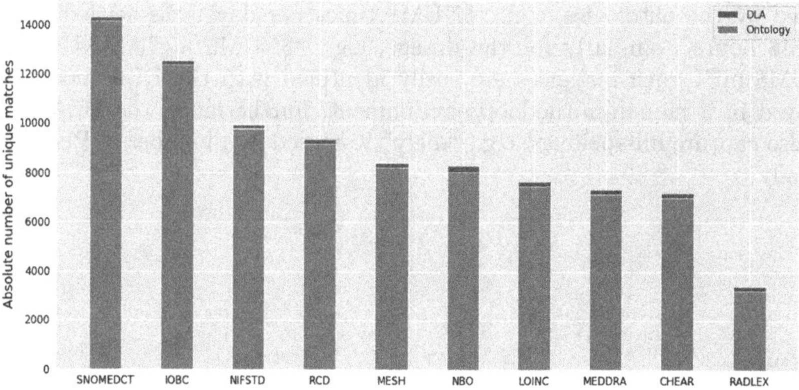

Fig. 8. Number of identified entities using BioPortal and DLA models in the whole document collection. (Color figure online)

In the second experiment, we show the importance of having a human-in-the-loop within the process of semantic annotation. The aim of this experiment is to highlight that regardless of the coverage that standard ontologies can provide - and in this use case BioPortal achieves very high coverage - the SMEs will always need custom entity extraction models which are application dependent. As DLA models are built directly on the corpus at hand and capture the subjective needs of the SMEs, their usefulness is perceived as high by the knowledge curators. Even a small dictionary of ~100 entities has a high number of matches and this is because the entities accepted by the human-in-the-loop for the dictionary are the ones which are highly relevant to them for the specific use case. The standard ontologies produce a higher number of matches, but that is also a result of their sheer size. Figure 8 depicts the number of unique entities identified in the top 10 ontologies (in orange color). The blue stacked bars show the fraction of entities that was not present in the ontologies and was matched using the DLA models. We can see that the models built using the DLA approach are able to identify a number of entities that are missed by the ontologies, which despite being small in absolute numbers, it is significant if comparing the size of the DLA models to the size of the ontologies. To quantify the contribution of the DLA models in relative terms, we count the average number of matches per document per each ontologies and calculate the fraction of the ontology they represent. Figure 9 depicts the average of this fraction on all the documents, grouped by each of the considered ontologies and the DLA models. For most of the ontologies the matches are basically contributed by 3% to 6% of the whole ontology, while the DLA models match more than 16% of its entities per document. In turns, this is perceived by the users as higher control on the annotation process, as the personalized model represent a concise and efficient view of the domain. Most of the entities that are not matched by the ontologies are result of the specificity of the annotation task by the SMEs. For example, a lot of phrases used to express the recommended frequency of usage for a medication are not covered by the ontologies, e.g., "NUM times per day", "as-needed", "every NUM hours", similarly for the dosage, e.g., "NUM mg", "NUM tsp", "NUM ml". Such instances are easily identified with the DLA model when deployed in a human-in-the-loop environment. Furthermore, the DLA models can also capture misspellings, e.g., "dialy" was used in a number of PIs, instead of "daily".

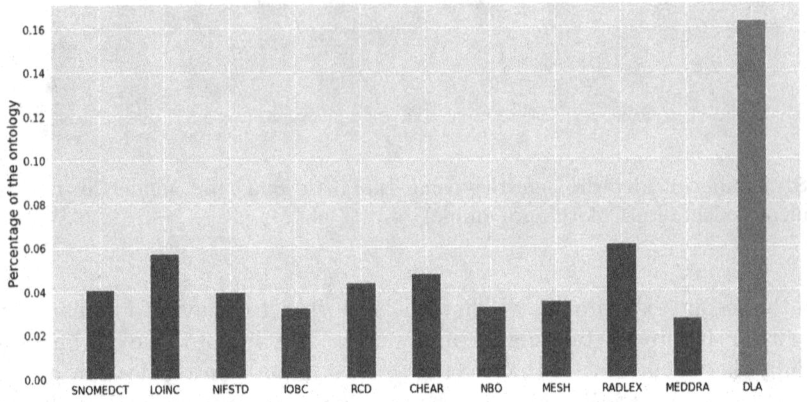

Fig. 9. Matched fraction of entities per ontology and DLA models per document.

6 Pilot Study and Lessons Learned

The pipeline and tooling described in this work are currently used internally by one of the IBM business units working on curating a pharmaceutical Knowledge Graph. The team involved in our pilot consists of 2 Medical Information Specialists and around 20 medical professionals - mainly pharmacists and a few nurses - that have the mission of synthesizing and summarizing various medical content, especially clinically-focused information on drugs, diseases, and toxicology management. Their primary and solely full time task is to perform this knowledge curation. The curated knowledge serves as Knowledge Base for point-of-care clinical decision support tools but also to create consumer-focused drug and disease information for patients who can be informed participants in their care.

Since its deployment on our internal cloud, the extraction pipeline has been used by the team to process between 4 to 15 documents per day. The team was previously only relying on built-in functionalities from Adobe Acrobat Reader, such as the diff tool, but since the deployment of our pipeline and after an initial comparison with their previous solution, the team entirely relies on our extraction pipeline. From the informal feedback that we gathered from the team, they identified two striking benefits of the extraction pipeline. First, the ability to compare different versions of medical documents to precisely identify and highlight the changes which are semantically relevant, while ignoring the multitude of changes that have no impact on the final KG. Second, the possibility to decide which annotations to visualize and when, so to reduce the information overload and to focus only on the current task at hand. The important lesson learned for us, by being the technology providers for the editorial team, was the importance of abstracting as much as possible from the semantic technology itself and focusing on providing the minimal but most useful annotations to the users. A key value for our user was the fact that we consolidated the knowledge and showed only the portion which was useful to the current user, for the particular task at hand. The clinical head of the team analyzed the time commitment of their team when using our extraction pipeline and stated that they saved a significant amount of time, up to 3.5 h per document when dealing with image PDF documents (which could take up to 8 h to review). Image PDF documents constitute 8% of their material and our extraction pipeline was the only available solution to semantically annotate and compare them as they had no alternative solution before.

7 Conclusions and Future Work

Accurate understanding of technical documents is crucial, especially when updating knowledge graphs where every error can be compounded by downstream analytics. This understanding often hinges on the context in which the information appears. Especially in the case of data formats such as PDFs, this leads to the costly requirement of human review of a large number of documents.

In this paper we showcase our human-in-the-loop pipeline to transparently deliver semantic annotations within PDF documents. Within-document annotations also allow to materialize personalized graphs on-the-fly on any selection of documents, document versions, annotation types, user permissions, etc. We enable the subject matter experts to rapidly create and train their own annotation engines, as well as using any readily available ontology based annotator, all within the PDF documents, without suffering disruption from changing tools or formats. While we showcase the use of the system with the use case of medical Package Inserts, the approach is applicable to many other scenarios, such as scientific publishing, the recruiting business - where many applicants' resumes are PDF files - legal contracts, electronic parts data sheets, material hazard data sheets, aircraft flight manuals, just to name a few. In all these scenarios it is crucial to be able to quickly train the extraction models and to deliver the results in a way that is familiar to the subject matter expert, as well as having ways to track changes between document updates.

References

1. Abekawa, T., Aizawa, A.: SideNoter: scholarly paper browsing system based on PDF restructuring and text annotation. In: COLING 2016, pp. 136–140 (2016)

2. Ahmad, R., Afzal, M.T., Qadir, M.A.: Information extraction from PDF sources based on rule-based system using integrated formats. In: Sack, H., Dietze, S., Tordai, A., Lange, C. (eds.) SemWebEval 2016. CCIS, vol. 641, pp. 293–308. Springer, Cham (2016). https://doi.org/10.1007/978-3-319-46565-4_23
3. Alba, A., Coden, A., Gentile, A.L., Gruhl, D., Ristoski, P., Welch, S.: Multi-lingual concept extraction with linked data and human-in-the-loop. In: Proceedings of the Knowledge Capture Conference, p. 24. ACM (2017)
4. Alba, A., Gruhl, D., Ristoski, P., Welch, S.: Interactive dictionary expansion using neural language models. In: Proceedings of the 2nd International Workshop on Augmenting Intelligence with Humans-in-the-Loop co-located with (ISWC 2018). CEUR Workshop Proceedings, vol. 2169, pp. 7–15. CEUR-WS.org (2018)
5. Barisevičius, G., et al.: Supporting digital healthcare services using semantic web technologies. In: Vrandečić, D., et al. (eds.) ISWC 2018. LNCS, vol. 11137, pp. 291–306. Springer, Cham (2018). https://doi.org/10.1007/978-3-030-00668-6_18
6. Coden, A., Gruhl, D., Lewis, N., Tanenblatt, M., Terdiman, J.: SPOT the drug! an unsupervised pattern matching method to extract drug names from very large clinical corpora. In: HISB 2012, pp. 33–39 (2012). https://doi.org/10.1109/HISB.2012.16
7. Collobert, R., Weston, J., Bottou, L., Karlen, M., Kavukcuoglu, K., Kuksa, P.: Natural language processing (almost) from scratch. J. Mach. Learn. Res. **12**(Aug), 2493–2537 (2011)
8. Garcia, A., Lopez, F., Garcia, L., Giraldo, O., Bucheli, V., Dumontier, M.: Biotea: semantics for Pubmed central. PeerJ. 1–26 (2018). https://doi.org/10.7717/peerj.4201
9. Gentile, A.L., Gruhl, D., Ristoski, P., Welch, S.: Explore and exploit. Dictionary expansion with human-in-the-loop. In: Hitzler, P., et al. (eds.) ESWC 2019. LNCS, vol. 11503, pp. 131–145. Springer, Cham (2019). https://doi.org/10.1007/978-3-030-21348-0_9
10. Gentile, A.L., Kirstein, S., Paulheim, H., Bizer, C.: Extending rapidminer with data search and integration capabilities. In: Sack, H., Rizzo, G., Steinmetz, N., Mladenić, D., Auer, S., Lange, C. (eds.) ESWC 2016. LNCS, vol. 9989, pp. 167–171. Springer, Cham (2016). https://doi.org/10.1007/978-3-319-47602-5_33
11. Kim, Y.: Convolutional neural networks for sentence classification. In: EMNLP 2014, pp. 1746–1751. ACL, October 2014. https://doi.org/10.3115/v1/D14-1181
12. Nathan, J.P.: The package insert. US Pharmacist **40**(5), 8–10 (2015)
13. Nuzzolese, A.G., Gentile, A.L., Presutti, V., Gangemi, A.: Conference linked data: the scholarlydata project. In: Groth, P., et al. (eds.) ISWC 2016. LNCS, vol. 9982, pp. 150–158. Springer, Cham (2016). https://doi.org/10.1007/978-3-319-46547-0_16
14. Piro, R., et al.: Semantic technologies for data analysis in health care. In: Groth, P., et al. (eds.) ISWC 2016. LNCS, vol. 9982, pp. 400–417. Springer, Cham (2016). https://doi.org/10.1007/978-3-319-46547-0_34
15. Roberts, K., Demner-Fushman, D., Tonning, J.M.: Overview of the TAC 2017 adverse reaction extraction from drug labels track. In: TAC (2017)
16. Segura Bedmar, I., Martinez, P., Sánchez Cisneros, D.: The 1st DDIExtraction-2011 challenge task: extraction of drug-drug interactions from biomedical texts. In: Proceedings of the 1st Challenge Task on Drug-Drug Interaction Extraction 2011 (2011)
17. Shotton, D.: Semantic publishing: the coming revolution in scientific journal publishing. Learn. Publishing **22**(2), 85–94 (2009). https://doi.org/10.1087/2009202

18. Staar, P.W.J., Dolfi, M., Auer, C., Bekas, C.: Corpus conversion service: a machine learning platform to ingest documents at scale. In: SIGKDD 2018, pp. 774–782. ACM (2018). https://doi.org/10.1145/3219819.3219834
19. Yuan, F., Liu, B.O.: A new method of information extraction from PDF files. In: ICMLC 2005, pp. 18–21. IEEE (2005)
20. Yuan, F., Liu, B., Yu, G.: A study on information extraction from PDF files. In: Yeung, D.S., Liu, Z.-Q., Wang, X.-Z., Yan, H. (eds.) ICMLC 2005. LNCS (LNAI), vol. 3930, pp. 258–267. Springer, Heidelberg (2006). https://doi.org/10.1007/11739685_27
21. Zeng, D., Liu, K., Lai, S., Zhou, G., Zhao, J., et al.: Relation classification via convolutional deep neural network. In: COLING, pp. 2335–2344 (2014)
22. Zhang, Z.: Effective and efficient semantic table interpretation using tableminer^{+}. Semant. Web **8**(6), 921–957 (2017). https://doi.org/10.3233/SW-160242

Use of OWL and Semantic Web Technologies at Pinterest

Rafael S. Gonçalves[1(✉)], Matthew Horridge[1], Rui Li[2], Yu Liu[2], Mark A. Musen[1], Csongor I. Nyulas[1], Evelyn Obamos[2], Dhananjay Shrouty[2], and David Temple[2]

[1] Center for Biomedical Informatics Research, Stanford University, Stanford, CA, USA
rafael.goncalves@stanford.edu

[2] Pinterest, San Francisco, CA, USA

Abstract. Pinterest is a popular Web application that has over 250 million active users. It is a visual discovery engine for finding ideas for recipes, fashion, weddings, home decoration, and much more. In the last year, the company adopted Semantic Web technologies to create a knowledge graph that aims to represent the vast amount of content and users on Pinterest, to help both content recommendation and ads targeting. In this paper, we present the engineering of an OWL ontology—the Pinterest Taxonomy—that forms the core of Pinterest's knowledge graph, the Pinterest Taste Graph. We describe modeling choices and enhancements to WebProtégé that we used for the creation of the ontology. In two months, eight Pinterest engineers, without prior experience of OWL and WebProtégé, revamped an existing taxonomy of noisy terms into an OWL ontology. We share our experience and present the key aspects of our work that we believe will be useful for others working in this area.

Keywords: Pinterest · Knowledge graph · OWL · WebProtégé · Ontology engineering · Taxonomy

1 Introduction

Pinterest[1] was founded in 2010, and is headquartered in San Francisco, California. Pinterest offers a visual discovery engine that helps people find things that they like, which might be things they would like to do, such as scuba diving, places that they might like to visit, such as tropical islands, garments that they might like to wear, such as Bohemia dress, and so on. More specifically, Pinterest offers users a collection of digital pin-boards, or simply boards (Fig. 1). Users, known as "Pinners", save bookmarks for Web content, known as *Pins*, to boards. A Pin can be shared amongst boards and is visualized by an image that summarizes what the Pin represents. Clicking a Pin takes a user to the underlying Web page that hosts the image and related content.

[1] https://www.pinterest.com.

C. Ghidini et al. (Eds.): ISWC 2019, LNCS 11779, pp. 418–435, 2019.
https://doi.org/10.1007/978-3-030-30796-7_26

Fig. 1. An example of a Pinner's home feed. The feed displays examples of Pins that the Pinner has saved to their boards and suggested Pins that they might also be interested in. Pins are comprised of a representative image, a title and a snippet of text. Clicking on a Pin will take the user to the Web content that the Pin represents or bookmarks.

Both Pins and Pinners are highly diverse and the amount of content is substantial—Pinterest hosts over 175 billion Pins and it has over 250 million monthly active users. To recommend the most relevant Pins to its users, and to achieve precise ads targeting, Pinterest defines a set of interests. These interests are simply terms that describe what each Pin/image on Pinterest is about, and what each user on Pinterest is interested in. The interests are organized in a hierarchical structure, called "the Pinterest Taxonomy". Behind the scenes, Pinterest categorizes both Pins and Pinners into one or multiple interests. By knowing what a user is interested in and what each Pin is about in the same categorization space, it becomes easier to provide personalized recommendations. Advertisers can also use the Pinterest Taxonomy to create Ads campaigns on Pinterest by selecting interests from the taxonomy. The selected interests essentially identify groups of Pinterest users who will be targeted by the campaigns.

In this paper, we describe the engineering process behind the Pinterest Taxonomy, and we discuss key aspects of the work carried out by the Pinterest and Protégé teams that we believe are relevant and useful to others working in this area. We discuss the use of OWL to model the content in Pinterest, and the benefits of using OWL over previous spreadsheet-based representations. We describe the WebProtégé collaborative editing environment that was used to create, maintain, and evolve the Pinterest Taxonomy, and we document the extensions to WebProtégé that we implemented to optimize the Pinterest taxonomy construction workflow at Pinterest.

2 Nomenclature

In what follows we define the nomenclature that we use throughout the rest of the paper. Figure 2 shows a schematic of the Pinterest nomenclature and represents an abstract view of the "Pinterest Taste Graph".

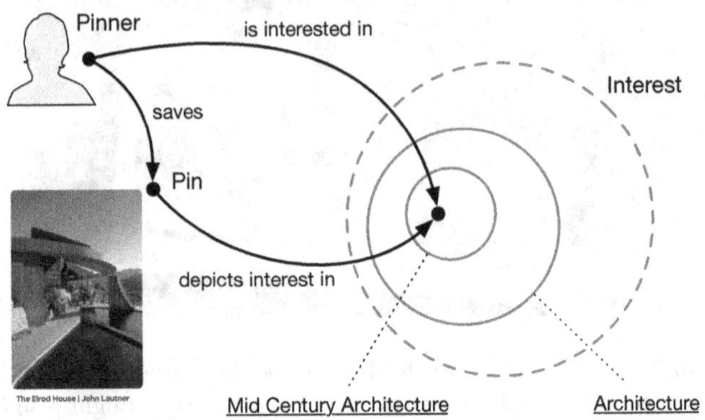

Fig. 2. A conceptual view of the Pinterest Taste Graph. A *Pinner* saves a *Pin* to one of their *Boards*.* The Pin depicts/represents one of the Pinner's *interests*. Here, the Pinner is interested in "Mid Century Architecture", which is an interest in "Architecture". Architecture is a top-level interest, which is known as a *Vertical*. The hierarchy of interests is known as the Pinterest Taxonomy, or "the taxonomy" for short. (*Note that the relationship of the Pin to the board is not shown here.)

Pin. An image, or visual bookmark on Pinterest that includes a description and links to an external URL.

Pinner. A Pinterest user who creates and/or saves Pins to their boards.

Interest. A concept that denotes what a Pin is about, or what a user is interested in. The Interest can be simply an answer to the question "What are you interested in?", which could be "Photography", "Cooking", etc. Interests can be very broad, for example, "Event Planning" or "Food and Drink", or specific, for example, "Scuba Diving", or very specific, for example, "DIY Pom Pom".

Board. A collection where Pinners organize their Pins in context as they plan. For example, a Pinner could create a board called *Italian Recipes* and add "Pizza Recipe", "Home Made Pesto Sauce" and "Veggie Lasagna" Pins to it.

Taxonomy. Extended from the scientific definition [1], the Pinterest Taxonomy is a hierarchical arrangement of interests. In OWL, the taxonomy roughly corresponds to the class hierarchy of an ontology.

Vertical. A top level node in the Pinterest Taxonomy and its sub-trees. Examples of verticals are "Women's Fashion", "Home Decor" and "Architecture". Figure 2 depicts a (very small) portion of the "Architecture" vertical.

Taste Graph. The Pinterest knowledge graph. The Taste Graph [6] is a graph formed by combining the Pinterest Taxonomy with nodes representing Pinners and Pins. Every Pinner node and every Pin node is associated with one or more Pinterest Taxonomy nodes.

WebProtégé. A collaborative cloud-based OWL ontology development environment. A WebProtégé user can log in to WebProtégé, create an ontology project, and then share the project with geographically distributed collaborators. Users see and discuss ontology changes in real-time.

3 From Pins, to Interests, to a Taxonomy, to an Ontology

Pinterest has come a long way in terms of understanding the Pins and users, and uses those to power its business. The company started out by keyword based understanding: extracting keywords from each Pin, doing clean ups, canonicalization, and labeling the Pins with these keywords. After that, based on users' engagement with the Pins, the users were labeled with some keywords too. Then Pinterest leveraged both the labels on the Pins and on the users to do recommendation and ads targeting.

Two years ago, Pinterest decided to enable an "interest" based ads targeting interface, which named the most popular keywords as interests, and organized them in a tree structure (a taxonomy) for advertisers to pick nodes from for their campaigns. For example, if Home Depot creates a campaign for the interest "Living Room", both the users interested in "Living Room" in general, as well as users interested in "Sofas", "TV Stands", "French Living Room Style", "Living Room Decor", etc., will all be exposed to the ads of this campaign. Having realized the potential that such a structured knowledge representation provides, Pinterest decided to investigate ways to (1) improve the quality of the taxonomy; (2) augment the scope of the taxonomy as needed to provide coverage for all Pinterest content; and (3) settle on principled and robust processes by which the taxonomy is constructed, maintained, and reviewed.

Given the wide diversity and the (sometimes highly) specific nature of the Pins hosted on Pinterest, existing public taxonomies such as the Google Product Taxonomy[2] are insufficient to fully describe Pinterest content. Thus, Pinterest decided to develop their own taxonomy, targeted at the kind of content that it hosts, and focusing on a specific business use-case: ads targeting. In the first version of the Pinterest Taxonomy, Pinterest had manually defined and organized ~400 interests in a 2 level hierarchy, most of which were very broad. Subsequently, Pinterest released a far more granular version, with ~6,000 interests organized in a 3 level hierarchy. This version was entirely curated in a spreadsheet that was generated based on terms from top queries in Pinterest. One year later, based on feedback from advertisers, Pinterest decided to improve the

[2] https://www.google.com/basepages/producttype/taxonomy.en-AU.txt.

taxonomy in terms of the quality and quantity of the interests in it. At that point, the Pinterest and Protégé teams begun working on an OWL version of the Pinterest Taxonomy.

Pinterest started out editing the Pinterest Taxonomy in spreadsheets. Soon after, the Pinterest Content team realized that it was difficult to visualize, keep track of changes, and associate interests with metadata. Thus, Pinterest decided to adopt a standard knowledge representation language and more appropriate tooling for collaborative taxonomy editing. Pinterest chose to use the Web Ontology Language (OWL) [2] to model their taxonomy, and WebProtégé [4] as the collaborative development environment.

Since the adoption of OWL and WebProtégé, Pinterest has greatly shortened the development cycle of the Pinterest Taxonomy. The new tooling has made it possible for Pinterest to build an end-to-end system in just two months. In this time span, Pinterest designed an OWL ontology in WebProtégé; built guidelines and workflows for human curation using WebProtégé; loaded the 6,000 interest taxonomy into WebProtégé; enriched it with 5,000 new interests extracted from user provided content; cleaned it up and re-organized it; and developed an engineering pipeline to consume the ontology, and use its content to populate a relational database for internal product consumption.

4 Key Requirements

The insights that Pinterest drew from building the initial versions of the Pinterest Taxonomy, and from advertisers' feedback, have provided us with concrete business requirements for this project. We list and discuss these requirements below. Subsequently, we enumerate the tooling requirements needed to fulfil the business requirements.

Business Requirements. The Pinterest Taxonomy will be used internally to categorize all the Pins and all the users, and externally to power Pinterest's ads targeting. To fulfill both of these use cases, the final knowledge representation needs to:

1. Be a single root tree structure, instead of a directed acyclic graph (DAG) for near-term downstream consumption. It should however be possible to evolve the taxonomy into a multi-parent DAG;
2. Provide support for adding attributes (facets) to the interests, in order to support multiple perspectives of the categorization and poly-axial classifications;
3. Match the Pinterest content, that is, it should include interests that depict a substantial number of Pins and exclude interests that Pinterest has little or no Pins for;
4. Contain no ambiguous interests—the interests' names should be clear on their own even after removing the context provided by the tree structure (i.e., the parents in the hierarchy), for example, "cricket" the insect versus the sport;
5. All children of the same parent should be mutually exclusive and collectively exhaustive (MECE); and

6. Quality of the interests is more important than quantity.

Tooling Requirements. To manage, curate and evolve the Pinterest Taxonomy, Pinterest needs a tool that provides:

1. The ability for multiple editors located in different geographical locations to work on the same project simultaneously;
2. A way to track which interests in the taxonomy have been reviewed;
3. The ability to efficiently reorganize the taxonomy—move an interest to a different branch, merge, rename or deprecate it;
4. A way to add annotations/metadata to one or multiple interests, e,g., sample Pins, a short description of the interest, synonyms, statistics and attributes of this interest;
5. Multi-lingual support, that is, support for adding labels in multiple languages and for displaying the full taxonomy in different languages; and
6. A friendly user interface (UI) to allow people to browse and search for interests in the taxonomy based on their annotations. The UI should provide the ability to share links directly to content in the taxonomy.

5 Ontology Modeling Experiments

We conducted several ontology modeling experiments. The goals of these experiments were: (1) To determine the kind of vocabulary defined in Sect. 2 that we would need for the project; (2) To settle on (best practice) conventions, for example, rules for consistent naming of the interests; (3) To experiment with editing workflows and define the curation instructions; (4) To evaluate WebProtégé as a tool to satisfy editing requirements; and (5) To see what gaps needed to be filled in terms of tooling.

5.1 Deriving a Seed Ontology

We used the 6,000 interests from the three-level taxonomy to bootstrap a starting ontology. There were several problems with the ontology output from this process:

Lack of Coverage. The interests were not enough to describe all of Pinterest's content. For example, it had 120 interests for "Men's Fashion", over 400 interests for "Women's Fashion", but no interests at all for "Children's Fashion".

Imbalanced Structure. The taxonomy was very broad and shallow. Moreover, it was inappropriately imbalanced with respect to the number of children per parent. For example, one vertical had only 2 child interests while another had over 80. This may feel odd to advertisers and may be harder to find the relevant interests.

Irregular Precision. Some areas of the taxonomy were too fine-grained. For example, the part of the taxonomy representing the “Art” vertical contained many interests of the form “11 × 17 posters” or “36 × 48 posters” (representing interests in very specific poster sizes).

Irregular Naming. The naming convention for the terms in the taxonomy was not uniform. Some terms were named in singular form while their siblings were named in plural form. There was also an inconsistent use of prefixes and suffixes.

5.2 Detailed Modeling Pilot Study

Having identified initial problems with the seed ontology, we honed in on two verticals, “Home Decor” and “Fashion”, in order to focus on more detailed modeling issues and to get a better feeling for development environment issues. We chose these verticals for the richness and variety of interests contained in them (to expose modeling issues) and for their prominence on Pinterest. We used seed lists of interests to start constructing ontologies representing these verticals.

Development Tools. During the pilot study phase, we used a number of tools for engineering and communication that we describe next.

Collaborative Editing Environment. We used WebProtégé and its collaboration features throughout the pilot experiment. We made use of threaded discussions to document editorial decisions and point to external references that were considered. We made heavy use of email and Slack notifications, which enabled timely responses to discussion within WebProtégé. We used the change tracking feature of WebProtégé to review recent changes when starting a modelling session, and we used the “live project feed” to monitor current activity.

Communication Tools. We used Slack for communication outside WebProtégé. Both the Pinterest and Protégé teams were already familiar with this tool for internal communication. Because WebProtégé supports “deep linking”, it was easy to paste links to entities in WebProtégé directly into Slack. We used Slack for any discussions unrelated to the ontology content, for example, to set up meetings, to discuss tooling matters, and to report and discuss software issues. We also held teleconferences on a regular basis.

In-person Meetings. We met face-to-face for extended periods of time at the start of the project, in order to make major decisions on workflow and tooling. We held a workshop meeting early in the pilot experiment to simultaneously work on the “Fashion” vertical in the same room. This enabled us to quickly assess usability and tooling issues, and it also helped us to quickly identify and discuss broad modeling issues.

Design Decisions and Modeling Choices. The modeling pilot study enabled us to settle on various modeling choices and engineering conventions:

Interests as Classes. We decided to represent interests as classes. This may seem odd, but *ontologically*, an instance of an interest represents someone's (a Pinner's) own particular, unique interest in something. Thus, classes in the ontology represent interests and not the actual subject of an interest. From herein we use interests and classes interchangeably.

Using classes for interests also side-steps the thorny issue of classes versus individuals. Suppose someone is interested in San Francisco. Ontologically, San Francisco, the place, is an individual. That is, there is just one San Francisco in the domain of discourse (the world). In the taxonomy, we do not explicate the fact that an *interest in San Francisco* represents an interest about San Francisco the place. While this may seem straightforward, the water is much more muddy when one thinks about things like recipes, computer games or cute videos of cats. Thus, focusing purely on interests as classes helps to keep the modelling clean and simple, and helps to avoid overly complex debates about modeling.

One more important benefit of modeling interests as classes is that interests can be easily specialized. This includes obvious cases of specialization, such as an interest in mid-century architecture is an interest in architecture. It also includes less obvious specializations, such as an interest in 1960's San Francisco is an interest in San Francisco.

Interest Descriptions. For each interest, we added a label (its preferred name), plus synonyms (if available) and definitions (where warranted). We recorded this information using the following annotation properties:

rdfs:label as the primary, preferred name/label for an interest in a given language.[3] Every label has a language tag, for example, @en.

skos:altLabel for recording synonyms. We encoded all known synonyms of each interest to support our search and presentation goals.

skos:definition to include a 1–2 sentence textual definition to clarify the meaning of an interest. This is important, as it provides a shared understanding among the team of what this interest is, especially when it is not a well-known term. Many of the definitions were copied from Wikipedia.

Domain specific annotation properties for both business usage and curation usage. For example, there are certain interests that are sensitive or brand related, and thus cannot (according to Pinterest policy) be exposed to advertisers. These interests are marked as noAds=true in order to identify them in the engineering pipeline and avoid exposing them in the targeting interface. We also used defined properties such as isHumanReviewed, to indicate whether an interest has been human reviewed or not, and to eliminate the possibility of curators reviewing previously reviewed interests.

Naming Conventions. We used title case names, with spaces, for interest names for example, "Garden Bench". Ontology engineering recommendations often state that singular noun forms should be used for entity names [7,8,10–12].

[3] Note that we could have chosen skos:prefLabel. We ensure that all labels are unique, so skos:prefLabel annotations could easily be generated from rdfs:label values.

However, we determined that it was necessary, and more natural, to use a mix of singular and plural forms based on the forms used in Pinterest's top queries.

We attempted to normalize the names of interests in a principled way. For example, under "Home Decor Styles" there are a large number of styles. Many of these were not uniformly named. Some were named ending with "Style" or "Styles" (for example, "California Style"), others were named ending in "Interior" or "Interiors" (for example, "Art Deco Interiors"), while others were named ending in "Decor" (for example, "Bohemian Decor"). In these cases, we settled on particular patterns, depending upon the context, and then normalized interests according to these patterns. Whenever we renamed a topic we endeavored to preserve the original name in a skos:altLabel annotation to keep the old name as a synonym.

Name Ambiguity. Some topic names in the original Pinterest taxonomy were used in different senses. For example, "Topiary" is both the activity of sculpting plants into three-dimensional shapes, and plants themselves that have been sculpted this way. We disambiguated them in the way that thesauri entries are disambiguated, for example, "Topiary (Plant)" and "Topiary (Gardening Activity)".

Interest Disambiguation. We frequently had to use the Pinterest text-search functionality to disambiguate obscure names. We struggled with ambiguous names like "privacy screen", "water scooper", "valances", among others. We made extensive use of Wikipedia for providing concise textual definitions for interests to aid curators during the review process. With an eye to advertising—one of the most important uses of the taxonomy—we also viewed external Web sites, such as Bed, Bath and Beyond, Crate & Barrel, IKEA and Walmart in order to compare their product categorization with the kinds of products that are represented by interests.

6 Production Tooling

Given the working relationship between Pinterest and Stanford, WebProtégé was the obvious choice for an editing environment. The pilot experiments that we carried out revealed that WebProtégé was able to meet the majority of the tooling requirements. However, we significantly enhanced WebProtégé to satisfy previously unmet requirements and, in places, to streamline existing cumbersome editing operations. In what follows, we describe the key aspects of WebProtégé in the context of the tool requirements for this project.

Support for Multi-user Collaboration and Sharing. WebProtégé is a cloud-based OWL ontology development environment where users perform editing and viewing tasks in a Web browser. It allows geographically dispersed users to collaborate in real-time.

When a change is made to an ontology, all collaborators see the change in real time. Changes are also tracked, in the form of axiom additions and removals.

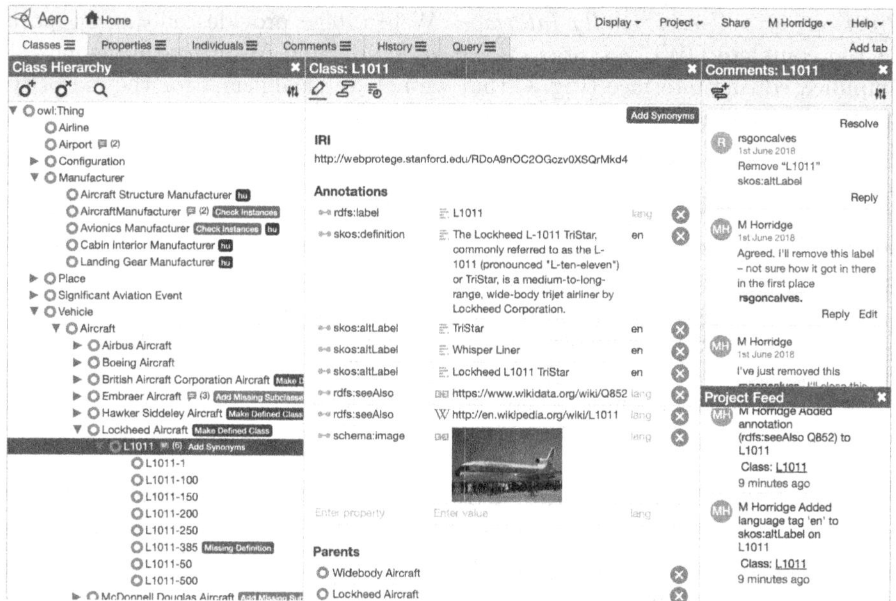

Fig. 3. The WebProtégé UI. The figure shows the main WebProtégé user interface displaying the 'Aero' project*. The left hand side displays the class hierarchy, containing various "tagged" classes. The center displays content for the selected class, in this case L1011. This center panel can be switched to display the history for the selected class. The right hand side displays threaded discussions for the selected class and recent editing and commenting activity. (*Note that, this project bears no relation to the Pinterest project. It is used here merely for illustration purposes.)

Information about a change is captured along with metadata about who performed the change and when the change was performed. The complete project change history is available for collaborators to peruse. Pinterest uses the change history to keep track of contributions by curators, and to carry out downstream analyses.

Crucially, WebProtégé users can be assigned different roles within the context of a project. This makes it possible to cater for workflows that comprise multiple teams with different responsibilities. In the case of the Pinterest project, there is a core team of editors surrounded by a larger group of reviewers/commenters. While the "under the hood" role management capabilities provided by WebProtégé are very fine-grained, the default user-interface supports high level coarse-grained privileges, namely "Manage", "Edit", "Comment" and "View". At the start of the project, it was not clear to us whether these privileges would be sufficient. However, as editing and refinement of the ontology proceeded, it became clear that these basic permissions worked well enough.

Provision of a User Friendly Interface. WebProtégé provides editing support for the complete OWL 2 syntax. However, by default, WebProtégé displays a simplified editing interface (Fig. 3) that we believe is sufficient for the majority of ontology projects [3].

This interface allows users to edit ontologies in a frame based style, specifying parents (`rdfs:subClassOf` under the hood), annotations, and relationships (`rdfs:subClassOf` with super classes that match specific patterns of class expressions under the hood) in an intuitive frame-like way. An image of this default user interface is displayed in Fig. 3.

So far, this simple interface has worked well for the Pinterest project, with the bulk of editing being annotation based editing and hierarchy editing. Pinterest ontology curators required little training in how to use the interface—they attended a one hour training session on the WebProtégé interface and ontology editing conventions.

Support for Ontology Reorganization. As mentioned previously, the initial input for the Pinterest ontology was a spreadsheet that had been derived from user data. This provided a seed taxonomy with at most three levels of depth and mixed bags of non-unique terms at each level. One of the perceived benefits of moving to OWL and using WebProtégé was that the ontology would be easier to browse and edit compared to the existing spreadsheet based approach. While this has largely proven to be true, we had to extend WebProtégé with two new features for streamlining the editing workflow.

The first feature that we added was a workflow to *merge entities.* This allows multiple entities to be selected and then merged into a target entity. This operation performs a number of complex steps under the hood, such as replacing references to the entities being merged with a reference to the target entity. It leaves merged entity IRIs intact, but deprecates them and preserves annotations on them, for record keeping purposes.

The second feature that we added was a *bulk move* operation. The initial cleanup step involved a significant amount of re-organizing edits to be performed, sometimes between large disparate branches of the taxonomy hierarchy. The new bulk move feature allows multiple entities to be selected and in the next step a new parent entity to be chosen for them. While simple, this feature proved to be much more effective and more reliable than using drag and drop.

Finally, both merge operations and move operations typically involve multiple atomic changes to achieve the desired outcome. WebProtégé bundles up these atomic changes into a single composite change operation, which can then be applied with a manually entered commit message that appears in the change history log of the project.

Support for Metadata Editing. Interest classes in the ontology are richly described with entity annotations. These annotations can be roughly split into two types: (1) *Content description annotations*, which provide synonyms, descriptions, visibility flags, and pointers to example Pins; and (2) *Status annotations*, which provide "housekeeping" information about the editorial status of

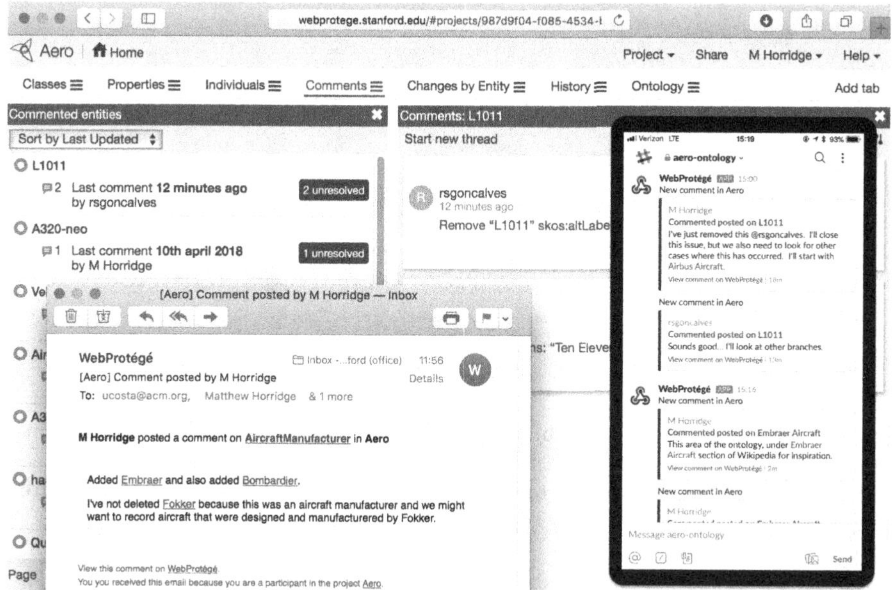

Fig. 4. Comments management and notifications. The main part of the figure shows the Comments tab. Comments can be sorted and viewed by entity. The lower left-hand side inset shows a notification email sent out to participants after a comment has been posted. The right-hand side inset shows integration with the chat app Slack.

classes. In both cases we quickly learnt that there was a reoccurring desire to apply edits to a large number of annotations at once. From switching a status flag from 'false' to 'true', to applying a consistent naming convention based on regular expressions. We therefore added a powerful bulk annotation editing interface to WebProtégé. This feature allows entity annotations to be "selected", using patterns, and then modified, deleted or augmented based upon the criteria used to select them.

Support for Reviewing and Quality Control. Besides offering real-time distributed editing capabilities, WebProtégé provides support for collaborative interaction in the form of "entity discussion threads" (Fig. 3, right hand side). Discussion threads can contain user mentions, links to entities and links to external resources.

This discussion functionality has been used for a number of purposes in the Pinterest project, including for filing interest related issues and for soliciting reviews of interest descriptions. Issues were sorted and managed via the "Comments" tab (Fig. 4), which provides basic functionality for sorting issues by creation or modification time and by entity, and largely proved sufficient for the task at hand.

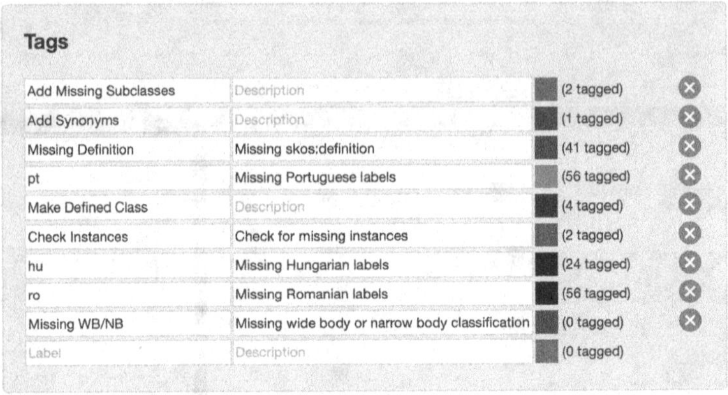

Tags

Label	Description	Tagged
Add Missing Subclasses	Description	(2 tagged)
Add Synonyms	Description	(1 tagged)
Missing Definition	Missing skos:definition	(41 tagged)
pt	Missing Portuguese labels	(56 tagged)
Make Defined Class	Description	(4 tagged)
Check Instances	Check for missing instances	(2 tagged)
hu	Missing Hungarian labels	(24 tagged)
ro	Missing Romanian labels	(56 tagged)
Missing WB/NB	Missing wide body or narrow body classification	(0 tagged)
Label	Description	(0 tagged)

Fig. 5. Tags management in WebProtégé. Each tag is assigned a label, an optional description and a color. Tags can be defined on a per project basis. These tags can then either be manually assigned to entities or they can be assigned in an automated live query-based way.

When discussions are posted to a project, collaborators are notified via email or Slack[4] (Fig. 4) so that they do not miss discussion posts that are relevant to them. Notification emails contain deep links to the interests being discussed so that it is possible to "jump" straight to the relevant portion of the ontology in WebProtégé. This proved to be an effective way of engaging members of the Pinterest knowledge management team in active discussion.

As part of the taxonomy quality control process, all classes representing interests require human review. Classes that require a review are flagged with annotations to indicate the review status. Early on in the project, Pinterest requested custom highlighting for classes, so that certain classes, for example those requiring a review, would stand out from other classes. To support this, we added "entity tags"[5] to WebProtégé.

Entity tags can be used to highlight entities in a colorful, enticing way in the WebProtégé user interface. Example entity tags are shown on the left hand side of Fig. 3, where there are tags for flagging missing definitions and missing Hungarian labels, among others. Multiple tags can be specified for a given project, as shown in Fig. 5, and multiple tags can be assigned to a single entity. Not only do tags "call out" entities in the user interface, they are also searcheable. Thus, it is possible to list and filter entities that have given tags.

We designed Entity Tags so that they could either be assigned to entities in a manual, explicit fashion, or assigned in an automated manner based on ontology content. Figure 6 shows the set up page for automated tag assignment. While a presentation of the full tagging capabilities is beyond the scope of this paper, it is possible to tag entities that match a given set of rules/criteria. This tagging

[4] https://slack.com.

[5] Recall that entities, in OWL, are classes, properties, individuals and datatypes.

feature supports complex, multiple conjunctive and disjunctive criteria, along with paths of values to be matched. Many types of matches are possible, such as matches by specific value, parts of values (regular expressions) and ranges. Furthermore, it is possible to use entity matching criteria to check constraints that involve multiple values, such as label uniqueness (in the context of a given language) and annotation value disjointness (to enforce rules such as preferred labels being disjoint from alternative labels).

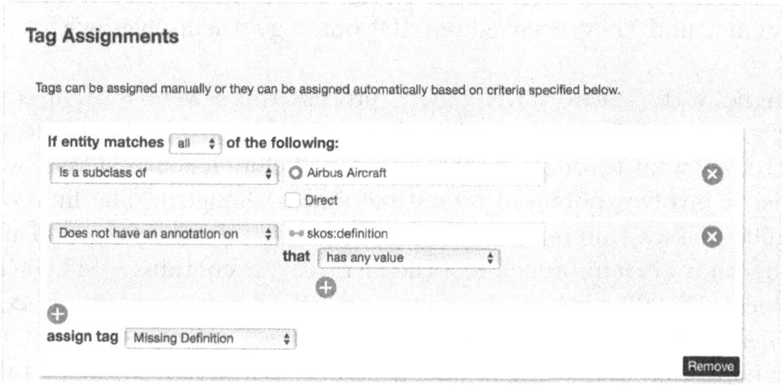

Tag Assignments

Tags can be assigned manually or they can be assigned automatically based on criteria specified below.

If entity matches all of the following:

Is a subclass of — Airbus Aircraft — Direct

Does not have an annotation on — skos:definition — that has any value

assign tag Missing Definition

Remove

Fig. 6. Automated tag assignment. Tags can be automatically assigned to entities based upon ontology structural criteria. Here, the criteria specify that any descendants of "Airbus Aircraft" that are missing a value for skos:definition will be tagged with the "Missing Definition" tag.

It is worth noting that the tagging functionality, that is, the entity matching criteria coupled with automated tag assignments, comes close to a SHACL Core [5] implementation in a user-friendly guise.

Support for Multi-lingual Editing and Viewing. WebProtégé has always had support for specifying IETF language tags [9] via auto-completion in the default editing interface. However, it soon became clear that the Pinterest curators required more elaborate functionality for viewing and checking language tags.

We first added support for a project default language tag setting. The default language is added to the labelling annotation when creating new entities. This saves a lot of clicking and typing when creating new interests.

We made significant changes to the rendering mechanism in WebProtégé so that it is possible to specify a list of *primary and secondary display languages.* Secondary display languages are used to derive secondary display names for entities, which are displayed along-side the primary display names in the various hierarchies (Fig. 7) and lists throughout WebProtégé. This provides a context and makes it easier for language specialists to perform translations.

Finally, we added rule templates, as part of the previously mentioned entity tagging functionality, so that it is possible to display colored indicators next to entities that are missing certain language tags (Fig. 7).

7 Production Development

There were eight Pinterest people involved in the development of the ontology, most of whom are not engineers and did not have any knowledge about OWL ontologies or WebProtégé. The eight ontology curators had a one-hour training session on how to use WebProtégé, and they were able to start curating content right away. Overall, it took the curators less than one month to build and finalize the ontology. After this first round of curation, some partner teams such as Ads and Sales reviewed the ontology, provided feedback and suggestions for improvements, and they even edited the ontology themselves with minimum training.

Throughout the entire development process there were ~2,000 comments spanning ~1,000 discussion/issue threads on interests, within WebProtégé. Overall the ontology went through 38,000+ revisions before its current version (where each revision involves potentially multiple axiom changes). The final ontology has ~11,000 classes (interests), 24 verticals (top-level interests), and up to 12 levels of depth in certain branches of the hierarchy. It contains ~145,000 axioms, out of which ~25,000 are logical axioms and ~95,000 are annotation axioms.

To consume the production ontology, Pinterest engineers built a Python-based pipeline that processes it and generates relational database tables for existing internal applications and other Pinterest tooling pipelines.

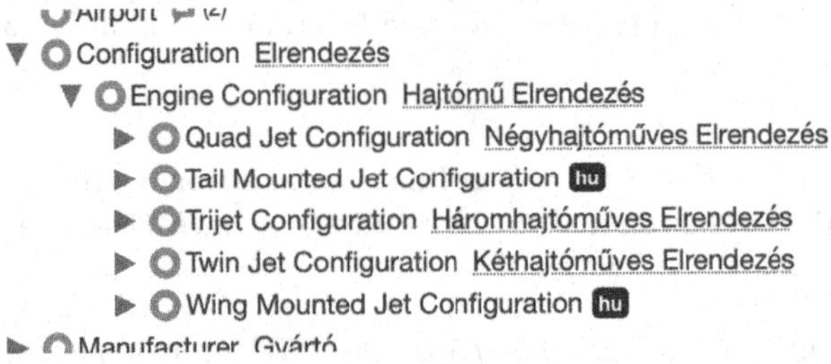

Fig. 7. An example of secondary language display names. The primary display language is "en" (English). The secondary display language is "hu" (Hungarian). The secondary display name is shown to the right of the primary display name. The colorful tag "hu" highlights classes that are missing the "hu" language tag.

8 Discussion

Throughout the development of the Pinterest Taxonomy, the Pinterest and Protégé teams encountered various challenges both in terms of modeling choices and tool support for ontology development. We describe some of these challenges below, and discuss how they will shape some future directions of our work.

Multiple Inheritance and Cross-Vertical Interests. Some interests would be best described with multiple parents. We frequently wanted to classify interests not only by their "primary type", but also by their intended role, their location, and the material that they are made from. For example, an interest in "Bathroom Lighting" is an interest in "Bathroom Decor". However, "Bathroom Lighting" could also be under "Light Fixtures". Allowing multiple parents for "Bathroom Lighting" would let advertisers of both bathroom design and lighting stores target Pinners who are interested in "Bathroom Lighting".

Multiple Relationship Types among Interests. Currently we only have one type of relationship between interest classes: **is-a**. For example, an interest in "Sandals" is an interest in "Shoes". However, we see a need for more relationships, for example, "Thanksgiving Recipe" (a "Food and Drinks" interest) and "Thanksgiving Decoration" (a "Home Decor" interest), plus "DIY Thanksgiving Card" (a "DIY and Crafts" interest) are all related to the Thanksgiving interest, so a Pinner interested in one before Thanksgiving time would highly likely be interested in the other two.

New Global Classes and Association with Interests. Besides categorizing Pins and users against interests, we can also categorize them into `Attributes`. For example, "Colors", "Brands" and "Materials". Since Pinterest powers shopping as well, we can imagine understanding supply and demand from the `Attribute` perspective would give Pinners more relevant products. `Attributes` should be defined as global (cross-vertical) classes, and they should be associated with applicable interests via appropriate relationships.

Richer Axiomatization. The ontology has gone through over 38,000 revisions in WebProtégé, each composed of potentially multiple axiom changes. The logical axioms used in the ontology are SubClassOf axioms. The current logical expressivity of the Pinterest Taxonomy falls under all three OWL 2 profiles: EL, RL, and QL. These profiles benefit from desirable computational properties, such as polynomial time (or less) worst-case complexity for core reasoning tasks. A next iteration of the Pinterest Taxonomy will make use of existential restrictions (i.e., SomeValuesFrom class expressions) to support faceted-based classification of interests. Such an extension would likely not go beyond the expressivity of OWL 2 EL, and would provide the benefit of automatically classifying interests by their asserted features, such as color and the materials things are made from, whilst preserving a primary axis of asserted classification that is required by some of the downstream consumers of the ontology.

9 Summary

During the past year's collaboration with the Protégé team, the Pinterest team have concluded that WebProtégé is by far the most suitable tool for developing the Pinterest Taxonomy. Not only has it proved to be a vast improvement upon the spreadsheet-based taxonomy curation, it has worked better than tools developed in-house. Since adopting WebProtégé, the curation and development cycle of the Pinterest Taxonomy has drastically shortened. With the old spreadsheet-based representation, it could have easily taken six months or longer to get to the same stage as we are today. The process would have been more error prone and far more tedious. WebProtégé facilitated the entire development process and allowed Pinterest to build out the Pinterest Taxonomy in only two months.

The flexibility of the OWL ontology representation allows the Pinterest Taxonomy to be easily expanded to a DAG. Adding further logical axiomatization to encode facets of interests offers the possibility of improving downstream search and recommendation applications. Besides the concrete outcome of an ontology, the use of WebProtégé has had a notable positive effect on strengthening the engagement of internal teams (from advertising and sales) with the Content Management team. Previously, it was a struggle to do this with the spreadsheet-based editing environment.

In October 2018, Pinterest released the newly developed Pinterest Taxonomy for interest-based ads targeting with over 1,500 new interests to target. The advertisers on Pinterest have overall expressed a positive impression of our work on the taxonomy. Additionally, Pinterest have determined that the new representation of their content has measurably increased revenue gains.

Finally, while there are a number of desirable improvements that we could make to the tooling and to the ontology itself, we hope that our experience and insights of using OWL and WebProtégé at Pinterest, to model real data from industry, are useful for the Semantic Web community.

Acknowledgements. We extend a huge thanks to John Milinovich (prev. at Pinterest), who played a pivotal role in establishing the collaboration between Pinterest and the Protégé team. We also thank Lance Riedel (Pinterest) and Brian Johnson (prev. at Pinterest), who steered the project in its earlier stages. The work described in this paper has been fully supported by Pinterest. Core WebProtégé work is supported by NIH NIGMS Grant GM121724.

References

1. Taxonomy. https://en.wikipedia.org/wiki/Taxonomy
2. Grau, B.C., et al.: OWL 2: the next step for OWL. Web Semant.: Sci. Serv. Agents World Wide Web **6**(4), 309–322 (2008)
3. Horridge, M., Tudorache, T., Vendetti, J., Nyulas, C.I., Musen, M.A., Noy, N.F.: Simplified OWL ontology editing for the web: is WebProtégé enough? In: Alani, H., et al. (eds.) ISWC 2013. LNCS, vol. 8218, pp. 200–215. Springer, Heidelberg (2013). https://doi.org/10.1007/978-3-642-41335-3_13
4. Horridge, M., et al.: Webprotégé: a collaborative Web-based platform for editing biomedical ontologies. Bioinformatics **30**(16), 2384–2385 (2014)
5. Knublauch, H., Kontokostas, D.: Shapes constraint language (SHACL). W3C Recommendation **11**(8) (2017). https://www.w3.org/TR/shacl
6. Milinovich, J.: Introducing the pinterest taste graph and enhanced targeting (2017). https://business.pinterest.com/en/blog/introducing-the-pinterest-taste-graph-and-enhanced-targeting

7. Montiel-Ponsoda, E., et al.: Style guidelines for naming and labeling ontologies in the multilingual web. In: Proceedings of the International Conference on Dublin Core and Metadata Applications (2011)
8. Noy, N.F., et al.: Ontology development 101: a guide to creating your first ontology. Stanford Knowledge Systems Laboratory technical report KSL-01-05 (2001)
9. Phillips, A., Davis, M.: BCP 47 - tags for identifying languages, September 2006. http://www.rfc-editor.org/rfc/bcp/bcp47.txt
10. Rector, A., et al.: OWL pizzas: practical experience of teaching OWL-DL: common errors & common patterns. In: Motta, E., Shadbolt, N.R., Stutt, A., Gibbins, N. (eds.) EKAW 2004. LNCS, vol. 3257, pp. 63–81. Springer, Heidelberg (2004). https://doi.org/10.1007/978-3-540-30202-5_5
11. Schober, D., et al.: Towards naming conventions for use in controlled vocabulary and ontology engineering. In: Proceedings of the Annual Bio-Ontologies Meeting, pp. 87–90 (2007)
12. Svátek, V., Šváb-Zamazal, O.: Entity naming in semantic web ontologies: design patterns and empirical observations. University of Economics, Prague, pp. 1–12 (2010)

An Assessment of Adoption and Quality of Linked Data in European Open Government Data

Luis-Daniel Ibáñez[1(✉)], Ian Millard[2], Hugh Glaser[2], and Elena Simperl[1]

[1] University of Southampton, Southampton, UK
{l.d.ibanez,e.simperl}@soton.ac.uk
[2] Seme4 Ltd., Southampton, UK
{ian.millard,hugh.glaser}@seme4.com

Abstract. The European Commission has adopted Linked Data principles and practices with the purpose of increasing the accessibility, interoperability and value of the data that is made available openly by European public sector organisations. This includes investment in metadata development for describing open datasets, catalogs of resources with persistent URIs, and the European Data Portal (EDP), which provides a single point of access, search and exploration of European open data. As the Public Sector Initiative (PSI) Directive is being revised, a critical question for the Commission is the extent to which open government data publishers have adopted Linked Data, and how they are applying the underlying technologies. In this paper, we undertake a quantitative analysis to support this. We explore if and how open data portals indexed by the EDP are using Linked Data and assess the quality of the datasets according to multiple dimensions.

Keywords: Linked Data · Open government data · Data quality

1 Introduction

Linked Data refers to a set of principles, technologies and practices that facilitate data integration. Publishers are encouraged to adopt them to make their data more useful [5]. Linked Data makes it easier for developers to access and combine datasets from different sources. To unlock the value of their data, publishers are advised to [5]:

1. use URIs to name things and relationships among things;
2. use HTTP URIs so those names can be looked up (a technique called *dereferencing*);
3. return useful information upon lookup of URIs, using open standards such as RDF; and

Supported by the European Data Portal, an initiative funded by the European Union.

C. Ghidini et al. (Eds.): ISWC 2019, LNCS 11779, pp. 436–453, 2019.
https://doi.org/10.1007/978-3-030-30796-7_27

4. include links to other URIs, so more things and relationships can be discovered organically.

Public sector organisations have embraced open data as a way to increase transparency and accountability of government services, boost innovation and foster participation [2]. For this purpose, they have set up so-called *open data portals*, which are web repositories where the data released by different government agencies can be searched, explored and downloaded. Open Data Soft, a technology provider in this space, estimates that there are more than 2600 such portals around the world.[1] To help track progress in open data publishing, Sir Tim Berners-Lee developed a 5-star deployment scheme, which features Linked Data as ultimate goal:[2]

1. Publish data under an open license.
2. Publish structured data.
3. Publish data using open formats.
4. Use URIs to denote things (matching Linked Data principles 1 to 3).
5. Link data to other data to provide context (matching principle 4).

Semantic Web (SW) technologies were chosen by the EC as the vehicle to achieve seamless and meaningful cross-border and cross-domain data exchanges between public administrations. Compared to other integration technologies, SW principles ensure data exchanged between public administrations is automatically recognised thanks to unambiguous, shared meaning, and setting the field for progressive and focused data integration among member states. Linked Data and the 5-star scheme are at the core of the open data strategy of the European Commission (EC), described in the Public Sector Information (PSI) Directive. This includes investment in the development and promotion of: metadata specifications such as DCAT-AP[3] to describe datasets; catalogs of resources with persistent URIs;[4] a data portal to host EC data;[5] as well as the *European Data Portal (EDP)*,[6] which provides a single point of access, search and exploration of open government data by various European public institutions. In November 2015, the EDP has started to harvest metadata from all national portals of the 28 EU countries and associated countries, the EC data portal, and a set of other sources such as geospatial portals. As the PSI Directive is being revised, policy makers need an overview of the adoption of their original recommendations by publishers, along the following lines:

(i) Are publishers using Linked Data? (ii) Are they using RDF or do they prefer other structured formats? (iii) Is the Linked Data they generate of enough quality to be queried and re-used?

[1] https://opendatainception.io/.
[2] https://5stardata.info/en/.
[3] https://joinup.ec.europa.eu/release/dcat-ap/12.
[4] http://data.europa.eu/URI.html.
[5] http://data.europa.eu/euodp/en/home.
[6] https://www.europeandataportal.eu/.

In this paper, we present a quantitative study that helps answer these questions. We analyse the use of Linked Data and the extent to which publishers indexed by the EDP follow the core principles. We explore the following themes: (i) the uptake of RDF as a publishing format, compared to structured and unstructured alternatives; (ii) the quality of the linked datasets, as an indicator of how well publishers implement Berners-Lee's deployment scheme; item and in comparison with previous quality assessments of the general *linked open data (LOD) cloud.*

Our contribution to the semantic web community is an up-to-date, empirically grounded reality check of the acceptance and uptake of arguably one of its core achievements - the principles, technologies and practices around Linked Data - in a critical early adopter sector, using a representative sample which includes 78 data portals, including all EU countries. We offer insight into how government publishers go about producing Linked Data and identify challenges and areas of improvement, which should inform the design of new supporting tools and techniques.

2 Related Work

The public sector has been one of the supporters of Linked Data from the beginning. There is a large body of literature documenting major open government data projects in different countries [6,15], compiling methodological guidance [16], and providing technical support [3,10,11].

Several studies have focused on empirical data quality assessments of different snapshots of the linked open data web. For instance, [7] looked at a corpus of more than one billion quadruples from almost four million documents acquired in 2010. [14] analysed best practice adoption in terms of linking, vocabulary usage, and metadata provision in different topical domains from a sample of 1014 datasets (including 183 from government) crawled in 2014. [4] evaluated the quality of a crawl seeded from the LOD cloud 2014 dataset of 130 datasets, totalling approximately 3.7 Billion quads. Our study applies a subset of the metrics used in these previous works on a much more recent (March 2019) corpus of open government datasets. Our study is also novel in the sense of analysing the unique perspective of a metaportal like the EDP, that by design is constrained to certain publishers and their catalogs.

Initiatives such as Open Data Monitor[7] and Portal Watch[8] keep track of a sample of web-based data portals and evaluate them according to criteria such as availability, conformance, retrievability, accuracy and metadata openness [13]. Our work complements them with a focused analysis of the quality of the datasets published as Linked Data on open government portals.

[7] https://opendatamonitor.eu/.
[8] https://data.wu.ac.at/portalwatch/.

3 European Data Portal

The European Data Portal (EDP) harvests metadata public sector open data portals across European countries. The aim is to improve access and discoverability, and hence facilitate re-use and value creation. The EDP is developed by the European Commission with the support of a consortium led by Capgemini, including INTRASOFT International, Fraunhofer Fokus, con terra, Sogeti, Time.Lex and the University of Southampton.

Following the DCAT and DCAT-AP specifications, EDP considers three main types of artefacts: (i) *catalogues*, which are curated collections of metadata about datasets; (ii) *datasets*, which refer to data published or curated by a single organisation and available for access or download in one or more formats; and (iii) *dataset distributions*, which are made in a specific format (CSV, PDF, RDF, etc).To harvest metadata, the EDP use dataset catalogues and APIs provided by open data publishers. The metadata can be accessed through several interfaces, including SPARQL[9].

EDP has implemented their own Metadata Quality Assessment (MQA) tool, based on a subset of the metrics in [13] and reports on the results of the SHACL validation of the mandatory DCAT-AP properties of the datasets they harvest. As per March 31 2019, all but three of the portals considered had achieved over 90% valid DCAT profiles. We refer the interested reader to the web page of MQA tool for further details.[10] In this study, we will focus on the datasets themselves, including two DCAT recommended properties: `dct:Format` and `dct:Publisher`.

4 Corpus and Methodology

4.1 Corpus

Our corpus has two parts. The first part consists of the collection of DCAT-AP catalogues, datasets and distributions harvested by the EDP, available through their SPARQL endpoint. We use this to compute a series of metadata-related metrics. The second part is made of all RDF distributions of all datasets harvested by the EDP. As the EDP stores only links to the distributions, we set up an acquisition process to download the data, including the following steps:

1. Acquire the available metadata of each dataset and its distributions, which are registered with the EDP.
2. Filter datasets having at least one distribution with the label `dct:format` property in the set {*n3, turtle, rdf+xml, ttl, rdf_trig*}. In Sect. 5.1 we will analyse in detail the different ways publishers used this property.
3. Attempt to download the RDF distributions of datasets extracted in the previous step. We register the Pay-Level-Domain (PLD) of the download URL and store it as the *host* of the dataset. As we will see in Sect. 5.2, not all publishers use the `dct:publisher` property in their metadata, therefore, we had to use the host to get an idea of the publisher.

[9] https://www.europeandataportal.eu/sparql.

[10] https://www.europeandataportal.eu/mqa/.

4. For distributions successfully downloaded in the previous step, parse and validate the RDF using the Raptor RDF library. 2.0.15.[11] Register any parsing or validation errors. Some distributions associated to a dataset represented slices of the same, and we considered them as one distribution in our calculations.

The corpus produced by this methodology has the following known bias factors, that we compare with those of previous studies. (i) Unlike [7,14], we did not use crawling to construct our corpus. Our approach was similar to [4], which used the LOD cloud DCAT descriptions as a starting point. (ii) We considered only datasets that included in their DCAT description the `dct:format` property. This means we miss some RDF datasets without this metadata. (iii) We did not consider SPARQL endpoints, as it was difficult to determine if they contained several other datasets besides the one linked in the distribution which is indexed by EDP. This means that we might have missed some datasets that do not come with a data dump distribution in RDF. As [4], we do not consider incorrect format tags. (iv) As we approximated publishers using the host's PLD, we might have lost some information about the actual publishers. Sometimes, multiple government agencies pool resources to develop and maintain a joint open data portal to manage economies of scale and encourage knowledge exchange - for instance, a city open data portal might host a dataset published by the local policy department, which is a different organisation than the city council.

We ran the acquisition tool on March 26 2019 and collected 6636 datasets with 8780 RDF distributions. Table 1 provides some descriptive statistics about the corpus. We identified 74 different hosts. The top-10 hosts with most RDF datasets are listed in Table 2. Most host names could be intuitively mapped to a data publisher or local data portal. We noted two PLDs, `dati.opendataground.it` and `nexo.carm.es`, where this is not clear. The former corresponds to the Italian municipality of Albano Laziale, and the latter to the Spanish region of Murcia. Three hosts were from Italy, six from Spain and one from the UK. We also noticed a fewer amount of contributors from France, Norway, Netherlands, Czech Republic, Austria and Finland, and none from catalogs of other EU countries.

Table 1. Descriptive statistics of our dataset corpus

Total datasets	6636	Total distributions	8780
Successful distribution download	8016	Failed distribution downloads	764
Successful distribution validation	6990	Failed distribution validation	1026
Datasets with at least one valid distribution	5856	Triples inspected	137, 208, 657

[11] http://librdf.org/raptor/.

Table 2. Top-10 host domains by number of datasets

Domain	# (%) of datasets
www.dati.lombardia.it	2836 (48.4%)
opendata.aragon.es	1252 (21.4%)
dati.opendataground.it (Comune AlbanoLaziale)	1011 (17.3%)
datos.gijon.es	357 (6.1%)
opendata.caceres.es	259 (4.4%)
www.dati.friuliveneziagiulia.it	172 (2.9%)
datos.santander.es	172 (2.9%)
nexo.carm.es (Region Murcia)	126 (2.2%)
opendata.camden.gov.uk	100 (1.7%)
datos.madrid.es	76 (1.3%)
Other 64 hosts	275 (4.7%)

4.2 Methodology

We analysed the corpus in terms of uptake, and along three quality dimensions: representational, contextual, and accessibility. We chose the metrics that allowed us to better assess re-usability and interoperability/interlinking, the main keywords of the PSI directive that the EC sought with the adoption of Semantic Web technologies.

Uptake. We measured the uptake of Linked Data by comparing the number of datasets in EDP that contained at least one distribution in a relevant format with the number of datasets that included at least one distribution in the following formats {*CSV, TSV, PDF, TXT, XML, XLSX, XLS, ODS, JSON*}, that is, other structured formats, plus PDF and TXT. We chose to ignore files made available as: (i) *ZIP*, as they are often provided as a convenience to download all different distributions in one go; (ii) image formats ({*PNG, JPG*}), as they are mostly used to visualise map data, and cannot be represented in RDF; (iii) APIs, as we did not consider SPARQL endpoints (their natural Linked Data counterparts) in our corpus; and (iv) *HTML*, as in most cases they link to external visualisations or dataset descriptions; and any other format tag. Our intention with this metric is to understand how many datasets are available in RDF with respect to other formats, providing a first measure of interoperability of the dataset landscape.

During our analysis, we noticed that publishers use a range of types as `dct:format` and `dcat:mediaType` values, which are currently not covered by the MQA tool implemented by the EDP. DCAT-AP guidelines recommend the use of the URI file type register operated by the Metadata Registry of the Publications Office of the EU (MRPO) to specify formats/media types.[12] We computed

[12] http://publications.europa.eu/resource/dataset/file-type.

the conformance to this recommendation, and report on the different ways data publishers are assigning this value.

Representational Quality. This dimension refers to how well the data is represented in terms of common best practices and guidelines. We considered the following aspects:

1. **Usage of well-known vocabularies.** Re-using vocabularies is key for increasing interoperability. Vocabularies for different domains are publicly available and can be found using tools such as Linked Open Vocabularies[13]. In our analysis, a vocabulary was considered to be used by a dataset if a term from that vocabulary appeared in the predicate position of a triple, or in the object position of an `rdf:type` triple. We relied on two sources for vocabularies: the list of from [14], and `prefix.cc` website. We report for each vocabulary the number of valid datasets that use it and the percentage with respect to the total. We also compared the relative percentage of vocabularies in our corpus with the one reported in [14] both for their overall corpus, and for their government datasets.
2. **Usage of proprietary and not well-known vocabularies.** Sometimes widely used vocabularies do not provide all the terms required to describe a dataset. Data publishers then resort to creating their own vocabularies to match their needs. Following [14] we considered a vocabulary to be proprietary if is used by only one dataset. However, unlike [14], we did not analyse datasets published by the same host as one dataset, which meant that a vocabulary defined by an organisation used in more than one of its own datasets would not be considered proprietary. Therefore, we also computed the set of hosts associated to each proprietary vocabulary. As a starting point, vocabularies that were not on `prefix.cc` were classified as *not well-known*.
3. **Usage of blank nodes.** The scope of blank nodes is limited to the document in which they appear, making them undesirable in Linked Data because they are impossible to re-use and interlink. Therefore, using them in datasets intended for public consumption is not advised. We computed the ratio of blank nodes against data-level constants as in [4,7]. Given a dataset D, the set of blank nodes in D $\beta(D)$, and the set of data-level constants $dlc(D)$, we defined the blank node ratio as $R = \frac{dlc(D) \setminus \beta(D)}{dlc(D)}$. A higher value of R means fewer blank nodes in D.

We chose these three metrics for the following reasons: usage of (not) well-known vocabularies quantify if publishers are using the vocabularies developed by the EC, and if not, what they are using instead. Use of blank nodes is recognized as limitative of interlinking and reuse [7].

Contextual Quality. This category refers to how well datasets were fit for the task at hand. In this category we considered *Provision of provenance information*

[13] https://lov.linkeddata.es/dataset/lov.

as indicator. Data provenance helps data consumers understand where the data comes from and who produces it. In the context of open government data, this dimension is particularly important, as publishers in this space usually have an official status. We captured this in two ways: (i) Count the number of DCAT profiles of all datasets registered in EDP that have a `dct:publisher` statement. This provided us with a general overview of how all publishers were using this particular type of metadata. (ii) Count the number of dcat profiles corresponding to datasets in our corpus that included a `dct:publisher` statement. This helped us understand how Linked Data publishers were using this type metadata.

We decided to use only `dct:publisher` as this is the property recommended by DCAT-AP, unlike in [4], who also included `dc:creator`. We did not consider other metrics in this category applied in the literature due to their dependence on the particular information need of the user conducting the search [4].

Accessibility. This dimension assesses the relative ease with which both machines and humans can re-use Linked Data resources. Within this space we computed the following metrics:

1. **Dereferenceability of vocabularies.** To enable applications to retrieve the definition of vocabulary terms, IRIs should be made dereferenceable. We report this metric for proprietary and not well-known vocabularies. We chose this particular metric as a natural complement to vocabulary usage. If publishers are using their own vocabularies instead of the EC ones, are they at least making them discoverable as well?
2. **Links to external datasets.** Links between datasets help data consumers query and explore datasets. From an EDP perspective, being able to combine datasets from different countries is of great value for producing EU-wide aggregations with a single SPARQL query. As [4], we counted an external link for each object's resource IRI in a triple that has a PLD different to the PLD of the host of the dataset. However, contrary to them, we did not check if the IRI was dereferenceable. For each detected external domain, we also computed the number of different hosts that published at least one dataset with an external link to it. We chose this metric as it quantifies the interlinking degree among datasets.

5 Results

5.1 Uptake

971,160 out of the 1,426,804 distributions registered in EDP include the recommended *dct:format* (68.4%). In terms of datasets, 384,128 out of the 860,294 contain at least one distribution with declared *dct:format* (44.6%). From these:

1. 476,377 distributions (44.9%) use the recommended MRPO vocabulary. For the sake of simplicity, we refer to the MRPO namespace as `mrpo`.

2. 127,015 distributions use *mrpo*, but with a wrong code at the end, *e.g.*, lowercase instead of uppercase, a non-existent format, or combinations of formats in a single IRI (e.g. `mrpo:ZIP+CSV`).
3. 154,216 distributions used a text literal. Most of them correspond to the codes of common file types.
4. 105,730 distributions used other IRIs. 96% of them came from one national open data portal that defined for each dataset an instance of the `dcterms:IMT` class with and an `rdfs:label` of the actual format. From a pure DCAT validation perspective, this is correct, as each IRI has the right type. However, this creates unnecessary entities and complicates the querying of different formats, as any aggregation then needs to be done on the text labels.
5. 108,082 distributions had a blank node, described by an `rdfs:label`. We noticed that Geoportals (portals that hold geographic information) were the most prevalent contributors of this metadata. These portals are aligned to the INSPIRE[14] metadata, specifically designed for geospatial data. In order to integrate metadata about geospatial data with the other types of data, the EC developed the GEODCAT-AP extension, and efforts were undertaken to map INSPIRE to it. According to the documentation, Geospatial data should use the filetypes from the MRPO register as format (or dcat:mediaType), or, in case of absence, use the type register of the INSPIRE project. We suspect that there is an issue on how geoportals export their INSPIRE metadata to GeoDCAT.

Regarding the optional `dcat:mediaType` property, 284,978 distributions (19.9%), with 114,990 datasets (13.3%) having at least one distribution with it. 98% of the distributions including *dcat:mediaType* also included *dct:format*. This is good, as DCAT-AP defines the former as a sub-property of the latter. However, similar to *dct:format*, we found that publishers have different ways of setting this value. Some of them use the full URL of the IANA mediaType, *e.g.*:

http://www.iana.org/assignments/media-types/text/csv

while others chose to use either the registry/name tag ('text/csv'), and a third group used the name ('csv'). According to the DCAT recommendation examples, the registry/name option is the correct one.

[4] measured this in their corpus using the *void:feature* property and found only 9 datasets including it. They recommended extending the metric to include DCAT properties, which is what we did here. However, we hypothesize that due to the existence of the DCAT-AP guidelines, PSI community is more prone to include this property than others.

Given the multiple ways that formats are declared, we decided to count datasets with at least one distribution on format F, with F the case insensitive value text label of each case identified above, i.e., the value of *skos:PrefLabel* for case (1) and (2), the literals for case (3), and the value of *rdfs:label* for cases (4) and (5). Figure 1 shows the comparison per each format. For this sample, RDF is still a minoritary format. Tabular formats (both open and closed) are

[14] https://inspire.ec.europa.eu/metadata/6541.

dominant, in particular CSV (over 100k datasets). RDF is approximately 5 to 6 times less common that non-tabular structured formats like XML and JSON.

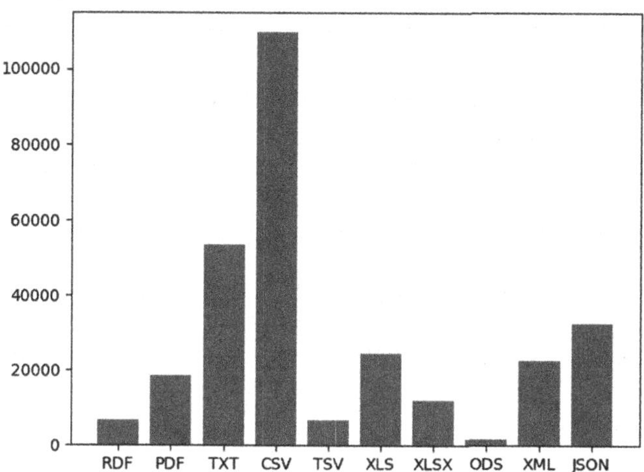

Fig. 1. Number of datasets with at least one distribution on each format

5.2 Basic Provenance Information

422, 058 datasets out of 838, 743 have a *dct:publisher* (50.3%). From the 5856 datasets with at least one resource in valid RDF format, we found that 2507 have a *dct:publisher* (42.8%). The latter result was a bit surprising for us, as we expected that organisations that are aware enough of Linked Data technologies to publish their data in RDF, would have their DCAT descriptions as complete as possible, even if *dct:publisher* is considered recommended instead of mandatory by the DCAT-AP specification. However, compared to the corpus in [4], where only 16.27% of datasets included this information, we can say that the PSI community is more committed to add it than others. Given the incompleteness of metadata on publishers, we chose use *hosts* as an estimation of publisher in the rest of our calculations.

5.3 Usage of Well-Known Vocabularies

Table 3 compares the percentage of well-known vocabularies in our corpus with the one reported in [14], both against the overall corpus and against datasets they categorised as Government. Overall, our corpus shows lower re-use percentage for all vocabularies, except for wgs84, when compared to the government slice. The sharpest differences are noted in the use of `dcterms` (−57% wrt (b)), `foaf` (−20% wrt (b)), `dcat` (−28% wrt (b)), `void` (almost nonexistent in our corpus), `cube/qb` (−53% wrt (b)), and `rss` (almost nonexistent in our corpus). The low

Table 3. Comparison of quotas of well-known vocabularies detected in [14] between (a) Full corpus of [14] (b) Government subset of corpus of [14] and (c) our corpus. We also add number of hosts and predicates detected in our corpus.

Prefix	(a)	(b)	(c)	# hosts	# predicates
rdf	98.22%	98.9%	83.54%	63	10
rdfs	72.58%	95.62%	87.18%	47	9
foaf	**69.13%**	**27.32%**	**7.53%**	43	20
dcterms	**56.01%**	**63.93%**	**6.10%**	47	45
owl	36.49%	23.49%	18.80%	18	5
wgs84	25.05%	7.10%	7.36%	19	4
sioc	17.65%	0.00%	0.00%	0	0
admin	15.48%	0.00%	0.00%	0	0
skos	**14.11%**	**20.76%**	**1.06%**	24	24
void	**13.51%**	**39.34%**	**0.91%**	13	13
bio	12.32%	1.09%	0.00%	0	0
cube/qb	**11.24%**	**61.74%**	**8.69%**	11	16
rss	**9.76%**	**54.64%**	**0.36%**	1	2
odc	8.48%	0.00%	0.00%	0	0
w3con	7.60%	0.00%	0.00%	0	0
doap	6.41%	2.73%	0.00%	0	0
bibo	6.11%	0.00%	0.10%	5	9
dcat	5.82%	28.41%	0.94%	12	12

usage of `dcat` and `void` in our corpus is expected, as by design there are few datasets that describe other datasets (EDP expects one DCAT-AP catalog per portal). The lesser usage use of `foaf` could be explained by our corpus not including many datasets that talk about people. The same argument could be made for `cube/qb`, as these vocabularies are almost exclusively used for statistical datasets. For `rss`, we believe it has stop being used as it was in 2014, as it is not dereferenceable anymore.

Table 3 also shows the number of different hosts that host data using that vocabulary, and the number of predicates from the vocabulary that are used across all datasets. Interestingly, although the number of datasets is low for **`foaf`**, **`dcterms`**, and **`skos`**, more than 30% of hosts use them. Furthermore, these vocabularies have the highest number of different predicates used.

Table 4 shows the top-10 vocabularies in terms of number of datasets, that exist in prefix.cc and were not already listed in Table 3. `xsd` and `dbpo` are the most prevalent in terms of datasets, while `vcard` and `dc11` the most popular in terms of number of hosts using them. We also found that `xhv` and `opensearch` are used in combination by a single publisher in the same relatively large number of small datasets to describe the results of an informative web page.

Table 4. Top-10 vocabularies in `prefix.cc` not listed on Table 3

Prefix	% datasets	# hosts	# preds.
`xsd`	17.3%	4	1
`dbpo`	13.25%	5	10
`apivc`	13.1%	2	4
`opensearch`	13.1%	1	2
`xhv`	13.1%	1	1
`sprx`	8.3%	1	5
`sdmx`	8.2%	1	3
`vcard`	4.4%	16	39
`dc11`	4.0%	18	31
`geonames`	2.2%	7	8

5.4 Usage and Dereferenceability of Other Vocabularies

Table 5 shows the most used not well-known vocabularies. Most of them are used by only one host, conforming to the definition of proprietary in [14]. However, only `Aragopedia`, `ontouniversidad` and `server1.avantic.net` were developed by data publishers (Spanish regions of Aragón, Cáceres, and Cádiz respectively). We highlight the popularity of `socrata.com/rdf/terms` both in number of datasets and different hosts. However, this is not a vocabulary per se: it is comprised of only one property, `socrata:rowID`, that is defined by default by the Socrata open data management tool in its CSV2RDF conversion utility. We can also infer from this that the original format of these datasets is CSV. Interestingly, the 3 predicates used from `open.vocab.org` are `csvHeader`, `csvRow` and `csvCol`, consistent with an attempt to export CSV to RDF. Finally, we note

Table 5. Top-10 not well-known vocabularies by dataset percentage

Vocabulary	% datasets	# hosts	# preds	Deref-able?
socrata.com/rdf/terms	52.6%	4	1	No
opendata.aragon.es/def/Aragopedia	13.0%	1	52	No
w3.org/2000/10/swap/pim/usps#	2.7%	4	4	Yes
data.press.net/ontology/stuff/	2.1%	2	5	Yes
opendata.caceres.es/def/ontomunicipio	1.7%	2	139	HTML
purl.org/ctic/infraestructuras/	1.1%	1	5	No
opendata.unex.es/def/ontouniversidad	1.0%	1	63	HTML
dublincore.org/documents/dcmi-box/	0.7%	1	4	No
open.vocab.org/terms	0.6%	1	3	HTML
server1.avantic.net/opendata/vocab/raw/	0.5%	1	206	No

that the `dcmi-box` namespace is incorrect. We believe the publisher meant to use the *dcterms:Box* property.

In terms of deferenceability, only and `uspe` returned an rdf+xml description, while `ontomunicipio`, `ontouniversidad` and `openvocab` returned HTML documentation. We are aware that both ontomunicipio and ontouniversidad have RDF versions, so the problem seems to be one of server configuration to return the right representation.

We found more than 3000 proprietary vocabularies, more than 95% of them non-dereferenceable at all. This surprisingly high number is mainly due to what it appears to be an incorrect use of the Socrata's RDF export from CSV utility[15], used by three of the top-10 contributors to our corpus (dati.lombardia.it, datifriulivenziagiulia.it, and opendata.camden.gov.uk). The utility sets a number of namespaces by default, including an auto-generated namespace based on the id of the resource, *e.g.*:

http://data.cityofchicago.org/resource/xzkq-xp2w/.

to which CSV headers are appended to create predicates. The default turns out to be quite unhelpful, as a different non-dereferenceable predicate is created for each column of each dataset, yielding an even less interoperable collection than the original set of CSVs. We found that more than 90% of the detected proprietary vocabularies correspond to this pattern. We also found that the Comune AlbanoLaziale portal (based on OpenDataGround[16]) has a similar functionality, that is also configured in a way that generates different predicates per each column header in a per-resource namespace.

5.5 Blank Nodes Usage

Figure 2 shows the distribution of the blank node ratios of datasets in our corpus. The median is very close to 1, meaning that the majority of datasets have none or almost none blank nodes. However, there is a sizable cluster of 485 outliers with $R \leq 0.1$, that is, 485 datasets with more than 90% of blank nodes.

We took a closer look at those extreme outliers. We found that they were all published by the Aragón region (opendata.aragon.es), as part of the first version of their project `Aragopedia`[17]. Datasets correspond to statistical observations of each of the 485 municipalities of the region. We contacted them about the issue, and they acknowledged that they were aware that the export was indeed faulty, and they were currently working on a fix. It was pointed out to us that both the XML v1 and RDF v2 distribution of these datasets were correct.

5.6 Links to External Providers

Table 6 shows the top-10 domains with more datasets linking to them, and the number of different hosts that use them. We also add to the table the

[15] https://dev.socrata.com/docs/formats/rdf-xml.html.

[16] http://www.evodevo.it/open-data-ground/.

[17] https://opendata.aragon.es/aragopedia/.

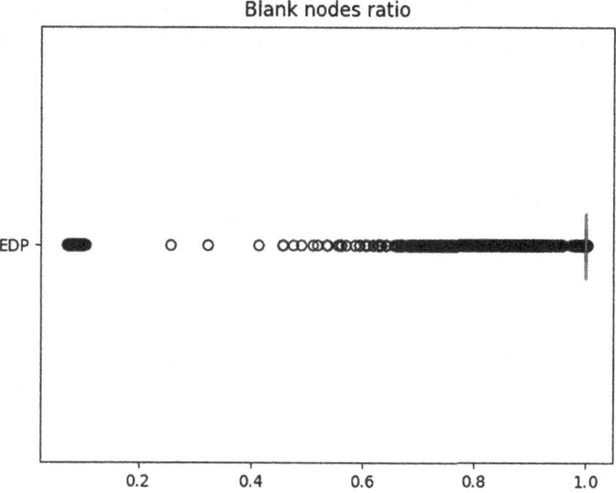

Fig. 2. Distribution of blank node ratio values for datasets in our corputs

`publications.europa.eu` domain to measure the usage in our sample of the controlled vocabularies defined by the EC. *w3.org* and *purl.org* are the most linked to by the most publishers. We also highlight the linking to DBpedia by close to 20% of the publishers, predominantly through the use of common vocabularies/predicates. There is very little linkage to `geonames.org`, which can be considered a bit surprising, as many of the datasets in our corpus are published by regions and municipalities, where we expect data about geographical places or with a spatial dimension. In this study we did not analyse the use of the `dct:spatial` property of DCAT-AP that could be used instead of including spatial statements in the dataset.

Concerning the use of government defined vocabularies, we highlight the presence of *reference.data.gov.uk* in many providers, suggesting that Linked Data publishers do use the definitions in the site: a vocabulary for time intervals, and for defining government offices. However, there is very little linkage both at dataset and publisher level with the *publications.europa.eu* domain, suggesting publishers are not using the controlled vocabularies provided by the EC.

6 Lessons Learned and Implications

In this paper we assessed the uptake of Linked Data principles on a large sample of open government datasets, made available via the European Data Portal. We measured the popularity of RDF against other publishing formats, and analysed the quality of the RDF datasets according to representational, contextual, and accessibility metrics. We list below main themes that emerged from the findings together with activities planned by EDP to address them to increase the interoperability of open government data:

Table 6. Top-10 domains with more datasets in our corpus linking to them, and number of different hosts where they are published. We add the no top-10 domain publications.europa.eu.

Domain	# datasets	# (%) hosts
w3.org	2467	55 (74%)
es.dbpedia	769	4 (5.4%)
purl.org	577	35 (47.3%)
reference.data.gov.uk	504	12 (16.2%)
data.press.net	123	2 (2.7%)
murciaturistica.es	122	1 (1.35%)
geonames.org	119	4 (5.4%)
www.gijon.es	117	1 (1.35%)
schema.org	73	7 (9.5%)
dbpedia.org	43	11 (14.8%)
publications.europa.eu	4	4 (5.4%)

1. **Recommended DCAT-AP properties are needed to facilitate automated quality analysis.** In our study, the limited use of `dct:format` meant that our sample may have missed some datasets. In the case of `dct:publisher`, we had to consider dataset hosts to identify publishers. Furthermore, the fact that publishers had different preferences for `dct:format` values made querying the data more difficult. The more publishers follow recommended practices, such as using `mrpo`, the easier it is to monitor uptake, identify challenges and propose solutions. In our corpus, we had first to investigate how the property was used (using OPTIONAL clauses, manual inspection etc.) to be able to derive the right query. This makes this sort of analysis more costly than it has to be, which in turn might mean less effective efforts to provide relevant standard updates and guidance.
   Follow-up actions. EDP will apply SHACL validation to recommended properties and encourage data publishers to follow the recommendations. For `dct:format`, EDP plans to perform the alignment and completion, and share the results with the publishers.
2. **RDF is a minority compared to other structured formats.** Our results suggest that RDF is very seldom the primary format of choice for open government datasets. Most datasets are in tabular format and then transformed to RDF.
   Follow-up actions. EDP needs to do more to engage publishers in reviewing the W3C recommendation for generating RDF from tabular data.[18] and kickstart discussions to add the recommendation to DCAT-AP.
3. **Vocabulary re-use is limited.** Our results suggest that publishers are having issues finding, using and/or aligning to vocabularies: from the different

[18] https://www.w3.org/TR/csv2rdf/.

ways of assigning values to `dct:format`, through the default parameters of Socrata's `csvtordf` conversion, to the low usage of the vocabularies defined by the EC.

Follow-up actions. Considering that lifting from tabular formats appears to be the best way to move forward, EDP will study the feasibility of applying recent research methods in this area [1,8] to find alignments to tabular headers. This could be done by intermediaries such as the EDP, by portals or the publishers themselves. Centralising the efforts at portal (or meta-portal level, like in EDP) creates economies of scale and guarantees more homogeneous results. Asking the publishers distributes the effort more widely, but additional care needs to be taken in providing clear guidelines for the choice and use of vocabularies, which will always leave some room for interpretation. In addition, portals and meta-portals need to consider the costs of coordinating individual lifting activities.

7 Conclusion and Future Work

In this paper, we conducted a quality assessment of the adoption and quality of Linked Data in the context of the European Data Portal, a portal that indexes European Open Government data. In this context Linked Data is used as a means to improve the re-usability and the interoperability of data assets within the European Union. We found that RDF is still a minority format. Most publishers that provided RDF versions of their datasets do so by taking advantage of capabilities of their portal software to convert CSV or XML datasets into RDF. However, they often do it without providing links to other datasets, or using well-known vocabularies. This suggests a gap between the numerous academic approaches to link CSV files to ontologies, and the tools used by open government data publishers. Besides the *technology readiness* gap, we also believe there is an organisational gap: on the one hand, data publishers may lack the contextual information of what other entities to link to; on the other, portals that only index metadata would need to download and process all datasets. Even if they can produce linksets or RDF versions of the datasets, there is the question how to manage their storage and update.

As future work, in addition to the recommendations outlined in Sect. 6, we would like to categorise the profile of data portal users to apply contextual metrics based on their particular information needs. Our quantitative results could drive the design and execution of a qualitative assessment of the discoverability and fitness for use of datasets in the portal, in the spirit of recent studies on Human Data Interaction in data portals [9]. Finally, we would like to explore the applicability of recent data portal models that integrate social tools common in collaborative software development infrastructures [12], to include dataset consumers in the loop with a view to improving dataset quality.

References

1. Alobaid, A., Corcho, O.: Fuzzy semantic labeling of semi-structured numerical datasets. In: Faron Zucker, C., Ghidini, C., Napoli, A., Toussaint, Y. (eds.) EKAW 2018. LNCS (LNAI), vol. 11313, pp. 19–33. Springer, Cham (2018). https://doi.org/10.1007/978-3-030-03667-6_2
2. Attard, J., Orlandi, F., Scerri, S., Auer, S.: A systematic review of open government data initiatives. Gov. Inf. Quart. **32**(4), 399–418 (2015). https://doi.org/10.1016/j.giq.2015.07.006
3. Bischof, S., Martin, C., Polleres, A., Schneider, P.: Collecting, integrating, enriching and republishing open city data as linked data. In: Arenas, M., et al. (eds.) ISWC 2015. LNCS, vol. 9367, pp. 57–75. Springer, Cham (2015). https://doi.org/10.1007/978-3-319-25010-6_4
4. Debattista, J., Lange, C., Auer, S., Cortis, D.: Evaluating the quality of the LOD cloud: an empirical investigation. Semant. Web **9**(6), 859–901 (2018). https://doi.org/10.3233/SW-180306
5. Heath, T., Bizer, C.: Linked data: evolving the web into a global data space. Synth. Lect. Semant. Web: Theory Technol. **1**(1), 1–136 (2011). https://doi.org/10.2200/S00334ED1V01Y201102WBE001
6. Hendler, J., Holm, J., Musialek, C., Thomas, G.: US government linked open data: semantic.data.gov. IEEE Intell. Syst. **27**(3) (2012). https://doi.org/10.1109/MIS.2012.27
7. Hogan, A., Umbrich, J., Harth, A., Cyganiak, R., Polleres, A., Decker, S.: An empirical survey of Linked Data conformance. J. Web Semant. **14**, 14–44 (2012). https://doi.org/10.1016/j.websem.2012.02.001
8. Kacprzak, E., et al.: Making sense of numerical data - semantic labelling of web tables. In: Faron Zucker, C., Ghidini, C., Napoli, A., Toussaint, Y. (eds.) EKAW 2018. LNCS (LNAI), vol. 11313, pp. 163–178. Springer, Cham (2018). https://doi.org/10.1007/978-3-030-03667-6_11
9. Koesten, L.M., Kacprzak, E., Tennison, J.F.A., Simperl, E.: The trials and tribulations of working with structured data: - a study on information seeking behaviour. In: Proceedings of the 2017 CHI Conference on Human Factors in Computing Systems, CHI 2017, pp. 1277–1289. ACM, New York (2017). https://doi.org/10.1145/3025453.3025838
10. Lopez, V., Kotoulas, S., Sbodio, M.L., Stephenson, M., Gkoulalas-Divanis, A., Aonghusa, P.M.: QuerioCity: a linked data platform for urban information management. In: The Semantic Web - ISWC 2012, pp. 148–163 (2012). https://doi.org/10.1007/978-3-642-35173-0_10
11. Maali, F., Cyganiak, R., Peristeras, V.: A publishing pipeline for linked government data. In: Simperl, E., Cimiano, P., Polleres, A., Corcho, O., Presutti, V. (eds.) ESWC 2012. LNCS, vol. 7295, pp. 778–792. Springer, Heidelberg (2012). https://doi.org/10.1007/978-3-642-30284-8_59
12. Neumaier, S., Thurnay, L., Lampoltshammer, T.J., Knap, T.: Search, filter, fork, and link open data: the ADEQUATe platform: data- and community-driven quality improvements. In: Companion Proceedings of the The Web Conference 2018, WWW 2018, pp. 1523–1526 (2018). https://doi.org/10.1145/3184558.3191602
13. Neumaier, S., Umbrich, J., Polleres, A.: Automated quality assessment of metadata across open data portals. J. Data Inf. Qual. **8**(1), 2:1–2:29 (2016). https://doi.org/10.1145/2964909

14. Schmachtenberg, M., Bizer, C., Paulheim, H.: Adoption of the linked data best practices in different topical domains. In: The Semantic Web - ISWC 2014, pp. 245–260 (2014). https://doi.org/10.1007/978-3-319-11964-9_16
15. Shadbolt, N., et al.: Linked open government data: lessons from Data.gov.uk. IEEE Intell. Syst. **27**, 16–24 (2012). https://doi.org/10.1109/MIS.2012.23
16. Villazón-Terrazas, B., Vilches-Blázquez, L.M., Corcho, O., Gómez-Pérez, A.: Methodological guidelines for publishing government linked data. In: Wood, D. (ed.) Linking Government Data, pp. 27–49. Springer, New York (2011). https://doi.org/10.1007/978-1-4614-1767-5_2

Easy Web API Development with SPARQL Transformer

Pasquale Lisena[1(✉)], Albert Meroño-Peñuela[2], Tobias Kuhn[2], and Raphaël Troncy[1]

[1] EURECOM, Sophia Antipolis, France
{pasquale.lisena,raphael.troncy}@eurecom.fr
[2] Vrije Universiteit, Amsterdam, The Netherlands
{t.kuhn,albert.merono}@vu.nl

Abstract. In a document-based world as the one of Web APIs, the triple-based output of SPARQL endpoints can be a barrier for developers who want to integrate Linked Data in their applications. A different JSON output can be obtained with SPARQL Transformer, which relies on a single JSON object for defining which data should be extracted from the endpoint and which shape should they assume. We propose a new approach that amounts to merge SPARQL bindings on the base of identifiers and the integration in the `grlc` API framework to create new bridges between the Web of Data and the Web of applications.

Keywords: SPARQL · JSON · JSON-LD · API

1 Introduction

The Semantic Web is a valuable resource of data and technologies, which is having a crucial role in realising the initial idea of Web. RDF can potentially represent any kind of knowledge, enabling reasoning, interlinking between datasets, and graph-based artificial intelligence. Nevertheless, a structural gap exists that is limiting a broader consumption of RDF data by the community of Web developers. Recent initiatives such as EasierRDF[1] are strongly pushing the proposal of new solutions for making Semantic data on the Web *developer friendly* [3,10].

We focus here on the output format of SPARQL endpoints, and in particular, query results in the JSON format [24]. This standard is part of the SPARQL W3C recommendation [12], introduced with the purpose of easing the consumption of the data by Web (and non-Web) applications. The format consists of a set of all possible bindings (of the form `<variable, value>`) that satisfies the query. This is not handy for efficient processing by clients, which would prefer nested objects (document-based data structures) rather than this representation of triples (graph-oriented data structures). An example of this is shown in Fig. 1.

[1] https://github.com/w3c/EasierRDF.

C. Ghidini et al. (Eds.): ISWC 2019, LNCS 11779, pp. 454–470, 2019.
https://doi.org/10.1007/978-3-030-30796-7_28

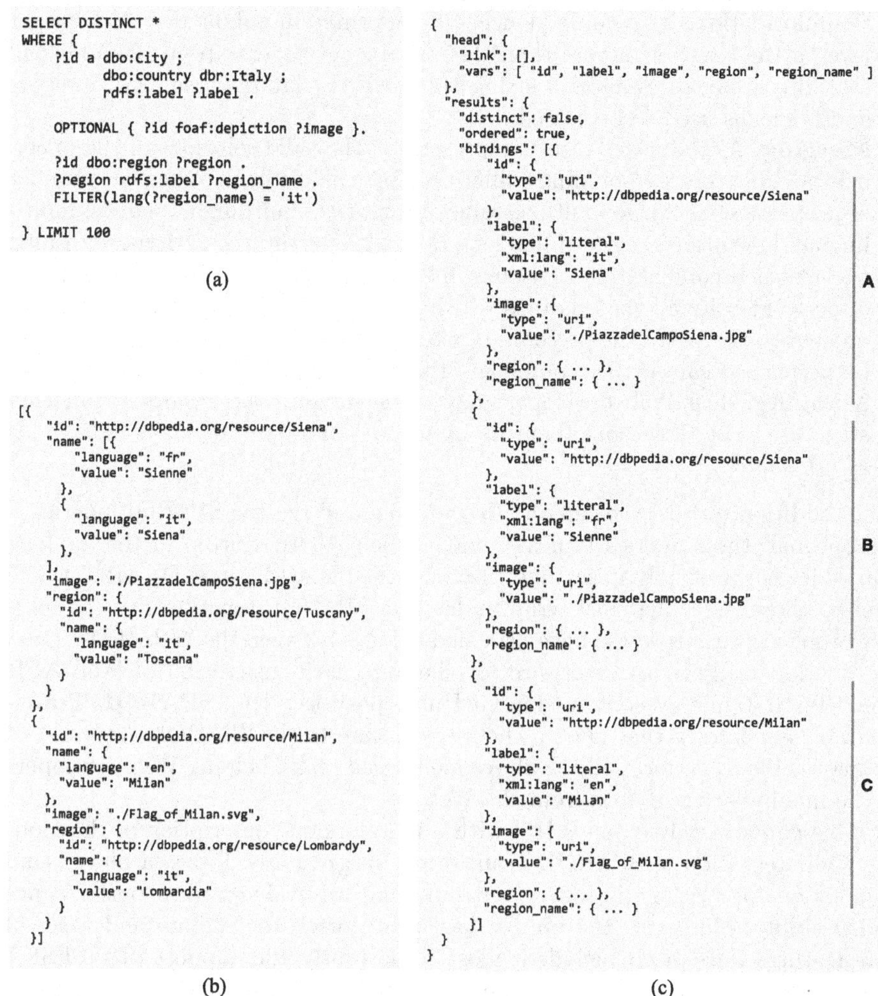

SELECT DISTINCT *
WHERE {
?id a dbo:City ;
dbo:country dbr:Italy ;
rdfs:label ?label .
OPTIONAL { ?id foaf:depiction ?image }.
?id dbo:region ?region .
?region rdfs:label ?region_name .
FILTER(lang(?region_name) = 'it')
} LIMIT 100
(a)
[{
"id": "http://dbpedia.org/resource/Siena",
"name": [{
"language": "fr",
"value": "Sienne"
},
{
"language": "it",
"value": "Siena"
},
],
"image": "./PiazzadelCampoSiena.jpg",
"region": {
"id": "http://dbpedia.org/resource/Tuscany",
"name": {
"language": "it",
"value": "Toscana"
}
}
},
{
"id": "http://dbpedia.org/resource/Milan",
"name": {
"language": "en",
"value": "Milan"
},
"image": "./Flag_of_Milan.svg",
"region": {
"id": "http://dbpedia.org/resource/Lombardy",
"name": {
"language": "it",
"value": "Lombardia"
}
}
}]
(b)
{
"head": {
"link": [],
"vars": ["id", "label", "image", "region", "region_name"]
},
"results": {
"distinct": false,
"ordered": true,
"bindings": [{
"id": {
"type": "uri",
"value": "http://dbpedia.org/resource/Siena"
},
"label": {
"type": "literal",
"xml:lang": "it",
"value": "Siena"
},
"image": {
"type": "uri",
"value": "./PiazzadelCampoSiena.jpg"
},
"region": { ... },
"region_name": { ... }
},
{
"id": {
"type": "uri",
"value": "http://dbpedia.org/resource/Siena"
},
"label": {
"type": "literal",
"xml:lang": "fr",
"value": "Sienne"
},
"image": {
"type": "uri",
"value": "./PiazzadelCampoSiena.jpg"
},
"region": { ... },
"region_name": { ... }
},
{
"id": {
"type": "uri",
"value": "http://dbpedia.org/resource/Milan"
},
"label": {
"type": "literal",
"xml:lang": "en",
"value": "Milan"
},
"image": {
"type": "uri",
"value": "./Flag_of_Milan.svg"
},
"region": { ... },
"region_name": { ... }
}]
}
}
A
B
C
(c)

Fig. 1. A SPARQL query (a) extracting a list of Italian cities with picture, label and belonging region, of which the URI and the Italian name are also requested. In the standard output of the endpoint (c), the city of Siena is represented by both object A and B, while the transformed output (b) offers a more compact structure.

Given this situation, we identify four tasks that developers have to fulfil:

1. **Skip irrelevant metadata.** A typical SPARQL output contains a lot of metadata that are often not useful for Web developers. This is the case of the `head` field, which contains the list of variables that one might find in the results. In practice, developers may ignore completely this part and check for the availability of a certain property directly in the JSON tree.
2. **Reducing and parsing.** The value of a property is always wrapped in an object with at least the attributes *type* (URI or literal) and *value*, containing

the information. As a consequence, this information is bounded at a deeper level in the JSON structure than the one the developer expects. In addition, each literal is expressed as a string value with a datatype, so that numbers and booleans need to be casted.
3. **Merging.** As the query results represent all the valid solutions of the query, it is possible that two bindings differ only by a single field. When the number of properties that have multiple values grows (i.e. multilingual names, multilingual descriptions, a set of images), the endpoint returns even more results, one for each combination of values. The consumption of such data requires often to identify all the bindings which represent a given entity, merging the objects on the URI. The presence of more variables on which the merging can be performed can further complicate the merging process.
4. **Mapping.** The Web developer may want to map the results to another structure – i.e. for using them as input to a library – or vocabulary such as *schema.org*.

In addition to this, the support for curating and reusing SPARQL queries is sub-optimal, these queries typically end up being hard-written in the application code. A specifically unsettling case of these Linked Data (LD) APIs, which refer to those APIs that just wrap underlying SPARQL functionality. To solve this problem, various works have provided bridges between the Web of Data and the developers. `grlc` is a software for the automatic generation of Web APIs from SPARQL queries contained in GitHub repositories [16]. **SPARQL Transformer**[2] is a library that gives a chosen structure to the SPARQL output. The library is able to perform all the above mentioned tasks, helping Web developers in the manipulation of data from the Web.

This paper largely extends [15] with a more organic description of the module, the integration of SPARQL Transformer in `grlc` and Tapas, a playground application for testing the query outcome and an evaluation on performance and usability. Moreover, the library has been ported to Python, and a set of new features have been included, most importantly the support of OFFSET (allowing pagination, e.g. in `grlc`) and language filtering for the management of multi-language APIs. The remainder of this paper is structured as follows: we propose a thorough review of other works which aim to ease the consumption of RDF data and their limitations in Sect. 2. We introduce the new JSON format for queries in Sect. 3, which feeds the SPARQL Transformer library detailed in Sect. 4. The work is finally evaluated in Sect. 5, while some conclusions and future work are presented in Sect. 6.

2 Related Work

The need for overcoming the issues about the usage of SPARQL output in real-life applications has inspired different works. One of the first proposed solutions

[2] SPARQL Transformer is available at https://github.com/D2KLab/sparql-transformer as a JavaScript library, while a Python implementation is available at https://github.com/D2KLab/py-sparql-transformer.

consists in a strategy for representing the SPARQL output in a tabular structure, to address the creation of HTML reports [1].

Wikidata SDK [14] takes care of the reduction and parsing tasks through a precise function[3] that transforms the JSON output to a simplified version by reading the variable names. However this implementation does not address the problem of merging.

The conversion of RDF data can rely on the *SPARQL Template Transformation Language (STTL)* [4]. Those transformation templates (as strings) are exploited for shaping the results of the SPARQL query. Moreover, STTL exposes a significant number of functions, especially when combined with LDScript [5]. Among the limits of this approach is the absence of any support for converting the results to JSON-LD. No merging strategy is also studied in this approach.

The W3C RDFJS Community Group[4] is heavily contributing to the effort of offering a tool to JavaScript developers for using RDF data. The major outcome of the initiative is a low-level interface specification for the interoperability of RDF data in JavaScript environments [2]. RDFJS brings the graph-oriented model of RDF into the browser, allowing developers to directly manipulate triples.

The `CONSTRUCT` query format – included in the W3C SPARQL Specification [12] – can be seen as a way for mapping the SPARQL results into a chosen structure, following one of the standard SPARQL output formats, including JSON-LD. An attempt has been realised by the command-line library `sparql-to-jsonld` [17]. The need for three different inputs – a `SELECT` query, a `CONSTRUCT` or `DESCRIBE` query, and a JSON-LD frame – indirectly proves that a sole `CONSTRUCT` for shaping JSON with non predefined structure is not sufficient. Indeed, the `CONSTRUCT` keyword can only generate triplesets, from which the generation of JSON tree-like documents is ambiguous. This is inconvenient for developers, and leads to the problem of how to change the structure of the query result. JSON-LD Framing[5] overcomes this problem, but, in our opinion, the combination is not easier for developers who would have to write and keep in sync the two parts (query and result shape). The complexity of writing a `CONSTRUCT` query – i.e. with respect to a `SELECT` one – can be an additional deterrent for its usage. Furthermore, literals are not parsed and they are always represented as objects, and aggregate functions are not supported.

JSON Schema is a format for defining the structure of a JSON object. Although it is a powerful tool for validation – for example – of forms and APIs, there are no evident benefits for JSON reshaping purposes [29].

The development of *SOLID* framework for decentralised LD applications [28] gives popularity to its module *LDflex*[6] for retrieving and manipulating Linked Data. LDflex allows the user to browse nodes in the graph by accessing to JS

[3] https://github.com/maxlath/wikidata-sdk/blob/master/docs/simplify_sparql_results.md.
[4] https://www.w3.org/community/rdfjs/.
[5] https://www.w3.org/TR/json-ld11-framing/.
[6] https://github.com/RubenVerborgh/LDflex.

properties. Thus, the paradigm of this module is different, consisting in navigating the graph following the links, rather than finding solutions to structured queries.

There is abundant work in SPARQL query repositories, which are typically used to study the efficiency and reusability of querying. For example, in [21] authors use SPARQL query logs to study differences between human and machine executed queries; in [13], these logs are used to understand the semantic relations between queried entities. Saleem et al. [23] propose to "create a Linked Dataset describing the SPARQL queries issued to various public SPARQL endpoints".

There is also a large body of Semantic Web literature on Linked Data and Web Services [9,20]. In [25] and the smartAPI [30], the authors propose to expose REST APIs as Linked Data, and enumerate the advantages of using Linked Data technology on top of Web services. In the opposite direction, the Linked Data API specification[7] and the W3C Linked Data Platform 1.0 specification, describe "the use of HTTP for accessing, updating, creating and deleting resources from servers that expose their resources as Linked Data"[8]. Our work follows this direction, and is more related to providing APIs that facilitate Linked Data access and query results consumption. The OpenPHACTS Discovery Platform for pharmacological data [11], LDtogo [19] and the BASIL server [6] use SPARQL as an underlying mechanism to implement APIs and provide Linked Data query results. Influenced by these works, `grlc` [16], a technology we extend in this paper, decouples query storage from API implementations by leveraging queries uniquely and globally identified by stable and de-referenceable URIs, automating the query construction process.

Recent works realised an interoperability between the GraphQL language[9] and RDF, performing in this way a conversion in JSON of the data in an endpoint [27]. The same syntax of GraphQL allows to produce a JSON object with different levels of nested nodes. Some of these solutions rely on automatic mappings of variables to property names (Stardog[10]), while others rely on a schema (HyperGraphQL[11]) or a context (GraphQL-LD [26]) which the developer is in charge to provide. None of those approaches implements any strategy for detecting and merging bindings referring to the same entity.

3 The JSON Query Syntax

As seen in the experiences reported in Sect. 2, the natural choice of format for defining and developing a transformation template involves JSON or its JSON-LD serialisation, which is usually added to the SPARQL query. The names of

---

[7] https://github.com/UKGovLD/linked-data-api.

[8] https://www.w3.org/TR/2015/REC-ldp-20150226/.

[9] https://graphql.github.io/.

[10] https://www.stardog.com/.

[11] https://www.hypergraphql.org.

```
1  {
2    "proto": {
3      "id" : "?id",
4      "name": "$rdfs:label$required",
5      "image": "$foaf:depiction",
6      "region": {
7        "id" : "$dbo:region$required",
8        "name": "$rdfs:label$lang:it"
9      }
10   },
11   "$where": [
12     "?id a dbo:City",
13     "?id dbo:country dbr:Italy"
14   ],
15   "$limit": 100
16 }
```

Listing 1.1. The JSON version of the SPARQL query in Fig. 1

```
SELECT DISTINCT ?id ?v1 ?v2 ?v3r ?v31 WHERE {
    ?id a dbo:City.                                    # 12
    ?id dbo:country dbr:Italy.                         # 13
    ?id rdfs:label ?v1.                                # 4
    OPTIONAL { ?id foaf:depiction ?v2  }.              # 5
    ?id dbo:region ?v3r .                              # 7
    OPTIONAL { ?v3r rdfs:label ?v31 .
        FILTER(lang(?v31) = "it") }                    # 8
}
LIMIT 100                                              # 15
```

Listing 1.2. The intermediate SPARQL query. The comments contain line numbers which identify which part of the JSON query in Listing 1.1 generates the statement.

the variables used should match between the template and the query, making the developing process error-prone.

Our proposal is to use a single JSON object, called *JSON query*, with the double role of declaring how to find the information (query) and which structure is expected in its output (template). These properties put the JSON query at a certain distance also from SPARQL `CONSTRUCT`, in which the query and the final structure are two distinct parts of the query.

The syntax of JSON queries consists of two main parts (Listing 1.1):

- the prototype definition, which describes the output structure, expressed as an object and introduced by the `proto` property;
- a set of rules to be included in the SPARQL query, defined through a set of properties starting with the `$` sign, e.g. `$where` and `$limit`.

JSON queries can be expressed in two different formats, producing coherently the output: plain JSON and JSON-LD. The latter foresees a slightly different syntax in order to return an output compliant with the JSON-LD specification. This version of the query allows to specify a JSON-LD context, and can be used for mapping the results into a chosen vocabulary. We refer to the documentation[12] for more details.

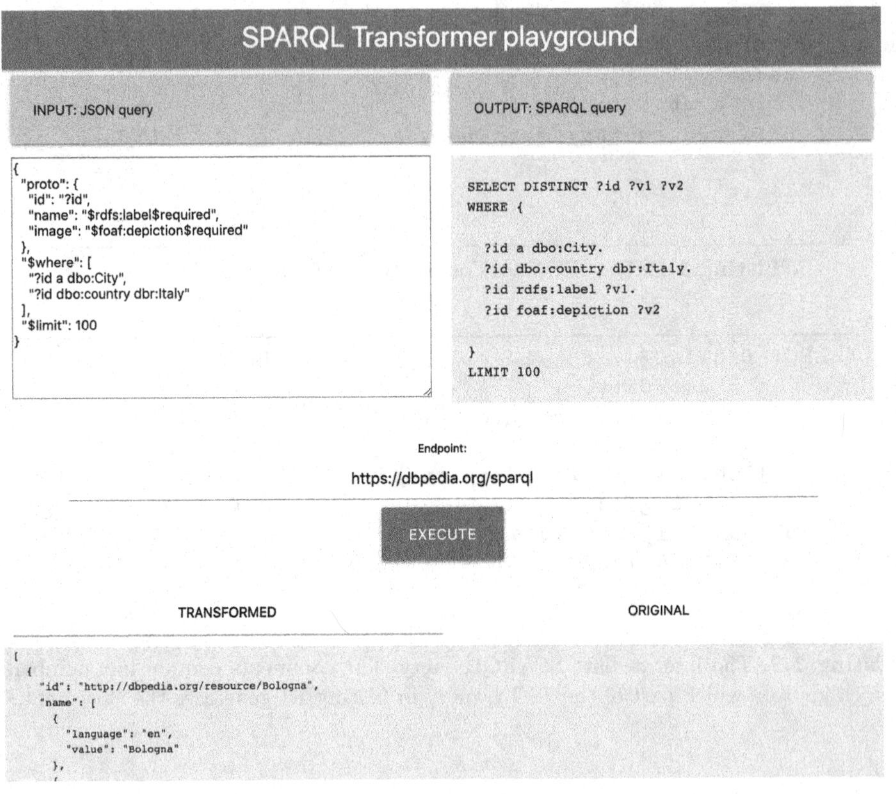

Fig. 2. User interface of SPARQL Transformer playground

A Web application called **SPARQL Transformer playground**[13] has been developed in order to quickly test JSON queries. The application is live converting the JSON into a corresponding SPARQL query, so that the user can appreciate every single change. In addition, it is possible to execute the query against a given endpoint, and the user interface offers the possibility of comparing the transformed output with the original one (Fig. 2).

[12] https://github.com/D2KLab/sparql-transformer.
[13] https://d2klab.github.io/sparql-transformer/.

3.1 The Prototype Definition

By prototype, we mean the common structure each object in output should respect. It is designed as an ordinary JSON object, in which the leaf nodes will be replaced by incoming data according to specific rules. In particular:

1. **variable nodes**, which start with a question mark "?" (like `?id` or `?city`), are replaced by the value of the homonym SPARQL variable;
2. **predicate nodes**, which starts with a "$" sign, are replaced by the object of a specific RDF triple;
3. **literal nodes**, which cover all the other contents, are not replaced and will be present as is in the output, regardless of the query results.

In the transforming process, SPARQL triples will be automatically generated from the prototype. Referring to case 2, the following syntax is used:

```
$<SPARQL PREDICATE>[$modifier[:option]...]
```

The first parameter is the SPARQL predicate, which can be a property or a property path, e.g. `rdfs:label`, `foaf:depiction`, etc. This kind of node will be replaced by the object of an RDF triple having as predicate the one given inline. As subject, the variable of the sibling *merging anchor* is selected if it exists; otherwise, the closer merging anchor among the parent nodes. The merging anchors are all the fields in the JSON introduced with the `id` property. If this variable does not exist, it is set to `?id` by default. In other words, each level in the JSON tree may declare a specific subject through the merging anchor, which will be the subject of all the predicates in the scope. Listing 1.1 includes two merging anchors at line 3 and 7: the former acts as subject of the name, image, and region; while the region name refers to the latter.

The role of the *merging anchor* is crucial for the following steps. In fact, two result objects having the same id will be considered as the same item and their properties will be merged. This will happen at each level of the JSON tree. This controlled way of aggregating SPARQL results ensures a more compact while not less informative output, ready to be used by Web developers.

Both variable and predicate nodes can accept some modifiers appended at the end of the string, separated by the $ sign. These elements are taken in account when writing the SPARQL query. For example, `$required` avoids the predicate to be considered optional (the default behaviour), while `$var` assigns a specific SPARQL variable as object (e.g. `$var:?myVar`), so that it can be addressed in other modifiers. Other possibilities include filtering by language (`$lang:it` or `$bestlang:en;q=1, it;q=0.7 *;q=0.1`) or sample those values (`$sample`).

3.2 The Root $-properties

A set of $-properties give access to the SPARQL features indicated by their name (`$limit`, `$groupby`, etc). These properties are directly assigned to the root of the JSON query object, and will not appear in the final output. Among them, some additional WHERE clauses – in the triple format – can be declared in the $where field. The $lang modifiers set the language chosen for all the $bestlang in the prototype. An exhaustive list of implemented $-properties is reported in Table 1.

Table 1. Supported root $-properties

Property	Input	Description
$where	string, array	Add where clause in the triple format
$values	object	Set VALUES for specified variables as a map
$limit	number	LIMIT the SPARQL results
$distinct	boolean	Set the DISTINCT in the select (default true)
$offset	number	OFFSET applied to the SPARQL results
$orderby	string, array	Build an ORDER BY on the variables in the input
$groupby	string, array	Build an ORDER BY on the variables in the input
$having	string, array	Allows to declare the content of HAVING
$filter	string, array	Add the content as a FILTER
$prefixes	object	Set the prefixes in the format "prefix": "uri"
$lang	string	Default language in the Accept-Language standard [8]

4 Implementation

The implementation of SPARQL Transformer relies on three main blocks, each one having a specific function (Fig. 3).

The **Parser** reads the input JSON query and parses its content. The prototype is extracted and a SPARQL variable – which here acts as a placeholder – is assigned to all the predicate nodes. Contextually, the SPARQL SELECT query (Listing 1.2) is generated: the predicate nodes are translated into WHERE clauses according to the rules defined in Sect. 3.1 and taking into account the modifiers. The root $-properties are parsed and inserted in the query, which is then passed to the **Query Performer**. This module is in charge of performing the request to the SPARQL endpoint and returning the results in the SPARQL JSON output format. The query performer can be replaced by the user with a custom one, for fulfilling different requirements for accessing the endpoint (e.g. authentication) or for integration into more complex environments (as done during the integration with grlc).

Finally, the **Shaper** accesses the results, discarding the side information included in the head field and directly accessing the bindings. The latter ones are applied to the prototype in sequence, matching the SPARQL variables to the placeholders separately for each binding. In this phase, the data-type of the binding is checked, eventually parsing the value to Boolean, integer or float.

When a result binding does not contain a certain value – which happens when the variable is `OPTIONAL` –, the property is removed from the instance. Then, the instances which have a common value for the merging anchor are identified and their properties are compared, in order to keep all the distinct values without repetition. Recursively, the same merging strategy is applied to the nested objects. Finally, they are serialised in JSON and returned as output.

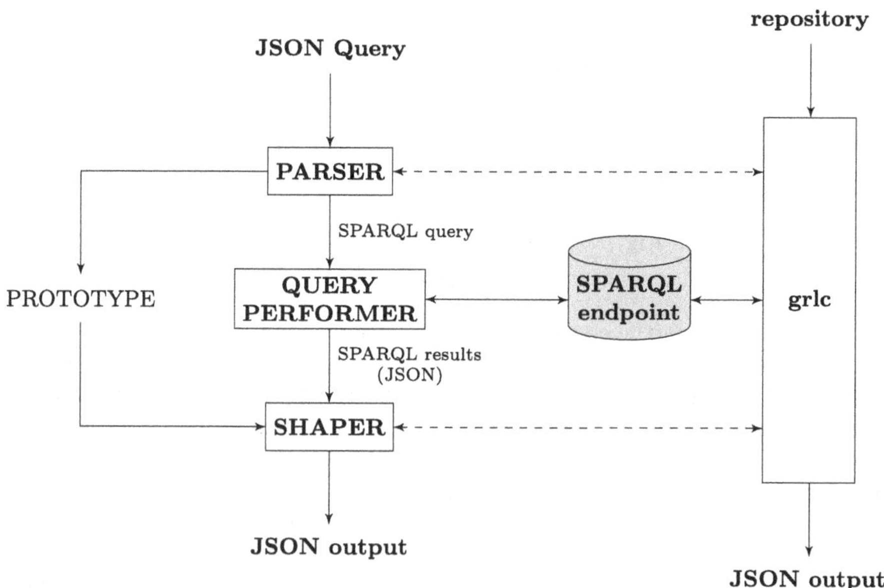

Fig. 3. The application schema of SPARQL Transformer

The SPARQL Transformer library is available in two different implementations in JavaScript and Python, published respectively on the NPM Package Manager[14] and the Python Package Index[15] (PyPI). The JavaScript version has been recently converted in an ECMAScript Module [7] and it is designed to both work in Node.js and in the browser. The Python version return a `dict` object, which can be directly manipulated by a script or serialised in JSON.

Since version 1.3, SPARQL Transformer is included in the `grlc`[16] framework, which is now able to generate Web APIs from the JSON queries contained in a given GitHub repository. The integration involved the Parser and the Shaper: the former is executed before each access to the SPARQL query, keeping in memory the prototype for being shaped once SPARQL results are back. The JSON query file can include the configuration options for `grlc` in an homonym

[14] https://www.npmjs.com/package/sparql-transformer.
[15] https://pypi.org/project/SPARQLTransformer/.
[16] http://grlc.io/.

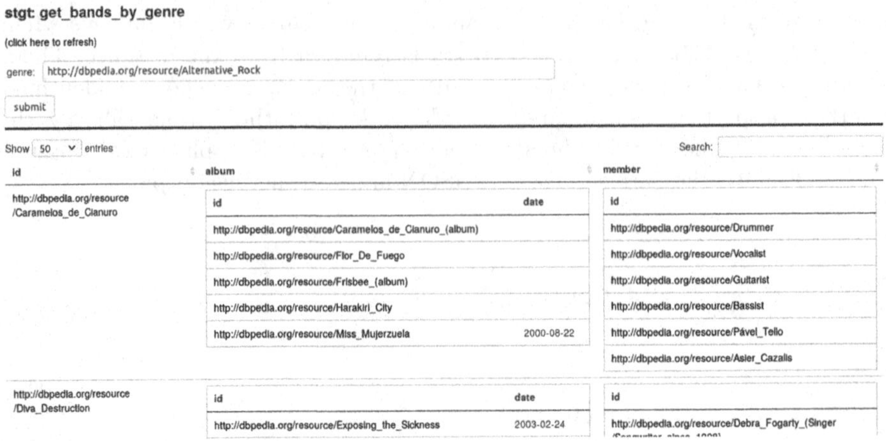

Fig. 4. Screenshot of the Tapas interface

field. For maximising the compatibility, the options can be specified as a YAML string or in JSON. The support to JSON queries includes all the features of `grlc`, such as the pagination and the selection of query parameters. In addition, a `lang` query parameter can change the value of the `$lang` property of the query, allowing the development of multi-language APIs. Further development involved the upgrade of `grlc` to the latest Python version.

Moreover, SPARQL Transformer queries are now also supported by Tapas[17]. Tapas is a small interface module implemented in HTML and JavaScript that reads the specification of an instance of a `grlc` API and turns it into a nice and simple HTML interface. The elements of the API specification are in a straightforward manner transformed into HTML form elements, which the user can fill in to access the service by pressing the *submit* button. Tapas asynchronously calls the API via `grlc` and shows the results at the bottom part of the same page using the YASR component of the YASGUI interface [22] to display the SPARQL query results in a user-friendly manner. We extended Tapas to also support SPARQL Transformer queries and display the results in an equally user-friendly manner. Unlike the flat tables produced by YASR for the common kind of SPARQL results, the nested results of a SPARQL Transformer query are shown as nested tables in Tapas. An example of this can be seen in Fig. 4, showing a screenshot of the query interface and its results for an exemplary SPARQL Transformer query about music bands, with the nested tables derived from the nested structure of the SPARQL Transformer results. Tapas together with `grlc` thereby allow us to automatically generate an intuitive interface for technically-minded end users just from the query file in a completely general and generic manner.

[17] https://github.com/peta-pico/tapas.

5 Evaluation

As evidence of *current* use, we have deployed this tool in two communities driven by H2020 projects which have adopted both SPARQL Transformer and `grlc`. MeMAD[18] uses it to generate automatically an API on top of a knowledge graph describing TV and radio programs which are also automatically annotated. The resulting semantic metadata is hence integrated in the professional Media Asset Management system Flow developed by Limecraft. SILKNOW[19] uses it to generate an API on top of a knowledge graph describing silk-related objects from 10 museums. The generated API is used to empower an exploratory search engine and a virtual assistant.

To provide evidence of *prospective* use of our approach, we carried out two kinds of evaluations:

- an experiment for measuring the compactness of the results and the execution time of SPARQL Transformer;
- a user survey on the preference of users on using a system that presents Linked Data query results through SPARQL Transformer, versus another that does so through traditional SPARQL results rendering.

5.1 Quantitative Evaluation

We test the Python implementation of SPARQL Transformer on a set of five queries detailed in the DBpedia wiki[20] in order to ensure a certain generality. The set involves different SPARQL features (filters, ORDER BY, language filtering, optional triples). Those SELECT queries have been manually converted into JSON queries—with 1 or 2 levels of objects in the JSON tree—, making sure that the transformed query was equal to the original one (variable names apart).

Each query has been resolved against a local instance of the English DBpedia[21], with a traditional SPARQL client for the SPARQL queries and with SPARQL Transformer for the JSON queries. Each execution has been repeated 100 times, with a waiting time of 5 s between consecutive executions, in order to obtain an average result as much as possible not correlated to any workload of the machine.

The results in Table 2 shows that the average execution time of SPARQL Transformer is slightly higher with respect to normal SPARQL queries, never surpassing 0.1 s (limit of the instantaneous feeling according to [18]). The difference in percentage, computed as $100 * (t_{sparql} - t_{json})/avg(t_{sparql}, t_{json})$, do not reveal any regularity in the time increment, even if some patterns suggest that it depends on the number of results and variables for each result. The same dimensions seem to impact also the gap in number of results, smaller in the JSON

[18] https://memad.eu/.
[19] http://silknow.eu/.
[20] https://wiki.dbpedia.org/onlineaccess, Sect. 1.5.
[21] The setup of the endpoint on a local machine relied on *Dockerized-DBpedia*, available at https://github.com/dbpedia/Dockerized-DBpedia.

query responses because of the merging strategy. It is interesting to point out that such difference exists between all valid combinations of values for requested variables and the number of real-world object described. This is evident in the first query, about people born in Berlin, in which the combinations of names in different languages and birth or death date in different formats almost double the number of results. As a consequence, the Prince Adalbert of Prussia[22] appears in 8 distinct (and even non-consecutive) bindings because of its four names and two versions of its death date, correctly merged in the more compact transformed version. The experiment is further detailed in the GitHub repository[23].

Table 2. Differences in number of results and execution time between SPARQL and JSON queries. For each query, is also reported the number of requested variables.

Query name	N. var	N. results			Time (ms)			
		json	sparql	diff %	json	sparql	diff	diff %
1. Born in Berlin	4	573	1132	49%	168	101	67	50%
2. German musicians	4	257	290	11%	61	49	12	22%
3. Musicians born in Berlin	4	109	172	37%	59	51	8	14%
4. Soccer players	5	70	78	10%	210	203	7	3.7%
5. Games	2	981	1020	4%	121	70	51	54%

5.2 User Survey

In order to evaluate the usefulness of the query results as presented by SPARQL Transformer to potential (technically-minded) end-users and developers and to compare them to a more traditional, table-centric provision of SPARQL query results, we conducted a user survey. We hypothesized that the level of nesting would play an important role, as classical SPARQL results are flat tables whereas the JSON structure of SPARQL Transformer allows for nesting.

We therefore constructed a pair of queries in SPARQL Transformer syntax and its corresponding plain SPARQL version for each of three levels of nesting: no nesting (Level 0), one nested structure (Level 1), and two nested structures (Level 2). These queries are all about bands and their albums and members, and they can be run through the DBpedia SPARQL endpoint. An example of two nested structures as found in Level 2 can be seen in Fig. 4 (the two nested structures being *album* and *member*). We then ran each of these six queries and stored the resulting JSON files (i.e. the files generated by SPARQL Transformer and the standard JSON files with the original SPARQL results, respectively). Moreover, we also ran these on Tapas to compare the user interface aspects

[22] http://dbpedia.org/resource/Prince_Adalbert_of_Prussia_(1811-1873).

[23] A notebook is available at https://github.com/D2KLab/py-sparql-transformer/blob/master/evaluation/test.ipynb.

Table 3. The results of the user survey

Type	Level	Preference for our system					Avg.	p-value	
		−2	−1	0	1	2			
JSON results	0 (no nesting)	6	6	4	13	26	0.85	0.0001980	*
	1 (one nesting)	5	5	3	21	21	0.87	0.000009063	*
	2 (two nestings)	3	9	5	17	21	0.80	0.0003059	*
Tapas interface	0 (no nesting)	4	8	3	19	21	0.82	0.0001275	*
	1 (one nesting)	3	10	2	20	20	0.80	0.0002685	*
	2 (two nestings)	4	7	3	16	25	0.93	0.00003589	*

that come with the different representations and nesting styles, and we made screenshots of the result tables. All these files, including queries, their results, and the Tapas screenshots, can be found online[24].

Based on these query results and screenshots, we then created a questionnaire, where we asked the participants for each of the six cases (JSON files and screenshots for each of the three nesting levels) whether they preferred SPARQL Transformer (referred to as "System A") or the classical SPARQL output (referred to as "System B"), displayed using the YASR component of YASGUI. The possible answers consisted of the five options *Strongly prefer B* (value −2), *Slightly prefer B* (−1), *Indifferent* (0), *Slightly prefer A* (1), and *Strongly prefer A* (2). We also asked the participants whether they consider themselves primarily researchers, developers, or none of these two categories, and we asked about their level of expertise with SPARQL and JSON. The questionnaire can be found online[25].

We then asked people to anonymously participate in this user survey via Linked Data related mailing lists (W3C SemWeb list), and internal group lists of Semantic Web groups at VU Amsterdam and EURECOM, in addition to the SIKS list addressing Dutch universities. The form was accessible for 5 days. In this way, we got responses from 55 participants (40 researchers, 9 developers, 6 others). Their level of expertise on SPARQL and JSON was mixed, with average values of 2.44 and 2.87, respectively, on a scale from 0 to 4. Eight participants had no knowledge of SPARQL at all, while only one participant had no knowledge of JSON.

Table 3 shows the results of the survey (the full table can also be found online[26]). We see that we got the full range of replies for all questions, but also that a clear majority prefers our system slightly (1) or even strongly (2). The average values for both types (JSON and Tapas) and all three nesting levels are between 0.80 and 0.93, i.e. close to the value that stands for a slight preference

[24] https://github.com/tkuhn/stgt/.
[25] https://github.com/tkuhn/stgt/blob/master/eval/questionnaire-form.md.
[26] https://github.com/tkuhn/stgt/raw/master/eval-results/questionnaire-results.ods.

of our system (1) and clearly above the value that stands for an indifference between the two (0).

To test whether the preference towards our system is statistically significant, we used a sign test in the form of a binomial test on the answers that were positive (preference of our system) or negative (preference of the existing system), excluding the zero cases (indifference). This test, therefore, does not take the distinction between slight and strong preference into account, but only which system was preferred. The final column of Table 3 lists the p-values of this test, showing that the effect is highly significant for all six cases.

The results, however, do not support our hypothesis that the level of nesting has an effect on the preference for our system. Throughout all nesting levels, the users expressed clear and significant preference for our system, but this preference did not increase with increased nesting levels.

6 Conclusion and Future Work

SPARQL Transformer offers to Web developers a different way of approaching RDF datasets. The adoption of a novel JSON format for defining both the query and the template makes it possible to realise self-contained files. When collected in a GitHub repository, these files can be easily transformed into Web APIs with `grlc`, completing the decoupling between query, post-processing and consumption in the application, and query results can moreover be presented in a simple and user-friendly manner via Tapas. The evaluation reveals that the restructuring and merging pipeline of SPARQL Transformer has an important impact in making the SPARQL results more usable and understandable by humans.

Differently from other works, SPARQL Transformer allows developers to use one single file for querying and mapping, and even with some limits – i.e. not being as expressive as SPARQL – can be of benefit for fast prototyping of web application.

Further development can improve SPARQL Transformer in order to fulfil a wider range of needs. The query support can be extended to other SPARQL operations, like ASK, INSERT and DELETE, going towards the realisation of full REST APIs on top of SPARQL endpoints. Aggregate functions (e.g. COUNT, SUM) should join the set of available features in the near future. We will further investigate the use of JSON frames, in order to extract the Shaper component from the library and make it available for standalone use.

Currently, the JSON syntax does not foresee any standard way for representing dates, which are therefore represented as plain strings. Alternative representations for dates should be found taking into account developer requirements, even listening and involving them in the final decision. Possibly, the solution should also involve other related data-types, like `xsd:gYear` or `xsd:duration`.

We plan to run another evaluation of this work, this time focused on the creation scenario, consisting in an interview on query writing with SPARQL Transformer and on API management with `grlc`.

Finally, we are currently planning to offer more customisation possibilities to users. Some examples include the choice of a different merging anchor (currently forced to `id` or `@id`); the possibility of ignoring language tags in the results (avoiding the presence of a language-value object); and the chance of distinguishing between IRIs (as resource references) and IRIs in lexical forms.

Acknowledgements. This work has been partially supported by the European Union's Horizon 2020 research and innovation program within the SILKNOW (grant agreement No. 769504) and MeMAD (grant agreement No. 780069) projects, and by the CLARIAH project of the Dutch Science Foundation (NWO). We want to thank Ilaria Tiddi for her support and suggestions on combining our work.

References

1. Abburu, S., Babu, G.S.: Format SPARQL query results into HTML report. Int. J. Adv. Comput. Sci. Appl. (IJACSA) **4**(6), 144–148 (2013)
2. Bergwinkl, T., Luggen, M., elf Pavlik, Regalia, B., Savastano, P., Verborgh, R.: Interface Specification: RDF Representation, Draft Report. Technical report, W3C (2017)
3. Booth, D., Chute, C.G., Glaser, H., Solbrig, H.: Toward easier RDF. In: W3C Workshop on Web Standardization for Graph Data, Berlin, Germany (2019)
4. Corby, O., Faron-Zucker, C., Gandon, F.: A generic RDF transformation software and its application to an online translation service for common languages of linked data. In: Arenas, M., et al. (eds.) ISWC 2015. LNCS, vol. 9367, pp. 150–165. Springer, Cham (2015). https://doi.org/10.1007/978-3-319-25010-6_9
5. Corby, O., Faron-Zucker, C., Gandon, F.: LDScript: a linked data script language. In: d'Amato, C., et al. (eds.) ISWC 2017. LNCS, vol. 10587, pp. 208–224. Springer, Cham (2017). https://doi.org/10.1007/978-3-319-68288-4_13
6. Daga, E., Panziera, L., Pedrinaci, C.: A BASILar approach for building web APIs on top of SPARQL endpoints. In: International Workshop on Services and Applications over Linked APIs and Data (SALAD), vol. 1359. CEUR Workshop Proceedings, Bethlehem (2015)
7. ECMA International: ECMAScript 2015 Language Specification, 6th edn, ECMA-262. Technical report, ECMA International (2015)
8. Fielding, R., et al.: Hypertext transfer protocol (HTTP/1.1): Header Field Definitions, RFC 2616. Technical report, Internet Engineering Task Force (2014)
9. Fielding, R.T.: Architectural styles and the design of network-based software architectures. Ph.D. Thesis (2000)
10. Gandon, F., et al.: Graph data on the web: extend the pivot don't reinvent the wheel. In: W3C Workshop on Web Standardization for Graph Data, Berlin, Germany (2019)
11. Groth, P., Loizou, A., Gray, A.J., Goble, C., Harland, L., Pettifer, S.: API-centric linked data integration: the open PHACTS discovery platform case study. Web Semant.: Sci. Serv. Agents World Wide Web **29**, 12–18 (2014)
12. Harris, S., Seaborne, A.: SPARQL 1.1 query language - W3C recommendation. Technical report, W3C (2013)
13. Huelss, J., Paulheim, H.: What SPARQL query logs tell and do not tell about semantic relatedness in LOD. In: Gandon, F., Guéret, C., Villata, S., Breslin, J., Faron-Zucker, C., Zimmermann, A. (eds.) ESWC 2015. LNCS, vol. 9341, pp. 297–308. Springer, Cham (2015). https://doi.org/10.1007/978-3-319-25639-9_44

14. Lathuilière, M.: `Wikidata SDK` (2015). https://github.com/maxlath/wikidata-sdk
15. Lisena, P., Troncy, R.: Transforming the JSON output of SPARQL queries for linked data clients. In: International Conference Companion on World Wide Web (WWW Companion), pp. 775–780. International World Wide Web Conferences Steering Committee, Lyon (2018). https://doi.org/10.1145/3184558.3188739
16. Meroño-Peñuela, A., Hoekstra, R.: grlc makes GitHub taste like linked data APIs. In: Sack, H., Rizzo, G., Steinmetz, N., Mladenić, D., Auer, S., Lange, C. (eds.) ESWC 2016. LNCS, vol. 9989, pp. 342–353. Springer, Cham (2016). https://doi.org/10.1007/978-3-319-47602-5_48
17. Mynarz, J.: `sparql-to-jsonld` (2016). https://github.com/jindrichmynarz/sparql-to-jsonld
18. Nielsen, J.: Usability Engineering. Elsevier, Amsterdam (1994)
19. Ockeloen, N., de Boer, V., Aroyo, L.: LDtogo: a data querying and mapping frameworkfor linked data applications. In: Cimiano, P., Fernández, M., Lopez, V., Schlobach, S., Völker, J. (eds.) ESWC 2013. LNCS, vol. 7955, pp. 199–203. Springer, Heidelberg (2013). https://doi.org/10.1007/978-3-642-41242-4_24
20. Pedrinaci, C., Domingue, J.: Toward the next wave of services: linked services for the web of data. J. Univ. Comput. Sci. **16**(13), 1694–1719 (2010)
21. Rietveld, L., Hoekstra, R.: Man vs. machine: differences in SPARQL queries. In: 4th Workshop on Usage Analysis and the Web of Data (USEWOD), Anissaras, Greece (2014)
22. Rietveld, L., Hoekstra, R.: The YASGUI family of SPARQL clients. Semant. Web **8**(3), 373–383 (2017)
23. Saleem, M., Ali, M.I., Hogan, A., Mehmood, Q., Ngomo, A.-C.N.: LSQ: the linked SPARQL queries dataset. In: Arenas, M., et al. (eds.) ISWC 2015. LNCS, vol. 9367, pp. 261–269. Springer, Cham (2015). https://doi.org/10.1007/978-3-319-25010-6_15
24. Seaborne, A.: SPARQL 1.1 query results JSON format - W3C recommendation. Technical report, W3C (2013)
25. Speiser, S., Harth, A.: Integrating linked data and services with linked data services. In: Antoniou, G., et al. (eds.) ESWC 2011. LNCS, vol. 6643, pp. 170–184. Springer, Heidelberg (2011). https://doi.org/10.1007/978-3-642-21034-1_12
26. Taelman, R., Vander Sande, M., Verborgh, R.: GraphQLLD: linked data querying with GraphQL. In: 17th International Semantic Web Conference (ISWC), Poster & Demo Track, Monterey, California, USA (2018)
27. Taelman, R., Vander Sande, M., Verborgh, R.: Bridges between GraphQL and RDF. In: W3C Workshop on Web Standardization for Graph Data, Berlin, Germany (2019)
28. Verborgh, R.: Decentralizing the semantic web through incentivized collaboration. In: 17th International Semantic Web Conference (ISWC), Blue Sky Track, vol. 2189, October 2018
29. Wright, A., Andrews, H.: JSON schema: a media type for describing JSON documents. Technical report, Internet Engineering Task Force (2017). https://datatracker.ietf.org/doc/draft-handrews-json-schema/
30. Zaveri, A., et al.: smartAPI: towards a more intelligent network of web APIs. In: Blomqvist, E., Maynard, D., Gangemi, A., Hoekstra, R., Hitzler, P., Hartig, O. (eds.) ESWC 2017. LNCS, vol. 10250, pp. 154–169. Springer, Cham (2017). https://doi.org/10.1007/978-3-319-58451-5_11

Benefit Graph Extraction from Healthcare Policies

Vanessa Lopez[1(✉)], Valentina Rho[1], Theodora S. Brisimi[1], Fabrizio Cucci[1], Morten Kristiansen[2], John Segrave-Daly[2], Jillian Scalvini[3], John Davis[3], and Grace Ferguson[3]

[1] IBM Research Dublin, Dublin, Ireland
vanlopez@ie.ibm.com
[2] IBM Watson Health, GHHS, Dublin, Ireland
[3] Payment Integrity (Truven Health Analytics), Ann Arbor, USA

Abstract. With healthcare fraud accounting for financial losses of billions of dollars each year in the United States, the task of investigating regulation adherence is key to reduce the impact of Fraud, Waste and Abuse (FWA) on the healthcare industry. Providers rendering services to patients typically submit claims to healthcare insurance agencies. Such claims must follow specific compliance criteria specified by state and federal policies. This paper presents an ontology-based system that aims to support the FWA claim investigation process by extracting graph-based actionable knowledge from policy text describing those compliance criteria. We discuss the process of creating a domain-specific ontology to model human experts' conceptualisations and to incorporate early-on the feedback of FWA investigators, who are the early adopters of our solution. We explore whether the ontology is expressive and flexible enough to model the diverse compliance processes and complex relationships defined in policy documents. The ontology is then used, in combination with natural language understanding and semantic techniques, to guide the extraction of a Knowledge Graph (KG) from policies. Our solution is validated in terms of correctness and completeness by comparing the extracted knowledge to a ground truth created by investigators. Lastly, we discuss further challenges our deployed semantic system needs to tackle in this novel scenario, with the prospect of supporting the investigation process.

1 Introduction and Business Scenario

The National Health Care Anti-Fraud Association estimates that the financial losses due to health care fraud in the US are in the tens of billions of dollars each year [1]. According to Truven Health research, approximately $125 to $175 billion is wasted each year on healthcare fraud and abuse [2]. The Health Care Fraud and Abuse Control

V. Lopez, V. Rho, T. S. Brisimi and F. Cucci—Equal research contribution. We would like to **acknowledge** Conor Cullen, Carlos Alzate, Spyros Kotoulas, Martin Stephenson, Pierpaolo Tommasi, Marco Sbodio, Denisa Moga and our OM: Tim Cooper, Mark Gillespie and Mark Goodhart for their support and insights.

C. Ghidini et al. (Eds.): ISWC 2019, LNCS 11779, pp. 471–489, 2019.
https://doi.org/10.1007/978-3-030-30796-7_29

Program (HCFAC), established under the Health Insurance Portability and Accountability Act (HIPAA), directs federal and state agencies to audit healthcare expenditure with the objective of improving the quality of care and recover tax payer dollars.

Medicare and Medicaid have been designated as high-risk federal programs [3], because of their size, complexity and susceptibility to improper payments. The *Program Integrity* investigation units established under the HCFAC aim to assert that the ***correct payment*** has been made for the ***correct member*** for the ***correct service*** to the ***correct provider***. Healthcare providers (hospitals, pharmacies, clinics etc.) submit claims to state and federally-administered health insurance agencies (such as Medicare or Medicaid) for services rendered to a patient. Policy guidelines set out which claims are permissible based on eligibility criteria for a particular service and generally accepted medical practices. Invalid claims are those that infringe policy criteria either intentionally (fraudulent) or unintentionally (providing services that are unnecessary, inefficient or inconsistent with accepted medical practices). FWA investigators need to prioritize investigations based on likelihood of recovery (dollars) and maximum return on investigation resources. However, understanding policy, consisting of hundreds of text pages describing *compliance criteria* that investigators have to review and refer to in an investigation for further recovery actions, is a manual and labor-intensive task. Investigation does not guarantee recovery, since the policy may turn out to be too vague to be enforced, or the recoverable amounts too low to warrant action – any of which take scarce investigation resources away from other recovery opportunities. Comprehensively understanding policy is a key step to ensuring recovery of inappropriately paid claims.

We present a semantic solution that extracts compliance knowledge from healthcare policy documents. This knowledge can facilitate FWA investigations in several ways - for example, helping in the development of claims-inspection algorithms. Semantics play a key role in extracting machine-readable knowledge about Benefit Rules from the human-oriented policy documents. ***Benefit Rules (BRs)*** describe structured compliance criteria, such as: eligible service providers (e.g. role: physician, nurse); eligible places of service (e.g., home, hospital); maximum billable units of service or equipment per-patient in a given period; services that should not be billed together for a patient on a single date, services (in)appropriate for a patient's age or gender, etc. An experienced team of ***FWA Investigator*** consultants, working with the state and federal government to help them meet their obligations under the HCFAC and to shape policy, acted as early adopters of our solution, providing robust evaluation feedback and ground truth data along the way.

Our **contributions** in this paper are twofold. First, we describe the lessons learned and the best practices adopted while working with investigators throughout the entire lifecycle: validating the value proposition; modelling a domain ontology with the purpose of supporting claims investigations; and capturing experts' feedback to build a **Ground Truth** (GT) on BRs, i.e., knowledge that an investigator would learn from policy text, enabling us to provide performance metrics that validate the accuracy and completeness of our solution's automatically extracted knowledge. Secondly, we describe the research challenges, design choices and the approach to build a semantic-based system that applies natural language understanding techniques to policy text to transform it into relevant, semantic, graph-based BRs, guided by the ontology.

The rest of the paper is organised as follows. Section 2 presents related work. Section 3 discusses the advantages as well as the challenges of using semantic technologies in our solution, while Sect. 4 gives an overview on the technical implementation. Section 5 presents a validation of the system *in-use* with policies from two different domains. We conclude with discussing and summarizing the ongoing work in Sect. 5.

2 Background and Related Work

2.1 Medical Claims Audit

The role of analytics to identify FWA in healthcare insurance claims has been explored in [4] through different analytical approaches on top of claims data (e.g., text mining, social network analysis, time series analysis).

Supervised and unsupervised data mining approaches to support fraud detection on claims data are presented in the surveys [5, 6]. For example, they are applied to detect anomalies in the utilisation of certain procedure codes, or to create a risk profile about providers to report to third-party payers (such as health insurance organizations like Medicaid/Medicare).

A significant differentiator of our approach with respect to claim-based state of the art analytical approaches is that this is the first system, that we are aware of, that aims to interpret unstructured policy with the purpose of supporting policy investigators' work. Investigator time is precious, and policy is vast, hard to understand and hard to relate to claims. Our goal is to extract BRs that can facilitate policy comprehension to support investigators on the analysis of potentially-inappropriate payments.

2.2 Knowledge Base Population

Ontology guided Information Extraction (IE) [7] and Knowledge Base Population (KBP) from text, has been addressed by both the computational linguistics and semantic web communities for several years (for a survey see [8]). For instance, the Text Analysis Conference (TAC) has a Cold Start KB evaluation track to build a KB from scratch, using just a predefined schema and a corpus of text [9]. Effective systems in these competitions combine many approaches such as rule-based relation extraction and distantly supervised linear and neural network extractors. Domain-independent relation extraction has been studied by a wide range of approaches, however relation extraction and KBP from text often requires building IE analytics to discover facts about entities in text for the domain, as generic models rarely work well on the customer specific data.

Statistical supervised IE approaches, based on term frequency and co-occurrence of specific terms, require substantial effort from domain experts to manually label each mention of an entity or relation on hundreds of documents. Background knowledge can alleviate the need for human supervision for domain adaptation. A *knowledge and linguistic-based* approach is presented in [10] to extract first, medical entities from sentences to determine their categories, and second, semantic relations between a pair of entities by using lexical patterns built semi-automatically using a corpus (PubMed) and six relations types from UMLS. *Distance supervision* approaches do not require manual data labeling, instead training data is provided in the form of entity pairs belonging to a specific relation [11]. For example, [12] exploits a partially populated KB and a corpus of text to train a set of deep learning classifier to find paraphrases, i.e. different expressions with similar meaning in text, and to augment and extend a partially populated KG. With the exception of [12], most state of the art approaches are only able to recognize explicit pairwise relations within the same sentence [13]. [13] explores a cross- sentence neural architecture for *n-ary* relation extraction, by building paths connecting two identified arguments through related entities in a biomedical domain.

An *ontology guided IE* approach is presented in [14], based on the linguistic platform GATE entities are annotated in documents (e.g., to capture facts about a company) and mapped into ontology concepts, and then documents that refer to the same entity (e.g., company) are cluster together using on a cosine similarity vector representation. PIKES is a frame-based framework to extract instances and relationships in text [15], each frame is a reified object connecting instances through properties describing their semantic role based on the FrameBase ontology. Semantics are often applied in the healthcare domain to integrate data from heterogeneous sources, model diverse business process, and to build declarative rules to capture measures on the quality of care expressing complex relationships [16].

We believe that recognizing the many explicit and implicit *N-ary* relationships needed to extract multiple BRs from a policy document requires substantial domain background knowledge and the ability to perform inference. In this paper we describe a first implementation that combines NLP, knowledge representation and ontology-guided reasoning, to automatically capture the complex BR relationships into a KG. Labelled data is required for evaluation only.

3 Semantics in Practice

3.1 Advantages and Challenges of an Ontology-Based Solution

Ontologies serve as explicit, conceptual knowledge models to share a common understanding of the information in a domain and make that knowledge available to information systems [17]. This knowledge includes machine-interpretable definitions of concepts and relations in the domain, makes domain assumptions explicit and separates the domain knowledge from the operational knowledge. In our scenario, the role of the ontology is central to guide the IE process and for visually representing auto-extracted knowledge to investigators for curation.

In the following, we describe the **advantages** to using a domain ontology as a foundation for our solution.

- **Interoperability:** the ontology is the only domain-dependent resource. It contains the schema of the relations and entities to be extracted from policy text, and the labels (surface forms) needed to match ontological resources to entities and relations in the policy. It also acts as central hub to link to other relevant domain sources. In particular: (1) medical codes used during the billing process to describe clinical procedures, such as the American Medical Association's CPT (Current Procedural Terminology) code set; (2) body parts, e.g. in the dental domain a procedure may be only applicable on a subset of teeth; (3) healthcare programs available for a specific State; and (4) eligible places of service. The ontology also links to medical taxonomies such as UMLS to define diagnoses or treatments, that are typically referred to by patient's *medical history* or *high-risk status*.

- **Flexible and incremental model:** it is not feasible to define a complete domain model a priori. We started by identifying high-value BR types with our investigators (for example, a Service Limitation subtype is shown in Table 1). We then extended the ontology incrementally to cover more BR subtypes, as well as new policy domains. As the coverage of the ontology increased, the extractor's ability to capture more-relevant knowledge and to infer missing relations also increased. Using semantics there is no need to impose a fixed BR template. Extractors can automatically instantiate a BR in the KG using any combination of criteria known in the ontology (property-values) as long as they are semantically consistent.

Table 1. Table with three BR examples based on a *Service Limitation* template, which describes unit or dollar limits for services for a single beneficiary on a date of service.

Policy text	Template	Ground truth (BRs)
Dental prophylaxis (i.e., teeth cleanings) is recommended every 6 months, and may be reimbursed twice per 12 months per member	Members who [*qualifying criteria*] can receive up to [*max units/monetary amount*] of [*list of applicable services*] per [*body part*] in [*applicable time period*] requires [*requirements*] unless [*list of non-applicable services*] and [*exclusions*]	[*qualifying criteria*] - all-members [*max units*] - 2 [*applicable services*] - prophylaxis [*time period*] - 12 month
Members determined to be at high risk for periodontal disease or high risk for caries (decay) is eligible for additional services. These services include [..] up to four (4) prophylaxis procedures		[*applicable services*] - prophylaxis [*member - high risk of*] - umls-caries, umls-periodontal-disease [*max units*] - 4
Fluoride rinse is not an acceptable treatment for any child member and will not be reimbursed		[*qualifying criteria - min age*] - 0 [*qualifying criteria - max age*] - 21 [*non-applicable services*] - fluoride-rinse

- **Semantically sound:** specific domain constraints can be defined in the ontology to ensure that consistent and meaningful BRs are extracted from a portion of text when consolidating multiple BRs and identifying information conflicts. For example, the content of a BR can span across different sentences in the same paragraph and/or other connected portions of the policy, e.g. section headings. In this scenario, the constraints in the ontology help in understanding when a BR can be enriched with contextual information or merged with another BR extracted from a connected sentence (see Sect. 4.2).

An ontological model can faithfully represent an expert Investigator's conceptualization and be sufficiently flexible to capture diverse compliance processes in knowledge graphs. However, a significant challenge is that **the knowledge graphs cannot be understood or curated by an Investigator**. Two important goals in our scenario were to enable investigators to curate the extracted knowledge and to create GT through an approachable user interface (UI). To achieve this goal, graph BRs are transformed in a user-friendly *flat*-representation (see Fig. 3), hiding the complexity of the underlying graph ontology (see Sect. 4.1). To help users understand extracted conditions, descriptive labels were added to the ontology for each field (i.e. condition) to be displayed. Users can curate the user-friendly representation of a BR by modifying, deleting or adding new fields and values.

Keeping track of the provenance of each BR is also a key requirement, not only to link the BRs in the KG to the original text in the policy, but also to reason about the origin of the information, e.g. which extractor extracted the BR, and to keep track of ontology updates. Ontology maintenance to reflect updates in policies and generalizability of the ontology is a challenge, e.g., context dependent default values, like a "fiscal year" may have different start and end date based on the state the policy applies to.

3.2 Ontology Definition and Ground Truth Collection with Investigators

Investigators expertise is crucial to understand the business area, to validate whether technical representations of BRs reflect the original policy accurately, and to assess the generalisability of this approach (schema) across policies from different geographies.

When processing unstructured data (text), the same information can often be represented and interpreted in many different ways. To collect a formal, abstract representation of domain knowledge from the Investigators, we adopted the following strategy:

- Investigators highlighted sentences containing BRs in the policy text and associated them with *BR templates*. The templates are abstract definitions of common BR patterns, expressed as a set of entities and relations. The templates are intended to be *transferable* - i.e. to generalize well to other policy areas and geographies.
- Guided by these templates, we (manually) created a first-draft of a formal ontological model (classes, relations and some instances) and began an iterative process of modeling, reviewing and incrementally improving the ontology with the Investigators. Investigators also helped identify other domain-related data sources, e.g. procedures codes, healthcare programs, body parts, places of service, etc.
- Using these templates, the investigators created a set of ground truth BRs from policies – a standard against which extractor output quality could be validated.

Table 1 showcases an example of a Service Limitation BR template and GT from policy text. These templates play the same role as *competency questions* (i.e., the set of questions that an ontology must be able to answer) typically used for ontology development, as they describe the ontology requirements to model different types of BRs.

4 Approach and Technical Components

We will introduce the components of the system, illustrated in Fig. 1 through the typical processing workflow. The first step when dealing with a new policy document, in PDF format, is to process it (1) together with its metadata in order to transform it in a machine-friendly tree structure in which the content is hierarchically organised, e.g. sections, paragraphs. After the document is ingested, the extraction service triggers the following steps: concepts annotation (2), based on the content of the BRs ontology and/or on external named entities annotators (NER) (Sect. 4.2); BRs extraction (3, 4), performed with different available extractors, currently WatsonX-based (3a) and SystemT-based (3b) (Sect. 4.2); across extractors consolidation and filtering (5) in order to merge the extracted rules and remove potential noise; BRs conversion (6) from the KG representation to a more user-friendly representation that can be easily displayed in the UI (8) to allow both the internal team and the investigators to inspect the extracted BRs, collect GT data and analyse the performance metrics computed on different extraction configurations (7). It's worth noticing that all the described components are domain independent, as they rely on the ontology to retrieve all the needed domain information. Existent KGs, e.g. some of the relevant types in the UMLS semantic network, are linked with the main ontology. External data in tabular form, e.g. relevant procedure codes, are normalised and lifted automatically (based on the creation of a file providing mappings between tabular columns and ontological entities) into a KG (0), following W3C recommendations [18], and linked to the ontology. All mentioned components are implemented as microservices and deployed on IBM Cloud. The ontology is currently loaded in-memory and accessed through the Jena Ontology APIs.

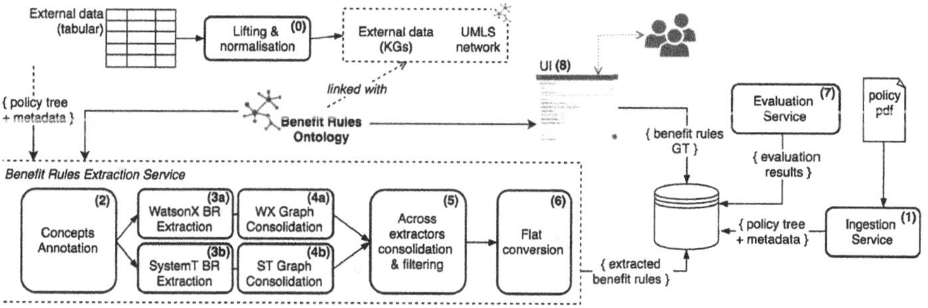

Fig. 1. Architecture of the system

4.1 Benefit Rules Ontology and Knowledge Graph Definition

The ontology has been iteratively and incrementally built pursuing two main goals: represent as correctly and unambiguously as possible the domain of interest, i.e. the BRs that are expressed in the policy text, and that is fit for purpose for the automatic IE, i.e. capturing the connections between the entities of interest and how they appear in text. The ontology was built based on the methodology described in [19] and the collaboration with a team of investigators. Based on the corresponding templates manually identified by the investigators (Sect. 3.2), we started by defining the class hierarchy, the object and data properties and semantic constraints that the ontology needs to cover. Different data sources, e.g. procedure codes, policy programs, places of service, have been identified and lifted in the ontology to populate the instances space.

Since the templates and the ontology are a commercially sensitive asset and they cannot be reasonably shared, we will focus the remaining of this section on a subset of it (see Fig. 2) that is meant to model the information encoded in the sentence *"Adult members may receive up to $1,000 in dental benefits per year (July1 through June 30)"*. The subset of the ontology used to model Service Limitations contains 21 object and 8 datatype properties of interest, 31 classes, 1034 individuals. The *Policy* class is the root node in the ontology. A *Policy* individual represents a document and may be associated with multiple *BenefitRule* individuals. A subtype of *BenefitRule* is created for each independent rule template we want to address, e.g. *BrServiceLimitation*. A subtype inherits all the properties of a generic BR class while at the same time allows us to capture the semantics particular to each. The principal BR properties modelled in Fig. 2 are: *service limitation,* that is meant to model a monetary or a unit limit range for a specific service under certain circumstances; *applicable services,* that model the services the BR applies to; *applicable time period*, represented in this case with *start* and *end date*, but that in other examples can be modelled as a frequency, e.g. "every 6 months"; *member eligibility*, to model all the eligibility criteria regarding the group of patients affected by the BR, in our example the only mentioned criteria was regarding the *age group* of the patient, but other criteria like the *enrolment* in a State plan, or the *history* of a particular disease, are covered as well. The ontology contains some pre-populated instances to model predefined nodes with default values, e.g. *adult* as an instance of *AgeRange* with predefined *min* and *max ages*.

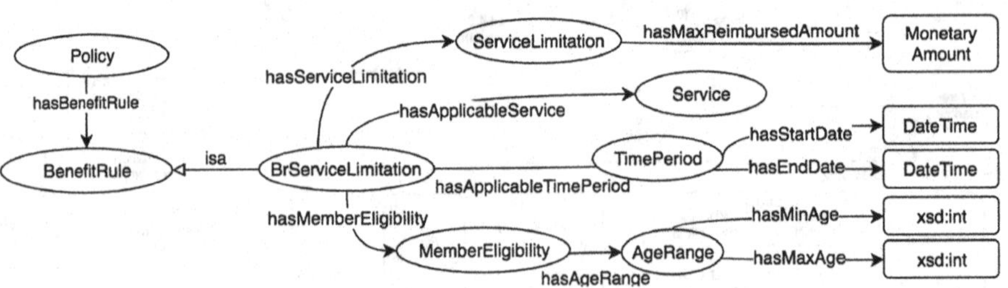

Fig. 2. Subset of the ontology to model the information in the policy text *"Adult members may receive up to $1,000 in dental benefits per year (July 1 through June 30)."*.

Different ontological constraints can be expressed on the ontology properties and will be used during the extraction process and enforced in the extracted KG, e.g. *owl: propertyDisjointWith*, *owl:minCardinality*, *owl:maxCardinality* or *owl:FunctionalProperty*. User-defined datatypes, associated to *entity types* extracted with the concept annotators ((2) in Fig. 1), are created to represent additional constraints that restrict the range of allowed datatype values to help in the disambiguation task, e.g., the string "$1,000" is annotated by the concept annotators as *MonetaryAmount* which is valid range for the datatype property *hasMaxReimbursedAmount*.

We divide classes and properties in the ontology in: *root*, e.g. *BenefitRule, hasMemberEligibilit; intermediate*, e.g. *TimePeriod, hasAgeRange;* or *leaf*, e.g. *Service, hasMinAge, hasService.* The user-friendly flat representation (Fig. 3) of a BR is created by taking all and only the leaf properties, also called *conditions*, in the BR with the corresponding range *values*. In order to be able to convert the KG into a flat representation without leading to ambiguities, the portion of the ontology that describes a BR type, i.e. the subgraph rooted in the *benefit rule type* class and generated by following the domain-property-range relations, must be in the shape of a tree; the proper ontological constraints are also added in the ontology to enforce the tree-shape of the KG as well. Given an instantiated BR, if the same *condition* has more than one different range value, these values are considered to be in disjunction with each other, e.g., if the BR mentions multiple *applicable services* we will consider the union of them. In contrast, two different conditions are considered to represent a conjunction, e.g. if both an *age* and a *history* of a particular disease are mentioned as eligibility criteria, the rule applies only to patients that are satisfying both criteria. A confidence score is assigned to each relevant KG statement. It is calculated based on the reliability of the applied extraction approach and the considered contextual information. Confidence information, as well as the approach used to extract each statement, are stored as reified statements.

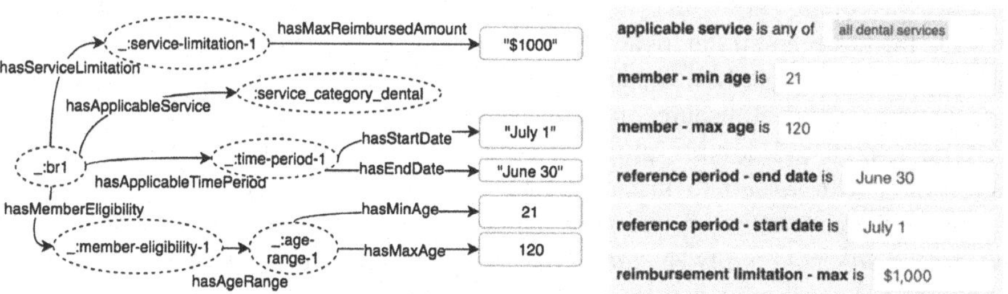

Fig. 3. KG of the BR (left) and the user-friendly flat representation (right) for sentence "Adult members may receive up to $1,000 in dental benefits per year (July 1 through June 30)."

4.2 Ontology-Based Information Extraction

Two extractors were implemented on top of two different NLP technologies WatsonX [20] and SystemT [21]. Due to space limitations we cannot give an in-depth description of the two, but we give an overview of how they work and discuss their capabilities in what follows. Currently, both extractors work at a sentence level, taking as input a set of concept annotations computed by entity annotators, e.g. UMLS annotator, and a custom concept annotator that exploits the surface forms present in the ontology, and returning a KG of BRs. Internally, a first graph consolidation step is performed in order to verify that the KGs are consistent with the ontology definitions.

WatsonX Approach. WatsonX is built as a classical NLP deep parsing pipeline implemented as an Apache UIMA application. Originally it was part of the IBM Watson system that won the Jeopardy challenge against human experts in 2011 [20]. It receives as input a sentence and identifies syntactic, morphological and semantic elements of the sentence, building a dependency parse tree (see example in Fig. 5). In a dependency tree, nodes are dependant of other nodes on the tree and that dependency is a labelled edge representing grammatical relations like *nominal subject, direct object, object of a preposition.* Dependency representations are useful for relation extraction because they can connect terms even if they are not subsequent in the original sentence.

From the dependency tree, a set of linguistic-based subtree extraction rules are executed in order to identify potentially interesting linguistic PAS (Predicate Argument Structure) tuples. These tuples represents relationships across the textual entities, in the form of <subject, predicate, object, object modifiers>, and other functional dependencies that can be expressed as linguistic rules over the dependency tree, such as a noun with object prepositions or adjective modifiers, e.g. in Fig. 5 <member, receive, $1000, up to>, <adult, member>, <$1000, benefits, dental>, <$1000, benefits, year>. Then, an ontology reasoning component translates functional dependencies in the sentences (PAS) to semantic relations, i.e. ontological statements. First, the textual entities in the PAS tuple are matched to ontological entities, based on a search over the entity labels. Second, PAS tuples are matched into a Graph Patterns (GPs).

The search of GPs across the combination of relevant entities and datatypes within a PAS is guided by domain-independent pattern templates. Given any of the combinations between the candidate entities matched in a PAS, the system searches for the patterns (or combinations) that better translate the PAS tuple, i.e. cover most of the terms in the tuple, and if the found GPs are semantically compliant with the ontology it adds them to the output KG. A pattern consists of variables (preceded by "?") that must bind to an ontological resource, parameters to substitute by the candidate matches of the type sought, e.g., a class, property, instance or datatype (in between <>) and the target variable (*?target*) to instantiate. In our example, for the PAS tuple <adult, member>, the pattern fired between the matched instance *adult* (of type *AgeRange*) and the class *MemberEligibility* is: *?target rdf:type <Class>. ?target ?property <Instance>*, that identifies *hasAge* as a valid binding for *?property*, resulting in the instantiated pattern *?target rdf:type <MemberEligibility>. ?target <hasAge> <adult>*. For other PAS tuples multiple combinations of patterns can be executed and intermediate nodes may be inferred in order to find a path between two resources connected in the ontology. A BR is then created by joining together all GPs obtained from the connected PAS tuples, i.e. those that have a *join* term. The resulting BR (shown in Fig. 3) can be consolidated with other BRs created from other subtrees in the sentence or across sentences.

SystemT Approach. SystemT is an industrial-strength declarative rule-based IE system. Borrowing ideas from database systems, commonly used text operations are abstracted away as built-in operators [...] and exposed through a formal declarative language called AQL (Annotation Query Language) [21]. The output of the execution of an AQL query is a set of tuples in tabular form (see example in Fig. 4). As a first step, the implemented extractor explores the ontology structure and annotations to dynamically generate, for each property of interest in the ontology, a corresponding set of extraction queries in AQL based on multiple property templates. These extraction queries aim at extracting candidate ontology pairs, i.e. <property, range>, based on the annotations resulting from the available concepts annotators, ((2) in Fig. 1). For example, given the annotations in Fig. 5, <receive, dental benefits> may be selected as a candidate pair for the *hasApplicableService* property. These queries combine different extraction approaches based on the characteristics of the target property, e.g. property type, range types, polarity, as well as the syntactic and semantic information available for the examined sentence. The property-range extraction approaches can be divided into two main categories: (1) semantic-based approaches, that make use of the results of a shallow semantic parsing of the input text[1], and they reason over semantic roles, actions and contextual information, (2) distance-based approaches, used as fall-back strategies when the semantic information is partial or missing, e.g. due to incomplete or grammatically incorrect sentences, and are based on the sequence and distance between a property-trigger and a corresponding candidate range annotation. For example Fig. 5, in a strategy of type (1) extracts the condition *'applicable service: dental benefits'* by taking into account the main action, its polarity and the connected theme (see Fig. 4), while a strategy of type (2) extracts the condition *'max reimbursement: 1000$'* by considering the proximity of the property's trigger *"up to"* and the candidate range value *"1000$"*.

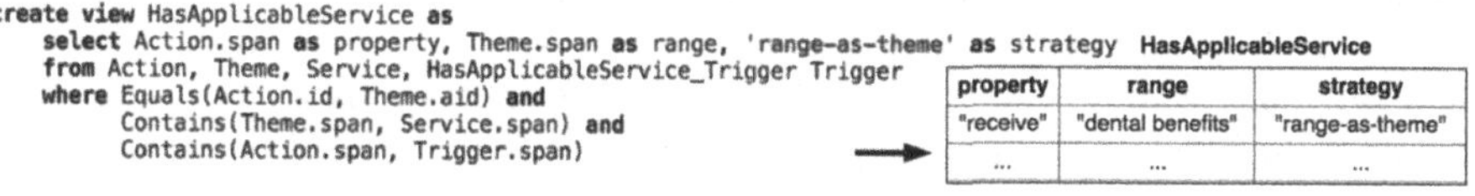

Fig. 4. Example of simplified AQL query and resulting tabular output

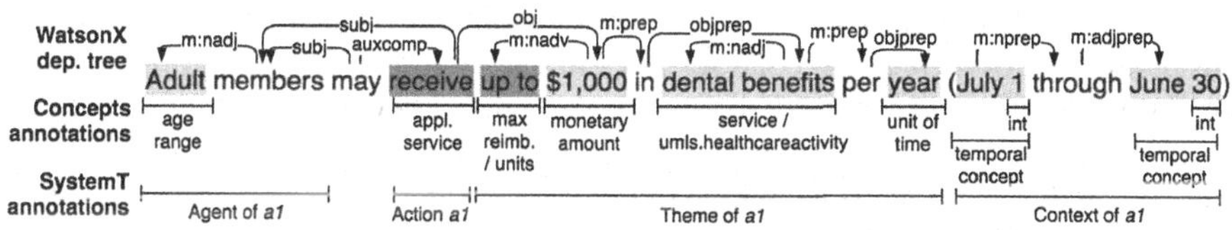

Fig. 5. Example of annotations extracted from the Concepts Annotation component and from the WatsonX and SystemT tools.

[1] The shallow semantic parsing of the sentence is performed through a natural language understanding capability of SystemT, currently under development, that computes and exposes information regarding the semantic roles present in the sentence, e.g. actions, agents, themes and contextual information of those actions, together with information regarding voice, polarity, etc.

All the applicable extraction queries are executed for each property of interest producing a set of candidate ontology triples where the domain can be inferred due to the previously described constraints on the ontology. The confidence score of each triple is dependent on the approach that generated the triple and on the information taken into account, e.g. semantic approaches are usually stronger than distance-based approaches and an explicit property trigger is stronger than an inferred trigger. As a last step, the extracted candidate pairs are then filtered and ranked, based on the associated confidence scores, in order to enforce the intuition that a specific span of text in the sentence can be associated only to a single condition in the resulting benefit rule, e.g. "1" can be either part of a date range or of a unit limitation. For each sentence, a BR is populated with all the selected triples.

Filtering and Consolidation. A fundamental step is the consolidation and filtering of the KGs created by the different extractors. This phase try to accomplish various goals: (1) enforce all the constraints expressed in the ontology, e.g. disjointness between two properties, min and max cardinality; (2) consolidate BRs extracted from different portions of the policy text, currently different sentences of the same paragraph; (3) consolidate BRs extracted by different extractors on the same policy text; (4) discard BRs that are noisy. We give an overview of the approaches adopted in the following.

Ontology Constraints Enforcement. The consolidation strategies that fall in this category are meant to find and solve ontological constraints violations, e.g. *max cardinality* constraints to enforce, for example, the presence of a single *age range* per BR. These are the main strategies executed in the internal consolidation stage for each extractor and are based on the statements' confidence scores.

Consolidation Across Sentences. These consolidation strategies are meant to merge information extracted from different sentences in a policy. Consider the example *"Adult members may receive up to $1,000 in dental benefits per year (July 1 through June 30). Emergency and denture benefits are not subject to this limit."* we would like to capture the information that *emergency benefits* and *denture benefits* are not covered by this rule. As a first implementation, assuming that the extractors capture the relevant information in two BRs, one per sentence, these BRs are merged if the resulting BR does not violate any ontological constraint. In our example, the merge will succeed extending the BR in Fig. 3 with the additional condition *excluded services*. Instead, if considering the following as second sentence in our example *"Emergency and denture benefits are not covered for children."* the merge would fail due to the conflict between the different *age range* conditions, i.e. *adults* and *children*. Currently, only the sentences belonging to the same paragraph of text are considered as candidate for this kind of consolidation, but we aim to improve the results of this strategy, e.g. by looking at explicit co-references between sentences.

Consolidation Across Extractors. When different extractors generate a BR for the same policy text, we want to output a consolidated result, if possible, to avoid repetitions and duplication. As a baseline strategy all BRs that are a subset of another BR from the same sentence are merged together. More elaborated strategies can be implemented i.e. to merge BRs that share most of the properties and can be merged without leading to (ontology) conflicts. More work is needed to implement strategies able to handle the disagreement between extractors, e.g., based on the confidence scores.

Noise Filtering. Finally, we implemented some filtering strategies to remove BRs whose structure are too simple to be valid, as such we filter out: (a) BRs with only one *root* property, e.g. describing only a *member eligibility requirement*; (b) sentences, and corresponding BRs, that do not contain any explicit *property trigger* (i.e., no ontological relation was detected across any of the entities mentioned in the sentence) for the specific BR type; (c) BRs that contain less than *n* condition values. Different strategies can be selected depending on if we want to maximise precision or recall.

5 Evaluation

Here we describe the ground truth, first set of metrics and evaluation framework used to assess the quality of the KGs extracted from policy text. To obtain a Ground Truth (GT), expert Investigators sampled pages from Medicaid policy documents and modelled an 'expected' set of structured BRs for them. The BRs were modelled using the same user-friendly 'flat' UI representation described in Sect. 4.1 (see Fig. 2). Guided by the ontology, this UI enables investigators to express policy knowledge by selecting structured combinations of conditions and entities or datatype values (to define BRs). Two investigators and a senior investigator lead worked together to create and agree on the GT, which was subsequentially peer-reviewed by a wider investigation team. To measure how well our approach generalises across different policy areas, Ground Truth was created for two areas: Physical Therapy and Dental Services. Once the investigators input the GT in the system, the evaluation framework is fully automated (configurable to use one or both extractors and different consolidation strategies). This enables us to incorporate and evaluate new policy domains.

Standard Precision(P) and Recall(R) metrics are adapted to measure the quality of extracted knowledge against the GT. However, in this scenario we cannot focus only on the quality of an individual pair of *condition* and *value*, but we need to consider the overall quality of the BRs extracted which combines multiple conditions and values. We focus our performance evaluation at both an overall knowledge-extraction (BR) level (how well the extracted BRs match the Investigators' expectations), as well as the contribution of individual elements (condition and values) to overall performance.

5.1 Performance Metrics and Results

The evaluation metrics are calculated by comparing automatically-extracted BRs to investigator-defined BRs (GT) on the same policy text. BRs are always compared in their 'flattened' form and are sorted based on the order they appeared in the policy text.

Ground truth BRs $R^{GT} = \left\{R_j^{GT}\right\}, j = 1,\ldots,n_{GT}$ are paired with those automatically extracted from the same policy text $R^E = \left\{R_i^E\right\},\ i = 1,\ \ldots,n_E$. They are identified as (a) Exact matches, if all condition-value pairs $\{c_k : v_k\}$, $k = 1,\ldots,L_i$ are identical; (b) Partial matches, if some conditions are missing or values of identical conditions differ, or (c) Not matched, if no identical condition was identified or if there was no rule coming from the same policy text. For every pair of partial matches BR $\left(R_j^{GT}, R_i^E\right)$, a similarity score S_{ji} is calculated (1) and the GT BR is matched to the extracted BR with the highest *similarity score*. This pair is then removed from each set before the process continues.

$$S_{ji} = \frac{\min(L_i, L_j)}{\max(L_i, L_j)} * \frac{1}{L_j} * \sum\nolimits_{k=1}^{L_j} score_{c_k} \tag{1}$$

where L_j and L_i are the sizes of R_j^{GT} and R_i^E correspondingly (i.e., how many conditions each BR consists of), $\frac{\min(L_i,L_j)}{\max(L_i,L_j)}$ represents a penalizing factor when the sizes of the two BR are not the same (rule length similarity). The score for each condition value pair $\{c_k : v_k\}$ is calculated (2)

$$score_{c_k} = \begin{cases} 0, & \textit{if } c_k \textit{ is captured in } R_j^{GT}, \textit{but not in } R_i^E \\ 1, & \textit{if } c_k \textit{ is captured in both } R_j^{GT}, R_i^E \textit{ and } v_k \textit{ is the same} \\ 0.5 + 0.5 * f_1 * \left(1 - \frac{1}{C_{a_k}}\right), & \textit{if } c_k \textit{ is captured in both } R_j^{GT}, R_i^E \textit{ and } v_k \textit{ differ} \end{cases} \tag{2}$$

Here, f_1 is the harmonic P-R mean generated by comparing the values of c_k in R_j^{GT} and R_i^E and $\{Ca_k\}$ is the number of semantically compatible candidate values a condition may have in the ontology (i.e., instances of the same type, such as all known medical programs), for datatypes Ca_k *is* 1.

Precision (P) measures the proportion of extracted rules that match the GT. Recall (R) measures the proportion of GT rules correctly extracted. f_1 combines these two. Specifically, they are defined as follows (3):

$$P = \frac{n^\circ \textit{ exact matches} + n^\circ \textit{ partial matches}}{n^\circ \textit{ extracted rules}} \qquad R = \frac{n^\circ \textit{ exact matches} + n^\circ \textit{ partial matches}}{n^\circ \textit{ GT rules}}$$

$$f_1 = 2 * \frac{P * R}{P + R} \tag{3}$$

In the GT, we have 50 manually created BRs extracted from 27 pages of Dental policy, and 25 manually created BRs extracted from 14 pages of Physical Therapy policy. The evaluation metrics for each scenario are presented in Table 2.

Table 2. Evaluation results: P, R, f_1, n° of exact and partial matches, average $score_{ck}$, n° of extracted BRs not matched to the GT (FP) and n° GT BRs not matched by extracted BRs (FN)

	P	R	f_1	n° exact	n° partial	Avg. s_c	FP	FN
Approach (dental policy)								
WatsonX only	**0.84**	0.54	0.66	4	23	0.5	5	23
SystemT only	0.70	0.66	0.68	5	28	0.56	14	17
Consolidated (subsets)	0.75	**0.82**	**0.78**	6	35	0.54	14	9
Consolidated (non-conflicts)	0.78	0.64	0.70	6	26	0.61	9	18
Approach (Physical Therapy)								
WatsonX only	0.**94**	0.64	**0.76**	6	10	0.63	1	9
SystemT only	0.64	0.72	0.68	4	14	0.56	10	7
Consolidation (subsets)	0.64	0.**84**	0.73	7	14	0.60	12	4
Consolidation (non-conflicts)	0.69	0.80	0.74	7	13	0.60	9	5

As expected, WatsonX deep-parsing, yields more precise BRs but also misses relations that were not captured from the dependency tree (e.g. because of ill-formed or complex sentences). SystemT applies a shallower NLP approach as well as different techniques to maximize recall. Two consolidation strategies are compared, the first one merges all BRs that are subset of another and the second one merges BRs if it doesn't lead to ontology conflicts. They offer a good compromise between (P) and (R). Combining both extractors increases (R) with a relatively small impact on (P). Further work could look at more sophisticated consolidation strategies that are able to leverage the confidence scores assigned by the extractors when merging statements across BRs, while detecting unresolved conflicts that require investigator input.

The evaluation framework also measures the contribution of individual elements to overall performance – specifically, P and R for each condition-value pair (see examples in Fig. 6), which helps with iterative enhancement and debugging of the extractors.

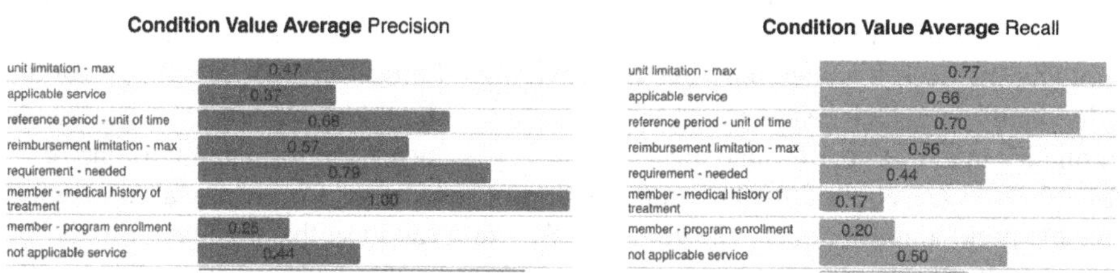

Fig. 6. Visualisation of P/R results on a subset of conditions when considering condition values.

5.2 Discussion

Here we look at areas where further work is likely to improve performance:

Automatic Extraction of Condition-Value Pairs: (1) a parse tree may not capture implicit semantic relationships present in policy text which can lead to failures capturing values. For example, a date range in brackets at the end of a sentence about waiver programs describes the period when that program is active. If the parse tree does not pick up the dependency, no values will be extracted for the relevant date range (in order to balance P & R, our extractors avoid making relational inferences in these cases); (2) Contextual values may be set outside of the sentence or paragraph being extracted - e.g. by titles like “Orthotics for Adults” or introductory sentences, or table headings (for text inside table cells). (3) Parsing errors can be introduced during the policy PDF ingestion which in turn lead to incorrect value extraction downstream in the extractors.

Mismatches Between GT and Extracted Condition-Value Pairs: (1) Some fields may have alternative valid representations leading to them being incorrectly measured as misses during the automatic evaluation - e.g. when the GT contains *‘1 year’* but an extractor gets *‘12 months’*; (2) Investigators modelling expected BRs (GT) may include knowledge that does not come from the policy text - e.g. modelling “high risk for caries” in the GT when they see a type of tooth surface in policy text that they happen to know is prone to caries. While extractors cannot make these inferences per-se, some progress may be achievable via an ontology hierarchy (specifically subclassOf and partOf). This could be used to infer some relationships, such as ‘anterior teeth’ from a reference ‘canine’ or ‘incisor’. More work is needed here, in particular for temporal expressions.

Invalid Condition-Value Pairs and BRs: (1) Paragraphs that mention relevant entities (e.g. a healthcare service and a program, or body parts) but do not describe limitations or other policy knowledge may still result in an BR being extracted, we describe these BRs as false positives or ‘noise’ and measure them via Precision (P). (2) Different extractors may produce conflicting BRs that cannot be merged. When this happens, one is selected and the other is measured as ‘noise’. For performance measurement, the one with the best-matching similarity score to the GT is selected; (3) A sentence may lead to two different BRs, for example, an ‘orthotic’ policy, expressing different service coverage for adults and children will be extracted as one BR for adult orthotics and another BR for child orthotics. Similarly two BRs may be consolidated into a ‘logical’ BR. For example, a unit limitation might refer to either a combination of procedures, implying the need to create only one BR covering all procedures, or to each procedure individually, in which case a separate BR limitation should be created for each. Due to ambiguity in text, two BRs may be have been erroneously consolidated into one (e.g., “Members [] are eligible for any combination of up to four (4) prophylaxes or up to four (4) periodontal maintenance visits”). We aim to address this challenge firstly, by more advanced BR consolidation strategies utilising confidence scores, and secondly by exploiting information redundancy in policies.

Human/Machine ‘Co-reasoning’: The goal of our work is to enable Investigators to collaborate and ‘co-reason’ with tools like these, not merely to automate knowledge extraction from policy text. A central element of this is empowering human Investigators to interact with, curate and use the extracted knowledge. This was the rationale for creating the UI (see Fig. 2) and ‘flat’ KG representation early on. These have been central to both iteratively reviewing extractor output with expert Investigators, as well as helping them to construct a GT to support formal performance measurement.

Informal feedback from the Investigators about the UI representation has been very positive. In particular, we were gratified to find that they could take new policy areas and rapidly construct high-quality GT for them after only a few hours of acclimatising to the UI tool. In large part, this is due to the ontology (and hence the UI) being driven by concepts and structure derived from on their own BR templates. In future, we hope to use this approach to speed up the process of obtaining formal GT for measuring performance on new policy domains. Specifically, by automatically extracting BRs and having Investigators manually curate them into a formal GT (rather than creating GT manually by hand).

Impact on the Investigators' Workflow: Computable policies in the form of benefit rules enables a wide range of downstream benefits that can have a significant improvement to the investigators workflow. Examples of this include:

- Investigators always have a large backlog of investigations and they lack objective data on which to prioritize the opportunity landscape. Automatically.constructed benefit rules could be executed against claims data to quantify systematic policy violations and support prioritization.
- Investigators need to provide strong evidence to support allegations of policy violations particularly for legal proceedings. Automatically constructed BRs can explicitly tie invalid claims to the policy constraints that they are violating.
- Additionally, through curation of the automatically constructed BRs we are building institutional knowledge on correct and complete policy BRs relevant for investigation cases. This enables consistency in policy reviews. The BR representation serve as a means for policy data insights, validation and sharing of knowledge across team members with varied levels of expertise and diverse skillsets. As such the BRs can inform development of new algorithms or enable modification of existing algorithms to make them more precise, targeted and complete.

6 Conclusion and Future Directions

We have developed a semantic system to extract a KG of *actionable* BRs from healthcare policies. The ontology is designed to balance expressiveness of the extracted knowledge with the ability to represent it in a simple, unambiguous, human-readable way to support policy comprehension and curation. The engagement with our target users (investigators) early in the development and throughout the continuous delivery process was key for the successful adoption of our semantic solution.

We presented a first validation of the semantic solution with investigators and showed solid progress in two vertical domains. Most of the effort required to generalise is on identifying external data linked to the ontology (i.e., instance data) that is state-specific, such as programs and codes that are not part of the federal code set. Nonetheless, we found a strong degree of re-usability in the core concepts between the two domains (i.e., same BR modelling was applicable), making this an excellent domain for the application of SW technologies. More BR types are being incrementally added for the next version of the system, thus incrementally improving the scope of information available to Investigators doing policy research. By tying together these BRs and the policy text from which they are derived, investigators can build the evidence necessary to make a case for recovery of inappropriately paid claims.

Further planning is in process to cover more policy areas and assessing both the value and viability of this technology for large-scale deployment across several domains. We aim to provide quantitative metrics on usability, increased productivity in the context of investigations (e.g., not just on time-saved but on whether this solution supports our users' prioritization of investigations that are likely to result in additional money recovery) and generalisability, scaled across policy domains. To this end, we hope to transition from manually-created GT to automatically extracted and manually-curated GT, which we expect to be considerably more efficient.

There is much room to improve performance, such as the ability to induce domain specific reasoning patterns. We aim to investigate approaches for classifying policy paragraphs that contain BRs (using labelled data collected via the UI), as this will reduce noise BRs by filtering out irrelevant paragraphs; as well as approaches for learning patterns not yet be explicitly captured in the ontology. We aim to experiment with unsupervised approaches to find paraphrases and to augment partially-populated KG. Finally, our hope is that extracting high-quality, computable representations of policy knowledge will ultimately lead to new, policy-informed ways of analysing claims data.

References

1. https://www.nhcaa.org/resources/health-care-anti-fraud-resources/the-challenge-of-health-care-fraud.aspx. Accessed Apr 2019
2. https://truvenhealth.com/media-room/press-releases/detail/prid/127/truven-health-analytics-professionals-receive-accredited-health-care-fraud-investigator. Accessed Apr 2019
3. https://www.gao.gov/key_issues/medicaid_financing_access_integrity/issue_summary. Accessed Apr 2019
4. Chandola, V., Sukumar, S.R., Schryver, J.C.: Knowledge discovery from massive healthcare claims data. In: Proceedings of the KDD, pp. 1312–1320 (2013)
5. Joudaki, H., Rashidian, A., Minaei-Bidgoli, B., Mahmoodi, M., et al.: Using data mining to detect health care fraud and abuse: a review of literature. Glob. J. Health Sci. **7**(1), 194–202 (2015)
6. Waghade, S.S., Karandikar, A.M.: A comprehensive study of healthcare fraud detection based on machine learning. J. Appl. Eng. Res. **13**(6), 4175–4178 (2018)
7. Wimalasuriya, D., Dou, D.: Ontology-based information extraction: an introduction and a survey of current approaches. J. Inf. Sci. **36**(3), 306–323 (2010)
8. Martinez-Rodriguez, J.L., Hogan, A., Lopez-Arevalo, I.: Information extraction meets the Semantic Web: a survey. Semant. Web 1–81 (2018, pre-press)
9. https://tac.nist.gov/2017/KBP/ColdStart/index.html. Accessed Apr 2019
10. Ben Abacha, A., Zweigenbaum, P.: Automatic extraction of semantic relations between medical entities: a rule based approach. J. Biomed. Semant. **2**(5), S4 (2011)
11. Mintz, M., Bills, S., Snow, R., Jurafsky, D.: Distant supervision for relation extraction without labeled data. In: Proceedings of ACL and AFNLP, vol. 2, pp. 1003–1011 (2009)

12. Glass, M., Gliozzo, A., Hassanzadeh, O., Mihindukulasooriya, N., Rossiello, G.: Inducing implicit relations from text using distantly supervised deep nets. In: Vrandečić, D., et al. (eds.) ISWC 2018. LNCS, vol. 11136, pp. 38–55. Springer, Cham (2018). https://doi.org/10.1007/978-3-030-00671-6_3
13. Peng, N., Poon, H., Quirk, C., Toutanova, K., Yih, W.: Cross-sentence N-ary relation extraction with graph LSTMs. Trans. Assoc. Comput. Linguist. **5**, 101–115 (2017)
14. Saggion, H., Funk, A., Maynard, D., Bontcheva, K.: Ontology-based information extraction for business intelligence. In: Aberer, K., et al. (eds.) ISWC/ASWC 2007. LNCS, vol. 4825, pp. 843–856. Springer, Heidelberg (2007). https://doi.org/10.1007/978-3-540-76298-0_61
15. Corcoglioniti, F., Rospocher, M., Aprosio, A.P.: Frame-based ontology population with PIKES. IEEE Trans. Knowl. Data Eng. **28**(12), 3261–3275 (2016)
16. Piro, R., et al.: Semantic technologies for data analysis in health care. In: Groth, P., et al. (eds.) ISWC 2016. LNCS, vol. 9982, pp. 400–417. Springer, Cham (2016). https://doi.org/10.1007/978-3-319-46547-0_34
17. Grimm, S., Abecker, A., Völker, J., Studer, R.: Ontologies and the semantic web. In: Domingue, J., Fensel, D., Hendler, J.A. (eds.) Handbook of Semantic Web Technologies, pp. 507–579. Springer, Heidelberg (2011). https://doi.org/10.1007/978-3-540-92913-0_13
18. W3C Recommendation. https://www.w3.org/TR/csv2rdf/. Accessed Apr 2019
19. Noy, N., McGuinness, D.L.: Ontology Development 101: A Guide to Creating Your First Ontology. Stanford Medical Informatics Technical Report SMI-2001–0880 (2001)
20. Kalyanpur, A., Boguraev, B., Patwardhan, S., Murdock, J.W., et al.: Structured data and inference in DeepQA. IBM J. Res. Dev. **56**(3), 10 (2012)
21. Chiticariu, L., Danilevsky, M., Li, Y., Reiss, F., Zhu, H.: Systemt: declarative text understanding for enterprise. In: NAACL-HLT, pp. 76–83 (2018)

Knowledge Graph Embedding for Ecotoxicological Effect Prediction

Erik B. Myklebust[1,2(✉)], Ernesto Jimenez-Ruiz[2,3], Jiaoyan Chen[4], Raoul Wolf[1], and Knut Erik Tollefsen[1]

[1] Norwegian Institute for Water Research, Oslo, Norway
ebm@niva.no
[2] Department of Informatics, University of Oslo, Oslo, Norway
[3] Alan Turing Institute, London, UK
[4] Department of Computer Science, University of Oxford, Oxford, UK

Abstract. Exploring the effects a chemical compound has on a species takes a considerable experimental effort. Appropriate methods for estimating and suggesting new effects can dramatically reduce the work needed to be done by a laboratory. In this paper we explore the suitability of using a knowledge graph embedding approach for ecotoxicological effect prediction. A knowledge graph has been constructed from publicly available data sets, including a species taxonomy and chemical classification and similarity. The publicly available effect data is integrated to the knowledge graph using ontology alignment techniques. Our experimental results show that the knowledge graph based approach improves the selected baselines.

Keywords: Knowledge graph · Semantic embedding · Ecotoxicology

1 Introduction

Extending the scope of risk assessment models is a long-term goal in ecotoxicological research. However, biological effect data is only available for a few combinations of chemical-species pairs.[1] Thus, one of the main efforts in ecotoxicological research is the design of tools and methods to extrapolate from known to unknown combinations in order to facilitate risk assessment predictions on a population basis.

The Norwegian Institute for Water Research (NIVA) is a leading Norwegian institute for fundamental and applied research on marine and freshwaters.[2] The Ecotoxicology and Risk Assessment programme at NIVA has through the last years developed a risk assessment system called RAdb.[3] This system has been applied to several case studies based on agricultural/industrial runoff into lakes

[1] Chemical and compound are used interchangeably.
[2] NIVA Institute: https://www.niva.no/en.
[3] NIVA Risk Assessment Database: https://www.niva.no/en/projectweb/radb.

C. Ghidini et al. (Eds.): ISWC 2019, LNCS 11779, pp. 490–506, 2019.
https://doi.org/10.1007/978-3-030-30796-7_30

or fjords. However, the underlying relational database structure of RAdb has its limitations when dealing with the integration of diverse data and knowledge sources. This limitation is exacerbated when these resources do not share a common vocabulary, as it is the case in our ecotoxicology risk assessment setting.

In this paper we present a preliminary study of the benefits of using Semantic Web tools to integrate different data sources and knowledge graph embedding approaches to improve the ecotoxicological effect prediction. Hence, our contribution to the NIVA institute is twofold:

(i) We have created a knowledge graph by gathering and integrating the relevant biological effect data and knowledge. Note that the format of the source data varies from tabular data, to SPARQL endpoints and ontologies. In order to discover equivalent entities we exploit internal resources, external resources (*e.g.*, Wikidata [21]) and ontology alignment (*e.g.*, LogMap [12]).

(ii) We have evaluated three knowledge graph embedding models (TransE [5], DistMult [23] and HolE [17]) together with the (baseline) prediction model currently used at NIVA. Our evaluation shows a considerable improvement with respect to the baseline and the benefits of using the knowledge graph models in terms of recall and $F_{\beta=2}$ score. Note that, in the NIVA use case, *false positives* are preferred over *false negatives* (*i.e.*, missing the hazard of a chemical over a species).

The rest of the paper is organised as follows. Section 2 provides some preliminaries to facilitate the understanding of the subsequent sections. In Sect. 3 we describe the use case where the knowledge graph and prediction models are applied. The creation of the knowledge graph is described in Sect. 4. Section 5 introduces the effect prediction models, while Sect. 6 presents the evaluation of these models. Finally, Sect. 7 elaborates on the contributions and discusses future directions of research.

2 Preliminaries

Knowledge Graphs. We follow the RDF-based notion of knowledge graphs [4] which are composed by RDF triples $\langle s, p, o \rangle$, where s represents a subject (a class or an instance), p represents a predicate (a property) and o represents an object (a class, an instance or a data value *e.g.*, text, date and number). RDF entities (*i.e.*, classes, properties and instances) are represented by an URI (Uniform Resource Identifier). A knowledge graph can be split into a TBox (terminology), often composed by RDF Schema constructors like class subsumption (*e.g.*, `ncbi:taxon/6668 rdfs:subClassOf ncbi:taxon/6657`) and property domain and range (`ecotox:affects rdfs:domain ecotox:Chemical`),[4] and an ABox (assertions), which contain relationships among instances (*e.g.*,

[4] The OWL 2 ontology language provides more expressive constructors. Note that the graph projection of an OWL 2 ontology can be seen as a knowledge graph (*e.g.*, [1]).

`ecotox:chemical/330541 ecotox:affects ecotox:effect/202`) and semantic type definitions (*e.g.*, `ecotox:taxon/28868 rdf:type ecotox:Taxon`). RDF-based knowledge graphs can be accessed with SPARQL queries, the standard language to query RDF graphs.

Ontology Alignment. Ontology alignment is the process of finding mappings or correspondences between a source and a target ontology or knowledge graph [10]. These mappings are typically represented as equivalences among the entities of the input resources (*e.g.*, `ncbi:taxon/13402 owl:sameAs ecotox:taxon/Carya`).

Embedding Models. Knowledge graph embedding [22] plays a key role in link prediction problems where the goal is to learn a scoring function $S : \mathcal{E} \times \mathcal{R} \times \mathcal{E} \rightarrow \mathbb{R}$. $S(s, p, o)$ is proportional to the probability that a triple $\langle s, p, o \rangle$ is encoded as true. Several models have been proposed, *e.g.*, Translating embeddings model (TransE) [5]. These models are applied to knowledge graphs to resolve missing facts in largely connected knowledge graphs, such as DBpedia [14]. Embedding models have also been successfully applied in biomedical link prediction tasks (*e.g.*, [2,3]).

Evaluation Metrics. We use (A)ccuracy, (P)recision, (R)ecall, (F_β) score to evaluate the models. They are defined as

$$A = \frac{tp + tn}{tp + tn + fp + fn} \tag{1}$$

$$P = \frac{tp}{tp + fp} \tag{2}$$

$$R = \frac{tp}{tp + fn} \tag{3}$$

$$F_\beta = (1 + \beta^2)\frac{PR}{\beta^2 P + R} \tag{4}$$

where tp, tn, fp, and fn stand for *true positive*, *true negative*, *false positive*, and *false negative*, respectively. Essentially, accuracy is the proportion of correct classifications. Recall is a measure of how many expected positive predictions were found by our model, and precision is the proportion of predictions that were correctly classified. F_β is a combined measure of precision and recall. $\beta = 1$ gives equal weight, while $\beta < 1$ favours precision and $\beta > 1$ favours recall. Here we use $F_{\beta=1}$ (F_1 in short) and $F_{\beta=2}$.

As the above metrics all depend on a selected threshold, we also use area under the receiver operating characteristic (ROC) curve (AUC) to measure and compare the overall pattern recognition capability of the prediction models. ROC is the curve of true positive rate ($^{tp}/_{(tp+fn)}$, i.e., recall) and false positive rate ($^{fp}/_{(fp+tn)}$), with the threshold ranging from 0 to 1 using a small step. AUC is the area under this curve, its values range between 0 and 1. Larger AUC indicates higher performance.

3 NIVA Use Case: Ecotoxicology and Risk Assessment

Ecotoxicology is a multidisciplinary field that studies the ecological and toxicological effects of chemical pollutants on populations, communities and ecosystems. Risk assessment is the result of the intrinsic hazards of a substance combined with an estimate of the environmental exposure (*i.e.*, Hazard + Exposure = Risk).

The Computational Toxicology Program within NIVA's Ecotoxicology and Risk Assessment section aims at designing and developing prediction models to assess the effect of chemical mixtures over a population where traditional laboratory data cannot be easily acquired.

Figure 1 shows the risk assessment pipeline followed at NIVA. *Exposure* is data gathered from the environment, while *effects* are hypothesis that are tested in a laboratory. These two data sources are used to calculate risk, which is used to find (further) susceptible species and the mode of action (MoA) or type of impact a compound would have over those species. Results from the MoA analysis are used as new effect hypothesis.

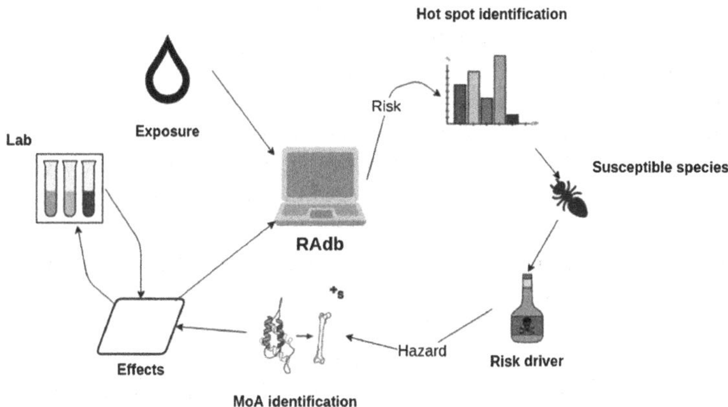

Fig. 1. NIVA risk assessment pipeline.

The effect data is gathered during experiments in a laboratory, where the population of a single species is exposed to a concentration of a toxic compound. Most commonly, the mortality rate of the population is measured at each time interval until it becomes a constant. Although the mortality at each time interval is referred to as *endpoint* in the ecotoxicology literature, we use *outcome* of the experiment to avoid confusion. Table 1 shows the typical outcomes and their proportion within the effects data. To give a good indication of the toxicity to a species, these experiments need to be repeated with increasing concentrations until the mortality reaches 100%. However, this is time consuming and is generally not done (*sola dosis facit venenum*). Hence, some compounds may appear

Table 1. The 10 most frequent outcomes in ECOTOX effect data.

Proportion	Abbreviation	Description
0.21	NR	Not reported
0.17	NOEL	No-observable-effect-level
0.16	LC50	Lethal concentration for 50% of test population
0.14	LOEL	Lowest-observable-effect-level
0.05	NOEC	No-observable-effect-concentration
0.05	EC50	Effective concentration for 50% of test population
0.04	LOEC	Lowest observable effect concentration
0.03	BCF	Bioconcentration factor
0.02	NR-LETH	Lethal to 100% of test population
0.02	LD50	Lethal dose for 50% of test population
0.11	Other	

more toxic than others due to limited experiments. Thus, when evaluating prediction models, (higher values of) recall are preferred over precision.

Risk assessment methods require large amounts of effect data to efficiently predict long term risk for the ecosystems. The data must cover a minimum of the chemicals found when analysing water samples from the ecosystem, along with covering species present in the ecosystem. This leads to a immense search space that is close to impossible to encompass in its entirety. Thus, it is essential to extrapolate from known to unknown combinations of chemical-species and suggest to the lab (ranked) effect hypothesis. The state-of-the-art within effect prediction are quantitative structure–activity relationship models (QSARs). These models have shown promising results for use in risk assessment, *e.g.*, [19]. However, QSARs have limitations with regard the coverage of compounds and species. These models use some chemical properties, but they usually only consider one or few species at a time. In this work we contribute with an alternative approach based on knowledge graph embeddings where the knowledge graph provides a global and integrated view of the domain.

Currently, the NIVA RAdb is under redevelopment, giving opportunities to include sophisticated effect prediction approaches, like the one presented in this paper, as a novel module for improving domain wide regulatory risk assessment.

4 A Knowledge Graph for Toxicological Effect Data

Risk assessment involves different data sources and laboratory experiments as shown in Fig. 1. In this section we describe the relevant datasets and their integration to create the *Toxicological Effects and Risk Assessment* (TERA) knowledge graph (see Fig. 2).

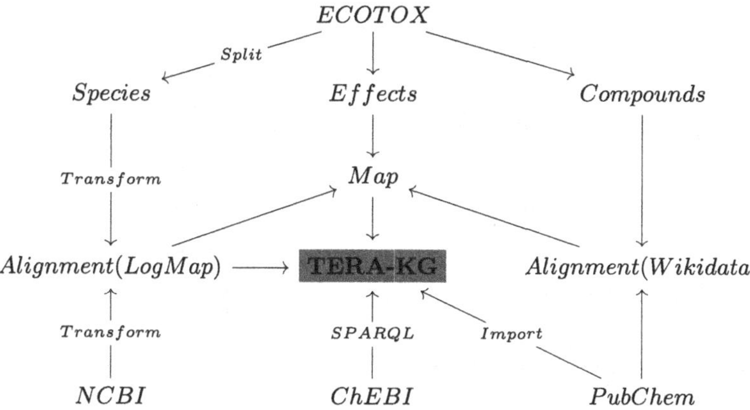

Fig. 2. Data sources in the TERA knowledge graph. Compound classification is available from PubChem. Chemical class hierarchy comes from the ChEMBL SPARQL endpoint. Compound literals are gathered from PubChem REST API and transformed into triples. ECOTOX and PubChem identifiers are aligned using the Wikidata SPARQL endpoint. ECOTOX and NCBI taxonomies are aligned using LogMap.

4.1 The ECOTOX Database

We rely on the ECOTOXicology database (ECOTOX) [9]. ECOTOX consists of $\sim$930k tests (or experiments) derived from the literature. Currently, an ECOTOX test considers the effect of one of $\sim$12k chemicals on one of $\sim$13k species. Which implies that less than 1% of compound-species pairs have been tested. The effect is categorised in one of a plethora of predefined outcomes. For example, the $LC50$ outcome implies lethal concentration for 50% of the test population. Table 1 shows the most frequent outcomes in ECOTOX.

Table 2. ECOTOX database entry examples.

test_id	reference_number	test_cas	species_number
1068553	5390	877430 (2,6-Dimethylquinoline)	5156 (Danio rerio)
2037887	848	79061 (2-Propenamide)	14 (Rasbora heteromorpha)

result_id	test_id	endpoint	conc1_mean	conc1_unit
98004	1068553	$LC50$	400	mg/kg diet
2063723	2037887	$LC10$	220	mg/L

Table 2 contains an excerpt of the ECOTOX database. ECOTOX includes information about the compounds and species used in the tests. This information, however, is limited and additional (external) resources are required to complement ECOTOX.

The number of outcomes per compound and species varies substantially. For example, there are 1,881 experiments where the compound used is *sulfuric acid*,

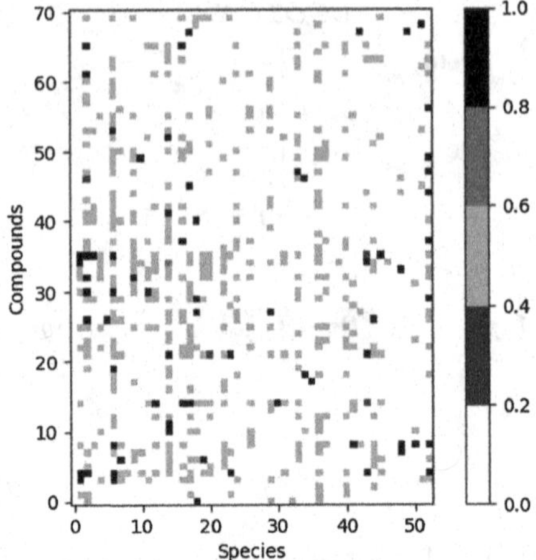

Fig. 3. ECOTOX effects data. x and y-axis represent individual species and chemicals sorted by similarity. Similarities are given by Eqs. (6) and (7) in Sect. 5.1. *i.e.*, chemicals $c_i \in C$ are indexed such that $S_{0,1} > S_{1,2} > \cdots > S_{n-1,n}$. Showing only chemicals and species that are involved in 25 or more experiments. Values relate to mortality rate of the test population, *i.e.*, LC50 corresponds to 0.5.

and 9,436 experiments where *Pimephales promelas* (fathead minnow) is the test species. The median number of experiments per chemical and species are 3 and 6, respectively. Figure 3 visualises a subset of the outcomes, here the zero values are either no effect or missing. This figure shows certain features of the data, *e.g.*, that compounds are more diversely used than species and that compound similarity is closely correlated to effects with regards to a species.

Currently, the ECOTOX database in used in risk assessment as reference data when calculating risk for a ecosystem. Essentially, comparing the reference and the observed chemical concentrations (per species). Since most compounds have multiple experiments per species, the mean and standard deviation of risk to a species can be calculated. However, if there is only one experiment for a compound-species pair we cannot calculate a standard deviation, such that the risk assessment is featureless. Therefore, estimating new effects is important to represent the natural variability of the effect data.

4.2 Dataset Integration into the TERA Knowledge Graph

Figure 2 shows the different datasets and their transformation that contribute in the creation of the TERA knowledge graph. For example Triples *(vii)*–*(ix)* in Table 3 have been created from the ECOTOX effect data.

Each compound in the ECOTOX effect data has a identifier called CAS Registry Number assigned by the Chemical Abstracts Service. The CAS numbers are proprietary, however, Wikidata [21] (indirectly) encodes mappings between CAS numbers and open identifiers like *InChIKey*, a 27 character hash of the

International Chemical Identifier (InChI) that encodes the chemical information in a unique manner. Hence, other datasets, such as PubChem [20], can be used to gather chemical features and classification of compounds. PubChem is already available as a knowledge graph and can be imported directly. However, the PubChem hierarchy only contains permutations of compounds. To create a full taxonomy for the chemical data, we use the ChEMBL SPARQL endpoint to extract the classification (provided by the ChEBI ontology [6]) for the relevant PubChem compounds. For example Triples *(v)* and *(vi)* in Table 3 come from the integration with PubChem and ChEMBL.

Table 3. Example triples from the TERA knowledge graph

#	subject	predicate	object
(i)	ecotox:group/Worms	owl:disjointWith	ecotox:group/Fish
(ii)	ncbi:division/2	owl:disjointWith	ncbi:division/4
(iii)	ecotox:taxon/34010	rdfs:subClassOf	ecotox:taxon/hirta
(iv)	ncbi:taxon/687295	rdfs:subClassOf	ncbi:taxon/513583
(v)	compound:CID10198308	rdf:type	obo:CHEBI_134899
(vi)	compound:CID10198308	pubchem:formula	''$C_7H_6O_6S$''
(vii)	ecotox:chemical/115866	ecotox:affects	ecotox:effect/001
(viii)	ecotox:effect/001	ecotox:species	ecotox:taxon/26812
(ix)	ecotox:effect/001	ecotox:endpoint	LC50
(x)	ecotox:taxon/33155	owl:sameAs	ncbi:taxon/311871

Aligning ECOTOX and NCBI. The species lineage in ECOTOX is not complete and therefore this (missing) information has been complemented with the NCBI taxonomy [16], a curated classification of all of the organisms in the public sequence databases (around 10% of the species on Earth). The tabular data provided for the ECOTOX species and the NCBI taxonomies has been transformed into subsumptions and disjointness triples (see first four triples in Table 3). Leaf nodes are treated as instance entities.

Since there does not exist a complete and public alignment between ECOTOX species and the NCBI Taxonomy, we have used the LogMap [11,12] ontology alignment systems to index and align the ECOTOX and NCBI vocabularies. ECOTOX currently only provides a subset of the mappings via its web search interface. We have gathered a total of 929 ground truth mappings for validation purposes. The lexical indexation provided by LogMap left us with 5,472 possible NCBI entities to map to ECOTOX (we focus only on instances, *i.e.*, leaf nodes). LogMap identified 4,681 (instance) mappings to ECOTOX (~40% of its entities) covering all 929 mappings from the (incomplete) ground truth, thus, an estimated recall of 100%. The mappings computed by LogMap have been included to the TERA knowledge graph as additional equivalence triples (see Triple *(x)* in Table 3 as example).

5 Effect Prediction Models

In this section we introduce the selected machine learning models to solve the effect prediction problem shown in Fig. 4. We use the known effects, denoted as *Affects* and *Not affects* in the figure, to predict whether or not new proposed chemical-species pairs are *true* (Affects) or *false* (Not affects).[5]

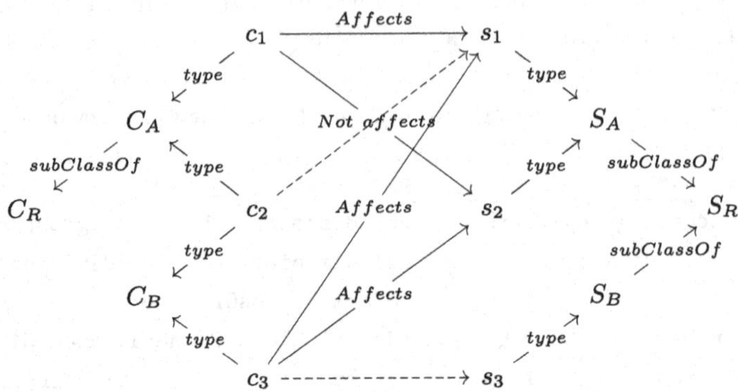

Fig. 4. The effect prediction problem. Lowercase s_j and c_i are instances of species and compounds, while uppercase denote classes in the hierarchy. Solid lines are observations and dashed lines are to be predicted. *i.e.*, does c_2 affect s_1?

Effect Data Sampling. A balance between positive and negative effect data samples is desired, therefore, we choose outcomes in categories (refer to Table 1): NOEL, LCp, LDp, NR-LETH, and NR-ZERO (p ranges from 0 to 100). We are only concerned about the mortality rate in experiments, consequently, we treat LC* and LD* identically. In addition, NR-LETH is treated as LC100. For simplicity, we treat the effects as binary entities. Hence, the outcome for a compound-species pair c, s is defined as

$$f(c,s) = \begin{cases} 1 & \text{if } (c,s) \in \text{LCp} \cup \text{LDp} \cup \text{NR-LETH} \\ 0 & \text{if } (c,s) \in \text{NOEL} \cup \text{NR-ZERO}. \end{cases} \tag{5}$$

For example, according to Fig. 4, $f(c_1, s_1) = 1$ (*i.e.*, c_1 affects s_1) and $f(c_1, s_2) = 0$ (*i.e.*, c_1 does not affects s_1), while $f(c_2, s_1)$ is unknown and thus a prediction is required for this chemical-species pair.

Knowledge Graphs. We rely on the TERA knowledge graph (see excerpts in Table 3 and Fig. 4) to feed the knowledge graph embedding algorithms. For simplicity we discard the ECOTOX species entities that have not a correspondence to NCBI. Note that we currently do not consider literals.

[5] The models are implemented with Keras [7]. Data and codes available from: https://github.com/Erik-BM/NIVAUC.

5.1 Baseline Model (M_1)

This (baseline) prediction model is based on the current prediction method used at NIVA. The basic idea of this method is to find the nearest-neighbour from the observed samples. In this context, the nearest neighbours are defined by hierarchy distance for species and similarity for compounds. Therefor, we first define a adjacency matrix for the taxonomy and a similarity matrix for compounds.

$$A_{i,j} = \frac{1}{|P(s_i, r)| + |P(s_j, r)| - 2|P(s_i, r) \cap P(s_j, r)| + 1} \tag{6}$$

where r is the taxonomy root, $P(x, r)$ is the classes in the path from x to r, and $|\cdot|$ denotes the cardinality. One basic approach to calculate the chemical similarity is using the Jaccard index of the binary fingerprints of the compounds [18]. Hence, the similarity matrix is defined as

$$S_{i,j} = J(c_i, c_j) = \frac{|(F_i)_2 \cap (F_j)_2|}{|(F_i)_2 \cup (F_j)_2|} \tag{7}$$

We define a matrix $E \in \mathbb{R}^{|C| \times |T|}$, where C and T denote the set of compounds and species respectively. E contains all the observed effects (training set):

$$E_{i,j} = \begin{cases} 1 & \text{if } (c_i, \text{ affects}, s_j) \\ 0 & \text{else} \end{cases} \tag{8}$$

We can then make the prediction with A, S, and E, as shown in Algorithm 1. The algorithm terminates when t_{max} neighbours are visited or $p > 0$.

5.2 Multilayer Perceptron (M_2)

Our second prediction model is a Multilayer perceptron (MLP) network with n hidden layers. The model can be expressed as:

$$\boldsymbol{y}^0 = [\boldsymbol{e}_c, \boldsymbol{e}_s] \tag{9}$$

$$\boldsymbol{y}^t = ReLu(\boldsymbol{y}^{t-1} W_t + \boldsymbol{b}_t) \tag{10}$$

$$\hat{y} = \sigma(\boldsymbol{y}^n W_n + \boldsymbol{b}_n) \tag{11}$$

where $t = 1, 2, ..., n$. $[\cdot, \cdot]$ denotes vector concatenation. $ReLu$ is the rectifier function and σ is the logistic sigmoid function. W_t are the weight matrices and b_t are the biasses for each layer. $\boldsymbol{e}_c, \boldsymbol{e}_s \in \mathbb{R}^k$ are the embedded vectors of c and s. For example $\boldsymbol{e}_c$ is defined as

$$\boldsymbol{e}_c = \boldsymbol{\delta}_c W_C \tag{12}$$

where $\boldsymbol{\delta}_c$ is the one-hot encoded vector for entity c, $W_C \in \mathbb{R}^{|C| \times k}$ is an embedding transformation matrix to learn.

```
Input: E, A, S, c_i, s_j
Output: p, effect prediction for c_i, s_j
i', j' ← i, j;
t_1 ← t_max;
p ← E_{i,j} ;                                 // 0 if no overlap between train and test
while t_1 > 0 do
    i' ← arg max_{k≠i} S_{i,k};               // find index of most similar compound
    A' ← A; t_2 ← t_max;                      // copy A and reset counter
    reset j;                                  // reset to j in input s_j
    while t_2 > 0 do
        j' ← arg max_{k≠j} A'_{j,k};          // index of closest specie
        p ← max(p, E_{i',j'});                // update prediction
        A'_{j,j'} ← 0;                        // set seen indices to zero
        t_2 ← t_2 − 1;
        if p > 0 then return p;
        i, j ← i', j';                        // update
    end
    S'_{i,i'} ← 0;                            // set seen indices to zero
    t_1 ← t_1 − 1;
end
return p;
```

Algorithm 1: Baseline prediction model algorithm (M_1).

A dropout layer is stacked after each hidden layer to prevent the network from overfitting. The model is optimised using ADAGRAD [8] with the following log loss function:

$$L(\boldsymbol{y}, \hat{\boldsymbol{y}}) = -\frac{1}{N} \sum_{i=1}^{N} \left[y_i \log \hat{y}_i + (1 - y_i) \log (1 - \hat{y}_i)\right] \tag{13}$$

5.3 Knowledge Graph (KG) Embedding and MLP ($M_2^\star$)

We have extended the MLP model (M_2) by feeding it with the TERA KG-based embeddings of c (*i.e.*, the chemical) and s (*i.e.*, the species), which encode the information of the taxonomy and compound hierarchies, among other semantic relationships. Note that the TERA knowledge graph also includes similarity triples about compounds. These triples represent pairs of compounds c_i and c_j where their similarity $S_{i,j}$ (as in Eq. 7) is above a threshold ϕ.

The embeddings are learned by applying the scoring function from one of DistMult [23], HolE [17], and TransE [5]. TransE was selected as it provides a very intuitive model. DistMult was included as it has shown state-of-the-art performance (*e.g.*, [13]), while HolE was considered as it also encodes directional relations. The score function for DistMult is defined as

$$S_D(s, p, o) = \sigma(\boldsymbol{e}_s^T W_p \boldsymbol{e}_o),\ W_p = diag(\boldsymbol{e}_p) \tag{14}$$

HolE uses a circular correlation score function, defined by

$$S_H(s,p,o) = \sigma(\boldsymbol{e}_r^T[\boldsymbol{e}_s \star \boldsymbol{e}_o]),\ \boldsymbol{e}_s \star \boldsymbol{e}_o = \mathcal{F}^{-1}[\overline{\mathcal{F}(\boldsymbol{e}_s)} \odot \mathcal{F}(\boldsymbol{e}_o)] \tag{15}$$

where $\mathcal{F}$ and $\mathcal{F}^{-1}$ are the Fourier transform and its inverse, $\overline{x}$ is the element-wise complex conjugate, $\odot$ denotes the Hadamard product. The final method is TransE, which has the score function

$$S_T(s,p,o) = ||\boldsymbol{e}_s + \boldsymbol{e}_p - \boldsymbol{e}_o|| \tag{16}$$

where $||\boldsymbol{x}||$ is the norm of $\boldsymbol{x}$. $\boldsymbol{e}_s$, $\boldsymbol{e}_p$ and $\boldsymbol{e}_o$ are the vector representation for the subject, predicate and object of a triple, respectively.

DistMult and HolE optimises for a score of 1 for positive samples and 0 for negative samples. Moreover, TransE scores positive samples as 0 and with no upper bound for negative samples. We modify the TransE score function to $S'_T = \tanh(1/S_T)$, such that $\lim_{S_T \to 0} S'_T = 1$ and $\lim_{S_T \to \infty} S'_T = 0$, to avoid modifying the labels.

The embeddings are used in the same network as the M_2 model. We train the embeddings and the classifier simultaneously using log loss and ADAGRAD. Training simultaneously will optimise the embeddings with regards to both the knowledge graph triples and the classifier loss.

6 Effect Prediction Evaluation

Sampling. We split the effect data 50%/50% for train/test. To prevent test set leakage, those training inputs that appear in the test set are removed, resulting in a 70%/30% split. $M_2^\star$ can be trained with the entirety of the knowledge graph, which is ignored under effect prediction. The negative knowledge graph samples are generated by randomly re-sampling subject and object of a true sample, while maintaining the distribution of predicates. We generate four negative samples per positive sample.

$\mathbf{M_1}$ Model Settings. We tested the performance of M_1 with 6 choices of nearest neighbour (5, 10, 20, 30, 40, 50). In addition to Algorithm 1, we tested an alternative technique for iterating over the data. However, Algorithm 1 yielded better results. The most balanced results were found when using 30 neighbours. When using more than 30 neighbours recall increases, but accuracy and precision suffer from a considerable decrease since the use of more neighbours increases the false positive rate.

$\mathbf{M_2/M_2^\star}$ Model Settings. The embedding dimension used in M_2 and $M_2^\star$ was based on a search among sizes 16, 64, 128 and 256. We found no difference between these parameters for M_2, therefor, 16 is chosen to aid faster training. $M_2^\star$ used a larger amount of entities and needs a larger embedding space to capture the features of the data. The performance plateaued at 128, hence, this was chosen. The models (M_2, $M_2^\star$) were trained until the loss stops improving for 5 iterations. For $M_2^\star$ we used different loss weights for the embeddings and

Table 4. Performance of the prediction models. $M_2^\star$ (S'_T), $M_2^\star$ (S_D) and $M_2^\star$ (S_H) stand for the MLP prediction models using TransE, DistMult, and HolE embedding models, respectively. *Above line*: ensemble averages of 10 clean tests. *Below line*: 10 fold cross validation on training set with standard deviation.

	M_1 $(t_{max} = 30)$	M_2	$M_2^\star$ (S'_T)	$M_2^\star$ (S_D)	$M_2^\star$ (S_H)
Accuracy	0.58	0.82	**0.83**	**0.83**	**0.83**
Precision	0.47	**0.76**	0.75	**0.76**	0.73
Recall	0.80	0.78	0.84	0.82	**0.87**
F_1 score	0.59	0.77	**0.79**	**0.79**	**0.79**
$F_{\beta=2}$ score	0.70	0.79	0.82	0.81	**0.84**
AUC	–	0.90	**0.91**	**0.91**	**0.91**
Accuracy	0.56 ± 0.01	$\mathbf{0.81 \pm 0.02}$	$\mathbf{0.81 \pm 0.02}$	$\mathbf{0.81 \pm 0.01}$	$\mathbf{0.81 \pm 0.02}$
Precision	0.55 ± 0.01	0.79 ± 0.04	$\mathbf{0.80 \pm 0.04}$	0.78 ± 0.03	0.79 ± 0.03
Recall	0.76 ± 0.03	0.84 ± 0.08	0.83 ± 0.08	$\mathbf{0.87 \pm 0.05}$	0.86 ± 0.02
F_1 score	0.65 ± 0.01	0.81 ± 0.03	0.81 ± 0.03	$\mathbf{0.82 \pm 0.01}$	0.82 ± 0.01
$F_{\beta=2}$ score	0.72 ± 0.02	0.83 ± 0.06	0.82 ± 0.06	$\mathbf{0.85 \pm 0.03}$	0.84 ± 0.01
AUC	–	$\mathbf{0.89 \pm 0.01}$	0.88 ± 0.01	$\mathbf{0.89 \pm 0.01}$	$\mathbf{0.89 \pm 0.02}$

the effect predictor. These weights were chosen such that the embeddings and effects are learned at similar rates. DistMult and HolE used 0.5 and 1.0 as loss weights for embeddings and effects models, respectively, while TransE used equal weights. We used a dropout rate of 0.2 and a similarity threshold of 0.5. Note that in $M_2^\star$ we simultaneously train the embedding models and the effect predictor. We perform *(i)* 10 fold cross validation on the training set, and *(ii)* a clean test on the unseen test set. This test consist of a ensemble of 10 models trained on the training set, each with a new set of random negative knowledge graph samples. We used an ensemble to limit the impact the random negative samples has on the results.

Evaluation. Figures 5a and b and Table 4 show the results of the conducted evaluation for the five effect prediction models. Figures 5a and b visualise the impact on accuracy and recall with different thresholds on the M_2–$M_2^\star$ prediction scores, while Table 4 presents the relevant evaluation metrics with a threshold of 0.5 for M_2–$M_2^\star$ and 30 neighbours for M_1. The results can be summarised as follows:

(i) M_1 is only slightly better than random choice, as the prior binary output distribution is 0.59 and 0.41. Thus it would not be appropriate for predicting effects. The false positive rate is also high, hence, M_1 would not be practical to use as a recommendation system.

(ii) M_2 is considerably better than M_1 and has balance between precision and recall. We suspect that this balance is due to random choice when the model has not previously seen a chemical or species. *i.e.*, a prediction close to the decision boundary when an input is unseen will maintain the false

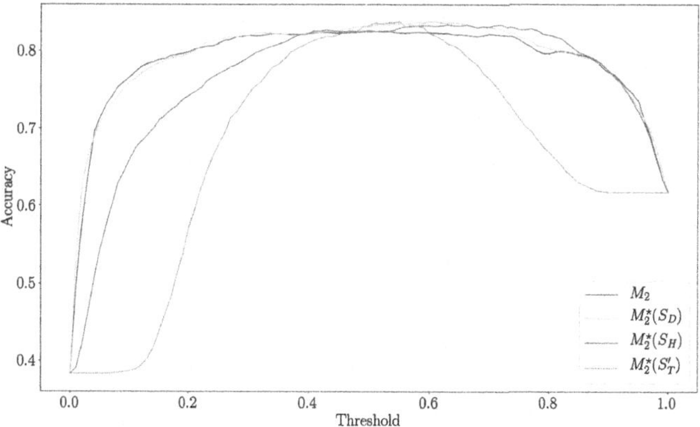

(a) Accuracy for the M_2 and $M_2^\star$ prediction models.

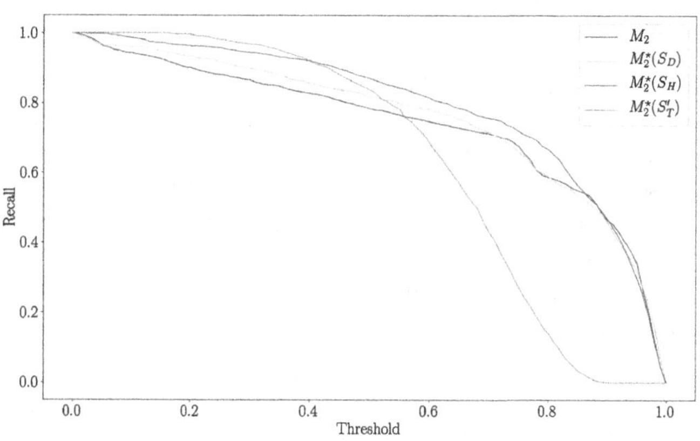

(b) Recall for the M_2 and $M_2^\star$ prediction models.

Fig. 5. Accuracy and Recall for the M_2 and $M_2^\star$ models with various thresholds.

negative/positive proportion, hence good for accuracy, not necessary for giving (interesting) recommendations to the laboratory.

(iii) Introducing the background knowledge to M_2, in the form of KG embeddings gives higher recall, without loosing accuracy. In contrast to M_2, $M_2^\star$ is more uncertain when unseen combinations are presented to the model (*in dubio pro reo*). Therefore, $M_2^\star$ is better suited to giving recommendations for cases where there is limited information about the chemical and the species in the effect data.

(iv) The best results in terms of recall, when using a threshold of 0.5 (see Table 4), are obtained by $M_2^\star$ with the embeddings provided by HolE (9 points higher than the M_2).

(v) As shown in Figs. 5a and b, lowering the decision threshold (0.30) would yield a higher recall (0.90) for the DistMult-based model, while maintaining the accuracy. TransE and HolE-based models have higher recall (0.97 and 0.94) at decision threshold 0.30, however, this comes at a cost of reduction in accuracy (0.74 and 0.79).

(vi) The highest overall $F_{\beta=2}$ score is 0.87, and is shared by all $M_2^{\star}$ models, albeit, at different decision boundaries, 0.34, 0.14 and 0.31 for models with TransE, DistMult, and HolE embeddings, respectively.

7 Discussion and Future Work

We have created a knowledge graph called TERA that aims at covering the knowledge and data relevant to the ecotoxicological domain. We have also implemented a proof-of-concept prototype for ecotoxicological effect prediction based on knowledge graph embeddings. The obtained results are encouraging, showing the positive impact of using knowledge graph embedding models and the benefits of having an integrated view of the different knowledge and data sources.

Knowledge Graph. The TERA knowledge graph is by itself an important contribution to NIVA. TERA integrates different knowledge and data sources and aims at providing an unified view of the information relevant to the ecotoxicology and risk assessment domain. At the same time the adoption of a RDF-based knowledge graph enables the use of *(i)* an extensive range of Semantic Web infrastructure that is currently available (*e.g.*, reasoning engines, ontology alignment systems, SPARQL query engines), and *(ii)* state of the art knowledge graph embedding strategies.

Prediction Models. The obtained predictions are promising and show the validity of the selected models in our setting and the benefits of using the TERA knowledge graph. As mentioned before, we favour recall with respect to precision. One the one hand, false positives are not necessarily harmful, while overlooking the hazard of a chemical may have important consequences. On the other hand, due to the limited experiments in terms of concentration (*i.e.*, effect data may not be complete), some chemicals may look less toxic than others while they may still be hazardous.

Value for NIVA. The conducted work falls into one of the main research lines of NIVA's Computational Toxicology Program (NCTP) to enhance the generation of hypothesis to be tested in the laboratory [15]. Furthermore, the data integration efforts and the construction of the TERA knowledge graph also goes in line with the vision of NIVA's section for Environmental Data Science. The availability and accessibility of the best knowledge and data will enable optimal decision making.

Novelty. Knowledge graph embedding models have been applied in general purpose link discovery and knowledge graph completion tasks [22]. They have also attracted the attention in the biomedical domain to find, for example, candidate genes for a disease, protein-protein interactions or drug-target interactions (*e.g.*, [2,3]). However, we are not aware of the application of knowledge graph embedding models in the context of toxicological effect prediction.

Future Work. The main goal in the mid-term future is to integrate the TERA knowledge graph and the machine learning based prediction models within NIVA's risk assessment pipeline. In the near future, we intend to improve the current ecotoxicological effect prediction prototype and evaluate the suitability of more sophisticated models like Graph Convolutional Networks. The TERA knowledge graph will also be extended with additional information about species (*e.g.*, interactions) and compounds (*e.g.*, target proteins) which is expected to enhance the computed embeddings and the effect predictions.

Resources. The datasets, evaluation results, documentation and source codes are available from the following GitHub repository: https://github.com/Erik-BM/NIVAUC.

Acknowledgements. This work is supported by the grant 272414 from the Research Council of Norway (RCN), the MixRisk project (RCN 268294), the AIDA project, The Alan Turing Institute under the EPSRC grant EP/N510129/1, the SIRIUS Centre for Scalable Data Access (RCN 237889), the Royal Society, EPSRC projects DBOnto, $MaSI^3$ and ED^3. We would also like to thank Martin Giese and Zofia C. Rudjord for their contribution in early stages of this project.

References

1. Agibetov, A., et al.: Supporting shared hypothesis testing in the biomedical domain. J. Biomed. Semant. **9**(1), 9:1–9:22 (2018)
2. Agibetov, A., Samwald, M.: Global and local evaluation of link prediction tasks with neural embeddings. In: 4th Workshop on Semantic Deep Learning (ISWC Workshop), pp. 89–102 (2018)
3. Alshahrani, M., Khan, M.A., Maddouri, O., Kinjo, A.R., Queralt-Rosinach, N., Hoehndorf, R.: Neuro-symbolic representation learning on biological knowledge graphs. Bioinformatics **33**(17), 2723–2730 (2017)
4. Arnaout, H., Elbassuoni, S.: Effective searching of RDF knowledge graphs. Web Semant.: Sci. Serv. Agents World Wide Web **48** (2018)
5. Bordes, A., Usunier, N., Garcia-Duran, A., Weston, J., Yakhnenko, O.: Translating embeddings for modeling multi-relational data. In: Advances in Neural Information Processing Systems 26, pp. 2787–2795. Curran Associates, Inc. (2013)
6. ChEBI-ontology: The European bioinformatics institute (2019). https://www.ebi.ac.uk/chebi/
7. Chollet, F., et al.: Keras (2015). https://github.com/fchollet/keras
8. Duchi, J., Hazan, E., Singer, Y.: Adaptive subgradient methods for online learning and stochastic optimization. J. Mach. Learn. Res. **12**, 2121–2159 (2011)
9. US EPA: Ecotoxicology knowledgebase (ECOTOX) (2019). https://cfpub.epa.gov/ecotox/
10. Euzenat, J., Shvaiko, P.: Ontology Matching, 2nd edn. Springer, Heidelberg (2013). https://doi.org/10.1007/978-3-642-38721-0
11. Jiménez-Ruiz, E., Cuenca Grau, B.: LogMap: logic-based and scalable ontology matching. In: Aroyo, L., et al. (eds.) ISWC 2011. LNCS, vol. 7031, pp. 273–288. Springer, Heidelberg (2011). https://doi.org/10.1007/978-3-642-25073-6_18

12. Jimenez-Ruiz, E., Cuenca Grau, B., Zhou, Y., Horrocks, I.: Large-scale interactive ontology matching: algorithms and implementation. In: The 20th European Conference on Artificial Intelligence (ECAI), pp. 444–449. IOS Press (2012)
13. Kadlec, R., Bajgar, O., Kleindienst, J.: Knowledge base completion: baselines strike back. CoRR abs/1705.10744 (2017). http://arxiv.org/abs/1705.10744
14. Lehmann, J., et al.: DBpedia - a large-scale, multilingual knowledge base extracted from Wikipedia. Semant. Web **6**(2), 167–195 (2015)
15. Myklebust, E.B., Jimenez-Ruiz, E., Rudjord, Z.C., Wolf, R., Tollefsen, K.E.: Integrating semantic technologies in environmental risk assessment: a vision. In: 29th Annual Meeting of the Society of Environmental Toxicology and Chemistry (SETAC) (2019)
16. NCBI-Taxonomy: The national center for biotechnology information (2019). https://www.ncbi.nlm.nih.gov/taxonomy
17. Nickel, M., Rosasco, L., Poggio, T.A.: Holographic embeddings of knowledge graphs. CoRR abs/1510.04935 (2015). http://arxiv.org/abs/1510.04935
18. Nikolova, N., Jaworska, J.: Approaches to measure chemical similarity – a review. QSAR Comb. Sci. **22**(9–10), 1006–1026 (2003)
19. Pradeep, P., Povinelli, R.J., White, S., Merrill, S.J.: An ensemble model of QSAR tools for regulatory risk assessment. J. Cheminform. **8**, 48 (2016)
20. PubChem: National Institutes of Health (NIH) (2019). https://pubchem.ncbi.nlm.nih.gov/
21. Vrandecic, D., Krötzsch, M.: Wikidata: a free collaborative knowledgebase. Commun. ACM **57**(10), 78–85 (2014)
22. Wang, Q., Mao, Z., Wang, B., Guo, L.: Knowledge graph embedding: a survey of approaches and applications. IEEE Trans. Knowl. Data Eng. **29**(12), 2724–2743 (2017)
23. Yang, B., Yih, W., He, X., Gao, J., Deng, L.: Embedding entities and relations for learning and inference in knowledge bases. CoRR abs/1412.6575 (2015)

Improving Editorial Workflow and Metadata Quality at Springer Nature

Angelo A. Salatino[1(✉)], Francesco Osborne[1], Aliaksandr Birukou[2], and Enrico Motta[1]

[1] Knowledge Media Institute, The Open University, Milton Keynes MK7 6AA, UK
{angelo.salatino, francesco.osborne, enrico.motta}@open.ac.uk
[2] Springer-Verlag GmbH, Tiergartenstrasse 17, 69121 Heidelberg, Germany
aliaksandr.birukou@springer.com

Abstract. Identifying the research topics that best describe the scope of a scientific publication is a crucial task for editors, in particular because the quality of these annotations determine how effectively users are able to discover the right content in online libraries. For this reason, Springer Nature, the world's largest academic book publisher, has traditionally entrusted this task to their most expert editors. These editors manually analyse all new books, possibly including hundreds of chapters, and produce a list of the most relevant topics. Hence, this process has traditionally been very expensive, time-consuming, and confined to a few senior editors. For these reasons, back in 2016 we developed Smart Topic Miner (STM), an ontology-driven application that assists the Springer Nature editorial team in annotating the volumes of all books covering conference proceedings in Computer Science. Since then STM has been regularly used by editors in Germany, China, Brazil, India, and Japan, for a total of about 800 volumes per year. Over the past three years the initial prototype has iteratively evolved in response to feedback from the users and evolving requirements. In this paper we present the most recent version of the tool and describe the evolution of the system over the years, the key lessons learnt, and the impact on the Springer Nature workflow. In particular, our solution has drastically reduced the time needed to annotate proceedings and significantly improved their discoverability, resulting in 9.3 million additional downloads. We also present a user study involving 9 editors, which yielded excellent results in term of usability, and report an evaluation of the new topic classifier used by STM, which outperforms previous versions in recall and F-measure.

Keywords: Scholarly data · Bibliographic metadata · Topic classification · Topic detection · Scholarly ontologies · Data mining

1 Introduction

Identifying the research topics that best describe the scope of a scientific publication is a crucial task for editors, in particular because the quality of these annotations determines how effectively users are able to discover the right content in online libraries.

C. Ghidini et al. (Eds.): ISWC 2019, LNCS 11779, pp. 507–525, 2019.
https://doi.org/10.1007/978-3-030-30796-7_31

A high-quality representation of research publications has also an effect on the performance of approaches to discovering and querying scientific articles [1], producing smart analytics [2], detecting research communities [3], extracting research entities [4], recommending publications [5], forecasting research topics [6], and so on.

Springer Nature (SN), the world's largest academic book publisher, produces for each new book a high quality list of relevant topics, which are used for describing the book content in the metadata. This task is particularly complex in the case of books covering conference proceedings, as these may easily contain over 100 different contributions, each of which may be relevant to several areas of research. As a result, the set of topics covered by the proceedings of a conference can be very large and it is not trivial to manually select a small number of topics that best describe the entire set of contributions. In particular, it is easy to miss the emergence of a new topic or to assume that some topics are still popular when this is no longer the case. For these reasons, this task has been entrusted to senior editors, which typically select a list of topics on the basis of their own expertise in the field, a visual exploration of titles and abstracts, and, optionally, a list of keywords derived from the call for papers of the conference in question. Hence, this process has traditionally been very expensive, time-consuming, and confined to a few expert editors. Moreover, the resulting topics may vary according to the background of the editor and the same topic could be referred to by means of different labels (e.g., LOD, Linked Data) or at a different abstraction level (e.g., Deep Learning, Machine Learning).

For these reasons, in 2016 we developed Smart Topic Miner [7], an application supporting Springer Nature editors in annotating publications in terms of a set of topics drawn from a large ontology of research areas in Computer Science [8]. Since then STM has been adopted by editors in Germany, China, Brazil, India, and Japan to annotate all book series covering conference proceedings in Computer Science, for a total of about 800 volumes per year. Over the past three years, STM has iteratively evolved in response to feedback from the users and has been extremely successful in both reducing costs and improving the quality of the metadata. It has drastically reduced the time used to annotate proceedings, from about 30 to 10–15 min for each volume, and allowed the task to be performed by junior editors or editorial assistants, ultimately achieving an overall 75% cost reduction. The resulting metadata have improved significantly the discoverability of the relevant books, resulting in about 9 million additional downloads. We believe that the evolution of this small prototype to a high impact system adopted by one of the main academic publishers constitutes an exemplary success story regarding the adoption of semantic technologies in large companies.

In this paper we introduce Smart Topic Miner 2 (STM 2), the most recent version of the tool, and describe the evolution of the system over the years, the key lessons learnt, and the impact on the Springer Nature workflow and on the discoverability of the relevant publications. We also present a user study on STM 2 involving 9 editors, which yielded excellent results in term of usability, and report an evaluation of the new research topic classifier, which outperforms the previous versions in terms of both recall and F-measure. The main novelties with respect to the earlier report on this work

[7] include: (1) a new approach to identifying research topics and producing an explanation for each suggested topic, (2) a new interactive interface, (3) a new capability for the system to take into account the annotation of previous editions of the conference in question, (4) the integration of STM 2 with the CSO Portal [8] and the SN editorial systems.

The paper is structured as follows. In Sect. 2, we discuss the evolution of STM and describe the latest version in detail. Section 3 presents the user study and the evaluation of the classifier. Section 4 describes the uptake and impact of STM, and Sect. 5 discusses the relevant work. Finally, in Sect. 6 we summarise the main results from this work and discuss our plans for further developing STM in Springer Nature.

2 Smart Topic Miner 2

Smart Topic Miner 2 is a web application that assists editors in classifying books and more in general any collection of research papers. Specifically, it takes as input XML files describing the metadata of one or more books and returns:

- A taxonomy of the relevant topics drawn from the Computer Science Ontology (CSO) [8], which is the largest taxonomy of research topics in the field;
- A set of relevant Product Marked Codes (PMCs), Springer Nature internal classification;
- An explanation for each topic, in terms of the text excerpts that triggered the topic identification;
- A list of chapters from the book annotated with topics from CSO.

The editors use an interactive interface to explore this output, check why specific topics were inferred by the system, compare them with the annotations produced in previous editions, and include or exclude specific topics or PMCs according to their expertise. The resulting sets of topics and PMCs are eventually included in the metadata of the publications. These are then used for classifying proceedings in digital and physical libraries and consequently improving the discoverability of the publications in SpringerLink and several other digital libraries and third-party sites. They are also used to power Smart Book Recommender [9], an ontology-based recommender system, which supports the editorial team in selecting the products to market at specific venues.

Figure 1 shows the STM 2 architecture, which consists of four main components: (i) the user interface, (ii) the parser, which elaborates the input files, (iii) the back-end which consists of five sub-components, and (iv) the knowledge bases.

A demo version of STM 2 is available at http://stm-demo.kmi.open.ac.uk.

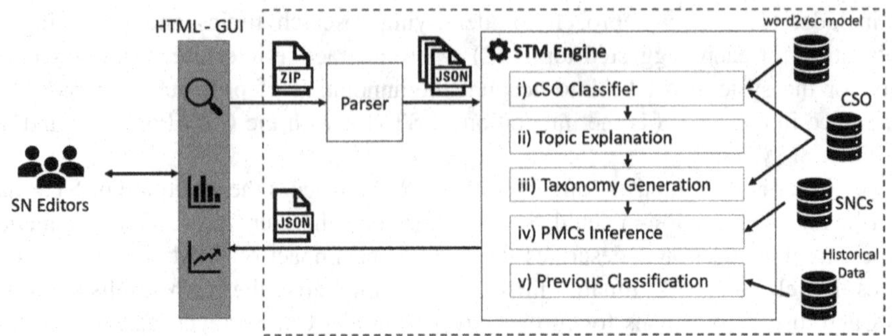

Fig. 1. The STM architecture

In the next subsection we summarize the evolution of STM over the last three years, and describe the current version, STM 2, in detail. In Sect. 2.2 we discuss the knowledge bases used by the system, in Sect. 2.3 we present the approach to infer research topics and PMCs, and in Sect. 2.4 we illustrate the user interface.

2.1 STM Evolution

Most of the features implemented in STM 2 were designed to address the feedback of the editors using this application since 2016. In this section we summarize the evolution of the system over the last three years by discussing the main changes and their rationale.

2.1.1 Back-End

A fundamental component of the STM back-end is the classifier used for detecting a set of topics for each chapter. In the original implementation, the STM classifier identified the label of the topics from the ontology (e.g., Linked Data) and then inferred all their super topics (e.g., Semantic Web, AI, Computer Science). However, an analysis of the output with SN editors revealed that our method was missing some variations of the labels that were not covered in the ontology. For this reason, we designed a new approach (the CSO Classifier 1.0 [10]) which selects all the ontology topics which have a Levenshtein similarity higher than a threshold with n-grams extracted from the text. A new meeting with the editors confirmed that this problem was solved, but revealed a more subtle issue: some topics were never explicitly mentioned and could be inferred just by considering the text as a whole. For instance, the abstract of a chapter about "online communities" never mentioned this label, a similar variation, or any of its subtopics in the ontology. However, it mentioned several related terms, such as the name of popular social networks and words related to network analysis. Hence, we recently created a new version of the CSO Classifier (2.0 [11], described in Sect. 2.3.2) that uses NLP and word embeddings to detect also implicit topics. This solution outperforms previous versions in terms of both recall and F-measure (see Sect. 3.2). Editors have also confirmed that the current output is now much more comprehensive, both at book and at chapter level.

2.1.2 User Interface

The user interface of STM 2 (Fig. 2) is visibly different from the 2016 version (Fig. 3). The first important change regards the way topics are presented. In the original version, the taxonomy was given as text in order to allow the editors to easily export the output. However, editors wanted to be able to interact with the topics for the purpose of requesting an explanation, renaming them, or inserting a missing sub-topic. Hence, we implemented a new interactive interface that displays the taxonomy as a tree and allows editors to right click on the topics to access a number of functionalities.

The second change is the introduction of a new input menu that allows the editors to load several books at once. Indeed, the proceedings of a conference can consist of 2–10 volumes, which need to be analysed together and will share the same topics and PMCs.

The third important change regards the way the editors control the granularity of the representation. Originally, STM used a set covering algorithm that, given a "granularity value" from 1 to 5, would return a more or less comprehensive version of the taxonomy. This solution had two main issues. First, the "granularity value" was arbitrary and there was no straightforward explanation on why a certain topic was included or not. Secondly, the editor needed to submit a new request to the back-end every time they

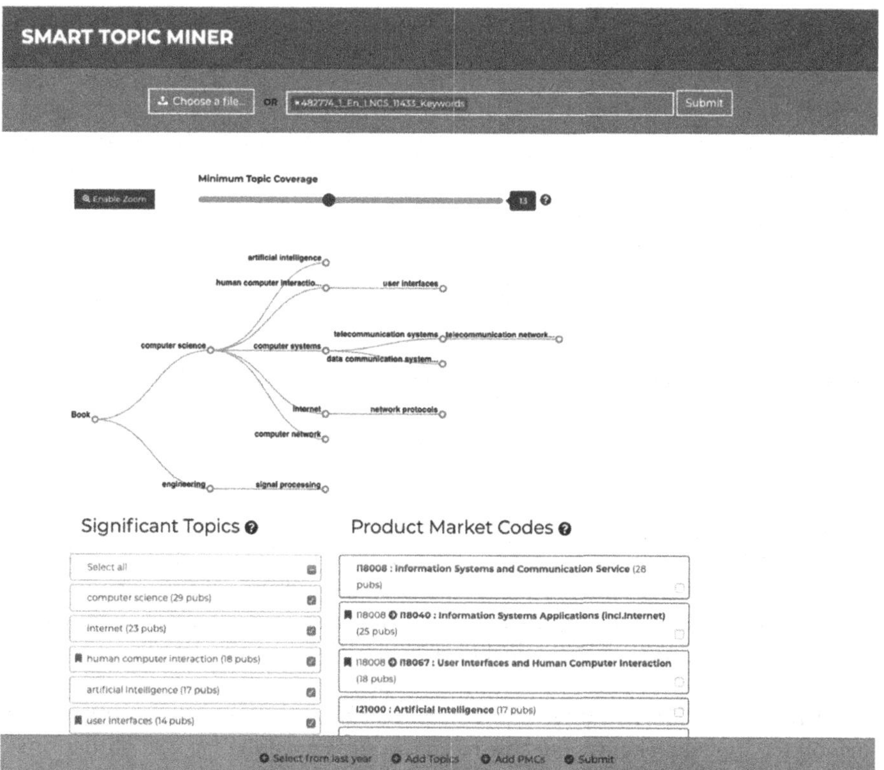

Fig. 2. Smart Topic Miner 2.0 interface.

had to change the granularity, which was quite time consuming. In STM 2 we addressed these issues by moving the process to the front-end. Now the back-end produces a taxonomy including all relevant topics, and the interactive interface shows only the ones associated with a minimum number of chapters. The user can change this value with a sliding bar, making the displayed taxonomy more or less inclusive. This solution was greatly appreciated by the editors, since it makes them feel in full control of the filtering mechanism. Interestingly, while the previous version produced arguably better summarizations of the taxonomies, editors prefer this simple solution since it produces a more predictable outcome. This suggests that transparency and understandability are of the utmost importance when supporting human experts in the exploration of automatically generated knowledge bases.

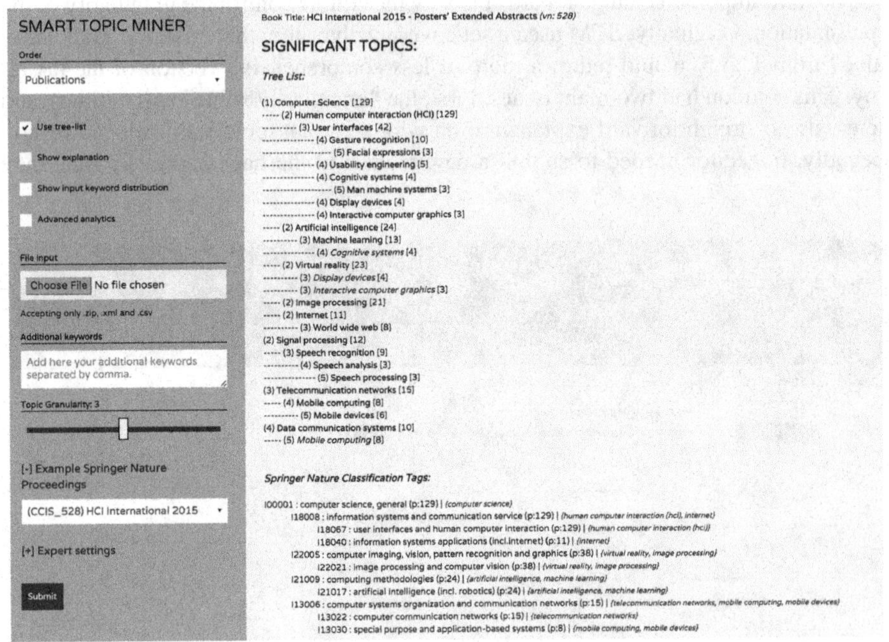

Fig. 3. Smart Topic Miner 1.0 interface.

The final change regards the left bar that used to include the main menu and all the options. The editors noticed that even if they did not typically use it after loading the proceedings, it was still taking a lot of screen space, reducing the area available for navigating the taxonomy of topics. More generally, we learnt that our users did not consider several settings that we included in the first version. For instance, many options for changing the parameters of the classifiers were considered too technical and opaque by the users. They preferred a simple and clean interface allowing them to focus on the topic taxonomy. For this reason, we removed the bar and all the superfluous settings and simplified the front-end as much as possible. The resulting interface is described in detail in Sect. 2.4.

2.1.3 Comparison with Previous Year Annotations

The previous version of STM only took in consideration the specific proceedings book loaded by the editor when producing the set of topics and PMCs. However, the proceeding books of previous editions may have been already annotated. The editors suggested that in some cases it would be easier for them if they could start from the annotations of previous editions, which had already been inspected and verified by an editor, and update them by taking in consideration new research trends for the conference. For this reason, STM now identifies the conference series, retrieves the annotations used for the previous edition, highlights these topics, and allows the editors to select them as default starting points. An additional advantage of this solution is that it clearly shows to the editors the fading or emerging topics in a certain venue. This information supports relevant editorial and marketing decisions, such as the publication of a book on the emerging topics.

2.1.4 Integration with the CSO Portal

Representing relevant topics as a taxonomy has always been one of the most appreciated functionalities of STM, since it provides an intuitive way to explore topics and their relationships. However, this taxonomy offers only a partial view of the original ontology, since it includes exclusively the most significant topics from the input books. Hence, editors had no way to examine the original ontology - e.g., for better understanding the nature of a topic or for assessing how good was the coverage of a certain venue with respect to a research field. A related problem was the lack of an automatic and robust mechanism for reporting potential mistakes in the knowledge base, such as an erroneous *subTopicOf* relationship that was causing incorrect inferences. We addressed these issues by integrating STM 2 with the CSO Portal, a web application that enables users to explore and provide granular feedback on CSO. This solution allows the editors to inspect each topic, read a brief summary extracted from DBpedia, check all related topics, and flag incorrect or dubious relationships.

2.1.5 Integration with Springer Nature Systems

The first version of STM was not integrated with the SN editorial system. Therefore, the editors had first to obtain a file with the publication metadata and import it in STM, then copy-paste the resulting set of topics and PCMs in an online form in order to submit them to the editorial systems. This process was time-consuming and not very robust. Hence, we integrated STM 2 with the SN metadata systems and production workflows, so that the editors can now load the metadata and submit the final annotations to the editorial system within the application interface.

2.2 Background Data

Smart Topic Miner relies on three main knowledge sources: (i) the Computer Science Ontology (CSO), (ii) the Product Market Codes (PMCs), and (iii) the metadata of Springer Nature publications. It also exploits a Word2Vec model trained on about 4.5M publications in Computer Science. We describe all of them in the following subsections.

2.2.1 The Computer Science Ontology

The Computer Science Ontology (CSO) [8] is a large-scale ontology of research areas that currently includes 14K topics linked by 162K semantic relationships. CSO is available through the CSO Portal[1], a web application that enables users to download, explore, and provide granular feedback on CSO at different levels. It was generated by running the Klink-2 algorithm [12] on a large dataset of research publications in the field of Computer Science [2]. Since it is regularly updated by re-running Klink-2 on recent corpora and integrating user feedback from the CSO Portal, it includes also emerging topics, which are not typically covered by human crafted taxonomies.

The CSO data model[2] is an extension of SKOS[3]. It includes three main semantic relations: *superTopicOf*, which indicates that a topic is a super-area of another one (e.g., Semantic Web is a super-area of Linked Data), *relatedEquivalent*, which indicates that two topics can be treated as equivalent for the purpose of exploring research data (e.g., Ontology Matching and Ontology Mapping, and *contributesTo*, which indicates that the research output of a topic contributes to another. CSO is licensed under a CC BY 4.0 and is available for download at https://cso.kmi.open.ac.uk/downloads.

2.2.2 Classification System at Springer Nature

The Product Market Codes is a three-level mono-hierarchical classification system used by Springer Nature to categorize proceedings, books, and journals. The Computer Science section includes 103 categories characterizing both research fields (e.g., *I23001 – Computer Applications*) and domains (e.g., *I23028 - Computer App. In Social and Behavioral Sciences*). This classification was recently updated by using an innovative ontology evolution approach [13] for selecting a new set of topics that best fit SN catalogue. The resulting identifiers are used in the metadata describing the contents for the Springer Nature website[4] as well as third-party libraries and bookshops.

We integrated CSO and PMCs by means of 332 relationships, so that every PMC is now associated to a set of related CSO concepts, as described in [7]. For instance, we mapped the *computer communication networks* category to CSO topics such as Network Security, Telecommunication Networks, Wireless Telecommunication Systems, Wireless Sensor Networks, and so on.

2.2.3 Metadata of Springer Nature Publications

STM 2 has access to a database of metadata contains titles, abstracts, keywords and other information describing about 50K books in the field of Computer Science, including 10K proceedings [14]. In this dataset each proceedings book is associated with an ID identifying its conference series, as well as with the topics and PMCs chosen by editors. This information is used by STM 2 to identify the previous edition of a conference and retrieve all relevant data.

[1] Computer Science Ontology Portal - https://cso.kmi.open.ac.uk.

[2] CSO Data Model - https://cso.kmi.open.ac.uk/schema/cso.

[3] SKOS Simple Knowledge Organization System - http://www.w3.org/2004/02/skos.

[4] Springer Link - https://link.springer.com.

2.2.4 Word2Vec Model

In order to support the classification of text, we trained a Word2Vec [15] word embedding model on a corpus extracted from the Microsoft Academic Graph (MAG), which is an heterogeneous graph containing scientific publication records, citation relationships, authors, institutions, journals, conferences, and fields of study. Specifically, we considered titles and abstracts of 4,654,062 English publications in the field of Computer Science. We pre-processed these data by replacing spaces with underscores in all n-grams matching the CSO topic labels (e.g., "semantic web" became "semantic_web") and for frequent bigrams and trigrams (e.g., "highest_accuracies", "highly_cited_journals"). These frequent n-grams were identified by analysing combinations of words that co-occur together (collocations), as suggested in Mikolov et al. [15]. This solution allows STM to better disambiguate concepts and treat terms such as "deep_learning" and "e-learning" as completely different words.

More details on how we trained the model and its parameters are available in Salatino et al. [11].

2.3 Back-End

The back-end processes one or more proceedings books according to five steps:

1. *Parsing of the metadata*, in which STM 2 extracts the metadata associated to each chapter;
2. *Topic Extraction*, in which STM 2 uses the CSO Classifier to map each publication to a selection of research concepts drawn from CSO;
3. *Generation of Explanations*, in which STM 2 generates for each topic the list of text excerpts that lead to its identification;
4. *Inference of PMCs*, in which the selected topics are used to infer a number of PMCs, using the mapping between CSO concepts and SN codes;
5. *Taxonomy generation and retrieval of previous annotations*, in which STM 2 produces a taxonomy of topics and retrieves the classification of the previous editions.

2.3.1 Parsing of the Metadata

In the first step, STM 2 extracts all XML files available within the input ZIP files. Then, for each XML file, it retrieves the metadata associated to each chapter: title, abstract, list of keywords, chapter id, volume number, and optionally the conference series identifier. In proceedings books, each chapter is typically a research paper accepted by a conference or a workshop.

2.3.2 Topic Extraction

At this stage, STM 2 extracts topics from the metadata of a book by running the CSO Classifier [11] on the title, abstract and keywords of each chapter. The CSO Classifier is a tool that we developed for automatically classifying research papers in terms of relevant concepts drawn from CSO. Figure 4 reports its workflow. It identifies topics by means of two different components, the syntactic module and the semantic module, then it combines their outputs and enhances the resulting set by including all relevant super-topics. Its pseudocode is available at https://cso.kmi.open.ac.uk/cso-classifier. In the following we briefly describe it; we refer the interested reader to [11] for additional details.

The *syntactic module* removes English stop words and collects unigrams, bigrams, and trigrams. Then, for each n-gram, it computes the Levenshtein similarity with the labels of the topics in CSO. Finally, it returns all research topics whose labels have similarity to one of the n-grams, which is equal to or higher than a threshold.

The *semantic module* uses part-of-speech tagging to identify candidate terms composed of a proper combination of nouns and adjectives and decomposes them in unigrams, bigrams, and trigrams. For each n-gram, it retrieves its most similar words from the Word2Vec model described in Sect. 2.2.4. For this task, the n-gram tokens are initially glued with an underscore, creating one single word, e.g., "semantic_web". If this word is not available within the model vocabulary, the classifier uses the average of the embedding vectors of all its tokens. Then, it computes the relevance score for each topic in the ontology as the product between the number of times it was identified in those n-grams (frequency) and the number of unique n-grams that led to it (diversity). Finally, it uses the elbow method [16] for selecting the set of most relevant topics.

The CSO Classifier aggregates the topics returned by the two modules and enriches them by inferring the list of all their super topics, exploiting the *superTopicOf* relationship within CSO [8]. For instance, given the topic "Neural Networks", it will infer "Machine Learning", "Artificial Intelligence", and "Computer Science". This feature allows us to capture both high-level fields and very granular research areas, in order to generate a comprehensive representation of the proceedings books. In order to exclude generic and ambiguous terms (e.g., "language", "learning", "component", etc.), the classifier does not consider the 3,000 most frequent words in the Word2Vec model.

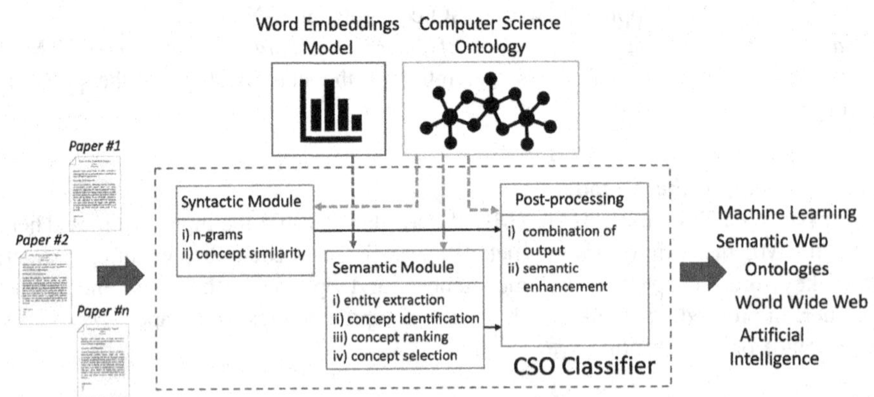

Fig. 4. Workflow of the CSO Classifier.

2.3.3 Generation of Explanations

Editors do not like to work with a black box. It is critical for them to be able to understand and verify why STM 2 identifies a certain topic. Therefore, STM 2 generates an explanation for each topic in terms of a distribution of text excerpts from which the topics was inferred. This process is important both for building trust in the system and for detecting possible mistakes. In order to produce these explanations, STM 2 first maps the topics with the portions of text that triggered them during the identification. It then associates the text excerpts of a topic to all its super-topics. Finally, it orders them by the number of chapters in which they appear. For instance, the explanation for the topic "Natural Language Processing" will be composed of fragments of texts and their frequencies such as *language processing (6), text mining (6), information extraction (4), keyphrase extraction (4), textual data (3), syntactic analysis (2)*, and so on. These explanations are one of the most appreciated features of STM 2. Indeed, editors reported that in several occasions they assumed that a suggested topic was wrong, but, after checking the explanation, they realized it was indeed addressed in several chapters.

2.3.4 Inference of PMCs

In this step, STM 2 uses the mapping between the PMCs and CSO to infer all relevant PMC identifiers. It does so by inferring each PMC that subsumes one of the topics in CSO according to the mapping described in Sect. 2.2.2. For example, if the Cryptography topic was yielded by the previous step, STM will infer the identifier 'I15033 - Data Encryption' (at the third level), 'I15009 - Data Structures, Cryptology and Information Theory' (second level) and 'I00001 - Computer Science, general' (root). It then associates to each identifier the total number of chapters covered by the associated topics to assist the editors in assessing its significance for the book under analysis.

2.3.5 Taxonomy Generation and Retrieval of Previous Annotations

Finally, STM 2 builds a taxonomy of topics, using the *subTopicOf* relationships in CSO. It then uses the conference series ID from the metadata to retrieve the topics and PMCs associated to the same conference in the previous year. This information will be displayed alongside the current list of topics and PMCs.

2.4 User Interface

The STM 2 interface (Fig. 2) is composed by three main components: (1) a top menu for loading the metadata of one or more books, (2) a main panel for inspecting and selecting topics and PMCs, and (3) a bottom menu for submitting the classification and accessing further options.

The main panel also consists of three main parts: (1) a taxonomy of CSO topics, (2) the main menu for selecting topics and PMCs, and (3) a list of chapters from the book. The taxonomy represents topics as nodes linked by their *superTopicOf* relationships from CSO. It includes by default all topics associated with a minimum number of chapters. The editors can control this value by mean of a sliding bar. For instance, in Fig. 2 the taxonomy includes all the topics which appear in at least 13 (out of 29) chapters. Topics can be collapsed or expanded and right clicking on one of them opens a contextual menu with several options:

- *Show Explanation*, which displays all relevant text excerpts;
- *Explore in CSO*, which allows editors to examine the topic in the CSO Portal, navigate CSO, and leave a feedback;
- *Rename*, which allows editors to change the label of the topic. For instance, "internet of things" has been renamed as "Internet of Things (IoT)";
- *Remove*, which allows editors to remove the topic from the output;
- *Add subarea*, which allows editors to add a new subarea to the selected topic.

The main menu displays topics and PMCs ordered by frequency and allows editors to select or re-rank them. The topics and PMCs used by the previous edition of the conference are marked with an icon.

The lower part of the main panel displays a summary of all the chapter/articles in the input books. STM 2 shows for each chapter its title, abstract, keywords, and the topics from CSO. It also highlights all text excerpts from the abstracts that triggered the identification of a topic.

The last component of the user interface is the bottom menu, which provides several functionalities that allow editors to interact with the classification outcome and export the final result. The button *Select from last year* allows editors to select all topics and PMCs that were used in the previous classification. The buttons *Add Topics* and *Add PMCs* allow the manual insertion of a topic or a PMC. All the edits are recorded by STM 2 and will be considered when generating a new version of CSO. Finally, the button *Submit* sends all the selected topics and PMCs to the editorial system.

3 Evaluation

In this section we discuss the results of a user study on STM 2 and report an evaluation of the classifiers used by STM over the years.

3.1 User Study

We performed a qualitative study on STM 2 to assess the quality of its output, the clarity of the explanations, the impact on the editor workflows, and the usability of the user interface[5]. To this end, we organized individual sessions with nine SN editors from Heidelberg, São Paulo, and Beijing. They had on average 4.8 years of experience as editors, and three out of nine had at least 7 years of experience. All of them claimed to have wide knowledge of the research topics in their fields, and seven have a significant knowledge of Springer Nature Classification. Three of them considered themselves also experts at working with digital proceedings.

We demoed STM 2 showing the new functionalities for about 30 min and then asked them to use the application for classifying several proceedings in their fields of expertise for about 30 min. We took advantage of this session to gather further feedback about new potential use cases. After the hands-on session the editors filled a three-

[5] The data collected during this evaluation are available for download at http://doi.org/10.21954/ou.rd.7951496.

parts survey about their experience. The first part assessed the editor background and expertise, the second part included seven open questions, and the third part was a standard System Usability Scale (SUS)[6] questionnaire to assess the usability of the application. Here we summarize their answers to the open questions.

Q1. How do you find the interaction with the STM interface? Four editors considered it "easy" to use, one of them found it "user friendly", two other editors were positive about it. Two editors found some minor issues: the first suggested that the explanatory tooltips could be made more readable, whereas the second argued that he would prefer to load the proceedings by filling in the acronym and the year of a conference (e.g., ISWC 2018) rather than the volume number (e.g., LNCS 11136 and 11137).

Q2. How effectively did STM support you in classifying books/publications? All the editors stated that the application had an extremely positive effect on their work, commenting that it was "quite effective", "very good tool", "extremely helpful", "useful", and so on.

Q3. What were the most useful features of STM? The most useful features included: the ability to explore topics at different granularities (five editors), the ability to automatically extract the list of topics and the list of PMCs (four editors), and the possibility to see previous conference classifications (one editor).

Q4. What are the main weaknesses of STM? Editors did not flag any particular weakness. Two editors pointed out that the main weaknesses of the previous version had been fixed. One of them pointed out that weaknesses might appear when used extensively.

Q5. Can you think of any additional features to be included in STM? The suggested features were: (1) the ability to suggest the primary PMC in the proposal phase, when the title and abstract of the chapters are not yet available (three editors), (2) the ability of saving a classification as work-in-progress and resume it later (two editors), and (3) the ability to see the rank of PMCs of the previous year classification (two editors).

Q6. How comprehensive/accurate do you consider the list of topics returned by STM? Six editors found the list of topics very accurate and comprehensive. Three junior editors claimed that they were not yet confident in assessing the quality of the outcome by themselves and usually relied on senior editors for a final confirmation before submitting.

Q7. How comprehensive/accurate do you consider the list of PMCs returned by STM? The answers were very similar to those for Q6. As before, six editors found the list very accurate, while three junior editors admitted they preferred consulting with senior editors to verify the quality of the outcome.

The SUS questionnaire confirmed the good opinion of the editors, scoring 82.8/100, which is equivalent to an A grade and places STM 2 in the 93% percentile rank[7]. Considering that the 2016 version obtained 76.6/100, equivalent to a B grade,

[6] System Usability Scale (SUS) - https://www.usability.gov/how-to-and-tools/methods/system-usability-scale.html.

[7] Percentiles of SUS - https://measuringu.com/interpret-sus-score/.

this result confirms that the changes applied over the years, responding to the editors' feedback, successfully increased the usability of STM. All editors felt very confident in using STM (with an average score of 4.3 ± 0.5) and thought that STM was easy to use (4.4 ± 0.72). In addition, they were happy to use STM frequently (4.6 ± 0.5) and did not think that it was complex to use (1.6 ± 0.7) or that they would need the help of a technical person to use it in the future (1.8 ± 0.6).

3.2 Classifier Evaluation

As discussed in Sect. 2.1.1, STM has used three classifiers in its lifecycle: (1) the STM Classifier in 2016, (2) the CSO Classifier 1.0 in 2018, and (3) the CSO Classifier 2.0 since 2019. The STM classifier, described in [7], identifies the label of the topics in the text. The CSO Classifier 1.0, described in [10], selects topics having a Levenshtein similarity higher than a threshold with a set of n-grams extracted from the text. The CSO Classifier 2.0, described briefly in Sect. 2.3.2 and more extensively in [11], uses NLP and word embeddings to identify also topics that are not explicitly mentioned in the text.

We evaluated these three methods on a gold standard of 70 research papers[8], each of them annotated by three domain experts. Table 1 shows the results of the evaluation. The STM classifier yielded the best performance in term of precision (80.8%), but the worst in term of recall. The CSO Classifier 1.0 obtained a marginally lower precision, but a higher recall. Naturally, the good precision of these methods derives from the fact that they focus on topics that are explicitly mentioned in the text. The CSO Classifier 2.0 outperformed the other solutions in both recall (75.3%) and F-measure (74.1%). The loss in precision is not so important in the context of STM for two main reasons. First, when aggregating the results from multiple publications (in several cases more than 100 papers) errors tend to cancel each other. Secondly, the resulting topics are manually checked by the editors, who prefer receiving a more comprehensive set and filtering out some mistakes rather than missing some interesting (and possibly emerging) topics.

Table 1. Precision, recall, and F-measure of the classifiers. In bold the best results.

Classifier	Precision	Recall	F-measure
C1: STM 2016 (STM Classifier) [7]	**80.8%**	58.2%	67.6%
C2: STM 2018 (CSO Classifier 1.0) [10]	78.3%	63.8%	70.3%
C3: STM 2019 (CSO Classifier 2.0) [11]	73.0%	**75.3%**	**74.1%**

[8] The gold standard is described in [11] and available at https://cso.kmi.open.ac.uk/cso-classifier.

4 Uptake and Impact

STM was introduced in Springer Nature in 2016 and has since been used routinely by their Computer Science editorial team to annotate all book series covering conference proceedings in Computer Science, including LNCS, LNBIP, CCIS, IFIP-AICT and LNICST, for a total of about 2,400 volumes over the last three years.

The adoption of STM has brought three main benefits. First, it halved the time needed for classifying a proceedings book from 30 to 10–15 min, saving more than 600 working hours since its introduction. Second, it reduced the complexity of this task, which traditionally was performed only by Senior Editors with a vast experience in the relevant research fields. This in turn allowed to entrust the annotation of new volumes to junior editors and editorial assistants, distributing the workload in the editorial team, freeing up the time of the senior editors. As a result, the overall cost of the annotation process is now about 25% of what it was before the introduction of STM. Finally, the adoption of a robust vocabulary for describing the content of these volumes resulted in a significant increment of the discoverability of relevant publications on SpringerLink, Springer Nature digital library.

Figure 5 shows the average number of yearly downloads for different kinds of SN books published in a specific year. The top line refers to proceedings books in Computer Science before (blue) and after (red) the STM adoption, the intermediate line (grey) refers to the other books in Computer Science, and the yellow line to all the other books. The dotted blue segment branching off the top blue line after 2015 represents the number of downloads for the proceedings books which was to be expected without STM, estimated on the basis of the downloads of other books in Computer Science. The average number of yearly downloads for Computer Science proceedings in Springer Link has doubled since the introduction of STM, increasing from 10K to 20K downloads. This rate of growth compares very favourably with the significantly lower 47% average yearly increase for other book series in Computer Science, which in the same period went up from 7.7K to 11.3K, and with other book series that grew from 6.5K to 10.2K. Hence, considering the expected download in 2016–2018 as a baseline, we estimate that the adoption of STM has resulted in about 9.3 million additional downloads over the last three years. In details, the rate of growth for books annotated with STM increased significantly from 563 (95% Confidence Interval in the range of 106-1019)/year to 2,093 (95%CI 1308-2877)/year ($p < 0.05$, with the two 95%CIs not overlapping). The gap in the number of downloads between CS Proceedings and other books in CS had a significant boost from the adoption of STM, jumping from a yearly rate of 324 (95%CI 1-789)/year in the 2004–2015 interval, to 2,092 (95%CI 1308-2878)/year after 2015 ($p < 0.05$, with the two 95%CIs not overlapping). In conclusion, while it may not be technically possible to establish a direct causal link between the introduction of STM and the subsequent increase in the number of downloads, all these evidences suggests that STM had a significant positive effect on the number of downloads. This may also indicate that the users are more successful in locating valuable content when it has been annotated with STM.

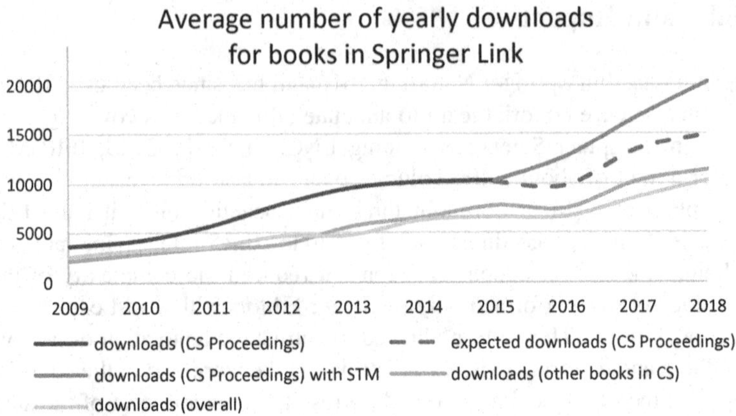

Fig. 5. Average number of yearly downloads for books published in a certain year. (Color figure online)

5 Related Work

In the last years the Semantic Web community produced a vast number of scholarly ontologies (e.g., SWRC[9], BIBO[10], BiDO[11], PROV-O[12], FABIO[13]) and bibliographic repositories in the Linked Data Cloud [17, 18] that can support the analysis of scholarly data. In particular, we saw the emergence of several approaches for linking textual entities to DBpedia, such as DBpedia Spotlight [19], Microsoft Entity Linking[14], BabelFly [20], Illinois Wikifier [21], KORE [22], AGDISTIS [23] and many others. Unfortunately, these systems could not be used for classifying research topics since DBpedia does not offer a particularly good representation of research topics. In particular, it does not contain some of the most recent or specific topics, and it does not structure them in a coherent taxonomy. For instance, the DBpedia entity "Deep Learning" does not currently have any relationship with "Machine Learning" or "Artificial Intelligence".

The task of annotating research papers according to their topics has traditionally been tackled either by using machine-learning classifiers, which assign to the text a number of pre-defined categories, topic models, such as LDA [24], or clustering methods [25, 26]. Here we will focus on the first category, which has the advantage of

[9] SWRC - http://ontoware.org/swrc/.

[10] BIBO - http://bibliontology.com.

[11] BiDO - http://purl.org/spar/bido.

[12] PROV-O - https://www.w3.org/TR/prov-o.

[13] FABIO - http://purl.org/spar/fabio.

[14] Microsoft Entity Linking - https://www.microsoft.com/cognitive-services/en-us/entity-linking-intelligence-service.

producing a clean set of formally defined research topics, and thus is usually preferred when it is possible to exploit a vocabulary or taxonomy topics, such as MeSH[15], PhySH[16], or CSO. For instance, Decker [27] introduces an unsupervised approach that generates paper-topic relationships by exploiting keywords and words extracted from the abstracts in order to analyse the trends of topics on different timescales. Mai et al. [28] describe an approach to subject classification which applies deep learning techniques on a training set of scientific papers annotated with the STW Thesaurus for Economics (~5K classes) and MeSH (~27K classes). Shen et al. [29] introduce a technique for concept-document tagging as one of the main components of Microsoft Academic Graph (MAG). Herrera et al. [30] present an approach to categorising the physics literature in terms of the codes from the Physics and Astronomy Classification Scheme (PACS), now replaced by PhySH. Ohniwa et al. [31] perform a similar analysis in the Biomedical domain using the Medical Subject Heading (MeSH). Semantic Scholar[17] is a relevant web application that uses machine language techniques to analyse publications and link them to a number of research areas[18].

Since the Computer Science Ontology is not yet routinely used by researchers, it was not possible to adopt supervised machine learning algorithms that would require a good number of examples for all the relevant categories. For this reason, we opted for an unsupervised solution that does not require such a gold standard.

6 Conclusions

In this paper we presented Smart Topic Miner, the tool adopted by Springer Nature editors for annotating all proceedings in Computer Science, and described its evolution over the years, the key lessons learnt, and the impact on the Springer Nature workflow. In particular, we showed how the integration of this ontology-based solution reduced drastically the time used to annotate proceedings and enhanced the discoverability of the relevant publications, resulting in more than 9 million additional downloads.

We plan to further improve STM and to work on different solutions for the automatic production of high-quality metadata describing the content of scientific publications. An important limitation of STM is that it uses exclusively CSO for representing the research topics, and therefore it can only classify publications in Computer Science. For this reason, we are now working on extending STM to consider multiple classification from different fields, starting from Engineering and Natural Sciences. We also intend to investigate methods for learning from the feedback of editors to increase the STM accuracy. Finally, we plan to develop a version of STM to be used by authors for classifying their own research papers when producing their camera ready. We believe that this solution could further improve the quality of the

[15] Medical Subject Headings - https://www.nlm.nih.gov/mesh/.

[16] Physics Subject Headings - https://physh.aps.org/.

[17] Semantic Scholar - www.semanticscholar.org.

[18] Topic extraction in Semantic Scholar - https://perma.cc/BP24-WTU7.

metadata and consequently foster the discoverability of the publications and the diffusion of the relevant scientific ideas.

References

1. Sinha, A., et al.: An overview of microsoft academic service (MAS) and applications. In: Proceedings of the 24th International Conference on World Wide Web - WWW 2015 Companion, pp. 243–246 (2015)
2. Osborne, F., Motta, E., Mulholland, P.: Exploring scholarly data with rexplore. In: Alani, H., et al. (eds.) ISWC 2013. LNCS, vol. 8218, pp. 460–477. Springer, Heidelberg (2013). https://doi.org/10.1007/978-3-642-41335-3_29
3. Osborne, F., Scavo, G., Motta, E.: Identifying diachronic topic-based research communities by clustering shared research trajectories. In: Presutti, V., d'Amato, C., Gandon, F., d'Aquin, M., Staab, S., Tordai, A. (eds.) ESWC 2014. LNCS, vol. 8465, pp. 114–129. Springer, Cham (2014). https://doi.org/10.1007/978-3-319-07443-6_9
4. Sateli, B., Witte, R.: Semantic representation of scientific literature: bringing claims, contributions and named entities onto the Linked Open Data cloud. PeerJ Comput. Sci. **1**, e37 (2015)
5. Khadka, A., Knoth, P.: Using citation-context to reduce topic drifting on pure citation-based recommendation. In: Proceedings of the 12th ACM Conference on Recommender Systems - RecSys 2018, pp. 362–366. ACM Press, New York (2018)
6. Salatino, A.A., Osborne, F., Motta, E.: AUGUR: forecasting the emergence of new research topics. In: Joint Conference on Digital Libraries 2018, Fort Worth, Texas, pp. 1–10 (2018)
7. Osborne, F., Salatino, A., Birukou, A., Motta, E.: Automatic classification of springer nature proceedings with smart topic miner. In: Groth, P., et al. (eds.) ISWC 2016. LNCS, vol. 9982, pp. 383–399. Springer, Cham (2016). https://doi.org/10.1007/978-3-319-46547-0_33
8. Salatino, A.A., Thanapalasingam, T., Mannocci, A., Osborne, F., Motta, E.: The computer science ontology: a large-scale taxonomy of research areas. In: Vrandečić, D., et al. (eds.) ISWC 2018. LNCS, vol. 11137, pp. 187–205. Springer, Cham (2018). https://doi.org/10.1007/978-3-030-00668-6_12
9. Thanapalasingam, T., Osborne, F., Birukou, A., Motta, E.: Ontology-based recommendation of editorial products. In: Vrandečić, D., et al. (eds.) ISWC 2018. LNCS, vol. 11137, pp. 341–358. Springer, Cham (2018). https://doi.org/10.1007/978-3-030-00668-6_21
10. Salatino, A.A., Thanapalasingam, T., Mannocci, A., Osborne, F., Motta, E.: Classifying research papers with the computer science ontology. In: International Semantic Web Conference (P&D/Industry/BlueSky). CEUR Workshop Proceedings, vol. 2180 (2018)
11. Salatino, A.A., Osborne, F., Thanapalasingam, T., Motta, E.: The CSO classifier: ontology-driven detection of research topics in scholarly articles. In: TPDL 2019: 23rd International Conference on Theory and Practice of Digital Libraries (2019)
12. Osborne, F., Motta, E.: Klink-2: integrating multiple web sources to generate semantic topic networks. In: Arenas, M., et al. (eds.) ISWC 2015. LNCS, vol. 9366, pp. 408–424. Springer, Cham (2015). https://doi.org/10.1007/978-3-319-25007-6_24
13. Osborne, F., Motta, E.: Pragmatic ontology evolution: reconciling user requirements and application performance. In: Vrandečić, D., et al. (eds.) ISWC 2018. LNCS, vol. 11136, pp. 495–512. Springer, Cham (2018). https://doi.org/10.1007/978-3-030-00671-6_29
14. Bryl, V., Birukou, A., Eckert, K., Kessler, M.: What is in the proceedings? Combining publisher's and researcher's perspectives. In: SePublica 2014. Semantic Publishing, Anissaras (2014)

15. Mikolov, T., Chen, K., Corrado, G., Dean, J.: Distributed representations of words and phrases and their compositionality. In: Advances in Neural Information Processing Systems, pp. 3111–3119 (2013)
16. Satopää, V., Albrecht, J., Irwin, D., Raghavan, B.: Finding a "Kneedle" in a haystack: detecting knee points in system behavior. In: ICDCSW 2011 Proceedings of the 2011 31st International Conference on Distributed Computing Systems, pp. 166–171. IEEE Computer Society, Washington (2011)
17. Peroni, S., Dutton, A., Gray, T., Shotton, D.: Setting our bibliographic references free: towards open citation data. J. Doc. **71**, 253–277 (2015)
18. Nuzzolese, A.G., Gentile, A.L., Presutti, V., Gangemi, A.: Conference linked data: the scholarlydata project. In: Groth, P., et al. (eds.) ISWC 2016. LNCS, vol. 9982, pp. 150–158. Springer, Cham (2016). https://doi.org/10.1007/978-3-319-46547-0_16
19. Mendes, P.N., Jakob, M., García-Silva, A., Bizer, C.: DBpedia spotlight: shedding light on the web of documents. In: Proceedings of the 7th International Conference on Semantic Systems - I-Semantics 2011, pp. 1–8. ACM Press, New York (2011)
20. Moro, A., Raganato, A., Navigli, R.: Entity linking meets word sense disambiguation: a unified approach. Trans. Assoc. Comput. Linguist. **2**, 231–244 (2014)
21. Cheng, X., Roth, D.: Relational inference for wikification. In: Proceedings of the 2013 Conference on Empirical Methods in Natural Language Processing, pp. 1787–1796. Association for Computational Linguistics (ACL) (2013)
22. Hoffart, J., Seufert, S., Nguyen, D.B., Theobald, M., Weikum, G.: KORE: keyphrase overlap relatedness for entity disambiguation (2012)
23. Usbeck, R., et al.: AGDISTIS - graph-based disambiguation of named entities using linked data. In: Mika, P., et al. (eds.) ISWC 2014. LNCS, vol. 8796, pp. 457–471. Springer, Cham (2014). https://doi.org/10.1007/978-3-319-11964-9_29
24. Blei, D.M., Ng, A.Y., Jordan, M.I.: Latent Dirichlet allocation. J. Mach. Learn. Res. **3**, 993–1022 (2003)
25. Duvvuru, A., Radhakrishnan, S., More, D., Kamarthi, S.: Analyzing structural & temporal characteristics of keyword system in academic research articles. Procedia-Procedia Comput. Sci. **20**, 439–445 (2013)
26. Wu, J., Choudhury, S.R., Chiatti, A., Liang, C., Giles, C.L.: HESDK: a hybrid approach to extracting scientific domain knowledge entities. In: 2017 ACM/IEEE Joint Conference on Digital Libraries (JCDL), pp. 1–4. IEEE (2017)
27. Decker, S.L., Aleman-Meza, B., Cameron, D., Arpinar, I.B.: Detection of bursty and emerging trends towards identification of researchers at the early stage of trends (2007)
28. Mai, F., Galke, L., Scherp, A.: Using deep learning for title-based semantic subject indexing to reach competitive performance to full-text. In: JCDL 2018 Proceedings of the 18th ACM/IEEE on Joint Conference on Digital Libraries, Fort Worth, Texas, USA, pp. 169–178. ACM, New York (2018)
29. Shen, Z., Ma, H., Wang, K.: A web-scale system for scientific knowledge exploration. In: Proceedings of ACL 2018, System Demonstrations, pp. 87–92. Association for Computational Linguistics, Melbourne (2018)
30. Herrera, M., Roberts, D.C., Gulbahce, N.: Mapping the evolution of scientific fields. PLoS ONE **5**, 3–8 (2010)
31. Ohniwa, R.L., Hibino, A., Takeyasu, K.: Trends in research foci in life science fields over the last 30 years monitored by emerging topics. Scientometrics **85**, 111–127 (2010)

A Pay-as-you-go Methodology to Design and Build Enterprise Knowledge Graphs from Relational Databases

Juan F. Sequeda(✉), Willard J. Briggs(✉), Daniel P. Miranker(✉), and Wayne P. Heideman(✉)

Capsenta Inc., Austin, TX, USA
{juan,will,miranker,wayne}@capsenta.com

Abstract. Business users must answer business questions quickly to address Business Intelligence (BI) needs. The bottleneck is to understand the complex databases schemas. Only few people in the IT department truly understand them. A holy grail is to empower business users to ask and answer their own questions with minimal IT support. Semantic technologies, now dubbed as Knowledge Graphs, become useful here. Even though the research and industry community has provided evidence that semantic technologies works in the real world, our experience is that there continues to be a major challenge: the engineering of ontologies and mappings covering enterprise databases containing thousands of tables with tens of thousands of attributes. In this paper, we present a novel and unique pay-as-you-go methodology that addresses the aforementioned difficulties. We provide a case study with a large scale e-commerce company where Capsenta's Ultrawrap has been deployed in production for over 3 years.

1 Introduction

Business users must answer critical business questions, optimize business decisions and deliver the answers as accurately and quickly as possible. The frequent bottleneck to delivering answers is the lack of understanding by business users of their large and complex enterprise databases. The handful of IT experts that fully understand the abstruse and inscrutable database schemas are not always available. Business users interfacing with both the IT staff and the database systems can entail communication problems due to lack of agreed terminology. The ultimate goal is to empower business users to achieve Self Service Analytics (SSA), which Gartner defines as "*a form of business intelligence (BI) in which line-of-business professionals are enabled and encouraged to perform queries and generate reports on their own, with nominal IT support.*"[1] Gartner predicts that

[1] https://www.gartner.com/it-glossary/self-service-analytics/.

At the time of submission, Capsenta was an independent company. It was acquired by data.world in mid 2019.

C. Ghidini et al. (Eds.): ISWC 2019, LNCS 11779, pp. 526–545, 2019.
https://doi.org/10.1007/978-3-030-30796-7_32

this year, 2019, the analytics generated by business users through SSA capabilities will exceed the analytics produced by professional data scientists[2].

Gartner crisply states that '*Self-service analytics is often characterized by [...] an underlying data model that has been simplified or scaled down for ease of understanding and straightforward data access.*' It should be evident to the reader (coming from the semantic web community) that semantic web technology, dubbed now as Knowledge Graphs, deliver precisely this value. Informally, we define a **Knowledge Graph** *as the result of data integration based on graphs where concepts and relationships are first class citizens and the data comes from inter-linking heterogeneous sources of data*[3]. Furthermore, we consider Ontology-Based Database Access (OBDA) [10] as a mechanism to implement Knowledge Graphs[4]. OBDA involve the development of an ontology as a formal conceptual model of a domain which uses the lingua franca of the business users and declarative mappings between select contents of the enterprise's databases and the ontology. The declarative mappings allow comfortable communication between business users and IT developers. Finally, business questions can be defined in terms of the ontology's logical abstraction instead of the individual heterogeneous source databases' physical structures. OBDA systems can support physical or virtual access to the data. Capsenta deploys Ultrawrap [11,14] as an OBDA system to deliver business-friendly data in the form of a Knowledge Graph over the inscrutable and heterogeneous databases. The resulting data is used by business users to achieve Self-Service Analytics.

The Semantic Web community continues to constantly provide evidence that semantic technology works in the real world (e.g. In-Use and Industry papers at ISWC, ESWC, Knowledge Graph Conferences[5]; renowned enterprises such as Google, Oracle, etc.; startups like Capsenta and data.world; European Projects such as Optique [7], etc.). Despite these successes, leading experts in semantic web, from both academia and industry, agree that the technology is still hard to deploy[6] because "systems are built such that they require PhD-type users to maintain"[7]. Given our experience of designing and building Knowledge Graphs with large scale customers in the e-commerce, oil and gas, and pharmaceutical domain since 2015, we agree! It is paramount that we devise ways to lower the barrier to entry in order to see the usage of semantic technology accelerate in industry.

[2] https://www.gartner.com/newsroom/id/3848671.

[3] It is important to acknowledge that the term "Knowledge Graph" was coined in a marketing blogpost by Google in 2012. Nevertheless, this term encompasses the work of the Semantic Web community from the early 2000s, which builds on the research combining Logic and Data that can be traced to the 1970s. See http://knowledgegraph.today for more details.

[4] Which nowadays is being called Virtual Knowledge Graphs.

[5] https://www.eventbrite.com/e/2019-knowledge-graph-conference-tickets-54867900367.

[6] https://lists.w3.org/Archives/Public/semantic-web/2018Nov/0036.html.

[7] http://www.juansequeda.com/blog/2019/03/22/2nd-u-s-semantic-technologies-symposium-2019-trip-report/, https://www.open-bio.org/2019/04/06/us2ts/.

In this paper, we argue that ontology engineering methodologies need to be extended to support Relational Database to RDF Graph (RDB2RDF) mapping engineering (Sect. 2). ***Our main contribution is an iterative pay-as-you-go methodology, that builds on existing ontology engineering methodologies and combines the engineering of Relational Database to RDF Graph (RDB2RDF) mappings. To the best of our knowledge, this is the first methodology that combines ontology and Relational Database to RDF Graph (RDB2RDF) mapping engineering*** (Sect. 3). It is important to note that this work can be applied in a straightforward manner to schema and mapping engineering for Property Graphs.

We define success if a business question is answered. The methodology is a means to success (i.e. answering business questions). Every time there is an iteration, it's because (1) an existing set of business questions have been answered successfully and (2) there are a new set of business questions to be answered. Therefore every iteration is an indication that more business questions are being answered, hence success has been achieved. Success is achieved without "*boiling the ocean*".

This paper provides a case study and a real world example with a large scale e-commerce company as evidence of how our pay-as-you-go methodology is successfully used to engineer an ontology and mappings which drives data for Self Service Analytics. This solution has been in production for the past 3 years (Sect. 4). We conclude with lessons learned and future work that we believe can inspire scientific research (Sect. 5).

2 Challenges

Per our real-world experience, the main challenges that must be overcome to design and build Knowledge Graphs from relational databases are **(C1)** Ontology Engineering: designing the ontology that models the domain experts's view of the world and **(C2)** Relational Database to RDF Graph (RDB2RDF) Mapping Engineering: defining mappings from the complex relational database schemas to the ontology. This is probably not surprising to a semantic web reader. However, what has been surprising to us is the ease of how one can fall into a "boiling the ocean" state when trying to combine these two tasks. This is evident when dealing with complex real-world enterprise relational database schemas.

(C1): Ontology Engineering. Engineering ontologies is difficult in and of itself. The field of Ontology Engineering was prolific throughout the 90s. Early seminal work by Fox, Gruninger, King and Uschold pioneered the field of ontology engineering [3,15,16], followed by a multitude of methodologies, notably METHONTOLOGY [2]. Research in this field continues to progress by focusing on the sophisticated use of competency questions [1,8], test-driven development [6], ontology design patterns [4], reuse [9], etc. to name a few. Furthermore, numerous ontologies have been designed so that they can be reused, such as Good Relations for e-commerce, FIBO for finance, Schema.org, and so on.

It seems to be a fair conjecture that C1 should actually not be challenge. This would be the case if the ultimate deliverable is just an ontology in isolation. However, populating an ontology with instances coming from a relational database, seems to be an afterthought and not a key component of existing ontology engineering methodologies. In the context of designing a Knowledge Graph from relational databases, both the ontology and the RDB2RDF mappings must be first-class citizens.

(C2): RDB2RDF Mapping Engineering. Let's assume that an ontology has been created via an established methodology. The next step is to map relational databases to the ontology in order to generate the graph data. A common theoretical practice is to bootstraps with the automatic direct mapping that generates a so-called *putative ontology* from the database schema [13]. This practice suggests approaching the problem as an ontology-matching problem between the putative ontology and the target ontology. In theory, this can work [5].

However, per our real-world experience, this has not yet (and may never) become practicable in the real-world for the following reasons: (1) Commonly, enterprise relational database schema are very large, consisting of thousands of tables and tens of thousands of attributes (Oracle EBS has +20,000 tables!). Schema developers notoriously use peculiar abbreviations which are meaningless. Commercial systems make frequent use of numbered columns with no explicit semantics (e.g. segment1, segment2, etc.). (2) Simple one-to-one correspondence between table-classes and columns-properties are rare. In all of our commercial deployments, complex mappings dominate: mappings with calculations, business logic that simultaneously considering database values. For example, the mapping to the target property *net sales* of a class *Order* is defined as gross sales minus taxes and discounts given. Tax rates can be different depending on location. Discounts can depend on the type of customer. A business user needs to provide these definitions beforehand. Thus, without clairvoyance, automating mapping is often simply not plausible. (3) It is not plausible that we will ever have copious amounts of schema to successfully train machine learning algorithms.

Early on in our practice we observed that ontologies and mappings must be developed holistically. That is, there is a continual back-and-forth between ontology and mapping engineering. Thus, ontology engineering methodologies must be extended to support RDB2RDF mapping engineering.

3 The Pay-as-you-go Methodology

Our proposed Pay-as-you-go Methodology address the two aforementioned challenges by combining ontology and RDB2RDF mapping engineering. At the center of the methodology are a set of prioritized business questions that need to be answered. The business questions serve as competency questions and as a success metric.

In the initial knowledge capture phase, the first business question is analyzed, understood, modeled into a minimal viable ontology, and mapped to a database. In the following knowledge implementation phase, the ontology and mappings are implemented in OWL and R2RML respectively. The resulting data can be (virtually or physically) accessed, validated and imported into one or more BI tools. In the final self service analytics phase the BI dashboards are used to answer the initial business questions. Once this initial iteration has occurred, the next business question is analyzed. If the next question can be answered with the current ontology and mappings, then we are done. Otherwise, the ontology is extended incrementally with its corresponding mappings. With this approach, the ontology and mappings are developed simultaneously in an agile and iterative manner: hence, pay-as-you-go.

The ontology expressivity we focus on is owl:Class, owl:DatatypeProperty (with domain and range), owl:ObjectProperty (with domain and range) and rdfs:subClassOf, thus RDFS without subproperties. We have found out that this expressivity is sufficient to address the BI needs for our customers. Furthermore, we have identified that the following terminology is well received: Concept rather than Class. Attribute replaces Data Property. Relationship is used in place of Object Property. We colloquially refer to Concepts, Attributes and Relationships as CARs.

This methodology was developed and refined over a number of customers, throughout the last 4 years. Furthermore, it builds upon the extensive work in ontology engineering over the past two decades. For example, common steps across all methodologies is to identify a purpose, define competency questions and formalize the terminology in an ontology language. Specifically, we are inspired and extend the notion of Intermediate Representations (IRs) from METHONTOLOGY [2].

We identify three actors involved throughout the process: **(1) Business Users** are subject matter experts who can identify the list of prioritized business questions, understand the business rules associated with the data and validate the integrity of the created data. **(2) IT Developers** understand database schemas, including how the data are interconnected. **(3) Knowledge Scientist**[8] serve as the communication bridge between Business Users and IT Developers.

The methodology is organized in three phases, with different expectations from each actor throughout the process: **(Phase 1) Knowledge Capture:** the Knowledge Scientist works with the Business User to understand the business questions, define an "whiteboard" version of the ontology and work with the IT Developer to determine which data is needed. This is documented in a knowledge report. **(Phase 2) Knowledge Implementation:** the Knowledge Scientist can now implement the ontology, mappings and queries based on the content from the knowledge report. **(Phase 3) Self-Service Analytics:** the Business User is now exposed to the data in a simplified and easy to understand view enabling straightforward data access with common BI tools. They can now create reports and dashboards to provide answers to new and existing business questions without having to further interface with IT.

[8] Traditionally, this role has been called Knowledge Engineer. We decided to call it Knowledge Scientist so it can be on-par with the title of the "Data Scientist".

Table 1. Knowledge report: concepts

Concept Name	The agreed name for the concept
Concept Definition	The agreed definition for the Concept
Concept ID	The ID that will uniquely identify the Concept and will from a URI
Unique ID of a Concept	The attribute from the Table Name/SQL query that uniquely identifies each instance of the Concept
Table Name or SQL Query	The Table Name or SQL query logic that represents the Concept

Phase 1: Knowledge Capture. The knowledge capture phase must accomplish two objectives: (1) Users must understand and clarify the business questions, and (2) Users must identify the data necessary to answer those business questions.

Step 1: Analyze Processes: The goal is to analyze and formalize existing processes because many these processes may have never been written down before. When a business question needs to be answered, we first need to understand the larger context: *what is the business problem that needs to be addressed? Is it currently being addressed, and if so, how?* Answering the following questions help achieve this goal:

What: What are the business questions? What is the business problem?
Why: Why do we need to answer these questions? What is the motivation?
Who: Who produces the data? Who will consume the data? Who is involved?
How: How is this the business question answered today, if at all?
Where: Where are the data sources required to answer the business questions?
When: When will the data be consumed? Real-time? Daily? Update criteria?

Step 2: Collect Documentation: In this step, the Knowledge Scientist focuses on the answers to the ***How*** and ***Where*** questions from the previous step. They identify documentation about the data sources and any SQL queries, spreadsheets, or scripts being used to answer the business questions today. They may also interview stakeholders to understand their current workflow.

Step 3: Develop Knowledge Report: The Knowledge Scientist analyzes what was learned in steps 1 and 2 and starts working with the Business User to understand the business questions, recognize key concepts and relationships from the business questions, identify the business terminology such as preferred labels, alternative labels, and natural language definitions for the concepts and relationships. At this stage, it is common to encounter disagreements. Different people use the same word to mean different concepts or different words are used to mean the same concept. The conversation is very focused on the business

Table 2. Knowledge report: attribute

Attribute Name	The agreed name for the Attribute
Attribute Definition	The agreed definition for the Attribute
Attribute ID	The ID that will uniquely identify the Attribute and will from a URI
Applied to Concept	The Concept for which this attribute is associated to.
Unique ID of a Concept	The attribute from the Table Name/SQL query that uniquely identifies each instance of the Concept
Table Name or SQL Query	The Table Name or SQL query logic that represents the Concept
Datatype	The expected datatype of the Attribute
Is NULL possible?	Can there be NULL values in the column name? Yes or No
If NULL?	If the column can have NULLs, then what is the default value ("NULL", "N/A", 0, etc.)

questions which helps drive to a consensus. Subsequently, the Knowledge Scientist works with the IT developer to identify which tables and attributes in the database contains data related to the concepts and relationships identified from the business questions. The conversation with IT is also focused.

Table 3. Knowledge report: relationships

Relationship Name	The agreed name for the Relationship
Relationship Definition	The agreed definition for the Relationship
Relationship ID	The ID that will uniquely identify the Relationship and will from a URI
From Concept	What Concept does this relationship come from (the domain)
Unique ID of From Concept	The attribute from the Table Name/SQL query that uniquely identifies the From Concept
Table Name or SQL Query	The Table Name or SQL query logic that returns the data for the Relationship. This query usually returns a pair of attributes which includes the IDs of the From and To Concept
To Concept	To what Concept does this relationship connect to (the range)
Unique ID of To Concept	The attribute from the Table Name/SQL query that uniquely identifies the To Concept

Table 4. Correspondence between knowledge report and OWL constructs

Knowledge Report	OWL Ontology
Concept	owl:Class
Concept Name	rdfs:label of the Class
Concept Definition	rdfs:comment of the Class
Concept ID	used to create the URI of the Class
Attribute	owl:DatatypeProperty
Attribute Name	rdfs:label of the Datatype Property
Attribute Definition	rdfs:comment of the Datatype Property
Attribute ID	used to create the URI of the Datatype Property
Applied to Concept	rdfs:domain of the Datatype Property
Datatype	rdfs:range of the Datatype Property
Relationship	owl:ObjectProperty
Relationship Name	rdfs:label of the Object Property
Relationship Definition	rdfs:comment of the Object Property
Relationship ID	used to create the URI of the Object Property
From Concept	rdfs:domain of the Object Property
To Concept	rdfs:range of the Object Property

An outcome of this step is a high-level view of the ontology– a whiteboard illustration. The final deliverable is a knowledge report which can be conveniently represented as a spreadsheet consisting of multiple tabs detailing the CARs (Concepts, Attributes and Relationships), with the corresponding SQL logic which serve as the mapping to the relational database. Subsequently there is a tab for each Extract, which is a definition of the tabular result that a Business User would like to have access. Each row in an Extract tab should list all the Attributes that will appear in the extract. The template for the knowledge report is shown in Tables 1, 2 and 3.

The diligent reader will notice that our notion of Knowledge Reports mimics the Intermediate Representations (IRs) from METHONTOLOGY. In the METHONTOLOGY conceptualization phase, the informal view of a domain is represented in a semi-formal specification using IRs which can be represented in a tabular or graph representation. The IRs can be understood by both the Domain Experts and the Knowledge Scientist, therefore bridging the gap between the business users informal understanding of the domain and the formal ontology language used to represent the domain. The Knowledge Scientist will report back to the Business User and IT developer and explain, using the knowledge report, how the business concepts are related and how they are connected to the data. If all parties are in agreement, then we can proceed to the next phases. Otherwise, the discrepancies must be resolved. These can be identified quickly due to the granularity of the knowledge report.

Table 5. Correspondence between knowledge report and R2RML constructs

Knowledge Report	R2RML Mapping
Concept: Concept ID	mapping to URI of the class in rr:Class
Concept: Unique ID of a Concept	rr:template
Concept: Table Name or SQL Query	rr:logicalTable
Attribute: Attribute ID	mapping to URI of the class in rr:predicate
Attribute: Unique ID of a Concept	rr:template
Attribute: Table Name or SQL Query	rr:logicalTable
Attribute: Column Name	rr:column
Relationship: Relationship ID	mapping to URI of the class in rr:predicate
Relationship: Unique ID of From Concept	rr:template
Relationship: Table Name or SQL Query	rr:logicalTable
Relationship: To Concept	rr:joinCondition

Phase 2: Knowledge Implementation. A key insight of METHONTOLOGY's Intermediate Representations, is that they ease the transformation into a formal ontology language. We build upon this insight. That is why the goal of the knowledge implementation phase is to formalize the content of the knowledge report into an OWL ontology, R2RML mappings, SPARQL queries and subsequently validate the data. As noted below, the different elements of the Knowledge Report has its correspondences to OWL and R2RML.

Step 4: Create/Extend Ontology: Based on the knowledge report, the Knowledge Scientist can create the ontology or extend an existing ontology. Table 4 details the correspondence between the elements of the knowledge report and constructs of OWL in order to create an OWL ontology using any ontology editor.

Step 5: Implement Mapping: Similar to the previous step, the Knowledge Scientist can create the R2RML mappings from the knowledge report. Table 5 details the correspondence between the elements of the knowledge report and constructs of R2RML in order to create an R2RML mapping.

Step 6: Extract Queries: Recall that an Extract is the definition of the tabular result that a Business User would like to access. A SPARQL SELECT query is the implementation of the Extract. The SPARQL query is executed in an OBDA system, such as Ultrawrap, using the R2RML mapping from the previous step.

Step 7: Validate Data: The final step is to validate the extracted data, resulting from the SPARQL query in the previous step. This data should also be validated by the business users. Suggested validation techniques are the following: sharing sample data to business users in a spreadsheet, creating sample visualizations in a BI tool, comparing the number of results in the extract with the source database to ensure they are the same, and checking the validity of NULL values.

After successful data validation with the business users, the data can begin to be used for Self-Service Analytics in the next phase. Otherwise, the root cause of the error must be found. This commonly in either in the SPARQL query or an R2RML mapping.

Phase 3: Self Service Analytics

Step 8: Build Report: A key component of Self-Service Analytics is for business users to use BI tools over a simplified view of the data. The ontology enables the simplified view but at the end, it is the tabular extract that the business user wants to access. Through our experience, the primary ways of BI tools access the extract are through uploads of csv files, special connectors developed for SPARQL or caching/materializing the result of a SPARQL query in a relational database. Once the extract(s) is available in the BI tool, the business user is enabled to build their business intelligence report.

Step 9: Answer Question: The BI report should answer the original business question (the **What** in Step 1). This report is shared with the stakeholders who asked the original business question (the **Who** in Step 1). If they accept the BI report as an answer to their question, then this is ready to move to production.

Step 10: Move to production: Once the decision has been made to move to production, we need to determine how the BI tools are going to access the extracts. If it is going to be through a SPARQL connector then it can be done live via the SPARQL endpoint. If the data is going to be accessed through a cache, the refresh schedule must be determined. Common refresh schedules are daily, weekly, monthly or on demand. Additionally, the time window of the extract needs to be determined. Is the cache going to update the entire extract, or is only yesterday's data going to be pushed to the cache? or last weeks? These questions must be answered before wide release.

4 An E-Commerce Case Study

Background: This case study is based on a Capsenta customer which is an e-commerce company selling health and beauty products in about a dozen countries. As in any large enterprise, BI is a key driver to help make critical business decisions. The customer had invested large amounts of time and money in an enterprise data warehouse (EDW) that integrated data coming from several of their multiple heterogeneous databases. The business users were skeptical of BI reports coming from the existing EDW. When comparing results between the EDW and those coming directly from the original source databases, the results were effectively different. Due to the lack of trust in the EDW's data, the business users decided to move off the EDW and start building BI reports by pulling data from the original source databases.

Challenge: To answer the business questions, the business users needed to create reports which required data from multiple, disparate, mostly inscrutable

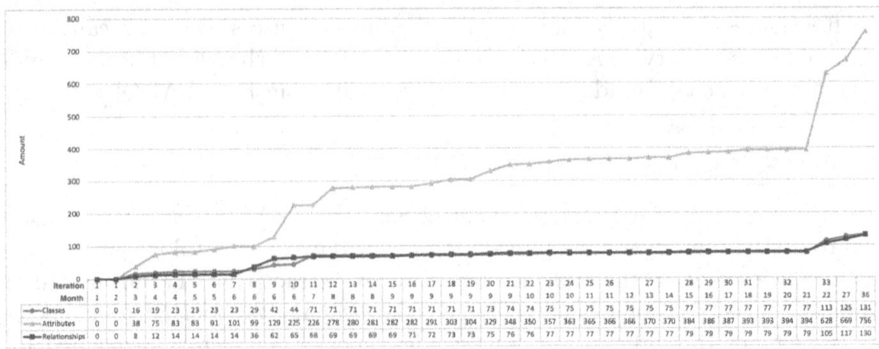

Iteration	1	1	2	3	4	5	6	7	8	9	10	11	12	13	14	15	16	17	18	19
Month	1	2	3	4	4	5	5	6	6	6	6	7	8	8	8	9	9	9	9	9
Classes	0	0	16	19	23	23	23	23	29	42	44	71	71	71	71	71	71	71	71	71
Attributes	0	0	38	75	83	83	91	101	99	129	225	226	278	280	281	282	282	291	303	304
Relationships	0	0	8	12	14	14	14	14	36	62	65	68	69	69	69	69	71	72	73	73

Iteration	20	21	22	23	24	25	26		27		28	29	30	31		32		33		
Month	9	9	10	10	10	11	11	12	13	14	15	16	17	18	19	20	21	22	27	36
Classes	73	74	74	75	75	75	75	75	75	75	77	77	77	77	77	77	77	113	125	131
Attributes	329	348	350	357	363	365	366	366	370	370	384	386	387	393	393	394	394	628	669	756
Relationships	75	76	76	77	77	77	77	77	77	77	79	79	79	79	79	79	79	105	117	130

Fig. 1. Analysis of iterations by month

relational database schemas. Business users would request data from IT and in return they would receive the results, typically, in a csv file. A small number of business users had sufficient SQL knowledge to extend SQL queries that were given to them from IT. However, given the complexity of the source relational schemas, these business users still needed to request help from IT. There was friction between the business users and IT due to lack of agreement on terminology and frequently the business users would not get the data they expected. Thus, IT was considered a bottleneck in delivering answers to business questions. When data coming from different databases needed to be combined, it would be ad-hoc merged locally either in Excel or in a MS Access database. Even though the business users had direct access to the multiple databases, which gave a feeling of ownership and control, the results were inconsistent and, hence, not trusted. When C-Level executives would ask business questions, multiple diverging answers were being provided because the business logic used to deliver the BI reports were severally and inconsistently implemented. Suffice it to say that the process of generating BI reports was ad-hoc, error-prone, time consuming and unscalable.

Furthermore, the company was in the process of bringing on board Tableau as a new, corporate-wide BI solution and IT executives feared that the current ad-hoc process could be detrimental to the implementation of Tableau and potentially it could suffer the same fate as the EDW.

Solution: The customer needed a consistent, understandable and trusted data view across the multiple relational databases such that BI tools (e.g., Tableau) could consume the data and a large number of business users could generate reports all using the same trusted data. Furthermore, the customer required an agile approach in order to start showing value quickly. Unsatisfied with the status quo of large scale enterprise data warehouse projects and not wanting to go down the same route again, the customer started looking into semantic technology.

The solution was to create an enterprise ontology which would then be mapped to the different relational databases. The OWL enterprise ontology would serve as the business user's common view and lingua franca. The R2RML mappings would ground the meaning of the business conceptualizations with data, thus serving as a means of communication between business and IT users. The business questions, represented in SPARQL queries, would be in the user-friendly terms of the enterprise ontology. Capsenta's Ultrawrap product family would be the OBDA platform that would tie together the ontology, mappings and queries. The results of SPARQL queries would feed different BI tools. The pay-as-you-go methodology was required in order to provide an agile development process which could quickly show the C-level executives that this wasn't going to be another multi-month, million dollar failure (i.e., their last EDW).

Results: In order to show the effectiveness of the technology and kick off the first iteration of the methodology, the goal was to replicate the most trusted BI report: the daily sales report that all C-level executives viewed every morning. There were three Business Users, two IT users and one Knowledge Scientist involved.

The daily sales report was being generated by one SQL query that a business user would execute every morning. The size of SQL query, in text, was 21 KB. Needless to say, this was a large SQL query. During the Knowledge Capture phase, we learned that the business user's SQL query was an extension of another SQL query created initially by an IT user. We observed multiple discrepancies between the Business and the IT user's SQL queries. The Knowledge Capture phase revealed that the daily sales report encompassed 16 concepts, 38 attributes and 8 relationships. Per the methodology, each CAR has a corresponding mapping. The customer was surprised to see how much knowledge was "hidden" within just one report.

Figure 1 depicts how the CARs evolved over 36 months and 33 iterations. Capsenta worked directly with the customer for the first 22 months. Afterwards, the customer took full control of the project, therefore we did not track all the iterations after month 22. The customer continues to deploy Ultrawrap and apply this methodology today. The following phases occurred.

(1) Rapid Growth Phase (Month 1–7): The first iteration took 2 months due to an initial ramp up of the project. The following 10 iterations took 5 months (approx one iteration every 2 weeks). During this phase, the ontology and mappings grew quickly because we were understanding the most important business concepts and how they were interrelated. The focus was to understand a proprietary order management system which consisted of three databases.

(2) Consistent Growth Phase (Month 8–22): 21 iterations occurred within the following 14 months (approx one iteration every 2.5 weeks too). The growth in the stage was consistent because, the focus was on adding attributes instead of concepts and relationships. The relational database underlying Oracle E-business Suite was integrated.

(3) Independent Growth Phase (Month 23–present): The customer was able to independently follow the methodology and continue to grow the ontology and mappings. As previously mentioned, we do no have data about the iterations during this time. Three additional relational databases were integrated: event management system, shipping database and a miscellaneous database that hosts spreadsheets.

Further analysis can be made from this data: **(A)** Concepts and relationships increased at the same rate because every time a concept is added, it is connected to another concept, hence a relationship is also added. On average, 2.2 concepts and relationships were added per iteration while the median is 0. The max number of concepts and relationships added in an iteration was 27 while the min was 0. **(B)** Attributes grew the most because this is where the actual data values from the source databases is coming from. On average, 11.2 attributes were added per iteration while the median is 2. The max number of attributes added in an iteration was 96 while the min was -2 (two attributes were eliminated). **(C)** The busiest month was Month 9 which had 7 iterations (an iteration every couple of days) focused on incrementing attributes. 66 new attributes were added. **(D)** Months 12, 14, 19 and 21 did not have any iterations because there was no new requests from business users, employees were on vacation, etc.

In every iteration, at minimum there was at least one Business User, Knowledge Scientist and IT user. At peak, there were three Business Users, three Knowledge Scientist and two IT users.

Before the start of this project (over 3 years ago), there were only a handful of BI developers. Today there are +20 active BI developers creating reports in Tableau. +100 business users are consuming these reports every day. Due to confidential reasons, we cannot provide details about the business questions that are being answered.

To further exemplify how the Pay-as-you-go Methodology is applied, we provide a real-world in-use example from the case study.

Round 1: Orders

Phase 1: Knowledge Capture. We start by asking the questions in Step 1 above, and fill in the appropriate answers:

What: How many orders were placed in a given time period per their status?
Why: Depending on whom is asked, different answers can be provided. Unaware of the source of the problem, the executives are vexed by inconsistencies across established business reports.
Who: The Finance department, specifically the CFO
How: A business analyst asks the IT developer for this information every morning.
Where: There is a proprietary Order Management System and Oracle E-Business Suites.
When: Every morning they want to know this number

The Knowledge Scientist gathers access to the database systems for the Order Management System and the Accounting System and learns that the Order Management System was built on an open-source shopping cart system and has been heavily customized. It has been extended repeatedly over the past years and the original architect is no longer with the company. Documentation about the database schema does not correspond to the production database schema. Furthermore, the database schema of the Order Management System consists of thousands of tables and 10 tables have the word "order" in the name with different types of prefixes (masterorder) and suffixes (ordertax). Finally, the Knowledge Scientist gets the SQL script that the IT developer runs every morning to generate the data that is then passed along to a business analyst. Also, the IT developer did not write this SQL script; it was passed to them from previous employees.

The Knowledge Scientist works with the Business User to understand the meaning of the word "order." Discussions with the business revealed that the definition of an *order* is if it had shipped or the accounts receivable had been received.

Together with the IT developer, the Knowledge Scientist learns that the Order Management System is the authoritative source for all orders. Within that database, the data relating to orders is vertically partitioned across several tables. The SQL scripts collected in the previous step provides focus to identify the candidate tables and attributes where the data is located. Only the following tables and attributes are needed from the thousands of tables and tens of thousands of attributes: `MasterOrder(moid, oid, masterdate, ordertype, osid, ...)`, `Order(oid, orderdate, ...)` , `OrderStatus(osid, moid, orderstatusdate, ostid, ...)`, `OrderStatusType (ostid, statustype, ...)` .

Together, they identify the business requirement of an order as all tuples in the MasterOrder table, where the ordertype is equal to 2 or 3. Note that in some SQL scripts, this condition was not present. This is the reason why the Finance department was getting different answers for the same question.

Furthermore, it is revealed that the table OrderStatus holds all the different status that an order has across different periods of time. In discussions with the business user, it is confirmed that they only want to consider the last order status (they do not care about the historic order statuses). This may have been another source of differing numbers because a single order can have multiple order statuses, but it is unique for a given period a time.

Table 6. Concept knowledge report for round 1

Concept Name	Order
Concept ID	Order
Unique ID of a Concept	moid
Table Name or SQL Query	select moid from masterorder m join order o on m.oid = o.oid where ordertype in (2,3)

The Knowledge Report is in Table 6, 7 and 8. Due to space limitation, a single CAR is shown. The extract consists of Order Number, Order Date and Order Status.

Phase 2: Knowledge Implementation. The ontology is the following:

```
ec:Order rdf:type owl:Class ; rdfs:label "Order" .
ec:orderDate rdf:type owl:DatatypeProperty ; rdfs:domain ec:Order ;
  rdfs:range xsd:dateTime ; rdfs:label "Order Date" .
 ec:hasOrderStatus rdf:type owl:ObjectProperty ; rdfs:label "has order status"
  rdfs:domain ec:Order ; rdfs:range ec:OrderStatus .
```

The following is an example R2RML mapping for the concept Order:

```
map:m1 a rr:TriplesMap ;
  rr:logicalTable  [ rr:sqlQuery  "select moid from masterorder m join
                             order o on m.oid = o.oid where ordertype in (2,3)" ] ;
   rr:subjectMap    [ rr:class     ec:Order ;
     rr:template  "http://www.e-commerce.com/data/Order/{moid} ] .
```

The SPARQL query to generate the extract is the following:

```
SELECT ?Order_Number ?Order_Date ?Order_Status
WHERE {
?x a :Order;
  :orderNumber ?Order_Number;
  :orderDate ?Order_Date;
  :hasOrderStatus [
     :orderStatusName ?Order_Status;
  ]
}
```

Sample data is provided to the business users and IT developer and validated.

Table 7. Attribute knowledge report for round 1

Attribute Name	Order Date
Attribute ID	orderDate
Applied to Concept	Order
Unique ID of a Concept	moid
Table Name or SQL Query	select moid, orderdate from masterorder m join order o where m.oid = o.id
Column Name	orderdate
Datatype	date
Is NULL possible?	No
If NULL?	N/A

Phase 3: Self-Service Analytics. The extract is now accessible in a BI tool. The Business User sees a very simple table with the accurate data that is needed in order to build the business intelligence report and answer the original query: "How many orders were placed in a given time period per their status?"

This data is now accessible to a large number of business users which before would have had to talk to IT in order to get the same or similar data. Assume the extract was cached in a table called `Orders`. Any business user can retrieve all the data about Orders by simply executing: `SELECT * FROM Orders`.

To get the exact same data directly from the database of the Order Management System, the business user would have to spend time with IT to determine the SQL query, which would have been:

Table 8. Relationship knowledge report for round 1

Relationship Name	has order status
Relationship Definition	An order has a Order Status
Relationship ID	hasOrderStatus
From Concept	Order
Unique ID of From Concept	moid
Table Name or SQL Query	select moid, ostid, max(orderstatusdate) from OrderStatus group by orderstatusdate
To Concept	Order Status
Unique ID of To Concept	ostid

```
SELECT m.moid as OrderNumber, o.orderdate as OrderDate,
       ost.statustype as OrderStatusName
FROM masterorder m
JOIN order o ON m.oid = o.oid
JOIN (SELECT moid, ostid, max(orderstatusdate)
     FROM OrderStatus GROUP BY orderstatusdate) os ON m.moid = os.moid
JOIN OrderStatusType ost ON os.ostid = ostid.ostid
WHERE m.ordertype in (2,3)
```

Round 2: Order Net Sales. In order to show the pay-as-you-go nature of the methodology, consider the following new request:

Phase 1: Knowlege Capture

What: What is the net sales of an order?
Why: Depending on whom is asked, different answers are provided. The net sales is dependent on at least 4 different aspects of each order and sometimes aspects of each individual line item. The departments and individuals reporting results are variously not applying all of the proper items, not applying them consistently or not applying them correctly (per the business' desired rules).
Who: The Finance department, specifically the CFO
How: A business analyst asks the IT developer for this information every morning.
Where: This is in the proprietary Order Management System.
When: Every morning they want to know the net sales of every order and also various statistics and aggregations.

In conversations with the Business User, the Knowledge Scientist learns that the business user gets a CSV file from IT. The business user opens it in Excel and applies some calculations. The Knowledge Scientist works with the business user to understand the meaning of the word "order net sales". It is then understood that the net sales of an order is calculated by subtracting the tax and the shipping cost from the final price and also adjusting based upon the discount given. However, if the currency of the order is not in USD or CAD, then the shipping tax must be subtracted. Working with IT, they identify another table that is needed: `ordertax`. It is noted that the ontology only needs to be extended to support two new Attributes: Order Net Sales and Order Currency as shown in Table 9. Finally the original Extract is extended with the two new attributes.

Table 9. Attribute knowledge report for round 2

Attribute Name	Order Net Sales
Attribute ID	orderNetSales
Applied to Concept	Order
Unique ID of a Concept	moid
Table Name or SQL Query	select moid, o.ordertotal - ot.finaltax - CASE WHEN o.currencyid in ("USD", "CAD") THEN o.shippingcost ELSE o.shippingcost = ot.shippingtax END as ordernetsales from masterorder m join order o on m.oid = o.id join ordertax ot on o.oid = ot.oid
Column Name	netsales
Datatype	float
Is NULL possible?	No
If NULL?	N/A

Phase 2: Knowledge Implementation. The existing ontology has now been extended with the following,:

```
ec:orderNetSales rdf:type owl:DatatypeProperty ; rdfs:domain ec:Order ;
  rdfs:range xsd:float ; rdfs:label "Order Net Sales" .
ec:orderCurrency rdf:type owl:DatatypeProperty ; rdfs:domain ec:Order ;
  rdfs:range xsd:string ; rdfs:label "Order Currency" .
```

The following is R2RML mapping for Order Net Sales

```
map:m3 a   rr:TriplesMap ;
  rr:logicalTable [ rr:sqlQuery  "select moid, o.ordertotal - ot.finaltax -
      CASE WHEN o.currencyid in (?USD', ?CAD) THEN o.shippingcost
      ELSE o.shippingcost = ot.shippingtax END as ordernetsales FROM ... " ] ;
  rr:predicateObjectMap  [ rr:objectMap  [ rr:column  "ordernetsales" ] ;
                                  rr:predicate  ec:orderNetSales ] ;
  rr:subjectMap [ rr:template  "http://www.e-commerce.com/data/Order/{moid}" ] .
```

The existing SPARQL query is extended as follows:

```
SELECT ?Order_Number ?Order_Date ?Order_Status ?Order_Net_Sales ?Order_Currency
WHERE {
?x a :Order;
  :orderNumber ?Order_Number;
  :orderDate ?Order_Date;
  :orderNetSales ?Order_Net_Sales;
  :orderCurrency ?Order_Currency;
  :hasOrderStatus [
     :orderStatusLabel ?Order_Status;
  ]
}
```

Phase 3: Self-Service Analytics. With the extended extract, the business users can further enhance the business intelligence report in order to answer the new question of this round.

5 Lessons Learned, Future Work and Conclusions

Knowledge Scientist: Success with the Pay-as-you-go Methodology depends on having a Knowledge Scientist– someone with a broad set of technical and social skills. Such people may be hard to find. We have learned that potential candidates have a technical background in data (SQL developers, etc.), know data modeling (UML, etc.), enjoy creating documentation, and commonly interact with business users. If looking internally, they are employees who have been at the organization for a long time and understand how the business functions. Potential candidates have dual backgrounds in computer science and arts (literature, music, etc.). Furthermore, the Knowledge Scientist should not be the Data Scientist. The Knowledge Scientist serves as a communication bridge between business and IT to understand the data. The Data Scientist works with the business to generate new insights and analysis with the data generated by the Knowledge Scientist.

Snowball Effect: It can sometimes take a while to get the ball rolling but once business users see the first bits of understandable data they get excited and want more. End users are empowered to ask questions that they had not even considered before with the status quo process. The Pay-as-you-go Methodology enables quickly adding more data in a way that business users can understand and easily access. The business benefit can be seen quickly and expanded. This feeds still more excitement for more data. The snowball gets larger and increasingly rolls down the hill faster. Additionally, the CIO can see tangible, early success (as opposed to the typical EDW) and feels comfortable funding the activities or expanding funding.

Manual Process: The amount of manual work and iterations could be seen as inefficient and expensive. We acknowledge this limitation. Regardless of the repetitions, we observe that when users understand the methodology, the iterations are faster. For example, the first iteration took 2 months, later on 4 iterations were done in one month. The repetitive process makes us reflect: what parts of the of methodology can we (semi-)automate? We find this a challenging problem because modeling can be seen as much of a science as it is an art.

Maintenance and Evolution: The ontology and mappings were created in an additive manner. In very rare cases we had to go back and make changes (in month 8, two attributes were eliminated). We attribute this to the fact that in the methodology clearly defines stages where there has to be reviews. If something is not clear from the beginning, we do not go further next step. We did not address the phenomena of schema changes and ontology evolutions. How should the methodology be adopted when there are database schema changes or if the ontology is updated outside of the methodology? What happens if these changes are monotonic or non-monotonic?

Ontology Expressivity: The ontologies that are generated with the Pay-as-you-go Methodology have a basic expressivity. One can consider that the limited expressivity is a limitation. In our case it was an advantage. For non-semantic aware customer, simple and less complexity reduced the barrier to entry. This has proven to be sufficient for the BI tasks of our customers. We acknowledge that this is not a methodology to create profoundly expressive ontologies. We believe there is opportunity to extend the methodology to support the engineering of more expressive ontologies.

Evaluation: In this paper, we presented a case study that shows 33 iterations over three years. Is this good? Is this bad? It is hard to provide an objective answer to this question. We believe it is critical to devise rigorous and thorough scientific evaluation methodologies for knowledge graph construction methodologies.

Tools: Existing tools have been designed for users with a strong background in semantic technologies. A clear need exists for ontology and mapping tools designed for non-semantic aware users. Furthermore, the tools need to be aligned with methodologies. Capsenta started out by developing Ultrawrap Mapper [14]. Subsequently, we developed Gra.fo (https://gra.fo), a visual, collaborative and real time knowledge graph schema/ontology editor. Both of these tools are in being integrated so they support this methodology. We believe it is paramount that tools are designed in conjunction with a methodology. We continue to refine the tools and techniques to be maximally useful to our non-semantic users while also exposing the much larger general business user and IT world to the valuable capabilities the semantic community has delivered.

At Capsenta, we now use the Pay-as-you-go Methodology, Gra.fo and Ultrawrap [11,14] in all customer engagements.

References

1. Azzaoui, A., et al.: Scientific competency questions as the basis for semantically enriched open pharmacological space development. Drug Discov. Today **18**(17–18), 843–852 (2013)
2. Fernandez-Lopez, M., et al.: Methontology: from ontological art towards ontological engineering. In: AAAI Symposium on Ontological Engineering (1997)
3. Gruninger, M., Fox, M.S.: Methodology for the design and evaluation of ontologies. In: Workshop on Basic Ontological Issues in Knowledge Sharing (1995)

4. Hitzler, P., et al. (eds.): Ontology Engineering with Ontology Design Patterns: Foundations and Applications. Studies on the Semantic Web, vol. 25. IOS Press/AKA, Amsterdam (2016)
5. Jiménez-Ruiz, E., et al.: BootOX: practical mapping of RDBs to OWL 2. In: Arenas, M., et al. (eds.) ISWC 2015. LNCS, vol. 9367, pp. 113–132. Springer, Cham (2015). https://doi.org/10.1007/978-3-319-25010-6_7
6. Keet, C.M., Ławrynowicz, A.: Test-driven development of ontologies. In: Sack, H., Blomqvist, E., d'Aquin, M., Ghidini, C., Ponzetto, S.P., Lange, C. (eds.) ESWC 2016. LNCS, vol. 9678, pp. 642–657. Springer, Cham (2016). https://doi.org/10.1007/978-3-319-34129-3_39
7. Kharlamov, E., et al.: Ontology based data access in Statoil. JWS **44**, 3–36 (2017)
8. Ren, Y., Parvizi, A., Mellish, C., Pan, J.Z., van Deemter, K., Stevens, R.: Towards competency question-driven ontology authoring. In: Presutti, V., d'Amato, C., Gandon, F., d'Aquin, M., Staab, S., Tordai, A. (eds.) ESWC 2014. LNCS, vol. 8465, pp. 752–767. Springer, Cham (2014). https://doi.org/10.1007/978-3-319-07443-6_50
9. Suárez-Figueroa, M.C., Gómez-Pérez, A., Motta, E., Gangemi, A.: Introduction: ontology engineering in a networked world. In: Suárez-Figueroa, M.C., Gómez-Pérez, A., Motta, E., Gangemi, A. (eds.) Ontology Engineering in a Networked World, pp. 1–6. Springer, Heidelberg (2012). https://doi.org/10.1007/978-3-642-24794-1_1
10. Sequeda, J.F., Arenas, M., Miranker, D.P.: OBDA: query rewriting or materialization? In practice, both!. In: Mika, P., et al. (eds.) ISWC 2014. LNCS, vol. 8796, pp. 535–551. Springer, Cham (2014). https://doi.org/10.1007/978-3-319-11964-9_34
11. Sequeda, J.F., Miranker, D.P.: Ultrawrap: SPARQL execution on relational data. JWS **22**, 19–39 (2013)
12. Sequeda, J.F., Miranker, D.P.: A pay-as-you-go methodology for ontology-based data access. IEEE Internet Comput. **21**(2), 92–96 (2017)
13. Sequeda, J.F., et al.: On directly mapping relational databases to RDF and OWL. In: WWW 2012 (2012)
14. Sequeda, J.F., Miranker, D.F.: Ultrawrap mapper: a semi-automatic relational database to RDF (RDB2RDF) mapping tool. In: ISWC Posters & Demos (2015)
15. Uschold, M., Gruninger, M.: Ontologies: principles, methods and applications. KER **11**, 93–136 (1996)
16. Uschold, M., King, M.: Towards a methodology for building ontologies. In: IJCAI 1995 Workshop on Basic Ontological Issues in Knowledge Sharing (1995)

Author Index

Printed in the United States
by Baker & Taylor Publisher Services